# Organizational
# Behaviour

University of Liverpool

# Organizational Behaviour

## Second edition

*Daniel King and Scott Lawley*

OXFORD
UNIVERSITY PRESS

# OXFORD
UNIVERSITY PRESS

Great Clarendon Street, Oxford, OX2 6DP,
United Kingdom

Oxford University Press is a department of the University of Oxford.
It furthers the University's objective of excellence in research, scholarship,
and education by publishing worldwide. Oxford is a registered trade mark of
Oxford University Press in the UK and in certain other countries

© D. King and S. Lawley 2016

The moral rights of the authors have been asserted

First edition 2013

Impression: 3

Published in the United States of America by Oxford University Press
198 Madison Avenue, New York, NY 10016, United States of America

British Library Cataloguing in Publication Data

Data available

Library of Congress Control Number: 2015955785

ISBN 978–0–19–872402–5

Printed in Great Britain by
Bell & Bain Ltd., Glasgow

# Acknowledgements

Writing a textbook like this is not something that can be done alone and we are grateful for the support and encouragement of many people who have contributed to its development. The original concept for the book arose out of our eight years of teaching at Nottingham Trent University. Therefore we would like to thank the thousands of students that we have had the pleasure of teaching over the last few years on the Foundations of Managing and Organizing module. Teaching you has been the inspiration for this book as we have sought to find ways of communicating our fascination with organizational behaviour to hundreds of students a year and make the subject come alive through our running case study. Similarly we would like to thank our colleagues at NTU who we have had the pleasure of teaching alongside and who have helped us develop the ideas that led to the foundations of this work and its development in this second edition.

We would like to thank Lucy Hyde and Antony Hey for their work in bringing the book to print, Sian Jenkins and Tomas Furby for their attention to detail throughout the copyediting stage, and Fiona Goodall for her work on the ORC. We would also like to express our gratitude to the many adopters of the book throughout the world and your guidance through the reviews in helping develop the book to the second edition.

We have found the input of the many people from industry who have given their time to help provide insights from their own working environment a huge help, particularly Alex Christie from Lendlease, Stephanie Dufner formerly of ALS Association, and Anthony Carey from Mazars.

Daniel is very grateful for Steph in giving up so much time over the summer whilst he was writing this new edition, and for Saffron, Ellerby, and Josh for putting up with him not always being around. He is also grateful for the ideas and support of family and friends in thinking through some of the ideas for the book.

Scott would like to thank colleagues past and present for their ideas and inspiration over the years, and all friends and family for their support during the writing of this book.

# How to use this book

## Running case:

**Running case:** transitions and new beginnings

It is 7:45 am and Simon Chance, the newly installed Chief Exe
Second-Chance Consortium, sits at his desk surveying his grou
The Second-Chance Consortium has just bought Junction H
proud heritage of strong customer service and a traditional appro
hotel for its high-class service, great food, and friendly but formal s
the hotel has undergone numerous changes of ownership and at
walls, worn carpets, and an antiquated computer system, Junctio
Chance's office is a bit like Junction Hotel—faded glory. A da

The fictional running case is set in Junction Hotel, and presents organizational problems and theories in a familiar context. We see issues from multiple perspectives and discover that there is often no 'one best way' to do things. The running case is closely integrated with the theories discussed in each chapter.

## Real life case boxes:

**Real life case:** the CEO who raised his firms' m
but is now being sued by his brother

In April 2015 Dan Price took a very controversial decision. He r
employees to $70,000 (£45,000) within three years (Cohen, 2015a
off (Gravity Payment, 2015). This would result in 70 out of the 120
having their salaries almost doubled (Torabi, 2015).
The co-founder of Gravity, a Seattle-based payment processing
(Cohen, 2015a) that he decided to do it after reading an article o
links between well-being and pay, which argued that emotional v

Organizational behaviour theories are played out in the real world every day. Contemporary examples from a range of sources (including businesses such as Vodafone, public sector institutions like the Metropolitan police, and not-for-profit organizations such as food cooperatives) help you make the link from theory to reality.

## Study and employability skills boxes:

**Study skills:** the difference between personal
an academically-informed perspective

My opinion

- uses my own taken-for-granted assumptions
- is based on gut reaction and personal opinion
- may often contain sentences such as 'I think that . . . '

An academically-informed perspective

- challenges received opinion and taken-for-granted assumptio

Each chapter contains skills tips to help boost your grades and your employability. These are linked to topics being discussed in the book, and further reinforce the relevance of organizational behaviour to real life.

**Theory in context:** henri Fayol and the profes

Henri Fayol (1841–1925) was a French mining engineer who
around a failing mine (Wren, 2001), he suggested that good man
lowing a set of general principles. Regardless of the person holding
would ensure efficient management across the organization. In h
*trielle et generale* (English translation, Fayol, 1949), he set out these

Management became a profession in itself (Pryor and Taneja, 2
becoming as important as training for production skills or other f
finance. In Chapter 3 we encounter Taylor, a fellow management

## Theory in context boxes:

Where do theories about organizational behaviour come from? What influenced the
theorists' thoughts and the resulting theories? The wider contexts of society, technology, politics, and economics are considered,
and you are encouraged to critically analyse
theories to deepen your understanding.

**Research insight:** The railway timetable Chia,
postmodern organizational analysis. Organizati

Chia (1995) examines the vast power of a simple bureaucratic inst
can order trains, passengers, and workers across a whole country
context of your own university studies and how they direct both yo
to hour.

One sheet of paper can represent the organization by structur
of space (different rooms), time (different time slots during the day
timetable slots). This small sheet of paper exerts power and cont

## Research insight boxes:

The body of academic literature on the
subject of organizational behaviour is vast.
This feature highlights seminal research
articles that made a significant contribution to the topic. The full reference is provided so you can follow up your textbook
reading with further research.

ager's time. If time is spent mired in issues of c
time for other aspects of managing the organi
controlling, but how about the planning, org

If you were the manager of an office of 100 peop
those workers on a day-to-day basis?

## Stop and think questions:

These short, reflective questions appear
throughout the chapters and encourage
you to consider the topics in light of your
own experience.

### Review questions

| | |
|---|---|
| **Describe** | According to Henri Fayol, what are the main five fu |
| **Describe** | What are the main features of bureaucratic organiz |
| **Explain** | Why does face-to-face management become more in size? |
| **Analyse** | What do you think is meant by the description of b sword?' |

## Review questions:

At the end of every chapter section, review
questions help you assess your understanding of the central themes and your
readiness to progress to the next part of
the topic.

### Further reading

Cottrell, S. 2011. *Critical thinking skills: Developing effective analysis an*
Basingstoke.
This popular study skills book gives some really useful material on the im
practical, as well as theoretical, ideas on how to improve in this area. Rea
this subject but also to other subjects on your degree course.

Bowell, T., and Kemp, G. 2002. *Critical thinking: A concise guide.* Routle
Another popular study skills book that stresses how to develop and build
strengths of an argument and how to develop your own.

## Further reading:

To take your learning further, reading lists
have been provided as guides to finding
out more about the issues raised within
each chapter and to help you locate the
useful academic literature in the field.

# How to use the Online Resource Centre

## www.oxfordtextbooks.co.uk/orc/king_lawley2e/

The Online Resource Centre that accompanies this book provides students and registered adopters of the textbook with ready-to-use teaching and learning materials.

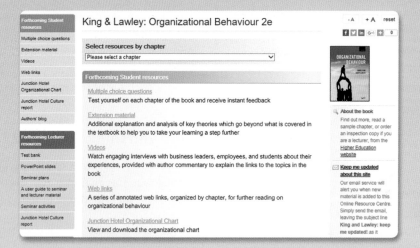

## Author blog:

The authors will provide fresh and newsworthy updates on relevant topics, thoroughly integrated with the textbook, with links to videos and other multimedia material on the Internet.

## For students

### Videos:

The world of work can sometimes seem far removed from the theories being discussed in the textbook. Business leaders, employees, and students are interviewed about their experiences, and an author commentary on each video clip explains the links to topics in the book.

## Extension material:

Additional explanation and analysis of key theories which go beyond what is covered in the textbook are available to help you to take your learning a step further.

## Multiple-choice questions:

A bank of self-marking, multiple-choice questions has been provided for each chapter of the text and includes instant feedback on your answers, cross-referencing the textbook to assist with independent self-study.

## Web links:

A series of annotated web links, organized by chapter, has been provided to point you in the direction of important material on organizational behaviour.

# For instructors

## Seminar resources:

A suite of fully developed seminar activities and tutor notes has been prepared for use in class. Activities are based around extension material from the running case and additional real-life case studies, articles, and video clips.

## Test bank:

A fully customizable resource containing interactive multiple-choice questions accompanied by answers and feedback with which to test your students.

## PowerPoint® slides:

Customizable PowerPoint® slides have been included for use in lecture presentations. Arranged by chapter theme, the slides may also be used as handouts in class.

# Guided tour of Dashboard

## Simple. Informative. Mobile.

Dashboard is a cloud-based online assessment and revision tool. It comes pre-loaded with test questions for students, a homework course if your module leader has adopted Dashboard, and additional resources as listed below. If your lecturer has adopted Dashboard and you have purchased the Dashboard Edition of the book, your standalone access code should be included and will provide instructions on how to sign up for the platform. If you have not purchased the Dashboard Edition or if you have purchased a second-hand copy, you can purchase standalone access online—visit www.oxfordtextbooks.co.uk/dashboard for more information.

**SIMPLE:** With a highly intuitive design, it will take you less than fifteen minutes to learn and master the system.

**MOBILE:** You can access Dashboard from every major platform and device connected to the Internet, whether that's a computer, tablet, or smartphone.

**INFORMATIVE:** Your assignment and assessment results are automatically graded, giving your instructor a clear view of the class's understanding of the course content.

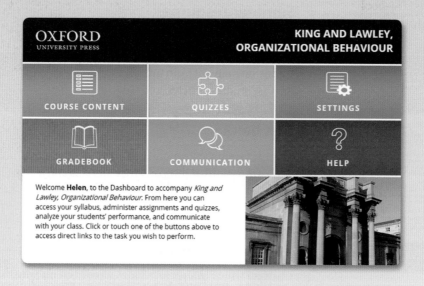

## Student resources

Dashboard offers all the features of the Online Resource Centre, but comes with additional questions to take your learning further.

## Lecturer resources

### Preloaded homework assignments and test bank

A preloaded homework course structured around the book is available, supported by a test bank containing a additional multiple-choice questions. Your students can follow the preloaded course, or you can customize it, allowing you to add questions from the test bank or from your existing materials to meet your specific teaching needs.

### Gradebook

Dashboard will automatically grade the homework assignments that you set for your students. The Gradebook also provides heat maps for you to view your students' progress which helps you to quickly identify areas of the course where your students may need more practice, as well as the areas they are most confident in. This feature helps you focus your teaching time on the areas that matter.

The Gradebook also allows you to administer grading schemes, manage checklists, and administer learning objectives and competencies.

# Contents

# Detailed contents

# Introducing organizational behaviour

*Transitions and new beginnings*

## Why read this introduction?

This chapter answers two key questions.

1. What am I studying? The chapter will give you an overview of the key themes within organizational behaviour (OB) to help you understand what they are and how they connect. This chapter aims to give you a good understanding of the key theories you will cover, and the underlying disciplines that they are based on.

2. How do I study OB? Studying OB is not simply taking in a series of theories that can then be reproduced in an essay or an exam. To gain a higher grade and really understand OB requires the ability to think critically, to question your own assumptions, and to apply the theories to real life contexts. Throughout this chapter we will look at some of these skills and how you can develop them, including the importance of critical thinking, the transition to degree level, and some top tips that will help you succeed in this subject.

## Introducing organizational behaviour

**Running case:** transitions and new beginnings—Simon Chance starts his reign

It is 7:45 am and Simon Chance, the newly installed Chief Executive of Junction Hotel and President of Second-Chance Consortium, sits at his desk surveying his group's latest acquisition.

The Second-Chance Consortium has just bought Junction Hotel, an upmarket, city-centre hotel with a proud heritage of strong customer service and a traditional approach. In its heyday people would flock to the hotel for its high-class service, great food, and friendly but formal style. Those days, however, are long gone and the hotel has undergone numerous changes of ownership and attempts to revive it. With paint peeling off the walls, worn carpets, and an antiquated computer system, Junction Hotel is in need of some real investment.

Chance's office is a bit like Junction Hotel—faded glory. A dark green leather chair from the 1940s sits in the corner—stylish but uncomfortable. Instead, Chance decides to use a chair from IKEA—not the most elegant design, but far more practical. The room is oak-clad, but some of the wooden panels are loose and a couple now have gaps in between them. 'I must fix that,' Chance muses. 'This place is a mess, nothing works properly, but I am sure we can turn it around.'

The Second-Chance Consortium is a venture capitalist company specializing in turning failed businesses into profitable enterprises. Simon Chance, a former footballer who retired early because of injury, reinvented himself as a business entrepreneur. Teaming up with his former agent and self-styled business guru Phil Weaver, Chance has led the consortium for six years, starting with the local football team and gradually building up a portfolio of successfully transformed firms. Chance feels confident that he can make the hotel a success. 'They just need strong leadership and a good strategy,' he thinks. 'I am sure that we can succeed here.'

At first glance, running an organization might seem straightforward. Television programmes such as *Dragons' Den* often give the impression that all you need is the right product, marketing, and finance to be successful. Equally, you might look at your own boss or the manager of a football team you support and think, 'why don't they just tell them to get on with it? If I were in charge we could quickly sort it out.' Yet, in practice, running organizations is more complicated.

Organizations can be difficult, challenging places, largely because they involve people. People can be unpredictable and complex as they have their own agendas (e.g. the desire to be seen as a success, fear of failure, etc.), beliefs (e.g. this is the right way to do things), identities (e.g. I am an accountant and this is how I do things), practices, and habits, all of which shape how they act.

To manage, or even work alongside, people you need to be able to understand how they think, what motivates them, what increases their commitment, how to organize them, and how to ensure they act in an ethical and sustainable way (Figure 1.1). Working with and managing people, therefore, is likely to be one of the most difficult and challenging things that you do.

People, therefore, are at the heart of this book; in particular we focus on how they are managed, motivated, trained, and led, and how they communicate. At the individual level we examine their personality, motivation, and learning; at the group level, how they are managed through teams and groups; and, at the organizational level, how they are led, impacted by power and politics, and affected by the organization's culture.

**Figure 1.1** The way individuals are managed.

**The rational organization**
- Bureaucratic procedures—following rules and regulations
- Taylorism—following set work procedures
- Rational organization today—Rational principles spread throughout society

**Contemporary trends**
- Globalization—working in a global world
- The service sector—emotional and aesthetic labour
- Corporate social responsibility—acting ethically

**The Social Organization**
- Social organization—power of peer pressure
- Groups and teams—managed through teamwork
- Organizational culture—changing hearts and minds

Ways in which the individual is managed

**Managing the organization**
- Change—top-down change
- Leadership—following the leader
- Power and politics—power games
- Communication—top-down communication

**Managing the individual**
- Individuals and personalities—through personality tests
- Motivation—becoming self-motivated
- Knowledge and learning—training and developing the individual

OB is also about how organizations are structured and run through systems and procedures, as well as how they relate to the wider, globalized world. Furthermore it is about society—or, more precisely, the impact that organizations have on the people that work for them, the communities around them, and society as a whole. It examines how organizations operate globally and also impact, for good and ill, society and the planet.

To study OB, therefore, is to really begin to understand how and why things happen at work, what is the most effective way of achieving things, and what impact this has on the people that work for organizations and the societies in which they operate.

**Running case:** understanding the complexity—our fictional case study, Junction Hotel

| | |
|---|---|
| **From:** | Phil Weaver |
| **Sent:** | 2 September |
| **To:** | Simon Chance |
| **Subject:** | Junction Hotel Report |

Hi Simon

I have done a full survey of the hotel, looking back at its accounts for the last five years and surveying the building, kitchen, and staff. Having stayed in the hotel overnight as part of the mystery shopper exercise I found the staff courteous and friendly, but the systems slow and cumbersome. Checking in took 20 minutes as they had lost my registration details, and we had to walk to the restaurant in order to pay my bill as the 'machine was not working'. The rooms were comfortable and fairly clean, but did seem to be of an inconsistent standard. I must say that the food at the restaurant was excellent and shows real class, but service was slow.

Overall, this hotel shows potential but there is much to improve. They are quite disorganized, some staff seem unmotivated and unclear in their tasks, and the service, while polite and professional, is not what you would expect.

Speak soon

Phil

Chance turns to the main report. The Second-Chance Consortium always create a comprehensive report when they take over a failing venture and collect good management data so that they can work out what to improve. Chance reads about the hotel's history and is interested to learn that back in its heyday, Junction Hotel hosted some stars from the stage and screen, its restaurant won awards, and it had successful conference facilities. As he reads more of the report, however, his mood changes. 'This won't be a quick fix,' he thinks, looking in detail at the problems that Weaver identified: poor systems, unmotivated staff, erratic schedules, no clear identity or purpose to the hotel, and running at a loss for the last five years. 'We need to sort this place out,' Chance thinks, staring out of the window. 'I'll get Weaver on the phone and work out our plan.'

What do you think are the key challenges that Simon Chance faces in transforming Junction Hotel?

Visit the Online Resource Centre to read the full report.

The complexity of organizations is often best understood in the context of familiar situations. In this book we will do this through our innovative fictional running case study, Junction Hotel. Instead of seeing theories as dry abstract models, in this book we use them as ways to make sense of the challenges the characters face. Through this case study we will learn about the hotel's characters, their personalities, backgrounds, and experiences, and the dilemmas they face. We will see their emotions, reactions, and different interpretations of the same event.

Applying theory to real situations is suggested by learning theorists, such as Kolb and Gibbs, to be far more effective. It helps us understand real dilemmas and challenges that managers, workers, or society face. Just think of it this way: a manager does not try to motivate their staff because a textbook says that they should do it; rather, they look at ideas surrounding motivation because they are facing a problem that they need to solve. The theories covered in this book were largely produced in response to challenges in real life. So, as you read the theory in this book try relating the theories to your own experiences—cases you know from real life—and to our fictional case, Junction Hotel.

# What is organizational behaviour?

So, what is involved in running and working in organizations? This book will be divided into five themes, each with their own focus and issues.

1. The rational organization.
2. The social organization.
3. Managing the individual.
4. Managing the organization.
5. Contemporary trends.

As we will see, these themes offer us a different perspective on what goes on within organizations and different ideas about how to manage them (Figure 1.2).

## Theme 1: The rational organization

Chapter 2: Rational organizational design and bureaucracy
Chapter 3: Rational work design
Chapter 4: Rationalization in contemporary organizations

**Figure 1.2**
Key themes in organizational behaviour.

---

**Running case:** 8:15 am Phil Weaver discusses his report with Simon Chance

'We need systems and procedures,' Weaver states boldly to Chance, 'like we had at the football club, to make this place run like clockwork.' Weaver animatedly discusses his plans with Chance. 'I've been looking at the booking-in procedure. I'm sure we could make it run quicker by streamlining it. Also, the cleaners seem to be getting away with murder—working slowly without set targets or procedures,' he continues, hardly taking a breath.

Getting out a grid drawn on a sheet of A3 paper, Weaver lays out targets for every individual and department, with measurements for every aspect of the hotel—from customer satisfaction through to room cleanliness. 'It's another Weaver masterplan,' Chance declares excitedly. Impressed, Chance picks up a document entitled 'Streamlining food production,' which has detailed step-by-step guides to peeling carrots through to cooking chicken. 'I've only just started,' Weaver states. 'I think we should work on the cleaners first. I'm sure that we could come up with detailed ways of doing everything in this hotel to make it run more efficiently.'

---

For well over 100 years, managers have dreamed of creating rational, logical, and efficient organizations. As we will examine in Chapter 2, by creating **bureaucratic** procedures, policies, and practices, they aim to create standardized, predictable, and efficient organizations so that management gain maximum control over, and efficiency from, workers.

This ambition for control was exemplified by Fredrick Taylor. As we will see in Chapter 3, Taylor (1911) believed that through scientific analysis he could discover the one best way of performing every task and through this approach create a more efficient, productive, and rational way of working.

**Bureaucratic** Describing the process of bureaucracy, sometimes used in a derogatory sense.

As we will examine in Chapter 4, such an approach continues to underpin so much of what we do today, from fast-food chains, such as McDonalds, and hotels such as Travelodge to the way in which you take out your library books. This rational approach has come to dominate the thinking of much of Western capitalism. Indeed, sociologist George Ritzer (2015) has described our society as **McDonaldized**, where the principles of the fast-food restaurant, and therefore rational production, have come to dominate more and more parts of society.

This approach has brought with it many positive features, with vast improvements in productivity enabling mass production, and has dramatically cut the cost of most consumer goods, making cars, televisions, clothes, and furniture affordable to many people.

But while these techniques of organization design achieve efficiencies, they are not without human costs—they can be boring, predictable, and routinized, and an imbalance of power between management and workers is created. This approach also transfers knowledge and power from the workers to the managers, creating systems that reduce the worker to a small cog in a very large machine. As Marxist theorist Harry Braverman (1974) argued, this rational approach deskills the workers and leaves them dehumanized in the process.

> **McDonaldization (of society)** The principles of efficiency, calculability, predictability, and control by which fast-food restaurants are managed and organized, as applied by Ritzer to other contemporary organizations.

## Theme 2: The social organization

Chapter 5: Discovering the social organization
Chapter 6: Managing groups and teams
Chapter 7: Organizational culture

---

**Running case:** 8:20 am Meg Mortimer prepares herself for the board meeting

Meg Mortimer sits at her desk in the little cubbyhole-cum-office behind the reception desk busying herself in readiness for the new day. 'I've seen it all before,' she thinks, as she prepares herself for the staff-wide meeting that morning. 'These new owners will come in with their grand plans and new procedures and try to lay their mark on the hotel, but they are not going to take us away from what we really are,' she thinks to herself, 'a caring and considerate hotel based on traditional quality service.'

Mortimer, the second-longest-serving member of the Junction Hotel team, started life as a cleaner and has worked through every position in the hotel to eventually become one of the senior managers. 'Owners come and go,' she thinks, 'but the Junction Hotel way will outlive any of them.'

---

> **Hawthorne studies** A series of studies which ran from 1924 into the late 1930s. Widely credited with discovering the human side of the organization.

While the principles and practice of the rational or formal organization continue to be highly popular, over the last eighty years there has been increasing recognition of the influence that the informal side of the organization has on actual practice. The informal organization sits beneath the surface, impacting what goes on in quite powerful, but often invisible, ways.

We will start with the **Hawthorne studies** in Chapter 5 and examine how they claimed to have 'discovered' that people are social beings who are influenced by the social norms of their peer group. Elton Mayo (1949) proposed that organizations should be seen as social spaces rather than machines, full of people with feelings and desires.

Chapter 6 will develop this view, illustrating how **groups** and **teams** have become increasingly important ways of managing people and increasing productivity. However, teamwork can be challenging, as it often fails to work as effectively as it might. Models such as Belbin's theory of group membership (2010) present techniques to make teams more effective.

Finally, in Chapter 7 we look at the social phenomenon of organizational culture—the behaviours, language, stories, and symbols of an organization that are enacted through the groups and teams within the organization. Again, we will see that culture is something that organizations seek to manage, but some argue that it is to a large degree beyond their control.

**Group** A collection of people with a sense of shared identity and something in common but *not* with a shared purpose.

**Team** A group who meet together with a common purpose and some degree of mutual interdependence.

## Theme 3: Managing the individual

Chapter 8: Personality and individual differences
Chapter 9: Motivation and the meaning of work
Chapter 10: Knowledge and learning

### Running case: 8:30 am Linda Wilkinson, Domestic Manager, arrives at work

Linda Wilkinson makes her way hurriedly across the car park of Junction Hotel, grabbing hold of her briefcase. 'Flipping traffic,' she mutters under her breath, 'the school run will be the death of me.' As she rushes past the boardroom window, she notices a man in his mid-50s staring into the distance. 'Is that Simon Chance,' she wonders to herself, 'the new owner of Junction Hotel, and who's he with?', looking at a smaller, earnest man pointing aggressively at some charts. As she does so, she catches a glimpse of herself in the window. Tall, blonde, and still quite elegant—or so her friends tell her—the forty-something mother of two notices the vomit stain left on her jacket's left shoulder by Sam, her youngest, as she dropped him off at nursery this morning. 'Grrrh,' she declares, slightly louder than she had intended. 'This is the last thing I need today,' she mutters. Her slight outburst alerts the man, who looks up at her. Trying to subtly hide her shoulder, Wilkinson smiles positively at him even though today she feels anything but positive. 'This is a big day,' she thinks to herself, 'I need to make a good impression and present myself as the manager-in-waiting.'

In the third theme we focus our attention on individuals within the organization and how they are managed. We begin in Chapter 8 by looking at theories of **personality**—what are the traits that make us all different, and can they be measured? We see how managers use such theories to create 'personality tests' that are used in procedures such as recruitment and appraisal.

Seeing people as having differences is also important when examining what motivates people to work harder; what motivates workers is the subject of Chapter 9. Maslow's hierarchy of needs (1943) is a familiar tool for analysing human **motivation**, but we discover that motivation is, in fact, a much more complex phenomenon—individual differences can relate not only to factors of personality, but also to the social factors that they bring in from their life outside the workplace.

**Personality** A set of characteristics and behaviour displayed by any individual.

**Motivation** The will and desire that a person has to engage in a particular behaviour or perform a particular task.

**Knowledge and learning** An aspect of organizational behaviour which emphasizes the importance of information, understanding and practical skills for organizational success. In particular it examines the capacity of the organization to share this knowledge in effective ways.

Finally, we turn our attention to **knowledge and learning** in Chapter 10. We will see that in the knowledge-intensive economy how knowledge is developed, captured, and distributed is an increasingly vital aspect that differentiates successful firms from those that fail. What, though, do we mean by knowledge? Is it a set of facts that can be learned or is it something that we acquire through experience?

# Theme 4: Managing the organization

Chapter 11: Changing the organization
Chapter 12: Leadership
Chapter 13: Power and politics in organizations

---

**Running case:** 10:00 am Simon Chance meets all the staff

Chance, followed closely by Weaver, walks purposefully into the conference room, reaches the podium, and surveys his expectant audience. All the staff of Junction Hotel are gathered, somewhat nervously, to hear from the hotel's new owner and Chief Executive Officer.

Chance starts by introducing himself and his consortium and explaining why they bought the hotel. He says that it has a proud tradition of quality customer service, but the world is changing and the hotel needs to change with it. He, with all their help, is going to transform this place, to bring it back to its former glory.

'Junction Hotel is going to feel like a new place,' he goes on to say, 'a new culture where hard work gets rewarded and the best people succeed. This is a clean slate for everyone and I am going to set the hotel on a new course.'

'This is an exciting time for all of us,' Chance continues, warming to his theme, 'but let's be under no illusions, it is going to be challenging. Some of you are going to find the changes that we put in place difficult. Some of you might not even want to come with us in this new direction. I respect that. But we have a direction,' he warned, 'and we will not be blown off course.'

'Over the next few months we will all need to pull together. Working together, I'm sure we can make Junction Hotel great again.'

Weaver then gets up, unravels his A3 sheets, and starts laying out the new direction for Junction Hotel.

---

**Change** The process by which an organization changes in practices, processes, culture, etc. in a planned or emergent fashion.

**Leadership** The process of leading or influencing the behaviour of others. In the broadest definition, it can be carried out by anyone in the organization.

Our fourth theme focuses on how the organization as a whole is managed. In a sense, the whole book is about organizational **change**, but we particularly focus on this topic in Chapter 11. We will see through that chapter that there are two major models of change: the emergent and planned approaches. While these focus predominantly on the role of the senior managers in organizations, we will see that how the rest of the staff respond to that change is critical in the organization's success. We also look at how theories of individual learning and development contribute to successful change and development on an organizational scale.

This brings us on to the issue of **leadership** and followership in Chapter 12. Leaders are seen as powerful people, vital for the success of the organization. While numerous theories have sought to identify what makes a great leader, recent theory has focused on the importance of followers for organizational success.

Far from the rational organization that we begin the book with, our final chapter in this theme will examine the more messy realities of organizational life, where organizational decisions are products of **power games and politics** between competing people (e.g. senior managers) or interest groups (e.g. workers and managers).

**Power games and politics** The process where one individual or group tries to gain advantage or get another individual or group to do things that they might otherwise not intend to do.

## Theme 5: Contemporary trends

> **Running case:** 10:48 am the meeting ends and all the staff leave the conference room

As they file out of the meeting, Graham Effingham, Junction Hotel's award-winning chef, goes on his phone and posts a quick blog post on his site. This is where he goes undercover and says what is really going on in the hotel, but without ever saying exactly where it is.

*Just come out the staff meeting with our new owners—arrrgh what a load of old clap-trap. I won't say the name of the new owners but all I can say is I think they have no chance.*

*They gave us all this talk about transforming the business, making it a place that people will be proud to come to and we would all feel excited by working for it. How it would be a hard journey, but if we all stick together (which I read as following what they say) then we will all be a success.*

*Nonsense—we've all been through this before with the last owners; it won't last. This lot, though, say they have a plan. The owner's side-kick had all these charts and tables about how we compare to other hotels—the man has an obsession with graphs and stuff, I can tell you. He kept on comparing us to more 'efficient' hotels, like Travelodge, saying that we can learn from them, or this European one Etap. It seems like a race to the bottom, I can tell you. Sounds like they are trying to turn us into a sweatshop!*

*Then, as we all left, we were given our department's A3—a set of targets that we are meant to achieve over the year. Mine is to cut the cost of the food by 30% and make it 23% quicker. 23% quicker, what the hell does that mean? I have to come back in a few weeks with a plan as to how we will do this and keep the costs 'reasonable,' otherwise they are going to look into getting our food from one of these catering suppliers. They only do processed food, not the direction we want to go!*

In the final theme we turn our attention to the contemporary issues that face organizations. We start, in Chapter 14, by exploring communication. We will see that communication is fraught with difficulty and represents a major challenge to effective organization. We will also discover that further issues emerge when technologies such as the Internet and mobile technologies are used to carry out communication. In Chapter 15, we examine **globalization**. As the recent global recession has demonstrated, we live, perhaps more than ever, in a highly interconnected and integrated world. Large multinationals have grown to become hugely powerful—in some cases bigger than many countries. However, the globalized economy brings with it its own challenges for management. As Hofstede (1980) noted,

**Globalization** Defined in many different ways, globalization is where activities take place on an increasingly global scale.

national culture presents multinational companies with significant challenges in managing the differences between cultures.

Chapter 16 looks at the rising **service sector**, which, in some senses, represents a continuation and, indeed, intensification of the rational approach we saw in the first theme. However, because it is customer-facing it carries the additional challenge of emotional and aesthetic labour in which employees have to manage their feelings and appearances, putting on an act in front of customers.

The recent financial crisis and corporate scandals have put the spotlight on our final theoretical chapter, **corporate social responsibility** (CSR). We will see some of the key ethical challenges that organizations face, how they respond to them, and the criticisms that campaigners and activists have about these responses.

**Service sector** Non-manufacturing industries, such as retail, leisure, transport, finance, and media.

**Corporate social responsibility** A contested term with different interpretations but generally taken to be the social and environmental responsibility corporations have towards their stakeholders.

# Organizational behaviour—an interconnected discipline

**Running case:** 11:15 am Weaver and Chance meet again in the boardroom

'Well, that went well,' says Weaver in a confident way, 'I think we really hammered home our message. This place needs a good shake-up and we're the people to do it. With our new targets and management practices Junction Hotel is going to be a very different place in a year's time when we have transformed them.'

Meanwhile, Linda Wilkinson is less jubilant as she talks to Meg by reception. 'They talk very positively,' Linda says with a sense of despondency, 'but they cannot just come here and impose their views on us like that.'

In our final chapter we draw all the issues together and look forward to the future challenges that face organizations. We will see that, while we have discussed all these topics as discrete entities, in practice they are highly interconnected and rely on each other.

It is, therefore, important to be aware of the connections between the themes as you read the chapters and prepare to write your essay or answer your exam questions.

# Key underlying theories

As will be apparent from the discussion, OB covers a wide range of issues. To do this it draws on a wide range of underlying disciplines (Figure 1.3).

- Sociology explores how society shapes people. It helps us understand that no action takes place in a social vacuum and helps us appreciate how individual experiences are part of broader society.
- Psychology seeks to measure, explain, and sometimes change human behaviour. It is often considered the science of the mind.

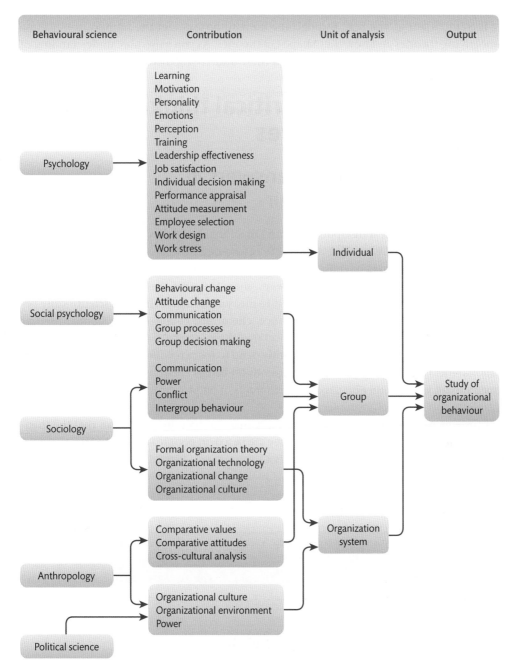

| Behavioural science | Contribution | Unit of analysis | Output |
|---|---|---|---|

Psychology → Learning / Motivation / Personality / Emotions / Perception / Training / Leadership effectiveness / Job satisfaction / Individual decision making / Performance appraisal / Attitude measurement / Employee selection / Work design / Work stress → Individual

Social psychology → Behavioural change / Attitude change / Communication / Group processes / Group decision making

Sociology → Communication / Power / Conflict / Intergroup behaviour → Group

Formal organization theory / Organizational technology / Organizational change / Organizational culture

Anthropology → Comparative values / Comparative attitudes / Cross-cultural analysis → Organization system

Organizational culture / Organizational environment / Power

Political science

Individual / Group / Organization system → Study of organizational behaviour

**Figure 1.3** The disciplines that underlie the study of organizational behaviour.

**Source:** Robbins, Stephen P.; Judge, Timothy A., *Essentials of Organizational Behaviour*, 10th Edition © 2010, p. 5. Reprinted by permission of Pearson Education, Inc., Upper Saddle River, NJ.

- Social psychology bridges sociology and psychology, and tries to understand the impact the group has on the outlook of the individual.
- Anthropology examines rites and rituals that shape how groups and cultures work.
- Political science examines the role of power within organizations.

Visit the Online Resource Centre for deeper analysis of the underlying theories.

It is important as you read through the book to be aware of the significance of these underlying theories and how they shape OB theories. As you gain more understanding of OB you will be able to distinguish between these underlying theories.

# The importance of critical thinking and multiple perspectives

## Why there are no right answers in organizational behaviour

The different theoretical disciplines within OB all make a variety of attempts to explain human behaviour. However, it is difficult to offer a definitive answer as to which view is correct because human behaviour is complex and subjective.

First, people do not act in predictable ways, share the same outlook, nor always behave as we would expect. Secondly, it is difficult to measure human behaviour scientifically because it is not controllable like, for instance, chemicals; people are not standardized or predictable. Thirdly, the different theoretical traditions each have their own questions and debates that interest them and, consequently, tend to focus on different features of organizational life. Finally, the 'right answer' depends on beliefs about whose interests organizations should serve—either managers/shareholders or employees/society (we have more to say about this in the following sections).

Consequently, within OB there are no right answers. This does not mean that the theories presented here are incorrect or that they are based on poor reasoning. In fact, there are many fascinating and insightful accounts of the subject. Rather, there are no definitive answers to the issues that we discuss. This makes OB a fascinating, although potentially somewhat complex, subject.

**Real life case:** the CEO who raised his firms' minimum wage to £45,000 but is now being sued by his brother

In April 2015 Dan Price took a very controversial decision. He raised the minimum wage of all his employees to $70,000 (£45,000) within three years (Cohen, 2015a) and also gave unlimited paid time off (Gravity Payment, 2015). This would result in 70 out of the 120 employees getting pay rises, with 30 having their salaries almost doubled (Torabi, 2015).

The co-founder of Gravity, a Seattle-based payment processing company, told the *New York Times* (Cohen, 2015a) that he decided to do it after reading an article on happiness. The article was on the links between well-being and pay, which argued that emotional well-being rose progressively until it reached $75,000. While above $75,000 a year brings pleasure, it does not increase happiness (Kahneman and Deaton, 2010).

The article made a deep impression on Price. He had heard many stories from his employees about how difficult it was to live off $40,000 a year, and he wanted to make a difference. Price stated he felt there was a 'moral imperative to actually do it ... I want everybody that I'm partnered with ▶

▶ at Gravity to really live the fullest, best life that they can' (cited in Torabi, 2015). To achieve this he decided to cut his own salary from just under $1 million to $70,000 (Torabi, 2015) stating that the 'market rate for me as a CEO compared to a regular person is ridiculous, it's absurd' (cited in Cohen, 2015a). He also felt it made business sense. 'I honestly believe that removing that distraction [of living from pay cheque to pay cheque] will significantly increase our ability to take care of our clients' (cited in Torabi, 2015). This has been reflected by some of the employees, who say that they are now working harder. For instance, one employee stated that they are willing to put in more hours. 'I never thought I would go to a job where I would want to work extra hours, but this is something that I, and everyone else, want to do,' said Ortiz, one of the employees. 'It's really inspirational to see so many people dedicating most of their day to this job' (cited in Elkins, 2015). Some also felt it was the start of a movement that aimed to reduce the differences between high and low earners. As Dan Price states, 'Income inequality has been racing in the wrong direction . . . I want to fight for the idea that if someone is intelligent, hard-working and does a good job, then they are entitled to live a middle-class lifestyle' (cited in Cohen, 2015b).

Yet a couple of months later, Dan Price was sued by his brother because as a minority shareholder he believed the increased wages of the staff were reducing the firm's profits. Dan Price was also struggling financially: he had to cut his own salary and rent out his house. He also faced criticism on Facebook, in letters, and in phone calls (Cohen, 2015b). Some customers left, feeling it was a political statement. Some employees also left. For instance, a former financial manager told the *New York Times*: 'He gave raises to people who have the least skills and are the least equipped to do the job, and the ones who were taking on the most didn't get much of a bump' (Cohen, 2015b). Others did not like the fact that the gap between the higher- and lower-paid was reduced, and some even questioned if they were really worth the increased salary.

Time will tell if Dan Price's experiment will prove successful and if he will repair the relationship with his brother. The case raises further organizational behaviour issues that we will cover in this book.

# The gap between highest- and lowest-paid

As co-founder and CEO of Gravity, Dan Price was earning around $1m a year, about 25 times more than the lowest-paid employee (who earned $36,000). Not only did Price say that it was difficult for the lowest-paid to live on $36,000 (approximately £23,275), but the gap between rich and poor was too high. As we will see in Chapter 17, this interest in inequality has been reflected more broadly, with critical theorists arguing that the importance of chief executive officers is overestimated and their pay is disproportionate for what they do. Critics of high executive pay argue that these executives are paid, on average, some 120 times more than their employees, 35 times more than hospital consultants and 162 times more than the average teacher (High Pay Commission, 2011). This gap between rich and poor creates higher levels of crime and even health problems (Wilkinson and Pickett, 2010). One possible solution to this issue is being tried in the USA, where companies are going to be forced to disclose the gap between the pay of CEOs and the rest of the workforce (Kasperkevic, 2015).

An alternative perspective argues that while Dan Price's position might be seen as a noble gesture, it is not a sustainable one. This perspective argues that getting high-quality senior managers is a significant challenge and, as we will see in Chapter 12, many leadership theories see the CEO as vital to increasing the long-term profits of the company. It is often argued there is a 'war for talent' (Peacock, 2010), with top people able to travel anywhere in the world; therefore, firms have to pay competitive salaries and bonus packages in order to attract and retain the best people. Furthermore, in a related argument, supporters of shareholder capitalism would argue that Dan Price did not have the right as CEO to make this decision alone because effectively he was spending shareholders' money (through the increase in wages), which was not (solely) his choice to make. Theorists such as Milton Friedman (see Chapter 17) therefore argue that it is immoral to spend shareholders' money on something just because you as a manager believe it is ethical.

## Motivation

Dan Price makes an interesting claim that having a minimum wage of around £45,000 will increase motivation and customer service. One argument drawn from psychology and behavioural economics, particularly the work of Daniel Kahneman, is that increases in feelings of well-being only continue up until around £48,000, and therefore a salary of this level will produce the maximum well-being for everyone.

However, does pay increase motivation? As we will see in Chapter 9, the link between pay and motivation is a highly controversial area. Indeed, it could be argued that far from increasing motivation, it might demotivate. This can be explained by Adams's Equity Theory (Adams, 1963), which argues that individuals will calculate the ratio of their inputs (time, effort, and skill) against the outputs (e.g. pay, job security). People compare their ratio of inputs to outputs with those of others, and if they feel someone is receiving greater levels of output in relation to their input then this will cause dissatisfaction. Therefore, highly skilled Gravity employees might experience the change as unfair because even though they received an increase in their wages, it was a smaller increase than the less skilled workers were receiving in proportion to their skill level.

As we have seen, many of the issues that organizational behaviour investigates are contested on grounds of either morality ('it is wrong to have too large a gap between rich and poor' versus 'it is wrong to spend shareholders' money') or effectiveness ('increasing satisfaction will increase productivity' versus 'the new wage structure will increase feelings of inequity between skill and wages'). Ultimately authors will take different positions on these debates because they hold fundamentally different assumptions about the world. Your job, therefore, in conducting this analysis is to understand these underlying assumptions first and then make a judgement based upon them. It is only by actually understanding these assumptions that it is possible to really make a judgement on the validity of the positions that theorists hold.

## The importance of analysis

It would be easy to read the preceding section and think 'well, anything goes in this subject. If there are no right answers, then it is just about opinion and all I need to do is put forward my opinion, as it is as valid as anyone else's.' While tempting, we believe such a perspective is dangerous for a number of reasons. Firstly, the ideas developed in this book are based upon years of research built up through numerous investigations, theoretical reflections, and analysis, and argued through many lectures, articles, and books. They are, therefore, more than simply opinions: they are built on reasoned arguments and investigations into actual practice. Secondly, they draw on (as we have seen in the preceding section) a variety of different underlying perspectives that are built on deep theoretical foundations. These are more than simply personal opinions or gut reactions, but reasoned arguments based on fundamentally different ways of thinking about and discussing the world. Finally, as we will explore in more detail in the following sections, these perspectives are built on wider theoretical reflections about the nature of societies and the roles that organizations should play in them.

## Study skills: the difference between personal opinion and an academically-informed perspective

My opinion

- uses my own taken-for-granted assumptions
- is based on gut reaction and personal opinion
- may often contain sentences such as 'I think that . . .'

An academically-informed perspective

- challenges received opinion and taken-for-granted assumptions
- is based on theoretical reasoning, evidence, academic literature, and evaluation of competing perspectives
- is based on the evidence
- may often contain sentences such as 'Research shows that . . .'

Therefore, while at first glance informed critical analysis might seem like simply stating your own opinion, in practice developing an academically-informed perspective is more rigorous, thoughtful, and evidence-based. While your personal opinion might, therefore, be a starting point, it begins with common-sense assumptions rather than evidence and theory and so you should be prepared to reconsider these views. Indeed, often the best essays are by students who have changed their view on a subject having read and really engaged with the academic arguments.

Because there are no set answers, we sometimes call this approach a 'contested' view. There are multiple perspectives because the issues that we are interested in cannot be 'solved' in any straightforward way and, consequently, it is an area of constant debate. The skill of a good analyst is to uncover these underlying assumptions and to see how they inform the research and how this perspective differs from alternatives. One of the central study skills that you will need throughout your time studying OB (and at university as a whole) is to be able to uncover the key underlying assumptions that inform the theories.

## The need to develop critical thinking

Developing your critical thinking skills is a long-term process of acquiring skills and also a mindset of approaching the world in a different way. As we can see from the real life case here, such an approach can be highly beneficial as it helps you to think more deeply and to be more innovative—something that employers throughout the world are increasingly looking for.

---

**Real life case:** innovative thinking in Singapore

In recent years the education systems of Singapore and China have come under increasing attention. Both countries have been praised for heading up the international league tables, with fifteen-year-old students from Singapore, South Korea, Japan, Hong Kong, and Shanghai around ten months ahead of UK students in English (Barber, 2012). This success is attributed to a highly-scripted teaching style and high levels of discipline and commitment from the students.

On the other hand, the focus on always being right and finding the right answers is increasingly being criticized in countries such as Singapore, who are actually changing their education approach (Ng, 2014). While for a long time their approach has been hugely successful in attracting multinational firms and making the country prosperous because 'Singaporeans are hardworking, loyal, and well-educated' (Economy Watch, 2011a), as the economy has developed questions are increasingly being raised about Singaporeans' ability to undertake more creative and innovative jobs. Recently, Steve Wozniak (Apple's co-founder) suggested that a rigid education system could stifle creativity and innovation: 'Singapore, teachers and employers are caught up with "the right answer," instead of the journey to get there and the creative solutions to other problems.' Wozniak's statement suggests that their education system, which praises students when they get the right answers, is, therefore, less able to prepare them for the more innovative thinking that creative jobs require. Being innovative and being able to solve complex problems (which people often produce) requires the ability to be prepared to think differently, to question one's assumptions, and to cope with uncertainty and doubt.

One of us (Daniel) discovered this when teaching in Singapore. At the end of a week of intensive teaching of OB to a group of Singaporean undergraduates, one of them came over to say that they both loved and hated the course. It made them think differently and question what they knew, and at the same time made them feel uncertainty and doubt. Studying OB can get us all to feel this way.

**Source:** Economy Watch (2011a, 2011b).

---

## So how do I develop critical thinking skills?

Teaching yourself to question things and also to learn in a different way can be a difficult, but exciting, process. At university your lecturers will want you to demonstrate a higher level of critical analysis than you may have encountered before and also a different approach to thinking. Rather than simply recounting the strengths and weaknesses of particular theories, they will be expecting you to look at the wider implications for our understanding of broader issues in society. This requires deeper thinking and engagement, opening yourself up to competing perspectives and interpretations of the world, and a readiness to engage in complex ideas. This can be particularly challenging given that, on the surface, OB seems little more than 'common sense'.

One example of the value of critical and analytical thinking is that it encourages us to go beyond these general assumptions to really examine the implications of these theories, not just for management practice but for society as well. This moves us to ask not only pragmatic questions, such as how things are done, but also wider ones, such as in whose interest they are conducted. This requires alternative ways of thinking.

---

**Real life case:** thinking outside the box

One of our students describes how she has struggled with wanting to find the *right* answer.

> I am a bit of a perfectionist really and I want to know the answers. At A-level I studied History—where there were a lot of dates and facts, Law—where there were many cases, and Business (where there was a lot of accounting)—where there were right answers. At university, studying organizational behaviour, I have realized that there are no right answers and I need to think outside the box.

---

You might find studying OB difficult and challenging, particularly if you come from a scientific or mathematics background, which tend to have 'correct' and 'true' answers. For many students, this desire for the right answers and anxiety about getting the wrong answer leads them to want to memorize and learn facts about theories, as these seem more certain and understandable. For instance, we have seen countless students put in details about when key theorists were born and when they died, or long descriptions of a theory, presumably believing this is the 'correct information'. However, it demonstrates very little understanding and often has a negative impact on their grade.

To really develop critical thinking requires asking different types of questions and focusing on different areas (Figure 1.4).

At the surface level is **description** (Figure 1.5). At this level you simply describe the theory, giving details of what it is, how it works, and its basic concepts. You will discuss the basic facts, models, or theories, and you will need to show familiarity with the theories, but little more. However, this level largely involves repeating back the theory. You do not need to do much thinking as you are merely reproducing what you have been told in lectures or in this book. You need this level as it is the foundation for the subject, but you need to remember that it is not enough at degree level.

**Description** A piece of writing that describes the theory or case study with little attempt at providing analysis. Often considered more superficial and therefore in student coursework results in lower grades.

| Description | Recalling and describing the theory: multiple choice questions, facts, recall, definitions, and models |
| Explanation | Applying to real life and own experience, and what the theory means for organizations in practice |
| Analysis | Considering strengths and weaknesses, exploring alternative viewpoints and the underlying assumptions |
| Critical analysis | How the theory challenges our fundamental understanding of OB. In whose interest is the theory? |

**Figure 1.4** Levels of critical thinking.

**Figure 1.5** The critical thinking iceberg.

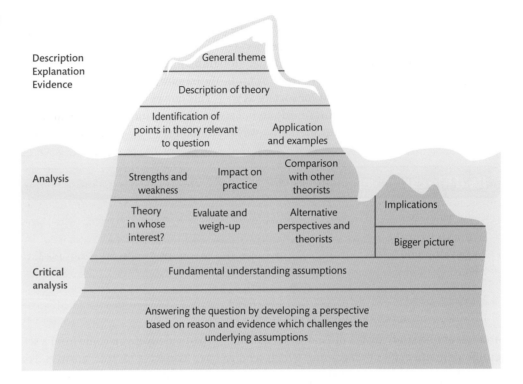

Description
Explanation
Evidence

General theme

Description of theory

Identification of points in theory relevant to question

Application and examples

Analysis

Strengths and weakness

Impact on practice

Comparison with other theorists

Theory in whose interest?

Evaluate and weigh-up

Alternative perspectives and theorists

Implications

Bigger picture

Critical analysis

Fundamental understanding assumptions

Answering the question by developing a perspective based on reason and evidence which challenges the underlying assumptions

**Explanation** In academic writing, the ability to explain a theory or perspective.

**Evidence** In academic writing, support for claims made.

The next level down is **explanation**, comprehension, and **evidence**. At this level you show that you really understand the theory and its relevance to the question and to real life practice. To do this you can apply the theory to an organization and show the implications for organizational practice. You can also identify the relevant points of the theory to the actual question asked. This shows a far deeper level of understanding, as it takes a stronger appreciation of what the theory entails in order to apply it to practice.

Within this level is also the application of theory. This is where you link what you have learned to actual organizational examples. In this book, this might either be to real life examples or to examples from the Junction Hotel running case. The idea here is to show that theories are not simply words on a page. They are tools that can both explain what happens in real life organizations and, furthermore, make recommendations for how organizations might solve particular management issues.

Application is based on what you know about the theories, including their strengths and weaknesses. For example, in Chapter 3 we introduce Taylorism, which outlines a way of designing work to make it more efficient. We sometimes ask our students to apply this to our running case. A very simplistic answer that we often hear is that 'Junction Hotel should introduce Taylorism because it would increase efficiency'. This is too simplistic and vague—it isn't good enough as an answer. Imagine if you presented something like this to a board of a company. They would rightly ask questions like 'how would it increase efficiency in our organization specifically?', 'what problems might its implementation cause for us?', or 'can you show evidence that it has worked in similar organizations?' Applying a theory thus moves from talking about general theoretical ideas to presenting them in the context of a specific organizational setting.

While this level shows a greater level of insight, it does little to question the assumptions that underpin the theories. It simply takes things for granted and does not show the deeper level of thinking that is necessary to make judgements about a theme.

Dropping below the surface is where we begin to **analyse** the theory. This level looks at the theory's strengths and weaknesses, identifying the advantages and disadvantages of the theory or the benefits and drawbacks that the theory offers. This form of analysis is common at post-16 qualifications (e.g. A-level) and demonstrates a stronger appreciation of the theory itself and how it works in practice.

The deepest level of **critical analysis** includes synthesis, comparison, evaluation, and creativity. It requires a much higher level of thinking because it does not merely assume that the theory is correct but looks as much at what the author does not say and who it impacts. Because of its greater complexity and more advanced level of understanding, this approach often gets higher marks. To achieve this you need to really understand the theory and its implications, read between the lines, and not accept things at face value but question everything. This also involves judgement, weighing-up of the relative merits of the theory, and then drawing conclusions to see if the perspective offered is fair and valid.

To develop your critical thinking, the following questions are useful when reading academic theory:

- What are its strengths and weaknesses?
- How does it compare with other theories?
- What evidence is it based on and is it reliable?
- What are the implications of the theory for practice?
- What are the underlying assumptions?
- Whose interest does it serve?
- What is its implication for answering the question?

As we can see, to really get to the heart of the issue and understand its significance we need to go beyond merely describing a theory and seek to understand its underlying assumptions.

Throughout this book are questions to get you thinking. 'Stop and think' questions appear throughout the chapters. They invite you to reflect on what you have just read and to put it in the context of your own thoughts and experiences. There are also review questions within the chapters. These have been structured to take your thoughts from simple description (at the top of the critical thinking iceberg) towards much deeper levels of critical analysis, which will be useful in your essays and exams. These review questions have been labelled 'describe', 'explain', 'analyse', and 'apply', as outlined in Table 1.1.

**Analyse** Widely associated with deeper intellectual thinking, it is the process of breaking things down into their constituent parts, investigating the underlying cause or basic principles.

**Critical analysis** To question the underlying assumptions of a perspective. In OB this may have particular emphasis on how power and inequality occur.

Table 1.1   The structure of the review questions

| | |
| --- | --- |
| **Describe** | These are the most basic questions. They invite you to recall and describe theory, providing basic facts, definitions, and models. |
| **Explain** | These go beyond basic definitions, explaining what theories actually mean, or why they are important for the study of organizations and management. |
| **Analyse** | Here you are invited to go much deeper, considering the strengths and weaknesses of theories, exploring alternative viewpoints and underlying assumptions, and showing how theories may have challenged existing and widely accepted viewpoints. |
| **Apply** | Here you are comparing theory with organizational examples, from both real life cases and the Junction Hotel running case. You may be asked to find evidence of theories in these examples, or even act as a consultant and make recommendations to organizations based on the theory that you have learned. |

# Degree-level analysis

Throughout this discussion you may have thought that much of this talk of analysis is familiar to you, as you have heard the terms 'analysis', 'evaluation', and 'application'. While post-16 (A-level) uses these terms, we require deeper and more engaged thinking to do well at degree level.

For instance, at post-16 analysis often consists of describing the strengths and weaknesses of a particular theory, and may compare it to other theories; at university, we are after a deeper examination of the implications of the theory to the fundamental assumptions of the discipline. Table 1.2 summarizes these differences.

Ultimately, at degree level, the emphasis for answers in essays and exams is on making an argument, based on theory, which responds directly to the question asked.

---

**Real life case:** making the transition to degree-level analysis

Having recently received back comments on her assignment for her OB module, one of our students has come to realize that the type of analysis required at degree level is deeper than she had previously been asked to do for A-level. 'Having read the assignment I thought that I was doing analysis by listing the strengths and weaknesses as we were asked to do at A-level. I now see that this was only part of what analysing means and you want us to think a lot deeper at degree level.'

The central intention here is that you will become independent critical thinkers who are able to develop arguments through critical analysis of others' positions.

---

Table 1.2  The differences between post-16 and degree thinking

|  | Post-16 | Degree level |
|---|---|---|
| How you use the theory | Reproduce material taught and show you understand which theorists are relevant | Digest the material and demonstrate understanding of its implications |
| What markers are looking for | Correct answers to hit the mark scheme | A critical response to the literature |
| Use of theory | Show understanding of the theory and both sides of the argument | Making an argument by writing within a school of thought, using accepted concepts and theoretical tools |
| Analysis is | Strengths and weaknesses of a theory | Questioning the underlying assumptions and their implications for the question |
| Evaluation is | Demonstrating understanding, comparing and weighing-up of both sides of the argument | Poviding own response to the question based on the theories in question |
| Material used | Given specific texts to investigate | Go out and undertake your own research |
| Paragraph structure | Key points, quote to back up, and then evaluate | Links together to make an overall argument that fully answers the question |

# Critical thinking: mainstream and critical views

Critical thinking can also mean a political view that asks you to question the underlying assumptions and values of theories for the purposes of understanding and challenging their impact on society—e.g. workers, the environment—and that is seen in opposition to mainstream theory. (Used in this sense, this is often called the 'critical management studies perspective'.)

The **mainstream**, or dominant view, represents the general established thinking about management. It is primarily interested in creating theory that helps to understand management practice better and generally to improve it. The mainstream perspective assumes that organizations exist to make profit and that the goal of management theory is to achieve performance, efficiency, productivity, order, and control. Furthermore, it supports hierarchy, managers' right to manage, and the idea that firms exist primarily for shareholders.

**Mainstream** The dominant or accepted view that emphasizes managers' right to manage and the central objective of organizations to make profits for shareholders.

The **critical** view argues that these mainstream views systematically favour elite interests at the expense of disadvantaged groups, for instance managers over workers; men over women; profit over society; and economic growth over the environment—arguing that this limits freedom of all (Grey and Willmott, 2005). The critical perspective suggests that there is a 'dark side' to organizations that these mainstream accounts rarely discuss.

**Critical** (as in 'critical management studies') A critical perspective, among other things, draws on Marxist theory and seeks to challenge the assumptions of mainstream management theory by stressing the impact that it has on employees and society.

While the critical perspective might seem negative, its proponents would argue that it is aiming at a more positive society. The critical perspective argues that organizations should exist for freedom and fulfilment, creativity and expression, and for the benefit of society, not just for shareholders. Critical perspectives therefore aim for emancipation (freedom from slavery). This form of critical thinking can be hard—it challenges many of our basic assumptions of the world—but it can also be highly transformative.

For whose benefit should the theory of OB be written? Management? Shareholders? Employees? Customers/Clients? Society?

---

**Study skills:** questioning taken-for-granted assumptions

When reading a theory, instead of taking the ideas for granted, the following questions can give you a more critical perspective.

- What are the underlying perspectives presented in the text?
- What are the taken-for-granted assumptions contained (but not expressed) in the theory?
- Whose interests are being served by this perspective?
- What issues are being glossed over or downplayed?
- What are the implications for power and control?
- What are the effects of the theory on people, society, and the planet?
- What other perspectives have been downplayed or ignored by this theory?

## Employability skills: the importance of critical thinking

Most people who study business and management degrees do get a job. Yet often we do not really consider what we need to do in order to achieve this. As an employer has stated in a fairly recent report: 'Academic qualifications are the first tick in the box and then we move on. Today we simply take them for granted' (Brown et al., 2003: 120). Therefore, while getting a good degree is essential, on its own—in this increasingly competitive market—it is not enough.

So, what is it that employers are looking for? While there can never be a definitive list, some of the common requirements of graduate recruiters are:

- professionalism or work ethic
- oral and written communication skills
- teamwork and collaboration skills
- critical-thinking or problem-solving skills
- generic skills rather than subject-specific skills
- abstraction (theorizing; using models, metaphors, and formulae)
- systems thinking (seeing the part in the context of the wider whole)
- experimentation (intuition and analysis)
- collaboration (communication and teamwork skills)                    Reich (1991, 2002)

You might be reading this and be thinking, 'but I have just got to university—why should I be thinking about this now?' Our experience, having been students ourselves and talking to thousands of students through teaching, is that your time at university goes by very quickly. While the next three or four years may seem a long way off, this time will fly by and you will wonder what you did with your time at university. Our key advice is that you start thinking about which skills you can improve now. You will find that your first year will pass very quickly and you will miss a golden opportunity that this first year at university presents: to begin to acquire the skills, experiences, knowledge, and self-awareness that will help develop you as a person and as a future employee. There are countless things that you could be doing to boost your experiences so that you are a step ahead when it comes to getting a job.

So how do you start building your employability? Throughout this book we will have a number of employability prompts to get you started thinking about these issues. You should then follow them up with material found in the Online Resource Centre, which will point you in the direction of further reading, activities, and advice that will enable you to construct your CV and gain skills and experience to help you get ahead. These include:

- self-test questionnaires
- video interviews with employers, students, and recent graduates
- employability tips
  —things to be thinking about now
  —short exercises to do now
- much more advice, and pointers to other websites and material.

# The links between study skills and employability skills

While we often think that the skills we need to study are different from those that we will use in a work situation, the links between the two are surprisingly similar, as we can see in Table 1.3.

Therefore, as you go through your university career it is valuable to develop these study skills as they are often transferrable to a work situation.

Table 1.3 The similarities between study skills and employability skills

| | Study skill | Employability skill |
|---|---|---|
| Time-management | Many assignments due at the same time A lot of study time and therefore personal responsibility Juggling paid employment, studying, clubs and societies, and personal responsibilities | Working on numerous projects in which you have to manage your own time and that of others |
| Synthesis of a lot of complex information | Reading dozens of academic articles and pulling out the key themes, arguments, and positions of the authors | Reading numerous reports, background briefings, and market research, and being asked to make sense of them |
| Working with ambiguous briefs | Getting an assignment brief and needing to work out what you need to do to get a good grade | Being given a loosely-defined task and be told to 'get on with it' |
| Writing for different audiences | Studying different modules with their various approaches to academic work such as referencing, analysis, and styles | Writing for different managers, for your staff, and to clients—all of which have different requirements |

Visit the Online Resource Centre for more information on transferable skills.

**Employability and study skills:** keeping a journal with evidence and examples of the skills you have developed at university and outside, and a diary to reflect on what you are learning

When you apply for most graduate jobs you will need to fill in an application form which will ask you for *evidence* that you have hit a number of requirements, such as teamwork, taking initiative, or project management. One way that you can significantly improve your chances is to keep a record of *actual examples* of you meeting any of these criteria. This could be through assignments at university—teamwork, working with different nationalities; or external activities, such as being involved in the football club (planning and organizing as you arrange matches and transport).

Studying OB is particularly useful in this regard, as the subject matter deals with many of the key skill areas that you will need at work. Therefore, as you read on topics such as motivation, leadership, and teamwork, consider your own experiences and how you can demonstrate examples of actual practice.

Throughout this book we will also offer study skills that give you opportunities to develop your abilities as a student. As you go through your course, it is really helpful to keep a diary in which you can honestly and openly reflect on what you would like to achieve in your working life and how you would like to get there.

# Chapter summary

## Running case: the day draws to a close

### Simon Chance's office (5.50 pm)

As early evening approaches, Simon Chance opens his diary and starts making a few notes to himself about his reflections on his first full day at Junction Hotel. The staff seemed friendly and generally professional, and seemed to take the meeting well. That chef, though (Effingham, he thinks he's called), looked a bit of a livewire and will need keeping an eye on. Everything here feels slightly chaotic, unmanageable even, Chance considers. Everyone goes about their jobs OK, but from where he is sitting they are not working effectively. It will take some doing to kick this lot into shape.

### The bar (10.00 pm)

As the kitchen staff's shift ends, Effingham, Josh, and Toby are sitting round the bar enjoying their evening 'nightcap'. 'What do you think about this new owner?' Josh asks Effingham. Effingham snorts, 'Same old management clap-trap, if you ask me. They come out with all these phrases and buzz words, "blue sky thinking, A3s, gold standard customer service", but they don't have a clue what it's really like.' Toby butts in, 'Yeah, I'd love to see him prepping for evening service or doing the breakfast run, then tell me all that management speak really means anything.' 'Yes,' Josh smiles, 'it's us who run the show really.'

As we have seen, organizations are fundamentally about people, and people can be complex and make organizational life messy. Rather than being rational and logical places, as we often like to believe, they can be full of emotion—pain, joy, excitement, disappointment, hope, fear, and anxiety—competing ambitions, and different perspectives. In view of this, instead of seeing the theories as abstract and separate from real life, OB is best understood by relating and applying it to concrete experience and practice. Our running case study, Junction Hotel, will give you an insight into how theories can play out in practice.

To sum up, there are no right answers within OB as it is a subjective discipline, born out of various theoretical disciplines and subject to different social and political perspectives. Therefore, to study OB effectively requires critical thinking and questioning: the ability to understand different perspectives and to seek to challenge your own assumptions.

It is also heavily linked to real practice. The employability and study skills therefore bring some of these issues to life as you develop your abilities for your university and employment career. Keeping a diary and working through the exercises in the book and the Online Resource Centre will help you to maximize your experience and gain a fuller understanding of the subject.

## Further reading

**Cottrell, S. 2011.** *Critical thinking skills: Developing effective analysis and argument.* **Palgrave Macmillan: Basingstoke.**
This popular study skills book gives some really useful material on the importance of critical thinking and offers practical, as well as theoretical, ideas on how to improve in this area. Reading this will be useful, not only in studying this subject but also to other subjects on your degree course.

**Bowell, T., and Kemp, G. 2002.** *Critical thinking: A concise guide.* **Routledge: London.**
Another popular study skills book that stresses how to develop and build arguments. It looks at how to assess the strengths of an argument and how to develop your own.

**Gallagher, K. 2010.** *Skills development for business and management students.* **Oxford University Press: Oxford.**
This study skills guide provides useful ideas on how to develop your all-round skills as a business and management student, including teamwork, presentation, and reading skills.

## References

Adams, J.S. 1963. Towards an understanding of inequity. *Journal of Abnormal and Social Psychology* 67 (5): 422.

Barber, M. 2012. Lessons on education from Singapore. *The Guardian*, 22 August.

Belbin, R.M. 2010. *Team roles at work.* Butterworth-Heinemann: Oxford.

Braverman, H. 1974. *Labor and monopoly capital: The degradation of work in the twentieth century.* Monthly Review Press: New York.

Brown, P., Hesketh, A., and Williams, S. 2003. Employability in a knowledge-driven economy. *Journal of Education and Work* 16 (2): 107–26.

Cohen, P. 2015a. One company's new minimum wage: $70,000 a year. *New York Times*, 13 April.

Cohen, P. 2015b. A company copes with backlash against the raise that roared. *New York Times*, 31 July.

Economy Watch 2011a. The trouble with the Singapore workplace. Available at: http://www.economywatch.com/economy-business-and-finance-news/the-trouble-with-the-singapore-workplace.21-07.html (last accessed 26 August 2015).

Economy Watch 2011b. Would Apple ever have been created in Singapore? Available at: http://www.economywatch.com/economy-business-and-finance-news/would-apple-ever-have-been-created-in-singapore.10-03.html (last accessed 30 July 2015).

Elkins, K. 2015. How one employee felt when the CEO announced her salary would double to $70,000 a year. *Business Insider*, 30 April.

Gravity Payment. 2015. Work with U. Available at: http://gravitypayments.com/about (last accessed 5 August 2015).

Grey, C., and Willmott, H. 2005. *Critical management studies.* Oxford University Press: Oxford.

High Pay Commission 2011. *Cheques with balances: Why tackling high pay is in the national interest.* Final report of the High Pay Commission.

Hofstede, G.H. 1980. *Culture's consequences: International differences in work-related values.* Sage Publications: Beverly Hills, CA.

Kahneman, D. and Deaton, A. 2010. High income improves evaluation of life but not emotional well-being. *Proceedings of the National Academy of Sciences* 107 (38): 16489–93.

Kasperkevic, J. 2015. Companies forced to disclose CEO-workforce pay gap. *The Guardian*, 5 August.

Maslow, A.H. 1943. A theory of human motivation. *Psychological Review* 50 (4): 370.

Mayo, E. 1949. *The social problems of an industrial civilisation.* Routledge: London.

Ng, J. 2014. The impact of children's learning during a curriculum reform in Singapore. *International Research in Early Childhood Education* 5 (1): 11–26.

Peacock, L. 2010. War for talent resumes as salaries climb. *Daily Telegraph*, 5 August.

Reich, R. 1991. *The work of nations.* Simon and Schuster: London.

Reich, R. 2002. *The future of success.* Vintage: London.

Ritzer, G. 2015. *The McDonaldization of society*, 8th edn. Sage: Thousand Oaks, CA.

Taylor, F.W. 1911. *The principles of scientific management.* Harper: New York.

Torabi, F. 2015. Why this CEO pays every employee $70,000 a year. *Time Magazine*, 23 April.

Wilkinson, R. and Pickett, K. 2010. *The spirit level: Why equality is better for everyone.* Penguin Books: London.

# Part 1
## The rational organization

# Rational organizational design and bureaucracy

*From direct to impersonal control*

## Chapter overview and learning outcomes

By the end of this chapter you should be able to:

- describe the main features of bureaucratic organization
- explain how bureaucracy is a form of rational organizational design that helps managers to control organizations as they grow in size
- analyse the negative effects of bureaucracy that Weber described as an 'iron cage'

- describe dysfunctions of bureaucracy, such as red tape and the bureaucratic personality
- analyse the balance between the positive effects of bureaucracy that make large-scale organization possible, and its dysfunctions and negative effects.

## Key theorists

| | |
|---|---|
| Max Weber | A sociologist who observed the increasing dominance of bureaucracy within society, noting its technical achievements but also its negative impacts on people |
| Henri Fayol | An industrialist known for outlining a rational, structured approach to bureaucratic organizational design and administration |

## Key terms

| | |
|---|---|
| Bureaucracy | Official aspects of an organization, such as the hierarchical structure, rules, procedures, and paperwork which allow control to be exerted over the whole organization |
| Rational organizational design | As championed by Fayol, the design of bureaucratic features in the most technically efficient way so as to achieve the organization's goals |
| Iron cage of bureaucracy | A phrase which summarizes Weber's critique of bureaucracy and rationality, suggesting that it is inescapable and leads to monotonous, dull routines |

# Introduction

**Running case:** 'a disorganized mess'

Simon Chance likes order and being in charge, but after a week with the management team he has inherited after taking over at Junction Hotel, he feels frustrated. 'This place is a disorganized mess,' he thinks to himself. 'No one seems to know what they are doing—it's unmanageable.'

The lack of formal organization is highlighted when Chance asks Meg Mortimer, the general manager, for an organization chart. 'Organization chart?' she says with a surprised tone. 'No, we don't have one of those. I know everyone here personally and we work together as a friendly little group.'

Mortimer has been at the hotel for over twenty-five years, from when it was a small organization. Although the hotel has grown and new staff have been taken on, she still tries to manage with a personal touch, as if it were still a small group of staff.

Chance soon realizes, however, that Mortimer delegates much of the hands-on management to her deputy, Linda Wilkinson. Wilkinson's role has grown over the years to include responsibility for the reception area, the cleaners, the waiting staff, the maintenance staff, and the fitness centre employees. Wilkinson also processes stock orders and similar paperwork—something she generally does in a rush whenever she finds some time.

While concerned about Wilkinson's workload, Chance also notes that Mortimer can't resist interfering in these everyday decisions, particularly with 'her girls': the cleaners and the reception staff. 'I know their jobs inside out,' Mortimer explains. 'I used to be a cleaner and was the main receptionist here for years!'

Chance decides to speak to Linda Wilkinson, who seems a little stressed. 'I feel sometimes that I run the place on my own—it's a lot for one person to do.' Chance presses her on Mortimer's interference: 'Meg feels that she needs to be involved in everything,' Wilkinson continues. 'Don't get the impression I don't value her input, but sometimes I would like to be left alone to get on with it.'

Chance notes that Wilkinson becomes more stressed when the conversation turns to the restaurant staff. 'The waiters are supposed to be managed by me. However, Graham Effingham . . . well, he thinks they work for him.'

Head chef Graham Effingham confirms the confusion over restaurant roles.

> I have official control over the chefs, but not the waiters. What's the point in that, especially when Linda is so overworked already? So, I tell the waiters what to do anyway—it gets the job done. Sometimes they don't like it and they go moaning to Linda when I shout at them, but needs must. They must be confused about who exactly is their boss, though. I wish I could just run the whole restaurant without any outside interference.

Chance starts to feel that things don't run as smoothly as Mortimer has suggested, sensing further problems with the role of David Hunter. Hunter, an old friend of Mortimer's, works part-time maintaining the company accounts. Mortimer often confides in Hunter and trusts his advice—he often chips in with his thoughts on running the reception area and procedures for stock ordering. 'To be honest,' chortles Hunter, 'who gets bonuses and pay rises is pretty much on my say-so.' Again, Wilkinson resents this interference in her work.

While Mortimer's presence seems to hold the hotel together, Chance can't help thinking that there are simmering tensions, many caused by a lack of a clear structure, with blurred roles and responsibilities. Furthermore, there is a lack of clear rules and procedures, and paperwork in the files is far from ordered. While Mortimer gives the hotel a veneer of being well-organized and managed, underneath the surface it is ad hoc and dysfunctional.

With a meeting with his team of investors imminent, and a clear instruction from them to get a grip on the hotel and make it profitable, Chance realizes that he needs to bring some coherent management and organization to the hotel.

# Control: From small- to large-scale organizations

It may seem like a statement of the obvious, but organizations need to be managed and organized in order to function effectively. Organizations are meant to be orderly places, in which managers at the top are in charge and staff do what is required of them—anything other than this may be seen as *dis*organized.

French industrialist Henri Fayol was one of the people who laid the foundations for our common-sense view of what orderly managing and organizing entails. Fayol (1949) provides a useful initial definition of the five main functions that managers perform, set out in Table 2.1. Many of Fayol's functions of management involve the management of people. In a small-scale organization, this can be done on a direct, personal, face-to-face basis by the owner in direct conversation with the workforce. This is the case with many organizations that we encounter regularly—the convenience store, the car workshop, the local café, the typical hairdressing salon, all usually small-scale, independent organizations with a handful of employees.

Managing this small group is done informally, performed daily on a face-to-face basis. It is a highly personal style of management. The owner will know all employees personally and by name. Rotas, holidays, and similar scheduling tasks will be sorted out in conversation and by informal negotiation between the owner and the team. The owner will know the personalities and characteristics of their staff, knowing who to reward as a good worker and, likewise, who might need a quiet telling-off from time to time. This personal style of management might work for a small enterprise with a handful of employees, but what if became successful and opened a second branch, then a third and a fourth? What if it grew to 100 employees, or 1,000, or even became a multinational enterprise employing tens of thousands of people across different continents? Could this personal style of management still be maintained? Coping with the size of a larger organization increases the need for greater forms of control.

Informal management in a hairdressing salon.

Table 2.1  Fayol's five functions of management (1949)

| | |
|---|---|
| Planning/forecasting | Looking to the future, trying to calculate and predict future circumstances (such as demand, competitors, etc.), and acting so as to be able to respond to this |
| Organizing | Building up the necessary structures, resources, and people to best meet the needs and goals of the organization |
| Coordinating | Bringing together the structure, human, and resource elements of the organization to act in harmony and towards the goals of the organization |
| Commanding | Giving orders and directions to people within the organization to maintain activity towards achieving the organization's goals |
| Controlling | Checking and inspecting work—monitoring and surveillance of work done rather than direct command |

**Real life case:** from small beginnings

Many of the large-scale and multinational companies that we know today began as small enterprises with a handful of employees; indeed, these humble origins are often presented as part of the history and folklore of these organizations. For example, Greggs the Bakers, which now has 1,600 stores in the UK, began as a single store in north-east England in the 1950s (Greggs, 2015). The UK-wide department store John Lewis, which currently has 90,000 employees (John Lewis, 2015), started out as a single drapery shop on London's Oxford Street in the 1860s (Butler, 2014). Aldi, the German multinational budget supermarket chain, is family-owned business which started with a single store run by the Albrecht family in Essen, Germany, in 1940 (Ruddick, 2013).

How do you think these well-known large-scale organizations have had to change and adapt their management styles as they have grown over the years from small-scale, single-branch companies?

Direct control  Face-to-face control of workers by a manager or owner.

Impersonal control  Control of workers that is not done face to face, for example through delegation or through rules and procedures.

Rational organizational design  The design of organizational structures and activities in order to achieve the organization's goals in the most technically efficient manner. Rational organization suggests an organization which is designed logically and systematically, even scientifically, so as to achieve its aims.

Bureaucracy  From the French *bureau*, meaning office; bureaucracy covers official, formal elements of rational organizational design, such as the hierarchical organization structure, the rules and procedures, and the official paperwork, which exert impersonal control over the organization.

The larger an organization becomes, employing more and more people, the more difficult it is to manage and organize in a personal, informal style. **Direct control** by one individual owner/manager at the top of the organization is no longer possible—the organization would become unmanageable and disorganized. This chapter examines how, as an organization grows in size, managers need to adopt more indirect, **impersonal control**, using, in particular, the bureaucratic structures and procedures which make up **rational organizational design**.

Rationality suggests that the structures and procedures of the organization are designed logically and methodically to achieve the organization's aims in the most efficient manner possible. Such impersonal, rational forms of organizational design and control are termed 'bureaucracy'.

## Aspects of bureaucracy

**Bureaucracy** refers to the formal structures and procedures that facilitate the management of an organization, in particular as a solution to the problem of diminishing control as an organization outgrows personal, face-to-face management.

Bureaucracy derives from the French word *bureau*, meaning 'office', and refers to what we might call the 'official' or formal side of the organization. In the following three sections of the chapter, we examine three particular aspects of bureaucracy.

- A **hierarchy**, or structure of offices, develops, with each level reporting to the level above and commanding the level below. Management is thus delegated from one level to another rather than one manager at the top trying to control the whole organization single-handedly. This hierarchy is often represented as an organization structure or chart, with each position within referred to as an **office** and the person holding the position as an official.

- Rules, procedures, and policies are instructions, usually written down, which govern activity across an organization. All officials must act in accordance with the rules, procedures, and policies that relate to the office they hold.

- Paperwork, such as forms, **records**, and timetables, is used within a bureaucratic organization to present and collate information about its people and processes in a manner that can be accessed and handled quickly and efficiently. Such paperwork makes up office work—filing, processing records, etc.—and is now done more and more through computer technology rather than using paper.

## A double-edged sword?

Elements of bureaucracy have existed for centuries, for example in the ranks and strict rules and regulations of armies (Morgan, 2006: 21) or in the hierarchical nature of religious organizations.

Visit the Online Resource Centre to see further examples of bureaucracies.

However, in the early 1900s, industrialization in the Western world saw the widespread emergence of large-scale organizations (see Thompson and McHugh, 2009: 19–27), for example the development of the factory system, as will be examined in Chapter 3. This linked with bureaucracy to create a particularly efficient form of rationalization (Ritzer, 2015: 38).

Fayol, who was managing and writing at this time, certainly saw bureaucracy as an issue of rational, technical design—achieving the optimum combination of a number of bureaucratic elements for the organization to achieve its aims. Max Weber, a sociologist writing at around the same time, also noted the technical efficiency of bureaucracy in achieving the aims of an organization, but he was critical of its effects upon humans and society. He saw it as trapping people in monotonous routines, taking away people's autonomy, and ensnaring us all in its 'iron cage' (Weber, 1968).

> **Study skills:** theory in its historical context
>
> It is useful to be able to contextualize theory—to understand the historical period that it came from and how other theories and practices developed from it. While much of the theory in this chapter developed in the early 1900s, in future chapters we draw out the relevance for contemporary organizations.
>
> Sometimes the date of publication of a text does not give the exact date of when it was written. It may refer to an edition published subsequent to the first edition, for example. Similarly, it may refer to a translation. This is the case with Fayol and Weber in this chapter. While they originally wrote in their own languages (French and German respectively) in the early 1900s, the translations into English did not appear until decades later.
>
> Thus, references to Fayol (1949) and Weber (1968), for example, refer to publication dates in the English translation rather than when the first texts were actually published. It is useful to understand the distinction between when a text is actually written and its date of publication.

The term 'bureaucracy' tends to be associated with negative connotations, such as red tape, inflexibility, and unthinking, petty officialdom. Bauman's (1989) analysis of the role of

**Hierarchy**  The levels and ranks of an organization. Any one level reports to the level immediately above and commands the level immediately below.

**Office**  A defined role within an organization.

**Records**  Information held by the organization relevant for bureaucratic functioning, including information about workers.

bureaucracy in making possible the Nazi holocaust of World War II brings out further sinister consequences of bureaucratic organization and control (see page 53).

What are your initial thoughts and reactions when you hear the word 'bureaucracy'?

We thus examine bureaucracy in the latter part of this chapter as a 'double-edged sword'. On one hand, bureaucracy allows for great achievements to take place—the large-scale organizations that we know today, and all that they achieve, would not be possible without bureaucracy. On the other hand, it brings considerable problems and dysfunctions of its own.

## Review questions

| | |
|---|---|
| **Describe** | According to Henri Fayol, what are the five main functions of management? |
| **Describe** | What are the main features of bureaucratic organization? |
| **Explain** | Why does face-to-face management become more difficult as an organization grows in size? |
| **Analyse** | What do you think is meant by the description of bureaucracy as a 'double-edged sword?' |
| **Apply** | How well do you think Fayol's five functions of management are being carried out in the Junction Hotel case? |

# Bureaucratic structure and hierarchy

## Running case: mapping the structure at Junction Hotel

Chance calls in Phil Weaver, a friend and trusted colleague from the football club that he ran. Weaver has a reputation as a fixer—his hard-headed, no-nonsense attitude is needed to bring some order and organization to the hotel. He will be seconded to work two days a week at the hotel to 'shake things up a bit'. While he will have a roving trouble-shooter role within the hotel, he will take a particular interest in the restaurant and the fitness centre, as these are areas that Chance wants to develop and make more profitable.

With Mortimer unable to provide an organization chart for the hotel, Chance and Weaver begin their work to bring organization to the hotel by sketching out the current organizational structure. As best they can, they try to show where each person fits into the structure—who reports to whom and what authority each person has. Their first attempt is shown in Figure 2.1.

Some problems are apparent immediately:

- too many chiefs at the top—there are too many levels of hierarchy with just one person occupying each level. Mortimer and Chance both seem to be running the hotel, and bringing in Weaver results in another level of management at the top.

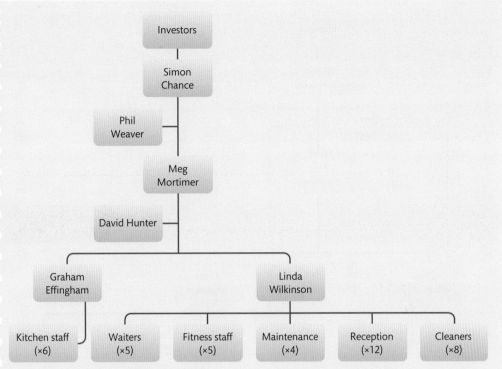

**Figure 2.1**  The current structure at Junction Hotel.

- Hunter assists Mortimer, but his actual role in the hierarchy is ill-defined—he seems to 'float around' at the side—the same can be said of the newly-introduced Weaver, who is assisting Chance.
- Linda Wilkinson seems to be overburdened with supervisory responsibility (34 people) in addition to the other tasks she performs.

While this chart outlines the official structure and associated roles and responsibilities at Junction Hotel, it doesn't tell the full story. People are acting in unofficial capacities not shown by the chart. Chance takes the original diagram and adds a series of dashed lines to show areas of control and supervision that are not officially defined, but which happen in practice (see Figure 2.2).

Mortimer intervenes regularly in the supervision of reception and cleaning staff. Hunter also tries to influence reception procedures, while Weaver now has responsibility for the development of the fitness centre. It is unsurprising that Wilkinson, although having a huge amount of official responsibility, is confused as to her exact power and authority within the hotel. This is shown with the waiting staff, in particular, where lines of authority are confused between Wilkinson and Graham Effingham. Effingham himself seems to have the future of his restaurant in the hands of Phil Weaver, even though the official organization structure suggests the restaurant is under Effingham's control.

Overall, there is a picture of confusion, with ill-defined, blurred roles and responsibilities coupled with an unevenly distributed hierarchy that is too narrow at the top and too wide at the bottom.

Chance and Weaver begin to think about restructuring the hierarchy.

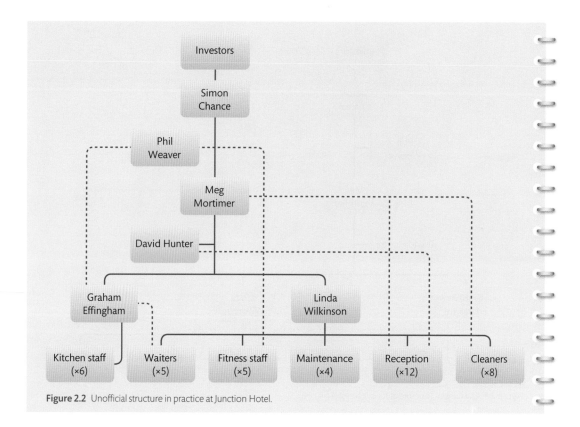

**Figure 2.2** Unofficial structure in practice at Junction Hotel.

The first element of bureaucracy that we examine is the official structure or hierarchy. A hierarchy develops as a response to the problem of maintaining control over people in an organization as it grows in size. Figure 2.3 illustrates such a situation.

The starting point is similar to the earlier examples of small-scale organizations, with a handful of employees managed directly on a face-to-face basis. But what if more employees are taken on? The organization moves to the middle position where the **span of control** of the manager—the number of employees that they supervise directly—has increased.

While a span of control of five was manageable, a much larger span of control becomes a handful, and stretches the abilities and capabilities of any one individual. Maintaining the personal relationships that existed beforehand is a lot more difficult—the manager may even be unsure of the names of some of the workers. Indiscipline and disorganization within the workforce may arise from this lack of control.

Furthermore, managing with such a large span of control is an inefficient use of a manager's time. If time is spent mired in issues of discipline and personal issues then there is little time for other aspects of managing the organization. The manager may be commanding and controlling, but how about the planning, organizing, and coordinating?

**Span of control** The number of workers controlled by a manager at any one particular level in a hierarchy.

If you were the manager of an office of 100 people, how would you command and control all of those workers on a day-to-day basis?

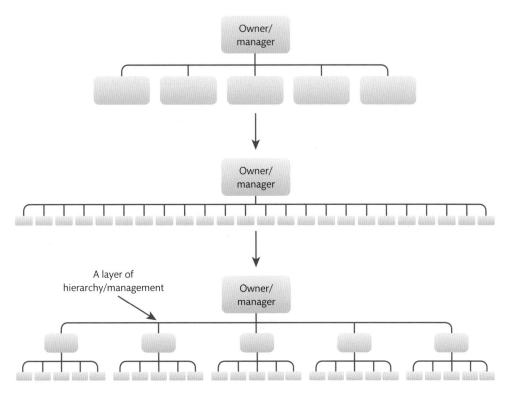

**Figure 2.3** Structure and hierarchy develop as an organization grows in size.

To solve the problem of control over a larger number of employees, managers will relinquish some of the personal, face-to-face control and instead **delegate** control through layers of management beneath them. The final part of Figure 2.3 shows the development of **organizational structure** and hierarchy:

- there is a level of management between the owner and the other workers
- day-to-day tasks, such as supervision, discipline, and calculating pay, are now delegated to the level of managers below
- commands need only be issued to managers at the level below, who will then pass the command down the hierarchy
- the owner no longer needs to even see, or have any contact with, the workers at the lower level
- the owner returns to a manageable span of control of five, as do each of the managers below.

When the span of control is too much at any one level, a further level of hierarchy can be introduced. In theory, and indeed in practice, this extension of levels of hierarchy will extend to organizations of any size. From a small factory to a multinational corporation, the principle of control through the hierarchical structure remains the same; only the number of levels differs. The larger the organization, the more levels of hierarchy will exist.

Between each of the levels in the hierarchy there is still personal, direct, face-to-face control. But, as orders and commands pass down the hierarchy, a form of control which is impersonal, indirect, and at-a-distance emerges.

**Delegate**  To pass a job, task, or order down to lower levels of a hierarchy.

**Organizational structure**  The roles and positions in an organization, often organized horizontally and vertically in the form of an organization chart diagram.

The hierarchical structure of the organization allows the owner control of the organization, albeit a form of control that now passes down through the levels of the hierarchy. It can also be seen as an efficient form of control in that the owner needs to deal only with the level of management below, freeing time for other management tasks to be performed.

## Vertical and horizontal differentiation

Vertical differentiation The process whereby a hierarchy creates a number of different layers of management within an organization.

Horizontal/functional differentiation The process whereby different parts of the hierarchy are grouped according to criteria, such as the function performed, the geographical area served, or the product or service provided.

The development of hierarchy creates **vertical differentiation**. Employees are separated and differentiated vertically from one level of the hierarchy to the next.

However, experience tells us that managers may also be differentiated by the specific responsibilities that they have within the organization. **Horizontal differentiation** occurs across the organization chart as different branches of the hierarchy are assigned different functions. Thus, horizontal differentiation is also known as functional differentiation.

Be they the head of the maths department in a school, the area sales manager for Europe in a manufacturing organization, or the director of finance for a local authority, managers are identified both by their level in the hierarchy and the specific area of the hierarchy over which they have responsibility. Horizontal differentiation might exist by:

- product, service, or area of activity—schools are organized according to subjects taught; local authorities are structured into areas for services, such as housing, social services, etc.

- specific function performed—manufacturing companies are often structured into departments for functions such as sales, marketing, production, human resources, finance, etc.

- geographical area—multinationals are structured along continental lines (e.g. European division, African division); an exporting company might be based in one country, but be structured according to the areas where it sells its products (e.g. UK sales, Scandinavian sales, etc.).

In practice most organizational structures will be a mix of these, with different means of horizontal differentiation at different levels of the vertical hierarchy. Figure 2.4 shows a

**Figure 2.4** A typical factory organization.

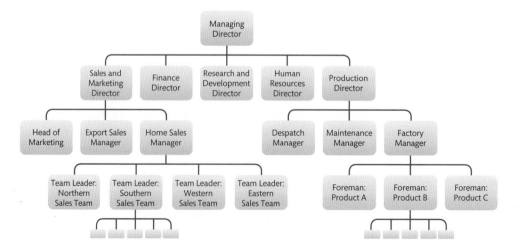

typical factory organization. Here, we see higher levels of the organization organized by function (sales and marketing, finance, etc.), home sales organized geographically (northern, southern, etc.), and the factory floor organized by product (Product A, B, C, etc.).

There is no one correct way in theory or practice in which any organization should be differentiated both horizontally and vertically. Different types of structure will be more appropriate in different circumstances.

---

**Real life case:** Telefónica's organizational structure

Telefónica is a multinational telecommunications group based in Spain. As with many multinational companies, it has a group holding company that owns and manages various national subsidiaries and divisions, some of which may even have different brand names (for example Telefónica owns national brands such as O2 in Germany and the United Kingdom and Movistar in Spain and South America). The group organizational structure shows that, beneath the Chief Executive Officer (CEO), the board level is organized both by function (e.g. group finance, group marketing, and group human resources) and by geographical areas, such as Brazil, Spain, and Germany. There are individual national divisions, which have their own particular organization structures headed by the member of the group executive board responsible for that area.

    The structure gives a clear line of command and control that can go from the CEO at the top down to an assistant in a mobile phone store in Germany or Paraguay or any of the other countries in which the company operates. While the CEO may never meet the vast majority of workers in the global organization, the structure still allows for command and control over the whole workforce.

**Sources:** Telefónica (2015); The Official Board (2015); Telefónica Deutschland (2015).

---

Visit the Online Resource Centre for a link to Telefónica's organization chart and examples of different organizational structures.

Compare the differences in the structures shown in the Online Resource Centre. Can you describe the structures using such terminology as 'span of control', 'hierarchy', 'horizontal differentiation', etc.?

# Roles and relationships

**Running case:** the new structure

A management team meeting is convened and Chance hands out a sheet of paper outlining the new structure (see Figure 2.5).

    Outlining his rationale for the new design, Chance makes the following points.

- The structure creates defined roles. Previously, people have taken on tasks because of who they were or who they knew, or had simply fallen into doing different jobs over time. Now, the role will take precedence, with staff being allocated to appropriate positions. Each role will have a written job description which will outline precisely the tasks to be performed.

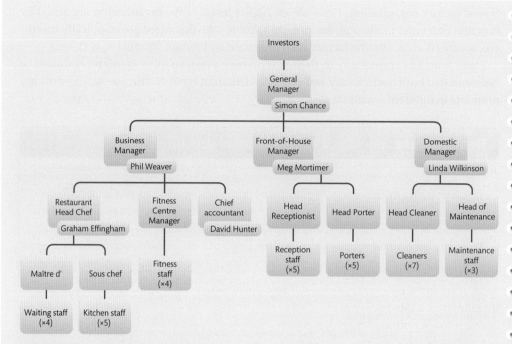

**Figure 2.5** The new structure at Junction Hotel.

- Chance will assume a more hands-on role as general manager. Beneath him, the managerial workload will be split more evenly, with new positions and levels of hierarchy being created.

- A front-of-house manager will have all responsibility for the reception area, including reception staff and porters. Given Meg Mortimer's tendency to concern herself with reception matters, she is deemed most appropriate for this role. From the receptionists and porters, there will be a promotion within each team to the positions of head receptionist and head porter, each reporting directly to Mortimer.

- Cleaners and maintenance staff will be the responsibility of a domestic manager, a role to be filled by Linda Wilkinson. Promotions within each of the two teams—cleaning and maintenance—will create another layer of hierarchy. Wilkinson will now have a definite and manageable workload. The lines of authority drawn out also mean that Mortimer no longer has a legitimate cause to interfere in the work of the cleaners.

- Phil Weaver will fill a new role of business manager, with responsibility for finance, marketing, and business development. The restaurant and fitness centre will fall under this part of the structure, as will the position of hotel accountant. Graham Effingham will remain as the head chef of the restaurant, with a sous chef and a maître d' forming a further level of hierarchy over the kitchen and waiting teams respectively. This clears up the confusion over who manages the waiting staff, placing them firmly under Effingham's control. One of the fitness centre staff will be promoted to manager of the fitness centre. Finally, David Hunter will report to Phil Weaver as chief accountant; his 'cosy' relationship with Mortimer will be broken up. Both Weaver and Hunter's uncertain roles within the organization are now clear and definite.

Looking at the changes made to the Junction Hotel structure, how would the changes improve the running of the hotel? Who do you think would be happy or unhappy with the changes made, and why?

Each position on the organization chart represents a role to be carried out by a person—the office indicated is to be held by a person acting in an **official** capacity. As such, the bureaucratic structure maps out the relationships between people acting in different official roles within the organization.

Lines of authority are shown—the structure demonstrates who a worker is controlled by and, likewise, who a worker has control over. It also shows the limits of such authority, namely who a worker has no legitimate authority over and to whom a worker is not answerable.

Horizontal differentiation specifies each role even further, with the specific task associated with each role defined. Positions within a bureaucratic structure will often have a written **job description** attached, which outlines the level or grade within the hierarchy of that position, and the specific tasks and duties that the office holder would be expected to perform. If you have ever applied for a job, then you'll know that the application pack usually includes such a job description.

The job description and tight definition of roles highlight a particular feature of the nature of bureaucratic structure. It is able to map out the set of roles and relationships within an organization and facilitate control over that organization, often with a diagram on a single sheet of paper. Alongside this broad overview it also exerts influence at a level of quite intricate detail within that structure, with tightly specified roles and relationships for any one person within it. Bureaucracy maps out both the large-scale general nature of the organization and the small-scale specifics within.

The existence of job descriptions indicates that bureaucracy needs more than just a structure in order to operate. In fact, written rules, procedures, and paperwork are just as important a part of bureaucratic functioning and control as the hierarchy and structure.

Visit the Online Resource Centre to see examples of job descriptions.

**Official** A person who fills a particular role in an organization. When working in that role, a person is said to be working in an official capacity.

**Job description** A document which outlines the formal duties and activities that the holder of a particular office will be expected to perform, and their place within the overall organizational structure.

## Review questions

| | |
|---|---|
| **Describe** | What is meant by 'hierarchy' in an organization structure? |
| **Explain** | How does hierarchy allow control to be exerted over a whole organization? |
| **Analyse** | What are the differences between exerting direct and indirect control? Which do you think would be easier to exert? |
| **Apply** | Using an actual organization structure, outline the differences between direct and indirect control between different levels. |

# Bureaucratic standardization—rules, policies, and procedures

**Running case:** implementing procedures

Running the organization is much more straightforward with the new structure in place. However, while Chance has delegated authority throughout the hierarchy, managers are implementing that authority in different ways and some staff are starting to complain that this is unfair.

- Meg Mortimer is authoritative, but she is seen to have her favourites when it comes to taking breaks or being able to leave early to deal with family issues. Meg's favourites also seem to be first in line when any opportunities for extra shifts or overtime come up.

- Linda Wilkinson is seen as a soft touch—cleaners and maintenance workers are taking extended breaks and seem to be allowed to leave early for spurious reasons. If workers are off sick, Linda takes their word for it, not insisting on any form of medical note. She doesn't keep a record of illness, leaving others in the organization to suspect that people are getting away with taking 'sickies'.

- Graham Effingham rules the restaurant with an iron rod, bawling out waiters and kitchen staff directly, and not going through the managers below him. He is unsympathetic to people who are off sick and often insists people work through breaks if there is a busy shift. If a shift extends beyond the set hours, Effingham sees this as a part of the job and does not award any extra money for overtime. He is even known to dock pay if he feels that work is not up to scratch.

Chance decides that, to even out conditions across the workforce, rules and procedures will be created and implemented. Two documents, entitled 'Pay and Working Hours Procedures' and 'Disciplinary Policy', are sent to the three managers below Chance, who are asked to implement the policies immediately.

The Pay and Working Hours Procedures specify a standard working day with defined hours and break times. Employees will sign in and out at the start and end of the day, and for all breaks taken. Managers will send this data weekly to David Hunter who will calculate pay and prepare pay packets. Absence will be reported directly to Hunter, who will get employees to provide appropriate evidence upon their return.

The Disciplinary Policy specifies expectations of staff behaviour, and a series of set offences with appropriate standard punishments is created. Chance wants to take discipline out of individual managers' hands as they seem to make up their own rules, which is at the heart of a lot of the unfairness felt by workers. Any disciplining of staff will, therefore, be referred to Chance directly in accordance with the new rules.

How might managers react to having to follow the rules and procedures outlined in the Junction Hotel case?

**Rules, policies, and procedures** Formal instructions that govern how particular activities in an organization are to be performed.

Bureaucratic structure is supplemented and enhanced by another aspect of bureaucracy: **rules, policies, and procedures.** Their aim is to standardize behaviours and activities throughout the organization, such that control is implemented in the same way at all levels across and up and down the hierarchy.

While the bureaucratic hierarchy allows the owner to control the organization in an indirect and more efficient manner, it can also be seen that there is a risk that at each level of

Table 2.2  Examples of rules, policies, and procedures in organizations

| | |
|---|---|
| Grievance | Policies which outline how workers themselves may pursue grievances—areas in which they are unhappy with how they are being managed |
| Finance | Procedures relating to expense claims, outlining what workers might legitimately claim (e.g. car mileage or transport costs), and a standard allowance for these |
| Equal opportunities | Policies that ensure equality of treatment on grounds such as gender, race, age, sexual orientation, and disability |
| Appraisal and promotion | Procedures for monitoring the standard of work that employees do, often done in a standardized appraisal procedure on an annual basis; such a procedure can then feed into decisions on promotion or pay increases |
| Recruitment and selection | Policies may cover aspects such as where a job is advertised, criteria for selecting candidates, and types of evidence required to demonstrate that candidates meet different selection criteria (see Chapter 8 for more on specific recruitment and selection techniques to match personalities to job descriptions) |

the hierarchy control is lost because of the way in which that control is *implemented* at levels below. Are all managers following their orders to the letter or are individual managers acting as they please? If workers hear that they are being treated unfavourably compared with other workers it can cause unrest and disruption.

Thus pay rates and scales are an example of a rule or procedure which may be implemented to standardize the way in which remuneration is offered across a whole organization. In some cases, pay scales are even standardized across a whole industry sector (e.g. in the UK's education system, local government, and health service). Payment rules and procedures extend beyond pay itself into other terms and conditions, such as working hours, holidays, sick pay, pension entitlements, etc., and take **discretion** out of individual managers' hands.

There are many other areas within modern-day organizations where activities will be controlled by a set of rules, or a policy or procedure which standardizes behaviour across the organization. See Table 2.2 for some examples.

What type of rules and procedures do you have to follow in your workplace? Do they help or hinder you in your work?

Here, we see an extra dimension of bureaucratic control. Not only is control delegated down through the hierarchy, but the autonomous action of any manager within that hierarchy is also now taken away. Instead, managers are controlled by adherence to the written rules and procedures. For the owner, this gives increased control and a standardization of behaviour across the organization.

In some cases, requirements for bureaucratic rules and procedures come not just from a desire for management control, but also from a legal imperative. This is the case in the UK, where workplace legislation (much of which originates at the level of the European Union) covers aspects of workplace management, such as equal opportunities, health and safety,

**Discretion** The ability of an individual to act according to their own independent judgement, rather than being told exactly what to do.

and disciplinary aspects (e.g. unfair dismissal and workplace bullying). Many bureaucratic procedures in workplaces are thus as much about ensuring compliance with such laws as they are about enforcing management control.

Visit the Online Resource Centre for further examples of rules, policies, and procedures.

**Human resource management (HRM)** The part of an organization that concentrates on policies and procedures relevant to the management of people within the organization (sometimes known as personnel management).

The work involved in implementing bureaucratic procedures relating to the human side of the organization leads to sections of the organization being devoted to this aspect of organizational functioning. Thus there is a whole organizational function, alongside functions such as marketing, production, and finance, which deals with **human resource management**.

In Chapter 4, with the example of the McDonalds restaurant chain, we will see how such standardization even takes place globally, not just with human resources policies but also with set instructions and procedures for performing particular work tasks.

## Review questions

| | |
|---|---|
| **Describe** | What is meant by 'rules, policies, and procedures'? |
| **Explain** | Why are rules and procedures needed to standardize behaviour across an organization? |
| **Analyse** | What effect do rules and procedures have on managerial discretion? |

# Bureaucratic records and paperwork

## Running case: for the record

Charged with running the new payroll and absence system, David Hunter is beginning to find the paperwork something of a burden. He is used to writing down information in a notebook as and when he receives it. Now, with clocking-on records and absence reports coming in daily, and pay cheques to prepare weekly, Hunter is becoming overwhelmed.

Some managers scribble their daily records on to a scrap of paper; others lay the records out as a well-ordered spreadsheet. There is no single format common to all organizations, but storing the scraps of paper in his notebook makes it increasingly difficult for Hunter to access and process payroll and absence information as more and more of it comes in. When asked for details of any specific employee, he finds he is wading through a mass of paper and this is taking up more and more of his time.

Hunter decides that a standard system of record keeping is needed. Opening a filing cabinet, he allocates a folder to each employee. On the front of each he creates a standard template to record details of the employee—name, address, date of birth, tax code, and any other relevant information. Furthermore, each employee is allocated an employee number.

A set of forms is created—one where managers can record clocking-on and clocking-off details for each employee, one for reporting absences, and one to record any disciplinary incidents. For each of these, the first box to be filled in is the employee number. Hunter can then file the forms immediately when received and access them rapidly when required.

The forms help Hunter to manage the payroll process much more efficiently; however, Simon Chance spots a further benefit. Every so often he asks Hunter to send up the file of a particular employee. Even if Chance doesn't know the employee personally, he can read the file and get a good picture of their working history, e.g. their absences, time taken on breaks, and disciplinary issues.

Even though the employees may be distant and unknown to Chance within the structure, their employee record makes them instantly visible to him.

What control over individual workers does the record keeping at Junction Hotel give to the managers?

While rules and procedures standardize aspects of workplace control, such procedures both necessitate, and are facilitated by, the keeping of records and **paperwork**. This is the final aspect of bureaucracy that we examine.

Bureaucratic paperwork is typified by the **pro-forma**—a set of fields and boxes that represent some aspect of the organization. For instance, employees will be represented in an organization as a set of fields and boxes on a form, each of which records a piece of information relevant to the organization. Such record keeping serves two purposes for management in controlling the organization.

- Firstly, many of the rules and procedures outlined in the previous section require information about the organization and its workers in order for those rules and procedures to be implemented. A payroll policy needs information about the hours worked by each employee; an absence policy needs to record frequency and reasons for absence, etc. If this information were unstructured (e.g. scribbled on scraps of paper) it would be difficult to manage. A pro-forma standardizes the information to be stored and thus makes it easy to access, retrieve, and use in implementing the policies that it supports.

- Secondly, a by-product of such record keeping is that a record is kept of an employee's activities that can be accessed at a later date. Such records allow added control through surveillance and monitoring of employees. While an employee might be 'lost' within a large organizational structure, referring to their records allows management to still cast an eye over their activity and exert control if, for example, there is a problematic absence record. (See Chapter 4 for a discussion of control through surveillance and the Panopticon.)

**Paperwork** Official documentation and record keeping within an organization.

**Pro-forma** A type of paperwork, sometimes called a form. It is a blank template with standard fields for different types of relevant information, which is filled in as a means of capturing information for the records of an organization.

## Real life case: the UCAS form

UCAS is the organization which handles applications for UK universities.

In dealing with the thousands of university applicants each year, UCAS has the problem of ordering a complex mass of individuals. They could ask people to turn up at their premises to discuss their university applications, but this would overwhelm their premises by the sheer weight of numbers ▶

USE BLOCK CAPITALS ON PAGE 1

**UCAS** APPLICATION FOR ENTRY IN **2013**

Attach your application fee and stamped, addressed acknowledgement card here with a paperclip

YOU MUST READ *HOW TO APPLY* BEFORE COMPLETING THIS FORM
Return completed form to: UCAS, PO Box 28, Cheltenham, Glos GL52 3LZ, UK

IMPORTANT
You must complete all the red sections, marked with an asterisk (∗). Your application will be delayed if you do not do so.

**1 PERSONAL DETAILS**
Title∗   Male (M)∗ Female (F)∗   Your date of birth∗   19   Age on 1 September 2013

Surname/family name∗
First/given name(s)
Preferred first name

Postal address∗
Line 1
Line 2
Line 3
Line 4
Postcode (UK only)   Country∗ (not UK)

Mobile phone number
Home phone number (including STD/area code)
email

Home address (if different from above)
Line 1
Line 2
Line 3
Line 4
Postcode (UK only)   Country (not UK)   Previous surname/family name at 16th birthday (18)

**2 ADDITIONAL DETAILS**
Fee code∗   Student support arrangements   Disability/special needs (including dyslexia)/medical condition∗
Occupational background∗ (22)   Parents' higher education   Enter ✔ if you **want** to receive correspondence in Welsh where available
Time in care   Representative's name (30)   Relationship (30)
Area of permanent residence∗ (30)   Residential category∗
Nationality∗ (30)   National identity∗ (UK applicants only)   Ethnic origin∗ (UK applicants only)   Date of first entry to live in the UK∗   Country of birth∗ (30)

|  | Start date | Duration | School year | Location | Sponsor |
|---|---|---|---|---|---|
| Activity 1 | M M Y Y |  |  |  |  |
| Activity 2 | M M Y Y |  |  |  |  |

**3 CHOICES IN ALPHABETICAL ORDER OF INSTITUTION CODE NAME**

| (a) Institution code name∗ | (b) Institution code∗ | (c) Course code∗ | (d) Campus code∗ | (e) Start date∗ | (f) Further details only if requested on Course Finder (20) | (g) Point of entry | (h) Live at home∗ | (i) Defer entry∗ |
|---|---|---|---|---|---|---|---|---|
|  |  |  |  | D D M M Y Y |  |  |  |  |
|  |  |  |  | D D M M Y Y |  |  |  |  |
|  |  |  |  | D D M M Y Y |  |  |  |  |
|  |  |  |  | D D M M Y Y |  |  |  |  |

If you have applied to any of the above institution(s) before, enter your most recent UCAS application number or Personal ID (if known)

**4A SCHOOL, COLLEGE, CENTRE AND UNIVERSITY EDUCATION∗** (40 per line)

| | PT, FT or SW | From∗ MM | YY | To∗ MM | YY |
|---|---|---|---|---|---|
| | | M M | Y Y | M M | Y Y |
| | | M M | Y Y | M M | Y Y |
| | | M M | Y Y | M M | Y Y |

**4B HIGHEST LEVEL QUALIFICATION ACHIEVED∗**
Honours degree level or above qualifications   Below honours degree level qualifications   I will have no formal qualifications

Form Number   Figures in brackets = maximum no. of characters, including spaces, allowed   ∗ Mandatory information   Page 1

**A UCAS form.**

**Source:** © Universities and Colleges Admissions Service.

and there is no way that an individual staff member could remember each potential student with whom they had had discussions. They could ask people to write a letter of application stating any relevant details. This would prevent the premises from being swamped, but how would they collate thousands of letters? Say they wanted to find all applicants for Midwest University; or say they ▶

wanted to find all applicants for Geography degrees, or all applicants over 25 years old. It would mean sifting through and examining closely every single letter among thousands to find the relevant details. Nothing would ever get done.

So, to make this task manageable, UCAS uses a number of bureaucratic mechanisms—the UCAS application, in particular. Rather than inviting unstructured letters, UCAS structures each individual in the shape of the UCAS application form (originally completed on paper but now online). Each individual is represented by the different fields that they fill in: age, predicted grades, gender, preferred universities, preferred courses, etc. Now, the mass of individual applicants is represented and structured in a way that makes their ordering, and, ultimately, allocation to different universities, possible. What was previously unmanageable is now manageable—it is the bureaucracy that allows information to be managed efficiently and, ultimately, for control to be exerted over the mass of student applicants for that year.

How does the use of a pro-forma at UCAS allow records to be processed efficiently (e.g. saving time and effort)?

The UCAS case shows how bureaucracy functions in both ordering and managing vast numbers of people, but also allows the record of any one individual within that mass to be pinpointed immediately. Bureaucracy can thus be used as an instrument for ordering and governing populations of whole countries.

Government bodies and organizations exist as massive bureaucracies, processing information and paperwork about their populations, with the intent of ordering and controlling that population in one way or another.

In the UK, the Driver and Vehicle Licensing Agency (DVLA) maintains records for all licensed drivers and their vehicles. Such records control who can and cannot drive, and even manage the exclusion of individuals from driving based on penalty points accrued or a lack of car taxation. Similar giant national bureaucracies keep records of our tax details and health records, etc. Privately-owned, commercial record-keeping organizations, such as Experian in the UK, keep similar records, for example about the financial history of an individual, for use in credit checks.

Visit the Online Resource Centre to see more on organizations that maintain records.

The use of bureaucratic techniques to manage a vast number of people is at the heart of so many organizations. Each individual is represented in a 'highly caricatured yet immediately available form' (Poster, 1995: 91). The paperwork and the records caricature an individual according to a standard set of entries on a pro-forma, which, at the same time, makes them visible, and their records easy to pinpoint and access, within a mass of similarly constituted individuals. This adds to the power of bureaucracy.

## Employability skills: information overload

In a world of 'information overload' (see Chapter 14 on 'Information, communication, and technology'), managing information is a vital workplace skill. Where previously this tended to be done in physical files and folders, there are now various forms of software which can help with the tasks of storing information, categorizing it, and making it available for easy retrieval at a later date. This might be for project management or for organizing your own notes.

Without such a level of organization and categorization of information in the workplace it is easy for information to become a confused mass. Even something as straightforward as email allows the creation of virtual folders so as to be able to keep information in a more manageable and easily accessible form.

## Review questions

| | |
|---|---|
| **Describe** | What is a pro-forma? |
| **Explain** | How does a pro-forma help to standardize bureaucratic records? |
| **Analyse** | How can bureaucratic records be used to control large numbers of people? |
| **Apply** | What do you think would happen if government bureaucracies such as the DVLA didn't exist? |

# The power of bureaucracy: large-scale control and rational design

**Running case:** great work

Phil—what you've done is great. Such simple ideas, but they give me so much control!

The various aspects of bureaucracy allow an organization, as it grows in size, to remain ordered and controlled rather than descending into chaos. With face-to-face control becoming more difficult, if not impossible, control is implemented through impersonal elements, such as the structure, rules, and paperwork. In that bureaucracy can achieve this control across large-scale organizations, even national populations, it creates tremendous organizational power.

It is difficult to think of organizations which do not have elements of bureaucracy to one degree or another: structure, rules, procedures, paperwork, etc. It underpins all large-, medium- and probably small-scale organizations that we know today—bureaucracy is 'ubiquitous and inevitable' (Watson, 2002: 239).

The ordering and controlling power of bureaucracy makes possible many achievements of organizations that we take for granted, but which, without bureaucracy, would simply be beyond human capability. Quite simply, the organizations that we know today would be incapable of operating without bureaucracy.

**Research insight:** The railway timetable
Chia, R. 1995. From modern to postmodern organizational analysis.
Organization Studies 16(4): 579–604.

Chia (1995) examines the vast power of a simple bureaucratic instrument—a railway timetable, which can order trains, passengers, and workers across a whole country. Think also about timetables in the context of your own university studies and how they direct both you and the university staff from hour to hour.

One sheet of paper can represent the organization by structuring it and breaking it down in terms of space (different rooms), time (different time slots during the day), and people (allocated to different timetable slots). This small sheet of paper exerts power and control over vast numbers. Without the timetable it would be impossible to run a university—it would be a disorganized mass of people milling around without direction.

# Fayol, bureaucracy, and the principles of management

As noted previously, bureaucratic structures, rules, and paperwork have existed for centuries; however, the particular power that they have brought to organizations since the early 1900s comes, in part, from the rationality of the design of bureaucratic structures, as promoted by the likes of Fayol.

Table 2.3 shows how the different elements of bureaucracy can be seen to allow Fayol's five functions of management to still be exerted as an organization grows in size and scale.

Fayol's work on bureaucratic organization design went along this rational route in that he saw it as playing an important part in achieving organizational goals in the most efficient manner possible. In other words, rational organizational design is about finding the most direct and efficient means to achieve organizational ends.

Table 2.3  Bureaucratic techniques and Fayol's five principles of management (1949)

| | |
|---|---|
| Planning/ forecasting | Standard rules and procedures make behaviour and actions more predictable across the organization and thus easier to plan for. Paperwork and records give data which can be used for forecasting, e.g. planning staffing requirements. |
| Organizing | A structure is created to meet the needs of the organization and to encompass the vertical and horizontal levels of hierarchy needed to achieve the organization's aims. Tightly defined job roles and recruitment procedures allow the development of an appropriately qualified workforce. |
| Coordinating | Standard procedures (e.g. for pay) make it easier to coordinate activities across the organization (e.g. through a payroll department). The bureaucratic structure and rules make clear what each person does and how they relate and report to each other across the organization. |
| Commanding | Command is delegated through the hierarchical levels of bureaucratic structure. Rules and procedures tell people what to do without a human commanding presence being necessary. |
| Controlling | Paperwork means that records of employee actions are kept, which can be used to monitor work performance and associated issues, such as absence. |

Fayol expanded his five general functions of management to create his general principles of management.

---

**Theory in context:** Henri Fayol and the profession of management

Henri Fayol (1841–1925) was a French mining engineer who became a manager. Having turned around a failing mine (Wren, 2001), he suggested that good management was a consequence of following a set of general principles. Regardless of the person holding an office, following such principles would ensure efficient management across the organization. In his 1916 work, *Administration industrielle et generale* (English translation, Fayol, 1949), he set out these principles.

Management became a profession in itself (Pryor and Taneja, 2010), with the training of managers becoming as important as training for production skills or other functions in the organization, such as finance. In Chapter 3 we encounter Taylor, a fellow management pioneer. Unlike Taylor, who concentrated on making individual work tasks more efficient, Fayol was interested in efficiency *at the level of the organization overall*.

However, work by both Fayol and Taylor was the basis for what became known in the UK as the **Classical Management School** (see Smith and Boyns, 2005)—a form of management that emphasizes rationality and searches for the 'one best way' to manage an organization. This is opposite to the disordered, ad hoc, and chaotic form of organization that might exist were it not for bureaucracy.

---

**Classical Management School** A set of theories of management which draws upon rational methods of managing and organizing. Having developed from the early 1900s, it encompasses a number of theorists and practitioners who advocated 'one best way' of management. Examples of management styles and techniques which the school draws upon include Fayol from this chapter, and Frederick Taylor from Chapter 3.

The principles of management numbered fourteen in total, although Fayol suggested that this was flexible—any principle that helped efficient management and control could be included. The principles promote the use of bureaucratic structures. Examples from his list include:

- a division of work where all tasks are specialized (as with vertical and horizontal differentiation), creating specific roles within the organization
- unity of command where each worker answers to only one manager, not several
- centralization, with **delegation** down through the ranks
- equity of treatment for all employees, as seen with rules and procedures
- order—everything to be in the right place at the right time, as seen with timetables
- subordination of interests—individual interests are secondary to those of the organization as a whole.

**Delegation** Passing a job, task, or order down to lower levels of a hierarchy.

 Visit the Online Resource Centre to see Fayol's full list of principles.

The power of bureaucracy seems to come from its rational approach to managing and organizing—not just in preventing disorder, but in making possible large-scale control and coordination that would otherwise be impossible without rational, bureaucratic instruments. However, rationality is a contested term—it has different meanings depending on your perspective. This contested nature is something we will encounter in the next section when we examine some of the critiques of bureaucracy.

### Review questions

| | |
|---|---|
| **Describe** | What is meant by the Classical Management School? |
| **Explain** | How does bureaucracy allow Fayol's five functions of management to be implemented over large-scale organizations? |
| **Analyse** | What do you think are the strengths and weaknesses of Fayol's approach to managing organizations which led to him being both 'revered and reviled' (Pryor and Taneja, 2010)? |

# Weber and the critique of bureaucracy

### Running case: what happened to the magic?

Chance feels that the new procedures enhance his power over the organization, standardizing both worker and managerial behaviour. However, while Chance is pleased with his work, reactions from Junction Hotel's staff seem hostile. What seemed perfectly rational to Chance as a means of running the organization efficiently is not necessarily perceived in the same way by others.

Meg Mortimer feels that she has been demoted, having to take her place alongside Linda Wilkinson in the hierarchy. The tightly written job descriptions limit her sphere of influence within the hotel and she is not happy that she will no longer be working closely with her friend David Hunter.

Linda Wilkinson feels disappointed. Although her workload has been reduced, she takes it as a slight on her performance that many areas she had managed are being taken away from her.

Graham Effingham is apoplectic—why does he find himself now a level below Linda Wilkinson in the hierarchy? Chance tries to reassure Effingham that the restaurant will be run almost as a separate unit under the guidance of Phil Weaver, and that the appointment of a maître d' and sous chef means, in fact, that Effingham has as many levels of hierarchy beneath him as Wilkinson and Mortimer. Effingham is still not happy, however, muttering about his reduced status within the organization.

Overall, there is a general lack of morale developing among the staff, especially as more and more policies and procedures are introduced to the hotel. Chance takes Meg Mortimer to one side to ask what the problem is. Mortimer replies:

> It's all this paperwork—there's too much drudgery and not enough working with people. I spend most of my time in that back office but I need to be around people—that's the part of the job I really love. And it's the same with the receptionists, too. We're meant to go out there, and be cheerful and welcoming to customers, but how can we show enthusiasm when we don't feel any?

> Last week you gave us another form to fill in, monitoring water usage for your environmental audit. I'm sure it's a great cause but it just adds to the drudgery. We are expected to go out there and create magic—really create the atmosphere for the customers. But how can we when the magic has gone?

While bureaucracy may increase the power and control of organizations and managers, and their ability to operate on a large scale, it does not come without consequences. Such consequences form the heart of the critique of bureaucracy from Max Weber. While Weber appreciated the power and technical efficiency of bureaucracy, he was also wary about its increasing dominance and negative effects within society.

> ### Theory in context: Max Weber and the study of organizations
>
> Max Weber is synonymous with bureaucracy. However, while he wrote in the early 1900s (at the same time as Fayol) it should be noted that *Weber was not a manager like Fayol* and thus had no interest in implementing bureaucracy within organizations so as to increase efficiency and control within them, *nor was he a management theorist.*
>
> As a sociologist, Weber was interested in a wide range of aspects of society (MacRae, 1974)—economy, religion, and music being examples. One interest (Weber, 1958) was in forms of authority and control within society, which led him to analyse bureaucracy in terms of its characteristics, its power, and its effects on people and society.
>
> It is sometimes suggested that Weber's work has met with a 'strange fate' (Perry, 1992) in management and organization theory, being viewed only in terms of how it can help organizations be managed more efficiently rather than recognizing the negative effects that he identifies. Thus, when Weber (1968) speaks of an 'ideal type' of bureaucracy, it is seen in some quarters almost as some form of blueprint for the design of organizations in a similar, technically-efficient sense to that suggested earlier by Fayol.
>
> The value of Weber's contribution, however, is found in his critique of bureaucracy, its dominance in society, and the effects that it has upon society.

Weber's (1958) studies of society led him to conclude that society at the time was moving from a grounding in tradition and religion towards rational, formal structures, such as bureaucracy. This was reflected in how authority operated in society. Where once power came from tradition (such as a hereditary position) or from the charisma and personality of an individual leader, Weber noted that authority was coming more from bureaucratic forms of authority, which he described as **rational–legal authority**.

**Rational–legal authority** According to Max Weber this is power that is legitimated by rules and procedures associated with an office rather than by traditional or charismatic means.

Rational–legal authority is where authority comes neither from tradition nor the charisma of an individual, but rather from the authority that they have due to the office they hold. Authority comes from the bureaucratic rules associated with that position. (See Chapter 12 on 'Leadership' and Chapter 13 on 'Power and politics in organizations' for more about power and authority in organizations.)

Noting the increasing dominance of rational, bureaucratic organizational forms within society, Weber (1968) outlined features of an 'ideal type' of rational, technically-efficient bureaucracy, including:

- functional division of labour (horizontal differentiation)
- hierarchical structure (vertical differentiation)
- rules and regulations
- impersonality—the separation of working lives from personal lives
- unbiased decision making, including recruitment, selection, and promotion.

The ideal type contains some now familiar aspects of bureaucracy and, indeed, has some aspects in common with Fayol. However, rather than being a prescription for efficient organizational design, Weber's model was a hypothetical abstraction of features he had observed in a number of bureaucracies. While noting it as a technically efficient 'ideal type', Weber did not suggest that his model was necessarily the right way to manage and organize.

## Formal and substantive rationality

For Weber, the **formal rationality** of the ideal type is but one type of rationality. It is a technical form of rationality which finds the most efficient means to achieving ends. *But this does not mean that pursuing those ends is rational in more human terms.* Weber proposed another form of rationality—**substantive rationality**—to take account of the effects of actions in human and ethical terms.

**Formal rationality** Technically efficient means of achieving particular ends without thinking of the human or ethical consequences.

**Substantive rationality** Rationality from a human and ethical perspective—if something is formally rational and efficient it does not make it substantively rational when considering its human and ethical consequences.

> **Research insight:** Modernity and the Holocaust
> Bauman, Z. 1989. *Modernity and the Holocaust*. Polity Press, Cambridge.
>
> In a compelling account of the Nazi Holocaust, Zygmunt Bauman (1989) asks how individuals working in death camps, where prisoners were killed in mass extermination chambers, could bring themselves to commit such horrific acts. His answer lies in the nature of bureaucracy.
>
> Dividing labour, and giving individuals just a small, tightly-defined role in the overall organization, made them become blinkered to the end result. In an organization with many levels of hierarchy, commands given from the top can seem very distant and impersonal from the bottom—orders and their consequences come without a human face.
>
> Thus, workers in death camps saw only their one small part in the process (it might be recording a name in a log book) rather than the overall end result.
>
> Bauman's work on the Holocaust reflects some of the dehumanizing aspects of bureaucracy that will be encountered later in this chapter. It also highlights different forms of rationality. In terms of formal rationality the Nazi death camps were perfectly rational—with a task set of killing many prisoners en masse, it achieved the most technically rational way of achieving this. But how can it be rational in human terms for an organization to exist to pursue such an ethically abhorrent act in such a ruthless and efficient manner?
>
> The case of the Holocaust highlights Weber's distinction between formal and substantive rationality. The fact that something is formally rational, i.e. technical and efficient, does not make it substantively rational, i.e. in human and ethical terms.

The Holocaust is a dramatic example, but we can think of examples in organizations today. In Chapter 17 ('Corporate social responsibility') we examine contemporary organizational arrangements that can be seen as ethically dubious, for instance by creating pollution or using sweatshop labour in the developing world. These may be formally rational in that they are the most efficient ways for an organization to operate, but are they substantively rational in terms of their effects upon humans or upon the environment?

Such issues also highlight Bauman's idea of individuals within an organization being distanced from the end result of that organization's activities. Does a sales assistant in a UK clothes shop feel personally responsible for the sweatshop conditions in which the clothes they sell were produced? Does a forecourt cashier in Sweden feel responsibility for pollution caused by oil spills on the other side of the planet? In both cases, the worker is a part of the same organization that created the problem, but their roles are so tightly defined and so distanced from the end results that they can potentially continue with a clear conscience.

Have you, in a workplace, ever performed a task that you thought to be wrong but continued because you were following orders or rules?

## Disenchantment—the loss of magical elements

**Disenchantment**
For Max Weber this was a loss of 'magical elements' in society, and suggests some of the dehumanizing elements of bureaucracy.

Weber noted a more general issue of substantive rationality, namely its negative effects on people and society. In particular, Weber (1958) noted that as society moved from religious and traditional views of the world towards more formal, bureaucratic procedures—both in religion and society generally—there was loss of the 'magical', enchanted elements in life. This removal of 'magical' elements in life was termed **disenchantment** by Weber. The magical is replaced with the rational, formal, and procedural.

While originally describing the loss of magical elements in society generally, 'disenchantment' is often interpreted as a dehumanizing and stifling effect of bureaucracy. It brings with it monotonous, repetitive routines, with people unable to act independently but instead bound by rules and procedures, becoming unthinking and detached from their work.

Have you ever done work that you have found repetitive, dull, and monotonous? How would you have made it more interesting?

Such disenchantment can be seen in the way in which following set rules and routines makes life predictable: rather than being spontaneous and creative, people simply follow rules.

## The iron cage of bureaucracy

**Iron cage of bureaucracy** Max Weber's observation of the increased presence of bureaucracy in society and its potential to trap people in its routines and procedures.

The phrase with which Weber (1958) is most commonly associated is the **iron cage of bureaucracy**. This stems from Weber's caution about the prevalence of bureaucracy within society and its potential negative effects.

How many aspects of your life are not governed by bureaucracy—rules, procedures, paperwork, timetables, etc.—in some form or another? How easy is it to escape from its influence?

For Weber, bureaucracy, even when he was writing in 1922, was coming to dominate more and more aspects of people's lives and of society in general. Thus, the 'iron cage' gives a sense of people being trapped—small, insignificant elements in large-scale organizations.

Such critiques of bureaucracy, which see bureaucracy as sinister and inhuman—an 'invisible enemy' (Bell, 2008: 65) that dominates people through its unquestioning, faceless rules and procedures, leaving people with very small, meaningless jobs and routines to pursue—are often seen in artistic and fictional portrayals of bureaucracy.

### Theory in context: the critique of bureaucracy in Brazil

In the dystopian film *Brazil* (dir. Gilliam, 1985), a typographical error on a form (caused by a fly landing on a typewriter) leads to the wrong person being arrested (Bell, 2008: 84). The film follows a low-level government employee who tries, with increasing frustration, to reverse the error. A powerful visual metaphor within the film is of the office exploding, scattering its paperwork across the landscape below. The arrested character tries to escape, but the flying paperwork catches up, covers him, and suffocates him.

Have you ever tried to get an error corrected by a large-scale organization such as an error with your phone contract or car insurance? How easy did you find it? Could the person you first spoke to deal with it by themselves?

The film *Brazil* resonates with Weber's concept of the iron cage, highlighting the unquestioning nature of the rules and procedures of bureaucracy, its dehumanization—literally suffocating a character in paperwork—and the inability to escape from bureaucracy.

The film also portrays bureaucracy's inflexibility and unquestioning nature in reversing something once it is formalized in paperwork. Such inflexibility suggests another area of critique beyond that of Weber—namely that bureaucracy may not *in practice* be efficient.

### Review questions

| | |
|---|---|
| **Describe** | What is meant by rational–legal authority? |
| **Explain** | What were the main problems that Weber found with bureaucracy? |
| **Analyse** | What is the difference between formal and substantive rationality? How can the Holocaust be discussed in terms of these two forms of rationality? |
| **Apply** | Which of Weber's critiques of bureaucracy applies most to the 'drudgery' encountered at Junction Hotel and why? |

# Dysfunctions of bureaucracy

### Running case: unintended consequences

Chance had thought that his rules, procedures, and paperwork would bring about a standardization and uniformity of behaviour among the Junction Hotel workforce. However, in practice, he finds a number of unexpected consequences.

- The fitness centre manager meticulously completes the paperwork related to attendance. On occasions, this leads to the fitness centre opening late as he tries to complete paperwork by the deadlines set.

- Effingham is upset at not being able to shout at staff. He feels it is part of the nature of kitchen work. In protest, he follows the disciplinary procedures to the letter, sending staff to Chance for the most minor infringements. At one point, all of the kitchen staff are waiting outside Chance's office to be disciplined while the kitchen lies empty with a restaurant full of unhappy customers waiting for their food.

- Meanwhile, the lax regime of Linda Wilkinson seems to continue. It is rumoured that she has told staff not to bother clocking in and that she will cover up any absences when she fills out the paperwork. She feels that this creates good staff relations, but also makes her own life easier—she doesn't have to spend time calculating absence rates and can get on with other management tasks.

- Check-in times at Reception have increased, despite the introduction of new procedures. It seems that the receptionists are so frightened that Mortimer will pick up on any deviation from procedures that they're following them to the letter, even when common sense suggests otherwise. On one occasion, a couple who, to all eyes, appeared to be over 70 years old were asked for proof of their year of birth to qualify for a pensioners' discount. As the woman reached for her bus pass, she strained her back and was taken to hospital, vowing loudly never to return as she was stretchered out past the, by then, massive queue in the foyer.

Looking at all the delays caused by the procedures, Chance wonders whether he is achieving efficient control over the organization after all. To his eyes, it seems like a return to the ad hoc dysfunctionality that he has tried to avoid.

While Weber presented a number of critiques of bureaucracy, he still noted the technical efficiency of the 'ideal type' of bureaucracy, albeit an ideal type that came with significant social consequences.

Remember, however, that Weber's ideal type was a hypothetical model, created without observing the workings of actual organizations. A number of organizational studies uncovered a difference between the ideal type of bureaucracy and how bureaucracies actually function. They found that, rather than making things rational and efficient, rules in bureaucracies either had unintended, inefficient consequences or were ignored in the name of the smooth running of the organization. Many of these **dysfunctions of bureaucracy** are still encountered today.

**Dysfunctions of bureaucracy** Unintended consequences of bureaucracy which lead to it not functioning in the efficient manner for which it is designed.

**Red tape** An unintended consequence of bureaucracy, where rules and paperwork get in the way of work and activities, rather than helping tasks to be performed efficiently.

## Red tape

The term **red tape** suggests negative connotations of rules and regulations getting in the way of an organization achieving its goals or where an organization puts in place a prohibitive amount of form-filling and 'check boxes' that must be ticked. Rather than promoting efficiency, bureaucracy has the opposite effect.

Red tape is typically characterized as being where paperwork and rules and procedures create extra work—they get in the way rather than helping with the work that people have to do. This is a typical source of contention in many professions—the feeling that paperwork and form-filling prevent people from doing their actual job.

---

**Real life case:** red tape in the UK public sector

A common complaint from workers in various areas of the UK public sector is that excessive bureaucracy—adherence to rules and regulations alongside the constant need to complete paperwork and provide data and information—was actually getting in the way of people doing their actual jobs. Two major reports highlighted how such red tape prevented people from doing front-line work in both the police force (Berry, 2010) and in social work (Munro, 2010). In the latter case, a problem arises where the burden of paperwork takes social workers away from one of the important tasks that they are meant to perform, namely protecting vulnerable children.

More recently, the UK Secretary of State for Education, Nicky Morgan, pledged to cut down on excessive bureaucracy and paperwork for school teachers, who found themselves overloaded with non-teaching activities such as marking, lesson planning, and pupil tracking. Adams (2015) reports that these requirements harm morale and recruitment within the profession, effects similar to Weber's disenchantment.

---

While bureaucracy may have a negative effect on individuals working in the public sector, private-sector businesses also complain that their ability to innovate and operate can be stifled by bureaucratic red tape. Visit the Online Resource Centre for a link to the Red Tape Challenge, a UK government initiative to identify and reduce red tape which has a negative impact upon businesses.

## The bureaucratic personality

Many of us may have encountered a 'jobsworth': an official who follows rules to the letter rather than thinking of the bigger picture or more reasonable outcomes. The jobsworth follows rules rigidly and inflexibly—to do otherwise is 'more than my job's worth'.

---

**Real life case:** the upside-down badge

Jobsworth stories where officials have implemented rules that seem petty and where people have been punished for seemingly minor infringements of the rules often make the news.

For example, in 2011 a pensioner with a disability in Nottinghamshire, UK, was fined £35 for parking in a disabled parking bay with the relevant accreditation badge displayed in the windscreen, but upside down (BBC News, 2011).

On one hand, the rules state that the badge must be legible. Following the rules to the letter, it was correct to issue the fine. However, the overall aim of the rules is to prevent people without the correct accreditation parking in a disabled bay. Here, we can interpret a mismatch between the spirit and aim of the rules, and their rigid implementation.

**Source:** BBC News (2011).

Disabled parking bay sign.

**Bureaucratic personality**
A tendency to follow rules to the letter rather than seeing the wider picture and making more common-sense judgements.

**Trained incapacity**
Where people are so used to their behaviour being controlled by bureaucratic rules and procedures that they become inflexible and unable to think for themselves and show initiative.

An unquestioning adherence to rules is an example of what Merton (1940) termed the **bureaucratic personality**. The rules are seen as important above all else, to the extent that 'conformity with the rules interferes with the achievement of the purposes of the organization' (Merton, 1940: 563). Rather than being guided by what would be of benefit to the organization overall, or to a particular client or customer of the organization, a bureaucratic personality suggests simply doing as one is told by the rules and procedures.

A similar unflinching adherence to rules and procedures is encapsulated by the phrase **trained incapacity**, which describes people so reliant on rules and procedures that they become inflexible and unable to act in any other way. If something new or different happens, they are so set in their ways that they are unable to adapt and deal with the change.

---

### Theory in context: 'computer says no'

A recurring sketch on the BBC comedy *Little Britain* depicts an office worker, variously working in a bank, travel agency, or hospital, who feeds information from customers into a computer which then makes decisions on her behalf. The catchphrase 'computer says no' depicts the clerk having no human input into the decision—it is all a result of information and procedures encoded within the computer system. When asked if decisions can be changed, she proves to be inflexible—unable to do anything beyond what the computer says. The character is portrayed as dehumanized, almost robotic, and is an example of the 'bureaucratic personality'.

---

 Visit the Online Resource Centre for links to video clips of the show.

**Work to rule** A form of industrial action where workers follow rules, regulations, and instructions precisely—this often results in the speed of work slowing considerably.

As with red tape, the notion of the bureaucratic personality suggests that, rather than being technically efficient, bureaucracy can have the opposite effect and hinder an organization in achieving its aims. Indeed, a common form of industrial action is the **work to rule**. Through following rules and procedures to the letter, work is actually slowed down dramatically—the instruments of bureaucracy are used against the organization.

## Bending the rules and exercising discretion

You may have heard the phrase 'rules are meant to be broken'. Many bureaucracies operate *despite* their rules—if people followed them to the letter they would get in the way of the organization running smoothly, creating too much red tape or inflexibility. In this respect, people are seen to operate not with a bureaucratic personality, but by interpreting and bending the rules where necessary.

Blau (1963) studied workers in a US business law enforcement agency. He found that workers would make informal adjustments to formal rules and requirements if it helped to get the job done or if the formal requirements were getting in the way. Workers who bent rules actually got jobs done more efficiently and achieved organizational goals better than those who followed rules to the letter.

Lipsky (1980) noted that discretion is required by social work professionals in applying rules in different cases. He suggests that they deploy a form of 'street-level bureaucracy', judging each case as it comes and in its own context, rather than applying rules to the letter. It is a more contextual, flexible application of rules and procedures than that of the rigid bureaucratic personality. Barton (2003) notes a similar exercise of discretion in police work. While the purpose of police work is ostensibly to enforce rules (or in this case laws), at street level officers use their own judgement and discretion as to which laws to apply and when. The best end result might come from a 'quiet word' rather than applying a particular law to the letter, which could inflame a sensitive situation.

The ultimate in bending rules is where they are ignored. Gouldner (1954) suggested that where rules are imposed and seen as unnecessary there might exist a **mock bureaucracy**—the rules exist on paper but are ignored in practice. Sometimes the phrase 'we have a policy' suggests that the policy exists but is not necessarily followed.

**Mock bureaucracy**
A situation where policies and rules exist, but are ignored.

## The inflexibility of bureaucracy

The examples in this section all show a distinction between the ideal type of bureaucracy and bureaucracy in practice whereby its rules, structures, and paperwork are used more flexibly. As we have seen, this flexibility can be necessary in order to get the job done—a rigid adherence to bureaucratic rules and procedures leads to dysfunctions, such as red tape and the bureaucratic personality (see Morgan, 2006: 26–7, for more on where bureaucracy may or may not be appropriate).

---

**Real life case:** Accenture ditches annual performance reviews

Accenture is a global management consultancy and professional services company headquartered in Ireland. In 2015 it announced, along with a growing number of Fortune 500 companies, that it would no longer be subjecting its employees to the bureaucratic demands of annual performance reviews (Cunningham, 2015a). These reviews are a form of appraisal, where employees are measured against a set of performance objectives. Employees have to fill in forms and paperwork to demonstrate how well they have met these targets and metrics. Data and records about employee performance are also fed into the process so that employees can be ranked against each other. For Vara (2015), such numerical classification and hierarchical ranking of employees makes performance review an example of the 'bureaucratic corporate cultures' of the twentieth century.

As with other bureaucratic techniques, performance review is a means of controlling and managing a large number of employees distributed across the globe. However, the CEO of Accenture, Pierre Nanterme, began to see problems with what he described as this 'maximum bureaucracy'. He suggested that rather than motivating people to perform better, as is the objective of a performance review process, it 'blocked' people, stifling them beneath a mass of metrics and objectives (Cunningham, 2015b). Even for workers with good performance reviews, there is evidence that the process can trigger disengagement and constrict openness to creativity and growth (Cunningham, 2015c). As Bright (2015) notes, performance review leads to people aiming their work effort towards meeting the objectives being measured—why do something that doesn't add to your performance measures? As such, a lot of the informal work and goodwill that organizations rely on is no longer done by employees as it isn't officially measured. ▶

>     While performance review, for Accenture, did not achieve its goal of improving performance, it was also wasteful in terms of the time and expense spent on filling out forms and carrying out evaluations. The new system, which involved giving more regular individual feedback to employees on specific projects undertaken, was aimed not only at being more relevant and effective but also at taking away 90% of the bureaucratic burden associated with performance review for over 300,000 employees (Cunningham, 2015c).

 Can you see any of the problems of bureaucracy discussed in this chapter in evidence in the Accenture case? Think about Weber's disenchantment, or some of the dysfunctions of bureaucracy such as red tape, the bureaucratic personality, bending the rules, and inflexibility.

 Visit the Online Resource Centre for more discussion of the dysfunctions of bureaucracy.

### Review questions

| | |
|---|---|
| **Describe** | What are the different dysfunctions of bureaucracy? |
| **Explain** | What is meant when bureaucracy is described as being inflexible? |
| **Analyse** | How might red tape prevent people from doing the work that they are employed to do? |
| **Apply** | In the Junction Hotel case, what type of bureaucratic dysfunctions can you see in the different actions of staff at the hotel? |

# Evaluating bureaucracy: a double-edged sword?

Bureaucracy can be seen as something of a double-edged sword. On one hand, it makes possible management and activity on a large scale that would otherwise be beyond human capability. The vast majority of the organizations that exist today would not be possible without bureaucracy. On the other hand, bureaucracy has negative aspects, both in its dehumanizing effects upon people and its dysfunctions.

That most, if not all, organizations employ some form of bureaucracy is a testament to its undoubted advantages:

- it not only allows for Fayol's five aspects of management (planning, organizing, commanding, coordination, and control) to take place, but it allows for them to be done efficiently on a large scale
- it solves the problem of keeping order within an organization as it grows in scale
- it creates clear roles and responsibilities, outlining clear lines of authority and the limits of that authority

- it allows for information about individuals in organizations, even whole populations, to be stored in a form that is easily manageable

- it ensures **impersonal fairness** within the organization, for example with equal opportunities; rules and procedures that are in place are intended to bring about equality and fairness in how workers are treated as much as to bring about control for management (see du Gay, 2000).

These advantages, however, come at the expense of some considerable disadvantages of bureaucracy:

- what might be rational in formal terms may not be substantively rational—bureaucracy is ethically neutral and simply a means to an end

- it can create negative human consequences—its routines and procedures are dehumanizing and disenchanting, in Weber's terms encasing society and people in an 'iron cage'

- its inflexibility creates inefficient dysfunctions, such as red tape and the bureaucratic personality, such that bureaucracy might be circumvented rather than adhered to rigidly.

> **Impersonal fairness**
> The idea that standardized bureaucratic procedures treat people equally and avoid the personal prejudice and preferences that individual managers might have.

## The death of bureaucracy?

An overall critique of bureaucracy is that its inflexibility leaves organizations unable to adapt to change, for instance to changes in the law, in the actions of competitors, or in the demand for a product or service (see Chapter 11 for more on organizations and change management; and Chapter 10 for the 'organizational learning' perspective where the emphasis is on developing creative, autonomous workers rather than workers simply following rules). This might not have been such a problem when Fayol and Weber were writing, when the world that organizations faced was seen to be more stable.

In Chapter 4 we will see a move from bureaucracy to post-bureaucracy. In response to a more dynamic, fast-changing world, organizations have developed more flexible structures and means of dealing with rules and paperwork than that suggested by the rigid, ideal type. From this perspective, dysfunctions have made bureaucracy, at least in the form described by Fayol and Weber, obsolete in the contemporary world.

However, it is wrong to proclaim the 'coming death of bureaucracy' (Bennis, 1966). Bureaucracy is used in all organizations in one form or another, even if it is not in the rigid type described by Fayol and Weber. In Chapter 4 we will also see how contemporary organizations not only make use of bureaucracy but also use it in, arguably, a more intensive way. In Chapter 16 (discussing service industries) we will see that rational forms of control are more than prevalent in modern-day service industries.

## Computers and bureaucracy

Bureaucracy is now usually implemented by computers rather than paperwork in filing cabinets. Given that bureaucracy is as much about holding and processing records and information as it is about structure, it is a task at which computers are adept. Indeed, the language used to describe how computer information is organized uses bureaucratic imagery, with 'files' and 'folders' an allusion to the paperwork of bureaucracy and its storage.

The bureaucratic power of organizations is helped greatly by the information processing power and speed of computers. Chapter 14 looks specifically at information and computer technologies. However, it is worth noting here not only that computers enhance the power of bureaucracy, but also

Traditional filing system.
**Source:** © Elena Elisseeva/123RF.

that their use in organizations very much reflects and enhances bureaucratic procedures. Furthermore, in a world dominated by computer networks, bureaucracy plays a role in ensuring that information communicated between computer networks is stored in a standardized format (Kallinikos, 2004: 18).

Computers also aid the monitoring and control function of bureaucracy. Paperwork and records store data about people, as do computer databases—at an organizational or governmental level. Such surveillance and its implementation through computer technology are explored in Chapter 4.

The earlier example of the UCAS application showed an image of a form on paper. This information is now computerised, with the forms being filled in online and immediately stored as records on a database. How does this help UCAS in processing the vast amount of applications that it receives each year? How do you think this helps universities and individual university applicants?

Early models of bureaucracy can be seen as somewhat inflexible and dated. However, aspects of bureaucratic design and functioning similar to these are a necessary part of the workplace today, as will be seen in subsequent chapters.

## Further reading

Morgan, G. 2006. *Images of organization.* Sage Publications: Thousand Oaks, CA.
    See Chapter 2 'Mechanisation takes command: Organizations as machines' for an overview of bureaucracy and how it fits in with other aspects of rational work design.

Pugh, D.S. 2008. *Organization theory: Selected classic readings.* Penguin Books: London.
    Contains extracts of original writings from Weber and Fayol (and other chapters relate to other theories in this book).

Pryor, M.G., and Taneja, S. 2010. Henri Fayol, practitioner and theoretician—revered and reviled. *Journal of Management History* 16(4): 489–503.
    A clear but critical introduction to Fayol's work and its relevance to contemporary management.

For the two reports mentioned in this chapter which examine red tape and bureaucratic dysfunctions in UK social work and policing, see:

Munro, E. 2010. *The Munro review of child protection.* Department for Education: London. Available at: http://www.education.gov.uk/munroreview/firstreport.shtml

Berry, J. 2010. *Reducing bureaucracy in policing.* Home Office: London. Available at: http://www.homeoffice.gov.uk/publications/police/reducing-bureaucracy/reduce-bureaucracy-police

## References

Adams, R. 2015. Nicky Morgan vows to end needless bureaucracy for teachers. *The Guardian*, 29 July.

Barton, H. 2003. Understanding occupational (sub) culture—a precursor for reform: The case of the police service in England and Wales. *International Journal of Public Sector Management* 16 (5): 346–58.

Bauman, Z. 1989. *Modernity and the holocaust*. Polity Press: Cambridge.

BBC News. 2011. Nottingham pensioner fined £35 for 'upside down' badge. Available at: http://www.bbc.co.uk/news/uk-england-nottinghamshire-13891422 (last accessed 10 August 2015).

Bell, E. 2008. *Reading management and organization in film*. Palgrave Macmillan: Basingstoke.

Bennis, W. 1966. The coming death of bureaucracy. *Think Magazine*, November–December: 30–5.

Berry, J. 2010. *Reducing bureaucracy in policing*. Home Office: London.

Blau, P.M. 1963. *The dynamics of bureaucracy: A study of interpersonal relations in two Government agencies*. University of Chicago Press: Chicago.

Bright, J. 2015. Accenture dumps annual performance reviews and emphasises freedom and trust. *Sydney Morning Herald*, 1 August.

Butler, S. 2014. John Lewis in party mood as 150th anniversary nears. *The Guardian*, 19 April.

Chia, R. 1995. From modern to postmodern organizational analysis. *Organization Studies* 16 (4): 579–604.

Cunningham, L. 2015a. In big move, Accenture will get rid of annual performance reviews and rankings. *Washington Post* , 21 July.

Cunningham, L. 2015b. Accenture CEO explains why he's overhauling performance reviews. *Washington Post*, 23 July.

Cunningham, L. 2015c. Accenture: One of world's biggest companies to scrap annual performance reviews. *The Independent* , 28 July.

du Gay, P. 2000. *In praise of bureaucracy: Weber, organization, ethics*. Sage: London.

Fayol, H. 1949. *General and industrial management*. Pitman: London.

Gilliam, T. 1985. *Brazil*. 20th Century Fox.

Gouldner, A.W. 1954. *Patterns of industrial bureaucracy*. Free Press: Glencoe, IL.

Greggs the Bakers. 2015. History. Available at: https://www.greggs.co.uk/about-us/history/ (last accessed 10 August 2015).

John Lewis Partnership. 2015. Our Founder. Available at: http://www.johnlewispartnership.co.uk/about/our-founder.html (last accessed 10 August 2015).

Kallinikos, J. 2004. The social foundations of the bureaucratic order. *Organization* 11 (1): 13–36.

Lipsky, M. 1980. *Street-level bureaucracy: Dilemmas of the individual and public services*. Russell Sage Foundation: New York.

MacRae, D.G. 1974. *Weber*. Fontana: Glasgow.

Merton, R.K. 1940. Bureaucratic structure and personality. *Social Forces* 18 (4): 560–8.

Morgan, G. 2006. *Images of organization*. Sage Publications: Thousand Oaks, CA.

Munro, E. 2010. *The Munro review of child protection*. Department for Education: London.

Perry, N. 1992. Putting theory in its place: The social organization of organizational theorizing. In: Reed, M., and Hughes, M. (eds) *Rethinking organization*. Sage: London, pp. 85–101.

Poster, M. 1995. *The second media age*. Polity Press: Cambridge.

Pryor, M.G., and Taneja, S. 2010. Henri Fayol, practitioner and theoretician—revered and reviled. *Journal of Management History* 16 (4): 489–503.

Ritzer, G. 2015. *The McDonaldization of society*, 8th edn. Pine Forge Press: Thousand Oaks, CA.

Ruddick, G. 2013. Aldi: A history of the low-cost supermarket. *Daily Telegraph*, 30 September.

Smith, I., and Boyns, T. 2005. British management theory and practice: The impact of Fayol. *Management Decision* 43 (10): 1317–34.

Telefónica. 2015. Executive team, June 1015. Available at: http://www.telefonica.com/en/about_telefonica/html/organisation/equipdirect.shtml (last accessed 10 August 2015).

Telefónica Deutschland. 2015. Management board of Telefónica Deutschland Holding AG. Available at: https://www.telefonica.de/company/management.html (last accessed 10 August 2015).

The Official Board. 2015. Telefónica. Available at: http://www.theofficialboard.com/org-chart/telefonica (last accessed 10 August 2015).

Thompson, P., and McHugh, D. 2009. *Work organisations: A critical approach*. Palgrave Macmillan: Basingstoke.

Vara, V. 2015. The push against performance reviews. *New Yorker*, 24 July.

Watson, T.J. 2002. *Organising and managing work: Organisational, managerial, and strategic behaviour in theory and practice*. Financial Times/Prentice Hall: Harlow.

Weber, M. 1958. *The Protestant ethic and the spirit of capitalism*. Scribner: New York.

Weber, M. 1968. *Economy and society: An outline of interpretive sociology*. Bedminster Press: New York.

Wren, D.A. 2001. Henri Fayol as strategist: A nineteenth century corporate turnaround. *Management Decision* 39(6): 475–87.

# 3 Rational work design
## Cutting costs, increasing control

## Chapter overview and learning outcomes

By the end of this chapter you should be able to:

- describe the principles behind Taylorist and Fordist rational work design

- explain how Taylorism and Fordism contributed to control over the workforce and the creation of more efficient forms of working

- analyse the effects that Taylorism and Fordism are said to have upon workers by reducing them to

'cogs in a machine,' including the critiques by Marx and Braverman

- explain the legacy of Taylorism and its prevalence in working methods today, such that they have been described as 'the most enduring social change of the 20th century' (Donkin, 2001: 159).

## Key theorists

| | |
|---|---|
| Frederick Winslow Taylor | An industrialist and one of the prominent pioneers of efficient, rational work design, Taylor developed the system of 'scientific management' |
| Henry Ford | An industrialist and pioneer of rational management techniques, Ford created systems of mass automobile production with his innovation of the moving assembly line |
| Frank and Lillian Gilbreth | Contemporaries and associates of Taylor, known particularly for developing the time and motion study and ergonomic work design |
| Karl Marx | A political philosopher who commented on the inequalities of power between capital and workers and the negative, alienating effects of capitalist work upon workers |
| Harry Braverman | From a Marxist perspective developed the deskilling thesis that criticized the loss of craft skills under rational production methods |

## Key terms

| | |
|---|---|
| Rational work design, rational production | The techniques developed by Taylor and Ford, among others; work is designed to achieve maximum efficiency, and organizations and workers are the tools used to achieve this efficiency |
| Capitalist working relationship | The relationship between capitalists, who pay wages, and labour, who work in return for those wages |

| Scientific management, Taylorism | The techniques pioneered by Frederick Taylor whereby work is broken down into small tasks which are then measured precisely and designed to be performed in the most efficient manner possible |
|---|---|
| Fordism | Rational work design, pioneered by Henry Ford, where work is designed for maximum efficiency; the worker remains stationary in front of a moving assembly line and repeats the same task |
| Efficiency | Getting more output from the same amount of resource input, e.g. time, money, labour |
| Deskilling | From the work of Braverman (1974), this is the loss of craft skills and expert knowledge experienced by workers when their jobs are simplified to fit in with rational work design |
| Alienation | From the work of Marx (1894/1981), this is a number of ways in which rational work design impacts workers negatively, isolating them from their skills, the final product, and their co-workers |

# Introduction

## Running case: the bottom line

Simon Chance is worried. Junction Hotel is not breaking even, and there are rumours of a budget hotel opening nearby. Furthermore, Chance is presented with a report by his investors, which makes for grim reading.

The executive summary states:

- having weathered a recession, the hotel industry is suffering—corporate customers are reducing spend on hotels
- prices need to come down to remain competitive and for the hotel to stay in business—*to afford that price reduction, Junction Hotel needs to reduce its costs*
- budget hotels are aggressively cutting costs, for example by removing free toiletries.

Chance has a dilemma. Junction is a luxury hotel—if they cut corners, then customers will complain and the hotel will lose its reputation. At the same time, low-cost competitors are taking business away from them.

Chance calls in business manager Phil Weaver, who has overseen many efficiency drives in his career. Weaver looks over the accounts and declares: 'You know, your biggest cost isn't shampoo or wallpaper or anything like that. Your biggest cost is your wage bill. That's the bottom line—it's losing you money and making you uncompetitive. *There's a lot of waste and inefficiency.*'

'There are plenty of opportunities to reduce your wage bill and still get the same job done. I've stayed here before and seen your cleaners stood around gossiping. Tell you what: let me have a closer look at what they do—I bet I can make them much more productive and bring down the wage bill.'

Chance looks queasy, 'I don't know,' he says. 'They do a good job—I wouldn't want to rock the boat. I don't think they would like you interfering in what they do.'

'The problem is you haven't got a clue what they do!' retorts Weaver. 'If you want this hotel to survive then you need to take *control*. It's not that you are just paying your cleaners—they are taking you to the cleaners! Let me have a go at getting them to work for their money.'

**Cost** is a concern for all managers. Recent global financial crises have led to companies and governments making efficiency drives, taking austerity measures, slashing budgets, and taking other actions in order to cut costs. The justification for government is to cut waste, reduce the deficit, and produce more efficient public services at better value for money. Businesses have also had massive cost-cutting exercises, which they claim are needed to cope during difficult economic times—possibly even to stay in business.

**Cost**  The amount in wages and materials that it costs to produce a good or provide a service.

We all like our money to stretch as far as it can, especially when on a tight budget. Think about how you minimize your own personal costs—shopping around, using comparison websites, and taking advantage of 'happy hours' and 'two-for-one'-type offers. All of these allow us to get more from our hard-earned money.

Even in times of economic growth, control of costs is an issue for business. Reduced costs can mean that lower prices can be charged (giving a competitive advantage) or increased profits can be reaped, leading to increased shareholder dividends. As will be seen in Chapter 4 ('Rationalization in contemporary organizations'), there are successful contemporary business models, such as budget hotels and airlines, which focus on price competition through intensive cost reduction. In Chapter 15 ('Globalization'), we see how international competition can undercut costs at home.

---

**Theory in context:** Wedgwood and costs

Cost control is not just a recent issue. In the eighteenth century, the pottery industrialist Josiah Wedgwood identified costs as a major area of measurement and control in setting market prices for his goods. Beforehand, pricing had been a result of educated guesswork, which had led to Wedgwood making a loss. While Wedgwood was a one-off pioneer in his own day, costs are now a major area of control for companies and organizations (McKendrick, 1970; Hoskin and Macve, 1986: 124; Morgan, 1990: 103–6).

---

One of the largest costs, if not *the* main cost for most organizations, is labour—the amount spent on wages (Simpson, 1999: 52). In this chapter, we examine how **rational work design** is applied to the **labour process** in order to create workers who are more cost effective. In other words, through the design of work itself, workers do more for the wages they are paid—they are more efficient and more productive.

Rational work design, as we will see in Chapter 4, is pervasive in today's workplaces. However, it developed from a period of rapid industrialization and the development of the factory system in the Western world around the early 1900s. Industrialists, such as Frederick Taylor and Henry Ford, designed work to be as efficient as possible. While Taylor and Ford are synonymous with rational work design (the terms **Taylorism** and **Fordism** being used, respectively, to describe their scientific management and assembly line innovations), they share the key features of rational work design with many other innovators of their time, which we summarize as:

- work is seen as a means of achieving a clearly defined end
- work is designed so as to achieve this end in the optimum or most efficient possible manner, both in terms of time and cost

**Rational work design**  The design of work tasks to achieve maximum efficiency and reduce costs.

**Labour process**  How work is designed and controlled by management.

**Taylorism**  The work process designed by Taylor, associated with the division of labour into small tasks, which are then redesigned to be performed as efficiently as possible.

**Fordism**  The use of a moving assembly line to mass produce goods.

- work is designed in a scientific manner, using measurement and calculation, as if designing a machine
- work is broken down into simple, repetitive tasks which take little or no skill to perform—a **division of labour**
- waste is designed out of the work process.

While rational work design might make workers more efficient and cost-effective, we will see that this comes at a cost. Workers are subject to increased managerial control and monotonous, simple work which leaves their skills superfluous to requirements. The chapter will look at critiques of rational work design from Karl Marx and Harry Braverman, examining the considerable resistance encountered when implementing such techniques.

Thus rational work design is seen not just as a technique for reducing the cost of labour, but also as a technique which attempts to exert control over workers. This struggle for control stems from the nature of the capitalist working relationship.

# The capitalist working relationship: cost and control

## Running case: Amy Turtle

Amy Turtle is in her mid-50s and has been a cleaner all her working life. She has been with Junction Hotel for ten years, and before that she was self-employed for twenty years. While she had enjoyed the independence of working for herself, she took on the position during a time when her client list was dwindling, and opted, instead, for a regular salary rather than the risk and hassle of managing her own business.

Her relationship with Linda Wilkinson is good—they are both old-timers at the hotel. With Wilkinson being busy enough with other tasks, she happily leaves the cleaning side to run itself, trusting Turtle to keep her eye on things. It's as if Turtle is still managing herself and, indeed, she resents any attempt by management to interfere in her cleaning work.

During her time at Junction Hotel, Turtle has developed a reputation as being a knowledgeable cleaner and a formidable character. She brings much experience and knowledge into the workplace, and is very much the 'queen bee' among the cleaners. Sometimes, she even brings in her own cleaning products to try out—she likes nothing more than the challenge of a new or mysterious stain to tackle.

Turtle socializes with the older cleaners and is a matronly presence with the younger ones. In the reorganization she is promoted to Head Cleaner. This very much reflects a role she has held informally for many years, whereby she is part supervisor—instilling fear in the younger cleaners who might stray—and part champion, sticking up for 'the girls' when necessary and taking their concerns to the management.

Rational work design needs to be understood in the context of changes that the early factory system brought about in the early 1900s. Prior to the factory system, manufacturing work was often based around the individual family household—the backyard workshop or furnace was commonplace (see Thompson and McHugh, 2009: 20). The work had a number of features which may seem unusual today other than for people who are self-employed:

- workers owned their own **means of production**—tools, equipment, etc.
- workers were independent and autonomous, i.e. they were their own boss—they decided their own working time, the amount they would sell goods for, the amount they would take as a wage or reinvest in the business, etc.

While many workers today might crave such independence, it comes with a degree of risk. The individual worker is exposed if, say, equipment breaks down and needs expensive repairs, or if orders drop suddenly. Furthermore, such production is inefficient—it doesn't take advantage of **economies of scale**, that is to say each piece of equipment or capital investment is not used to its optimum.

See the Online Resource Centre for a description of how the textile industry in Nottingham, UK, developed from home-based working into industrial, factory-based production.

The factory system took advantage of economies of scale. Rather than having individual workers, each independently investing in their own small-scale equipment, a factory brought together a group of workers in one space, operating large-scale equipment (see Simpson, 1999: 48). The initial outlay on equipment might be more expensive, but for the number of workers that can use that equipment it works out less than each of them buying their own equipment individually.

The shift to the factory system brought about a new working relationship.

- Workers no longer owned their own means of production. Factories required massive capital outlay, beyond the means of any one individual worker. Factory owners, either wealthy individuals or groups of shareholders, were, thus, capitalists, providing that initial outlay and owning the means of production.
- Capitalists paid a wage to workers who would work in their service within the factory. Workers lost their previous independence and autonomy—their working hours would be dictated and their tasks set, and they would have no control over the price of goods or investment decisions, etc. Their role was simply to turn up and do a day's work.

Thus, the **capitalist wage–labour** relationship is an exchange (Figure 3.1). The capitalist who owns and invests **capital** in a company pays a wage to workers. In return for this wage, workers supply their **labour**.

The capitalist wage–labour relationship gives rise to a need for management. Workers are directed in what to do, what time to arrive, when to leave work, etc. All of this needs to be implemented by management. But where would management appear in Figure 3.1? On one hand, management are the agents of capital, doing their bidding in directing workers. On the other hand, managers are not owners. Just like the people they direct and control, they too are wage labourers.

**Means of production** Tools, premises, and other property used to manufacture goods.

**Economies of scale** Cost reduction that comes from producing a product in large amounts.

**Capitalist wage–labour relationship** The relationship between capitalists, who pay wages, and labour, who work in return for those wages.

**Capital** Investment in a business to set up the means of production, often used as a term to refer to business owners or capitalists who make that investment.

**Labour** Any person who works in return for a wage; the term is used to refer to such workers collectively.

**Figure 3.1** The capitalist wage–labour relationship.

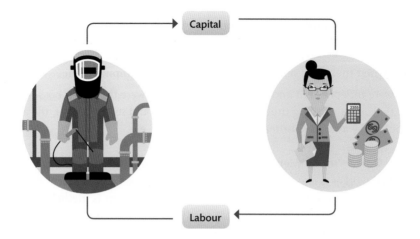

## Tensions in the capitalist wage-labour relationship

This relationship between capital and labour, fairly new at the time the factory system first developed, might seem like a simple exchange, but a fundamental tension lies at its heart: capital and labour want different things and have different priorities.

Capital has an interest in getting the most work for the wages they pay, i.e. in obtaining maximum efficiency. This means the employees working to their maximum possible output and not wasting time and effort. It is here that such techniques as rational work design act in the favour of capital by maximizing what effort they get for their labour costs.

However, as we saw in Chapter 2, what might be rational from one perspective may not be from another. Workers have an interest in not being worked necessarily to the optimum, but in taking regular breaks, having holidays and paid sick leave, etc. All of these conflict with the capitalist's desire to maximize effort in return for the wage (Figure 3.2).

As we will see, from a Marxist perspective the capitalist working relationship becomes one of a battle of control between two conflicting sets of interests as much as it is an exchange of effort in return for wages—one which can result in conflict and resistance. **Industrial action**, such as strikes, is often a result of disagreements over aspects of the capitalist working relationship, such as pay and working conditions, etc.

**Industrial action** Any action taken by workers in a dispute between capital and labour.

**Figure 3.2** Conflict in the capitalist wage–labour relationship.

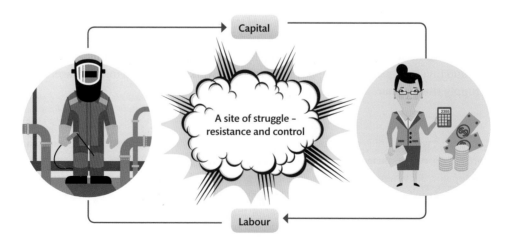

A site of struggle – resistance and control

In the following sections we see how rational work design was used by Taylor, Ford, and their contemporaries not just as a means of gaining **efficiency** for the wages paid, but also as a means of asserting control from the side of capital in the wage–labour relationship. The Marxist critique, examined later in the chapter, recognizes how conflict might be an inevitable outcome of such control given the tensions inherent in the relationship.

**Efficiency** The minimization of cost, doing the same for less input of time and money.

## Review questions

| | |
|---|---|
| **Describe** | What are the main features of the capitalist wage–labour relationship? |
| **Explain** | Why was the factory 'a revolutionary organisational form' (Simpson, 1999: 48)? |
| **Analyse** | Why might workers not want the same things as capitalists in the wage–labour relationship? |
| **Apply** | How can the employment of Amy Turtle (a) before and (b) after she joined Junction Hotel be explained in terms of the capitalist wage-labour relationship? Do you think that the hotel is getting the most from her for the wages that they pay her? |

# Frederick W. Taylor: efficiency and control

**Running case:** initial observations

Phil Weaver shows his notebook, in which he has made his initial observations of the cleaning process, to Linda Wilkinson.

*Amazing—no method or routine. Cleaners put in pairs, given list of rooms to do then left to get on with it—all of them approach the task in different ways and have had different training in how to clean. Lots of gossiping—with each other and with guests. Turtle might tell the younger ones off but she covers up for them in front of management—she looks after her own first. Best of all—they deliberately speed up the morning shift to get an extra 30 mins gossiping time over lunch. If they can work that quickly they should be doing more. Problem is, no management to be seen—there's no control over them: they are a law unto themselves.*

Wilkinson gives him a knowing smile and replies, 'Phil, don't you think I realize that? Thing is—they are happy, the job gets done, and I get an easy life'. Weaver, however, is getting more and more frustrated: 'That's 30 minutes when they could be doing something else—30 minutes you are paying them for.' 'Look,' says Wilkinson more seriously, 'I learned my lesson a few years back. I did ask Amy whether they would be able to squeeze a few more rooms in before lunch but she blinded me with science—told me how long different processes would take. She outlined different ways of tackling different stains, all built up from her years of experience, and talked about the dangers from various different bacteria if she didn't clean properly and thoroughly. In the end, I gave up.'

'This is nonsense!' yells Weaver. 'You have no control over these workers. If anything, they control you and, as a result, you are getting far less out of them than is possible for the wages you pay.'

'Let me have a look at this more closely,' says Wilkinson.

Taylor's rational work design innovations transformed how organizations operated, and they still have a major impact on how we live and work today. His *The principles of scientific management* (Taylor, 1911), developed in the early 1900s in the Philadelphia steel industry, identified a set of techniques that came to be known simply as 'Taylorism'.

**Scientific management** The use of scientific techniques to design work to be as efficient as possible.

For Taylor, as suggested by the term **scientific management**, there was a *science* of management and the organization was to be managed as if it were a machine. An industrial engineer by training, he saw management problems just like mechanical and engineering problems. In the words of his biographer, Taylor saw the world through the eyes of both an economist and an engineer (Copley, 1923a: xviii).

In this respect, Taylorism is often seen as being simply about efficiency, minimizing waste and increasing output. However, such attempts at efficiency are directed within the capitalist wage–labour relationship at people rather than machines. And, while Taylor wanted to design organizations like machines, people do not necessarily behave in the same precisely controllable manner.

> **Theory in context:** Taylor's obsessions
>
> Bahnisch (2000) notes that a number of commentators have written about the 'obsessional' and 'neurotic' nature of Taylor's personality and his desire for control. His meticulous attention to detail crossed over into aspects of his private life, such as positions for sleeping and steps to be taken when dancing. His hobby of golf was also addressed with a similar attention to detail, with Taylor devoting time to designing golf clubs and even analysing different types of grass which would provide the optimum performance on the putting green (Copley, 1923b). It is this obsession and attention to detail that he took into his workplace experiments, and which feeds into many rational management techniques that exist today.

## Taylor's 'problems' of control over labour

When Taylor first began working in a factory environment, he viewed the existing approach to work as rather amateurish, governed by traditions and habits—all of which were controlled by the workers. The management, Taylor thought, had little control over what was happening and did little to influence the work process.

Visit the Online Resource Centre for more information on the early factory systems.

In *The principles of scientific management*, Taylor (1911) identifies a number of problems with how work at that time was organized, which indicate that his concerns were as much about control as they were efficiency. In that people do not behave and are not easily controlled like machines, this presented a number of problems of control over labour which, for Taylor, got in the way of the efficiency that he craved.

## Non-standard and unpredictable labour

In the Philadelphia steel industry, where Taylor worked, there was a mix of people within his factory. They came from different craft traditions, each with their own ways of performing jobs; furthermore, many had a variety of cultural backgrounds, languages, and, indeed, attitudes to work (Jaffee, 2001: 51; Thompson and McHugh, 2009: 29). Workers could certainly not be seen as standard units that would behave and be controlled in the same way as would components in a machine.

## Craft knowledge and power

**Craft knowledge** is where workers have specialist expertise in the work that they do. This was a problem for Taylor because it meant that they held power over him as a manager. He did not know the work as intimately as his workers and, thus, when he asked a question about how long a process would take or how much it would cost he relied, to a large extent, on them being truthful about their expert knowledge.

Workers would use their craft knowledge to create a **rule of thumb** (Taylor, 1911: 16)—the estimate that workers would give for the time a job would take. This was the workers controlling the work process—they could blind management with science, take longer to do tasks, and even demand higher wages because their skills were not easily replaceable.

> **Craft knowledge** Knowledge of a particular skill, often the result of a long period of training or apprenticeship.
>
> **Rule of thumb** A rough estimate of the time needed to perform a task, based on a worker's expert knowledge of that task.

Have you ever had to take your computer or car to be repaired? When you are given a quote for the amount that the repairs will cost and the time that it will take, are you in a position to argue back and negotiate? The mechanic or engineer has an advantage over you because of their expert knowledge, which you are not in a position to dispute.

## Soldiering

Taylor believed that a typical worker was inherently lazy, lacking the motivation to work other than picking up a wage at the end of the day: 'this man plans to do as little as he safely can . . . to do not more than one-third to one-half of a proper day's work' (Taylor, 1911: 13).

However, while this natural individual **soldiering** (ibid.: 13) was one thing, the fact that workers were organized in tightly-knit gangs led to a more systematic form of soldiering, with pressures from co-workers to 'underperform'. Using their expert knowledge and the 'rule of thumb' they could cover for each other, overestimating to management the time that it would take to complete a job and thus improving their own conditions of work by making more time available, leaving room for breaks, and thus not working to the optimum.

> **Soldiering** Techniques used by workers to create time for themselves during the working day. Soldiering means that workers are not working at the most efficient level possible.

From Taylor's perspective, the drive to control workers for greater efficiency and his frustration with workers' own control over the work process was understandable. However, looking back at the nature of the capitalist working relationship, it is also understandable why workers wanted to maintain and exert that control—they maintained autonomy over the pace and nature of their work, earned extra time in the form of breaks, and generally helped to maintain some balance in their side of the working relationship. It was with Taylor's innovations in scientific management that this balance would be changed more firmly in favour of management.

## Review questions

| | |
|---|---|
| **Describe** | What is meant by craft knowledge? |
| **Explain** | How does craft knowledge give workers power over management? |
| **Explain** | How did human labour present a problem for the ways in which Taylor wished to control an organization? |
| **Analyse** | What were Taylor's central assumptions about how an organization should be managed? How did his background as an engineer influence these assumptions? |
| **Apply** | How do you think Taylor would view the power held by Amy Turtle and the cleaners at Junction Hotel? |

# Scientific management: finding the 'one best way'

## Running case: the one best way

Weaver observes the cleaners, running about with a clipboard, timing workers with a stopwatch, and measuring the distances they walk from room to room. He even sets up a video camera to record cleaners as they go around a room. When he plays it back, he can make further detailed measurements of the work process, analysing the pictures with some specialist computer software.

He starts taking cleaners to one side to practise different movements, demonstrating a series of basic moves which they should perform every time they clean a toilet, and constantly measuring and refining the moves to make them more and more efficient and reduce the time taken to clean one toilet.

Similar routines are devised for such tasks as making beds, replacing towels, and cleaning all parts of the room. In each case, the task is broken down into a set of pre-defined movements which Weaver then refines to make more efficient. In all cases, wasted movements are to be eliminated—including stopping and gossiping mid-way through a shift.

Everything has its right place in the room—the TV remote, the kettle, sachets of tea and coffee, writing paper, etc., with the aim of standardizing the process and removing any variability in the job.

Weaver also suggests that equipment and fittings could be designed to make the process even more efficient. Items would be laid out on the trolley in the order in which they would be placed in the room, for example toiletries first, and tea and coffee second. Trolleys should be big enough to accommodate all the linen and equipment needed so as to avoid wasteful trips down to the laundry or the store cupboard to reload.

Eventually, following all of his observations and work redesigns, Weaver presents the 'one best way' to clean a room, proudly written down in a training manual given to all cleaners. Whereas a room previously took an average of 30 minutes to clean, Weaver sets a target of 15 minutes per room.

Taylor firmly believed that for any job there was **one best way** to perform it. The four principles of scientific management that he outlined not only increased the efficiency with which a job was performed, but also put power in the hands of management by understanding exactly what work people did to make a product and creating the standard one best way for workers to then perform that task. The four principles, which we will examine in turn in this section, are (based on Taylor, 1911):

One best way
Rational management techniques that propose the one most efficient way to perform any task.

- *work is broken down into small, repetitive actions—a division of labour*; these are analysed scientifically, through a time and motion study, and redesigned so that they are performed to their optimum efficiency with minimal waste
- *workers are selected scientifically* for each role, with the most suitable workers then being trained so as to work to the optimum efficiency
- *work is divided between management and workers*, with management taking responsibility for the design and planning of the work
- *management and the workforce cooperate* to achieve the task in hand.

## The division of labour

Scientific management begins by breaking a job down into a series of simple repetitive tasks—a division of labour. A worker ceases to manufacture a product from start to finish, for example making a whole wheel. Instead, the worker is one of many who perform one repetitive and simple task in a chain, for example inserting a spoke in a wheel.

Have you ever assembled a piece of flat-pack furniture? Even though you may have no previous experience or skill in furniture-making, the way in which the job is broken down into small, manageable tasks with a set of basic instructions means that you are able to assemble your new bookcase. Now imagine that you and a group of friends had 100 flat-pack bookcases to assemble. What would be the most efficient way to do this? Would you each sit and make bookcases individually from start to finish, or would you use a form of division of labour, where each of you specializes in just one task, performing that one task on each of the bookcases?

Taylor was neither the first nor the only person to use the division of labour, but the degree to which he then scientifically analysed the work process marks him out.

Visit the Online Resource Centre for a description of economist Adam Smith's earlier observations of the division of labour.

Taylor was interested in designing work that eliminated waste movements and created the most efficient way to perform a task. This might be through instructing workers on what moves to make, or designing machinery and the physical layout of the factory to minimize waste movement. Work was designed like a machine, and workers were managed as if they were a part of that machine, using precise, scientific measurement and calculation.

Time and motion study  Rational work design where tasks are measured and timed, and redesigned to maximize efficiency.

Taylor was a pioneer of the **time and motion study**, a technique still used in modern-day organizations. This involved closely observing and measuring every movement made by a worker using a stopwatch and measuring tape for every movement made.

The most famous example of this given by Taylor (1911: 43ff) was the story he recounts of the Dutch labourer, Schmidt, in *The principles of scientific management*. He speaks (in mostly disparaging terms) of how he observed this labourer's movements in shovelling pig-iron—a very basic task—and redesigned the work to be performed at the optimum efficiency. At the Bethlehem Steel Works, where these observations took place, the number of pig-iron handlers required for the same task was reduced from 600 to 140 (ibid.: 71)—representing a massive reduction in labour costs. In return for this punishing and monotonous work, Taylor increased pay, but by a level which was more than offset by the efficiency gains.

## The Gilbreths: time and motion study

The work done by Schmidt was very basic, unskilled labouring. However, the same principles of scientific management could, according to Taylor, be applied to any task in hand. Taylor cites with approval the work of his contemporaries Frank and Lillian Gilbreth, who studied the work of bricklayers. They looked not just at the motion of bricklaying, but also the position of the bricks and tools next to the bricklayer so as to further decrease waste motion. They were reported to have designed the process of laying one brick from an initial observation of eighteen individual moves down to just five. The resulting efficiency gain saw bricklayers move from laying 120 bricks per hour to 350 (Taylor, 1911: 81).

The Gilbreths were, arguably, the experts at time and motion study, extending it into a number of different areas—not just factory work but also retail work and office work, such as typing. In their quest for measurement and efficiency, and using a grid and stopwatch, they filmed people performing their work and then analysed and redesigned their movements to enable them to perform their tasks more efficiently (Price, 1992: 61).

### Theory in context: home life

As with Taylor, the Gilbreth's brought their desire for efficiency into their home life. Two of their twelve children wrote a book about their home life (Gilbreth and Carey, 1949), which was made into the Hollywood film *Cheaper by the Dozen* (dir. Lang, 1950). Among anecdotes of home life in the book, the children were invited to submit sealed bids for household chores, such as washing-up. Furthermore, a gramophone player was placed in the bathroom so that family members could listen to language-learning records—no time was to be wasted time.

After the death of Frank Gilbreth, Lillian Gilbreth performed similar work in department stores, introducing time and motion studies to work that requires a greater variety of movement than a simple, repetitive task (Graham, 2000).

The time and motion study will be familiar to many workers today, sometimes masquerading under such names as 'Organization and methods'. The same ideas apply—work is observed, measured, and timed with the aim of eliminating waste movements. Either the job itself is redesigned, or the equipment and layout are redesigned so as to eliminate such movement. The redesign can be quite practical: for example a bank worker who has to constantly walk to a safe at the back of the office could have the safe moved closer to save time and effort (and thus increase their efficiency). A whole science of **ergonomics** is devoted to making the working environment adapt as efficiently and conveniently as possible to the humans who will use it.

While this chapter focuses on rational work design as a means of increasing efficiency and control in fairly routine, repetitive tasks, the work observation methods and ergonomic redesign of work tasks pioneered by the Gilbreths are far more widespread.

See the Online Resource Centre for examples of how such techniques are used in highly skilled jobs where precision is important, such as surgery, and in improving performance at the most highly-skilled levels in sport.

**Ergonomics** The design of workplace environments and tools to best fit the movements of the human body.

---

**Study skills:** time-management

As a student you may see the need to be efficient with money, but are you also efficient with your time? Do you work out any particular methods for tasks such as cleaning a room, making a meal, or writing an assignment which help you to complete them more quickly and avoid wasting time?

A key study skill is time-management: the ability to plan time around your university work and other competing demands, such as work and social life. Many of our students who have not done as well as they have hoped on essays will openly admit that poor time-management contributed to their poor grade.

Time-management isn't just about not starting an essay the night before a deadline. It involves getting materials for the essay, which can involve a wait for library books. It also involves knowing the availability of tutors and when they are available to help—they are unlikely to be able to answer questions at the very last minute, for example.

---

# Scientific selection of employees

Taylor's design of work went beyond work and equipment. He also believed that particular people were better 'fits' for different jobs. In a sense, with work designed like a machine, certain people made better 'components' for different types of work. Referring back to Schmidt, it is obvious from Taylor's own work that this hefty individual was better suited for the work he did than others might be. Thus, for Taylor, a **scientific selection** and training of individuals for jobs was just as important as the work design itself.

**Scientific selection** Defining the precise characteristics of the ideal candidate for a job.

# Workers work, managers manage

This idea of workers simply 'fitting in' is shown by a second aspect of the division of labour under scientific management. While there was a *horizontal* division of labour on the shop floor (i.e. a division of work tasks) there was also a *vertical* division of labour between management and workers (see Figure 3.3). This builds on the bureaucratic organization

**Figure 3.3** The horizontal and vertical division of labour.

Horizontal division of labour
*Work divided into simple, individual, specialized tasks*

structure developed in Chapter 2 in that it now shows where knowledge of the production process resides within that structure.

Management do all the planning—the work measurement, work design, and so on—and the workers then do simply as they are told. There is a separation between the mental work, the thinking, and the physical work on the shop floor. In other words, there is a **separation between planning and doing**. Taylorism began to introduce levels of management based around the work design—functional foremanship meant that supervisors were assigned to specific tasks rather than the more informal and ad hoc arrangements under the internal contracting system.

> **Separation of planning and doing** Tasks designed by management, with workers having no input other than to perform those tasks.

## Workers and managers cooperate

A final aspect of scientific management, as described by Taylor, is that it requires the cooperation of workers and management. However, as we see in the next section, such cooperation is more a relationship of control and, furthermore, one where Taylor encountered resistance rather than cooperation.

### Review questions

| | |
|---|---|
| **Describe** | What are the four principles of scientific management? |
| **Explain** | How do time and motion studies increase efficiency? |
| **Analyse** | What is meant by a 'separation of planning and doing?' What does this imply for the roles of managers and workers? |
| **Apply** | Think of an organization that you know. Are there any areas where scientific management principles are applied or are there any areas where scientific management principles might improve efficiency? |

# The fall and rise of Taylorism

> ### Running case: resignation letter
>
> Dear Linda,
>
> With great regret, I am writing to offer my resignation from my job at Junction Hotel.
>
> I used to have a job here where I had great pride in my work. I felt part of a family and felt valued, both for my knowledge and my experience.
>
> Now I feel completely demoralized, and would rather opt for early retirement than continue to work here.
>
> I feel so sorry for the other girls—they are not happy. They have no control over what they do and when. Everything is dictated to us, there's no room to breathe. And as for all of that checking up—it feels like we're in the army on parade. I used to love this job—now every task is simply given to us step by step.
>
> Best wishes
>
> Amy

Today, there are few workplaces that do not employ Taylorist techniques to some extent; indeed, as will be argued in Chapter 4, rational work design is alive and well, and more prevalent and intensive than ever. However, it was not always so; indeed, there was initial resistance to Taylorism from both workers and factory owners. In part, this came from the nature of the work, but also the degree to which it enabled managers to exert control.

## Control through Taylorism

It was not just efficiency that was increased by scientific management. The rational work design that he pioneered also gave a solution to the problems of control over labour that he had earlier encountered.

1. *Standardization.* By designing and defining precisely the nature of work, down to its most basic movements, Taylor was able to increase uniformity and predictability—work was standardized, minimizing the variable nature of human labour that Taylor so feared. It no longer mattered that people came from various craft traditions, all with their own particular ways of performing a task. With a tightly-defined and prescribed task much of this variability in the labour force could be overcome.

2. *Individualization.* Rather than work being organized in gangs under the patronage of a subcontractor, workers were now individualized: that is to say, they had the one task that they performed, having been selected and trained for that task. Again, this regained some control for Taylor as he was able to bypass the soldiering and control which came from groups of workers.

3. *Surveillance.* Individualization brought about another type of control—a more internalized form of control. Whereas workers underwent direct supervision, it is not difficult to see that if a worker is assigned to one small element of the work process and that element is

defective or not being produced to speed, the culprit is easy to single out (see the section on 'Panopticism, surveillance, and control' in Chapter 4).

4. *Knowledge.* The power that workers had from their craft knowledge was effectively rendered redundant. Atomizing the work process means that workers only have knowledge of their one small part of the job. The separation of planning and doing means that knowledge of the overall process resides with the management—those who do the calculations and then plan the work process. So, the control that workers had over the pacing and other aspects of their work are now gone and are held by management.

5. *Skill.* Similar to knowledge, the level of skill required to perform a job is diminished greatly by scientific management. Previously, managers relied on the craft skills of workers; this meant that workers were valuable and often irreplaceable—a source of power. With skill replaced by a simple, repetitive task, workers become more expendable—they can be replaced easily by other unskilled labour. Again, this gives greater bargaining power to management.

# Resisting Taylorism: workers and managers

**Running case:** the showdown

Phil Weaver is summoned to Simon Chance's office, where Chance stands with Linda Wilkinson. Chance is enraged: 'What have you started here? We've got our best cleaner resigning, the rest of them are unhappy. We all used to get on so well. Now it feels like civil war'.

'Maybe so,' replies Weaver, 'but I've done what you asked—they are working more efficiently and with such routinized jobs they are easy to control'.

Wilkinson is uncomfortable. Yes, there is more control over the cleaners, but it seems to be Weaver who is exerting it, not her. She can see much more trouble ahead.

Evidence suggests that during Taylor's lifetime, the adoption of his techniques was piecemeal rather than swiftly and across the board (Clegg et al., 2005: 21). Workers were keen to defend their craft traditions (see Braverman, 1974, on deskilling). In the UK this combined with factory owners and a ruling class, who preferred a conservative approach to maintain stability and avoid upheaval in the workplace, rather than going for wholesale change and adopting Taylor's more 'modern' techniques (Whitston, 1997: 2).

Workers, factory owners, and even governments had their own doubts about rational working techniques. In 1912, the US congress launched an inquiry into Taylorist techniques following a strike at the Watertown Arsenal, a munitions factory where such techniques were being used (see Kanigel, 1997: 459–84). The report from the inquiry declared Taylorism to be a failure, with time and motion studies being banned in all US defence plants.

It is perhaps surprising given the fame of Taylor's techniques today that he was, in fact, eventually sacked from his position at Midvale. Although he had brought about efficiencies in production, they came at a price—notably industrial unrest, which, as we will see later in the chapter, also beset Henry Ford's assembly line (p. 83). For the factory owners, the hassle of this unrest simply wasn't worth the efficiency gains.

Taylor spent the rest of his time as a consultant, taking his scientific management ideas into other workplaces and industries.

# The rise of Taylorism

## Running case: all hands on deck

As if things aren't bad enough for Weaver, most of the cleaners have walked out in support of Amy Turtle. Simon Chance and Linda Wilkinson are facing rooms that need cleaning and no cleaners to do the work. 'You've got a lot to answer for, Weaver,' snarls Linda Wilkinson.

'Right,' says Weaver. 'You two get a couple more of the management team, roll your sleeves up and we'll show the cleaners a thing or two.'

Despite not being experienced cleaners, Weaver is able to demonstrate the cleaning routines from the cleaning manual. 'All of the knowledge of cleaning is in here,' he states, 'no more relying on Amy and her experience.'

They quickly pick up the simple tasks and set to work cleaning the hotel rooms from top to bottom. And, to their surprise, they learn the tasks fairly easily, getting the job done in not much less time than the usual cleaning team.

A potential crisis is averted. Chance knows that the management can't do this every day—he needs to patch things up with the cleaners—but, at the same time, he sees the value in Weaver's techniques—anyone can now do this work.

From such an initial slow take-up, and outright resistance and controversy, the techniques of Taylorism gained ground in the USA so as to become 'conventional wisdom' (Whitston, 1997: 2) in management by the end of World War I.

Indeed, wartime was a time where the benefits of Taylorism could be demonstrated. As the (male) workers in the factories were away fighting, the women at home were the people who came to work in factories which produced guns, tanks, and other machinery needed for the war effort. They were unskilled but, given the deskilled nature of Taylorist work, were able to be productive with little training. Taylorism could now claim to have been used for patriotic purposes (Kanigel, 1997: 487). Despite the considerable criticism faced by Taylorism, Grey (2005: 41) points out that it also created the tanks which overcame Nazi Germany.

Different countries embraced Taylorism in different ways. Often it had to blend in with their own national culture. Thus, within the USA, the UK, France, Germany, and even Russia and Japan, Taylorist techniques came to dominate the factory floor, albeit taking different routes and time spans to be implemented (Copley, 1923a: xx–xxii; Nelson, 1992: 16ff).

**Real life case:** Taylorism in Soviet Russia

An interesting case in the spread of Taylorism is its success in Soviet Russia. Taylorism was very much a product of the capitalist West and the USA, so it is curious to see that it was also embraced by the communist regime in Soviet Russia. In the early days of the Russian revolution, then Soviet President Lenin, despite initial scepticism towards scientific management, named Taylor directly as an example to follow in industrial production (Jaffee, 2001: 61; Grachev and Rakitsky, 2013: 518).

While having a different political ideology from that of the West, the Soviet regime still had an interest in efficient mass production. However, whereas Taylor denigrated the role of the worker, in the Soviet Union the hard worker was celebrated as heroic. This was particularly the case with Lenin's successor Stalin, who glorified the heroic worker as an icon of the Soviet system. The hard work of one particular worker, Alexei Stakhanov, was held up as exemplary. Taylorism in the Soviet Union (and to an extent in Communist China) was implemented through the lens of the Stakhanovite movement, which promoted the idealized, heroic factory worker (Donkin, 2001: 154; Jaffee, 2001: 61; Grachev and Rakitsky, 2013: 521).

Visit the Online Resource Centre for more detail on the effects of national cultures on Taylorism.

### Review questions

| | |
|---|---|
| **Describe** | How did Taylorism allow management to exert control over workers? |
| **Explain** | Why was Taylorism not taken up instantly by all organizations? |
| **Analyse** | If Taylorism helps managers to increase efficiency and control, why may management be reluctant to implement Taylorist techniques? |
| **Apply** | Do you think Taylorist techniques are beneficial to the cleaning department at Junction Hotel, or do they cause more disruption than good? |

# Henry Ford and the assembly line

**Running case:** the laundry factory

Weaver looks for further areas of the cleaning work process that he can redesign, including automating the laundry room, where towels and bed linen are laundered each day. However, he realizes that operations at Junction Hotel are on too small a scale to justify such an outlay on equipment. He begins to think that he has done all that he can to make the cleaning side of the hotel as cost-effective as possible when an email from an old golfing partner arrives in his inbox.

**To:** phil_weaver@junctionhotel.com
**From:** bob.smith@laundromation.co.uk

**Subject:** Of interest???

Phil—long time, no speak. I hear you are in the hotel business—my new venture might interest you, especially as far as your laundering costs go. How about a round of golf next week and then I'll show you around?

Bob

Weaver visits his friend's new business, Laundromation, which is effectively a factory for processing laundry on a large scale. Clients, such as local hotels, leisure centres, and restaurants, have their dirty linen picked up by Laundromation and, in return, a fresh batch of clean linen is delivered. The task is *outsourced* to the laundry factory.

Inside the factory, Weaver looks around in admiration. At one end, vans dump dirty laundry into a chute where it goes on to a conveyor belt. Workers place the laundry into giant washing machines and then into driers. As dry, clean laundry emerges from the driers, workers remove and sort it—there is an individual conveyor for each type and size of laundry, along which workers stand and fold each item as it passes. Workers are trained, in a Taylorist fashion, how to fold an item in the speediest fashion possible and they become expert at this. A worker can spend the entire day standing in one position folding the same types of towel.

At the end of each conveyor belt the products are stacked so that van drivers can pick up individual orders easily, load them on to a trolley, and pack them into the van for delivery.

'You see,' says the factory owner, 'by creating a laundry factory on this scale I can do the job a lot more efficiently. Think what you spend on wages, laundry equipment, etc., and all the hassle of having to supervise your cleaners. I can do it for you at less cost. On this scale I can do the job far more cheaply per towel than you could ever do in-house'.

From a manager's perspective Taylorism made great gains, increasing efficiency and shifting control firmly in favour of management. These changes in control and efficiency are taken even further by Henry Ford's development of the moving **assembly line**.

At first glance there are many similarities between Taylor's scientific management and the assembly line Ford used to manufacture the Model T car at his Detroit plant in 1913. While there is nothing to suggest that Ford and Taylor ever met, these two industrialists were both working in the USA in the early part of the twentieth century and were certainly aware of each others' work. Ford faced the same issue of variability in the workforce as Taylor; indeed, much of Ford's workforce was made up of immigrant labour from Europe, many of whom did not speak English but could be trained easily to perform this very basic and standardized work (Beynon, 1984: 36).

However, while Taylor split the work process into its component parts, Ford's innovation was to then place these tasks in the order they needed to be completed and create the *moving* assembly line for his Highland Park car plant in Detroit. In other words, while Taylor's attention focused on a specific task performed by an individual, *Ford's interest was in a whole sequence of tasks which went into the manufacture of a finished product.*

**Assembly line** An automated conveyor that moves a product in front of workers who perform a small, repetitive task on each product that passes before them.

## Theory in context: development of the assembly line

Ford's inspiration for the moving assembly line came from butchery. On a visit to an abattoir, an aide of Ford witnessed the way in which carcasses were dismembered in sequence. With the fresh carcass hanging from a pulley, it was moved along in a line in front of various butchers who each took their own particular cut of meat in turn—not so much an assembly line as a disassembly line.

Ford realized that the assembly line allowed each butcher to become specialized in one particular task. However, unlike Taylor's system, by being on a pulley the carcass would come to the worker, rather than the worker travelling to it. This made the process quicker and more efficient. Ford wondered whether the process could be reversed and applied to making products. Placing his workers in two lines in the order of which component they added to the car, Ford had a chassis mounted on a trolley which was wheeled slowly in front of the workers who, in turn, did their small part in putting the car together—the prototype for the automated moving assembly line (Donkin, 2001: 147–8).

The extent of the breakdown of a task exceeded that of Taylor. For instance, even the job of inserting a nut and bolt could be broken down (one man inserts a bolt, one man places a nut on to the bolt, and one man tightens the bolt). Components were designed so as to facilitate easy and speedy assembly in this manner.

The moving aspect of the assembly line increased efficiency. Workers did not have to move from the spot to perform their tasks—the work simply passed by in front of them. The assembly line system is also sometimes termed a 'flow-line' system. Work flows along the line and at each point the worker performs a highly specialized task, often with machinery specially designed for that one specific task (e.g. tightening a nut on a wheel) (Figure 3.4).

A modern assembly line system.
**Source:** Vladimir Salman /123RF.

Think back to the earlier flat-pack example. How could you organize mass production of such furniture using assembly-line techniques? How much more efficient would this make the process?

The Fordist assembly line certainly increased the efficient production of the Model T. The first Model Ts—made by stationary assembly in 1909—were produced at a rate of approximately 14,000 a year at a cost of $950 per car. By 1916, and the move to a fully automated assembly line, over half a million cars were being made with cost being reduced to $360 per car (Donkin, 2001: 148).

Ford's system worked because his main product, the Model T car, was highly standardized. Ford is famously reported to have said of the Model T: 'Any customer can have

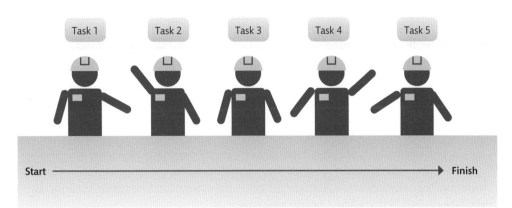

**Figure 3.4** Efficiency on the assembly line.

a car painted any colour that he wants so long as it is black' (Ford and Crowther, 1922: 71). The standardized nature of the product, in this case the colour, is vital to the efficiency gains made by the assembly line—too many variations and the line has to be stopped and started again, e.g. to set up a different colour of paint. The fewer variations there are in the product, the more costs are kept down.

The Model T Ford.

## Fordism and mass production

The Fordist system can only operate under large economies of scale, known as **mass production**. Think of the costs involved in setting up the car factory and all of its specialized equipment—the assembly line is a large-scale, capital-intensive undertaking. Such an initial capital outlay requires massive costs per unit if only a few cars are produced.

But mass production needs people to buy the cars. Part of Ford's revolution was to create a change in society, as well as the workplace, towards **mass consumption**. Cheaper mass-produced cars were more affordable to the public, thus increasing the demand for them. Beforehand, car ownership was out of the financial reach of many—especially the unskilled workers who made up Ford's workforce. Now, with cars retailing for below $600 (Raff and Summers, 1987: 64), and with Ford encouraging a savings scheme among his workers, car ownership by the masses was possible.

Mass production and consumption is a legacy that endures from Ford; indeed, mass-produced objects constitute so much of our daily lives that Donkin describes Taylorism and Fordism as 'the most enduring social change of the 20th century' (Donkin, 2001: 159). It is not just cars, but most electrical items, computers, and clothing that are produced and consumed *en masse* using the assembly line system or some form of derivative.

Mass production   The production of a large volume of a standardized product, often making use of an assembly line.

Mass consumption   Large-scale purchasing of a product by consumers within society.

## Real life case: surgical assembly lines in Russia and India

It is not only unskilled work that can be subject to an assembly line process. In 1985, a Moscow eye surgeon, Syvastoslav N. Fyodorov, developed an assembly line technique for performing cataract operations, going as far as to describe his clinic as a 'medical factory'. Rather than a conveyor belt, patients on trolleys are moved along as different parts of the process are performed. Similar techniques have been used in India with the resulting efficiency savings making vital healthcare procedures available to a largely poor population. The techniques are also being extended to procedures such as heart surgery.

With medical procedures there is a limit to how much the assembly line can be used. Only the most basic, standard procedures are amenable to this. Whereas the Fordist factory led to deskilling, the skills of the surgeon are still needed for more complex cases.

**Sources:** Schmemann (1985); Matthews and Nemtsova (2006); Morris (2010).

Visit the Online Resource Centre for a link to a video news report about production line heart surgery in India.

While its origins are in heavy industry, the assembly line has been applied to many other tasks which have repetitive, standardized elements. Food production often follows an assembly line pattern, for example the supermarket sandwich originates from a standardized component—the triangular piece of bread (The Food Programme, 2010). In white collar work, the idea of a 'paper factory' has also emerged, where administrative tasks, such as processing forms, move along a series of stages where simple operations are performed at each (Baldry et al., 1998).

Visit the Online Resource Centre for a link to the podcast of this radio broadcast about sandwich production lines.

Just how much of an impact does the assembly line have on your everyday life? What items that you are wearing or using in your home, workplace, or place of study have been mass-produced on an assembly line? Without the assembly line we would not have affordable cars, computers, or electrical goods, etc. In other words, our modern way of life would be unrecognizable.

## Review questions

| | |
|---|---|
| **Describe** | What are the main features of the assembly line? |
| **Explain** | How does the assembly line draw upon, but also intensify, the techniques of Taylorism? |
| **Analyse** | Why does Fordism need mass production and consumption to realize its efficiency gains? |
| **Apply** | What modern-day industries can you think of which use assembly line techniques? |

# Rational production: the Marxist critique

**Running case:** cogs in a machine

Babs Davies is off to clean again, but is looking to work elsewhere.

**Babs Davies:** I used to love working at Junction. Now I don't even feel like a human being there.

**Debbie Smith:** Feel the same. Since they let that consultant in there's no room to breathe—everything is watched and we're ordered about. Feels like I'm under a microscope all the time. And the work is just boring now. I feel like my soul has been taken away from me.

**Andy James:** You've got it lucky. Try coming to work at Laundromation—hot, steamy, folding the same towels day in day out: that's soulless for you.

**Babs Davies:** Well, if the rumours are true I might be looking for a job there. Weaver wants to out-source half of our work to you—there's going to be job cuts if that's the case.

**Debbie Smith:** Tell me about it, love. Feel like we're just cogs in a machine these days.

Fordism offers many of the forms of control seen under Taylorism in a more intensified form. The speed of work on the assembly line was controlled simply by the *speed of the line itself*; workers would have to perform their individual tasks as and when each car appeared in front of them. The system ties workers more than ever to being a part of the machine, to the point of controlling them to remain at the line and perform their task, not pausing or taking unauthorized breaks for fear of their one unperformed task being detected later down the line.

Go back to the five features of Taylorist control earlier in the chapter. How do you think the Fordist assembly line intensifies each of these five forms of control? How would you feel working under such circumstances?

The intensification of work by Ford was not without its problems. Ford also recognized that work in his factories was monotonous and dehumanizing. Indeed, Ford had to pay a decent wage to get people to work in his factories. While subject to certain stringent qualifying conditions, the $5 day far exceeded the $2.34 that unskilled workers could previously hope to earn (Raff and Summers, 1987: 69).

These problems were not isolated within the factory gates. They had a resonance in wider society, as reflected in various artistic media of the time.

**Theory in context:** cultural critiques of Ford

Charlie Chaplin's (1936) silent film *Modern Times* is a satire on the human effects of assembly line work. In a memorable scene, Chaplin's worker performs a repetitive task as the speed of the line is increased. Hypnotized by the repetitive task and unable to keep up with the speed of the line, Chaplin is carried along into the heart of the machinery. The imagery is deliberate—Chaplin's character has been reduced, literally and figuratively, to being a 'cog in the machine'.

▶ A similar negative view of the factory system and its effects upon individuals was presented by the Mexican artist Diego Rivera. Commissioned by Henry Ford to produce a set of murals for the Ford headquarters in Boston, Rivera produced a set of paintings where the imagery of the machine was dominant, the people reduced to small, sullen, expressionless beings. Ford was so incensed by this portrayal of his factory system that the murals were destroyed, never to be exhibited.

In the novel *Brave New World*, Aldous Huxley (1932) presents a world where people are in danger of losing their own identity—a world run by a god named Henry Ford. In this novel it is not cars that are mass produced, but humans themselves. At the lowest levels of society are 'epsilons'—humans produced as workers in mass bundles.

Common to all three of the works described here are critiques of Ford and Taylor suggesting that humans lose their individuality, their humanity even, in the face of organizations which are run as massive machine-like entities. What is rational in terms of organizational efficiency is not necessarily rational in terms of the effects upon humans themselves. The observations of the likes of Chaplin, Rivera, and Huxley suggest a mode of organization that is inherently **dehumanizing**—workers become components in a larger industrial machine. Beynon's (1984) study of work on the Ford production line has many quotes from workers talking not just about the boredom of the work, but its complete lack of interest and meaning (compare it with the meaning and identity that people take from work as discussed in Chapter 9).

**Dehumanization**
Work that reduces people to part of a machine-like process, ignoring their human attributes. Widely associated with rational work design that was criticized by Harry Braverman.

# Rational production: Marx's critique of capitalist production

## Running case: on strike

### Midshires Gazette

#### Fresh walkout leaves laundry factory in a spin

Laundry services company Laundromation Ltd has suffered from the latest in a series of walkouts over working conditions. Problems began on last night's night shift when workers downed tools, bringing a halt to all activity in the plant.

Laundromation provides contract laundry services to a number of local organizations, including hospitals, sports centres, and hotels. It is understood that over half of today's scheduled deliveries have not taken place.

Simon Chance, the owner of Junction Hotel, said: 'This is the third time this month it has happened. We're left with no towels, no clean linen, no tablecloths—how are we supposed to run a hotel? It feels like we're hostage to the poor industrial relations at Laundromation.'

Andrew Rook, head of the regional branch of the Collectivity union, outlined the reasons for the actions: 'Work has been increasingly intensified. The conveyors which carry the laundry to workers are being speeded up week by week as the company takes on more contracts. We're being expected—forced—to work harder for no extra money.'

> Bob Smith, Managing Director of Laundromation, said, 'We are sorry for the disruption this is causing to our valued customers. I should point out that this action is being organized by a few militant workers in one small section of the factory. At Laundromation we pay highly competitive wages. I would have expected that workers would be grateful for a full order book in such difficult economic times and would work to make sure that we retain our current customer base.'

Karl Marx saw the desire for efficiency as an inevitable part of the capitalist working relationship. In competitive markets, with capitalists demanding high returns on investment in order to keep investors and shareholders happy, the pressure is on managers to reduce all costs, including labour, meaning that work needs to be as efficient as possible. A Marxist view suggests that this causes a conflict of interest: the accumulation of profits is done at the expense of workers, who see their conditions of work and rewards from the capitalist working relationship deteriorate.

Karl Marx (1964) suggested that the capitalist working relationship produced **surplus value**. By working more efficiently workers help to increase profits, but this is enjoyed by capitalists rather than the workers themselves. Conversely, workers experience, through the pursuit of efficiency, a deterioration in their own conditions of work and see their craft skills depleted and replaced with monotonous, repetitive, and dehumanizing tasks.

> **Surplus value** Profit that capitalists gain over and above the wages they pay to workers.

For Marx, this relationship is fundamentally unequal. Whereas workers previously owned their own means of production, determined their own pace of work, and decided how much they took from the business for their efforts, these terms—wages, hours, and working conditions—are now set by management. Management have the power to do this because they are acting on behalf of capital—the power of the money, property, and equipment tied up in the business. Each individual worker relies on this for their wage—effectively their ability to live, eat, and be housed. However, should they object to the working conditions and wages set they are effectively powerless—management have the ability to hire and fire.

Have you ever worked in a job where you have felt unhappy with something, such as pay, working hours, the type of work you have to do, or your relationship with your boss? How much power have you felt (or not felt) to do something about it? What might have given you more power in the situation?

## Marx and alienation

Karl Marx (1894/1981) took a different view of the nature of workers than that of Taylor and Ford. Rather than being naturally lazy, workers were, for Marx, naturally creative—they had a desire to transform the world around them. Furthermore, work was, for Marx, fundamentally a social rather than an economic activity. Factory working systems, however, laid to waste a lot of this human potential, trapping workers in dull, monotonous working routines, often in isolation from other workers.

The result, for Marx (1894/1981), is that there are a number of negative effects upon workers, which he terms **alienation**.

> **Alienation** In capitalism, the estrangement of people from a number of human qualities, noted particularly by writers such as Marx and Braverman as a consequence of rational work design.

1. Workers are alienated from the product. Rather than having a defining role in planning and creating the product, they only play one small part in the production process, with

planning done by the capitalists. The worker may not even see the end product, and may not have a role in selling and realizing the profits.

2. Workers are alienated from the production process. Work becomes a series of dull, repetitive, meaningless tasks performed solely for money. There are no intrinsic rewards in the job. Craft skills become redundant as work is deskilled.

3. Workers are alienated from the human species or their 'human essence'. Work is dehumanizing in that the natural human desire for creativity is taken away and workers become 'cogs in a machine'.

4. Workers are alienated from other humans. Work becomes an economic transaction in return for a wage rather than a social activity. Workers are individualized in the production process and also separated from management.

 Visit the ORC to view a short animation that introduces Marx's concept of alienation.

## Braverman and deskilling

**Deskilling** The obsolescence of workplace skills caused by rational work design or the introduction of new technology.

Such a waste of human potential is echoed in Braverman's (1974) **deskilling** thesis. At a basic level this means a degradation in the nature of work, from workers having highly valuable craft skills to being reduced to performing monotonous tasks requiring no skill whatsoever. Deskilling is something that Braverman witnessed first-hand as a worker in the print industry, seeing his own skills replaced by new technology.

Braverman (1974) suggested two particular areas of deskilling:

* organizational deskilling represents the overall knowledge of the production process being held by management and taken away from the brains of the workers

* technological deskilling represents the means by which the design of tasks removes the need for workers' skills; indeed, it can even replace them with technology and thus lead to job losses.

As with Marx, for Braverman the pursuit of efficiency inevitably led to deskilling and the degradation of work. For both it creates a conflict of interest between workers and capital—a fundamental tension at the heart of the capitalist working relationship.

**Trade unions** Membership organizations which collectively represent the interests of a group of workers.

How much knowledge and skill do you need to perform a task on a production line? How much would you know about other tasks which go into making the overall product? How would you feel working on a production line and being told what to do all day?

**Collective action** Any form of resistance against management taken by a group of workers.

## Conflict in the capitalist working relationship

**Strike** A form of collective action where workers withdraw their labour.

Marx's conclusion is that such alienation and the inequality of the capitalist working relationship leads, inevitably, to conflict between capital and workers. The formation of **trade unions**, which are able to take **collective action**, such as **strikes**, can be seen as an attempt to reintroduce collective power to the workforce—power which was lost through the control mechanisms of Taylor and Ford.

Ford's factories were certainly plagued by industrial unrest, and unionization was heavy in his factories (see Beynon, 1984). Even with the $5-a-day wage, the boring, monotonous work was still resisted fiercely. The nature of his production system left it vulnerable to the so called 'spanner in the works': with all parts of the work process interdependent in a line, it only took a problem in one small area to bring production to a halt.

Strikes, sabotage, and even riots were commonplace. Ford himself had an abrasive approach to industrial relations. Beynon (1984: 49) described how, in one period of industrial unrest and rioting, Ford considered arming the non-striking workers with the intention of them turning on the strikers.

Visit the Online Resource Centre for more detail on attempts to reintroduce collective power.

Resistance doesn't necessarily take the form of organized action, such as strikes. If people opt out of the job—resigning, looking for work elsewhere, etc.—this too is a sign of resistance against the organization. When Ford wanted to add 100 people to the line it was necessary to hire 963 people because initially they were skilled mechanics who did not like the unskilled task of simply pulling the lever on a machine (Crawford, 2006: 20). Ford's plants had, on average, a labour turnover rate of 370%—almost four people a year for each position (Raff and Summers, 1987: 63). In other words, each job changed hands every ten weeks.

In this section we have seen that the introduction of rational production techniques came at the cost of a great amount of conflict. In the final section we assess this against the possible advantages of such production techniques.

## Review questions

| | |
|---|---|
| **Describe** | What is meant by alienation? |
| **Explain** | Why might work in Ford's factories be described as 'dehumanizing?' |
| **Analyse** | What does Marx mean when he says that the capitalist working relationship favours the side of capital? |
| **Apply** | What examples of strikes and industrial action have you seen recently in the news? What are the reasons for such action taking place? |

# Evaluating rational work design

## Running case: some positive reactions?

Phil Weaver is in an ambiguous position in the eyes of the management at Junction Hotel. His work with the cleaning department has demoralized the workforce to the point that it caused the crisis of the walkout. And yet these same techniques created the means by which the management have been able to cope with the crisis.

On further analysis, some cleaners have not joined in the walkout and later claim that they don't mind Weaver's techniques.

'Look—I know exactly what I have to do,' says one cleaner. 'When Turtle ruled the roost you were open to her moods and she undoubtedly had her favourites. Now I know just what to do and how my work will be judged, full stop. I much prefer it that way—it's not open to personalities.'

Another cleaner, a student, adds: 'I don't want to come here and think. I'm just after a bit of extra cash to get through my studies. Work now is great—I just come in and get on with the job. There's no hassle.'

While rational working techniques are subject to much critique, in many ways they mirror how we often routinize tasks in our own lives (Morgan, 2006: 26). Maybe you take part in sports—how do you learn to perform that sport better? Are there advantages to be gained from breaking down movements into smaller parts and analysing them so as to be able to perform them more effectively? Perhaps you have a job around the house, such as making the beds—do you devise a standard routine, with each stage of the process performed in a particular order, that helps you to perform it more efficiently?

Which tasks in your day-to-day life do you approach by using rationalized techniques?

In this section we examine both the advantages and the disadvantages of rational work design.

### Employability skills: work simulation

Many job selection processes, especially at assessment centres (see Chapter 8) involve some form of practical work simulation. So called 'in-tray exercises' involve dealing with a series of tasks that might be encountered during the job itself.

The chances are that the task will not be deskilled and repetitive, as with Taylor and Ford's work. Nevertheless, the assessors may well be looking for you to devise some sort of system and routine for dealing with the tasks as you go along. Do you, for example, group together similar tasks so that they can be dealt with more efficiently together? If you have a complex task to repeat several times, do you break it down into more manageable stages?

Such routines show a methodical and efficient way of working rather than taking each task randomly and without any forethought into how it will be performed.

Not all workers react negatively to rational work designs, such as Taylorism and Fordism. In Chapter 9 we will see that some people prefer a straightforward task, whereby they can come into work, do a clear and simple job without having to put in too much thought, and collect their wage at the end of the day.

Furthermore, the standardization and simplification of rational work design can be seen to have a number of positive effects for workers.

• Simplifying the task opens up work to people who might otherwise have been unable to participate in the job market. Both Taylor and Ford employed unskilled workers.

In the case of Ford's factories we have seen that many of the workers spoke different languages, but they could still learn quickly the simple tasks undertaken in his factories.

- An unheralded aspect of the Gilbreth's work is their attempts to design jobs in such a way that workers with physical disabilities are able to participate in paid work (Gotcher, 1992). While the Gilbreth's work was focused on bringing injured World War I veterans into the workplace, work and task design is used by contemporary organizations to ensure compliance with relevant legislation concerning the employment of people with disabilities (see Equality and Human Rights Commission, 2015).

- Rational working methods bring in an element of fairness. Where previously the conditions of work, pace and standard of work expected, payment, and even being hired or not were open to the whims of individual managers, now they are standardized and formalized, and can be applied equally across the workforce. In this respect, there is a link between rational work design and the bureaucratic rules and procedures examined in Chapter 2.

## Rational work design: advantages and disadvantages

### Running case: denouement

Simon Chance sits down a few months after the walkout and analyses the situation.

The cleaning department will never be the same again. Where once it had larger-than-life characters who had Junction Hotel running through their veins, now it has part-timers and students walking around like robots. Yes, they are more compliant, easy to control, and easy to replace if they become uncontrollable, but a little something has been lost.

At the same time, Chance realizes that his wage bill is considerably reduced. Rooms are being cleaned much more quickly. There is the odd short-cut being taken and there are a few more complaints from guests, but, overall, the job is being done.

Chance feels there are lessons to be learned for the rest of the hotel. Efficiencies need to be spread, but Chance decides to minimize the overall influence of Weaver as his methods are too extreme and the consequences on the workforce too great. But, at the same time, there are areas throughout the organization where rational work design can be used to some extent to make things more efficient.

For Gareth Morgan (2006: 26), Taylorism is seen as a strength when there is a straightforward task performed in a stable, unchanging context, and where precision is important. In other words, Taylorism and similar rational work designs are ideal when there is a very machine-like environment in which the tasks are performed. This includes having people within the work process prepared and happy to work as if a part of a machine.

While Morgan saw rational work design as being fine for stable working environments, equally its rigidity makes it difficult for coping with changing circumstances or where a large variety of different products rather than one standard product are produced. In

Chapter 4, we will see how, with such a changeable environment existing in the modern day, rational techniques such as Taylor's and Ford's are seen by some people to be somewhat unsuitable and out of date. This does not, however, mean that rational work design has necessarily been superseded. Indeed, we will see in Chapter 4 that in modern-day organizations, such as the fast-food restaurant, the techniques of rational work design and the bureaucratic procedures that we saw in Chapter 2 are alive and well and more intensified than ever.

## Review questions

| | |
|---|---|
| **Describe** | Under which circumstances does Gareth Morgan suggest rational work design works best? In which circumstances is it unsuitable? |
| **Explain** | How can rational work design be used to increase fairness in the workplace? |
| **Analyse** | Rational work design can bring about cost savings for an organization, but what human costs do you think it creates? |
| **Apply** | Are there any areas of Junction Hotel where rationalization could be applied? How would you apply it, and what would be the potential benefits and problems? Are there any areas where you would definitely not apply rationalization within the hotel? |

# Chapter summary

Rational work design encompasses techniques from, among others, Taylor and Ford. Taylor's scientific management addressed issues of organizational control and efficiency by meticulously breaking down the work process into small, discrete tasks. These tasks were then analysed scientifically—through measurement and calculation—and redesigned to be as efficient as possible. This made the process more efficient and gave management much more control over workers—a process intensified by the moving assembly line of Henry Ford.

However, as observed by theorists such as Marx and Braverman, and writers and dramatists such as Huxley and Chaplin, rational production also had negative effects. It created boring, monotonous work, and it also loaded the capitalist working relationship heavily in the favour of management. Skills gained through craft knowledge, apprenticeships, and experience became worthless and degraded as deskilling took place, with the knowledge of the overall production process moving from individual workers to levels of management.

The overall advantages and disadvantages of rational work design are summarized in Table 3.1.

Table 3.1  Advantages and disadvantages of rational production techniques

| Advantages | Disadvantages |
|---|---|
| Increase in production efficiency when there is a simple, standardized product to be produced | Inefficient and inflexible for product ranges with plentiful variation or where market conditions require rapid changes |
| Increase in control over a large number of factory workers | Workers lose autonomy and control over their day-to-day activities |
| Tasks and expectations for workers are clear, simple, and unambiguous | Workers lose craft skills and expertise |
| Workers can participate in the labour market regardless of skill, experience, language and, in some cases, disability | Work is dull, monotonous, and unfulfilling |
| Fair treatment/equality of opportunity—workers are hired and paid according to pre-existing standards; minimizes potential for favouritism that existed with previous factory systems | Can be inefficient if the alienating and intensive nature of work causes widespread resistance |
| Provides efficient goods or services in times of need (e.g. war, poverty) | Interdependence of work tasks leaves the assembly line prone to a 'spanner in the works' |
| Allows goods to be mass produced at a price that would otherwise be unaffordable to the public | Humans are reduced to being 'cogs in a machine' |

## Further reading

**Beynon, H. 1984. *Working for Ford*. Penguin: Harmondsworth.**
  Considers the developments of Taylor and Ford, bringing in a critical edge to examine the deskilling and degradation of work.

**Donkin, R. 2001. *Blood, sweat and tears: The evolution of work*. Texere: New York.**
  Chapters 10 and 11 provide a readable and accessible introduction to Taylor and Ford, set in the historical context of the factories where their systems were introduced.

**Kanigel, R. 1997. *The one best way: Frederick Winslow Taylor and the enigma of efficiency*. Little, Brown and Company: London.**
  A lengthy but thorough introduction to the life and work of Taylor.

**Mousa, F., and Lemak, D. 2009. The Gilbreths' quality system stands the test of time. *Journal of Management History* 15 (2): 198–215.**
  Introduces the work of the Gilbreths and discusses how it is still found in contemporary workplaces.

## References

Bahnisch, M. 2000. Embodied work, divided labour: Subjectivity and the scientific management of the body in Frederick W. Taylor's 1907 'Lecture on Management'. *Body and Society* 6 (1): 51–68.

Baldry, C., Bain, P., and Taylor, P. 1998. Bright satanic offices: Intensification, control and team Taylorism. In:Thompson, P., and Warhurst, C. (eds) *Workplaces of the future*. Macmillan: Basingstoke, pp. 163–83.

Beynon, H. 1984. *Working for Ford*. Penguin: Harmondsworth.

Braverman, H. 1974. *Labor and monopoly capital: The degradation of work in the twentieth century*. Monthly Review Press: New York.

Chaplin, C. (dir.) 1936. *Modern times*. United Artists: New York.

Clegg, S., Kornberger, M., and Pitsis, T. 2005. *Managing and organizations: An introduction to theory and practice*. Sage: London.

Copley, F.B. 1923a. *Frederick W. Taylor, father of scientific management*, vol. 1. Harper and Bros: New York.

Copley, F.B. 1923b. *Frederick W. Taylor, father of scientific management*, vol. 2. Routledge/Thoemmes Press: London.

Crawford, M.B. 2006. Shop class as soulcraft. *The New Atlantis*, Summer: 7–24.

Donkin, R. 2001. *Blood, sweat and tears: The evolution of work*. Texere: New York.

Equality and Human Rights Commission 2015. Work place adjustments. Available at: http://www.equalityhumanrights.com/your-rights/employment/work-place-adjustments (last accessed 26 August 2015).

Ford, H., and Crowther, S. 1922. *My life and work*. Garden City Pub Co.: Garden City, NY.

Gilbreth, F.B., Jr., and Carey, E.G. 1949. *Cheaper by the dozen*. William Heinemann: London.

Gotcher, J.M. 1992. Assisting the handicapped: The pioneering efforts of Frank and Lillian Gilbreth. *Journal of Management* 18 (1): 5–13.

Grachev, M. and Rakitsky, B. 2013. Historic horizons of Frederick Taylor's scientific management. *Journal of Management History* 19 (4): 512–27.

Graham, L. 2000. Lillian Gilbreth and the mental revolution at Macy's, 1925–1928. *Journal of Management History (Archive)* 6 (7): 285–305.

Grey, C. 2005. *A very short, fairly interesting and reasonably cheap book about studying organizations*. London: Sage.

Hoskin, K.W., and Macve, R.H. 1986. Accounting and the examination: A genealogy of disciplinary power. *Accounting, Organizations and Society* 11 (2): 105–36.

Huxley, A. 1932. *Brave New World: A novel*. Chatto & Windus: London.

Jaffee, D. 2001. *Organization theory: Tension and change*. McGraw Hill: Singapore.

Kanigel, R. 1997. *The one best way: Frederick Winslow Taylor and the enigma of efficiency*. Little, Brown and Company: London.

Lang, W. (dir.) 1950. *Cheaper by the dozen*. Twentieth Century Fox.

Marx, K. 1894/1981. *Capital: A critique of political economy*, vol. 3 (transl. David Fernbach). Penguin: London.

Marx, K. 1964. *Economic and philosophic manuscripts of 1844*. International Publishers: New York.

Matthews, O., and Nemtsova, A. 2006. Medical meccas: Eye surgery assembly line. *Newsweek International*, 30 October.

McKendrick, N. 1970. Josiah Wedgwood and cost accounting in the Industrial Revolution. *The Economic History Review* 23 (1): 45–67.

Morgan, G. 1990. *Organizations in society*. Macmillan: Basingstoke.

Morgan, G. 2006. *Images of organization*. Sage Publications: Thousand Oaks, CA.

Morris, C. 2010. 'Production line' heart surgery. *BBC News*, 2 August. Available at http://www.bbc.co.uk/news/health-10837726 (last accessed 20 August 1015).

Nelson, D. 1992. Scientific management in retrospect. In: Nelson, D. (ed.) *A mental revolution: Scientific management since Taylor*. Ohio State University Press: Columbus, pp. 5–L 39.

Price, B. 1992. Frank and Lillian Gilbreth and the motion study controversy 1907–1930. In: Nelson, D. (ed.) *A mental revolution: Scientific management since Taylor*. Ohio State University Press: Columbus, pp. 58–76.

Raff, D., and Summers, L. 1987. Did Henry Ford pay efficiency wages? *Journal of Labour Economics* 5 (4): 557–86.

Schmemann, S. 1985. Moscow eye doctor hails assembly-line surgery at clinic. *New York Times*, 2 July.

Simpson, I.H. 1999. Historical patterns of workplace organization: From mechanical to electronic control and beyond. *Current Sociology* 47 (2): 47–75.

Taylor, F.W. 1911. *The principles of scientific management*. Harper: New York.

*The Food Programme*. 2010. The sandwich. BBC Radio 4, 17 October [radio programme]. Available at http://www.bbc.co.uk/programmes/b00vc508 (last accessed 20 August 2015).

Thompson, P., and McHugh, D. 2009. *Work organisations: A critical approach*, 4th edn. Palgrave Macmillan: Basingstoke.

Whitston, K. 1997. Worker resistance and Taylorism in Britain. *International Review of Social History* 42: 1–24.

# 4 Rationalization in contemporary organizations

## Chapter overview and learning outcomes

By the end of this chapter you should be able to:

- describe Ritzer's McDonaldization and other examples of contemporary forms of rationalization

- explain how post-Fordism and post-bureaucracy are examples of a trend away from rationalized forms of organization in contemporary society

- explain how computer technology allows rational techniques to exert increased control and surveillance in organizations, such as in call centres

- analyse the different degrees to which rationalization is used in different contemporary organizations, and the extent to which this is desirable for different organizations.

## Key theorists

| | |
|---|---|
| Daniel Bell | American sociologist who suggested that the economy was moving away from manufacturing towards a 'post-industrial' society |
| George Ritzer | American sociologist who examined the hyper-rationalized techniques of the fast-food restaurant, using the term 'McDonaldization' to describe their use in many contemporary organizations |
| Michel Foucault | French philosopher who used the prison metaphor of the Panopticon to examine how power is exerted through the surveillance methods that rational management techniques in organizations produce |

## Key terms

| | |
|---|---|
| Rationalization | Methods for increasing the efficiency of work, drawing on techniques of bureaucracy (see Chapter 2) and of rational work design, such as Taylorism and Fordism (see Chapter 3) |
| Post-industrialism | A perspective that suggests that, in response to a more changeable and unpredictable environment, organizations are moving away from rationalization to more flexible forms of managing and organizing; encompasses both post-bureaucratic and post-Fordist perspectives of management |
| McDonaldization (of society) | A perspective (Ritzer, 2015) which recognizes the continued use of rationalization in contemporary organizations, as typified by the work design of the fast-food restaurant |
| Panopticon | Based on a seminal prison design, a metaphor for the levels of control and surveillance in contemporary rationalized organizations |

# Introduction

**Running case:** the business trip

Heading down to London for a business trip, Simon Chance thinks about the degree to which he can introduce rationalization at Junction Hotel. Do nothing, and the hotel becomes disorganized and wasteful—ultimately it may not even survive if work-related costs are not kept under control. Go too far and workers become like robots, demotivated because of boring and repetitive work. In a business where guests and workers are constantly in contact, this would not give the best impression. 'Rationalization has efficiency benefits,' thinks Chance, 'but at the end of the day we're not a factory, we're a hotel—and a luxury hotel at that.'

Chance decides to make his trip a fact-finding mission about rationalization in other hotels and organizations. Arriving at his first hotel, a luxury hotel, he begins to write some notes.

*Hit the jackpot here, this hotel is top-end luxury, a massive room with two balconies overlooking a park.*

*Service at reception is polite and attentive, although all done through a standard computerized procedure, with a key card eventually being issued. At least the staff aren't identikit—they are always happy to pass the time of day, no matter how trivial the request.*

*So, here I am sat on the balcony. Interesting that, though well-turned out, the rooms use identical furnishings. Indeed, they are identical across the chain—I've stayed in another of these elsewhere. It doesn't detract though, it's good quality stuff.*

*Just ordering breakfast for tomorrow—very similar to most other hotels. I hang the order on a pre-printed form on the door. And the cleaning seems to be pretty much as we designed it back at Junction, all quite efficient. But they do take time to put a lovely little tuck into the end of the toilet roll ...*

A life of luxury?
**Source:** Edvard Nalbantjan / 123RF.

To what extent does the luxury hotel use rationalization? Are there any areas where you think it would be inappropriate for their area of the market?

In the previous two chapters on bureaucracy (Chapter 2) and rational production (Chapter 3), you could be forgiven for thinking this a book about history rather than contemporary management. Rational techniques in those chapters emerged from the heavy industry of the early 1900s: the bureaucratic structures and techniques, as witnessed by Weber, or the methods of efficient production developed by Taylor and Ford. In this chapter we ask if such *historical* ideas are still relevant *today*?

The chapter begins by examining post-bureaucratic and post-Fordist theories, which suggest that today's world is different—it is no longer dominated by manufacturing industry and is much more dynamic and changeable. It is suggested that the **rationalization** of Taylor and Ford's era is no longer appropriate for this contemporary world.

> **Rationalization** Work that is designed to achieve maximum efficiency and reduce costs, encompassing aspects of bureaucracy and the scientific design of work.

However, while such movements away from rationalization have been evidenced over the past decades, it would be hasty to suggest that it is obsolete. Rationalization is present today, just as it was in the Industrial Revolution, in industries other than the manufacturing settings in which it originally flourished, and often in more intensified forms. In this chapter we examine a number of examples of contemporary rationalization.

• George Ritzer has noted that the McDonalds restaurant chain is a hyper-efficient organization which uses rationalized techniques that have their roots in scientific management, bureaucracy, and the assembly line. The organizational techniques of the fast-food restaurant are found in many modern-day organizations, to the extent that Ritzer (2015) has suggested that today's society is 'McDonaldized'.

• Many organizations also employ their own particular models of cost-cutting and minimization. We examine examples of contemporary efficient organization such as 'no-frills' and 'value engineering'.

• As much as rationalization is about *efficiency*, we also saw in Chapters 2 and 3 that it allows management to exert *control* over the workforce. Computer technology allows contemporary organizations to exert such control even more intensively. Michel Foucault's (1977) metaphor of the Panopticon is used to examine the means by which rational organization is used to control and exert surveillance over contemporary organizations, which we apply to the example of the call centre.

When first formulated in the Industrial Revolution, rationalization was very much presented in a **one best way** formulation. This chapter concludes that while there may no longer be 'one best way' to manage and organize, and while rationalization may not be appropriate for all organizations, it is still ever-present in the contemporary organizational world.

**One best way** Rational management techniques that propose one most efficient way to perform any task.

# The demise of rationalization?

**⊸ Running case:** the hotel restaurant

Just got in from dinner with an old friend down in the hotel restaurant. It was expensive but worth it for the exquisite nature of both the food and the service—I just hope I can get it through expenses!

The maître d' showed us to our seats. Even though he was obviously serving others, he had a gift when at the table of making it seem like we were the only customers in there.

The food was outstanding and, after we'd ordered, the chef actually came to the table to ask just how we wanted it cooked. Although the menu set out the dishes on offer that day, the chef was able to customize the dish for each of our individual requirements. He chatted to us about how he operated the kitchen:

'Nothing is set in stone,' he said, 'it's not just that customers might want different things, sometimes a particular food will be unavailable at market, or out of season, and I have to be ready to change the menu around at the drop of a hat. Not just me—all of the kitchen staff have to be ready to react as and when necessary. All of that comes from training, knowing our food, and having a passion for cooking.'

With my professional hat on, I asked the maître d' a bit more about how the place was managed. 'Not very much,' was the reply, 'they try to keep rules and regulations to a minimum. We're all encouraged to meet up, try out new ideas, make suggestions—anything that helps improve what we offer to customers. Overall, we're trusted as professionals with expertise and an interest in our work. The chef actually makes sure that the staffing of different shifts is always changed around so that people don't get stuck in their ways. Instead, we are always learning and sharing ideas with different people.'

As I left, I couldn't help thinking about the restaurant at Junction. Could we keep Graham Effingham forever, or is this the sort of thing he aspires to? Certainly, if we did anything to downgrade his restaurant and the quality of food and service, he'd be off.

How is management in this example different to rational forms of management encountered in Chapters 2 and 3? What benefits does it bring to the restaurant?

In the previous two chapters, ideal-type bureaucracies and Taylor's scientific management have been presented as examples of a 'one best way' approach to managing and organizing. However, it has also been suggested (see Chapter 3) that such 'one best way' approaches are only valid in certain circumstances, for example with a standard product and stable environmental conditions.

**Environment** The world outside of an organization which can have an impact upon that organization.

We first examine the idea of an organization's **environment**, and the impact that it has. We see that the environment that is facing organizations has become more unstable and changeable since Fordism and Weber's theories of bureaucracy were first formulated, and we examine trends from Fordism and bureaucracy towards more flexible post-Fordist and post-bureaucratic theories of management.

However, we also see that while the nature of organizations and their environments may have changed, arguments for post-Fordism are accompanied by arguments for neo-Fordism, where rationalization is still used, in some cases in more efficient forms than when the first assembly lines were developed.

## The organization and its environment

The concept of the organizational environment suggests that organizations are not hermetically sealed; they interact with, and are affected by, things going on around them. The **PEST model** (Figure 4.1) splits the environment into four sectors:

**PEST model** A model which breaks an organization's environment into four sectors: political, economic, social, and technological.

- political—government policies and laws
- economic—e.g. the state of the economy, demand, exchange rates, etc.
- social—consumer tastes, fashions, and opinions
- technological—current technology and innovation.

The environment impacts organizations, which might have to react and make changes. For example, in many countries, a factor in the political sector of the environment has been to ban smoking in public places. This has forced changes upon a number of organizations such as pubs and restaurants, which have had to create, for example, outdoor smoking areas.

The impact of the environment is the starting place for an argument which suggests the retreat of rationalized forms of organization.

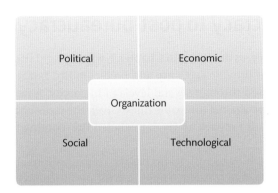

**Figure 4.1** The PEST model.
**Source:** Edvard Nalbantjan / 123RF.

# The contemporary environment

An initial example of an attack on the 'one best way' approach can be seen in the set of theories developed around the 1970s, known as **contingency theory** (e.g. Thompson, 1967; Woodward, 1958). These studies took Weber's ideal type of bureaucracy (see Chapter 2) as a lead, but concluded that rather than one ideal type, there were a number of different ideal types of bureaucratic structure and functioning, depending on the environment facing the organization. Environmental variables, such as uncertainty, the technology used by an organization, and the size of the organization, demanded different types of bureaucratic organization—organizational design was about making the best 'fit' between the organization and its environment. While contingency theory moves away from one ideal type of bureaucracy, it is still quite rational in its focus, matching the ideal organizational structure to a set of variables.

> **Contingency theory** Suggests that the best structure for an organization is determined by factors such as environmental uncertainty, the organization's size, and the technology that the organization uses.

In the 1980s, much greater shifts in the nature of the environment facing organizations were in evidence. Western economies moved from a manufacturing focus to a **post-industrial** society (Bell, 1973), one which is dominated by service industries (see Chapter 16) and, more recently, where information technologies mean that information transfer and organizational activity takes place at instantaneous speed through global networks (see Chapter 14).

> **Post-industrial** A move in society and economy away from the dominance of manufacturing, towards a more flexible, service-based economy.

The contrast between the contemporary environment and that facing Weber, Taylor, and Ford is described by Clegg and Baumeler (2010) as a shift from the static, unchanging nature of 'iron cages' of bureaucracy to a world that is fast-moving, changeable, and in constant flow. Rather than static and stable, Bauman (2000) describes our contemporary world as a fluid world of **liquid modernity**. Alongside the control and standardization of bureaucracy, organizations, workers and consumers experience a more uncertain and precarious side to life (Kociatkiewicz, 2014).

> **Liquid modernity** Bauman's characterization of modern-day society as dynamic, changeable, and flexible.

With such a turbulent, dynamic, changeable, and uncertain environment, 'one best way' approaches begin to creak at the seams. They can be seen as dinosaurs—inflexible and slow to react. In contrast, more flexible, nimble organizations are able to cope better and gain advantage in such situations. It is thus suggested that there has been movement from bureaucracy to post-bureaucracy, and from Fordism to post-Fordism.

Visit the Online Resource Centre for more detail on the contemporary environment.

# From bureaucracy to post-bureaucracy

**Bureaucracy** From the French *bureau*, meaning 'office', bureaucracy covers official, formal elements of rational organizational design, such as the hierarchical organization structure, the rules and procedures, and the official paperwork, which exert impersonal control over the organization.

**Post-bureaucracy/post-bureaucratic organization** A trend away from rigid, bureaucratic rules and structures in organizations towards more flexible and less hierarchical, rule-driven organizations.

**Red tape** An unintended consequence of bureaucracy, where rules and paperwork get in the way of work and activities, rather than helping tasks to be performed efficiently.

**Trained incapacity** Where people are so used to their behaviour being controlled by bureaucratic rules and procedures that they become inflexible and unable to think for themselves and show initiative.

**Matrix structure** An organizational structure that combines a traditional functional hierarchy with separately-managed project teams that draw people from across different functional departments.

Traditional **bureaucracy**, as described in Chapter 2, with its rigid structures and fixed rules and procedures, might provide certainty and predictability, but it is not quick to react. Orders have to be passed through several levels of hierarchy. A need to change a procedure rapidly may run up against inflexible rules. Given the more changeable nature of the environment, Bennis, as far back as 1966, predicted the 'coming death of bureaucracy' (Bennis, 1966).

A move towards **post-bureaucratic** forms has seen organizations attempt to design structures which are more flexible and which minimize the dysfunctions of bureaucracy, such as **red tape**, where rules get in the way of people doing their work, and **trained incapacity**, where strict rules and regulations mean that people do not think for themselves and are unable to change and adapt to new situations (see Chapter 2).

## Matrix structures

An example of a move away from the traditional bureaucratic hierarchy is the **matrix structure** (see Figure 4.2). While there are heads of different departments, such as finance or sales, there are also heads of different projects. A project might be any task or area of focus for the organization, such as a particular product or service that the organization offers. For example, in Figure 4.2, Project A might be the development of a new project. There is a head of the project who coordinates staff from across the production, finance, and sales departments to bring their particular knowledge and expertise to that project.

The matrix organization means that, rather than being in one fixed work group, people move between different teams. More knowledge and information can be shared across the organization as people shift between teams (see the section on 'Organizational learning' in Chapter 10) and specialists with particular knowledge can be brought into particular project groups where they are needed.

The matrix organization shifts away from bureaucracy in that it breaks one of Fayol's principles of management (1949, see Chapter 2): that of unity of command, where people have just one line manager. While this moves away from the rigidity of bureaucracy, it also brings the danger of confusion as to who is in charge of any one individual and that individual having divided loyalties between their different 'bosses'.

**Figure 4.2**  A typical matrix structure.

Visit the Online Resource Centre for an example of how matrix structures have been used and adapted by the global technology firm Cisco.

## The post-bureaucratic organization

While the matrix structure begins to introduce some elements of flexibility to organizational structure, post-bureaucratic organizations are those which go even further in minimizing bureaucratic structures and rules and regulations. The aim of such organizations is to promote creativity, innovation, and rapid response among their workers when required.

The goal of such organizations is to focus on the competencies of their workers and how they can be used for particular tasks, rather than fitting people into official positions or roles with strict definitions of what they should be doing during their working day. Furthermore, the post-bureaucratic organization tries to foster dialogue and discussion among its workers in order to share ideas and innovations.

---

**Real life case:** Oticon—the 'spaghetti organization'

Oticon, a Danish technology firm specializing in hearing-aid equipment, is often held up as an example of what a purely post-bureaucratic organization might be like. In order to promote flexibility and innovation within the company, it restructured away from a traditional hierarchy and got rid of traditional bureaucratic features, for example:

- All paperwork is scanned when first received and stored on computer. The paper itself is shredded and, as a symbol of the intent to remove paperwork, the shredded paper is put into a clear plastic chute that passes from roof to floor in the middle of the canteen.

- There are neither job titles nor fixed roles. Departments and similar examples of bureaucratic structure are removed, and in their place are 'projects' to which any interested people from any part of the organization might contribute.

- Formal offices and dividing walls have also been removed; even fixed desks no longer remain. Instead, workers have their own trolley which contains their computer and other essential items.

In Oticon we can see a move away from formal structures and towards movement and fluidity—rather than structure, the organization is interlinked like spaghetti. As people move around with their trolleys, they are more likely to speak with other members of staff, share ideas, and come up with new innovations. Rather than working in pre-existing departments and within a pre-existing structure, people cluster together to work on particular projects. Rather than being directed top-down, workers are left to self-organize.

**Source:** Burnes (2000: 319–27); Jaffee (2001: 161–2); Larsen (2002).

---

Visit the Online Resource Centre for a discussion of the advantages and disadvantages of Oticon's spaghetti organization.

While the lack of rules and structure at Oticon may seem unusual compared with many of our working lives, a similar lack of rules and structure can be seen in the Googleplex, the headquarters of Google (see Chapter 11), and with the lack of hierarchy in Holacracy (see Chapter 12). In both cases, these are organizations that wish to promote technical innovation and respond rapidly when change is needed, and not have rules and structures getting in the way.

Is a post-bureaucratic form suitable for all organizations? Are there some types of organization where it would not work?

> ### Employability skills: the post-bureaucratic worker
>
> Working for a post-bureaucratic organization such as Oticon or Google might seem like an ideal job—very few rules, the ability to work on projects that you like, and, in the case of Google, the ability to turn up to work at whatever time you want in the morning (see Chapter 11)—it's very different from working the regular 9 to 5.
>
> Such work, however, has its own pressures. There is often a pressure to perform—to demonstrate the ability to innovate by coming up with the goods. And with such a lack of formal control and rules, a lot of self-discipline is required in order to keep focused on tasks relevant to work.
>
> Such pressures are evident in a recent policy announced by Richard Branson which, in a bid to increase productivity and creativity, has allowed workers at Virgin Group's headquarters to take unlimited holidays, *as long as they get their work done*. As Branson puts it in his blog, 'It is left to the employee alone to decide if and when he or she feels like taking a few hours a day, a week or a month off' (Branson, 2014).
>
> Would you as an employee rush to take advantage of this loosening of management control? Barker (1993) argues that getting rid of management direct control can lead to more subtle and intensive form of control because other members of the team and the individuals themselves self-discipline. This is what Sewell calls responsible autonomy (Sewell, 1998), where workers are given freedom so long as they hit their targets. Given that many workers feel a sense of job insecurity, as Anne Perkins (2014), writing in *The Guardian*, states, Branson's offer 'should be enough to keep most workers chained to their desks forever. If the first condition for taking time off is deciding you wouldn't be missed, it sounds scarily like an invitation to the boss to make it permanent' (Perkins, 2014). Indeed, this more flexible form of working means that you have to self-discipline and therefore control yourself more. If by taking a holiday you are leaving other people in your department in difficulties, or a project not finished, imagine the pressure not to take a holiday when you know that you will be responsible for a potential project failure.

Visit the Online Resource Centre for more on unlimited holidays at Virgin.

## From Fordism to post- and neo-Fordism

In the 1980s, many Western economies were in recession. Manufacturing was in decline and the service sector became more dominant. Furthermore, new computer technologies were able to produce goods in a more customized way than the mass-produced assembly line, and tastes in consumption were also becoming more fragmented towards niche and specialist markets, rather than standardized, mass-produced goods.

At the same time, the economy of Japan was becoming more successful. Western organizations, including Ford, began to look at Japanese forms of organization, which were much more successful in comparison.

One response to these changes has been a move away from the traditional Fordist assembly line, where work is highly controlled and jobs are fragmented into small tasks which require little skill. **Post-Fordism** is seen as a break with the deskilling and highly controlled nature of Fordism and Taylorism, instead valuing the skills and knowledge of workers and allowing them autonomy in how they organize their work.

While post-Fordism doesn't suggest any one particular form of organization, a number of examples of managing and organizing demonstrate post-Fordist characteristics.

> **Post-Fordism** A break away from Fordism and towards management techniques which use the skill of workers and grant autonomy to workers, emphasizing communication and competencies, rather than command and control.

- In Sweden, Volvo moved away from the assembly line to manufacturing cars in small teams. Workers received training in a wider, and deeper, level of skills, and the teams largely managed themselves, with representatives from teams also involved in decision-making at a higher level in the organization (Rehder, 1994).

- Flexible specialization (Piore and Sabel, 1984) was observed in clothing manufacturing in Italy, where an industry would cover a geographical area within which were small, specialist firms of trained workers, concentrating on high-quality, niche production.

- Ford themselves introduced elements of work organization that can be described as post-Fordist. As we will see in Chapter 10, Japanese firms welcome suggestions and input from shop-floor workers, whereas the traditional Fordist model is one where workers are at the bottom of a hierarchy and do as they are told. In the 1980s, Ford instigated an 'After Japan' programme, to move away from top-down management and engage workers in participative management, whereby they had a say in decisions, and in team work, with cross-functional teams as would be found in a matrix structure like the one we saw earlier in this chapter. The intention was to generate trust and cooperation, moving away from the Fordist 'management by fear' (Starkey and McKinlay, 1994).

Visit the Online Resource Centre for more analysis of these examples.

## Post-Fordism or neo-Fordism?

> **Real life case:** you could have your lunch off the floor
>
> When you think of a car factory what do you imagine? Noise, dirt, oil, grease, mess? Certainly our popular perception leads us to the impression that car manufacturing is quite a dirty and messy environment. This view is wrong. In our interview, Joe Greenwell, the Chairman of Ford in Britain, states: 'Don't think of the car industry as some grubby manufacturing environment . . . there are no grubby manufacturing environments anymore . . . you could have your lunch off the floor. It is a very different, uncluttered, quiet, air-conditioned environment where technicians abound and there is a very high degree of automation'.
>
> This is not just at Ford but throughout the car industry. For instance, Volkswagen's Phaeton factory in Dresden, Germany, is called Gläserne Manufaktur—the factory made of glass. This transparent factory has glass walls so that the whole production process can be seen. The process is so clean the floors are made of Canadian maple and the workers even wear white overalls (see AutoMotoTV, 2010). ▶

> ▶ All the parts come in on a tram and are then delivered to the appropriate location by robots guided by magnets. The entire floor is a giant conveyor belt moving very slowly. Each workstation is powered via the floor. The whole process is also computerized so that it monitors everything that goes into the vehicle and will even know if a single screw is missing and when the car is ready to go to the next stage. The car is even moved round by a machine to suit the technician's body as they put in the parts.
>
> Car manufacturing has come a long way in 100 years.
>
> **Source:** Author interview with Joe Greenwell, Ford in Britain, 2012.

Visit the Online Resource Centre to view videos of modern car factories in action and for the full interview with Joe Greenwell.

**Neo-Fordism** A form of rational organization which combines Fordist efficiency and control with the ability of computer technology to introduce flexibility into the work process.

While trends away from the rationalization of Fordism have been observed with post-Fordism, **neo-Fordism** suggests Fordism being developed in ways which combine Japanese techniques and culture, but retain the drive for efficiency of traditional Taylorism and Fordism. Typical of this is the Toyota Production System (TPS, also known as Toyotism) used by Japanese car manufacturers Toyota. Work tasks are designed to be efficient and to minimize waste with the same degree of calculation and precision as Taylor's scientific management. Added to this are techniques than further minimize waste, but in more flexible ways than Taylorism. For example, with the Japanese **just-in-time** system, components are delivered as and when necessary, rather than wasting space in store rooms (Jaffee, 2001: 135ff; Towill, 2010). See Chapter 7 for more about the culture of Japanese management.

Visit the Online Resource Centre for more information about Toyotism and how it both compares with and differs from traditional Fordist production.

**Just-in-time management** A form of management that tries to promote efficiency by reducing the amount of stock that an organization holds, with components delivered as and when needed.

**Lean management** A contemporary form of Taylorist rational organization that attempts to eliminate from organizational processes waste or anything that does not add value.

In neo-Fordist organizations, computer technology helps to control large volumes of production, but rather than Fordist, standardized products, the technology allows for changes to the set-up to be made quickly. Thus, neo-Fordist organizations combine mass production and economies of scale with the ability to react more flexibly than a Fordist assembly line. With neo-Fordist organization comes a ruthless desire for efficiency and the minimization of waste, typified by contemporary techniques such as **lean management** which have developed from Toyotism. Lean management seeks not only to eliminate waste from the production process, but also to evaluate all processes and activities for the value that they add, and to eliminate all activities that fail to add value to the organization.

Under neo-Fordism, workers generally have a better working environment than the traditional noisy, dirty factory. Furthermore, they often have a wider variety of tasks than the one repetitive task of the traditional assembly line. Instead, they engage in job rotation or job enlargement (see Chapter 9), and such worker flexibility is a key feature of the Toyota Production System (Dohse et al., 1985). However, in a manner similar to their counterparts from the traditional Fordist assembly line, they often perform repetitive and tightly-controlled tasks, with little autonomy over their own work.

## Summary

In this section we have seen two contemporary and seemingly contradictory trends.

- On one hand, post-bureaucracy and post-Fordism suggest a 'retreat from rationalization' and a movement towards more flexible forms of organization with skill and autonomy returned to the workers.

- On the other hand, neo-Fordism achieves flexibility through technology, but this technology is used to make work processes efficient and to exert precise control over the tasks that workers perform.

While both trends are able to co-exist, we see that rationalized techniques are still very much in existence in contemporary organizations. They may not follow the 'one best way' prescription of rationalization in the Industrial Revolution era, but the drive for efficiency still exists—in many cases in more intensified forms. The following three sections of the chapter examine contemporary rationalization in organizations. In examples such as the fast-food restaurant and the call centre we see elements of neo-Fordism—a variety of tasks are performed by workers, but these tasks are designed to be performed as efficiently as possible and the workers are highly controlled.

Visit the Online Resource Centre for a case study of the currently evolving technology of 3D printing, and how this can be seen in terms of post-Fordist and neo-Fordist perspectives.

### Review questions

| Describe | What have been the main changes in the environment that faces organizations since the time of Taylor and Ford? |
| --- | --- |
| Explain | What is meant by post-Fordism and post-bureaucracy? |
| Analyse | What are the differences between post-Fordism and neo-Fordism in the way that they have each developed from Fordism in the contemporary era? |
| Apply | How would you describe the work at the luxury restaurant in the case study in terms of post-Fordism and post-bureaucracy? |

# Fast-food restaurants and 'McDonaldization'

### Running case: the fast-food restaurant

At the moment, I'm sitting in a fast-food restaurant. It wasn't planned but I'm running a bit late, so I stopped here to grab a quick lunch. The contrast between this and last night's dining experience couldn't be more pronounced.

*Went up to order my food—it felt like I was talking to a machine and it seemed like the till they were using was feeding them lines to say. There certainly didn't seem to be any thought going on between the assistant's ears; indeed, at one point I ordered a black coffee and was asked 'Do you want milk with that?'*

*I observed as my order was put together. With burgers being deposited down chutes and fries being scooped into cartons, my meal was eventually presented on a tray—it felt like I was the last station on an assembly line.*

*It's not the most comfortable dining experience ever. I am sitting on a hard plastic chair, having to share a table with other (not well-behaved I hasten to add) diners. A cleaner is going around mopping the floor and actually mopped under my chair as I was sitting on it!*

*Well, I am getting out of here as quickly as possible—can't believe I am expected to even deposit my rubbish in the bin myself. Do they not have waiters here?*

*Still, it did the trick of getting me fed as quickly as possible, and the cost is a fraction of what was spent last night. I can only imagine what would happen though if I tried to go back to our place and suggest Effingham run his restaurant like this—he would erupt!*

For George Ritzer (2015) rationalization is not a relic of the past, but is alive and well and is exemplified by the McDonalds fast-food restaurant. McDonalds is a global organization which employs rational techniques to the optimum for the rapid mass-production and service of food. If you have ever worked, eaten at, or even managed in a fast-food restaurant, you will realize that there are few levels in the organization that escape this intensive and pervasive cocktail of rationalization. For example:

- putting together a burger is broken down into small, repetitive tasks which can be learned easily and rapidly by untrained staff, in a similar manner to Taylorism; a burger is 'assembled' from simple components in a manner similar to a Fordist factory (Ritzer, 2015: 143)

- the service encounter, where orders are taken, is often done according to a pre-planned set of steps, with the till giving operators lines to say or prompting them as to what they should ask the customers (ibid.: 116–17)

- manuals outline procedures for almost all aspects of work within the organization (ibid.: 118); for example, there are step-by-step instructions on how to perform a mundane task, such as cleaning a toilet

- much of the work of management involves implementing bureaucratic rules and procedures that come centrally from the organization (some of which are identical in all restaurants worldwide) or filling out predesigned forms for such things as pay and stock ordering.

## Characteristics of McDonaldization

**McDonaldization (of society)** The principles of efficiency, calculability, predictability, and control by which fast-food restaurants are managed and organized, as applied by Ritzer to other contemporary organizations.

Ritzer (2015) describes **McDonaldization** as an extension of the rationalized techniques first described by Weber and Taylor. He outlines four principles that characterize the organization of fast-food restaurants, all of which can be seen to have their origins in rationalized techniques of bureaucracy and scientific management (see Chapters 2 and 3 for more explanation of these). Table 4.1 summarizes these principles.

Table 4.1  Principles characterizing the organization of fast-food restaurants

| | |
|---|---|
| Efficiency | Getting something done in the optimum manner, with as little waste as possible in the shortest amount of time and with the least cost input in terms of wages and resources, as was the basis for Taylorism and Fordism |
| Calculability | Emphasising what can be measured and calculated so as to achieve that efficiency, as with Taylor's time and motion studies |
| Predictability | Eliminating variability and unpredictability, through standardized products and work processes, as with Taylorism and Fordism, or through standardized bureaucratic rules and procedures |
| Control | Commanding workers through bureaucratic rules and hierarchy, but also by making work as simple as possible and, where possible, replacing humans with technology |

(Based on Ritzer, 2015: 14–16)

In this section we examine these four principles as Ritzer applies them to the fast-food restaurant.

## Efficiency

Fast-food restaurants have efficiency inscribed in their DNA—not just in the production of food, but at just about every level and function of the organization. It is even a part of the language and marketing of the restaurant (*fast*-food, *express* tills, etc.). Efficiency not only benefits the company, it is what customers come to expect from a fast-food restaurant—speedy and efficient service.

Every task is designed to be as efficient and to create as little waste as is possible. Think about the process of putting together a burger and, in particular, the role of the folding box into which it is placed (based on Ritzer, 2015: 43–4):

- the two (pre-sliced) halves of bread for the burger are placed in each half of the box
- on top of the bottom half are placed the meat, sauces, (pre-shredded) lettuce, and other items
- in a final flourish of efficient work design, the box is closed—there is no need to place the bread on top of the burger, the act of closing the box simultaneously, and with no extra time or effort, also puts the bread in place.

This may seem a trivial example, saving just fractions of a second, but the aim of a fast-food restaurant is to serve people quickly and in volume. If fractions of a second are saved not only in closing the box, but at all stages of making a burger, and this is replicated thousands of times during a day, then the fractions of a second add up to big efficiency savings.

Visit the Online Resource Centre for a comparison of fractional time savings in making burgers and designing racing cars.

Similar efficiency can be found in the service encounter, where the till is designed to make processing the order and communicating it to kitchen staff as efficient as possible.

There is a separate button for each item on the menu, so there is no need to waste time training staff to know the prices of different items or to look them up on a separate menu.

> ### Real life case: working for free
>
> When you go to a fast-food restaurant, think about how you actually do some of the work and, furthermore, do that work for free.
>
> Within the restaurant you act as waiter, taking your own tray of food to the table, and as a cleaner, emptying your tray into a bin. This is all work which would otherwise take up the paid time of members of staff. In some fast-food restaurants, there are 'express' tills where the customer keys in the order, pays by card, and then collects their food. Yet another job—that of the till operator—is now performed for free by the customer (Ritzer, 2015: 70–2).
>
> Craig Lambert (2015) describes such work as 'shadow work'—a series of unpaid and unseen jobs that we perform daily. Whether using self-service checkouts, printing out boarding passes for a flight, or booking a hotel through an online booking service, we are doing a job that previously someone else was paid a wage to do for us (Bennett, 2015)
>
> All of this helps businesses such as fast-food restaurants to run more efficiently. Indeed, getting work done for free rather than paying a wage is, perhaps, the ultimate in efficiency and cost-saving.
>
> **Source:** based on Ritzer (2015: 70–2).

How do you feel about performing work for free at a fast-food restaurant? Is it worth it if the cost savings lead to a reduction in price? Can you think of any other organizations where you do similar work for free?

Efficiency also comes from simplifying the product range in a similar way to Henry Ford limiting his Model T car to one colour so as to avoid halting the production line to change the paint set-up (see Chapter 3). Unlike a luxury restaurant where a meal is chosen and cooked individually, a fast-food restaurant has a limited number of products and options. While it is possible in a fast-food restaurant to order a burger without, for example, gherkins, it requires the burger to be produced individually away from the main 'production line'. While this may be done occasionally, if every customer wanted a similar customization, it would take more time and the process would become less efficient.

## Calculability

Is a fast-food restaurant the type of restaurant that you would go to in order to impress a business client or, perhaps, for a romantic first date? Certainly, it would be difficult to emphasize the quality of a fast-food restaurant compared with, say, a Michelin-starred restaurant. Not only is the food of the Michelin restaurant in a completely different league, there is also a difference in the quality of the experience. You would not be expected to clear away after yourself in a Michelin-starred restaurant, nor would there be someone cleaning the floor underneath your table as you eat!

For Ritzer (2015: 73), if quality cannot be marketed, then fast-food restaurants emphasize quantity—the amount that you get for your money. This can be seen in the names of products—the Big Mac, the Whopper, the Supersize menu.

**Theory in context:** *Supersize Me*

The documentary film *Supersize Me* (dir. Spurlock, 2004) focused on the health impacts of eating nothing but fast food. The film-maker, Morgan Spurlock, ate nothing but McDonalds food for a month and followed a rule that when asked if he wanted to 'supersize' a meal he would have to agree.

The film saw how his health declined as a result of this. McDonalds, in response, claimed that their food is not meant to be eaten at all meals and should be part of a balanced diet (McDonalds, 2004).

Calculability also extends to work design in fast-food restaurants—hardly surprising given their origin in Taylorist techniques based around measurement and calculation. While much of the work process is based around calculating the optimum efficiency with which to perform a task, the emphasis on what can be measured can also be seen with 'live' orders on a screen behind the service area, with a clock ticking to show how long has elapsed since the order was taken.

## Predictability

Many of you may have travelled abroad and found yourself in an unfamiliar environment where you don't know the language, the local customs, or the local foods. The sight of a set of golden arches on the front of a McDonalds restaurant can be a welcome sign of familiarity, where the nature of the food is known instantly—even ordering is simple, as a phrase such as 'Big Mac' is universal.

Ritzer (2015: 79) suggests that McDonalds restaurants exhibit predictability—a lot of what they do is identical, whether the restaurant be in Birmingham, Beijing, or Berlin. Such predictability comes about as a result of using the standardized routines and work patterns of bureaucracy.

- The interiors of fast-food restaurants for any one chain often look very similar—what Ritzer describes as 'predictable settings'. The predictable setting is not just about marketing and image; there are efficiencies from buying fixtures and fittings in bulk, and from having a standard design for a restaurant rather than employing individual designers each time (ibid.: 82) (see also the global standardization of organizational environments in Chapter 16).

- As we have seen, fast-food restaurants have a standard range of products and the procedures for making these products are also standardized. Furthermore, conditions are placed on suppliers for the potatoes, meat, etc. that they provide. The end result is that there is a predictable and familiar range of products which look and taste identical wherever they are consumed (ibid.: 15).

- The behaviour of employees, who are all trained using the same manuals and procedures, is also predictable from one restaurant to another (ibid.: 115–17).

Many fast-food restaurants are global organizations, and so there is predictability and standardization on a global scale—the same settings, products, and behaviours worldwide. (However, see Chapter 15 for examples of where McDonalds do have to adapt for national markets.)

## Control

McDonaldization exhibits Taylorist control (see Chapter 3) and also bureaucratic control through its meticulous use of manuals and procedures for tasks throughout the organization.

Ritzer (2015: 123) outlines further areas where control is exerted and the independent, autonomous activity of workers is minimized. As much as possible is pre-prepared before it even reaches the restaurant, for example the aforementioned pre-shredded lettuce, so there is less for workers to do and fewer mistakes that they can make.

Control in a fast-food restaurant.

A major aspect of control is exerted by replacing 'human with non-human labour' (Ritzer, 2015: 122ff)—getting a machine to perform the task where possible. For example, the judgement on the length of time to cook fries is not left to humans as it may be with a trained chef; instead, a timer beeps to tell the operator when to remove the fries. As previously seen, technology at the till takes away human judgement from the service encounter, prompting the till operator what to say or ask next. The express till replaces operators completely with a machine.

# The 'McDonaldization' of society

The four aspects of McDonaldization connect with each other to produce a form of contemporary rationalized organization that is efficient on a global scale. Even small elements of the work process that might go unnoticed can contribute to this process. Think of the scoop that is used to place fries in a carton—it contributes to all four aspects of McDonaldization:

- it is an *efficient* way of transferring fries to the carton
- it *calculates* the portion size that goes into the carton
- it allows *predictability* in that the same portion size is served every time
- it *controls* the worker, preventing them from producing variable portion sizes each time.

When Ritzer refers to the 'McDonaldization of society' he does not mean that society is becoming overrun with fast-food restaurants, but that the rationalized organization and management techniques found in fast-food restaurants are found in *many other* types of contemporary organizations worldwide. McDonaldization, for Ritzer, is thus defined as:

> The process by which the principles of the fast-food restaurant are coming to dominate more and more sectors of American society as well as the rest of the world.

> (Ritzer, 2015: 1)

## Examples of McDonaldized organizations

There are many other types of organization that can be described as having been Mc-Donaldized, displaying similar characteristics of efficiency, calculability, predictability, and control to those found in fast-food restaurants.

- Banks employ standardized procedures and have similar, predictable branch settings. Efficiency is gained from getting customers to do work for free through online banking and cashpoints. Technology controls and performs many tasks, such as balance transfers or paying bills, which used to be done by cashiers in handwritten ledgers (Ritzer, 2015: 67).

- Multiplex cinemas have a standard, predictable appearance across a chain, and are made more efficient by maximizing the number of screens within the building. Again, the customer does some work, and technology takes control through online and automated ticket booking.

- Parker and Jary (1995) describe McDonaldization in universities, where courses are divided into standardized modules and assessments such as multiple choice assessments, which are designed for speed and efficiency, often using technology such as a scanner to mark the assessment (see also Ritzer, 2015: 77).

Visit the Online Resource Centre for more examples of McDonaldized organizations.

What other examples of McDonaldized organizations can you think of? How do they display characteristics of efficiency, calculability, predictability, and control?

### Study skills: university rules and procedures

There was a time when universities were exclusive organizations that very few people could hope to reach. Students would have regular one-to-one tutorials with eminent professors, discussing academic issues and work in depth.

Nowadays, such a situation exists only at the very top institutions. Mass higher education means that many more people are able to go to university, but it also means that there is less personal contact with tutors—contact is in larger seminar groups that are timetabled automatically.

As with other organizations as they grow in size, universities have to use bureaucracy and rationalized techniques to manage the organization. Parker and Jary's 'McUniversity' (1995) reflects this rationalization.

Part of the rationalization of university life involves a wide range of rules and procedures, for example:

- exceptional circumstance procedures for dealing with illness or similar problems

- degree classification procedures for bringing together module marks into a final degree classification

- assessment briefs and marking schemes

- academic misconduct procedures, e.g. for dealing with plagiarism.

Many of these rules and procedures are there to help students, and most have an impact on their academic achievement. It often surprises us that many students are unaware of even basic procedures, such as the requirements for an essay, let alone what to do if an extension is needed because of illness—many never read the undergraduate handbook that is given to them at the start of their studies!

Being aware of the various procedures that affect your life as a student is a great help in getting the most out of your studies—understanding exactly what is required of you, what help and assistance is available to you, and how your work will be assessed allows you to focus on your studies much more clearly.

### The 'iron cage' of McDonaldization

**Iron cage** Max Weber's observation of the increased presence of bureaucracy in society and its potential to trap people in its routines and procedures.

While Ritzer first described the concept of McDonaldization, this does not mean that he supports or advocates it as a form of management and organization. Indeed, Ritzer echoes Weber's concerns with the **iron cage** of rationality (see Chapter 2) to suggest that there now exists an 'iron cage' of ever-present McDonaldization. Following Weber, Ritzer (2015: 132ff) cautions against the 'irrational' aspects of rationality—the difference between what might be formally rational for an organization in terms of efficiency and what is substantively rational: the effects in human terms.

**Disenchantment** For Max Weber this was a loss of 'magical elements' in society, and suggests some of the dehumanizing elements of bureaucracy.

Ritzer (2015: 137–8) uses Weber's concept of **disenchantment**—a loss of the 'magical aspects' of life (see Chapter 2) as more and more organizations and aspects of life become standardized and routinized. An example or symptom of this today can be found in campaigns against 'identikit' high streets, where the same chains, rather than independent retailers, can be seen in high streets across the country—the implication being that in being standardized, individual towns lose something of their character (Judd and Kirby, 2005).

### Deskilling and McJobs

Restaurant work is often linked with high levels of skill and even artistry. Top chefs train for years to get to their level and have a great deal of personal pride and identity linked to their work. A further critique of McDonaldization parallels Braverman's (1974) **deskilling** thesis which critiqued the loss of workers' skills under Taylorism (see Chapter 3).

**Deskilling** The obsolescence of workplace skills caused by rational work design or the introduction of new technology.

Fast-food restaurants deskill food production. No longer is it a highly-trained art form; instead, it involves performing a repetitive task which can be learned in a couple of hours. As with Taylorism, knowledge of the overall production process rises to the management levels which design the overall work process. Individual workers are left with a very limited knowledge of one very simple task and their autonomy is reduced, as is the amount of control that they can exert—a troublesome worker is easily replaced, and their replacement can be trained and put in place within the day.

**McJobs** Deskilled jobs found particularly in service industries, such as the fast-food restaurant.

Such is the impact on the nature of work in fast-food restaurants that the phrase **McJobs** (Etzioni, 1986) has entered the common parlance to describe simple, repetitive jobs with little job satisfaction, often performed by younger workers in the service sector (although see Gould, 2010, who suggests that there are some benefits for workers of 'McJobs', including the ability to work flexible hours around an individual lifestyle).

 Visit the Online Resource Centre for a link to a discussion about work in the fast-food industry.

## Summary

The notion of McDonaldization outlines some characteristics that are prevalent in many contemporary organizations, not just fast-food restaurants, and makes the link between rational techniques in such organizations and those developed during the Industrial Revolution. However, we should be cautious of taking the phrase 'McDonaldization of society' to apply to *all* contemporary organizations. Indeed, a volume by Smart (1999) outlines a number of instances where resistance against McDonaldization takes place—we will see some examples of these in Chapter 15.

In the following section we examine some further models of contemporary rationalization.

### Review questions

| | |
|---|---|
| **Describe** | What are the four main features of McDonaldization? |
| **Explain** | How does McDonaldization originate within and further develop more traditional forms of rationalization, such as bureaucracy and scientific management? |
| **Analyse** | How could McDonaldization be described as a trade-off between quantity and quality? |
| **Apply** | What aspects of McDonaldization can you see in organizations with which you are familiar? |

# Contemporary models of rationalization

**Running case:** budget hotel

I'm now in a budget hotel and, after the luxury of the previous hotel, this is a bit of a shock to the system.

At check-in, the queue extended to the front door and was managed by a temporary aisle of the sort used outside nightclubs.

Customer service was perfunctory—there was a job to do in processing the queue as quickly as possible. The check-in process was efficient. Despite the long queue, I soon had my key card, which gave me access to the lift and, finally, my room.

The room was almost identical to other rooms that I've experienced in this budget chain. It's interesting to see no door on the wardrobe—it certainly cuts costs: fewer raw materials to make the things in the first place, no moving parts to require repair should they go wrong, and no door for the cleaners to have to open and reach inside.

Tea and coffee was provided. The small kettle was hard-wired into the wall. Next to it were receptacles for the tea/coffee sachets—almost to a preset size so that the cleaners can just drop in the required amount very quickly. There was soap, but no other toiletries—I had to purchase those for myself from reception.

Food was to a set menu—not very much choice, just a standard, and limited, range and served in the bar area. Reception staff seem to double-up as bar and waiting staff.

Check-out required no human interaction; the key card was simply dropped into a slot on the reception desk. Had I wished to store baggage I would have needed to purchase a token and then place it myself into a set of lockers put aside for the purpose. Normally, hotels will store left-luggage for free; here, it is an optional paid extra—and I had to go and collect it for myself.

Obviously, this place reduces its costs well, but I'm not sure we could go this far with Junction Hotel—the service and luxury is what our customers want.

Can you list the methods by which the budget hotel saves costs?

Many organizations that we use on a regular basis run on a rationalized business model of saving costs and increasing efficiency—in some cases their main business strategy is cost minimization in order to compete on price. In this section we examine some examples of these, such as supermarkets, no-frills airlines, budget hotels, and flat-pack furniture retailers.

All of these could be described as 'McDonaldized' in Ritzer's terms and do exhibit some of the characteristics of McDonaldization. However, each also has their own particular ways of implementing rationalized techniques, which are worthy of examination in their own right. While this section does not cover all examples of contemporary rationalization it highlights rationalization in a number of familiar organizations.

## 'No-frills' rationalization and value engineering

There was a time when air travel was seen as glamorous—the province of celebrities and the well-off. Now, it is relatively cheap thanks to the development of budget airlines such as Ryanair, EasyJet, and German Wings.

**No-frills** A model of organizational cost reduction which offers a basic product, charging customers for anything extra to this basic offering.

Such airlines are described as **no-frills** airlines. While they may cut costs in the labour process, their main cost-cutting strategy is to simply eliminate costs that are not essential to providing the basic service of a seat on a plane. If a customer incurs any further optional costs, they pay for them as and when. Where previously the price of an aeroplane seat would include extras, such as a meal and a baggage allowance, budget airlines strip the offering down to the most basic necessities at the lowest price possible.

**Value engineering** A form of cost analysis that compares the cost of an item or process against its perceived value.

A similar pricing and cost minimization model is found in the budget hotel industry. Davis (2007) notes how a budget hotel company, such as Travelodge, engages in **value engineering**—a meticulous analysis of where costs are incurred and whether they can be pared down.

---

### Real life case: value engineering at Travelodge

Famously, Travelodge does not offer shampoo in its rooms—it means that they save on the cost and are able to offer the room at a lower price. If people want shampoo or similar optional extras, they can buy them at an extra cost. Travelodge's own website gives the reasons for this:

- Our hotels are equipped with everything you need for a good night's sleep.
- Unlike other hotel companies we don't provide a trouser press, chocolates on pillows, toiletries or other unnecessary items.
- We keep things simple and consistent because we understand that all you want is a restful place to sleep. This keeps our costs down and therefore we can offer rooms for much less than other hotels.

**Source:** Travelodge Ireland (2015).

---

Visit the Online Resource Centre to see a variety of ways in which hotels use 'no-frills' offerings, and how other industries use value engineering.

Are there any other industries or organizations where you have seen a 'no-frills' model in operation?

# Flat-pack rationalization

> ### Real life case: 'we hate air at IKEA'
>
> Flat-pack furniture is most associated with the Swedish global retailer IKEA, whose standardized stores offer the same standard range globally, although the flat-pack technique is used by other manufacturers and retailers. Being able to flat-pack the furniture saves on storage space and space on delivery vehicles, and thus saves costs (IKEA, 2003). Indeed, as Chaudhuri (2015) suggests, IKEA obsesses about its packaging, working to shave fractions of a millimetre off the size of their packaged goods so as to maximize the number that can go into a delivery vehicle. In this way, the transportation cost per unit drop.
>
> Chaudhuri (2015) outlines how a redesign of the packaging of the IKEA Ektorp sofa reduced the packaging size by 50%, resulting in over 7,000 fewer truck journeys annually. In addition to the environmental benefits of fewer journeys, the costs savings were passed on as a price reduction of 14% on that item. Stefansson (2008) similarly notes how a move from bagging packs of tea-light candles loosely and randomly meant that there was a lot of air within the sealed bags which equated to wasted space. Arranging the candles in neat stacks before packaging them more tightly and reducing the amount of wasted air allowed 30% more packages to be placed on a pallet, reducing transportation by 18,000 pallets per annum. It is in this respect that Peter Agnefjäll, CEO of IKEA, suggests that 'We hate air at IKEA' (Chaudhuri, 2015).

The example of IKEA above shows similarities to McDonaldized efficiency: whereas McDonalds strives to save fractions of a second, IKEA strives to reduce fractions of a millimetre. In both cases these factor up in huge cost savings. Removing excess air from packaging also links with value engineering, as Peter Agnefjäll states: costs that add no value to the end product are designed, or engineered, out of the process (Chaudhuri, 2015).

Other than efficiencies in the packaging process, there are rationalized aspects of flat-pack furniture which allow costs to be minimized and the product to be sold much more cheaply than high-end bespoke furniture (see also Ritzer, 2015: 17–19).

- As we saw in Chapter 3, flat-pack furniture is designed to be packed as small, individual parts which can be assembled easily, just as Taylor designed work tasks. The customer does the actual work of assembling the goods themselves, so saving the manufacturer the costs of assembly, and there is no need for the expensive skills of trained furniture-makers at any point in the process.

- Tasks are simplified so much that the instruction sheet can be provided simply as a set of diagrams rather than words. This means that exactly the same package is stored in all countries, and so there is no need to translate and print different instruction booklets for each country. Economies of scale are global.

- It is not just products that are standardized. Standard components, such as shelves and screws, can be used across a number of products.

# Barcode technology and rationalization

When you go to the supermarket, you may see the barcode on each of the products as a type of electronic price tag. While this is true, the barcode allows a supermarket to do far more than calculate prices at the till. Much of the rationalization in supermarkets is a result of the technology associated with barcodes, allowing the supermarket to make efficiencies and reduce costs in a number of ways (see also Ritzer, 2015: 71–2).

The ubiquitous barcode.

- The barcode is printed on each individual product by the manufacturer and so the work of pricing up individual items does not need to be done in the supermarket. When a price change is required, the price can simply be altered on the computer system. In fact, it can be done not just for one store, but for all stores across the country—a massive efficiency gain in terms of the time that it would take nationally to apply labels to all individual products.

- Rather than keying in individual prices for items, the supermarket cashier simply waves the goods in front of a barcode reader. The checkout often has a conveyor belt—it is as if the cashier is simply one part in an assembly line with the customer placing goods at one end and packaging them at the other.

- The act of scanning the barcode not only adds up the total bill for the customer, it simultaneously reduces the store's inventory for that product. There is much less need for stocktaking to be done by staff and, indeed, stock ordering can be done automatically by the computer system. The simple act of passing a product in front of a till feeds into a national distribution and supply system.

- Self-service tills have become commonplace in supermarkets, with the customer doing the work of a cashier and scanning the items for themselves. In future, it may be that barcodes can be replaced by radio-frequency tags—these have the capabilities of barcodes but with the added advantage that they need not be scanned individually: a whole trolley can be 'read' in one go.

The example draws from large-scale supermarket chains. Which of the techniques and characteristics mentioned have you experienced in other, possibly smaller, stores?

While the use of a barcode and associated computer technology enhances the capabilities of a supermarket in getting a large and increasing volume of customers through the store as efficiently as possible, it also leaves it vulnerable. If one area of the rational system is disrupted then it can stop the system overall from functioning.

One such disruption, which is probably familiar to many of you, can happen with barcodes. A customer is being served at a till. On one item the barcode is ripped and cannot be read by the scanner. The customer knows the price of it and the cashier also knows the price. But the only way that it can be input is by scanning the barcode—without it the transaction cannot take place. During this time the customer, and anyone else in the queue, is made to wait and become frustrated by what seems to be a rigid following of procedure rather than having the issue resolved in the quickest way possible.

When working well, the barcode produces an efficient system, but the demands of the system are such that, when it breaks down, it can suffer from similar issues of 'red tape' as seen in Chapter 2, where the system and its rules and procedures actually get in the way of work being done efficiently.

## Barcodes, information, and tracking

### Real life case: Ebuyer

Many online retailers have warehouses from which their orders are dispatched—a massive operation for some of the larger companies.

Ebuyer, a UK-based electronics retailer, demonstrates how it can deliver orders the following day if they are ordered up until 11 pm. At the heart of this efficient process is its partly-automated warehouse, where goods can be picked out within 15 minutes, travelling along conveyor belts, with the barcode being scanned at all stages as a means of tracking the product.

**Source:** Ebuyer (2008).

Visit the Online Resource Centre to view a video of what goes on in the warehouse.

Barcodes are not just used as a type of product label in supermarkets; they can be used for tracking a product or a person. When a parcel is delivered to your house, the courier may scan a barcode on the label—this barcode will have been scanned at several points on its journey as a means of tracking the product. You can even follow its progress for yourself by typing in the order number on the courier's website and then receive an automatic notification to your smartphone when the item has been delivered.

While this allows for an efficient handling of products for despatch, tracking a product also allows an organization to track where the worker handling that product has been and how efficiently they are working. It allows for surveillance and control over the workers.

This can lead to an intensification of work. Hencke (2005) notes how in some warehouses, workers have devices strapped to their arms which direct them to the next product to pick up. In a Taylorist sense, wasted movement can be minimized—the computer system can identify the nearest worker to the product so that it can be retrieved in the quickest time possible, to the extent that Spicer and Cederström (2015) suggest such technology provides a 'time-and-motion utopia' where employees can be tracked on a second-by-second basis.

Visit the Online Resource Centre for some examples of automated warehouse work and the use of tracking devices.

Rather than just accessing existing information on a database, barcodes and computer systems allow for information to be generated about a worker's performance, and allow for control to be exerted over that worker. It is to these issues of surveillance and control in the contemporary rational organization that we turn in the next section.

## Review questions

| | |
|---|---|
| **Describe** | How do the organizations discussed in this section cut costs and create efficiencies? |
| **Explain** | How do barcodes facilitate both efficiency and control? |
| **Analyse** | How do you think Frederick Taylor (see Chapter 2) might have been able to use barcode technology in his factories had it been available to him? |
| **Apply** | While value engineering is often associated with budget hotels, how might it still be applied in a luxury hotel such as Junction Hotel? |

# Panopticism, surveillance, and control

## Running case: the credit card statement

**MIDTOWN BANK**

| Credit card statement | S. CHANCE (Business a/c) | Card No. 4567 887 999988 |
|---|---|---|
| Date | Vendor | Amount |
| 1/2/2011 | Midtown Trains Online Booking | 57.89 |
| 1/2/2011 | Hurryup.com Hotels Online | 70.00 |
| 1/2/2011 | Budgetshack | 34.00 |
| 5/2/2011 | Marks & Spencer (St Pancras) | 5.50 |
| 5/2/2011 | House of Fraser (Oxford Street) | 120.00 |
| 5/2/2011 | City Casino, Leicester Square | 100.00 |
| 5/2/2011 | Bunny's Soho | 120.00 |
| 5/2/2011 | Luxhotel restaurant | 180.00 |
| 6/2/2011 | Fastburgers, Euston Road | 4.00 |
| 6/2/2011 | Budgetshack Hotels | 20.99 |
| 7/2/2011 | Mr Florists | 23.00 |

How much of Chance's business trip can we retrace from this credit card statement? Is there anything on here that he may wish to hide (and does this explain the final entry on the list for when he got home)?

The French philosopher Michel Foucault (1977: 228) is renowned for his statement that '[P]risons resemble factories, schools, barracks, hospitals, which all resemble prisons'. Foucault doesn't mean that people are kept under lock and key when in school or in hospital; his quote refers to how all of these organizations exert power and control through the use of **surveillance**.

Foucault suggests that an early prison design which permits surveillance, the **Panopticon**, is a model on which similar types of surveillance and control are exerted in organizations more widely. Although Foucault died before the advent of call centres, we will examine them as an exemplar of such panoptic power within organizations.

From within Foucault's work, we find some parallels with the way in which control is exerted in the rational organization, whose design facilitates surveillance over people within organizations. This surveillance is intensified by computer and database technology.

> **Surveillance** The observation, either overt or covert, of people to gain information about them or to exert order and control over them.
>
> **Panopticon** A prison design that allows surveillance to take place efficiently over all prisoners, used as a metaphor for surveillance and control in organizations as a whole.

# Foucault and the Panopticon

> **Research insight:** Discipline and punish
> Foucault, M. 1977. *Discipline and punish: The birth of the prison.*
> Pantheon Books: New York
>
> The French philosopher Michel Foucault (1926–84) was not interested specifically in organizational issues, but was interested in how control and order were maintained historically in society as a whole.
>
> Foucault begins with a gruesome description from 1757 of Damiens the regicide (murderer of the king) being hung, drawn, and quartered in Paris. Today, says Foucault, control and punishment in society are not so torturous and direct; instead, power operates by more subtle means, and this power operates at the level of individual organizations and institutions.
>
> The exemplar of this is the prison design of the Panopticon, which exerts power not directly and physically, but through more indirect means of surveillance. The design of the Panopticon, according to Foucault, is a blueprint for power and surveillance in many organizations that are a part of our daily lives.
>
> The Panopticon is an architectural design for a prison building originally proposed by legal and social reformer Jeremy Bentham (1748–1832). It was built so that cells were arranged in a circle around a central watch tower.
>
> In the Panopticon, every prisoner is instantly *visible* and thus open to surveillance (the word surveillance links with the idea of visibility—*surveiller* being the French word for 'watching over'). Its design means that at any one time a prisoner can be selected and observed from the central tower. The prisoner does not know at any one moment whether they are being observed, but the fact that they *might* be observed at any given moment makes them behave as the guards would wish—control is internalized within the prisoner.
>
> The design of the Panopticon allows for a massive efficiency gain in terms of staffing the prison. One guard can maintain order over hundreds of prisoners from the central watch tower, rather than many guards needing to exert direct control over the prisoners. Thus the Panopticon encompasses two aspects of rational organization—efficiency and control.

Visit the Online Resource Centre for more detail about the original Panopticon.

## The modern-day Panopticon

The same type of power through surveillance operates in modern-day CCTV systems. When we are in a store or town centre covered by CCTV cameras, we do not know if the pictures are being observed at any one time, but it is the fact that they *might be* which makes a potential miscreant behave. Again, we internalize control and power rather than having it exerted upon us face to face.

Modern-day surveillance.

The image of a security guard sitting in front of a bank of CCTV screens that show different areas of the store or town centre is perhaps not too different to the prison guard in the Panopticon looking at a grid of individual cells. In both cases, an efficient system to exert power and control is in place. The advantage that CCTV has over the Panopticon is that even if the security guard misses something as it happens, it is preserved on film to be looked at later. Technology can thus be seen to enhance the power and surveillance abilities of the Panopticon.

Think about how you are controlled when you drive. A speed camera may not even be switched on, but you are not to know this as you approach it. To what extent does the speed camera make you internalize power and control? Are speed cameras a form of modern-day Panopticon?

## Organizational Panopticons

In a prison setting, the structure of the Panopticon allows for surveillance to be exerted that brings about two benefits which, no doubt, would interest managers in other types of organization.

- It allows for control to be exerted over the organization where otherwise chaos and unpredictability might ensue.
- It allows for this to be done in a highly efficient manner.

Maybe it should come as no surprise that Bentham based his idea for the Panopticon as a prison on an idea that his brother—a factory owner—had for redesigning his own factory (Hume, 2004: 270). Just as control over a large number of prisoners presents an organizational problem, so might control over a large number of workers in a factory.

Production systems based around Taylor's ideas, such as the assembly line or the McDonalds restaurant, can be seen to display panoptic principles. Workers are given individual, simple tasks. This improves the efficiency of the production process, but also helps to increase surveillance over each individual worker. If a product is being made with component number 49 incorrectly attached, it does not take much to locate the cause of the problem—it is the worker whose sole job is to attach component 49.

## The call centre as an organizational Panopticon

A rationalized, efficient form of contemporary organization that has been described as operating in a manner similar to a Panopticon (Fernie and Metcalf, 1998) is the call centre. Whenever we interact with many large-scale organizations by telephone (our bank or insurance company, for example) more often than not this call is handled by a call centre—a part of the organization designed specifically for dealing with telephone calls, or even an outside organization that is subcontracted to handle calls.

The **call centre** is a model of rationalization that handles a large volume of telephone calls in as efficient a manner as possible. Calls are automatically directed to operators—the operator does not pace their own work. When a call is finished, the system automatically directs the next call to them. In some respects it is similar to the assembly line—the pace of work is dictated by the line or, in this case, the computer system. Work is passed before the worker and has to be attended to there and then—there is no room for a rest or a breather.

> **Call centre** An organization or department set up to handle a large volume of telephone calls, often managed efficiently using rationalized techniques.

Such intensive work regimes are further controlled by the degrees of surveillance within the call centre, which exhibit a number of characteristics similar to the Panopticon.

- The physical layout of a call centre—workers having their own individual booths—is visually remarkably similar to the layout of the Panopticon. Workers can be watched, as with the guard in the Panopticon, so anyone leaving their booth for a cigarette or toilet break can be spotted instantly.

- While an operator might be tempted to deal with a rude customer by telling them in no uncertain times where to go, they are prevented from doing this by the possibility that a supervisor may be listening in to their conversation. As with the Panopticon, this is not a constant, direct, face-to-face level of control—it is the fact that at any one moment the supervisor might be listening which leads the operator to internalize power and control and behave accordingly.

- Call data is recorded electronically—targets for the number of calls handled per hour can be set and reviewed on a computer by a supervisor. To increase the efficiency of a call centre, the target number of calls per hour can be increased—similar to increasing the speed of the assembly line. Computer data can also be used to review and monitor performance. For example, data can indicate the time spent away from the computer. There are instances where a maximum toilet time is given and the computer data can monitor if people take longer (Hencke, 2005).

While not all call centres control and monitor workers to such an extent, and there are examples of how such a system can be resisted (see Bain and Taylor, 2000), the potential for electronic monitoring and surveillance leads Fernie and Metcalf (1998) to describe the call centre as an 'electronic panopticon', where supervisory power has been 'rendered perfect'.

In what ways in your life in general, beyond the workplace, are you under surveillance? How can your behaviour be observed even after it has taken place?

## The electronic Panopticon and 'dataveillance'

The final aspect of control created within the call centre—the use of electronic data—makes a link back to bureaucratic control (the keeping of records) and rational work design (the calculation of standards and workplace targets). Panoptic power becomes not just about physical observation but also about how information is generated and recorded about workers and used to judge their performance, especially when stored in an electronic form (Simpson, 1999: 69).

The ways in which organizations generate data about people, putting them into categories and measuring them against targets, was an interest of Foucault—especially where such targets are used as a means of control.

 Visit the Online Resource Centre to read more on how data can be used as a means of control.

---

**Real life case:** credit ratings

Many of us are used to having our credit rating checked when we apply for a loan, for example, or sign up to a mobile phone contract, but do you know how such ratings are calculated?

Credit rating agencies are companies that hold masses of data about all individuals—especially their financial history. They have records of credit cards held, loans taken out, and other financial products held. Furthermore, they have records of how well people have kept up with their payments—do they have an unblemished record or have they missed several months of payments in a row? (Lewis, 2015).

From all of this data held, the credit rating agency is able to exercise surveillance in that they can see your entire financial history and from that make decisions about whether or not you are a worthy credit risk.

---

In the contemporary world we are used to a lot of information being generated and held about us. As we will see in Chapter 14, vast amounts of data are held in computer networks and shared between organizations. Terms such as **dataveillance** and the **electronic Panopticon** are used to describe the ways in which data can be used by organizations to exert control and surveillance over individuals in a manner similar to the Panopticon. Such control and surveillance has two important aspects:

**Dataveillance** Surveillance brought about by examining electronic data which is held about individuals.

**Electronic Panopticon** The ability to monitor our lives through the amount of electronic data and records held about us.

- Anything that we do that is recorded on a computer system—websites visited, tweets sent, etc.—is potentially discoverable at a later date. Politicians have found this to their cost when emails that they thought were private are uncovered months later and leaked to the press (e.g. Pearse, 2012). It also means that anything which links to a computer system is recorded—bank withdrawals, credit card payments, card swiped through door entry systems, etc. There is a lot of electronic data held about us that could potentially come back to haunt us.

- Such data can be used not only for surveillance—to find out what we have been doing—but also to make decisions about us. While credit-rating agencies assess our creditworthiness, insurance companies use data to assess the degree of risk that we pose as drivers, for example, comparing us with data held on other individuals (Poster, 1995).

The Panopticon thus shows how surveillance and control not only affect us in the workplace, but also are used to exert power and surveillance over us by organizations in society generally. While the Panopticon was first conceived of as a rationalized prison design centuries ago, Foucault shows how its surveillance and ordering mechanisms are just as relevant to rationalized organizations today.

## Review questions

| | |
|---|---|
| **Describe** | How did the Panopticon exert control over prisoners? |
| **Explain** | How is surveillance used as a means of power and control in contemporary organizations and society? |
| **Analyse** | What did Foucault mean when he said that prisons are a blueprint for power and control in many other organizations? |
| **Apply** | What examples of surveillance in your own workplace or university can you identify? How do you feel about being watched like this? |

# Chapter summary

## Running case: the email

**From:**    Simon Chance
**To:**        Management Team
**Subject:**  A tale of two hotels

Colleagues,

As you know, I have been away on business and, during that time, I stayed in two contrasting hotels. One is a luxury outfit like our own, the other was a cheap and cheerful budget hotel.

I've attached a report with my reflection on the two. In brief, as you may expect, the budget place has more examples of rationalization in order to gain efficiency. Now, that's great for costs, but it's at the expense of the overall experience. Of course we can't go down that route as a luxury hotel.

However, even the luxury place still rationalizes to an extent—it's a matter of finding where it's feasible and appropriate.

So, I want all of you to look at your areas of responsibility and send me back a report detailing where rationalization is possible and where it would simply ruin things.

Thanks,

Simon

Simon Chance is considering the extent to which he will bring in rationalization to Junction Hotel. Given that it is a hotel with a luxury reputation, to what extent do you think rationalization is appropriate for the organization overall? Where do you feel that rationalization would be most appropriate and why?

In this chapter we have seen two different trends describing the degree to which rationalization is found in contemporary organizations.

- On one hand, there are post-Fordist and post-bureaucratic models which adopt more flexible, less rigid, and less controlled models of organization, and which can be seen as a trend away from rationalized forms of managing and organizing.

- At the same time, neo-Fordism, McDonaldization, panoptic surveillance, and other contemporary forms of organization have shown that rationalization is still used today, in some cases in more intensive and widespread form than in the days of Taylor and Ford, when it was first developed.

These two trends are not mutually exclusive—they coexist and, thus, there are a variety of forms of organization which use different degrees of rationalization. Rather than a 'one best way' approach to rationalization, it is a matter of using rationalization in the most appropriate way for any one particular organization (see Morgan, 2006: 26–7).

For example, post-bureaucratic forms of organization are appropriate in an organization where creativity and innovation require workers to have autonomy and flexibility. But for a fast-food restaurant, which requires conformity and the ability to do a simple task repetitively in order to operate efficiently, it would be wholly inappropriate—a fast-food restaurant does not want its staff to spend time being creative and devising new menus! And while some people may want the convenience and efficiency of a fast-food restaurant, at other times people desire the much less rationalized approach, and the greater attention to individual detail and quality, of a Michelin-starred restaurant.

Figure 4.3 brings together in one framework different categories of work, and the degree to which that work is rationalized. The diagram locates type of work according to:

- *variety of work*—does a worker do a wide variety of tasks, or just a small number of repetitive tasks—or even just one?

- *discretion in work*—the degree of control that a worker has over their own work. Do they have high discretion, with a large amount of autonomy and independence, or low discretion, where their work is very tightly controlled?

**Figure 4.3** Work categorization framework.

**Source:** © John Bratton, Peter Sawchuk, Carolyn Forshaw, Militza Callinan and Martin Corbett, *Work and organizational behaviour*, published 2010. Reproduced with the permission of Palgrave Macmillan.

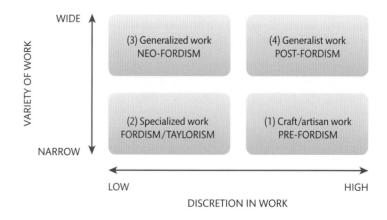

The diagram shows how different types of work coexist, displaying different degrees of rationalization. For example, we could relate the framework to the food industry, showing how different types of work in that industry relate to the types of work in the four quadrants.

1. Pre-Fordism is craft or artisan work, where a worker exercises a skill or craft on a small scale. They work independently and so have high discretion, and they work on a small variety of tasks. An example might be a dairy farmhouse kitchen, where one person makes a small amount of speciality cheese.

2. Fordist production is specialized work. A single task is performed, and workers are highly controlled and so have low discretion. Some food factories mass produce food on assembly lines. A worker on such a line may have just one repetitive job, for example sprinkling icing sugar on to cakes as they go past on the line.

3. Neo-Fordist production is generalized work, where a worker performs a wide variety of general tasks, but the tasks are simple and highly controlled and so the worker has low discretion. A fast-food restaurant would be an example of this: a worker rotates between jobs such as serving customers, cleaning tables, and making burgers, but each of these jobs is designed to be simple and highly controlled.

4. Post-Fordism is generalist work. A person with expert knowledge performs a wide variety of tasks and does so relatively autonomously, i.e. with high discretion. The head chef of a restaurant is an example of this, using their knowledge and expertise to produce any of a wide variety of dishes, creating the menu themselves each day.

The example listed shows the variety of work in an industry, but Noon et al. (2013: 165) suggest that such a variety can be seen even within one organization. Can you find examples for each of the four types of work shown in Figure 4.3 in Junction Hotel or in a similar type of workplace?

In this chapter we have examined the differing degrees of rationalization that exist in contemporary organizations and how these exist alongside trends away from rationalization. Moves towards, and away from, rationalization will also be reflected in future chapters, for example:

• Perspectives such as the learning organization (Chapter 10) and emergent change (Chapter 11) lean towards a more post-bureaucratic, less rationalized view of organization, where organizations need to be flexible in order to respond rapidly to change and maintain competitive advantage. Furthermore, perspectives that emphasize the social side of the organization (Chapter 5) and the importance of groups and teamwork (Chapter 6) move us away from the rationalized view of organizations as machines and people as cogs within them.

• Nevertheless, by examining work organization in the service sector (Chapter 16), global standardization and subcontracting (Chapter 15), and the issue of sweatshop labour in factories in the developing world (Chapter 17), we see examples where rationalization is still prevalent and widespread.

## Further reading

Noon, M., Blyton, P., and Morrell, K. 2013. *The realities of work: Experiencing work and employment in contemporary society, 4th edn*. Palgrave: Basingstoke.
Chapter 6 is a good overview of Fordism, post-Fordism, and neo-Fordism.

Ritzer, G. 2015. *The McDonaldization of society, 8th edn*. Pine Forge Press: Thousand Oaks, CA.
The classic, and accessible, overview of the McDonaldization thesis.

Gould, A.M. 2010. Working at McDonalds: Some redeeming features of McJobs. *Work, Employment and Society* 24(4): 780–802.
Presents arguments for and against 'McJobs'.

Fernie, S., and Metcalf, D. 1998. *(Not) hanging on the telephone: Payment systems in the new sweatshops*. Centre for Economic Performance, London School of Economics and Political Science: London.
A study which likens call centres to the Panopticon and also looks at the Panopticon concept itself.

## References

AutoMotoTV. 2010. Volkswagen Phaeton: Die gläserne Manufaktur Dresden. Available at: https://www.youtube.com/watch?v=sFV5EnsRgvw (last accessed 13 August 2015).

Bain, P., and Taylor, P., 2000. Entrapped by the 'electronic panopticon'? Worker resistance in the call centre. *New Technology, Work and Employment* 15(1): 2–18.

Barker, J.R. 1993. Tightening the iron cage: Concertive control in self-managing teams. *Administrative Science Quarterly* 38(3): 408–37.

Bauman, Z. 2000. *Liquid modernity*. Polity Press, Blackwell: Cambridge, UK, and Malden, MA.

Bell, D. 1973. *The coming of post-industrial society: A venture in social forecasting*. Basic Books: New York.

Bennett, O. 2015. Rage against the machine. *Management Today*, July/August.

Bennis, W. 1966. The coming death of bureaucracy. *Think Magazine*, November/December: 30–5.

Branson, R. 2014. Why we're letting Virgin staff take as much holiday as they want [blog post]. Available at: http://www.virgin.com/richard-branson/why-were-letting-virgin-staff-take-as-much-holiday-as-they-want (last accessed 13 August 2015).

Bratton, J., Sawchuck, P., Forshaw, C., Callinan, M., and Corbett, M. 2010. *Work and organizational behaviour*. Palgrave Macmillan: Basingstoke.

Braverman, H. 1974. *Labor and monopoly capital: The degradation of work in the twentieth century*. Monthly Review: New York.

Burnes, B. 2000. *Managing change: A strategic approach to organisational dynamics*, 3rd edn. Financial Times/ Prentice Hall: London.

Chaudhuri, S. 2015. IKEA can't stop obsessing about its packaging. *Wall Street Journal*, 17 June.

Clegg, S., and Baumeler, C. 2010. Essai: From iron cages to liquid modernity in organization analysis. *Organization Studies* 31(12): 1713–33.

Davis, E. 2007. Value engineering. *BBC News*, 21 May. Available at http://www.bbc.co.uk/blogs/thereporters/evandavis/2007/05/value_engineering.html (last accessed 13 August 2015).

Dohse, K., Jurgens, U., and Malsch, T. 1985. From 'Fordism' to 'Toyotism': The social organization of the labour process in the Japanese automobile industry. *Politics and Society* 14(2): 115–46.

Ebuyer. 2008. Ebuyer order process . Available at: https://www.youtube.com/watch?v=PbaVy02u_9s (last accessed 13 August 2015).

Etzioni, A. 1986. The fast-food factories: McJobs are bad for kids. *Washington Post*, 24 August.

Fayol, H. 1949. *General and industrial management*. Pitman: London.

Fernie, S., and Metcalf, D. 1998. *(Not) hanging on the telephone: Payment systems in the new sweatshops*. Centre for Economic Performance, London School of Economics and Political Science: London.

Foucault, M. 1977. *Discipline and punish: The birth of the prison*. Pantheon Books: New York.

Gould, A.M. 2010. Working at McDonalds: Some redeeming features of McJobs. *Work, Employment and Society* 24(4): 780–802.

Hencke, D. 2005. AA to log call centre staff's trips to the loo in pay deal. *The Guardian*, 31 October.

Hume, L.J. 2004. *Bentham and bureaucracy*. Cambridge University Press: Cambridge.

IKEA, 2003. From supplier to store. Available at: http://www.ikea.com/ms/en_GB/about_ikea/press_room/distribution.pdf (last accessed 13 August 2015).

Jaffee, D. 2001. *Organization theory: Tension and change*. McGraw Hill: Boston.

Judd, T., and Kirby, T. 2005. Clone attack: The two sides of high street UK. *The Independent*, 7 June.

Kociatkiewicz, J. 2014. Life in the liquid organization: Control and ambiguity in organizational experience. In:Kociatkiewicz, J., and Kostera, M. (eds) *Liquid organization: Zygmunt Bauman and organization theory*. Routledge: London, pp. 58–70.

Lambert, C. 2015. *Shadow work: The unpaid, unseen jobs that fill your day*. Counterpoint: Berkeley, CA.

Larsen, H.H. 2002. Oticon: Unorthodox project-based management and careers in a 'spaghetti organization'. *Human Resource Planning* 25: 30-7.

Lewis, M. 2015 . Credit scores. MoneySavingExpert.com. Available at: http://www.moneysavingexpert.com/loans/credit-rating-credit-score (last accessed 13 August 2015).

McDonalds. 2004 . McDonald's UK position on *Super Size Me* press release. Available at: http://web.archive.org/web/20071012135323/http://mcdonalds.co.uk/pages/global/supersize.html (last accessed 13 August 2015).

Morgan, G. 2006. *Images of organization*. Sage Publications: Thousand Oaks, CA.

Noon, M., Blyton, P., and Morrell, K. 2013. *The realities of work: Experiencing work and employment in contemporary society*, 4th edn. Palgrave: Basingstoke.

Parker, M., and Jary, D. 1995. The McUniversity: Organization, management and academic subjectivity. *Organization* 2(2): 319.

Pearse, B. 2012. Jeremy Hunt should quit over 'hacking advice' email, says Ed Miliband. *The Guardian*, 21 May.

Perkins, A. 2014. Richard Branson's 'unlimited holiday' sounds great—until you think about it. *The Guardian*, 25 September.

Piore, M.J., and Sabel, C.F. 1984. *The second industrial divide: Possibilities for prosperity*. Basic Books: New York.

Poster, M. 1995. *The second media age*. Polity Press: Cambridge.

Rehder, R.R. 1994. Saturn, Uddevalla and the Japanese lean systems: Paradoxical prototypes for the twenty-first century. *International Journal of Human Resource Management* 5(1): 1–31.

Ritzer, G. 2015. *The McDonaldization of society*, 8th edn. Pine Forge Press: Thousand Oaks, CA.

Sewell, G. 1998. The discipline of teams: The control of team-based industrial work through electronicand peer surveillance. *Administrative Science Quarterly* 43(2): 397–428.

Simpson, I.H. 1999. Historical patterns of workplace organization: From mechanical to electronic control and beyond. *Current Sociology* 47(2): 47–75.

Smart, B. 1999. *Resisting McDonaldization*. Sage: London.

Spicer, A., and Cederström, C. 2015. What companies should ask before embracing wearables. *Harvard Business Review*, 20 May.

Spurlock, M. (dir.) 2004. *Super Size Me*. Palisades Tartan (UK).

Starkey, K., and McKinlay, A. 1994. Managing for Ford. *Sociology* 28(4): 975–90.

Stefansson, G. 2008. Case Study: IKEA—Increased transport efficiency by product and packaging design. European Commission Bestlog Project.

Thompson, J.D. 1967. *Organizations in action*. McGraw Hill: New York.

Towill, D. 2010. Industrial engineering the Toyota Production System. *Journal of Management History* 16(3): 327–45.

Travelodge Ireland. 2015. Everyday low prices—how we do it. Available at: https://www.travelodge.ie/everyday_low_prices/ (last accessed 13 August 2015).

Woodward, J. 1958. *Management and technology*. HMSO: London.

# Part 2
## The social organization

# Discovering the social organization

*The Hawthorne studies and the human side of the organization*

## Chapter overview and learning outcomes

By the end of this chapter you should be able to:

- describe the basic features of the Hawthorne studies

- describe how the Hawthorne studies challenged many of Taylor's assumptions

- explain how the Hawthorne studies led to the foundations of organizational behaviour (OB), challenging the rational perspective and introducing the power of the social organization

- describe the power of the informal organization

- analyse whether the results of the Hawthorne studies increase worker *freedom* or *control* over workers

- analyse the assumptions that Mayo's interpretation of the Hawthorne studies were based on and explore other perspectives.

## Key theorists

| | |
|---|---|
| Elton Mayo | Seen as the founder of human relations, a key figure in the Hawthorne studies and one of the founders of OB |
| Fritz Roethlisberger and William Dickson | The writers of the largest account of the Hawthorne studies, which comprises over 600 pages of highly detailed description of the research |
| Mary Parker Follett | Alongside Lillian Gilbreth, a key female early-management theorist; she was a political scientist, social work pioneer, speaker, and advisor to leaders concerning the relations between workers and management |
| Daniel Bell | A key social theorist after World War II, who wrote extensively about post-industrialization and its impact on society; provided a key critique of Mayo |

## Key terms

| | |
|---|---|
| Social organization | The underlying belief that the social relations between people are a key factor in shaping how people act in organizations |
| Hawthorne studies | A series of studies that ran from 1924 into the late 1930s; widely credited with discovering the human side of organization |
| Human relations | Born out of the Hawthorne studies, human relations aims to understand and prescribe changes in workplace behaviour based on the importance of group norms, communication, and supervisory skills |

# Introducing the social side of the organization

**Running case:** too much to do and not enough time

Nina Biagini, Junction Hotel's maître d', looks at the pile of napkins piled in front of her: 250 to fold before the restaurant opens at 5 pm; 400 glasses also need to be cleaned; and then all the silver cutlery needs to be polished. 'We are never going to be ready for tonight's Rotary International meal, and we need to be on the top of our game with all these business leaders coming,' she thinks. 'This is just the start of it,' she says to herself, 'what with our busy season coming up, this place is going to be carnage if we don't get it sorted. We need help.'

Feeling anxious that the restaurant will not be ready in time, Biagini phones Weaver to get an extra pair of hands. 'What?' Weaver blasts down the phone. 'We can't afford more people. Look, I'll get you help today, but I can't keep bailing you out like this . . . I'll tell you what,' he continues, in a calmer manner. 'I'll come down and work out how to make this process more efficient so this doesn't happen again.'

Weaver feels confident he can achieve the same efficiencies for the restaurant as he did for the cleaners. So, sitting in his office, he devises detailed napkin-folding instructions, including starching the cloths before they are used, how to sit them in the right way to minimize movement, and how to fold them in the exact order. 'One hundred and twenty napkins folded an hour per person . . . easy!', he concludes.

Excited with his new procedure, Weaver is confident this will increase efficiency, thereby making prep-time stress-free. However, when he shows it to the restaurant team the reaction is not as he hoped. 'We're not robots,' Naomi and Saffron complain. 'Weaver should try doing this job day in, day out and see if he can do it. We get tired and it's cold in here—not like in *his* office, which is comfortable with the radiator on.'

---

This chapter is about the importance of the human side of the organization. It tells the story of a fundamental transformation in management theory and practice from a Taylorist view (see Chapter 3), which saw organizations as purely mechanical, formal, measureable, and rational machines, to one that revealed the significance of informal relations between people. This view, which we will call the **social** side of the organization, has led to the interest in the importance of teamwork, organizational culture, motivation, and leadership—all of which feature heavily throughout the rest of the book. In other words, this chapter is about the introduction of a new way of thinking about organizations that stresses the importance of the informal, human side of the organization.

> **Social** The human side of the organization, in particular the relations between people at work.

The findings from the Hawthorne studies have been credited with humanizing management practice. People are not nameless cogs in the machine, following rules and procedures in mechanical, predictable, and routine ways. Rather, this view states that for people to work effectively, they should feel wanted and be treated as human beings. According to this view, the informal group, rather than being a problem as Taylor assumed, becomes a resource used by management to increase productivity. Consequently, to be productive it is possible—indeed, essential—to treat people as human beings. Management can, therefore, be humanized.

This chapter is about the Hawthorne studies, one of the most important pieces of research to introduce this way of thinking. The Hawthorne studies, particularly as they were popularized by Elton Mayo, are widely credited as introducing a revolution in management thinking, offering a magic cure—an end to conflict between the worker and the manager, producing harmony and progress.

At the time it sent shockwaves across business circles, fundamentally challenging both management practitioners and the emerging university Business School. To our twenty-first century eyes, however, the ideas that the social side of the organization is important, that we are influenced by peer pressure, that teamwork is important, and that employees respond better when managers pay attention to them are unlikely to shock. They have become an accepted part of management thinking and practice. This chapter is about the emergence of a new way of thinking and its continued importance for management today, showing how these ideas arose.

## Chapter outline

This chapter starts with describing the key studies as they are normally described. As you will read, these started with assumptions that would fit comfortably within a Taylorist framework—that the levels of lighting and worker fatigue impact employee output. However, as the studies progressed, the researchers began to realize the importance of the informal behaviour of the group. These findings lead to a change in assumptions in how to manage people.

However, this typical account of the Hawthorne studies is not all it appears. While Mayo and his colleagues stated that they 'discovered' the social side of the organization and that workers are naturally cooperative, a number of critics have argued the the way Mayo interpreted his data was highly ideological. These critics of Mayo claim that the research methodology and interpretation of findings were flawed. Furthermore, they argue that the results of the Hawthorne studies have been used by management as a better way of controlling workers, rather than empowering the workers as Mayo and his colleague claimed. The latter part of the chapter will examine these criticisms, drawing attention to the political and social consequences of the Hawthorne studies. This chapter will not only look at the studies but also seek to demonstrate the importance of understanding the historical context of research, and of using critical analysis to see other perspectives of well-known studies.

The existence and strength of the criticisms of the Hawthorne studies presented, however, should not detract from the positive benefits that the findings of the Hawthorne studies have presented to management theory and practice. In comparison with the dehumanizing impacts of Taylorism, an awareness of the significance of the human side of the organization certainly presented a step forward. However, from the workers' point of view, as we will argue in this chapter, it still offers a way that management can control workers—potentially in ways that we do not even see.

## Background to the Hawthorne studies: from the mechanical to the social

The Hawthorne studies were a series of six experiments carried out between 1924 and 1932 at the Western Electric Company in Cicero, on the periphery of Chicago, Illinois, USA. It has been considered one of the most significant pieces of research in the history of OB, not

**Table 5.1**  The dates of experiments in the Hawthorne studies

| No. | Name | Dates | Description | Findings |
|---|---|---|---|---|
| 1 | *Illumination* | 1924–April 1927 | Tested how different levels of light impacted productivity | No clear correlation between lighting levels and output |
| 2 | *Relay I* | April 1927–June 1929 | Assessed the impact of rest periods on productivity | No clear correlation between rest periods and output |
| | | | Tested fatigue and monotony thesis | No clear correlation between fatigue and output |
| 3 | *Relay II* | August 1928–January 1929 | Tested effects of wage incentive on output | No notable increase in output from wage incentive but not sustained |
| 4 | *Mica Splitting experiment* | October 1928–September 1930 | Duplicated relay assembly room, but without wage incentive | Same pattern for first year then declined; output more to do with **psychological** issues than wage incentives |
| 5 | *Interview programme* | September 1928–February 1929, extended into 1931 | Link between morale and supervision, improvements in employee–supervisor relations and the attitude of staff | Workers often have obsessive and irrational views; social groups have powerful influence over the actions of individuals |
| 6 | *Bank wiring observation* | November 1931–May 1932 | The role of the group in determining output | The informal group is key to impacting behaviour |

**Psychological** Arising from the mind or emotions.

only for the size of the research, but also because of the implications it holds for our understanding of management theory and practice today.

The Hawthorne works was a large factory, which has been described as being like a small city with over 29,000 (over 40,000 at its peak) employees. At the time it was 'America's largest manufacturer of electrical products', in particular making telephones for Alexander Graham Bell (Hassard 2012: 1438). These telephones required highly-skilled workers to put together the fiddly systems. The main experiments and their findings are shown in Table 5.1.

While the Hawthorne studies are closely associated with Elton Mayo, the fullest account is provided by Fritz Roethlisberger, a professor at Harvard, and William Dickson, the Chief of Employee Relations at the Hawthorne Works. Their book *Management and the worker* (1939) provides a highly detailed (over 600 pages) and often fascinating account of every experiment, including the methods used, the often surprising reactions of the staff, the questions that the perplexing results raised for the researchers, and how the research led to alternative interpretations of management problems and potential solutions. We will concentrate on the key events, interpretations, and debates.

Visit the Online Resource Centre for a full account of the research. It is worth reading about this research in some depth, as much of its significance lies in the detail.

# The experiments

## Experiment 1: testing the link between lighting levels and output—the illumination experiments

**Running case:** Weaver explores the impact of heating

Looking at the results, Weaver is concerned that the restaurant team are not as effective as he thought they could be. On paper, they should fold at least 120 napkins an hour, but they are still only folding 80. Weaver feels confused and decides to investigate further.

Visiting the restaurant, Weaver starts to watch how the restaurant team work, noting their body movements, the way they arrange the napkins and glasses, and the way they perform their tasks.

'It is a little cold in here,' he thinks. 'I wonder if they can't move their fingers properly.' Asking Nina Biagini why this is, she states that when there are no customers they do not have heating. Weaver thinks this might be the cause of their slow work. Inspired by his time and motion studies, he starts recording the output and heating on a graph, asking them how they feel about the temperature as he does it. 'If we can find the right temperature,' he thinks to himself, 'then we can maximize the output.'

In 1924, a small group of researchers aimed to uncover the links between lighting levels and employee output. By trying to create a 'science of seeing' they thought they would discover the optimum levels of lighting needed to maximize productivity and, owing to their funding from General Electric—one of the world's largest manufacturers of light bulbs—the research would also lead to increased sales of light bulbs to industry (Donkin, 2001: 165).

This research, conducted just over a decade after Taylor had published *The principles of scientific management*, was set firmly within the scientific management tradition. Indeed, Alexander Church, a 'Taylorist' and a supporter of scientific management, had already stated his belief that poor lighting caused a strain on workers and that high-intensity lighting lifted workers' spirits. Frank Gilbreth (see Chapter 3) was also worried that the reflection on surfaces caused tiredness among workers (Donkin, 2001: 165). Thus, the first research shared Taylorist assumptions that physical conditions are an important area for *scientific* research.

Aiming to improve efficiency, they believed that creating the right inputs (in this case physical conditions) would increase output (the workers' productivity). Armed with measurement devices to assess the strength of lighting and record sheets to measure output, the researchers recorded the levels of lighting and set about monitoring and adjusting the levels of lighting and output.

The assumption that the correct physical conditions, such as lighting, can improve employee output is widely held today. Many offices are designed to be 'light and airy', maximizing the amount of natural daylight and supplementing it with suitable artificial light, where necessary, believing that it energizes the workers.

How important do you find the levels of lighting to your feelings of energy, well-being, and levels of productivity?

The researchers fully expected to find a pattern between the lighting levels and output; however, the results shocked them. Instead of seeing a direct correspondence between light levels and employee output as they expected, the 'output [levels] bobbed up and down' in rather confusing ways.

Unable to find a link between lighting and output, they became more scientific and set up a **control group**, for which they kept lighting levels the same, and an experiment group, for which they adjusted the

A modern office designed to maximize daylight.
**Source:** skdesign/123RF.

> **Control group** Used in scientific research, a control group does not receive any intervention and therefore is seen as representing the population as a whole. The control group is used as a standard of comparison to the research group who do receive intervention.

lighting. However, again, to their bafflement both groups' productivity went up in 'almost identical magnitude' (Roethlisberger and Dickson, 1939: 16). Lighting, it seemed, did not matter. Still trying to establish a link, they set up a third experiment in which they reduced the lighting to levels where the workers 'were hardly able to see what they were doing' (ibid.: 17). Even at this level efficiency remained high. At one point they even said that they had changed the light bulbs for brighter ones when they had not and productivity went up.

The researchers, particularly as recounted by Roethlisberger and Dickson (1939: 17), therefore began to question their original assumption that lighting was an important component to productivity, concluding it was 'more "psychological" than real'. They needed to look for other factors involved in increasing productivity.

## Review questions

| | |
|---|---|
| **Describe** | What happened in the illumination study? |
| **Explain** | Why did the researchers conclude that productivity was more psychological than real? |
| **Analyse** | Why did a focus on lighting levels reflect Taylorist assumptions? What were the underlying assumptions the researchers held, which led them to conclude lighting was a key factor? |

# Experiment 2: testing the link between fatigue and output—the Relay I assembly test room

## Running case: if it's not heating then what is it?

Weaver meets Nina Biagini to discuss the preparations for the busy Christmas period. 'We are making some improvement, but the level of heating does not seem to make any difference,' Biagini states. 'Yes, it is odd,' replies Weaver. 'I mean you would have thought that when we dropped the heating back to the original level, their performance would have dipped again. There must be more we can do. In a couple of weeks' time we are going to have three sittings a day, so we are going to have to work extra hard to keep up.'

'But we will never be able to achieve that,' Biagini responds. 'They barely keep going for two hours, let alone for four. They get exhausted doing the same thing over and over again.'

Suddenly, Weaver has a brainwave. 'Exhaustion, you say. I think you might be on to something.'

As the initial experiment suggested, lighting was only a minor factor in employee output. The researchers, continuing in a scientific mindset, believing there must by other physical factors that impacted productivity. Their next assumption was that fatigue was the problem, assuming tired workers would produce less. They therefore aimed to discover scientifically the ideal balance between work and rest.

The role of fatigue was already a subject of much research with concern that operators, particularly the munitions workers of World War I, working seven days a week with only one day off per month, were often so tired that they were found asleep at their lathes (Gale, 2004).

The researchers took a group of six women, who were making telephone circuits, from the large factory and put them in a special unit to study them. Trying to control the experiment scientifically, they decided that the women needed to be highly experienced so that productivity increases could not be attributed to improvements in skill, but could be confirmed as a result of what they were testing—the balance between work and rest. Crucially, for their later findings, they also decided to make the research environment as friendly, cooperative, and natural as possible so that they could get closer feedback on the results. We will return to why this was significant in the section on 'The importance of group norms'.

## Theory in context: gender in the Hawthorne studies

One of the fascinating aspects of the Hawthorne studies is the role that gender played. Throughout Roethlisberger and Dickson's (1939: 182) account they referred to the six women in the relay assembly room as 'girls'. The language that they used indicates it was not a relationship of equals.

As with many aspects of working life at the time, men decided levels of pay, hours, or even if women could have a job. In this experiment it was men who decided that the women should work in a separate special room away from the large factory; it was men who decided that the women were talking too much; it was men who decided when it was acceptable for the women to talk; it was men who carried out physical examinations and asked questions as to the women's eating habits, bedtimes, and activities outside of work; and it was men who decided the meaning of the discussions that the women had. Indeed, as Marks argues, when the research was intrusive, it was the women who were investigated, whereas when they decided to avoid manipulation the researchers decided to select men as their subject matter (Marks, 1999).

This gendered relationship even extends to the language that the researchers and commentators used. For instance, Elton Mayo (1933) argued that it revealed the existence of 'Social man', which replaced the previous assumption of 'Economic man'. While you may dismiss the use of *man* in this context as semantics, as simply a difference in the meaning of the word, the choice of words reflects the assumptions that were prevalent at that time—that the world of work revolved around male assumptions of the world. We will be using the more gender-neutral 'social person' for the remainder of this chapter, as it represents a more inclusive perspective.

The work the women did was mind-numbingly boring. For instance, to put one of the relays together, the worker had to perform thirty-two separate operations for each hand and to make one every minute for nine hours a day for five-and-a-half days a week. They had little hope of promotion or even variation in the job (Gillespie, 1991).

Imagine that you did this kind of work—how would you feel? How would you cope with the monotony?

The primary objective of the research was to discover the ideal pattern of work and rest. To test this they started by keeping everything constant for a few weeks and then experimenting with different break periods. Table 5.2 shows that by the eighth period they had started shortening the working day and then, by the eleventh period, even removing the Saturday morning shift.

To their surprise they discovered that regardless of how long the rest periods were or when they were taken, output constantly rose. Even when they returned to the original pattern output was higher than ever. The researchers concluded, contrary to their assumptions, that there was no simple correlation between output and rest patterns.

So why did the output levels not correspond to the rest periods? To find the answer, the researchers devised a number of hypotheses, such as better lighting and ventilation, reduction in overall fatigue, reduction in monotony of work, and increased pay.

Centring on their hypothesis that fatigue was the most important factor, the researchers went to some lengths to test the physical condition of the workers. This included regular physical examinations of the workers' blood pressures and **vascular skin reaction** to test their level of fatigue. They even compared the results with marathon runners, believing that stamina was vital for work.

**Vascular skin reaction** A white line on the wrist created by a blunt instrument which disappears more quickly when the person is fatigued.

While they still assumed that physical conditions were important, they also began to notice—which became important for later studies—that the atmosphere and mental attitude in the group improved. At first, they had prevented the women from talking, but as the study continued they allowed them to talk to each other more. Indeed, the researchers felt they needed to create a more harmonious atmosphere in order to undertake the tests they wanted. They came to realize that the 'girls' enjoyed the less formal test room with no formal bosses present and increased freedom. Over the course of the study they noticed

Table 5.2  Rest patterns

| I | Standard | VIII | As VII stop 4:30 |
|---|---|---|---|
| II | Standard | IX | As VII stop 4:00 |
| III | Standard | X | As VII |
| IV | 2 × 5 minutes | XI | As VII Sat. am off |
| V | 2 × 10 minutes | XII | Standard |
| VI | 6 × 5 minutes | XIII | As VII |
| VII | 1 × 15 and 1 × 10 minutes | | |

that antagonism between the group members was replaced by banter and joking. Attendance improved and they worked well together. The women, by being allowed to talk, managed to overcome some of the monotony of the job and found a way of working that best suited them.

What do you think about these tests? Are they a good way of capturing this information or do they treat people more like robots?

### Real life case: fatigue at work today

While the Hawthorne studies rejected the fatigue hypothesis, it is still a key debate within research and practice. In 2007 a survey claimed that nearly 40% of Americans experienced fatigue over a two-week period, costing employers an estimated $101 billion a year (Ricci et al., 2007). In the UK, fatigue is estimated to cost between £115–240 million per year in accidents alone. This can also be a problem for office workers unable to switch off, with a recent survey stating that more than half of British workers checking their emails while on holiday (O'Conor and Cahillane, 2015).

One popular strategy is to encourage naps, where even a brief nap of 7–10 minutes (Lovato and Lack, 2010) has benefits. The Japanese company Okuta allows workers a 20-minute power nap at their desk. 'Inemuri—or "sleeping while present"—is considered the preserve of employees exhausted by their commitment to hard work, rather than a sign of indolence' (McCurry, 2014).

Research has focused on the importance of breaks away from work and the best way to use them (Fritz et al., 2013), sleep and energy management strategies, such as taking frequent forms of physical exercise (Fritz et al., 2011), or micro-breaks such as drinking water or having a snack (Zacher et al., 2014). However, researchers have found that these physical strategies seem less important, and energy levels feel higher when the work seems more meaningful. Therefore, learning something new or doing something that will make a colleague happy are ways of increasing vitality, making work feel more meaningful rather than trying to conserve energy (Fritz et al., 2011). Researchers are calling on firms to train their staff to learn how to take effective breaks and develop areas so that they can go outside to take hourly micro-breaks to refresh themselves (Zacher et al., 2014).

### Review questions

| **Describe** | What happened in the fatigue experiments? |
|---|---|
| **Explain** | Did the fatigue experiments prove any link between the rest time and productivity? |
| **Analyse** | Why do you think it is significant that the research was largely carried out by men on women? Why might the gendered nature of words matter? |
| **Apply** | Which of the strategies described in the real life case on fatigue at work today would be desirable or practical for Junction Hotel? |

# Experiments 3 and 4: testing the link between pay and output—Relay II and the Mica Splitting experiment

The second relay experiment and the Mica Splitting experiment shifted the focus of the Hawthorne studies dramatically. For the first time the researchers began to examine the *psychological* and *social* factors that influenced how people behaved, rather than just the *physical* ones. They therefore became interested in what made them a team and how individual behaviour arose out of the nature of the group. It was, therefore, a shift in focus from the individual to the group.

This change in focus laid the foundations for an area of research known as **'Human Relations'**, an academic school of thought which examines the *social relations* between people, the *motivation* of workers, and the impact that *employee satisfaction* has on output and productivity. Rather than seeing workers as 'cogs in the machine', this approach saw workers as social beings, with a need for belonging within the group. This approach acted as a precursor to modern-day *human resource management*.

Workers in the relay assembly department.
**Source:** © Baker Library Historical Collections, Harvard Business School.

> **Human Relations** A movement emerging out of Organizational Development that studies the behaviour of people in groups.

However, these two experiments did not begin by examining the social relations between group members; rather, they held another Taylorist assumption: that increased pay levels would increase output—an attempt to establish a link between another set of inputs (bonuses) and output.

At first it seemed that their assumptions were correct because after giving the workers a bonus, output rose sharply. However, to their puzzlement, this rise did not continue. The results, though, proved to be inconclusive, as the experiment had to be cut short. Other groups in the factory got wind of the scheme and felt it was unfair that this 'social group' were getting preferential treatment and they 'wanted similar consideration' (Roethlisberger and Dickson, 1939: 133). Fearing upset, the rest of the factory managers demanded that the experiment was ended—showing the importance of social factors.

The researchers continued their investigations into whether increased output could be attributed to a wage increase; therefore, in Experiment 4—the Mica Splitting Test Room—they tried replicating Relay II, but without the bonus scheme. To their surprise the first year's results mirrored Relay II with a sharp increase in productivity, even without the bonus. However, in the second year output declined. The researchers believed this was because rumours were spreading that jobs were to be transferred to another city, concluding that the employees' 'fears and anxieties so completely overshadowed the experimentally introduced changes' (ibid.: 153). This suggested to the researchers that it was not wage incentives that impacted their performance, but the employees' attitudes (e.g. fear of job loss). Again, we can see the importance of social factors.

As pay did not seem a significant factor, the researchers began to consider other explanations. What mattered more was employees' morale, their relationships with their supervisors and each other, and their personal backgrounds. Most importantly, they concluded that the Relay Assembly Test Room was a '"group" story' where the members acted as a team: they did not have bosses but cooperated and worked together. By contrast, they thought that the Mica Splitting Test Room 'was a story of "individuals"' who were self-sufficient and did not feel the need to work together' (ibid.: 156). They thought that individual behaviour was 'rooted in [shaped by] their personal and social background' (ibid.: 171). In other words, the Relay experiment was successful because the members cooperated and saw themselves as part of a team, whereas the less successful Mica Splitting Test Room subjects were individuals who did not bond.

Why do you think the researchers at the Hawthorne studies began to see the importance of the relationship between group members to their overall levels of productivity?

# Experiment 5: interview programme—discovering the importance of a personal life

**Running case:** listening to the staff

Faced with the confusing results from Weaver's experiments, Nina Biagini is asked to interview the restaurant staff and find out how her team feel about working in the restaurant.

'Right, Isabella, I have been asked by the senior management team to find out the level of staff satisfaction at Junction Hotel. We want to have a happy team, as well as a productive one, so today I want to know your views of working at Junction Hotel. Don't worry, your views will be kept anonymous—we just want to know what you think.'

A little taken aback, Isabella smiles at Biagini. 'Oh, me, well,' pausing before laughing nervously, 'how long have you got!' Isabella begins by cautiously saying that she really enjoys working for Junction Hotel: 'they are all good fun' and 'supportive when you're having a bad day, although I didn't like Weaver watching us like that'. She then goes on to say that she is finding life at home a little hard at the moment: 'there's always so much to do and I feel a little harried,' she confesses to Biagini. She's just fallen out with her son and isn't talking to her husband—'he's just so distant,' she says with a faraway look in her eye. Listening to all this Biagini starts to feel a little uncomfortable—'I feel more like a counsellor than a manager,' she thinks. Rounding off the discussion, Isabella turns to Biagini—'oh, sorry, I hope I didn't go on to much. Thanks so much for listening'.

Having established the importance of the social side of the organization, the next set of experiments began exploring employees' attitudes to work. Undertaking a large interview programme, the researchers thought that gaining an insight into how employees viewed work and their relationship with their supervisors would unlock ways of increasing productivity. What they found, however, was that it was the interview itself, particularly being listened to, that the employees really responded to.

The researcher team conducted one of the largest investigations of employee attitudes ever undertaken, with an enormous 10,300 interviews lasting between 30 minutes and 1.5 hours, all of which were fully transcribed. This was a very time-consuming task as, on average, an hour-long interview can take at least five hours to transcribe. This produced hundreds of pages of detailed personal information, providing an amazing insight into the mindset of these ordinary American workers during the 'Great Depression'. Even today the size and level of detail of this study is hard to match, and it gave a comprehensive insight into the lives of ordinary workers.

The researchers took the thousands of comments and sorted them into categories, such as work conditions, attitudes to supervisors, and the nature of their jobs, and divided them into favourable and unfavourable groups. They discovered the workers disliked certain working conditions, such as the washrooms and the smoke and fumes, but strongly approved of the benefit plan and vacations. Men seemed more interested in economic security, whereas the women were more focused on working conditions. This, they thought, would help the management understand how workers felt and therefore how to manage them.

However, the researchers were surprised (and often frustrated) that the interviewees would become fixated on what they considered irrelevant issues in their personal lives. Employees would recall personal events, sometimes from years before, with full emotion as though it was yesterday. The researchers surmised that doing repetitive factory work gave 'a great deal of time for preoccupation' (Roethlisberger and Dickson, 1939: 133), resulting in the workers being 'obsessive' and 'irrational'. This brooding on their personal lives, they considered, made the workers less productive.

Eventually, though, rather than dismissing their home lives, the researchers began to see that what happened at home shaped employees' experiences at work. For instance, being treated unfairly by a supervisor at work at the same time as feeling unfairly treated at home (e.g. by a husband) made them over-react to the criticism (ibid.: 310–11). The researchers concluded that supervisors need to understand people's home situations to manage them better. Furthermore, being part of a group with 'human comradeship and social conversations' (ibid.: 324) helped employees manage their emotions.

These interviews revealed that workers' personal backgrounds and experiences shape how they perform. Unlike Taylorism—where the worker was little more than a cog in a machine—the Hawthorne studies revealed the importance of understanding employees' personalities and, most significantly, of them working in groups.

## Real life case: listening to your staff can reduce their stress

A recent UK government report has found that one in three workplace absences is now due to stress (Hope, 2013). This mirrors a previous Chartered Institute of Personnel & Development (CIPD) report, which found that stress is now the biggest cause of workplace absenteeism, overtaking the physical problems of back strain and cancer (Peacock, 2011). To counteract this, CIPD researcher Dr Jill Miller stated that managers could help relieve the stress by listening to their staff. Speaking on the ▶

Attentive managers can help reduce stress.
**Source:** Rob Marmion /123RF.

BBC's *Today* programme (BBC News, 2011), in a move that echoes the findings of the Hawthorne studies, she said in times of increased stress increased communication was important: 'even if people do not have all the answers to tell employees, managers can still be there to be supportive and to be really talking about employees' worries, and this reveals the key role for line managers'. Using emotional intelligence (the ability to recognize your own and others' emotions) is seen as a way of teaching employees to manage their stress and through it create happier employees (Treanor, 2015).

**Sources:** CIPD (2011); Peacock (2011); BBC News (2011).

Do you think it is realistic to expect that employees always separate their personal life and working life? Do you think managers manage better when they understand their staff's personal lives?

# Experiment 6: Bank Wiring Observation Room—the power of the group

**Running case:** slow down, you'll put us out of a job

'Hey Speedy, what are you trying to do—put us all out of a job?' Isabella jokes to Naomi as she sees Naomi's napkin-folding rate on the whiteboard in the staff room. 'One hundred and twenty-five an hour . . . you'll kill yourself working as hard as that.'

The final set of experiments produced some of the most startling results to academics and managers at the time. It revealed that the informal group, by producing **group norms** and informal rules, controlled behaviour and output more powerfully than rewards (e.g. bonuses) or supervisory influence. In other words, it was the discovery of the power of the informal, social organization.

The researchers' interest was sparked in this area because, during the interview programme, employees that were seen as working too hard were called 'dumb', picked on, given nicknames, and excluded from social activities by their fellow employees. In one particular case the supervisor, rather than praising and trying to protect the productive worker (as rationally he should), feeling powerless and believing the productive worker caused disharmony, gave him extra jobs to reduce his output.

The idea that workers were systematically restricting output was hardly a shock. Fredrick Taylor called this phenomenon 'soldiering' (Chapter 3), arguing that workers systematically tried to restrict their output. However, the investigators decided that rather than trying to get rid of these informal behaviours, they would investigate them.

The researchers decided to watch closely the behaviours of one particular group. This time the group was all male: nine wiremen who placed wires in the correct location (a skilled job); three soldermen who soldered the wires (a less skilled job); and three well-educated inspectors who tested the units to make sure there were no errors. The researchers wanted to investigate these two themes:

- Does the group restrict output and, if so, how?
- What is the relationship between the supervisors and the group?

> **Group norms** The unwritten rules that shape peoples' behaviour within a group.

## The role of the group in restricting output

Officially, each worker was meant to make 7,200 units per day, for which they would receive a bonus. However, surprisingly from the viewpoint of the researchers, they seemed to restrict their effort.

Investigating further, the researchers discovered informally that the workers believed making between 6,000 and 6,600 units a day represented 'a day's work'. While those that did not produce enough were 'bawled' at by the supervisors, if they made above the (unofficial) average they were excluded from the group and nicknamed 'Shrimp', 'Runt', 'Slave', and 'Speed King', and even '**binged**' to indicated they were breaking group norms. As one worker put it, those that 'loaf along are liked better than anybody else' (Roethlisberger and Dickson, 1939: 418). The workers' personal relationships were highly complex, full of tension, animosity, teasing, and, at times, physical violence (Figure 5.1).

From this observation the researchers stated the group had the following informal rules.

1. You should not turn out too much work. If you do, you are a 'rate-buster'.

2. You should not turn out too little work. If you do, you are a 'chiseller'.

3. You should not tell a supervisor anything that will react to the detriment of an associate. If you do, you are a 'squealer'.

4. You should not attempt to maintain social distance or act officious. If you are an inspector, for example, you should not act like one (ibid.: 522).

The researchers saw that the group was, in fact, two **cliques**, each with different ways of behaving and different output levels. In order to fit in with one group, workers had to behave in a particular way (see Table 5.3).

They concluded that the group internally controlled members' behaviour but, at the same time, protected them from external management interference. The workers, they thought, were more motivated by their need to belong to the group than by what management said to them or by financial incentives. In short, the group controlled the behaviour of its members through *group norms*.

**Bing** A phrase used during the Hawthorne studies meaning flicking the ear or arm of the person working too hard.

**Cliques** Exclusive groups.

**Figure 5.1** Pressure on employee to perform.

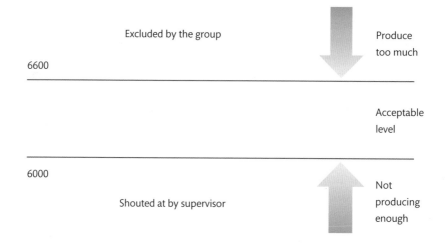

Table 5.3  Behaviour of the two cliques

| Clique | 1 | 2 |
|---|---|---|
| Output | High | Low |
| Personal behaviour | Sensible | Messing around |

# The importance of group norms

One of the central findings of the Hawthorne studies, particularly in Elton Mayo's interpretation, was the power of group norms. The group norms provide the rules or standards of conduct that group members have to adhere to in order to fit in. They act as unwritten rules that guide behaviour and help members gain a sense of belonging, providing group members with a framework of how to behave and a shortcut to know how to react to a given situation.

In general, nobody dictates these rules directly; we are left to pick them up through subtle cues from other members, such as jokes at our expense and being excluded from conversations. In particular, we often learn these rules when we break them.

Group norms are powerful because if we want to belong to the group and, in particular, gain high social status within it, we have to stick to them. Very few people violate them as this ultimately means being excluded from our peer group, leaving the individual feeling isolated and without social and emotional support.

Group norms can provide stability to the group by providing an accepted way of behaving. However, they can also be controlling, as there is pressure to go along with the views of the group, even when it might be at odds with your personal views. This can be particularly difficult when working in, say, a sexist or homophobic environment.

## Difficult position of the supervisor

**Running case:** Nina Biagini goes to Phil Weaver's office

'You are still not hitting the targets,' Weaver complains. 'They should be able to fold at least 140 napkins an hour if they followed my plan . . . look, they are only hitting 80. And look at Naomi, she was folding 125 an hour, and now that the chart has gone up she has fallen down to the same level as the rest of them.' Biagini looks downcast. 'It's not as easy as that,' she states. 'I just feel powerless in front of them. Naomi is a good worker, but the rest just drag her down to their level.'

'Why don't you just tell them what to do?' Weaver asks. 'It's not as easy as that,' Biagini replies again. 'You see, if I start having a go at them it will make our relationship difficult and really tense. Then, if I want them to do anything extra, like stay at the end of the shift to clear up or deal with a difficult customer, then they will just say no.'

Table 5.4  The supervisor's dilemma

| Supervisor action | Let them get away with it | Middle ground | Report to foreman |
|---|---|---|---|
| Consequence of action | Not perform task effectively | Try to balance group and management needs | Be a 'grass' and lose the sympathy of the group |

The Wiring Bank Observation Room also demonstrated how weak the supervisor's position was. Because he relied on the group's goodwill to get the job done, he had to maintain friendly relations with them. However, as a representative of management he had to keep costs down and keep production levels high. This was particularly evident in how he recorded individuals' work and workers' bonuses. The wiremen pressurized him to record higher figures, but management wanted to keep the records low. If he followed the groups' interest he was not doing his job properly, but if he tried to impose the management's priorities he faced losing the sympathy of the group, making the working relationship difficult. He was, therefore, under pressure from two directions, as shown in Table 5.4.

The researchers concluded that the supervisor could not change the group purely by the force of his personality. In fact, he was a victim. Indeed, we could argue, following Karl Marx (see Chapter 3), that the supervisor was as much exploited by capitalism as the workers.

This was demonstrated through the results obtained by the two supervisors during the study. The first supervisor was lax about certain rules and could be considered almost part of the group. His replacement was stricter, more authoritative, and rules- and output-focused. Surprisingly, the group were more productive under the first supervisor.

Roethlisberger and Dickson (1939: 531) believed the workers restricted output for a number of reasons. In part, it was because they did not understand the bonus scheme; they thought the workers also acted 'irrationally', choosing to believe that the management might lay people off as productivity rose, but Roethlisberger and Dickson claimed the workers had no concrete evidence of this. The workers were not lazy (as Taylor assumed) or in conflict with managers (as Marx assumed), and the supervisors were not ineffective. Such a view 'mistake[s] symptoms for causes and [is] to neglect the social factors involved' (ibid.: 548). Their key finding was that the informal group controlled output and behaviour, often in ways that went against the interests of the organization *and* the individual employee.

## Review questions

| Describe: | What are group norms? |
|---|---|
| Explain: | Why should a manager be aware of group norms to be effective? |
| Analyse: | How do Roethlisberger and Dickson claim their work is different from Taylor's views? |
| Apply: | How do group norms serve to reduce productivity among the waiting staff at Junction Hotel? |

# The implications of the Hawthorne studies

## Running case: team meeting

Nina Biagini gathers all the waiters and waitresses together. 'We are the "restaurant team",' she declares. 'If we are going to move forward then we need to work together as a team.' She opens the meeting asking for a 'full and frank' discussion, and airing of views.

The waiters and waitresses begin cautiously, with everyone being respectful, but after 15 minutes they begin to share more of their thoughts and feelings. Nina Biagini, alongside Meg Mortimer, listens attentively to what everyone is saying, nodding throughout the discussion.

At the end of the discussion Nina Biagini thanks everyone for their involvement. 'We are one big team,' she states, 'and all need to work together'.

The results of the Hawthorne studies are widely credited with transforming management theory and practice. They challenged the dehumanizing Taylorist approach by showing it was possible, and even desirable, to be concerned with the interest of the workers. They showed the significance of the informal organization and the power of the group in controlling individual behaviour. Most importantly, they also claimed to provide a more humane approach to management (see Table 5.5). Particularly in the hands of Elton Mayo, who, as we will see, wrote some of the most influential interpretations of the Hawthorne studies, they shifted attention away from focusing simply on the processes towards trying to understand and satisfy employees' needs. To their supporters they offered a better and more enlightened form of management based around harmony and cooperation, laying the foundation for OB today. Most of all they provided a shift in assumption from people as simply economic beings solely interested in their own private benefit, to social beings who want to belong to groups.

The key implications will be discussed in the following sections.

## A note on the alternative layout

Observant readers will notice for the rest of this chapter the layout is a little different from the rest of the book. For the remainder of the chapter the headings 'Claim X' and 'Critical perspective X' will be used to assess the Hawthorne studies' research. As with all research

Table 5.5  Comparison of Taylorism and the Hawthorne studies

|  | Taylorism | Hawthorne studies |
| --- | --- | --- |
| Focus | Individual | Groups |
| Labour/capital relations | Conflict | Harmony |
| Management is ... | Dehumanizing | Humane and caring |

and theories, the Hawthorne studies were based on assumptions about human nature and the way that society operates or should operate. These assumptions shaped (consciously and unconsciously) the way that the research was carried out, the decisions about which findings were considered important, and the way the results were interpreted and presented. Uncovering these assumptions helps us to better understand the research and judge it for ourselves. We will, therefore, look at each of the key claims that the research was based on (which we will label Claim X) and some of the challenges that later researchers have made to either the research itself or the manner in which it was interpreted (which we will call Critical perspective X).

It needs to be made clear that the existence of these assumptions does not make the research invalid. Indeed, all research and theory is based on assumptions. We are, therefore, focusing on the Hawthorne studies in this chapter and highlighting these assumptions as a way of encouraging you to think more critically about *all* research and theory that you read.

## Discovery of the 'social person'

The Hawthorne studies are widely credited with discovering the 'social person'—the underlying belief that people are governed by social needs, such as belonging to a group, rather than economic needs and self-interest, which Taylorism and other rational theories are based upon. This, they argue, explains why the employees preferred to stick to the norms of the group rather than make the rational, economic decision to work a bit harder and receive more pay.

Elton Mayo, one of the key researchers and popularizers of the Hawthorne studies, argued that the classic 'economic man' thesis provided a negative view of human nature. He called it a 'rabble hypothesis', a view which sees humankind as a horde of unorganized individuals motivated solely by self-interest (Mayo, 1949 [1975]). The Hawthorne researchers argued for a richer and more rounded view of human nature, which understands the 'relations of mutual interdependence' between people (Roethlisberger and Dickson, 1939: 569). In other words, they argued for a more complex view of workers' lives, concentrating on personal histories, group interactions, and the bonds that develop between people (Figure 5.2).

This, therefore, provided a fundamental reconsideration of human nature and a completely different view on how to manage people.

*Contribution to OB:* This more complex view of workers opened the door to studying organizational culture (Chapter 7), the importance of personality (Chapter 8), and motivation (Chapter 9) as a way of understanding why people behave how they do in organizations. It therefore introduced a richer and more complex view of human behaviour.

## Management can harness the power of the group

A key implication of the 'social person' thesis was understanding how the group fundamentally influences individual behaviour and restricts output. This phenomenon had already been identified by Fredrick Taylor, who regularly complained that groups restricted individual output. His solution was to break the power of the group by individualizing tasks.

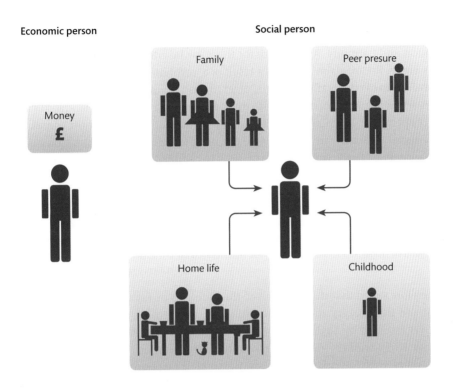

**Figure 5.2** The fuller understanding of the social person.

The Hawthorne researchers concluded that although the Taylorist solution might techni-cally 'make the employees more efficient', it would 'unwittingly deprive them of those very things which give meaning and significance to their work' (Roethlisberger and Dickson, 1939: 418): the sense of social belonging.

This 'social person' perspective therefore 'reformulated' management's problems (ibid.: 569) by seeing the informal group as 'a necessary prerequisite for effective collaboration' (ibid.: 559) instead of a problem. In other words, the group could be used to aid production rather than to stop it.

*Contribution to OB:* This insight has led to considerable attention being placed on the role of teams and groups (see Chapter 6) and the power of group norms—the informal codes of conduct that shape behaviour. It also has implications for leadership and management (Chapter 12), as it draws attention to how to influence the group rather than particular individuals.

## There is harmony of interests between workers and managers

The Hawthorne researchers were able to make these bold claims about the power of the group based on their belief that if people were left to their own devices, groups would *natu-rally* develop their own spontaneous social organization with their own values and objec-tivities which would be 'more likely to be in harmony with the aims of management' (Roethlisberger and Dickson, 1939: 418).

This view was strongly pushed by Elton Mayo. He argued that people naturally strive for cooperation and harmony. As evidence for this view he cited the increased output in the Relay Assembly Room, claiming it was a result of a 'revolutionized supervisor' who formed a cohesive group of cooperative workers, eager to push production on to a higher level and acting in 'wholehearted cooperation with management' (Mayo, cited in Handel, 2002: 100).

This cooperation, Mayo argued, was feasible because all human action comes from a need for social solidarity: in other words, the need to belong to a group. Consequently, when managers act fairly, workers have no need to complain as they are working for collective interests.

This allowed them to make the following bold claim:

> Producing an article at a profit and maintaining good employee relations are frequently regarded as antithetical [opposite] positions. The result of the studies which have been reported indicated, however, that these two sets of problems are interrelated and interdependent.
>
> (Roethlisberger and Dickson, 1939: 552)

They therefore stated that they had solved the problems of Taylorism and Marxism. Management and the workers' interests, according to this view, no longer need to be seen in conflict (as assumed by Taylorism or Marxism). Rather, organizations can only be more productive when workers' needs are taken into consideration. Mayo, through the Hawthorne studies, therefore sought to redraw the capitalist working relationship by claiming that workers and management did not need to be in conflict (Figure 5.3).

*Contribution to OB:* Mayo presents organizations as places of potential harmony and cooperation. However, as we will see in Chapter 13, those from the political left, such as Steven Lukes, disagree by stating that the labour–capital relationship is always fundamentally in conflict—even when it does not appear so at first glance.

## The nature of leadership needs to change

One of the fundamental shifts in management practice that the findings of the Hawthorne studies produced was to change the way we see management. While Mayo believed

**Figure 5.3** Mayo's redrawn capitalist working relationship.

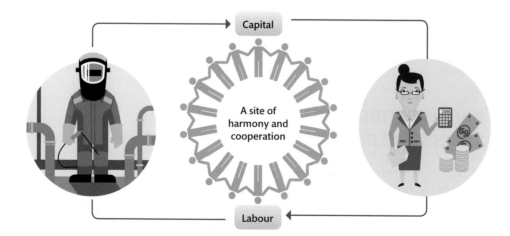

harmony and cooperation could be achieved, he argued that this spirit of cooperation is not inevitable. It requires improved communication with leaders listening to their group. Mayo offers us this prescription:

> Before every change of program, the group is consulted. Their comments are listened to and discussed; sometimes their objections are allowed to negative a suggestion. The group undoubtedly develops a sense of participation in the critical determinations and becomes something of a social unit.
>
> (Mayo, 1933: 39)

According to Mayo, managers therefore need to work on transforming the nature of the group, rather than particular individuals, by listening to workers and overcoming any objections.

*Contribution to OB:* The Hawthorne studies showed the importance of *soft skills* in management and leadership, such as listening to staff and understanding their views before a change is made. They therefore have implications for our understanding of leadership (Chapter 12) and how to manage change (Chapter 11).

---

**Employability skills:** the importance of soft skills

The Hawthorne studies demonstrated the importance of managers treating their employees as people: listening to them, understanding group norms, and responding to individual and group concerns. To be an effective manager you need to be able to understand and respond to these 'social issues'. Therefore, as well as gaining the technical qualification of your degree, it is important to develop these so-called soft skills. University offers many possibilities for this, such as group work and seminars where you have the chance to work with others and improve your communication skills; joining clubs and societies where you can be on committees, plan events, and learn to work as a team; and volunteering, where you can work with different types of people in the community. Such experiences are not only great for your CV, but also excellent for self-development.

---

What activities can you do to increase your skills, experience, and confidence in these areas?

## An alternative view of human nature

The Hawthorne studies thus produced a fundamentally different way of seeing human behaviour and human nature. Table 5.6 compares this with the rational organization approach.

To the supporters of the Hawthorne studies, they are a symbol of a new way to manage, away from a path of conflict and soul-destroying work performed by isolated individuals to new practices based on cooperation, harmony, and understanding of employees' needs while still increasing production.

*Contribution to OB:* as we stated in at the start of this chapter, these studies represent one of the most significant studies in OB and one of the foundations of the discipline.

Table 5.6 Difference between the rational approach and the human relations approach

| Key theorist | Fredrick Taylor | Elton Mayo |
|---|---|---|
| Human nature | Economic person | Social person |
| Why people act | In rational best interests | Irrational and governed by sentiment |
| Employee motivation | Economically motivated | Socially motivated by belonging needs |
| Mentality of researcher | Engineer | Psychologist |
| Approach to organization problems | Mechanically fix with technical solutions | Social engineer to get people working together |
| Restrictions to output | Worker laziness<br>Physical condition, e.g. fatigue<br>Soldiering | Power of informal organization in creating norms that regulate behaviour |
| Solution to output restrictions | Individualize work by breaking tasks down to increasingly simple tasks | Collective collaboration |
| Management control workers by ... | Managing every aspect of the task<br>Time and motion studies | Gaining loyalty of the group, shaping its beliefs to work towards common outcomes |
| Relation output and employee satisfaction | Unrelated—employees are just told what to do; they are all replaceable | Inter-related—employees need to be satisfied to be productive |

## Review questions

| **Describe** | What are the key implications of the Hawthorne studies? |
|---|---|
| **Explain** | How did the Hawthorne studies challenge pre-existing assumptions of management theory and practice? |
| **Analyse** | How do the Hawthorne studies offer a different view of human nature? How does this affect how they recommend that staff are managed? |

# Critics of the Hawthorne studies: understanding critical analysis

**Running case:** leaving the meeting

As they filed out of the meeting Naomi was glowing. 'It is really nice to see management taking an interest in us as people. I mean, we do a good job here and it is nice to be noticed.' Saffron looked at her in a surprised manner. 'They just want us to work hard and produce more without paying us more. I'm not falling for that one. Do you think they are really that interested in us?'

As we have seen, the results of the Hawthorne studies have been used to claim that people are naturally cooperative, and harmony between management and workers is not only desirable, but also possible. In short, particularly in Mayo's hands, it provided a fundamentally different way of looking at the world.

The Hawthorne studies have been called part of the 'creation myth' of OB—one of the central studies the field is based on. Yet as scholars of OB it is important that we do not take these findings at face value, but question how the research was constructed and interpreted, its circumstances and background, and what assumptions it was based upon. To do this we need to examine the research methods themselves, the interpretation of the findings, the context of the research, and the background and values of the researchers carrying out the research. The rest of this chapter will carry out this task.

It is important to note that the following criticism made of Mayo and the Hawthorne studies could equally be levelled at other theories, such as Taylorism. All academic theories have inbuilt assumptions upon which they are based and can be examined from alternative 'critical' perspectives. This does not mean that we should discount their findings. While some of these findings were based on small samples and, arguably, the pre-existing beliefs of the researchers, the social side of the organization is undoubtedly a vital component of organizational life. Moreover, although, as we will argue, it potentially gives managers increased control over the workers, it does offer the potential for a more humane form of management than pure Taylorism.

## Study skills: the importance of thinking critically—assessing academic theories

Where do your beliefs about management come from? How often do you stop to question them or look for alternatives?

We tend to think that our beliefs about management and organizations are based on common sense. Yet the views we hold today have not always been accepted. Indeed, a quick examination of the history of management theory reveals that people in other times held quite different perspectives to ours. In fact, our common-sense certainties might seem to them to be highly controversial or even wrong. For instance, fifty years ago many thought women incapable of working in the boardroom. Today, such a view would be unacceptable.

So where do our ideas come from and what influences them? One source is academic research. It is not only the research itself that is important, but the way that it has been received, interpreted, and used. As such, our beliefs are, in part, a product of past debates, where the winning perspective has become accepted as true and is today's common sense.

However, quite often the origins of the research get lost in time and we are only left with the conclusions that become filtered into practice and accepted without question. In the next section we will argue that it is important that we are aware of this background not only because it gives us a deeper understanding of the theories themselves, but also because it allows us to question their assumptions and challenge the things that we take for granted.

For the remainder of the chapter we will be assessing the Hawthorne studies *analytically*, taking the argument apart by seeing the *assumptions* that they are based upon. We will see whether the *research methods* and the *conclusions* they drew were valid, and whether the *evidence* they presented stacks up. We will be exploring this *critically* by examining it from other viewpoints and seeing how these ▶

▶ alternative perspectives, based on different *assumptions*, may lead to different conclusions. The chapter will lay the foundations for some *debates* which we will examine in the rest of this book.

This chapter aims to encourage you to *think critically*. This means not taking things at face value, being able to weigh up the evidence, and being able to understand the implications of a perspective. By doing so its aim is to help you be a better student and also potentially a better manager. Not taking things for granted will help you learn to think more deeply and not accept things as they are given—to see things from other perspectives and understand the assumptions behind the views people hold.

# The assumptions of the Hawthorne studies assessed

## Claim 1: workers are naturally cooperative and harmonious and form groups spontaneously (testing assumptions 1, 2, and 3)

The findings of the Hawthorne studies, and particularly Elton Mayo's interpretation of them, are based on the discovery of the 'social person', who is naturally cooperative and seeks harmony. Mayo based his argument on the experiences witnessed in the first Relay Assembly Room experiment, which he stated saw a smooth and rapid change in the attitude of the staff who became, in his words, a 'team that gave itself wholeheartedly and spontaneously to co-operation in the experiment' (Mayo, 1949: 64).

However, to make this interpretation Mayo was forced to downplay and even ignore key findings that did not fit his perspective. The departments and participants used for the study were specifically selected to be cooperative, and the supervisors tried to make the relationships as smooth and friendly as possible. It cannot, therefore, be assumed that people naturally want to be cooperative.

This selection for cooperation even went as far replacing two 'uncooperative' workers in the Relay Assembly Room experiment who were 'talking too much' and 'lacked attention to their work'. To his funder, Mayo reported that one worker had '"gone **Bolshevik**" and had to be dropped' (cited in Bramel and Friend, 1981: 872). In his account Mayo ignores these features, simply saying they 'retired' (Mayo, 1949). They were replaced by two new, enthusiastic employees, both of who were immediately more productive than the ones they replaced.

Mayo also downplayed the significance of the arguments between the workers and managers. Roethlisberger and Dickson's research showed the workers often actively resisted management, slowing down output, and stating that if they had their rest periods back they would increase productivity. Management responded by threatening to take away perks, such as lunch breaks. As Bramel and Friend state:

> The workers were quite consciously adopting a strategy intended to induce the experimenters to return quickly to the preferred conditions. If the workers had in fact had the kind of trust in management's good intentions that Mayo claims, would they have found it necessary to resist the experimenters so actively in this period? The picture we get, instead, is of a group of rather wary workers engaged in a continuing skirmish with management and determined not to be taken

**Bolshevik** An insult indicating that a person is a Russian communist; in other words, that they are troublemakers who want revolution.

advantage of. Rather than become a part of the company 'team', they became a team of their own, rather coolly looking out for their own economic interests in an adversary relationship with management, regardless of how much they may have personally liked certain members of the research team.

(1981: 874)

The increase in productivity, rather than being assumed to have come about through cooperation, could equally be seen as a result of stern discipline, e.g. replacing difficult staff (Carey, 1967) and the use of coercion rather than naturally-produced cooperation.

*Critical perspective 1:* the Hawthorne researchers, particularly Elton Mayo, were highly selective in what evidence they reported; findings that did not fit their view were ignored.

**Study skills:** implication of this perspective

We need to be careful in assuming that what people report is the only interpretation of the findings. We should not take research at face value.

## Claim 2: workers are more motivated by social needs than financial ones (testing assumptions 1 and 2)

Mayo, like Roethlisberger and Dickson, claimed that the group members were more motivated by the need to fit within the group than by financial needs. Concerns that if workers increased production it would lead to others losing their jobs were dismissed as 'irrational' because they stated there was no evidence that this would be true.

However, the research took place in the 1930s, which saw the deepest and most prolonged depression of the twentieth century. During this time there were very high levels of unemployment and little social security, producing mass poverty. Clegg and Dunkerley believe of the Hawthorne studies that 'Restriction of output by voluntary norms was a rational response by primarily economically-oriented agents to the increasingly likely prospect of unemployment' (1980: 131). In other words, there were genuine fears that increasing production would mean that other workers would be sacked as higher production did not necessarily mean higher sales. They were responding rationally to their economic situation.

Also, as Carey (1967) convincingly argues, much of their own data demonstrates the significance of wage incentives in creating increases in productivity.

*Critical perspective 2:* the Hawthorne researchers dismissed economic reasons as irrational; however, given the context, the employees' views could be seen as quite logical.

**Study skills:** implication of this perspective

The ideological position of researchers shapes how they interpret their findings. If you believe that economic reasons motivate action, then you are more likely to see this. If you believe it is social factors, then this evidence may seem stronger. Understanding the underlying beliefs of the researcher can be a key way of engaging in critical analysis, as it allows you to challenge these views. See Chapter 1 for more details on how to develop critical thinking skills.

# Claim 3: the findings of the Hawthorne studies can be replicated in management practice (assumption 5)

The findings of the Hawthorne studies are rightly considered significant because they were one of the first sets of experiments to examine real people in a real factory rather than in a laboratory. Therefore, it is claimed that what the researchers discovered can be applied to management practice.

However, the actions of the participants cannot be considered 'natural'. Throughout the study the research subjects were constantly observed, with their level of output recorded every 30 minutes. This form of observation changes behaviour. The implication is that the very act of measuring the output meant that the workers were better able to adjust their output.

## The Hawthorne effect

**Hawthorne effect** The very act of observation changes behaviour.

This phenomenon was labelled the **Hawthorne effect** by Henry Landsberger. He concluded that the very act of someone observing a person changes their behaviour (Landsberger, 1958). There are two key ways in which this phrase has been used. Firstly, it denotes the increase in productivity that is seen to result from psychological and social factors. Secondly, it points to the impossibility of researching what people *actually* do because the very act of observation (and particularly monitoring performance) changes behaviour. The research findings cannot therefore be assumed to represent what people *naturally* do.

Imagine yourself at work (or writing a university assignment) on a normal day. Now think how you would act if someone watched everything that you did. Would you act the same? Would you still take sneaky breaks, check Facebook, or talk to your friends at work in the same way?

Despite the extent of the research as a scientific experiment, it was poorly controlled. One of the key focuses of the research—the changes of human behaviour under supervision—only emerged later in the study, meaning that the researchers had to make assumptions about the workers' early behaviour rather than actively studying it. Equally, in the Bank Wiring Experiment, the researchers did not have a control group and therefore they did not know whether output would have gone up anyway.

The sample size is very small (six for the Relay Assembly Room and thirteen for the Bank Wiring Observation Room). While this gave the researchers unprecedented access and a highly detailed account of workers' daily interactions, it is a mistake to claim that the findings of the research are true for all societies over human history.

*Critical perspective 3:* the results of the findings are influenced by the researchers being present and the small sample size. Very large claims have been made on what is a small amount of evidence.

## Study skills: implication of this perspective

Because it involves people, any process of social research will be influenced by the way that it is researched and the presence of the researcher. This is unavoidable. Consequently, we need to be aware that research results are influenced by the way the research is carried out.

# Claim 4: the research 'discovered' the social person (assumption 1)

Roethlisberger and Dickson present the Hawthorne studies as a *journey of discovery* where they began their enquiry believing in essentially (although never named) Taylorist assumptions, but, because of the evidence, they came to discover 'social man'. This, '*revelatory* narrative' as Hassard calls it, is common in most 'textbooks on organization and management theory' (2012: 1433). However, both Roethlisberger and Mayo had pre-established assumptions which shaped their research findings and which are often not recounted in textbooks.

Roethlisberger had a strong disliking of Taylorism, calling its effects 'repugnant'. Wickström and Bendix argue that he used the Hawthorne studies as a platform to provide an alternative scientific basis to management (Wickström and Bendix, 2000). Equally, Mayo (1949) had a strong preference for cooperation and harmony and a strong dislike of conflict, which he saw as a 'social disease'. Even before the Hawthorne studies, he had already concluded that 'Social and psychological ills could be traced back directly to failure to establish stable systems of cooperation. Individuals must feel that their work is socially necessary and must be able to see beyond their group to the society' (Smith, 1998: 231). Indeed, Mayo's personal beliefs were formed prior to the Hawthorne studies and were not being discovered through the research evidence (O'Connor, 1999).

Even in the first experiment, the researchers were '*already* aware that "human factors could influence production and thereby interfere with the experimental results"' (Gillespie, 1991, cited in Hassard, 2012: 1434). Furthermore rather than discovering the 'social person' this view was already known within American industry (Nyland and Bruce, 2012). A book by Whiting Williams (1920) had already put forward the discovery that workers form groups to protect themselves from management (Muldoon, 2012).

In exploring the historical archives, John Hassard argues that the organizational culture (see Chapter 7) of the Hawthorne plant was quite unusual. Being a very large factory and the dominant employer, it was like its own city. It contained its own hospital, fire brigade, running track, and school; many social events such as dances and concerts were run by the Hawthorne Club. It also operated a form of 'welfare capitalism' where the workers received higher pay, pensions, health care, and sports facilities. The workers mostly lived near each other, making it feel like a 'family culture' (Hassard, 2012). The implication of this, Hassard argues, is that far from being a revelation, or also replacing engineering thinking with psychological perspective, the 'human relations' philosophy was already being promoted by Western Electric.

*Critical perspective 4:* rather than *discovering* the 'social person', both Roethlisberger and Mayo, in particular, had long-held views about the importance of cooperation, harmony, and the need for spontaneous forms of organization. In the Hawthorne studies, rather than revealing 'social man', the 'social man' perspective was the lens through which the research findings were interpreted.

## Study skills: implication of this perspective

Academic theories are based on the underlying assumptions set by the theorists which shape the results that they present. It is important to seek to understand these perspectives and read other researchers' interpretations of them to gain a fuller picture of their research.

# Claim 5: the Hawthorne studies represent a progressive alternative to Taylorism (assumption 5)

It is often claimed by its supporters that the result of the Hawthorne studies is a more humane and holistic approach to managing people. It certainly offers some benefits. Listening and responding to the needs of employees and focusing on teamwork provides a more rounded view of the worker, and a more supportive and person-centred form of management. However, it has been widely criticized for also being a stronger form of control.

One of Mayo's earliest critics was the sociologist Daniel Bell, who argued that Mayo did little to challenge the key assumptions underlying Taylorism and that the focus should be on increasing productivity. For Bell, all Mayo really did, to quote Bell's title, was *Adjusting men to machines* (1947).

Mayo's attention on employees' needs, Bell argued, was just another way of controlling them. He did this, Bell stated, by treating anyone who challenged harmony (for which he meant the manager's view) as showing evidence of psychological problems. Bell argued, like many other critical theorists, that such harmony was not possible because workers and management have divergent interests. Consequently, the labour/capital conflict cannot simply be solved by improving communication between the workers and managers.

Bell went further by stating that people only work because their human spirit has been tamed and they have been trained to desire consumption rather than meaningful human relations. In an early critique of consumer society he said that we are obsessed with our next purchase. This has resulted in a diminished view of work and social society. 'The belief in man as an end in himself has been ground under by the machine, and the social science of the factory researchers is not a science of man but a cow-sociology' (Bell, 1947: 88). In Bell's view, to offer a true break from Taylorism, Mayo should have explored how work could be created to expand human freedom and spontaneity. Mayo therefore 'fail[ed] to consider whether work offers other possibilities for the expansion of human spontaneity and freedom' (Waters, 1996: 52).

Bell's view is supported by a more recent article by Bruce and Nyland (2011). They argued the Hawthorne studies offered 'a new way to control workers to accept less, while claiming that workers needed psychological counselling about their relations at work that only management could administer' (Bruce and Nyland, 2011: 386).

According to such theorists, the use of psychological counselling offered managers a powerful tool to access the hidden world of employees' unconscious drives and use them for their own purposes. It offered the promise of harmony and cooperation, but only on management's terms and interests rather than on the employees' terms. '[C]ooperation in the Mayo perspective', according to Baritz (1974: 113), 'is the relationship involving happily unorganized (nonunionized) workers who unthinkingly and enthusiastically comply with the wishes of management towards the achievement and maintenance of its economic objectives'.

The research was also a way of trying to suppress trade unions at a time where there were company spies to identify labour activists (Hassard, 2012). Indeed, within the 600 pages of Roethlisberger and Dickson's book (1939) there is only one short statement on trade unions. Mayo himself was a known anti-trade union academic. According to Mayo's research and welfare capitalism, giving employees benefits could be interpreted as a way of stopping the workers from trying to overthrow capitalism.

## Theory in context: the philosophical underpinnings of Mayo's theory

Mayo did not restrict his claims on the benefits of the Hawthorne studies to a more considerate form of management—he saw it as a way of *saving* Western civilization.

Modern society, he argued, was characterized by increasing numbers of unhappy people who are fragmented into groups that are 'not eager to co-operate wholeheartedly with other groups' (1949: 7). The root cause of this, Mayo argued, was the Industrial Revolution. Led by large corporations, it brought rapid changes in technology which, although they produced material comfort, did so at the expense of a 'destruction of individual significance' (1949: 7). Through this the social ties of what Mayo called *established* society—the structures of families, communities, and traditional authority—were broken, producing a new *adaptive society*, which, Mayo argued, had abandoned its traditional effort for cooperation, leading to potential chaos.

According to Mayo, one result of this was that worker unhappiness and industrial disputes have a psychological root, rather than an economic one. He argued that an increasing number of unhappy workers had obsessive personalities and did not wish to cooperate. Workers had irrational, or what Mayo called 'non-logical', mindsets. Individual unhappiness was often as a result of their personal lives or childhood which, when not listened to by managers, reinforced their problems. Mayo saw the interview programme as a therapeutic release of pent-up emotion. It gave workers an opportunity to get rid of useless emotion which enabled them to collaborate better with other workers. An interview 'clears lines of communication of emotional blockage' (1949: 72) to allow the development of cooperation and teamwork.

> Thus, individual happiness and the social 'growth and health' of society are dependent not upon freedom from unreasonable restraint nor upon any rational calculus of pleasure and pain, nor upon the opportunity for self-development, but upon whether or not the individual has a sense of 'social function'.
>
> (Bendix and Fisher, 1949: 313)

The solution to these problems, believed Mayo, was the training of an administrative elite—what we would now call management—who could learn how to manage people. '[C]ollaboration of an industrial society cannot be left to chance,' Mayo argued (1949: 8). Current training and research, Mayo argued, had seen considerable advancements in technical expertise (e.g. Taylorism), but social skills had not kept up with this, leading to an imbalance. This administrative elite could be trained in these social skills—which Mayo called the ability to secure cooperation of people—and learn how to manage people. In doing so Mayo was liked by managers as he legitimized their role and their position in society (Child, 1996).

## Review questions

| | |
|---|---|
| **Describe** | What is the Hawthorne effect? |
| **Explain** | Why do some commentators believe Mayo did not 'discover' the social person? What are the implications of this? |
| **Analyse** | Why does Mayo's interpretation of the Hawthorne studies results not necessarily produce a more humane form of management practice? |

# Suppression of industrial democracy

While Taylorism is often demonized as oppressive to, and controlling of, workers, there were a number of theorists, writing at the same time as Elton Mayo, who were seeking to supplement this with industrial democracy. These progressive Taylorists, such as Mary Parker Follett, wanted workers to choose their own representatives and to be involved in management decisions. Having just endangered their lives in defence of democracy in World War I, as John Dewey argued, it seemed ironic that they then returned to a system of 'industrial and economic autocracy' (Dewey, 1982: 85). These Taylorist democratists supported the growth and development of unions (Bruce and Nyland, 2011). Mayo, with the support of Rockefeller money, had a strong distrust of such moves.

> There is another difficulty for me in Miss Van Kleeck's [a member of these progressive Taylorists] approach to the investigation—she seems to assume that a 'democratic' method of managing industry is necessarily appropriate . . . If it means that industry is to develop a two-party system and to determine any issues that arise by discussion and compromise then it would seem that such a method would revive and accentuate a situation of class conflict. This is indeed exactly what has happened in Australia—the country that has provided a 'shocking example' of how things should not be done in industry.          (Mayo, 1929, cited in Bruce and Nyland, 2011: 397)

## Theory in context: Mary Parker Follett

Mary Parker Follett was one of the earliest management theorists, a writer, speaker, and consultant who, alongside Lillian Gilbreth (see Chapter 3), was one of earliest women to influence OB. She had an interest in social work, psychology, administration, learning, teamwork, and, our interest here, democracy. Follett argued not only for local government democracy through things like neighbourhood forums, but also for more industrial democracy.

Follett believed that conflict was inevitable, but rather than imposing power 'it is possible [for management] to develop the conception of power-with, a jointly developed power, a co-active, not a coercive power' (Follett, cited in Fox and Urwick, 1973: 72). The only way, thought Follett, to resolve conflict is not through one side having victory, or through compromise, but as the integration of interests. Like Mayo, she believed that managers should work with a group. But unlike Mayo, who thought that conflict of any sort was abhorrent (Child, 1996), Follett believed that conflict could be constructive. As a result she argued that the manager's role should be as a facilitator: 'we are beginning to think of the leader not as the man [sic] who is able to assert his individual will and get others to follow him, but as the one who knows how to relate the different wills in a group so that they will have driving force' (Follett, cited in Fox and Urwick, 1973: 247). She also differed from Mayo, who considered ordinary employees to be governed by 'sentiment'. Instead, Follett believed employees could be rational, and would be able to find mutually acceptable solutions.

Mayo's work, John Child argues, proved more popular because it 'appealed directly to managers' as it 'legitimated their authority' (Child, 1996: 88). Unfortunately this has overshadowed Follett's contribution, which, Child asserts, 'derived from a more profound social, political, and psychological understanding of relationships' (Child, 1996: 89). As Parker and Ritson put it: 'Follett offered an impressive spectrum of contributions to management thought that were well ahead of the practices and theories of her day and which anticipated many subsequently emerging management theories and practices' (Parker and Ritson, 2005: 1342–3).

Mayo saw elites, particularly managers, as having the right to manage. Mayo's conclusions to the Hawthorne studies and his 'theory of human relations' were 'based almost entirely on his own political interpretation of worker motivation' (Bruce and Nyland, 2011: 385). Rather than a neutral investigation, Mayo's work could be seen as a highly political attempt to crush moves towards industrial democracy and give elites more power.

*Critical perspective 5:* while the Hawthorne studies present a more holistic view of human nature, critics say that Mayo and his colleagues did not challenge the fundamental assumptions of the capitalist working relationship; indeed, arguably, it intensified it. Its aim was the psychological control of the workers. In taking this approach it even diverted attention away from a more democratic form of management.

Why might Mayo's interpretation of his findings be supported by management? Think about how a critical perspective may challenge this view.

> **Study skills:** implication of this perspective
>
> It is important to understand the underlying assumptions and politics behind a management theory. Research rarely sits in a vacuum and can be a product of things like funding, the power of journal editors, or what universities want to promote. All researchers on management and organizations have political and social views, but not all research reveals it. As you read the research you can begin to understand the authors' views by trying to explore whose perspective they are on (i.e. the worker or the managers), or what they are trying to support (i.e. increased efficiency or increased autonomy for the workers).

## Summing up

While the Hawthorne studies represent a substantial move forward towards a humane form of management practice, we have seen the critics, particularly of Mayo, state that the theories produced are, in fact, a more subtle form of control. Mayo and his colleagues were selective in their evidence, dismissed and psychologized rational alternative perspectives held by the employees, and, rather than changing management control, actually reinforced it. One of the key criticisms is that rather than discovering through research the social side of the organization, these were Mayo's long-held beliefs. It is to this we now turn.

## Funding the Hawthorne studies

Another underlying influence on the Hawthorne studies was the funding they received, and the social and political circumstances under which they were conducted. A large part of the funding for the research, and particularly for Elton Mayo's role at Harvard Business School, was from the Rockefellers—a highly influential and wealthy family of American businessmen. Bruce and Nyland claim that 'Mayo could conceivably be considered as a mere puppet or servant of far greater power: the Rockefellers' (2011: 388). They argue that 'Mayo simply and shrewdly tuned into what he believed his benefactor wanted to hear' (2011: 391), twisting his personal biases to meet the needs of John Rockefeller.

Because of the Great Depression, many factory owners were scared that workers and trade unions would try to overthrow capitalism and produce a new society. As a consequence, many business leaders were 'seeking to find a way to resolve industrial conflict without jeopardizing their status as the central locus of organizational authority' (O'Connor, 1999: 120).

According to this view, Mayo used his scientific evidence as a way of justifying the prejudices and interests of his funders (Bruce and Nyland, 2011), and therefore constructed knowledge that aided managers to the detriment of the workers. Indeed, Mayo, Baritz argues, believed that 'America's managers were remarkable men without prejudice'—an 'elite which had the ability and therefore the right to rule the rest of the nation' (Baritz, 1974: 200). The findings of the Hawthorne studies, particularly as popularized by Mayo, were appealing to these ruling elites because they explained social problems as results not of economic inequalities but of irrational thinking on behalf of the worker. Mayo argued that society needed an 'administrative elite' capable of creating cooperation and producing harmony. Consequently, instead of being undermined by these social problems, these powerful people's interests were actually enhanced by them. It 'presented business leaders both with an insidious means of monopolizing authority in the workplace and the wider community, as well as a justification for this monopoly founded on the assertion that the minds of workers are not suited to management or political decision making' (Bruce and Nyland, 2011: 384). Bruce and Nyland argue that the findings of the Hawthorne studies therefore reinforced the right of managers to manage by demonstrating their need to solve social problems. Mayo's widely criticized pro-management bias, therefore, was, at least in part, a product of the funding he received.

## Review questions

**Describe**    Who funded the Hawthorne studies?

**Explain**    What is the relevance of who funds a piece of research?

**Analyse**    What is the significance of the historical context (the Great Depression and post–World War I) to the way that the Hawthorne studies' findings have been interpreted?

# Chapter summary

In this chapter we have explored in some depth the contribution of the Hawthorne studies, particularly as popularized by Elton Mayo. We have seen that these studies have been highly influential in the history of management thought, introducing new ways of seeing organizations as social organizations governed by informal dynamics. These studies laid the foundations for investigations of issues such as teamwork, culture, personality, motivation, and leadership, which we will explore in the following chapters.

The Hawthorne studies have certainly offered a more positive view of human nature and a way of managing people. By introducing the social side of organization, they opened up management theory and practice to the importance of the informal organization, and showed that it was possible—even desirable—for managers to embrace this side of the organization. This meant that managers no longer had to be restricted to simply looking at processes and managing people through coercive approaches of targets and punishments, but through a more positive view of getting teams to work together. This approach has laid the foundations for the study of teamwork (which we will see in Chapter 6), as well as interest in organizational culture (Chapter 7) and reappraising the role of leadership (Chapter 12).

However, the Hawthorne studies have also been widely criticized for deepening management control over the psychological realm of organizational life, controlling workers' thoughts and feelings—reducing their capacity to resist. By studying people's thoughts and feelings, management is able to turn these insights to their advantage by manipulating them towards management goals.

The Hawthorne studies therefore remain one of the most significant and powerful influences in management today. In particular, they raise the question of whether informal or social organization is an area which creates a more humane form of management, or a stronger and more subtle form of control?

## Further reading

**Roethlisberger, F., and Dickson, W. 1939.** *Management and the worker.* **Harvard University Press: Boston.**
Provides the most comprehensive and in-depth account of the Hawthorne studies. It gives very detailed descriptions of the Hawthorne studies from the researchers that led the research.

**Mayo, E.  1949 [1975].** *The social problems of an industrial civilisation.* **Routledge: London.**
Mayo popularized the Hawthorne studies to a wider management audience. This book gives a background to many of his ideas, and his broader thoughts on management and society.

**O'Connor, E. 1999. The politics of management thought: A case study of Harvard Business School and the Human Relations School.** *Academy of Management Review* **24(1): 117–31.**
This provides a really interesting account of the early development of the human relations movement as led by Elton Mayo. It helps explain the social context in which the Hawthorne studies emerged and the part Mayo played in popularizing it.

**Bruce, K., and Nyland, C. 2011. Elton Mayo and the deification of human relations.** *Organization Studies* **32(3): 383–405.**
This article shows the importance of the funding that Mayo received in developing the Hawthorne studies and the influence that it had on the findings.

**Hassard, J. 2012. Rethinking the Hawthorne studies: The Western Electric research in its social, political and historical context.** *Human Relations* **65(11), 1431–61.**
Provides an interesting historical analysis of the context of the Hawthorne studies

## References

Baritz, L. 1974. *Servants of power: History of the use of social science in American industry.* Greenwood Press: Westport, CT.

BBC News. 2011. Job stress 'worse in public sector'. Available at: http://news.bbc.co.uk/today/hi/today/newsid_9607000/9607686.stm (last accessed 13 June 2012).

Bell, D. 1947. Adjusting men to machines. *Commentary* 3: 79–88.

Bendix, R.C., and Fisher, L.H. 1949. The perspectives of Elton Mayo. *Review of Economics and Statistics* 31(4): 312–19.

Bramel, D., and Friend, R. 1981. Hawthorne, the myth of the docile worker, and class bias in psychology. *American Psychologist* 36(8): 867–78.

Bruce, K., and Nyland, C. 2011. Elton Mayo and the deification of human relations. *Organization Studies* 32(3): 383–405.

Carey, A. 1967. The Hawthorne studies: A radical criticism. *American Sociological Review* 32(3): 403–16.

Child, J. 1996. Commentary Follett: Constructive conflict. In: Graham, P. (ed.) *Mary Parker Follett: Prophet of management*. Harvard Business School Press: Boston, pp. 87–95.

CIPD (Chartered Institute of Personnel and Development). 2011. Absence management survey. Available at: http://www.cipd.co.uk/hr-resources/survey-reports/absence-management-2011.aspx (last accessed 13 June 2012).

Clegg, S., and Dunkerley, D. 1980. *Organization, class and control*. Routledge: London.

Dewey, J. 1982. Internal social reorganization after the war. In: Boydston, J.A. (ed.) *John Dewey: The middle works, 1899–1924*, vol. 11, pp. 73–86. Southern Illinois University Press: Carbondale, IL.

Donkin, R. 2001. *The history of work*. Palgrave Macmillan: London.

Fox, E.M., and Urwick, L. (eds) 1973. *Dynamic administration: The collected papers of Mary Parker Follett*. Pitman: London.

Fritz, C., Ellis, A.M., Demsky, C.A., Lin, B.C., and Guros, F. 2013. Embracing work breaks: Recovering from work stress. *Organizational Dynamics* 42(4): 274–80.

Fritz, C., Lam, C.F., and Spreitzer, G.M. 2011. It's the little things that matter: An examination of knowledge workers' energy management. *Academy of Management Perspectives* 25(3): 28–39.

Gale, E.A.M. 2004. The Hawthorne studies—a fable for our times? *QJM: An International Journal of Medicine* 97(7): 439–49.

Gillespie, R. 1991. *Manufacturing knowledge: A history of the Hawthorne experiments*. Cambridge University Press: Cambridge.

Handel, M. 2002. *The sociology of organizations: Classic, contemporary and critical readings*. Sage: London.

Hassard, J. 2012. Rethinking the Hawthorne studies: The Western Electric research in its social, political and historical context. *Human Relations* 65(11): 1431–61.

Hope, C. 2013. One in three absences at work due to anxiety and stress, official Government survey finds. *The Telegraph*, 26 June.

Landsberger, H.A. 1958. *Hawthorne revisited*. Cornell University Press: Ithaca.

Lovato, N. and Lack, L. 2010. The effects of napping on cognitive functioning. In: Kerkhof, G., and Van Dongen, H. (eds) *Human sleep and cognition: Basic research*. Elsevier: Oxford.

Marks, S.R. 1999. The gendered contexts of inclusive intimacy: The Hawthorne women at work and home. In: Adams, R.G., and Allen, G. (eds) *Placing friendship in context*. Cambridge University Press: Cambridge.

Mayo, E. 1933. *The human problems of an industrial civilization*. Macmillan: New York.

Mayo, E. 1949 [1975]. *The social problems of an industrial civilisation*. Routledge: London.

McCurry, J. 2014. Japanese firms encourage their dozy workers to sleep on the job. *The Guardian*, 18 August.

Muldoon, J. 2012. The Hawthorne legacy: A reassessment of the impact of the Hawthorne studies on management scholarship, 1930–1958. *Journal of Management History* 18(1): 105–119.

Nyland, C. and Bruce, K. 2012. Democracy or seduction? The demonization of scientific management and the deification of human relations. In: Lichtenstein, N., and Shermer, E. (eds) *The right and labor in America: Politics, ideology and imagination*. University of Pennsylvania Press: Philadelphia.

O'Connor, E. 1999. The politics of management thought: A case study of Harvard Business Schooland the Human Relations School. *Academy of Management Review* 24(1):117–31.

O'Conor, L. and Cahillane, L. 2015. Are we ever really 'out of the office'? *The Guardian*, 7 July.

Parker, L.D., and Ritson, P. 2005. Fads, stereotypes and management gurus: Fayol and Follett today. *Management Decision* 43(10): 1335–57.

Peacock, L. 2011. Stress overtakes cancer as main form of sickness absence. *Daily Telegraph*, 5 October.

Ricci, J.A., Chee, E., Lorandeau, A.L., and Berger, J. 2007. Fatigue in the U.S. workforce: Prevalence and implications for lost productive work time. *Journal of Occupational and Environmental Medicine* 49(1): 1–10.

Roethlisberger, F., and Dickson, W. 1939. *Management and the worker*. Harvard University Press: Boston.

Smith, J.H. 1998. The enduring legacy of Elton Mayo. *Human Relations* 51(3): 221–49.

Treanor, J. 2015. 'How to use emotional intelligence to combat stress', *HR Magazine*.

Waters, M. 1996. *Daniel Bell*. Routledge: London.

Wickström, G., and Bendix, T. 2000. The 'Hawthorne effect'—what did the original Hawthorne studies actually show? *Scandinavian Journal of Work, Environment and Health* 26(4): 363–7.

Williams, W. 1920. *What's on the worker's mind*. Scribner's Sons: New York.

Zacher, H., Brailsford, H.A., and Parker, S.L. 2014. Micro-breaks matter: A diary study on the effects of energy management strategies on occupational well-being. *Journal of Vocational Behavior* 85(3): 287–97.

# Managing groups and teams

*From managing the individual to managing the collective*

## Chapter overview and learning outcomes

By the end of this chapter you should be able to:

- describe why teamwork has become a central feature of organizational life
- explain the link between teamwork and productivity
- analyse the factors needed to produce an effective team
- explain how teamwork can lead to greater surveillance and control
- explain how groupthink can have negative implications on teams.

## Key theorists

| | |
|---|---|
| Meredith Belbin | A British management researcher best known for his classification of team roles |
| Bruce Tuckman | An American psychologist best known for his categorization of stages of group formation |
| Jon Katzenbach and Douglas Smith | American management consultants and organizational theorists |
| Irving Janis | An American social psychologist who pioneered the groupthink theory |

## Key terms

| | |
|---|---|
| Group | A collection of people with common bonds but *not* a shared sense of purpose |
| Team | A group who meet together with a common purpose and mutual interdependence |
| Groupthink | A psychological phenomenon which limits the range of alternatives being considered because there is an overwhelming desire for consensus |
| Cohesiveness | Where the group members feel bound together, often feeling as though they share a similar fate |
| Group dynamics | The underlying (and often unconscious) processes which shape the way group members react to each other |

# Introduction

**Running case:** confusion in the kitchen

Linda Wilkinson walks into the kitchen. 'It's chaos in here,' she thinks. 'Not only are they not getting the food out on time, but they are arguing about it as well.'

Despite the restaurant having an award-winning chef and a great menu, the last few months have seen an increase in customer complaints and, recently, a few negative comments in the local paper. Despite the reputation that head chef, Effingham, holds personally, and the hotel being in such a great building, Wilkinson worries that the standard of their day-to-day service is slowly eroding their image.

Looking round the kitchen Wilkinson begins to see why. All the chefs seem to be working very hard, cooking their individual items and putting them on the 'pass' (where the food is checked by the head chef before going out to the customers) when they are done. However, they work in a haphazard order, with some items being completed long before the rest of the table's order is finished, leaving food to go cold.

The tickets (the orders on slips of paper) are also stacking up. Food is going out to different tables at different times, with some customers waiting only 10 minutes and others waiting well over an hour.

Effingham, as the head chef, is barking orders to the chefs, Josh, Toby, and Ella, who are doing their best to keep up with the standards he demands. As they cook they present the food to him ready to be served—if it is not up to the standard Effingham expects, he sends it back. 'We are trying to win an award here,' he can be heard muttering repeatedly to himself. 'We'll never make it with that standard of food.'

Wilkinson also notices the front of house team darting in and out, picking up plates but looking confused as to what to do with them. 'Where is that one for?' she asks Isabella, one of the most experienced waitresses. 'Umm, Table 17, I think,' and she rushes out, only to come back two minutes later looking frantic with the same food.

'What are you doing, girl?' Effingham shouts at her. 'That chicken is for Table 7—come on, you should know that.'

'But we've served Table 7,' Isabella stammers. 'For goodness' sake,' Effingham shouts, 'look, it is written here, Table 7.'

Even more worrying is that the waiting team keep taking orders for items that have sold out and then having to return to the customer to take alternative requests. Getting annoyed with each other, the kitchen and waiting staff can be heard from the restaurant shouting at each other.

'This is getting embarrassing,' Wilkinson thinks to herself. 'What should be the flagship part of the hotel is disorganized chaos. I thought we were meant to be a team!'

'Are you a good team player?' The next time you apply for a job you will probably be asked a question about your teamwork skills. Teamwork is increasingly an essential skill for most jobs. It is one of the building-blocks of modern organizations (Hackman, 2002), particularly in modern flat organizations. From being in the 'customer service team' through to being part of the 'senior management team', being a good team member is now seen as a central requirement in modern working life. As multinational company Philips state:

> Speed and Teamwork lie at the heart of every improvement initiative. Each and every individual within Philips knows that only by fully cooperating and working together will we be able to perfect our business processes.
>
> (Philips 2015)

**Figure 6.1** Teamworking skills.

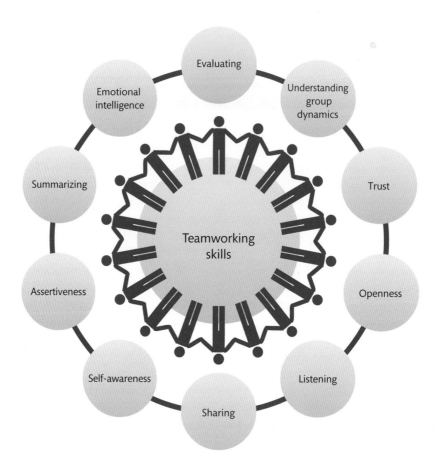

It is not just at work that we are in groups and teams. In our personal lives we might be in sports or pub quiz teams or on a student committee. Even organizing a night out with friends requires essential teamwork skills of listening, understanding others, cooperation, and negotiation.

So why do companies seem to value teamwork so highly? Teamwork is considered linked to increased creativity, problem-solving, and an organization's success. Being part of groups and teams increases employee satisfaction because they fulfil many of our 'social needs' (Mueller, 1994), giving us our sense of belonging and identity (Figure 6.1). Teamwork is therefore often presented as a universal, unquestioned good (Learmonth, 2009).

However, being in a team can be hard and getting a team to work together genuinely is often challenging. People can fall out, not pull their weight, have competing interests and ideas, have personality clashes, and end up as a dysfunctional team where nobody feels a sense of common identity or commitment to the team's goals. The results of this kind of dysfunctional teamwork are often demonstrated on the TV show *The Apprentice*. Regularly the contestants fall out as an individual tries to do everything him/herself. When they reach the boardroom we see the results of the team breakdown: blame, a lack of trust, in-fighting, and a lack of common vision.

So what makes teams work well and why is this so hard to achieve? This chapter looks at what some academic theory says makes 'high performance teams' and some of the barriers that stand in the way of achieving this. It also questions this 'cult' of teamwork (Coutu, 2009) and examines the dark side of teamwork.

## Study skills: doing group work at university

Do you like doing group assignments at university? While many people enjoy working in teams, we know from experience that many students say they find it frustrating, particularly when others do not seem to be 'pulling their weight'. To get around this problem, many students simply divide up the tasks equally and then do them individually before putting them together in a single document. While this might feel quick and easy, it can cause problems because the work is inconsistent in terms of quality and the information presented. Importantly, this approach means many of the benefits of group work, such as creative thinking, alternative perspectives, and encouragement and support, get lost.

So how do you create a better group assignment? As the chapter will demonstrate, to make group work more effective it helps to have a shared vision of what you group wants to achieve, and spend some time building trust and communication between group members so that ideas can flow freely and new insights can be generated.

Teamwork skills are important for employability and take time to develop. University is a good location to practise them. Some of the key things you can work on are listening skills, facilitation skills, and understanding of group dynamics. Writing a diary where you reflect on how the group has worked together and how you could work better within the group can be useful to help you personally develop. Joining clubs and societies can also be good ways of demonstrating your teamworking skills and answer that important interview question, 'Are you a good team player?'

Visit the Online Resource Centre for some further practical tips on team working.

# The difference between groups and teams

While in everyday terms we tend to use the words 'groups' and 'teams' interchangeably, the academic literature often gives them quite specific meanings (although these are not universally agreed). **Groups** exist when there is commonality but *members do not necessarily work together for a common purpose*. Groups cover wider situations, such as a group of friends. The term **team** is seen as having a *more specific purpose* and function. They rely *more on each other*, have a greater sense on *collective vision*, and are *mutually accountable*. A summary of the differences is shown in Table 6.1.

**Group** A collection of people with a sense of shared identity and something in common but *not* with a shared purpose.

**Team** A group who meet together with a common purpose and some degree of mutual interdependence.

Table 6.1  Differences between teams and working groups

| Team | Working group |
|------|---------------|
| Collectively accountable | Individually accountable |
| Plan together, collaborate, collectively decide future actions | Share information and different perspectives |
| Focus on team goals and outcomes | Focus on individual goals and outcomes |
| Work together on collective tasks | Work on individual tasks which sometimes are done in connection with others |

---

**Real life case:** we need to talk about Kevin

Having just scored 326 runs for his county, England cricket international Kevin Pietersen might well have expected to be able to get his place back in the England cricket team. Having scored his triple century, the undoubtedly talented batsman walked off the field declaring he was 'ready to play for England' (BBC 2015a). Yet, that evening he met with Andrew Strauss, the England Director of Cricket, and was told there would be no recall and that it was 'hard to see' any set of circumstances where he should be recalled (*The Independent*, 2015).

Why was this? Pietersen clearly has talent, and on this basis alone many said he should be in the team (Jenkins, 2015). Yet, talent alone does not seem to be enough. Pietersen has been accused of not being a team player, of falling out with his teammates and of writing an autobiography that was highly critical of the people around him (*The Independent*, 2015). For Lord MacLaurin, the former Chair of the England and Wales Cricket Board, a lack of teamwork is destructive. 'If you're running a team, whether in business or in cricket, you have to have trust in all the players and quite clearly over the years, sadly, Kevin Pietersen hasn't shown trust and I don't think there's any room for anybody like that in the England side' (BBC, 2015b).

---

**Employability skills:** teamwork

Are soft skills like teamwork important? A recent survey by Hay Group found that although 93% of employers think they are important, 51% of graduates believe that people skills actually get in the way of getting the job done (Hay Group, 2015). In another recent survey, the British Chamber of Commerce stated that 57% of businesses do not find graduates sufficiently skilled in teamwork. Commenting on these findings, John Longworth, Director General of the British Chambers of Commerce, said 'Firms need young people that are resilient, good communicators and understand how to work as part of a team' (British Chambers of Commerce, 2015). Therefore, while getting a good degree is vital for getting interviews, demonstrating teamwork and interpersonal skills is increasingly essential for getting a job.

So how do you develop your teamwork skills? University is a good time to build your teamwork experience, particularly through outside activities. Spend five minutes thinking about the activities that you regularly engage in and the teamwork skills that you have developed and those you still need to develop. For instance, you might have organized a charity fundraising night or done a Duke of Edinburgh's award, which requires teamwork. For each area can you think of one or two good examples of each?

 Visit the Online Resource Centre for more details and some related activities.

# What is a team?

The origin of the word 'team' is a set of animals yoked together (pulling a cart), emphasizing the *common purpose* and *mutual interdependence* of the team members.

Within the academic literature there are numerous definitions of teamwork. Two of the popular ones are:

> A team is a collection of individuals who are interdependent in their tasks, who share responsibility for outcomes, who see themselves and who are seen by others as an intact social entity embedded in one or more larger social systems.
>
> (Cohen and Bailey, 1997: 241)

> . . . small groups of interdependent individuals who share responsibilities for outcomes for their organization . . .
>
> (Sundstrom et al., 1990: 120)

The origin of the word 'team'.
**Source:** Margo Harrison/123RF.

Most academic definitions stress the importance of mutual reliance, interdependence, and accountability that group members feel when working together.

## Real life case: the teamwork behind the ice-bucket challenge

In August 2014 you may have done something very odd: taken out your mobile phone and asked a friend to record you saying you were going to donate to an ALS charity (supporting research into amyotrophic lateral sclerosis and, in the UK, into motor neurone disease) and then saying the names of a few friends you wanted to nominate, only to have a bucket of ice-cold water poured over you (invariably followed by you screaming at the shock of the pain). The 'Ice Bucket Challenge', as it became known, had swept through social media. Many people's Facebook and Twitter feeds were full of videos of people pouring water on their heads and nominating their friends. Soon celebrities, politicians, and business leaders such as Anne Hathaway, Alex Salmond, and Bill Gates were getting into the act.

For the team behind the challenge, this was a major job. The ALS charity, which normally would receive only 10 enquiries a day, suddenly had to field over 200. In an interview for this textbook, Stephanie Dufner, then the ALS communications manager, told us they had to work 14 hours a day, and 6 hours at weekends, answering individual and media enquiries (Dufner, 2015a). The attention the Ice Bucket Challenge received meant they had to constantly update the Frequently Asked Questions, answering questions on the charity's stance on issues like animal testing and stem cell research, and clarifying miscommunication on social media. Dufner states in an article in *The Guardian* that 'This required me to work with my colleagues in communications and marketing and other departments to formulate consistent messaging that answered these questions in a timely manner' (Dufner, 2015b). They had to constantly keep social media up-to-date. For a small organization at the centre of a worldwide media spotlight, this required them to work together and support each other at a faster pace than they had ever been used to. 'I recall a sense of camaraderie that occurred during the challenge' Dufner told us (Dufner, 2015a). They also needed excellent communication to keep each other up to date with what was going on.

What sort of teamwork challenges do you think that the team from ALS faced?

Often thrown together with strangers, business people need to get along, understand each other, and even provide emotional support and encouragement. They need a common vision, sense of trust, and cooperation to work together effectively as a team.

## Review questions

| | |
|---|---|
| **Describe** | What are the differences between groups and teams? |
| **Explain** | Why is teamwork important? |
| **Apply** | What problems with teamwork are there in the running case at the start of this chapter? |

# The variety of teams

So far we have used the word 'team' in quite a generic way; however, in practice the nature of teams is quite diverse. Different teams can be placed along a range of different continuums, as shown from left to right in the following tables.

While each of the teams in Table 6.2 is officially a team, some, like the supermarket checkout team, have very little interaction or interdependence, and are a team in name only. Others, like in the hospital theatre, are completely interdependent and require high levels of cooperation.

Table 6.3 shows different levels of formality. The informal group can be a vital place to discover informal rules, careers advice, tacit knowledge (see Chapter 10 for more details), and cultural insights. As you build your career it is useful to spend time developing these networks with others in your field, both within and outside of your company. They can also be places in which you can get mentored and supported as you take the first steps in your career.

Teams can also be fixed and permanent, or more temporary in nature, as shown in Table 6.4.

Table 6.2  Independent-to-interdependent continuum

| Independent: Same tasks | Independent: Different tasks | Independent: Specialist | Interdependent: Specialist | Interdependent: Same tasks |
|---|---|---|---|---|
| Supermarket checkout team | Manufacturing team | Hospital theatre | Project team | Gymnastics team |
| While called a team, in practice they act as independent people doing their own tasks with little interaction. | Everyone in the team does their own task in order on the production line. | Each person does their own job, but they have to work together as they operate on the patient. | All work together and share information using specialist skills to tackle problems. | All are completely dependent on each other. |

Table 6.3  Formal-to-informal continuum

| Formal team | Semi-formal team | Informal work group | Informal group |
|---|---|---|---|
| Committees, project teams, or sales teams | Working group around a specific area | Conversations around the water cooler | Group of sales representatives that meet in the pub |
| Established by management, they are officially recognized and have particular tasks or responsibilities. | A team that comes together to work on a particular problem but that is not formally constituted by management. | Gossip, exchange inside information, personal views on events, and career tips. | Fulfil personal needs of friendship and mutual support. |

Table 6.4  Permanent-to-temporary continuum

| Permanent team: fixed roles and positions in the team | Temporary team: arranged around a specific project and then disbanded |
|---|---|
| Senior management team | Construction project |
| While the membership of the team might change, the roles and functions are generally quite stable.<br><br>They have the advantage of common understandings of how to achieve tasks and understandings of each other. However, this potentially creates challenges, e.g. personality clashes, and deep-seated group dysfunction as the group members are focused on **interpersonal relationships** as well as the task. | To tackle a specific task or be together for a limited period of time, team members come together around a particular project: for instance, teams of specialists brought in to tackle a problem.<br><br>They have to quickly form working patterns and hierarchies, and are therefore often more task-focused. This can make them quite productive, but they do not have the deeper levels of trust and cooperation that established functioning teams can have. |

Interpersonal relationships  The way group members relate to each other.

Table 6.5  Physical-to-virtual continuum

| Physical meeting | Meeting in temporary locations | Virtual meeting |
|---|---|---|
| Domestic management team | Regional management team | An international management team |
| Meetings in offices or visits by sales representatives. Such meetings are very useful for getting informal information through conversation and establishing rapport. | Meetings in areas such as airports. Sometimes business people fly in to an airport, conduct the meeting, and then leave again. | Video-conferencing, email, and use of software like Microsoft Live Meeting or Skype.<br>Sometimes team members never meet, as they all work on different parts of the project or in various countries. |

While the emergence of new technology has increased the possibilities of virtual meetings, many managers still prefer physical meetings, particularly to establish initial contact. However, the rise of technology does save time and reduce carbon emissions (see Table 6.5).

Some teams can be based on location, or can cross national and cultural boundaries, as shown in Table 6.6.

Table 6.6  Domestic-to-multinational continuum

| Cross-cultural teams or trans-national teams | Local or regional team |
|---|---|
| Multinational company | Domestic company |
| From different cultures and often across different time zones, languages, and cultures. These teams increase the pool of expertise and perspectives that can be drawn upon, but face the challenges of cultural differences. | They require less travel, a reduction in project time, less potential communication and cultural differences, but possibly more limited perspective and available talent. |

## What the team does

Our last categorization is not so much a continuum as three different types of teams. According to Katzenbach and Smith (1993) there are three key categories of teams, those that:

- *do things*—make a product, conduct a service, or market a product
- *run things*—such as managers who devise the organization's strategy and mission statement
- *recommend things*—such as problem-solving teams.

# Does teamwork increase productivity?

**Running case:** Linda Wilkinson meets Graham Effingham

After the service has finished, Linda Wilkinson meets Graham Effingham.

'Look, Graham, we need to get the whole of the restaurant team working together. It is a complete shambles at the moment. You have some skilled individuals but you're not getting the best out of them. We currently have 90 covers a night. We should be doing 130 and have the potential for 180. The food is great, but we are getting a reputation for slow and erratic service, and that isn't going to get any better unless we work together. I want us to run a smooth, slick service and produce food that we are all proud of without you all running around like headless chickens.'

Effingham, taken aback, begins to protest. 'How can you say that? I've won awards for my cooking,' he retorts, pointing to the plaque on the wall.

'I'm not talking about you as a chef, or the food—which is great,' Wilkinson replies calmly, 'but it's the way the whole restaurant is functioning. We're just not getting food out quickly enough or in the right order—we're beginning to get a bad reputation.'

'Well, it's not me you should be talking to, is it?' Effingham responds with a menacing stare. 'The problem isn't the kitchen, it's with them. They cause us chaos. I mean Nina and her lot, they are just completely clueless sometimes. It's like trying to cook blindfolded. Not only do they tell the customers wrong things about the food and put in orders for things that we have sold out of, but they even keep changing the menu, allowing customers to change the food. I had Josh last week pulling mushrooms out of the risotto, that's just crazy. They should try cooking for a week!'

Armed with this information, Wilkinson goes over to speak to Nina Biagini, the maître d', who is sitting with her team in the opposite end of the bar. 'Ha, is that what he said?' Biagini replies indignantly. 'It's his lot that are in chaos. We can only put on the tables what we are given. Effingham just spends his time shouting at everyone—my guys and girls can't stand being in there. We're the ones having to go and see customers and apologize for the slow service—it's painful sometimes. And then whenever they go in the kitchen they just get shouted at if they dare say anything about speeding things up. My crew are all good people and we like to put customers first. Effingham and the other chefs never have to face customers. I agree with you it's getting bad, but Effingham is the problem. He's more worried about winning awards and his personal reputation than serving ordinary customers.'

Returning to her office, Wilkinson begins to jot down some notes to herself.

*It's the restaurant as a whole. The service is a mess, there is no communication between the front of house and the kitchen: things in the wrong order and they get in each other's way. They also drink in separate groups at the end of the night.*

Can you get more done by working together or by working alone?

Common sense would suggest that a tug of war team will do better than an individual alone. However, this isn't always the case. Studies have shown that a team of 8 pulls 50% less per person than individuals (Harkins et al., 1980). Harkins et al. claim that when in a team, individuals try less—a phenomenon known as **social loafing**.

However, Norman Triplett (1898) looked at cyclists pedalling around a track. He found that those who pedalled around in groups went faster than those that pedalled alone. Cycling in a group increased performance, which has come to be known as **social facilitation** theory.

> **Social loafing**  A term which describes people who, when working in groups, do not work as hard because, often unconsciously, they rely on others to do the task.
>
> **Social facilitation**  The tendency that individuals have to work harder when being watched by others, particularly on simple tasks.

From your experience of being involved in teams, do you work harder or slack off? Why do you think this is the case?

## The benefits of teamwork: more than the sum of its parts

Since the 1980s there has been explosion of interest in teamwork, with supporters arguing it offers a more productive, creative, satisfying, and empowering way of working that encourages workers to participate more (Procter and Mueller, 2000).

Teams are vital for sharing and retaining knowledge. They increase the range of knowledge to tackle a problem, with advocates arguing they produce more accurate and creative answers because team members bring with them a breadth of knowledge, perspectives, and skills, and challenge each other's views, which leads to better decisions. Also, when one member leaves or is off sick, all of the team's knowledge does not disappear with them.

## Real life case: breaking the silos—working in teams in the car industry

In traditional hierarchical organizations (which we saw in Chapter 2) different functions within the business were kept in their distinct groups and rarely worked together. We have seen this perspective in the classic Taylorist model, where the designer works independently from the person actually producing the product. This, though, created what Joe Greenwell, the former chairman of Ford in Britain, calls 'silos'—separate areas which rarely connected with each other. This resulted, he stated, in some communication and design problems, as the designers would design things that could not be manufactured easily. UK car manufacturing 'tended to be silo based' with the associated risk of 'turf wars' and a rather redundant rivalry, particularly between engineering and manufacturing. What began to happen, and is now close to standard practice, is to have manufacturing engineers co-located alongside product development engineers, both placed at the plant so they can both work together to produce solutions.

As a consequence, these 'functional chambers' began to disappear and working in cross-functional teams has become the norm. In the car industry, this move towards stronger teamwork came from the problems of UK manufacturing in the 1970s (the industrial disputes and poor productivity) and the emergence of Japanese manufacturing and productive development processes, such as the Toyota production system and Total Quality Management.

Products are now co-produced by designers, engineers, marketers, and lawyers. According to Joe Greenwell, 'There are no more silos. There is collective responsibility . . . instead of engineering heads passing over to manufacturing and bickering there is a chief programme engineer and then cross-functional teams' (Figure 6.2).

Working in these cross-functional teams has been beneficial to Joe Greenwell's career, as it has increased the network of people he can work with and developed his skills as a leader. It has also given him a greater awareness 'and a natural instinct' for what is happening across the organization.

**Source:** Author interview with Joe Greenwell, former Chairman of Ford in Britain, 2012 (see Online Resource Centre for the full interview).

**Figure 6.2** The move from silos to cross-functional teams.

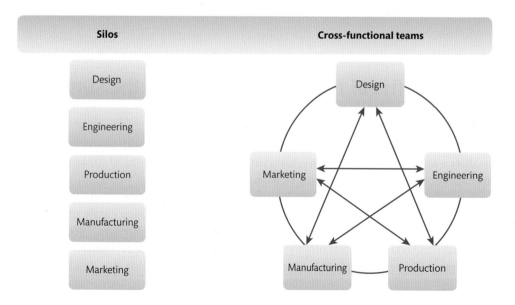

Table 6.7 Benefits of teamwork

| Benefits of teamwork to employees | Benefits of teamwork to organizations |
|---|---|
| • More meaningful work<br>• Sharing of responsibility and of the ups and downs of the challenges that are faced<br>• Learning from others (increasing skills by working alongside others)<br>• Job enrichment and rotation (working as part of a team means that you can do a variety of jobs and therefore not be bored doing just one)<br>• Belonging needs—feeling part of a group<br>• Increased autonomy as team becomes responsible for tasks (do not need to always go to a manager), which can help people feel more involved and interested in their jobs<br>• Motivation—emotional and psychological support | • Better quality decision making and problem solving by drawing on a wider range of skills<br>• Transfer of skills and technical expertise<br>• Reduced dependency on particular individuals<br>• Task requirements, e.g. designing jobs where impossible for one individual to work independently<br>• Increased time utilization—peak/trough jobs<br>• Task responsibility for the whole process rather than an 'it's not my job' attitude<br>• Delegation of authority so people take more responsibility for the outcome<br>• Group becomes responsible for improving their practice<br>• Faster decision making and increased commitment |

Teamwork supporters also claim that this change increases commitment by creating social bonds between the team members, giving greater **camaraderie**, emotional support, and a sense of shared purpose. Team members can learn from each other, gain alternative perspectives on how to tackle problems, and even suffer less stress (West, 2004). Further benefits of teamwork in general are shown in Table 6.7.

> **Camaraderie** A sense of togetherness and bonding.

## The challenges of teamwork

> **Theory in context:** nearly half of all employees feel their organization does not support their teamwork
>
> Despite the importance and benefits of teamwork, a survey by consultancy firm Cedar of 2000 UK employees states that a third of workers dread coming to work because of poor teamwork environment: 47% say that their organization does not support teamwork and 37% prefer to work by themselves. Furthermore, 42% of people aged 18–24 preferred working by themselves. Many businesses, the survey suggests, do not encourage people to work effectively in teams, and employees get frustrated by having to correct the 'sloppy mistakes' of colleagues. Teamwork is certainly difficult.
>
> **Sources:** HR Grapevine (2013); Onrec (2013); Xenergie Consulting Ltd (2013).

Teamwork is not always a recipe for success. Poorly performing teams can be highly dysfunctional. They often lack trust, fear conflict, lack commitment, and avoid accountability, and members do not care about results or feel little ability to influence them. Often, instead of expressing ideas openly, members of these teams avoid direct conflict at all costs, either making compromised decisions that nobody is satisfied with and/or having latent conflict

Table 6.8  The challenges of teamwork

| Challenges of teamwork for employees | Challenges of teamwork for organizations |
|---|---|
| • Personality clashes<br>• Frustration of ideas<br>• Breakdown of trust<br>• Reliance on less conscientious or less skilled members | • Employees becoming unproductive<br>• Personality clashes and dysfunctional activity<br>• Time-consuming practices<br>• Lack of shared identity and purpose |

which comes out in the form of politics, back-biting, and personal resentment, or withdrawal from the group (see Table 6.8).

## Why is teamwork difficult?

In order to gain the significant benefits that can arise from teamwork, teams often have to overcome a number of problems. The first is that of social loafing.

In the 1970s Bibb Latané and his colleagues (Latané et al., 1979; Harkins et al., 1980) conducted a series of experiments to investigate whether people worked harder in groups or individually. To test this, in a first experiment, they asked people as individuals and then as groups to shout as loud as they could and in a second experiment to clap as loudly as they could.

They discovered that people were louder individually than they were in groups. However, they argued this was not because people decided to put in less effort, as they believed they worked as hard in the group as individually. Rather, unconsciously they tried less hard. The researchers called this phenomenon social loafing (Latané et al., 1979).

This built on earlier research by Max Ringelmann, an agricultural engineer who found that, working alone, an agricultural student could pull a weight of 85 kg but a team of seven could only pull 450 kg instead of the 595 kg they should have been able to pull.

Why did this happen? Latané et al. suggest that individuals put more effort into tasks where they know they can be personally identified and less when they think their contribution will be lost in a crowd. They also argue that in teams we only work as hard as we need to and therefore reduce effort where we feel we do not need to. Therefore, when individuals feel their contribution particularly matters they will try, but when they feel it is less important they try less hard.

Reflecting on your own experiences in teams, which do you think captures your experiences better—social loafing or social facilitation theory? Why is this? Do some groups make you want to work harder *for* the team and others to work *only* when you are personally identified?

A related phenomenon is called **shirking** or **free-riding** (Schnake, 1991). This occurs when individuals purposely live off the efforts of others, for example a student who does not attend any meetings or put in any work for a group assignment but turns up on the day of the presentation and expects to get the same grade as everyone else. The larger the group, the more opportunity for free-riding exists, as individuals can feel able to get away with doing less.

Shirking or free-riding  An individual who does not pull their weight but is carried by other members of the group.

## Review questions

| | |
|---|---|
| **Describe** | What is free-riding? |
| **Explain** | How can teamwork improve performance? |
| **Analyse** | What are the challenges in getting effective teamwork? Does this mean that managers cannot automatically assume people will work well in a team? |
| **Apply** | What benefits did increased teamwork at Ford bring to the organization and to individual workers? How had 'working in silos' prevented this team working? |

# Creating a high performance team

**Running case:** Wilkinson calls Effingham and Biagini together

'Right, I've called you both together because we need to sort this out. We have got a lot of potential in this restaurant, but we are failing and the customers are beginning to turn against us. We are not serving anywhere near the numbers we should.'

'Well, it is nothing to do with us,' Effingham replies indignantly. 'My team are great, and the food quality is great.'

'Nobody is saying that the food that is produced is not great,' Wilkinson responds a little defensively. 'It's just not getting served quickly enough.'

'Well, that's her lot, then,' Effingham huffs.

Nina Biagini looks shocked at Effingham. 'Us? Come on, get real, we aren't the ones cooking it all so slowly.' 'Exactly,' Effingham huffs back. 'We do our best,' Biagini continues, 'but if it's not cooked quickly enough then there is not much we can do.'

Sensing a row brewing, Wilkinson intervenes. 'Look, this isn't a blame game here. The simple facts are that as a unit we are not getting the food out quick enough. I have spent a lot of time studying what goes on in the restaurant as a whole, and things have to change, starting with you two.' Effingham and Biagini look towards each other in a surprised manner. 'You are both at loggerheads constantly, and it's working its way down through the rest of the restaurant. A restaurant is a team game—we all need each other to perform—and that starts with you two. I want us working as a high performance team, trusting, relying, and working with each other.'

'If you became a team then you could do something really great,' Wilkinson continues evangelically. 'You know, share ideas, learn from each other, work collectively, be committed to each other, and support each other's personal development. Look, you need each other to succeed. You need to start thinking as a team.'

'Umm . . . ,' replies Effingham, softening somewhat. 'I do concede that sometimes things are not that coordinated and we could work better together. Maybe I could go as far as involving the waitresses and waiters a bit more socially, but I'm still in charge round here,' he finishes firmly.

'Well, maybe we could try and understand the chef's position a little more,' Biagini continues in the same spirit. 'We do need each other and we could work better together.'

'This is my baby, my restaurant, my reputation at stake,' Effingham states, trying to retain his authority.

**Table 6.9** The differences between working groups and high performance teams (based on Katzenbach and Smith, 1993)

|  | Working groups | High performance teams |
| --- | --- | --- |
| Focus of performance | Individual | Group |
| Task relationship | Independent | Interdependent |
| Approach | Takes personal approach | Committed to a common approach |
| Who takes responsibility | Personal responsibility | Group responsibility and high trust |
| Outcome | Is the sum of its parts | Magnified—is more than the sum of its parts |

While many of us say that we work in teams, Katzenbach and Smith argue that, in practice, true teams are rare, as most of us actually are in what they call *working groups*. High performance teams, they state, are special, as everything is focused on the team. Members are highly reliant on each other and focus on team outcome rather than individual outcomes. In contrast, working group members work largely independently and focus on individual performance. Table 6.9 sets out the main differences between working groups and high performance teams.

To become a high performance team requires substantial effort; high levels of commitment, trust, and cooperation; and a team focus for all members. This is challenging, as it requires a move away from thinking individually to being open with others and sharing success and failure. It therefore requires a 'leap of faith' to put one's fate in the hands of others.

Working groups can be effective, as the best ones 'come together to share information, perspectives, and insights, to make decisions that help each person do his or her own job better' (Katzenbach and Smith, 1993: 89). Consequently, Katzenbach and Smith say that where 'there is no performance need for the team approach, efforts spent to improve the effectiveness of the working group make much more sense than floundering around trying to become a team' (1993: 90).

To become a high performance team, Katzenbach and Smith argue that the group will go through four stages (Figure 6.3).

1. The *pseudo-team*. They have the need to be a team (i.e. would benefit from working together), but they have not achieved it as they are not focused on collective performance. Consequently, there is actually a drop in performance as 'their interactions detract from each member's individual performance without delivering any joint benefit' (1993: 91). They are, therefore, less than the sum of their parts.

2. The *potential team*. They try to improve performance, but need greater clarity on purpose, goals, and approach to work, and 'ha[ve] not yet established collective accountability' (1993: 91). They are about as effective as a working group, as they gain some benefits of teamwork but have to spend longer communicating.

3. The *real team*. A great leap in productivity is made here. They become a small group with complementary skills and a common purpose that members aspire to. Particular goals are an integral part of this purpose—specifics are clearly understood, there is

**Figure 6.3**
Katzenbach and Smith's teamwork performance curve.

**Source:** Katzenbach and Smith (1993). Reproduced by permission of Harvard Business Publishing.

a commonly-agreed working approach, and members are mutually accountable. Katzenbach and Smith believe that the key to achieving a real team is a focus on performance rather than personal chemistry (1993: 61).

4. The *high performance team*. Teams that achieve this level are rare but highly productive. They are like *real teams*, but with greater levels of trust and commitment to each other's personal growth, professional development, and success. They work on the model that 'if one of us fails, we all fail' (1993: 66). They have interchangeable skills, greater flexibility, shared leadership, a deeper sense of purpose, and even greater humour and more fun. High performance teams have 'a deeper sense of purpose, more ambitious performance goals, more complete approaches, fuller mutual accountability, and interchangeable as well as complementary skills' (1993: 79).

A comparison of high performance and poor performance teams is given in Table 6.10.

Think of teams that you have been involved in—what stage of the team performance curve do you think they are or were at?

Table 6.10  Comparing high performance and poor performance teams (based on Ket De Vries, 1999)

| High performing teams have: | Poor performing teams have: |
| --- | --- |
| • Members who respect and trust each other<br>• Members who protect and support each other<br>• Members who engage in open dialogue and communication<br>• Members who share a strong common goal<br>• Members who have strong shared values and beliefs<br>• Members who subordinate their own objectives to those of the team<br>• Members who subscribe to 'distributed' leadership | • A lack of a clear sense of direction<br>• Insufficient or unequal commitment to the group<br>• A lack of skills in key areas<br>• Incohesive or outright hostility among group members (Katzenbach and Smith, 1993)<br>• Unresolved goals<br>• Personal conflicts<br>• Poor leadership |

For a group to move to a team therefore requires stronger bonds of cooperation, trust, and interdependence in terms of tasks, knowledge, and cognitive/emotional needs.

> **Real life case:** the Dutch national football team
>
> A clear example of the importance of teamwork can be seen in sport. For many years, the Netherlands have had some of the most talented football players in the world, particularly in the 1970s when they played 'total football'. Yet, despite their brilliant, breathtaking football playing, they often lost to inferior opponents in championships and had nothing to show for all their talents. The often-cited cause for their failure was reported to be infighting within the team (in 1974) or because certain players refused to go to the World Cup (1978). They were certainly less than the sum of their parts!
>
> **Sources:** Winner (2001); Taylor (2010); Rich (2012).

# Building an effective team

> **Running case:** Linda Wilkinson gathers the entire restaurant staff together
>
> 'Welcome to the first restaurant team meeting,' declares Linda Wilkinson, as she paces up and down in front of the front-of-house and kitchen staff. 'You might have wondered why you're here.' 'You're telling me,' Effingham whispers to Toby, who sniggers. 'Well, we felt,' says Linda, continuing to look directly at Effingham as if to keep him in his place, 'that we really want the restaurant to work together—you are one big team. So today we are launching "Team Junction Restaurant".'
>
> 'We all need to work together and act as one big unit if we are going to achieve our mission—providing high quality service to the customer.'
>
> 'As members of "Team Junction Restaurant" you all need to work together and rely on and trust each other—if we are to succeed, we succeed together; if we are to fail, we fail together.'
>
> 'This is a chair from Malawi in eastern Africa,' Wilkinson continues, pointing to a carved wooden chair. 'What I love about it is it shows everyone doing their job but being part of one big community. Everyone is important, from the lowliest basket carrier to the most senior chief. If you remove any one of them the whole thing would come crashing down—this is how I see "Team Junction Restaurant": one big community.'

As we have seen earlier, teamwork is central to most organizations but is difficult to get right. A group of individuals cannot simply be put together and be expected to become a team, which sadly is often the case (Katzenbach and Smith, 1993). So, how do you build a successful team? Unfortunately, despite the numerous attempts by academics, business consultants, and managers to discover a formula to create a well-functioning team, there is no single, quick-fix solution (Katzenbach and Smith, 1993) (Figure 6.4).

To build an effective team requires finding the right people with the right technical and teamworking skills, with a sense of commitment to each other, and then setting the right environment for them to succeed. It also requires the team members to cooperate, trust,

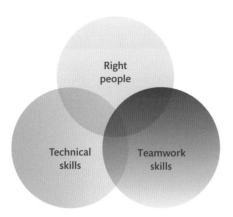

**Figure 6.4** What makes an effective team?

and be committed to each other, and to take collective ownership of problems. It is to the question of how to develop these aspects that we now turn.

## Review questions

| **Describe** | What are the four stages in becoming a high performance team? |
|---|---|
| **Explain** | What is the difference between the working group and a high performance team? |
| **Analyse** | Why do Katzenbach and Smith counsel that a working group should not always try to become a high performance team? |
| **Apply** | What stage of Katzenbach and Smith's teamworking cycle do you think Junction Hotel are at? |

# Skills balance

To create a successful team, it is essential to have the right balance of the skills and knowledge for the team to carry out the tasks they need to complete. In some settings this will be achieved by having specialists who carry out specific tasks (such as an orchestra where each person carries out one task). In other environments, these skills might be spread across the team. Some organizations, such as the UK's National Health Service (NHS), conduct a skills audit matrix to decide whether the team is equipped with the necessary skills. While sometimes the team leader will be able to build the team from scratch, often they are required to develop these skills within the existing team; therefore, it is important to identify potential within the current members' skills potential or gaps that need to be filled by new members.

Visit the Online Resource Centre to see the NHS skills audit matrix in detail.

Have a think about your skills and what you can bring to a team. What are your greatest strengths and how can you use them?

**Real life case: Strengthscope™**

Strengthscope™ offer a tool marketed to business professionals which allows individuals, teams, and organizations to assess the strengths that each individual team member holds and map these strengths across the whole team, seeing who has what strengths. Rather than looking at technical expertise, such as accounting, they look at work-based strengths, such as courage, emotional control, compassion, decisiveness, self-improvement, and critical thinking. With a skilled facilitator, they believe that a team can be made more effective by tapping into the strengths (sometimes hidden in normal working arrangements). Unlike traditional appraisal systems which look at rectifying weaknesses, they seek to build on individuals' strengths in relation to others. They claim that using their system can lead to:

- improved team communication, problem-solving, and focus on results
- heightened appreciation of, and respect for, individual differences
- enhanced accountability for delivering team goals
- higher levels of team morale and enhancement
- increased confidence and resourcefulness to overcome performance blockages
- improved understanding of the team's weaker areas and ways to manage or mitigate these.

**Source:** www.strengthscope.com

Visit the Online Resource Centre for more detail about this tool.

As we will see in Chapter 8, such personality tests should come with a health warning, as some researchers are sceptical of their ability to capture the 'essence' of a personality. Such tests also require considerable levels of trust within the team, as members reveal private information about how they see themselves and how others see them.

# Team roles

**Running case: teamwork results**

Linda Wilkinson stands in front of Team Junction Restaurant. 'Right, each of you has an envelope which contains a report about your teamworking skills. There are no superior roles—everyone is equally important. What we need to do is merge you into a team. Over the next week I will be meeting all of you to discuss your role and how we can all work better together.'

'Plant,' declares Toby in a slightly puzzled way. 'Oh, I get it,' he declares as he reads more. 'I always told you I'm creative! What are you, Josh?' 'Monitor Evaluator,' Josh replies, in a more muted fashion. 'Goody-two-shoes,' Toby mocks. 'Effingham, what are you?' 'Shaper,' Effingham replies, barely able to hide his smirk. 'Told you I'm the one to get things going round here—right, let's get on with some real work and stop this nonsense!'

Team-role theorists argue that in order to get the optimum output of technical skills, a team only reaches its full potential when it has a balance of team roles. The central premise of all these systems is that for a team to function effectively, the team needs a number of roles fulfilled. The most popular of these theories is provided by Meredith Belbin (2010), who devised his famous Team Role Inventory (Figure 6.5). These different roles are useful for the

**Figure 6.5** Belbin's team role summary descriptions.
**Source:** Belbin® 2015 www.belbin.com

## BELBIN®

# Team Role Summary Descriptions

| Team Role | Contribution | Allowable Weaknesses |
|---|---|---|
| Plant | Creative, imaginative, free-thinking. Generates ideas and solves difficult problems. | Ignores incidentals. Too preoccupied to communicate effectively. |
| Resource Investigator | Outgoing, enthusiastic, communicative. Explores opportunities and develops contacts. | Over-optimistic. Loses interest once initial enthusiasm has passed. |
| Co-ordinator | Mature, confident, identifies talent. Clarifies goals. Delegates effectively. | Can be seen as manipulative. Offloads own share of the work. |
| Shaper | Challenging, dynamic, thrives on pressure. Has the drive and courage to overcome obstacles. | Prone to provocation. Offends people's feelings. |
| Monitor Evaluator | Sober, strategic and discerning. Sees all options and judges accurately. | Lacks drive and ability to inspire others. Can be overly critical. |
| Teamworker | Co-operative, perceptive and diplomatic. Listens and averts friction. | Indecisive in crunch situations. Avoids confrontation. |
| Implementer | Practical, reliable, efficient. Turns ideas into actions and organises work that needs to be done. | Somewhat inflexible. Slow to respond to new possibilities. |
| Completer Finisher | Painstaking, conscientious, anxious. Searches out errors. Polishes and perfects. | Inclined to worry unduly. Reluctant to delegate. |
| Specialist | Single-minded, self-starting, dedicated. Provides knowledge and skills in rare supply. | Contributes only on a narrow front. Dwells on technicalities. |

group as, for instance, the Resource Investigator in Belbin's model is often good at kick-starting projects, but loses interest after the initial enthusiasm has passed, whereas the Completer Finisher is not as good at these initial phases but can bring a project to completion.

To perform well, a team needs a good balance of all these roles. The theory states that every person has a series of traits that lead them to have a preference for one particular role, but also to be capable of one or two back-up roles should the team's work demand it.

Each role has strengths and allowable weaknesses, e.g. the price that has to be paid for the strength. For instance, in the Belbin model the Shaper role is dynamic and has a strong drive which can push through ideas; however, this can lead to that person offending people's feelings and being provocative.

Each individual discovers their team roles through completing a self-assessment inventory, which can be supplemented by assessments by managers, colleagues, and those you manage.

This approach has become a mini-industry in itself, with many paid-for online assessment exercises as well as numerous books, games, and group activities based on similar models.

While Belbin's is the most famous, others include the Team Management Systems (TMS Global, 2012) model and Peter Honey's (2001) five team roles.

 Visit the Online Resource Centre to read more about these models.

According to Fisher et al. (2001), the background of Belbin's model is a combination of the need for clearly defined roles that are matched to specific individuals, drawn from bureaucratic theory (see Chapter 2), and the desire to involve team members in decision making, which originates in the human relations approach (Chapter 5).

Despite their popularity, concerns exist over their validity and usefulness. Furnham et al. (1993) argue that Belbin's original research was based on limited evidence, and the questionnaires are vague and do not necessarily relate to how people behave within a team. Negative personality traits like neuroticism are not included in the models, despite the fact that they have significant impact on team performance. Most troubling is that the questionnaires rely on self-reporting, which is not a dependable way to discover how we act. Fisher et al. go as far as to argue that these measures are 'psychometrically unsound' (2001: 142), and Anderson and Sleap (2004) state that they take little account of gender.

### Real life case: team roles in action

Completing these types of personality tests can have powerful effects on people's sense of identity. As a placement student, one of us had a manager who completed a Belbin-style questionnaire and was quite taken by the result: 'Daniel, some academics have done some research on me and discovered I am a driver [this particular team-roles version of a shaper],' he said, waving a 40-page report. 'I am really dynamic, see things that others do not see, and will drive the group onwards. This does mean that I tread on people's toes and can upset people . . . but that's just who I am. You know,' he continued reflectively, 'at first I did not believe it, as it did not seem like me. But over time I have realized that it really summed up who I am.'

What is interesting is his response to this 'research', which was actually little more than a self-assessment exercise and a couple of observation exercises. Instead of simply reflecting his team role, he began to identify himself as that character. In other words, instead of discovering the truth about himself, he began to mould himself into the type of team role personality that the report described.

What type of team role do you normally adopt—do you know what this team role is and how you can utilize it to your advantage?

# Personality clashes

**Running case:** tensions rise in the kitchen

Despite Linda Wilkinson's best efforts, on Friday night when service resumes, the tensions between the kitchen and the front of house still continue. Orders keep being misplaced, and arguments are breaking out between the kitchen and the waiters. Concerned that the heads of the kitchen and front of house are still at loggerheads, Wilkinson decides she needs to intervene.

'He just thinks he's God's gift,' Biagini complains. 'He is more bothered about winning that wretched award than serving customers. It is just not right.' Looking away from Wilkinson, Biagini mutters, 'I just can't really cope with him. He's arrogant and loud-mouthed, just not the type of person I can work with. I don't want my team being treated like that.'

Concerned, Wilkinson goes to visit Effingham. 'If you can't stand the heat, then you need to get out of the kitchen,' he replies gruffly as Wilkinson tentatively raises Biagini's concerns. 'Look, the kitchen is a tough environment. We can't be pussyfooting around being bothered by a waitress's feelings. They should just concentrate on getting the orders right.'

Wilkinson looks on in despair. Despite her best efforts, things seem more difficult than she ever thought.

Even when a team has the right balance of skills and roles, some teams fail because of personality differences (see Chapter 8). The root cause of these clashes, many personality researchers state, is the imbalance of personality traits within the group. What is necessary, they argue, is to get the correct balance of personality characteristics and make sure that no individual dominates. For instance, extraverts can be positive influences, as they are sociable, enthusiastic, energetic, and optimistic. However, Barry and Steward's findings (1997, cited in Barrick et al., 1998: 381) suggest that 'teams may be more effective when there is greater variance among member levels of extraversion, so that complementary roles of leading and following are carried out'. Similarly, high levels of emotional stability can be important to create a well-functioning team as it promotes a relaxed atmosphere, reduces anxiety, and promotes cooperation. However, as is often documented in the creative industries, sometimes a clash of personalities or having a group with heightened emotional sensibilities can lead to more creative work, even if this is difficult to sustain in the long term.

These personality researchers see personality traits as relatively fixed and knowable. They devise complex numerical formulas to capture the personalities within a team and work out their ideal balance (see Barrick et al., 1998, as an example). This offers interesting possibilities for managers when they set up a team.

However, as we will see in Chapter 8, other personality perspectives see personality as more changeable over time (see Chapter 8 for an in-depth discussion of personality traits). There are serious questions as to the validity of reducing personalities down to a set of numbers (as these studies tend to) and whether people act as these computer models predict.

Have you ever fallen out with someone during a team exercise? Why do you think this was, and how much of it was down to a clash of personalities?

As we have seen, to become a team rather than a group, the members need to feel they belong together and have a common purpose. Consequently, to be successful team, members need to feel that their fate is tied in with that of the team.

# Social identity theory

Social identity theorists (Abrams and Hogg, 2001) argue that an individual has two identities: (i) personal identity, which comprises personal and social beliefs, and (ii) group identity, which comprises the benefits of belonging to the team. Ideally, these identities will be aligned, but if not, the team membership identity should be stronger.

To make this change, such theorists argue that individuals need to be 'de-individualized' (Abrams and Hogg, 2001), transformed from thinking and feeling like an individual to feeling 'psychologically intertwined with the group's fate' (Mael and Ashforth, 1995: 310). In other words, their primary identity is that of a member of the team rather than as an individual (Tajfel and Turner, 1986). This shifts their outlook from 'my task' to 'our tasks', thus thinking as a team and being committed to the collective output.

---

**Employability skills:** creating a team's collective identity

If you take on the role of managing a team one of the central ways that you can get people to work together is to get them to adopt the language and the perspective of the team rather than seeing themselves as individuals.

Therefore, rather than speaking to, or praising, individuals, a team spirit can be encouraged by praising the team collectively and getting them to spend time together, as this collective mentality helps form the bonds within the team.

Things that help are using 'we' rather than 'I', referring to the team as a whole rather than individuals, and responding to requests by the team as a whole rather than from one individual.

In short, your role is to develop a team perspective rather than an individual outlook.

---

## Review questions

| | |
|---|---|
| **Describe** | What are Belbin's team roles? |
| **Explain** | Why is it important according to Belbin to have a balance of team roles within any one team? |
| **Analyse** | What are the strengths and weaknesses of Belbin's model? Do you think that people fit into such defined roles within a team? |
| **Apply** | In the running case, what effects are personality clashes having upon teamwork? |

# Tuckman's stages of group formation

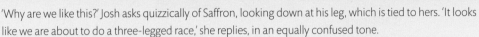

**Running case:** the three-legged race

'Why are we like this?' Josh asks quizzically of Saffron, looking down at his leg, which is tied to hers. 'It looks like we are about to do a three-legged race,' she replies, in an equally confused tone.

'I've gathered you all together,' Linda Wilkinson declares, 'to get us all working together'. She looks across at her staff, who are all in a line, in pairs—one from the kitchen, the other front of house—with their legs tied together. 'Over the last few months we have been working against each other. Today, we want to be working as a team. In pairs, you need to complete the obstacle course, carrying your uncooked egg and the balloon to the finish line. We have a trophy for the winner and a booby prize of cleaning out the deep-fat fryer for the loser.' With that, she blows her whistle and begins the contest.

At first, the restaurant staff, all feeling a little silly, go through the obstacle course reluctantly, not wanting to be seen as too enthusiastic for what they all collectively feel is a little embarrassing. However, after the first circuit, Effingham shouts 'blow this' and suddenly makes a dash for the front, dragging Biagini with him. 'Come on, Nina, you're with the kitchen team now,' he shouts as they charge for the front. Sensing the change in attitude, Saffron calls to Josh, 'Come on, we can beat them.' Suddenly, the race gets going.

As they go round for the second time Linda Wilkinson looks on in great delight. For the first time the two departments seem to be genuinely working together. For the open parts of the course the more cavalier attitude of the chefs seem to drive them forward, whereas when they come to the obstacle section the front-of-house workers guide them through better.

They then move on to a blindfolded obstacle course, where one of the pairs has to guide their partner around the field avoiding various items while the other is blindfolded. Finally, they have to build a tower.

'Well, I've not had so much fun in ages,' declares Effingham as they reflect on events in the bar afterwards. 'You know what,' he says, looking directly at Biagini, 'I was impressed with how you guided me around that blindfold course. You really made it clear what to do.' Biagini smiles. 'You weren't so bad yourself. You really had a good eye for that tower.' Effingham picks up the trophy. 'Yep, we won this together.'

To build a sense of identity, organizations often engage in team-building activities, the most famous of which was developed by Bruce Tuckman (Tuckman, 1965; Tuckman and Jensen, 1977).

Tuckman's model lays out the path to high performance. The central concept is that teams have to go through stages in order to become mature and function effectively. A fully mature team, he argued, functions well because they have established norms of behaviour and trust.

Tuckman argued there are two key factors: interpersonal relationships and **task orientation**. These two factors shape the members' behaviours within the team (what we will call group dynamics) and how the team deals with different perspectives, communication, conflict, leadership, and trust (Figure 6.6).

In Tuckman's model teams, go through five stages: forming, storming, norming, performing, and adjourning.

**Task orientation**
Focusing on tasks rather than on people.

**Figure 6.6** Tuckman and Jensen's (1977) team formation.

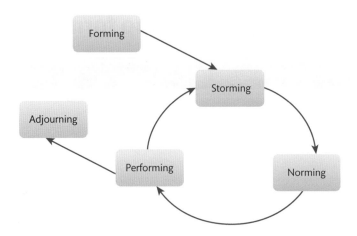

## Stage 1: forming

During this initial stage, team members often feel lost, apprehensive, and uncertain of how to behave. Tuckman describes this as the orientation stage, as team members are looking to work out how the group functions. They look for ground rules and a leader to tell them what to do to reduce their anxiety. They also try to reduce this anxiety by creating irrelevant discussions on peripheral problems and over-intellectualizing issues as a way of avoiding making decisions. At the formation stage, team members are normally polite and tentative, to avoid saying anything that offends others.

## Stage 2: storming

This politeness does not last too long, and after a while the group members become hostile and begin infighting. At this stage, the group lacks unity and often gets polarized over key issues. Many resist becoming members of the group, seeking to retain their individuality, and conflict arises as the differences between personal goals and group goals are revealed (see social identity theory earlier in the chapter). This often leads members to become defensive, negative, or aggressive, or to withdraw—what Wilfred Bion (1961) calls fight or flight. Members often clash with one another as the 'pecking order' is established. The initial leaders do not always survive this period.

## Stage 3: norming

The norming stage occurs when the group begin what Tuckman calls 'a "patching-up" phase' (Tuckman, 1965: 392) where the 'group norms and values emerge' (ibid.). At this stage, group conflicts are being resolved and a sense of togetherness forms, and what Tuckman calls 'we-feelings' emerge. At this stage the group becomes a cohesive unit where the members accept the group and 'idiosyncrasies of fellow members' (ibid.: 386). Of core importance here is that the group members want the group to exist and therefore value harmony as central. Emotions are still high at this stage, but they are more focused on achieving the tasks.

## Stage 4: performing

At this stage the group has bonded; interpersonal issues are solved, the group structure is accepted, and the group has matured. The group, therefore, is focused on problem-solving and dealing with tasks. Members provide each other with mutual support and strong interpersonal bonds.

## Stage 5: adjourning

This is the stage where the team is dissolved, either because the team members leave or the task is complete. This can be a difficult stage for team members, as they will have felt a personal connection with the team and can feel like mourning the death of it.

Think of a group that you have been a part of. Can you see the five stages of Tuckman's model in action? How closely does Tuckman's model replicate your experiences?

## The changing role of the team leader

Not only does the role of the team change over time, but also, as we will see in Chapter 12, how the leader acts also needs to adjust. An effective team leader style will need to act in a *telling* manner to the *forming team* to give them certainty. As they reach the *storming* stage the leader's role is under most threat as they can become the victim of the team infighting. They therefore need to sell the team a vision of the future. In the *norming* stage they need to develop more *participatory* decision making processes to help the team develop its norms. As the team reaches the *performing* stage the leader needs to *delegate* to the team, as members have increased commitment and experience. Overall, the team leader moves from a position of cop (controlling the team) to coach (facilitating their growth and development).

---

**Real life case:** team-building exercises

'Drum circles' have been used as team-building exercises. By taking part in one of these drum circles team members are said to develop synergy, camaraderie, and increased well-being. As one drum circle website (drumcircle.com) states: 'As the team begins to play music together a common language emerges and communication improves. Individuals become a team and the team becomes a thriving community'. Another (activerythmology.co.uk) claims: 'One of the things people learn is how to work together and to do this they first have to listen and respond. They automatically want to make the improvised music sound better, so without realising it they adjust their playing and their relationships to one another. The mixed sounds of a drum circle co-operating to make a harmonious whole is a great metaphor for the benefits of team work building in real life—which can be pointed out in a training exercise if appropriate'.

> Drawn from both websites, some of the benefits of drum circles are said to be:

- teach team-building in a unique way
- stimulate creative thinking
- promote cooperation among participants
- demonstrate the individual effect on the larger whole
- encourage clear communication
- develop communication skills
- motivate interaction between participants
- define common ground
- provide a playful vehicle for experiential learning.

**Sources:** http://www.drumcircle.com/team-building/index.html   http://www.activerhythmology.co.uk/

# Developments of Tuckman's model

Rickards and Moger (1999, 2000) developed Tuckman's model by reducing the five stages to three (Figure 6.7). They argue that between each pair of stages there is a barrier, which acts like a glass ceiling and which needs to be broken to progress.

The first barrier is interpersonal forces, where the group develops its norms. This barrier is weak and so is easy to break, resulting in around 85% of teams achieving this. Once they reach the second stage, they establish the group and function quite effectively. They do not become a high performance team or what Rickards and Moger (1999) call the 'dream team' until they smash the second barrier and break out of conventional expectations. Very few groups go through this barrier.

The implication is that it is relatively easy for a team to reach normal performance levels but difficult to reach high performance ones. Rickards and Moger suggest training to help the teams break through these barriers.

Observations of organizational practice, however, state that groups do not necessarily follow these stages. Rickards and Moger's own experiences of teams are that they 'never seemed to achieve a satisfactory level of coherence' (2000: 277). Ed Kur goes further, arguing that the linear direction of Tuckman's model is misplaced. He suggests that 'teams move

**Figure 6.7** Team development model.

**Source:** © Rickards, T. and Moger, S. 2000. Creative leadership processes in project team development: An alternative Tuckman's stage model. *British Journal of Management* 11: 273–83, Wiley-Blackwell.

from moderate to high levels of performance, then into dysfunctional conflicts, through self-assessment and back to high performance' (1996: 32). Rather than stages of development building on each other, the team has 'faces', or personalities, which rotate. Therefore, rather than being static 'even the highest performing, most empowered and most productive teams periodically put on the other faces' (Kur, 1996: 33). A team might have a 'performing face' and then have a negative experience which makes them reassess their mission (the forming face) before returning to the 'performing face' again.

- *Informing face:* shared mindset; debating, exploring, and testing values.
- *Forming face:* clarifying mission; getting to know each other and expectations.
- *Storming face:* confusion and anger with way things are, or misalignment with hopes for the group and what it has become.
- *Norming face:* group rules with a focus on harmony.
- *Performing face:* team with high trust, energy, and innovation (based on Kur, 1996).

One of the great strengths of Tuckman's model is also, arguably, its weakness. It is very straightforward and easy to understand, and this has led it to be applied widely. However, it is too simplistic: it represents group development as clear-cut stages. The stages are idealized and they do not necessarily represent what happens in reality.

## Theory in context: the background to Tuckman's model

Even though Tuckman's model is very popular, there is very little actual evidence for it. Indeed, it was not based on direct research or even accounts of business practice. Rather, Tuckman created a **hypothesis** based on synthesizing fifty published studies of group development. Rather than being about work organizations, the majority of these studies were based on therapy groups, whose main purpose is to learn from the experience of being in groups. The few studies that were conducted in an organizational setting, Tuckman notes, often missed the storming stage, as the teams were more focused on the tasks they needed to complete than the social processes involved in becoming a group that the therapy groups focused on.

Hypothesis A proposition that needs to be tested.

Teams in work organizations, Tuckman argues (1965; Tuckman and Jensen, 1977), therefore develop this pattern.

- *Forming:* As in the earlier description, members are uncertain, but they reduce uncertainty by making judgements about each other based on the roles they occupy outside of the team, e.g. other accountants they have met. This, Tuckman concludes, 'is somewhat suggestive of testing'.
- *Storming:* while in an organization there is still some rebellion, opposition and conflict are not personal as in therapy groups, which most of Tuckman's theory was based on. Therefore, in organizations, teams tend not to go through the storming stage.
- *Norming:* group members discover what they have in common and there is a growth of interlocking friendships, role interdependence, increased harmony, and establishment of group norms. A key task activity is in feeling able to exchange ideas.

- *Performing:* there is positive interdependence and emphasis on task achievement; the group develops its own subculture.

Consequently, while there are similarities, groups in organizations act in a more muted way than Tuckman's hypothesis suggests. Furthermore, in real life, teams generally have more fluid membership that has evolved over many years and therefore do not go through the cycles that Tuckman describes. Groups today are often more diverse, with a wide range of backgrounds leaving Lembke and Wilson to suggest it is 'difficult to apply traditional group dynamics models' (1998: 927) to modern organizational life.

## Study Skills: the importance of understanding the background

Although Tuckman's work has been highly influential, the way that it is often used (and is often presented in textbooks) is largely based on a simplified version of his original article. Appreciating that the original article was based on therapy groups rather than groups in work organizations and that it was only a hypothesis rather than a proven theory can make us more cautious about applying it to work organizations. Often research in organizational behaviour originates from other fields (e.g. Maslow's hierarchy of needs in part is based on primatology, see Chapter 9, and Lewin's three leadership styles originate from researching mask-making by 10-year-old children, see Chapter 12). Showing an awareness of this background, and how it may not always be as straightforwardly relevant to work organizations, can give you a more subtle understanding of the theory and can clarify the challenges of using it in practice.

Why do you think that groups in organizations seem to go through the stages a bit differently to therapy groups?

## Review questions

| | |
|---|---|
| **Describe** | What are the five stages of Tuckman's model? |
| **Explain** | How has group formation in actual organizational practice differed from that suggested in Tuckman's model? |
| **Analyse** | Does researching the group processes in therapy groups necessarily translate to work organizations? What are the implications of Tuckman's model being a hypothesis? |
| **Apply** | Have a quick search online to see what other types of team-building activities there are. What claims do these websites make about their effectiveness, and do you think they are justified? |

Group dynamics  The processes involved in interaction between group members, with particular emphasis on the tensions, conflicts, and adjustments that occur.

# Group dynamics

Tuckman's work derives from a theory called **group dynamics**. This perspective argued that groups have their own dynamic, or we might say personality or patterns that exist independently of a single individual. These patterns are powerful forces, as they shape the way that the group and individuals act.

According to group dynamic theory, groups operate at two levels: the task level, the work tasks a group needs to complete, and the group processes, the underlying way the group behaves. These group processes or dynamics exist outside of the conscious awareness of the group members, but shape the way they interact and behave.

Group dynamics theory was named by Kurt Lewin and developed by, among others, Gustave Le Bon (2009). Wilfred Bion (1961) and Lewin argued that 'the group to which an individual belongs is the ground for his perceptions, his feelings and his actions' (Allport, 1948: vii). In other words, the group you belong to provides the basis for how you see the world, what you judge to be acceptable and unacceptable, what you aspire to, and how you interpret events. The group could thus be thought of as a lens through which we interpret the world.

Furthermore, it is argued that it is 'usually easier to change individuals formed into a group than to change any one of them separately' (Lewin, 1947: 76, cited in Burke et al., 2008). Therefore, he claimed, the leader should focus on changing the team rather than any one individual.

## Unconscious group dynamics

Some group dynamics theorists stress the importance of the **unconscious** processes that shape the group behaviour. Developing this notion from psychoanalytical theory, such as that of Sigmund Freud and Melanie Klein (see Freud and Riviere, 1927; Likierman, 2001), they argue that the group is shaped by unconscious forces that members of the group are largely unaware of.

Wilfred Bion (1961), one of the earliest to put forward this view, argued that group behaviour occupies the three basic assumptions shown in Table 6.11.

These three 'basic assumptions' shape the way that the group acts. They create defensive positions that unconsciously protect group members from harm. Bion states they are

**Unconscious** From psychology, particularly psychoanalysis, the area of thinking that is not directly available to the conscious mind, and is below the level of personal awareness.

Table 6.11 Bion's dynamics of group behaviour compared with Tuckman's (1965) stages of group formation

| Bion's three basic assumptions | | Cf. Tuckman's model |
|---|---|---|
| **Dependency** | Group aims for security by looking for a leader to remove all anxieties and solve their problems. The leader is seen as god-like and can do no wrong. If the leader does not miraculously achieve this then they will look for a new leader. | Forming |
| **Flight/Fight** | The group tries to preserve itself at all costs; it either fights or runs away from a common enemy, or directs this energy inwards where the group argues and falls apart. The group ignores all other activities when it is in this phase. | Storming |
| **Pairing** | Two people dominate the group, and talking to each other is considered by the individuals and group as sexual. The group hopes that they will produce a new leader to save them. | Norming |

primitive in origin and provide the emotional energy of the group. They provide an essential conflict within team members between the need to belong and the frustration felt by having to conform. Bion argues that the group needs to mature to become an effective or what he calls a 'sophisticated' group, where it is more cooperative and not controlled by these basic assumptions. Bion's work draws from psychoanalytical theory and can be difficult to grasp. However, it does alert us to the challenges of creating a well-functioning team, as groups are often shaped by unconscious assumptions that members are only dimly aware of.

### Review questions

| **Describe** | What is group dynamics theory? |
| --- | --- |
| **Explain** | What is meant by 'unconscious' group dynamics? |
| **Analyse** | What are the implications of these unconscious group dynamics for our understanding of how groups and teams form? |

# Decision making in groups: opportunities and challenges

A common form of group that exists in many organizations is a committee or decision-making group. This is often a formal collection of people, like a senior management team or a staff team, where individuals from across the organization come together to make decisions on the future direction of the organization or to solve problems. Groups like this can be powerful because different views can be presented, leading to more informed decisions than if made by a single person (i.e. a departmental leader). However, group decision-making can be hard, as often these different perspectives can be in conflict and passions can run high.

How effective groups are at decision making can depend on the type of task. Steiner argued that the success of a group can be a combination of the nature of the task, the resources group members have available, the motivation of the group, and the patterns the group develops (Steiner, 1966). Research has shown that groups are better at making decisions than an individual alone because they have a wider variety of perspectives. However, for conjunctive tasks, which are group tasks everyone must contribute to, the group is normally only as effective as the least capable member (Frank and Anderson, 1971; Steiner, 1966).

One long-standing solution is for groups to have a discussion, followed by a decision taken either by the chair of the meeting or by a group vote. While this can lead to quick decisions, often alternative perspectives can be stifled, particularly if there is a domineering chair. The other approach is through consensus decision making. This approach, led by a facilitator, seeks to draw out as wide a range of views as possible, to encourage group members to truly listen to opposing perspectives, and to achieve consensus, where all group members feel happy with the decision taken (Hartnett, 2010). While this approach might be slower to achieve, its proponents argue that it creates a shared sense of ownership and more creative solutions than traditional group decision making.

> **Research insight:** Can groups make better decisions?
> Shore, J., Bernstein, E., and Lazer, D. 2015. Facts and figuring: An experimental investigation of network structure and performance in information and solution spaces. *Organization Science* 26(5): 1432–46.

Does working in large groups improve or diminish problem solving and decision making? One factor that academic research has investigated states that it depends on how interconnected and similar group members are (Shore et al., 2015). One key perspective argues that connecting people together improves problem solving by increasing coordination; however, other research argues that it can also encourage unproductive behaviour resulting in exploitation, even for simple tasks (Lazer and Friedman, 2007). Recent research by Shore et al. argues that large networks of people are better at collecting information but are less effective at making decisions and problem solving (Shore et al., 2015). This is because when members of these networks share information and are aware of each other's theories, they do not search for alternative solutions. The researchers argue that a more effective way is for information to be collected at a large group level and then problems to be solved within small groups or pairs. They also claimed that more diverse groups are better at generating ideas than those with similar views. One of the implications of this is next time you are working on a collective project it can be useful to work in large groups to collect information but better to establish small groups to look for solutions. Also look for different people to work with who have different skills and interests from yours so that you can generate new, original insights.

# Strong bonds: the dangers of a close team

> **Running case:** Team Junction Restaurant sitting together at the end of the night
>
> 'Well, I must say, I'm in shock,' Effingham declares to Biagini. 'I really thought that tonight would work. I just can't see why it didn't.' Biagini smiles at him. 'Nor me. It seemed such a good idea—a toga night with all the customers dressing up for Valentine's night with our Roman menu and a Venus and Mars waiting team! We had put so much effort into the layout of the restaurant tonight and the statues. With only ten bookings, three of which were couples who did not even dress up, tonight was a disaster. Where did we go wrong? It seemed such a good idea at the team meeting.'

As we have seen, most team theories see a successful team as having strong bonds, where individuals should see their identity primarily as team members and should be loyal, committed to the team's purpose, and sharing similar outlooks. This can be highly beneficial: without competing perspectives decision making is quicker, as members do not need to explain what they mean each time a decision is made or try to understand each other's perspective. However, such a close relationship can cause problems.

Over-conformity potentially stifles creativity and growth. With everyone sharing the same basic assumptions, alternative viewpoints do not get debated and therefore opportunities, or risks, can be ignored. Strong teams can therefore have collective beliefs or delusions which result in outside evidence either being ignored or being interpreted in such a way as suits the group's mindset.

Amanda Sinclair argues that the emphasis on consensus and the assumptions that mature teams are task-focused narrows the definition of what a team is. In particular, she argues that what appears to be consensus is often a result of downplaying division, as political pressure is placed on non-conforming members. 'Behaviour which recognizes and defers to the dominant power-holders in the group is likely to be labelled constructive or task-orientated, while behaviour which challenges that power is labelled disruptive and counter-productive' (Sinclair, 1992: 621).

# Groupthink

Have you ever been part of a group and thought that the group was making a wrong decision but did not speak out? Within academic theory, this is called *groupthink*. Groupthink (Janis, 1971) occurs when powerful social pressures are put upon group members to think in a particular way, or not to voice concerns or alternative viewpoints.

Groups that suffer this problem have a tendency to minimize conflict and therefore do not explore alternative options. They also often stick to agreements that the group has committed to, even if they turn out to be the wrong options. Janis argued that this results in a 'deterioration in mental efficiency, reality testing, and moral judgments as a result of group pressures' (1971: 84).

> The more cohesive the group, the greater the inner compulsion on the part of each member to avoid creating disunity, which inclines him [sic] to believe in the soundness of whatever proposals are promoted by the leader or by a majority of the group's members.
>
> (Janis, 1971: 85)

## Theory in context: the background to groupthink theory

Irving Janis devised the concept of groupthink to explain US foreign policy fiascos, such as the 'failure to be prepared for the attack on Pearl Harbor, the Korean War stalemate and the escalation of the Vietnam War' (1971: 84). The most famous example was the botched Bay of Pigs invasion.

The US government was trying to overthrow the Cuban leader, Fidel Castro, but they did not want anyone to know it was them. Therefore, they trained 1,400 Cuban exiles to invade the Bay of Pigs, as the CIA believed the invasion would cause an uprising in Cuba.

The Cuban flag.

However, the planned uprising did not happen because the invasion was some 80 miles from where people lived. The Cuban exiles were massively outnumbered, without air support, enough ammunition, or even an escape route, leaving most to surrender or be killed. It ended in massive failure. ▶

> ▶ Some could argue that this was a failure of planning, organizing, and thinking. 'How could we have been so stupid?' President Kennedy was heard muttering regularly to himself afterwards, reflecting on the Bay of Pigs fiasco. It was, he said, a 'colossal mistake' which ended in complete failure (Dallek, 2004: 367, 375).

Janis (1971) states that the Bay of Pigs fiasco was a result of groupthink, particularly of over-confidence and not accepting evidence to the contrary of assumptions. According to this theory, the danger is not that the group member will not reveal criticisms, but that they will not even think them, will not carry out careful scrutiny of the ideas, and will reject any misgivings that they might have. Groupthink, Janis argued, has the following characteristics:

1. *Illusion of invulnerability*—the group overestimates its power, is over-optimistic, takes extraordinary risks, and ignores warnings.

2. *Construction of rationales to avoid warnings and negative feedback*—being selective with information and discounting ideas that contradict their perspective.

3. *Belief in inherent morality of their group*—feeling morally justified in the actions they take.

4. *Stereotyped view of the enemy*—as evil, stupid, or ineffective.

5. *Pressure on opponents*—attacking anyone who puts forward an alternative viewpoint.

6. *Self-censorship*—avoiding deviation from the group consensus and minimizing personal doubts.

7. *Illusion of unanimity (consensus)*—taking the false view that anyone silent is in agreement, which prevents disagreements from arising.

8. *Tendency to become mindguards*—protecting themselves and the leader of the group by stopping the discussion or not passing on information.

Have you been involved in a team that you felt demonstrated elements of groupthink? How did you feel about it, and what were the consequences of this?

**Real life case:** groupthink in banking

There have been numerous examples of groupthink occurring in the financial sector.

- In May 2015 six banks were fined a total of $5.7 billion for manipulating foreign exchange markets. The traders used chatrooms, describing themselves as 'The Cartel', to manipulate the markets (Titcomb, 2015). It appears that although the traders knew they were breaking the rules they reinforced each other's belief that they were not going to get caught.

- In late 2001, Enron, an American commodities company, went bankrupt despite claiming a profit of over $100 billion the previous year. Enron's board exhibited signs of groupthink and appeared to be among the last to know about Enron's collapse. The group shared a similar background, felt cohesive, had a superstar culture, and believed that they were changing society. These features meant that they did not ask sufficiently probing questions about how the company was operating (O'Connor, 2002; Sims and Brinkman, 2003). ▶

- The banking crisis of 2008 saw evidence of collective delusion, with traders believing that the stock market would always rise and that complicated financial models would continually produce profit. When Paul Moore, HBOS's Head of Regulatory Risk, challenged their practices, saying they were too risky, he was criticized and then sacked (BBC, 2009; *Daily Telegraph*, 2009).

All of these financial scandals demonstrate elements of groupthink. Very senior, intelligent, and well-paid people failed to question the practices that they were engaged in.

A 2010 parliamentary report (UK Parliament, 2010) argued that 'the lack of diversity on the boards of many, if not most, of our major financial institutions, may have heightened the problems of "group-think" and made effective challenge and scrutiny of executive decisions less effective'.

The chair of the committee, John McFall, argued that a solution would be to introduce more women. 'Diversity at the top is one way to challenge potentially dangerous "group-think"' (UK Parliament, 2010).

The result of groupthink is that members look at very few options, fail to consider the costs of decisions, do not take into account what outside experts say, or do not consider how opponents might react. Believing in their own righteousness and invulnerability, they can make a decision that might be perceived by an outsider as a bad one (Janis, 1971). For instance, in the Iraq war many members of the Bush administration were convinced that the Iraqis would be so pleased to see them that they would be welcomed with open arms. They failed to consider that many would not like a foreign occupying force and would resist it; therefore, they did not properly plan for the aftermath of the war, with what some commentators have argued to be disastrous consequences (Fox News, 2004; Badie, 2010).

### Research insight: The Abilene paradox
Harvey, J. B. 1988. *The Abilene paradox and other meditations on management.* Jossey-Bass: New York.

The Abilene paradox states: 'Organizations frequently take actions in contradiction to what they really want to do and therefore defeat the very purposes they are trying to achieve' (Harvey, 1988: 19). This occurs when a group collectively makes a decision that actually goes against the preference of any individual. It is a failure to manage agreement and has six stages:

1. Agree privately as individuals the nature of the problem the organization faces.

2. Agree privately as individuals the steps to take.

3. Organization members fail to communicate accurately their desires or beliefs to each other, but do the opposite.

4. With inaccurate information they make contrary decisions to what they want to do.

5. By making counterproductive decisions members become frustrated and angry, form subgroups, and blame each other—particularly blaming leaders.

6. This cycle repeats itself and becomes more intensive.

To check that they are not falling into the trap of 'groupthink', Wilkinson suggests that group members should ask each other 'Are we going to Abilene?' to make sure that the decision is really desired by the group.

To overcome groupthink Janis recommends:

1. Encouraging *critical evaluation* in every member.
2. Encouraging an *impartial stance* at the beginning of the meeting to create open-mindedness.
3. *Evaluation groups* for decisions.
4. Discussing decisions with *outsiders* and reporting back.
5. Inviting *outside experts to question decisions*.
6. Members playing *devil's advocate* for key decisions.
7. Considering *rivals' reactions* to a decision.
8. Occasionally dividing into two groups and returning to discuss different perspectives.
9. 'Second chance' meetings to express remaining doubts.

The concept of groupthink therefore makes an important challenge to the underlying ideas of teamwork by warning of the dangers which occur when people share perspectives that are too similar and reject dissenting voices. While the examples that Janis gives are quite extreme in their consequences (potentially costing thousands of lives and billions of pounds), groupthink often occurs on a more mundane level when members of a team, despite their personal misgivings, go along with decisions that outsiders would question. All teamwork requires a balance between coherence/**conformity** and dissent/creativity—the challenge is to get the balance right.

> **Conformity** Everyone in the group thinking and acting in the same way.

## Decision making in teams: the risk-shift phenomenon

When we are in groups we tend to take more risky decisions than we do when alone. This is called the 'risk-shift phenomenon'. This occurs because when we are in groups we feel more secure and responsibility is spread across the group, and individual members do not want to let others down. By listening to others in the group who are more open to risk, individual members move towards greater risk.

### Review questions

| | |
|---|---|
| **Describe** | What is groupthink? |
| **Explain** | Why does groupthink happen? |
| **Analyse** | What are the implications of groupthink to our understanding of teamwork? Do you think that Janis's advice on overcoming groupthink is helpful? |
| **Apply** | What evidence of groupthink can you find in the real life case of the banking crisis? |

# Does teamwork produce increased freedom?

**Running case:** clearing up

Isabella phones her boyfriend Steve. 'Hi, Steve, it's me. Look, I know its Valentine's night and I promised you a night out, but we're having to clear up after tonight's meal. Oh, it was such a disaster. Nobody came, so we are going to all go out to drown our sorrows. I was involved in the planning for this, so I feel I need to help clear up the pieces. Look, I know I'm letting you down, but I really feel I owe it to this lot to stick together. I've got tomorrow night off—I'll make it up to you, I promise.'

One of the great claims made about teamwork is that it gives the potential for greater freedom and autonomy for the team members. As we can see in Figure 6.8, the greater skill level of the team members, the more freedom (or empowerment) the team can have.

When team members have low skill levels, being part of a team can give greater variety through *job rotation*. In firms such as McDonalds, relatively unskilled workers can change roles, e.g. making fries, then putting burgers together, etc., which makes the job more

**Figure 6.8**
Empowerment
continuum.

**Source:** Reproduced
from *Management*, Daft
et al., 2001, South
Western. Reproduced by
permission of Cengage
Learning.

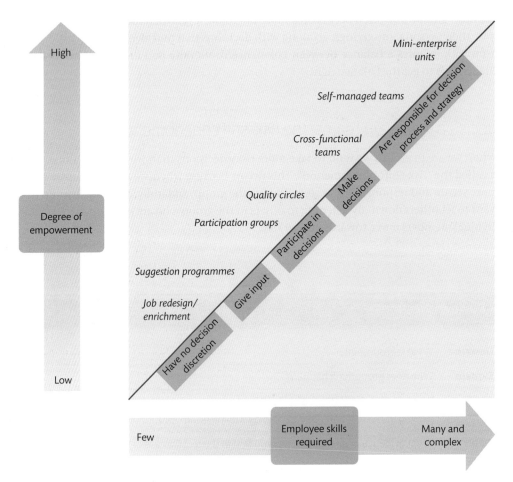

interesting. This concept, like *job enrichment* (see Chapter 9), gives the workers more opportunity to use skills and, as Herzberg believed, increases motivation (Paul et al., 1969).

Employees can also be involved in recommending changes through suggestion programmes. These schemes, however, give them little opportunity to implement the changes, as a *recommending team* (e.g. a group of managers) makes the final decision.

A strong level of empowerment can be achieved by employees forming **quality circles** (Marks et al., 1986). Members of these groups are ordinary members of staff (e.g. from production or service delivery) who meet together for a few hours a week or month and discuss solutions to work-related problems and then present them to management. In doing so they aim for continuous improvement, from health and safety through to production processes. Quality circles therefore combine the *recommending team* and the *doing team*. While quality circles have not lived up to their promise since the 1980s (Lawler and Mohrmann, 1985), they can be effective ways of bringing about improvements lead by the employees themselves.

**Interdisciplinary teams** or **multifunctioning teams** have, in recent years, become increasingly popular and used in areas such as social services, health, and policing (Schofield and Amodeo, 1999). They are often used in skilled professions and have more autonomy as they can make decisions. Interdisciplinary teams can be powerful in that they draw together multiple skills and diverse knowledge to tackle complex problems, but they are also challenging to work in because different professions within the team often hold competing understandings of problems and can, therefore, find it difficult to establish a common language.

Such teams may draw people in from many different professions. For example, doctors, nurses, occupational therapists, mental health nurses, and others may come together to talk about a patient, offender, or drug addict and to make sure that all the different services are sharing information and working together to deliver 'joined up services' rather than piecemeal delivery where the services sometimes work in contradiction to each other (Robinson and Cottrell, 2005). Within businesses, multifunctioning teams might come together to discuss the launch of a new product or service.

> **Quality circles** A group of workers who come together, often under the supervision of a leader, to identify, analyse and solve organizational problems.

> **Interdisciplinary team or multifunctioning team** A team of people that is comprised of people coming from different disciplines. This approach can produce a wider perspective and knowledge but can also produce greater conflict.

---

**Real life case:** making multi-function teams work can save lives

If you are about to go for an operation, one of the last things that you would probably think about is how good the teamwork is among the surgical team. But maybe you should. The operating theatre is a complex location with consultants, anaesthetists, and nursing staff all having to work together to ensure that the patient stays safe throughout the procedure. One of the challenges is that each of these professions has different professional training and expertise that can sometimes conflict. Intensive care theatres in particular can be stressful places where emotions run high, and conflict can result between these professionals (Coombs, 2003). This inter-professional conflict has been claimed to lead to high levels of medical errors, particularly due to communication and teamwork (Buttigieg, West and Dawson, 2011), which potentially put patients' lives at risk (Baldwin and Daugherty, 2008). Indeed, it 'is thought that half of adverse events in surgery are avoidable and "the majority" are due to poor communication, decision making and teamwork' (Smith, 2014).  ▶

▶ A hospital on the east coast of the US has sought to tackle this problem by delivering communications training to help the different professionals try to understand each other, using a group dynamics expert to understand the group processes that were occurring and help aid individuals' self-understanding of how their behaviour impacted others. By coaching, modelling positive behaviour, and understanding the group dynamics, the hospital has reported better outcomes for all (Eiser, 2015).

Simon Paterson-Brown, a fellow of the Royal College of Surgeons of Edinburgh, states that 'It's all about being aware of what's going on and communicating with the nurses and junior staff, allowing other people to speak up in theatre and say, "I think you're getting this wrong; this isn't right." All of these things we didn't really do in surgery. Consultants in the past didn't really like to be questioned by their junior staff' (cited in Rimmer, 2014). Time will tell how easy it will be to change the power dynamics to enable junior staff to speak up, but achieving this result will be critical to help improve the outcomes for everyone involved.

Visit the Online Resource Centre to watch some videos on teamwork.

**Empowered** The process by which the workers are given greater power and autonomy. Critics suggest this approach also places a greater burden on workers.

**Self-managed teams** A team, often of professionals or highly qualified people, who manage themselves.

**Empowered** or **self-managed teams** have increased autonomy and higher skill levels (Cohen and Ledford, 1994). The key trait of these teams is they have the authority to solve their own problems and directly respond to the needs of their customers. These teams do not have managers telling them what to do: the group makes decisions and has collective responsibility for its actions. This can be done by rotating the leader or by using collective decision making processes. Self-managed teams can often set their own hours, the planning of tasks, and even their own budgets.

Self-managed teams can be more productive because they can make quicker decisions, create stronger bonds between team members as they tackle challenges collectively, and increase commitment as the team members have more freedom to experiment and have an increased say in how things are run. 'In theory, ownership, responsibility and involvement in the strategic direction [by self-managing teams] are likely to lead to more rapid development and implementation of the strategy by workers dealing directly with customers' (Dunphy and Bryant, 1996: 692).

However, such teams can be harder to manage, particularly initially, as their management requires managers to be able to trust the team to work well together, be committed to the aims of the team and customers, and be skilled in the task that they are doing. It can also be challenging for managers schooled in traditional 'command and control' practices, as it requires a different relationship with the team. It has been described as moving from 'cop' to 'coach', or 'controlling' to 'involving' (Lawler, 1986). The senior manager's role is to set the parameters for the group, such as its vision, objectives, and key milestones, whereas the team works out the operational details, such as the most effective way to perform the tasks and meet the objectives.

Thus, teamwork proponents argue that teamwork simultaneously enables increased organizational performance, improves in employees' working lives, and even solves alienation within society.

# Is teamwork a way of enhancing control?

**Running case:** Josh asks Isabella to help out in the kitchen

'Can you give me a hand?' Josh, the chef, calls over to Isabella the waitress. 'We really need to get this food prepped before we go home so it is ready for the breakfast team in the morning'. 'It's not my job . . .' Isabella stammers before Josh interrupts. 'Teamwork,' he states knowingly. 'We are all one big team now.' Sensing her reluctance, he carries on. 'Look, if you give me a hand with this then maybe I'll help you lay the tables for the morning when we are done.'

The use of teamwork is claimed to increase autonomy and participatory decision making and to enable staff to form positive social bonds with colleagues (Mueller 1994). However, more critical voices have questioned if teamwork can be presented as unequivocally positive. Returning to the example of the operating theatre, Rachael Finn challenges the view that teamwork really equalizes the balance between surgeons and other medical staff. She argues that while teamwork gives the image of everyone working together equally, in practice the language of teamwork can be used as a resource that reinforces the powerful, privileged position of surgeons (2008).

Other critical theorists claim that self-managed teams can result in **downsizing** by removing layers of management and making the team take on these responsibilities (Dunphy and Bryant, 1996). This, they argue, increases the burden on ordinary members of staff as they become more responsible for delivering products and services, but without additional pay. They argue that this is an intensification of work as employees come to be seen as more responsible for solving problems—traditionally a manager's domain. Barker (1993) and Sewell (1998) thus argue that it can actually represent a stronger form of control, producing what Sinclair calls the tyranny of teamwork (1992).

Barker argues that, on the surface, *self-managing teams* represent a shift in power from management to workers. 'Instead of being told what to do by a supervisor, self-managing workers must gather and synthesize information, act on it, and take collective responsibility for those actions' (Barker, 1993: 413).

This can result in increasing their commitment as employees feel responsible for completing a task. As one of the employees in Barker's study states, 'Under the old [bureaucratic and hierarchical] system, who gave a hoot if the boards shipped today or not? We just did our jobs. Now we have more buy-in by the team members. We feel more personal responsibility for the product' (1993: 422).

While at first glance it might appear that management have given up control, Barker argues that, in fact, self-managed teams represent a more subtle and intensive form of control. Team members, he argues, control each other's actions. 'Team members rewarded their teammates who readily conformed to their team's norms by making them feel a part of the team and a participant in the team's success. In turn, they punished teammates who had bad attitudes . . . with guilt and peer pressure to conform' (1993: 425). For instance, the increased levels of responsibility mean team members missing their children's school plays, working weekends, and starting work at 5.00 am to meet production schedules, because they feel more responsible. Control is thus intensified because more experienced members

**Downsizing** Reducing the size of the workforce.

of staff watched and disciplined the less experienced and reinforced the rules and group norms, and staff self-disciplined by taking personal responsibility. This resulted in the experienced staff feeling like unpaid supervisors and suffering burnout, and the new staff feeling like they were constantly being watched. This creates a stronger 'iron cage', as termed by Weber (see Chapter 2), this time not of bureaucracy but of the discipline of the team.

Teamwork, therefore, could be seen as a way of shifting the responsibility from managers on to the shoulders of staff, what Sewell (1998) calls *responsible autonomy*. Workers have freedom so long as they hit the targets set and use their discretion for the good of the organization.

At a deeper level, teamwork changes the outlook of employees: 'management is concerned not only with changing the way in which employees work but also the way they think' (Knights and McCabe, 2000: 1494).

## Review questions

| | |
|---|---|
| **Describe** | What are self-managed teams? |
| **Explain** | Why can self-managed teams be harder to manage? |
| **Analyse** | Why can teamwork increase freedom *and* at the same time control? |

# Chapter summary

**Running case:** Linda Wilkinson, Nina Biagini, and Graham Effingham sit down for an end-of-day drink

'It all is running a lot smoother now,' Linda Wilkinson says with satisfaction, watching the waiting staff and chefs working together to clear the last of the tables after another busy day of service. 'It almost runs itself.' Graham Effingham smiles. 'Yes, it's good to see. We now do 150 covers a night. We run well as a team.' 'It wasn't always like that,' Nina Biagini interjects. 'We took a while to gel, didn't we? But I must say I like working here now. It didn't always feel so good.' The three managers look on as their staff, or team members as they now call them, systematically work calmly together, clearing up the tables and laying out for the breakfast sitting. 'Sometimes,' Biagini says wistfully, 'I almost wonder if they need us at all.' Effingham nudges her in the ribs. 'Don't let Weaver hear you say that,' he says half-jokingly, 'or you'll be down the job centre in the morning!'

Teamwork is widely presented as being positive for both employees and organizations. Management theorists have long argued that it increases productivity, creativity, and employee satisfaction (Procter and Mueller, 2000). When it works well, it helps create more imaginative and successful products and services, combining the skills, experience, and different outlooks of people from different backgrounds and areas within the company to gain a wider and more creative perspective. Creating *high performance teams*, Katzenbach and Smith (1993) claim, will lead to significantly higher productivity. It is little wonder, then, that being able to demonstrate teamworking skills will be an essential part of your working life.

Given the claims for teamwork, organizational theorists, consultants, and managers have, therefore, spent a lot of time developing models and ideas of how to make teams function effectively. *Belin's team roles* seek to capture the variety of traits a team needs to have to function well, where each role has a strength and allowable weakness. However, as we have seen through this chapter, teamwork can be a challenge. It requires trust, accountability, an openness to other people's ideas, and an ability to rely on each other and to share a common outlook. *Social identity theory* argues that to be part of a team requires the ability to forgo an individualistic outlook and to see yourself as part of a team. This can be a painful and challenging process, as it can mean giving up personal ideas and putting faith in other people. *Tuckman's stages of group formation* demonstrate the difficult path team members have to take, by going through the forming, storming, and norming stages before they are performing. Using team-building activities can be a way of breaking down barriers and helping individuals begin to gel as a team.

Despite these efforts, there still appears no 'magic bullet' to make teams function fully, and teamwork can be challenging for even the most experienced manager. As teams form tight bonds, they can encounter difficult emotional and psychological experiences that many people try to avoid. As a result, it can be challenging for teams to achieve all the results expected of them. Indeed, there is a danger that teams can develop too similar a mindset and as a result suffer from *groupthink*, where they begin to feel invulnerable and do not take into account outside perspectives.

Despite its positive aspects, teamwork can also be thought of as another form of control. The use of the word 'teamwork' can be hard to resist, as it hides the more subtle differences in power between team members (Finn, 2008). Furthermore, as Barker (1993) argues, teamwork is a form of surveillance as team members watch each other, controlling each other's effort and output. This can result in employees working harder. The manager is, therefore, replaced by team members: ten pairs of eyes rather than just one.

Therefore, while teamwork is very common in organizations it is also highly challenging to carry out well. You cannot simply put people together and assume that they will function as a team. Rather, effective teams require considerable effort and skill to build the trust needed to work well.

## Further reading

**Tuckman, B., and Jensen, M. 1977. Stages of small-group development revisited.** *Group & Organization Management* **2(4): 419–27.**
Tuckman's classic text describes the key stages of his group formation model. It also provides an interesting insight into the background of the theory.

**Katzenbach, J.R., and Smith, D.K. 1993.** *The wisdom of teams: Creating the high performance* ***organisation.*** **McGraw-Hill: Maidenhead.**
Provides an interesting account of how to create a 'high performance' team from a manager's viewpoint.

**Belbin, R.M. 2010.** *Team roles at work.* **Butterworth-Heinemann: Oxford.**
Describes one of the most popular teamwork models and gives some practical insight into how the theory works in practice.

**Janis, I.L. 1971. Groupthink.** *Psychology Today* **5(November): 43–6, 74–6.**
A classic account of groupthink with some interesting historical accounts.

**Barker, J.R. 1993. Tightening the iron cage: Concertive control in self-managing teams.** *Administrative Science Quarterly* **38(3): 408–37.**
Provides an interesting critical perspective on why teamwork can be a stronger form of control.

## References

Abrams, D., and Hogg, M.A. 2001. Collective identity: Group membership and self-conception. In: Hogg, M.A., and Tindale, S. (eds) *Blackwell handbook of social psychology: Group processes*. Blackwell Publishers: Oxford, pp. 425–61.

Allport, G.W. 1948. Foreword. In: Lewin, G.W. (ed.) *Resolving social conflict*. Harper & Row: London.

Anderson, N., and Sleap, S. 2004. An evaluation of gender differences on the Belbin Team Role Self-Perception Inventory. *Journal of Occupational and Organizational Psychology* 77(3): 429–37.

Badie, D. 2010. Groupthink, Iraq, and the War on Terror: Explaining US policy shift toward Iraq. *Foreign Policy Analysis* 6(4): 277–96.

Baldwin, D.C., Jr., and Daugherty, S.R. 2008. Interprofessional conflict and medical errors: Results of a national multi-specialty survey of hospital residents in the US. *Journal of Interprofessional Care*, 22(6): 573–86.

Barker, J.R. 1993. Tightening the iron cage: Concertive control in self-managing teams. *Administrative Science Quarterly* 38(3): 408–37.

Barrick, M.R., Stewart, G.L., Neubert, M.J., and Mount, M.K. 1998. Relating member ability and personality to work-team processes and team effectiveness. *Journal of Applied Psychology* 83(3): 377–91.

BBC 2009. The choice. BBC Radio 4, 3 November. Available at: http://www.bbc.co.uk/programmes/b00nk2c2

BBC 2015a. Kevin Pietersen: England hopes boosted by triple century. Available at: http://www.bbc.co.uk/sport/0/cycling/32696838 (last accessed 10 July 2015).

BBC 2015b. Lord MacLaurin: Kevin Pietersen is not a team player. Available at: http://www.bbc.co.uk/sport/0/cricket/32771616 (last accessed 10 July 2015).

Belbin, R.M. 2010. *Team roles at work*. Butterworth-Heinemann: Oxford.

Bion, W. 1961. *Experiences in groups and other papers*. Tavistock: London.

British Chambers of Commerce 2015. Young people need more support to make transition from education to work, says BCC. Available at: http://www.britishchambers.org.uk/press-office/press-releases/young-people-need-more-support-to-make-transition-from-education-to-work,-says-bcc.html (last accessed 1 August 2015).

Burke, W., Lake, D.G., and Paine, J.W. (eds) 2008. *Organization change: A comprehensive reader*. Jossey-Bass: San Francisco.

Buttigieg, S.C., West, M., and Dawson, J.F. 2011. Well-structured teams and the buffering of hospital employees from stress. *Health Service Management Research* 24: 203–12.

Cohen, S.G., and Bailey, D.E. 1997. What makes teams work: Group effectiveness research from the shop floor to the executive suite. *Journal of Management* 23(3): 239–90.

Cohen, S.G., and Ledford, G.E. 1994. The effectiveness of self-managing teams: A quasi-experiment. *Human Relations* 47(1): 13–43.

Coombs, M. 2003. Power and conflict in intensive care clinical decision making. *Intensive and Critical Care Nursing* 19(3): 125–35.

Coutu, D. 2009. Why teams don't work. *Harvard Business Review* 86(9): 64–72.

Daft, R.L. 2001. *Organization Theory and Design*, 7th edn. South-Western Publishing: Cincinnati.

*Daily Telegraph* 2009. HBOS whistleblower Paul Moore: Evidence to House of Commons 'Banking Crisis' hearing, 11 February. Available at: http://www.telegraph.co.uk/finance/newsbysector/banksandfinance/4590996/HBOS-whistleblower-Paul-Moore-Evidence-to-House-of-Commons-Banking-Crisis-hearing.html

Dallek, R. 2004. *John F Kennedy: An unfinished life*. Penguin: London.

Dufner, S. 2015a. Working during the Ice Bucket Challenge. Personal communication with Daniel King.

Dufner, S. 2015b. What I learned during the Ice Bucket Challenge: Be ready for anything. *The Guardian*, 1 July.

Dunphy, D., and Bryant, B. 1996. Teams: Panaceas or prescriptions for improved performance? *Human Relations* 49(5): 677–99.

Eiser, B. 2015. Improving physician–nurse teamwork *Hospitals and Health Networks*, 12 March.

Finn, R. 2008. The language of teamwork: Reproducing professional divisions in the operating theatre. *Human Relations* 61(1): 103–30.

Fisher, S.G., Hunter, T.A., and Macrosson, W.D.K. 2001. A validation study of Belbin's team roles. *European Journal of Work and Organizational Psychology* 10(2): 121–44.

Fox News 2004. 'Group think' led to Iraq WMD assessment, 11 July. Available at: http://www.foxnews.com/story/0,2933,125123,00.html

Frank, F., and Anderson, L.R. 1971. Effects of task and group size upon group productivity and member satisfaction. *Sociometry* 34(1): 135–49.

Freud, S., and Riviere, J.T. 1927. *The ego and the id authorized* (transl. J. Riviere). Hogarth Press: London.

Furnham, A., Steele, H., and Pendleton, D. 1993. A psychometric assessment of the Belbin Teamrole Self-perception Inventory. *Journal of Occupational and Organizational Psychology* 66(3): 245–57.

Hackman, J.R. 2002. *Leading teams: Setting the stage for great performances.* Harvard Business School Press: Boston.

Harkins, S.G., Latane, B., and Williams, K. 1980. Social loafing: Allocating effort or taking it easy. *Journal of Experimental Social Psychology* 16: 457–65.

Hartnett, T. 2010. *Consensus-oriented decision-making.* New Society Publishers: Gabriola Island.

Harvey, J.B. 1988. The Abilene paradox: The management of agreement. *Organizational Dynamics* 17(1): 17–43.

Hay Group 2015. The business/graduate divide: Are poor 'people skills' stifling UK graduates' potential? Available at: http://www.haygroup.com/uk/Press/Details.aspx?ID=46164 (last accessed 13 July 2015).

Honey, P. 2001. *Improve your people skills.* Chartered Institute of Personnel and Development: London.

HR Grapevine 2013. Businesses that fail to support team working risk productivity fall. Available at: http://www.hrgrapevine.com/markets/hr/article/2013-01-30-businesses-that-fail-to-support-team-working-risk-productivity-fall (last accessed 10 July 2015).

Janis, I.L. 1971. Groupthink. *Psychology Today* 5(November): 43–6, 74–6.

Jenkins, S. 2015. Talent is talent—England needs Kevin Pietersen. *The Guardian*, 12 May.

Katzenbach, J.R., and Smith, D.K. 1993. *The wisdom of teams: Creating the high performance organization.* Harvard Business School: Boston.

Ket De Vries, M. 1999. High-performance teams: Lessons for the Pygmies. *Organizational Dynamics* 27(3): 66–77.

Knights, D., and McCabe, D. 2000. Bewitched, bothered and bewildered: The meaning and experience of teamworking for employees in an automobile company. *Human Relations* 53(11): 1481–517.

Kur, E. 1996. The faces model of high performing team development. *Leadership and Organization Development Journal* 17(1): 32–41.

Latané, B., Williams, K., and Harkins, S. 1979. Many hands make light work: The causes and consequences of social loafing. *Journal of Personality and Social Psychology* 37(6): 822–32.

Lawler, E.E. 1986. *High-involvement management: Participative strategies for improving organizational performance.* Jossey-Bass: San Francisco.

Lawler, E.E., and Mohrman, S.A. 1985. Quality circles after the fad. *Harvard Business Review* 63(1): 65.

Lazer, D., and Friedman, A. 2007. The network structure of exploration and exploitation. *Administrative Science Quarterly* 52(4): 667–94.

Learmonth, M. 2009. 'Girls' working together without 'teams': How to avoid the colonization of management language. *Human Relations* 62(12): 1887–906.

Le Bon, G. 2009. *The crowd: A study of the popular mind.* Classic Books International: New York.

Lembke, S., and Wilson, M.G. 1998. Putting the 'team' into teamwork: Alternative theoretical contributions for contemporary management practice. *Human Relations* 51(7): 927–44.

Likierman, M. 2001. *Melanie Klein: Her work in context.* Continuum: London.

Mael, F., and Ashforth, B.E. 1995. Loyal from day one: Biodata, organizational identification, and turnover among newcomers. *Personnel Psychology* 48: 309–33.

Marks, M.L., Mirvis, P.H., Hackett, E.J., and Grady, J.F. 1986. Employee participation in a Quality Circle program: Impact on quality of work life, productivity, and absenteeism. *Journal of Applied Psychology* 71(1): 61–9.

Mueller, F. 1994. Teams between hierarchy and commitment: Change strategies and the 'internal environment'. *Journal of Management Studies* 31(3): 383–403.

Onrec 2013. Businesses that fail to support team working risk drop in productivity, 30 January.

Available at: http://www.onrec.com/news/news-archive/businesses-that-fail-to-support-team-working-risk-drop-in-productivity (last accessed 20 July 2015).

O'Connor, M.A. 2002. The Enron board: The perils of groupthink. *University of Cincinnati Law Review* 71: 1233.

Paul, J.P., Robertson, K.B., and Herzberg, F. 1969. Job enrichment pays off. *Harvard Business Review* 45(March–April): 61–78.

Philips 2015. Quality and business excellence. Available at: http://www.philips.com/about/company/businesses/businessesexcellence.page (last accessed 20 July 2015).

Procter, S.C., and Mueller, F. (eds) 2000. *Teamworking.* Macmillan: Basingstoke.

Rich, D. 2012. Netherlands v Germany: Oranje feeling the squeeze. *The Independent*, 13 June.

Rickards, T., and Moger, S. 1999. *Handbook for creative team leaders.* Gower Press: Farnborough.

Rickards, T., and Moger, S. 2000. Creative leadership processes in project team development: An alternative to Tuckman's stage model. *British Journal of Management* 11(4): 273–83.

Rimmer, A. 2014. Surgical trainees will be taught about communication and teamwork. *BMJ Careers*, 27 August. Available at: http://careers.bmj.com/careers/advice/view-article.html?id=20019002 (last accessed 15 July 2015).

Robinson, M., and Cottrell, D. 2005. Health professionals in multi-disciplinary and multi-agency teams: Changing professional practice. *Journal of Interprofessional Care* 19(6): 547–560.

Schnake, M.E. 1991. Organizational citizenship: A review, proposed model, and research agenda. *Human Relations* 44(7): 735–59.

Schofield, R.F., and Amodeo, M. 1999. Interdisciplinary teams in health care and human services settings: Are they effective? *Health and Social Work* 24(3): 210–19.

Sewell, G. 1998. The discipline of teams: The control of team-based industrial work through electronic and peer surveillance. *Administrative Science Quarterly* 43(2): 397–428.

Shore, J., Bernstein, E., and Lazer, D. 2015. Facts and figuring: An experimental investigation of network structure and performance in information and solution spaces. *Organization Science* 26(5): 1432–46.

Sims, R., and Brinkman, J. 2003. Enron ethics (or: Culture matters more than codes). *Journal of Business Ethics* 45(3): 243–56.

Sinclair, A. 1992. The tyranny of a team ideology. *Organization Studies* 13(4): 611–24.

Smith, R. 2014. Surgeons are to be tested on 'people skills'. *Telegraph*, 23 August.

Steiner, I.D. 1966. Models for inferring relationships between group size and potential group productivity. *Behavioral Science* 11(4): 273–83.

Sundstrom, E., De Meuse, K.P., and Futrell, D. 1990. Work teams: Applications and effectiveness. *American Psychologist* 45(2): 120–33.

Tajfel, H., and Turner, J.C. 1986. The social identity theory of intergroup behaviour. In: Worchel, S., and Austin, W.G. (eds) *Psychology of intergroup relations.* Nelson-Hall: Chicago, pp. 7–24.

Taylor, D. 2010. World Cup 2010: Holland hope for harmony from their feuding stars. *The Guardian*, 13 June.

*The Independent* 2015. Andrew Strauss: No England recall for Kevin Pietersen. *The Independent*, 11 April.

Titcomb, J. 2015. Banks fined £3.7bn for rigging foreign exchange markets. *The Telegraph*, 20 May.

TMS Global 2012. Available at http://www.tms.com.au (last accessed 26 November 2012).

Triplett, N. 1898. The dynamogenic factors in pacemaking and competition. *American Journal of Psychology* 9: 507–33.

Tuckman, B. 1965. Developmental sequence in small groups. *Psychological Bulletin* 63(6): 384–99.

Tuckman, B., and Jensen, M. 1977. Stages of small-group development revisited. *Group & Organization Management* 2(4): 419–27.

UK Parliament 2010. Report calls for more women in City to challenge group-think. Available at: http://www.parliament.uk/business/news/2010/04/report-calls-for-more-women-in-city-to-challenge-group-think/ (last accessed 25 June 2012).

West, M.A. 2004. *Effective teamwork: Practical lessons from organizational research.* Blackwell: Oxford.

Winner, D. 2001. *Brilliant orange: The neurotic genius of Dutch football.* Bloomsbury Publishing: London.

Xenergie Consulting Ltd 2013. Staff performance hit as leaders fail to develop team working. Available at: http://www.xenergie.com/staff-performance-hit-as-leaders-fail-to-develop-team-working/ (last accessed 20 July 2015).

# Organizational culture

*The hidden side of the organization*

## Chapter overview and learning outcomes

By the end of this chapter you should be able to:

- describe what organizational culture is
- describe why 'organizational culture' has become a popular term within management practice and academic theory
- explain how organizational culture shapes the behaviour of organizational members
- explain how managers try to change culture
- analyse the extent to which managers can change culture
- analyse whether managing through culture represents greater freedom or increased control.

## Key theorists

| | |
|---|---|
| Tom Peters and Robert Waterman | Popular management writers and consultants who spearheaded interest in organizational culture as a management resource. They argued that organizations need a 'strong culture' to be successful. |
| Edgar Schein | Schein provided one of the first real models of organizational culture. His model presents organizational culture at three levels which are progressively harder to access, but are more significant the deeper down they are. He believes culture is significantly influenced by the founder and leadership, and that by following the ten-step programme it can be changed. |
| Charles Handy | Business guru and writer Handy is well-known for developing a typology that proposes four types of culture. |
| Linda Smircich | Smircich sees culture as something that the organization either <br> • *has*—something that is a possession of the organization that managers (and others) can control, or <br> • *is*—an integral part of the organization. |
| Hugh Willmott | A critical management theorist who argues that there is a dark side of organizational culture—a form of slavery and control. |

## Key terms

| | |
|---|---|
| Organizational culture | The collective behaviour exhibited by members of an organization, often seen as comprising values, beliefs, practices, history, and traditions |

| Mission statement | The stated aim of the organization—often with the intention of inspiring the employees and differentiating them from others |
| Cultural typology | A classification of the type of organizational culture |
| Cultural change | Often driven by management or consultants with the intention of making the organization more productive; sees culture as a possession that management can control |

# Introduction: learning a new culture—new situation, new rules

## Running case: first day nerves

Sue Marshall looks into her mirror, preparing for her first day working at Junction Hotel. 'What will people be like? Friendly, I hope. Am I dressed correctly?' she says, looking down at her new suit. 'Not too formal, I hope, but I need to be taken seriously. This is an important job for me.'

Sue Marshall still feels nervous but tries to relax. 'How should I act when I get there? They seemed friendly when I looked round, but you never know. Linda Wilkinson said they are one big happy family.' Sue hopes this is true, but she's heard rumours about the head chef, Effingham. Her friend Isabella said he shouts and swears. 'I do hope that Isabella was just saying that to scare me. I'm not sure if I'll fit in if that's the case. Oh well, only one way to find out . . .'

 Think back to when you started a new job, school, or university—how did you feel? What were your hopes and fears? What were your first few days like? Did anything seem strange in the way people talked or behaved?

Going into any new social situation can be unsettling. We do not know what the people will be like, how to behave, what to wear, and what to say. We often worry whether people will like us and whether we will like them—in short, will we fit in?

Learning how to fit in could be thought of as adapting to the organization's culture. We largely do this without consciously thinking about it. We look for clues in the appearance of buildings, the company's reputation, and how they come across during the interview. The culture might be spelt out in policy documents, mission statements, official histories, induction packs, and dress codes. However, we also look to the less obvious things, such as the jokes and stories, the subtle put-downs, or the praise people receive. Through observing these subtle clues we pick up the unwritten rules of behaviour and learn how to fit in.

## Employability skills: learning to fit into the organization's culture

Successful people are often the ones who manage to fit within the company's culture. Put simply, if you want to be seen as successful at work you need to learn and adapt to your organization's culture—it will not adapt to you.

▶ There are a number of things that you can do to fit in better:

- research the culture before you apply to make sure that you can fit in—talk to people who work there or read up about the organization

- when joining, spend the first few weeks observing the culture to pick up clues on how it works, focusing particularly on:

  - the norms and patterns of behaviour: how other people act within the organization

  - the formal *and* informal aspects of culture—do not just follow what the official culture management try to promote, but also be aware of how your colleagues respond to what people say and do

- be aware that there is often more going on than first meets the eye, and that within different departments there might be more than one culture within the organization

- build and maintain strong relationships with key people within the organization, particularly those that can act as mentors and supporters.

However, it is also important not to become too drawn into the culture or to accept it unquestioningly. A strong organizational culture can shape what you believe, potentially teaching you to think in ways that go against the values you held before joining the organization. Therefore, while it is important to learn the organization's culture it is also vital to gain critical distance from it so that you are not drawn into it. Talking to people from outside of work can be helpful in giving you some perspective on what is going on in your own organization.

What is organizational culture? At its most basic level, it is the way things are done and the values held within an organization, the characteristics that make an organization unique. Culture shapes how people think and behave. This has led many managers, consultants, and academics to see organizational culture as a resource to increase performance and commitment.

However, some critical theorists argue that a strong culture can have a dark side, acting as a trap, with little room for resistance. This can end up producing what critical theorist Hugh Willmott has called a type of slavery, to 'exploit, distort and drain the dwindling cultural resource of caring, democratic values' (1993: 541).

Throughout this chapter we will debate whether managing through culture offers increased freedom or greater (and more insidious) control. Is it a resource that management may use, or is it beyond the scope of any individual or group?

# What is organizational culture?

**Running case:** Sue Marshall arrives at Junction Hotel

Sue Marshall arrives at Junction Hotel reception. It seems smaller than she remembers. 'Can I help?' the smartly-dressed receptionist asks. Marshall notices the receptionist's understated make-up. 'I'm here to start work,' Marshall replies nervously. 'Oh, you must be Sue—we've been expecting you. I'm Mandy,' the receptionist says, breaking out into a broad smile. 'I do hope that you enjoy working here. Come with me.'

They walk at a gentle pace through the corridor and down a hall. The thick-pile carpet gives off an air of quality, thinks Sue as she walks next to Mandy. As they walk, Mandy engages Sue in polite conversation. 'She seems friendly enough,' thinks Sue. 'I might just fit in here.'

At its simplest, organizational culture is defined as 'the way we do things around here' (Deal and Kennedy, 1982: 4), the common practices, attitudes, behaviours, beliefs, and values that are shared between organizational members (Schein, 2010). Organizational culture could be likened to organizational 'glue'.

Here are some popular definitions:

- 'Culture is the system of such publicly and collectively accepted meanings operating for a given group at a given time' (Pettigrew, 1979: 574)
- 'the collective programming of the mind which distinguishes the members of one organization from another' (Hofstede, 1991: 262)
- 'the basic assumptions and beliefs which are shared by members of an organization, that operate unconsciously, and that define in a basic "taken-for-granted" fashion an organization's view of itself and its environment' (Schein, 2010). Schein also defines culture as 'a set of basic assumptions [that] defines for us what to pay attention to, what things mean' (2010: 32).

However, as with many of the subjects in this book, there is no consensus on what organizational culture is, how it operates, or its importance to organizations. Indeed, as Frost et al. argued as far back as 1991, researchers 'do not approach the phenomena they do study from the same theoretical, epistemological, or methodological points of view' (1991: 7).

# Why study organizational culture? The rise of management interest

**Running case:** Simon Chance attends a business seminar

Simon Chance has just come back from a business seminar 'Harnessing your culture—your secret weapon for success' at his local Business Link. He is excited. The speaker, an influential American, talked passionately about how he turned his food manufacturing business from a small-scale enterprise into a market leader through changing his firm's culture, by focusing on the customer and excellence in everything. His enthusiasm was infectious. The American described how they got everyone working together around a common mission and how, through that, productivity went up.

Chance is impressed. He likes the idea of a unified culture where everyone shares the values of high quality at affordable prices. He looks at the leaflet he picked up at the seminar and starts to read it . . .

Why do you think Chance would want to change the culture of Junction Hotel? How would you go about finding what the culture of the organization is?

In 1982 two management consultants for McKinsey's, Tom Peters and Robert Waterman, published a book that caused a storm within management circles. *In search of excellence* became a global hit, selling over 3 million copies within its first four years, and was commonly seen in boardrooms, airport lounges, and business schools. This phenomenal success led to 'organizational culture' becoming the **buzzword** for businesses.

At the book's heart was the claim that *excellent* companies had one key thing in common: a strong set of shared values which put the customer at the heart of the operation.

Buzzword  A phrase which is a fad for a period of time.

Successful firms, Peters and Waterman argued, were defined by strong, unified cultures; a bias for action; being close to the customers; innovation; being value driven; and having autonomy in decision making. 'In fact', Peters and Waterman state, 'we wonder whether it is possible to be an excellent company without clarity on values' (1982: 280).

They were not alone in this interest in culture. Indeed, from the late 1970s academics and consultants such as Deal and Kennedy (1982) and Geert Hofstede (1991) all argued that organizational culture is central to business success. For instance, '[t]o be successful', Tichy argues, 'a company's culture needs to support the kind of business the organization is in and its strategy for handling that business' (1982: 71). As Cameron and Quinn have argued, 'Virtually every leading firm you can name, small or large, has developed a distinctive culture that is clearly identifiable by its employees' (2006: 4–5). This can be summed up in a quote that is attributed to Peter Drucker: 'culture eats strategy for breakfast' (cited in Kahle and Gurel-Atay 2013: viii).

Indeed, as far back as the 1960s Tom Watson, Jr., the former president of IBM, claimed that 'in order to survive and achieve success, [an organization] must have a sound set of beliefs on which it premises all its policies and actions' (1963: 5, cited in Posner et al., 1985: 294). He went on to say these beliefs 'must always come before policies, practices, and goals. The latter must always be altered if they are seen to violate fundamental beliefs' (1963: 72–73). Culture and shared values, therefore, were seen as central for organizational success. As Google executives Eric Schmidt and Jonathan Rosenberg have recently stated, 'culture and success go hand in hand' (2015: 23).

# Do strong cultures equal strong performance?

**Running case:** Simon Chance looks at changingculture.info.uk

Simon Chance looks through the changingculture.info.uk website.

'If your people continue to act and think as they now do, will you be able to achieve the results you need? If your answer is no,' the website continues, 'then changing your organizational culture is not simply an option—it's essential. Organizational culture,' he reads on, 'can be the difference between success and failure, change or stagnation … Changing your culture can drive spectacular results by capitalising on your greatest asset, your people … You can change the way that people think and act … become more competitive and focused … be the best in your field … To succeed, you must win the hearts and minds of your staff. changingculture.info.uk develop winning corporate cultures with shared beliefs and passion for the organization where all the energy of the company pulls in the same direction.'

Great stuff, thinks Chance. The staff seem committed, but I'm not sure I have won their 'hearts and minds'? Maybe I should give culture change a go?

Management consultants' interest in organizational culture hangs on one central claim: getting the right culture increases productivity. It does this by creating a shared sense of purpose, increasing staff motivation (Peters and Waterman, 1982) and commitment (Deal and Kennedy, 1982), reducing conflict, enhancing the smooth running of the organization, and producing higher levels of productivity, quality, efficiency, and morale (Cameron and Quinn, 2006).

Some very bold assertions have been made to support this claim. Deal and Kennedy claim 'we estimate that a company can gain as much as one or two hours of productive work per employee per day' (1982: 15). Similarly, Collins and Porras argued that visionary companies outperformed non-visionary companies by about 1,500% over 64 years (1994). With figures like this, it is easy to see why managers and management consultants get excited. Getting the organizational culture right, its proponents claim, is essential for organizational success. As Google executives Schmidt and Rosenberg argue, the 'power of a great culture… can make each member of the company better. And it can make the company ascendant' (2015: 65).

There are many cultural change consultancies that make bold claims. Visit the Online Resource Centre for links to some of them.

### Review questions

| | |
|---|---|
| **Describe** | What is organizational culture? |
| **Explain** | What is meant when culture is described as 'the way we do things around here'? |
| **Analyse** | Why do you think managers have taken a great interest in organizational culture? How could changing culture benefit them? |
| **Apply** | Go to the Online Resource Centre and follow the link to culture change consultancies. Why do you think they see culture as so important? What claims do they make regarding the impact that they can make on organizational performance? Do you think the claims are justified? |

Indeed, as Cameron and Quinn argue, while anyone can buy machinery or set up and design production processes and distribution networks, what makes an organization successful is the right culture (2006). This claim is even more relevant in service- and knowledge-intensive work, which rely almost entirely on their staff for success.

In a recent article, Boyce et al. (2015) look at the relationship between culture and the performance of 95 car dealership franchises over 6 years. They conclude that culture 'comes first' and that it is a consistent predictor of customer satisfaction and sales. Similarly, Kotrba et al. (2012) argue that there is a close connection between culture and effectiveness, particularly for organizations that could be consistent but adaptable.

**Research insight:** Does organizational culture really make a difference? Posner, B. Z., Kouzes, J. M., and Schmidt, W. H. 1985. Shared values make a difference: An empirical test of corporate culture. *Human Resource Management* 24(3): 293–309.

With the rising interest in corporate culture, and optimistic claims for its significance, researchers began to look for evidence that it was really making a difference. This early research asked 6,000 managers (of whom 25% replied) about their personal values and expectations, and how they matched those of the firms they worked for.

▶ They found that where there was **congruence** between personal and organizational values there was less conflict, more ethical decision making, more satisfaction with work, less tension in home lives, reduced anxiety, increased ability to cope with pressure, and increased productivity and commitment. For instance, those with high-value congruence were less likely to take a promotion if they felt unsure about their ability to handle the job.

They advised companies to select, train, reward, and counsel new staff in the light of their shared values to maximize the chances of them fitting in. Managing culture they argued, was, therefore, a key responsibility of managers.

**Congruence** To correspond or match.

### Real life case: Google

Google have not only transformed the way that we use the Internet, they are also heralded, by *Fortune* magazine, as the best place to work in the world (*Fortune*, 2015). Why is that? Google are well known for their trendy, playful, and even weird office designs with slides for staircases, caravans as meeting rooms, and video-games and playrooms (Fast Company, 2015; also see Chapter 11 on Googleplex), but the phenomenon goes deeper than that. According to Google's senior vice-president for people operations Laszlo Bock, Google's culture is based on seeing work as a calling and giving people 'more trust, freedom, and authority than you are comfortable giving them' (2015: 53). This is echoed by Google executives Schmidt and Rosenberg, who say that for Google to be successful the employees 'need to *care* about the place they work and Google succeeds by giving people "responsibility and freedom"' (Schmidt and Rosenberg, 2015: 29 and 52, italics in original). Part of this freedom comes with the company's tolerance for dissent, encouraging strong opinions and creating 'an environment where all employees feel valued and empowered' (2015: 42). They tell a story of how in 2002 Larry Page, Google's co-founder, was unhappy with the ads that were appearing on the Google searches because they were largely unrelated to what he had searched for. On a Friday afternoon he printed the search results he received, wrote 'THESE ADS SUCK' at the top of the page, pinned it to the noticeboard by the pool table, and left. On Monday at 5:05 am a search engineer sent an email agreeing with Page and offered a diagnosis and solution. The engineer and colleagues had spent the weekend trying to solve the problem, and they were not even in the team responsible for the original problem. This solution was the foundation to Google AdWords, the key money-making tool for Google. Schmidt and Rosenberg state that the fact these engineers 'spent their weekends transforming someone else's problem into a profitable solution speaks to the power of culture' (2015: 29).

**Sources:** Schmidt and Rosenberg (2015); Bock (2015).

# From managing machines to managing dreams: a new way to manage organizations

This focus on organizational culture led to considerable hype predicting that organizations would be transformed. These management gurus presented a tantalizing, almost messianic, vision of businesses changing from the top down, from hierarchical control with all the problems of conflict we saw in Chapters 2, 3, 4 to a culture of harmony and productivity, where workers and management come together around shared values.

---

**Theory in context:** responding to the rise of Japanese manufacturing

The rising interest in organizational culture occurred at a point when the USA's position as the economic superpower was being challenged by the rise of Japanese firms. For example, Harley Davidson was challenged by Honda's smaller, more efficient bikes (Ouchi, 1981).

The Japanese culture was seen as key in their success. For instance, Peters and Waterman recounted a story of a 'Honda worker who, on his way home each evening, straightens up windshield wiper blades on all the Hondas he passes. He can't stand to see a flaw in a Honda!' (1982: 37). In contrast, some US workers were seen as purposely destructive. For example, one worker described how 'he would go home at night chuckling to himself about the things he had thought up during the day to mess up the system. He'd leave his sandwich behind the door panel of a car, for example…Or he would put loose screws in the compartment of the frame that was to be welded shut' (Cameron and Quinn, 2006: 15).

---

**Real life case:** Hitachi's consensus-building culture improves decision making

Hitachi is one of the world's most successful manufacturing companies, making everything from televisions to the Bullet Train. Like fellow Japanese giant Toyota (see Chapter 4), they work on a principle of *nemawashi* (which roughly translates as consensus-building). 'It means we don't mandate change,' says HR director Stephen Pierce. Rather, they work to 'persuade and influence them in order to create change' (Jeffery, 2014). This consensus-building approach means decisions are made in a 'bottom-up and top-down model'. Pierce states 'the top people still make a call when they need to, but it ensures a greater degree of engagement before you get to that point' (Jeffery, 2014).

Hitachi's corporate values are core to how they work and develop leaders. Kazuo Furukawa, president of Hitachi, states that they 'use them as criteria to assess our managers' progress' (cited in EgonZehnder, 2015). Hitachi's basic credo states 'harmony, sincerity and pioneering spirit, to instill a resolute pride in being a member of Hitachi, and thereby to contribute to society through the development of superior, original technology and product' (Hitachi, 2015). 'Those who fail to acquire these personal skills,' Furukawa states, 'will not be recognized as Hitachi men and women' (cited in EgonZehnder, 2015).

---

In view of the ascendancy of Japanese firms, American business dominance was seen as being under threat and in need of reviving. The interest in organizational culture was presented as a way for US firms to reassert their dominance and confidence. As Deal and Kennedy put it: 'a strong culture has almost always been the driving force behind continuing success in American Business' (1982: 5).

According to this view, managers' roles had to change fundamentally. They no longer simply controlled 'hard' financial measures, structure, and strategy, but needed to manage 'soft', less measurable aspects of visions and values, mission and purpose, unifying the

Table 7.1  Rational and cultural management (based on Peters and Waterman, 1982)

| Rational management | Cultural management |
|---|---|
| • Hard | • Soft |
| • Rational argument based on facts and figures | • Emotional appeal through shared values |
| • Managed through budgets, strategy, and targets | • Managed through shared values and purpose |
| • Management control imposed on workers via rules, procedures, and systems of accountability | • Workers control themselves through shared beliefs and values |
| • Formal communication through newsletters, emails, etc. | • Informal communication through symbols and stories |
| • Formal authority structures and hierarchy | • Reliance on informal opinion leaders, traditions, accepted practices, and sense of mission |
| • Control, monitoring, and evaluation | • Trust, commitment, and autonomy |

workplace around core values everyone believed in. Table 7.1 presents a summary of these contrasts.

Managing through culture and values presented a new, more innovative and exciting way of managing. Tom Peters (2001) later called it 'soft stuff that determines what really gets accomplished and how well it gets done. It turned out to be a revolutionary message'.

## Theory in context: culture producing a new form of worker

Peters and Waterman (1982) argued that managing through culture would produce a radical alternative to the standard bureaucratic model that stressed rules and regulations and carrot-and-stick motivation. They thought this would be replaced by organizations where freedom and autonomy ruled, governed through a shared sense of values and purpose. This, they claimed, would produce a different type of workplace and with it a new type of worker.

The idea was simple. If the worker was released from the constraints of bureaucratic standardization and given something to believe in, the organizational members would be committed to the mission of the organization and work harder as a consequence. Peters and Waterman (ibid.) pronounced that 'The individual', so dehumanized by Taylorism, 'still counts'.

Peters and Waterman offered a vision where workers would love their company and believe in its values. Gone was Taylorism with its standardization and uniformity, top-down command-and-control management, and repetitive tasks. In its place was a shared sense of vision and values, mission and purpose.

The workers' personalities and individuality, so disliked by Taylor, would be rediscovered and harnessed for the organization's benefit. Peters and Waterman thought a new society could be created around individual autonomy and freedom, governed by shared values. As Sewell later commented, 'direct control of the labor process is no longer seen as necessarily the most effective way to realize organizational goals' (1998: 401).

Organizational culture therefore promises that the worker can be productive *and* have increased job satisfaction. The conflict between labour and capital, Peters and Waterman argued, is solved because there is no longer a conflict between the workers' interests and that of the organization.

Such a move was needed, its proponents argued, because the nature of society was changing. From the 1960s, respect for authority began to diminish and workers were less accepting of hierarchical relations. Indeed, Deal and Kennedy argued that the loss of faith in large-scale institutions, such as government and church, meant that 'corporations may be the last institutions in America that can effectively take on the role of shaping values' (1982: 16).

**Real life case:** Zappos—delivering happiness the Zappos way

Zappos, the US online shoe retailer, was founded in 1999 and was sold to Amazon in 2009 for $1.2 billion. It is not just their phenomenal growth that has made the headlines, but their culture.

They call themselves the 'Zappos family' and place an emphasis on fun and having 'wow' elements (Zappos, 2015). Their CEO, Tony Hsieh, comes to work in jeans and a t-shirt and earns only $36,000 per year (Wei, 2010). They have a chief happiness officer and a culture evangelist, Donavan Roberson, who argues that they invest money in 'building a culture dedicated to the happiness of our people' (cited in Michelli, 2012: 71). Managers are asked to spend 10–20% of their time socializing with employees. They run competitions and games for employees and provide perks such as free food. They conduct regular staff surveys and have unusual practices. For example, when an employee logs in to the computer system, in addition to their password, they are shown a random photo of another employee and are asked to name them. After they answer, a brief profile of that employee is shown 'so that everyone can learn more about each other' (Hsieh, 2010: 173). They also have an online culture book where employees can submit uncensored photos and ideas about Zappos' culture (Zappos Insights, 2015) and write about it in blogs (blogs.zappos.com). This leads Tony Hsieh to claim that 'everyone at Zappos lives by the 10 Core Values' (Hsieh, 2010: 162). These values include 'Pursue Growth and Learning' and 'Deliver WOW Through Service', as well as more unusual ones like 'Be Passionate' and 'Create Fun and a Little Weirdness'.

Hsieh states, 'Our employees know that our number one priority at Zappos is our company culture' (2010: 171). Employees are recruited not only for the skills they offer but if they fit with Zappos culture (compare with recruitment at Pret a Manger, as described in Chapter 8). 'I know Zappos has a well-defined technical education curriculum, and if the person fits our values regarding learning and growth, we can teach the technical aspects of the job,' states Markel, director of casual lifestyle at Zappos (cited by Michelli, 2012). All new employees (right up to senior leaders) have to go through a one-month induction process that was originally designed for entry-level jobs, in order to give everyone a common experience. It includes an overview of the ten core values and the history behind each value, presentations from senior managers, and four weeks of customer service training. This training culminates in answering the phone to actual customers for two weeks (Michelli, 2012). There is a further check to see if employees fit; after their induction, newly oriented employees are offered one month's salary to leave if they do not feel they fit with the culture (Taylor, 2014).

Why do Zappos try to recruit for cultural fit? Would you like to work at Zappos? Visit the Online Resource Centre for more information on Zappos.

### Review questions

| | |
|---|---|
| **Describe** | What are rational management and cultural management? |
| **Explain** | What are the key claims about why cultural management increases performance? |
| **Analyse** | In what way does managing through culture shift the manager's role? |
| **Apply** | Can you describe the key features of the cultures at Hitachi and Zappos? How do these cultures benefit each organization? Do you think they might have any drawbacks? |

# How to understand culture

**Running case:** Chance wonders whether cultural change will work at Junction Hotel

Impressed with the claims that changingculture.info.uk make about the importance of organizational culture, Chance decides to delve a little deeper. 'It would be great to get the staff all sharing the same vision of Junction Hotel and all our energy directed towards making the hotel a success,' he muses.

'The first thing you need to do,' he reads on the website, 'is to diagnose what your existing culture is. Take our free self-diagnostic test,' the website suggests, 'and find out what your culture is'. OK, thinks Chance, it can't do any harm.

Completing the survey, Simon Chance clicks on the result: 'A Role Culture'. 'Umm . . .,' thinks Chance. 'I guess so, although I'm not sure it is really like that. Anyway, what can I do with this information?' At the end of the result page, Chance reads: 'if you want more information and to talk through your result, phone this number'. He decides to give them a call.

The consultants explain that the culture survey is only a snapshot of the organization and it is only based on his perspective. 'To really understand what is going on,' Mark Wickham continues, 'a full survey of the organization is necessary. This will give you a chance to understand how your staff view Junction Hotel'.

A popular way of understanding and trying to change an organization's culture is to use a cultural classification, also known as a typology. These **typologies** are useful in that they provide a way of quickly capturing an overall impression of the organization and allow it to be compared to other organizations. There is no single 'best culture'. Rather, the role of managers is to fit the organizational culture with the external environment.

**Typologies** A system of classification of traits that organizations have in common.

## Deal and Kennedy's typology

One of the first such models was provided by Deal and Kennedy (1982) (see Table 7.2). They argued that an organization's culture is a product of the environment in which they operate—in particular the amount of risk key activities carry and the speed of feedback that workers receive. For example, a car sales person generally gets quick feedback (someone either buys or does not buy a car), but the risk of a single transaction is fairly small, producing a work hard/play hard culture. If someone works in a government bureaucracy it has a low risk and slow feedback, producing a process culture. Each of these cultures has their own strengths and weaknesses. It is important to match the culture to the right environment.

**Real life case:** stockbrokers in a tough-guy macho culture

The financial markets have received considerable attention over the last few years as people have tried to make sense of what caused the financial crisis that hit much of the world in 2008. Some commentators (e.g. Dewatripont and Xavier, 2012; Wilson, 2012) have begun to criticize those who work in 'the City' (of London) and Wall Street (in the US) of taking too many risks. They have argued that they ▶

▶ take a very short-term approach, gamble unnecessarily with other people's money, and claim bonuses far beyond their true value.

What happened in 2008 would not have been a shock to those that had followed the numerous exposés of the City in recent years. Films, such as Oliver Stone's *Wall Street*, and books, such as Michael Lewis' (1989) *Liar's Poker* and Venetia Thompson's (2010) *Gross Misconduct*, have portrayed working in the City as a high-risk, adrenaline-fuelled, masculine environment where 'greed is good'.

The macho world of the financial markets.
**Source:** Cathy Yeulet /123RF.

Dealing with millions of pounds of trade in stocks and shares, bonds, and other complex financial products, life in the City is highly stressful, with millions potentially lost in a single day. It is, therefore, high-risk and fast-feedback, producing a *tough-guy macho culture*. Thompson (2010: 54) states that the 'broking floor is arguably the most aggressive, male-dominated environment that anyone could work in. Brokers often have to communicate by shouting to be heard above everyone else. Swearing at each other and smashing things is accepted—not officially, of course, but if a broker smashes a phone, no one notices'.

She also states the work had a strong social element where avoiding 'drinking at lunchtime was virtually impossible' (ibid.: 55). As gaining clients was vital to the success of a broker, entertaining them was an essential activity. 'Getting [the powerful clients] to agree to spend an evening with you, or maybe even a weekend, was therefore a contest in itself, with different brokers competing to secure the best clients for the best events. They had seen and done it all before and had the same jaded reaction, even if you offered a VIP helicopter trip to the Monaco Grand Prix' (ibid.: 57–8).

**Table 7.2**  The link between culture and feedback (Deal and Kennedy, 1982)

|  | | |
|---|---|---|
| **Fast** | **Work hard/play hard**<br>• Fun-focused<br>• Performance and action driven<br>• Strong customer focus<br>• Small risks<br>• High energy level<br>• Example—sales and manufacturing | **Tough-guy macho**<br>• Quick decision making<br>• High risk—all or nothing<br>• Highly driven people<br>• Individualistic<br>• Competitive—low teamwork<br>• Example—stockbrokers, media, sports, and construction |
| **Speed of feedback** | **Process culture**<br>• Bureaucratic—clear rules that must be followed<br>• Highly regulated<br>• Often need for precision<br>• Status orientated<br>• Takes years to discover if decision was correct<br>• Example—government bureaucracies | **Bet-your-company culture**<br>• Long-term outlook<br>• High-risk and high-cost decisions but years before outcome is known<br>• High planning, technical expertise and diligence throughout<br>• Examples—pharmaceutical firm devising a new drug, oil companies |
| **Slow** | | |
| | Low                    Degree of risk                    High | |

Based on Deal, T. and Kennedy, A., *Corporate Cultures: The Rites and Rituals of Corporate Life* (1982). Reproduced by permission of Perseus Books.

Visit the Online Resource Centre for an extended profile of stockbroker culture.

Which of Deal and Kennedy's cultural typologies do you think that stockbrokers fit? To what extent do you think the culture might explain the action of large banks and their role in the financial crisis?

## Charles Handy's typology

Another typology is offered by Charles Handy in his book *Gods of management* (2009). Handy argues that organizations should try to match their type of culture to the external needs of the organization. He offered the following four cultural categories based on Greek gods (Table 7.3, adapted from Handy, 2009).

Table 7.3  Handy's four cultural categories

| Power culture—Zeus | Role culture—Apollo |
|---|---|
| • Power and decision making concentrated on the centre, e.g. founder/manager<br>• Control of centre becomes weaker as firm grows, so normally split into subdivisions<br>• Tough and competitive environment<br>• Few set rules, as is more about power and choosing people who think in similar ways<br>• *Examples*—family firms, new businesses, and small entrepreneurs | • Bureaucracy in its purest form<br>• Roof—senior management decision making<br>• Pillars—functional units<br>• Staff do their roles<br>• Authority based on position in hierarchy<br>• Predictable<br>• Works well in predictable environments, but is difficult to adapt to change<br>• *Examples*—civil service and high street banks |
| **Task culture—Athena** | **Personal or cluster culture—Dionysius** |
| • Focus on getting the job done<br>• Temporary project teams to meet task needed, then disbanded<br>• Expertise is central<br>• Control through allocation of people and resources<br>• *Examples*—project management, construction, and advertising | • Consensus management; power is shared<br>• Individual freedom is key<br>• Exist for the members<br>• No collective goal<br>• Reject formal hierarchies<br>• *Examples*—self-help groups and architect partnerships |

## Quinn and Rohrbaugh's competing values framework

Our final framework was developed by Quinn and Rohrbaugh (1983; see Cameron and Quinn, 2006) and is used to assess not only organizational culture but leadership, communication, and employee selection. Like the other frameworks, it divides culture into four distinct types (see Table 7.4). The key dimensions on the horizontal axis are if the organization is inward-focused on the organization or outward, in favour of customers. The vertical axis shows whether the control is with management (at the bottom) or autonomy is with the staff (at the top). Each of the four therefore represent opposite sets of assumptions.

Table 7.4  Competing values framework

| | Flexibility and discretion | |
|---|---|---|
| | **Clan (late 1960s onwards)** | **Adhocracy (information age)** |
| Internally-focused and integrated | • Like a family organization<br>• Shared values and cohesion<br>• Teamwork and employee empowerment, friendly place to work<br>• Customers are partners<br>• Leaders are mentors/parent figures<br>• *Example*–PeopleExpress | • Ad hoc–temporary and specialized, disbands when the task is complete<br>• No centralized power–power flows from individual to individual<br>• Emphasis on individuality and risk-taking and creativity<br>• *Example*–software development, think-tanks |
| | **Hierarchy (from 1900 onwards)** | **Market (from 1960s onwards)** |
| | • Bureaucratic culture<br>• Clear lines of decision making<br>• Stable and efficient<br>• Standardized rules and procedures with no discretion<br>• Environment is stable<br>• Leaders are good organizers<br>• *Example*–McDonalds and Ford | • Organization functions as a market with competition<br>• Aims to reduce transaction costs<br>• Profit is key; highly results-orientated<br>• Meeting customers' needs<br>• Customers competitive for best price<br>• Leaders are highly competitive<br>• *Example*–General Electric |
| | Stability and control | |

*(Right axis label: Externally-focused and differentiated)*

(Adapted from Cameron and Quinn, 2006).

It is interesting to note that these cultures also reflect the organizational structure (see Chapter 2), as they involve how decisions are made and how power operates within the organization.

# Cultural typologies assessed

Cultural typologies are popular because they provide a quick way of capturing what an organization is like, its strengths and weaknesses, and comparing it to other organizations. However, they should be treated with caution.

They tend to generalize rather than provide specific descriptions of how a culture operates. Organizations do not necessarily fit neatly in categories, and applying these typologies in a rigid way can mean we lose sight of some of the features that make an organization unique. These typologies also focus on the structural elements of the culture and tend to ignore the more mundane, everyday aspects of organizational life. Their accuracy also depends on the ability of the individual to successfully understand the culture and match it to the framework. Finally, they present organizations as having a unified, homogeneous culture and thus miss some of the subtleties between departments or different sites. They therefore provide a useful frame of reference but should only be used as a starting point for analysis.

 Visit the Online Resource Centre and complete the culture diagnostic test for an organization you know well. How well do you think it represents the organization?

### Review questions

**Describe**   What is a cultural typology?

**Explain**   How might a manager use a cultural typology?

**Analyse**   What are the strengths and weaknesses of cultural typologies?

**Apply**   Can you apply the cultural typologies in this section to some of the real life cases throughout this chapter? Can you apply them to Junction Hotel as a whole? Do different cultural types exist in different parts of the hotel?

## Edgar Schein's cultural iceberg

Schein sees culture as being like an iceberg, where the important parts of the culture occur below the surface (Figure 7.1 and Table 7.5). The things near the top are the easiest to change, but have the least significance. The further one goes down the iceberg the deeper ingrained the culture is and the less conscious the participants are of it. These levels are harder to change but have greater impact.

At the top are physical artefacts, such as the building or staff uniforms. They express certain aspects of the culture, but they are open to interpretation by the observer. The middle layer represents the **intangible** beliefs or values of the organization. Schein

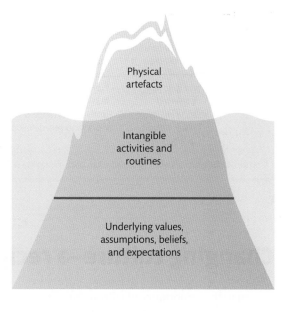

**Figure 7.1** Schein's cultural iceberg.
**Source:** © Schein, *Organizational Culture and Leadership*, 2010, John Wiley & Sons Inc.

Intangible  Something that you cannot touch.

believes that these often start from the founder or leader and are passed on to the organizational members through mission statements or strategy. The deepest level holds the strongly held values and assumptions. For Schein, underlying assumptions are the essence of culture. Changing them can result in anxiety and defence mechanisms, but 'unless one digs down to the level of the basic assumptions one cannot really decipher the artefacts, values, and norms' (Schein, 2010: 59).

Changing culture is, therefore, a complex process. Because much of culture is unconscious it can be hard to change; however, this is not to suggest that it is impossible to change. Schein argues that by following a ten-step process, cultures can be understood in a single day (2010: 348) and begin changing quickly after that.

Can you apply Schein's model to an organization or workplace that you know?

Table 7.5  Schein's cultural iceberg (based on Schein, 2010)

| Level | Description | Examples | Analysis | Ability to change |
|---|---|---|---|---|
| **Artefacts** | What one sees and hears | Physical environment Language Technology Clothing Emotional display Myths and stories about the organization | Visible, but hard to decipher Cannot rely on alone, as observer will project their own feelings and reactions | Relatively straightforward but also fairly superficial and therefore not going to change the culture dramatically |
| **Espoused beliefs and values** | Beliefs and key practices spoken initially by leader/ founder and then validated by the group | What people say in particular situations Mission statements Strategies and goals | Stated assumptions shared by the group Often leave many aspects of behaviour unexplained | The leader can change this level and may be good at training new members how to behave |
| **Basic underlying assumptions** | Regular solution to a problem, it becomes taken for granted; preferred solution, any other option inconceivable | Values that guide behaviour Values shared and therefore reinforced Fundamental aspects of life, human nature, nature of truth, importance of family, work, and self-development, etc. | Unconscious, taken for granted, not discussable; anything that challenges this produces defence mechanisms | Very difficult to change as often unconscious and completely taken for granted |

© Schein, *Organizational Culture and Leadership*, 2010, John Wiley & Sons Inc.

# Changing culture—a recipe for success

Owing to the importance of culture for organizational performance, many cultural change consultants offer step-by-step guidelines to change culture by:

- diagnosing the current culture
- deciding what needs changing
- transforming the culture to its new way of operating
- entrenching the new culture in the way that the organization works.

The underlying assumption within these typologies and management change frameworks is that culture is management's property, something tangible, knowable, and controllable. This perspective assumes that senior managers, with the support of a consultant, can diagnose what the culture is, change it, and control it in the way that they want. Seeing culture in this way views it as a resource that is used and manipulated by the management to increase commitment and to enhance performance. Culture, therefore, is a tool that can be used to increase profitability.

## Review questions

**Describe**   What are the main features of Schein's cultural iceberg?

**Explain**   In what way do typologies and management change frameworks see culture as management's property?

**Analyse**   What are the implications of managers seeing culture as a tool for organizational practice? What are the potential negative repercussions of seeing culture as a property that managers can control?

**Apply**   Can you apply Schein's model to the real life cases in this chapter? Which parts of the model are easy to describe and which are more difficult?

---

**Research insight:** Practical guides to changing organizational culture
Cameron, K., and Quinn, R.E. 2006. *Diagnosing and changing organizational culture.* Jossey Bass: London.

Cameron and Quinn offer a popular, and quite practical, guide to changing organizational culture. This guide includes a range of tools, such as questions, surveys, and instruments, for organizational managers to use in diagnosing and changing their organization's culture, and a framework in which managers can understand the basic assumptions and communication style within the organization.

Their key tips include:

- identifying what can be changed easily
- changing it and then publicizing it—so that everyone knows what has happened
- identifying illustrative stories of the type of culture you want to produce
- measuring change so people know what to focus on
- holding a funeral for the past approach of the organization and celebrating that past—this helps employees gain closure on the old culture
- focusing on process.

This approach is quite simple and, as we will see in Chapter 11, it is questionable whether change can occur through such a linear approach.

---

Schein provided an alternative model of changing organizational culture—the ten-step approach, which is outlined in Table 7.6.

While there are many models that claim to be able to change culture, as we will see in the following sections, in practice, culture is often more complicated than these recipe-book approaches suggest.

Table 7.6  Schein's ten-step approach to changing organizational culture (based on Schein, 2010)

| Stage | Aim | Description |
|---|---|---|
| 1 | Obtaining leadership commitment | Changing the culture is a major undertaking; therefore the leadership need to be committed |
| 2 | Selecting groups for interviews | Consultant works with leadership to select representative groups, including **subcultures** |
| 3 | Selecting an appropriate setting for the group interviews | Comfortable setting with the right equipment |
| 4 | Explaining the purpose of the meeting | Leadership set out the key purpose; outside consultant introduced |
| 5 | Giving a short lecture on how to think about culture | Explain cultural iceberg and the importance of the organization's history |
| 6 | Eliciting descriptions of the artefacts | Ask most recent employee what it felt like entering the organization; all members contribute; look at issues such as dress code, way of addressing the boss, how people get rewarded (takes about an hour) |
| 7 | Identifying espoused values | The consultant explores why they do what they do; aim is to elicit statements that are commonly agreed (takes about an hour) |
| 8 | Identifying shared tacit assumptions | Taking the artefacts and espoused values and pushing deeper, particularly where the practices contradict the conscious values (1–2 hours) |
| 9 | Identifying cultural aids and hindrances | Break into subgroups and refine understanding of steps 6–8; explore whether the culture aids or hinders the problem the organization is trying to address |
| 10 | Reporting assumptions and joint analysis | Aim for consensus on what is important and implications for what the organization wants to do; aim to get as clear a view as possible, then explore how to manage culture to achieve the organization's aims (half a day minimum) |

(Adapted from Schein, 2010: 340–48)
© Schein, *Organizational Culture and Leadership*, 2010, John Wiley & Sons Inc.

**Subculture** A localized culture with its own set of values and behaviours that reflects, but is distinct from, the wider culture.

# The manager changing culture: the role of founders and organizational leaders

**Running case:** cultural change report

**To:** s.chance@junctionhotel.net
**From:** m.wickham@changingculture.info.uk
**Subject:** Culture change at Junction Hotel—Report
*Junction Hotel Current Culture Report*

Dear Mr Chance

Many thanks for choosing *changingculture.info.uk*. We are delighted to attach your full report for Junction Hotel's corporate culture. We had a good response rate for the survey, with 73%

of staff taking part. The full report gives extensive detail about the culture, but the headline issues are:

- only 23% of staff could name Junction Hotel's mission statement and most of them were managers
- 37% of staff felt that they identified with the hotel
- 76% felt that they enjoyed being part of the hotel
- 27% felt that they were listened to.

Getting the right culture can mean long-term success for your firm, a more committed workforce, higher productivity, and increased job satisfaction. I suggest that we arrange a meeting next week to discuss what contribution *changingculture.info.uk* can offer Junction Hotel.

With very best wishes

*Mark Wickham PhD*

*changingculture.info.uk*—bringing cultural change to UK business, for profits and people

Chance looks at the email in shock—this was not the result he was expecting. He had always thought that people valued working at Junction Hotel and that they shared the same vision, but the survey results seem to be saying something altogether different. He calls in Linda Wilkinson for a chat, as she has the ear of the staff.

'What do you think of this? Shocking, isn't it—don't the staff care?' asks Chance. 'I think…,' stammers Wilkinson, 'that they value the organization, but not in the same way that you do'. 'Oh,' Chance responds somewhat indignantly, 'what do you mean?' Wilkinson looks up at him. 'Well, sometimes,' she responds hesitantly, 'we don't always include them in what we do.' 'So what are you saying?' Chance asks positively. 'That we need a strong shared culture?' Linda looks back somewhat quizzically, 'Yes, something like that,' she says.

Visit the Online Resource Centre to read the full report.

For many writers the most significant figures for establishing or changing the culture are the **founders** and leaders of the organization. As Edgar Schein has argued, 'organizations begin to create cultures through the actions of founders who operate as strong leaders' (2010: 242). The personality of the founder sets the environment for the first members of staff. 'Typically, the founders and his or her successor's leadership helps shape a culture of shared values and assumptions guided and restricted by the founders' personal beliefs' (Bass and Avolio, 1993: 114).

> **Founder** The person who established the organization.

As the firm grows, the founder's ability to directly influence the staff might diminish, but their influence is often sustained through stories and myths about their actions. These stories can provide the organization with a sense of history and purpose and a framework within which to operate (see the following sections for more discussion on the power of stories). Founders' stories provide powerful ways to communicate the values of the organization and give the company a sense of tradition and purpose.

## Real life case: founders' stories

For some firms the way in which they were founded has taken on almost mythical status. Bill Hewlett and Dave Packard, the founders of Hewlett Packard (HP), one of the world's biggest information technology firms, and also the founders of 'Silicon Valley', began their firm's life in a humble garage. ▶

> ▶ They were innovative in their products and management approach, creating a decentralized and egalitarian system, which has become known as 'the HP way' (Packard, 1995):
>
> 1. We have trust and respect for individuals.
>
> 2. We focus on a high level of achievement and contribution.
>
> 3. We conduct our business with uncompromising integrity.
>
> 4. We achieve our common objectives through teamwork.
>
> 5. We encourage flexibility and innovation.
>
> Both Hewlett and Packard were highly innovative, with a focus on profits but also on charitable activity (giving most of their fortunes away to charity). However, in more recent times, some have claimed that HP has lost its way (Burrows, 2003; and Malone, 2007). HP, they claim, has lost its focus on innovation, and workers are scolded for working late (Bandler and Burke, 2012). During his brief stint as CEO, Leo Apotheker argued that 'HP has lost its soul' (Yarrow, 2011).

# How leaders can change culture

**Running case:** Chance looks for solutions

'So what can we do about this?' enquires Chance of Wickham, the culture consultant. 'Our staff do not seem to share the same passion for Junction Hotel as I do. I thought it was obvious what we stand for,' Chance continues. 'We need a few quick hits,' Wickham suggests. 'You need to put across your vision for the hotel, show the staff what is important. You are the most important person in the organization. They will follow you.'

Although the organizational founder certainly has significant influence, as they leave or the organization grows, their influence diminishes and the organization's managers gain more influence. In Edgar Schein's (2010: 257) words, leaders 'create the conditions for culture formation'. Similarly, Bass and Avolio (1993: 113) claim 'The characteristics and qualities of an organization's culture are taught by its leadership and eventually adopted by its followers'. Indeed, as Selznick argues, leaders can be seen as the embodiment of organizational values (cited in Schein, 2010).

Schein argues that, given the influence of the leaders, they have to be consistent in their actions; otherwise their influence on their followers is diminished. He suggests that they have the following tools to change culture:

*Primary embedding mechanism*

- What leaders pay attention to, measure, and control on a regular basis
- How leaders react to critical incidents and organizational crises
- How leaders allocate resources
- Deliberate role modelling, teaching, and coaching
- How leaders allocate rewards and status
- How leaders recruit, select, promote, and excommunicate

*Secondary articulation and reinforcement mechanisms*

- Organizational design and structure
- Organizational systems and procedures
- Rites and rituals of the organization
- Design of physical space, facades, and buildings
- Stories about important events and people
- Formal statements of organizational philosophy, creeds, and charters

(Schein, 2010: 246)

Quinn (1984, see Cameron and Quinn, 2006) argues it is important that the leadership style matches the culture as represented in the competing values framework, as otherwise they will not be effective.

One of the most powerful ways that leaders can influence their culture is through symbolic acts and powerful stories. These stories have powerful effects in that they transmit the values that the leaders hold and communicate to members what they deem important. As Smircich and Morgan argue, 'Through words and images, symbolic actions and gestures, leaders can structure attention and evoke patterns of meaning that give them considerable control over the situation being managed' (1982: 263). 'The reason culture is important is because top management can directly influence culture through activities and symbols' (Daft, 1986: 486). In other words, leaders, through their actions, can shape the culture of the organization.

| Hierarchy | • Coordinator<br>• Organizer<br>• Administrator |
| Adhocracy | • Entrepreneur<br>• Innovator<br>• Risk-taker |
| Market | • Decisiveness<br>• Production<br>• Achievement |
| Clan | • Participative mentor<br>• Facilitator<br>• Parent-figure |

(based on Cameron and Quinn, 2006)

It is not just in the academic literature that these views are popular. Management consultant Dan Look argues that instilling a strong sense of culture is a key role for leadership. He claims that 'in the long term, culture is the only strategic differentiator'. Leaders are key to achieving this because 'culture is reinforced by everything a leader does' (cited in Roper, 2015a). Peter Cheese, the chief executive of the CIPD, agrees, stating: 'Where does culture start? At the top' (cited in Roper, 2015b). However, leaders are often not very good at managing culture: 'Managers often don't understand the culture because they are not very good at listening to employees' (Roper, 2015b). While these senior practitioners see the value of culture, they argue that many leaders are not sufficiently skilled at utilizing it.

**Real life case:** Lendlease—the importance of the founders' values

Founded in Australia in 1958, Lendlease is an international property and infrastructure group that specializes in world-leading developments, investment management, and construction project management. Its projects include everything from roads and bridges to state-of-the-art buildings and hospitals, including the iconic Sydney Opera House, the 2012 Olympic Games Athletes' Village in London, and the National September 11 Memorial and Museum in New York City. Like many ▶

▶ companies, it has core values including respect, collaboration, trust, and integrity (see *Lendlease: Our Values*, http://www.lendlease.com/worldwide/about-us/values).

These beliefs can be traced back to the company's Dutch-born founder Dick Dusseldorp, who recognized the responsibility his company had to society, arguing: 'Companies must start justifying their worth to society, with greater emphasis placed on environmental and social impact rather than straight economics.'

Alex Christie, Lendlease's head of human resources, said: 'It was this statement that embedded our governing principles and defined how we do business. For example, there are times when we have decided not to work on projects or with clients because they have not been aligned with our sustainability and ethical standards. We are also encouraging tenants at the International Quarter, our new commercial development on the Olympic Park, to embrace agile and flexible working, with new offices designed to improve productivity and wellbeing' (Christie, 2015).

The Lendlease Foundation was set up within the company by Dusseldorp in 1983 to specifically nurture and support the development and benefit of all employees—as well as a social responsibility to communities. The Lendlease Foundation continues to gain momentum to this day, with designated employee representatives in each region running new policies, programmes, and community initiatives across the globe.

The company runs a family intern programme, continues to increase the diversity of its employee base, and hosts a yearly personal development programme in Tasmania for employees from across its regions. More recently it introduced Wellbeing Leave, a policy which gives employees the opportunity to take time off work to focus on their own mental and physical health.

Lendlease's company website states 'Dick Dusseldorp dreamt of building an organisation that would be measured not just on its financial returns, but on its positive contribution to the environment and society... He also believed the wellbeing and best interests of his employees was paramount. More than 50 years later, this is where our focus remains' (see *Lendlease: Working at Lendlease*, http://www.lendlease.com/worldwide/careers/working-at-lend-lease).

The influence of the founder's key values, particularly the importance of stakeholders (rather than just shareholders), is key. Clark, who wrote *Finding a common interest* (Clark, 2002), a book about Dick Dusseldorp, argues that Lendlease's 'entire corporate culture—that has been embedded in the company from the start... begins with its founder Dick Dusseldorp' (2002: 9).

Christie added: 'There is a strong business case for us to take the health and wellbeing of our employees seriously. Recent initiatives such as Wellbeing Leave are good examples of Dick's philosophy. It is a proactive investment in the health and wellbeing of our employees, and acknowledges the importance of a balanced work–family life. A healthier, happier workforce is naturally a more productive and engaged one—and less likely to take regular sick leave' (Christie, 2015).

## Review questions

| | |
|---|---|
| **Describe** | How does Schein suggest that culture can be changed? |
| **Explain** | How do founders and leaders influence the culture of their organization? |
| **Analyse** | How significant do you feel a founder's story is for the shaping the culture in the long term? |

# Changing layout, changing cultures

**Running case:** a tour of Junction Hotel

Mandy Armfield leads Sue Marshall through a tour of Junction Hotel. 'This, obviously, is the front of house. You'll get a chance to meet the girls later—we're a friendly bunch.' Sue notices a computer, which must be for booking in, a board with every room number, and a list. 'Oh, that,' Mandy says, noticing Sue's attention on it, 'that's for the maintenance team'. 'It's all very organized in here,' Sue comments. 'Oh yes, we like to keep on top of things. In here, this is our office—we call it our cubby-hole. It's not much, but we like it.' Sue looks in amazement: a tiny room with no natural light, one desk with an old-looking computer, and a couple of mugs of tea. 'We come here for a gossip,' Mandy says with a wink.

Continuing on, Sue is shown some of the plush bedrooms, one with a four-poster bed, the dining room with staff busily preparing for the lunchtime meal, and the kitchen, which is incredibly organized with colour-coordinated chopping boards and lists of the week's meals. They then take a right turn through a door which says staff only and go up some stairs. The light flickers on the staircase, the carpet is threadbare, and paint is peeling off the walls. Seeing Sue's face Mandy moves to reassure her: 'Oh, this is just a short-cut to the meeting rooms. We don't let customers or the board come in this way.' 'What about us?' Sue wonders. They proceed through what Sue imagines is the staff room, which has a few old magazines in the corner next to the coffee machine. Back through another door, they return to the plush carpet and are faced with a large oak door with the label 'Simon Chance's Office' on it.

In the office, Sue Marshall looks around at the oak-panelled walls and the luxury deep-pile carpet. In the corner Jenny Hyam, Simon Chance's secretary, sits on a small swivel chair in front of a pine veneer desk—'IKEA,' thinks Sue as she assesses the scene. Rows of box files, all neatly ordered, are on shelves behind Jenny's desk, colour-coded and alphabetically arranged. Jenny has a picture of her holding a small child—her daughter, Sue assumes—in a pretty red dress. Jenny looks over at Sue. 'He won't be long now,' she says calmly. 'Mondays are always a busy day for Mr Chance.'

The oak panelling continues throughout the boardroom, which has a large mahogany table in the centre. Looking down on the room are ten austere-looking men captured in oil paintings with plaques beneath giving their names and dates. The door opens and Simon Chance pops his head round. 'You must be Sue,' he says shaking her hand firmly, 'pleased to meet you. I would love to stay and chat, but we are making a lot of changes at the moment and I am rather busy. Maybe we can catch up at the end of the month—I'd love to hear your views on the place.' And with that, the phone rings and he rushes back into his office.

One of the ways managers try to change the culture is to change the physical surroundings. As Turner and Myerson (1998: 1) state, 'workspaces themselves usually reflect the style and personality of the organization'. The design and layout reflect the culture that the organization wants to project to the outside world. They also reflect 'who and what is valued in the organization. For example, arranging offices by rank so that the highest-level executives occupy the top floor(s) and/or the largest and most nicely appointed office space (e.g., corner offices with large windows) and lower-level employees occupy successively lower floors and smaller offices, conveys the message that the organization places a high value on status' (Ornstein, 1989: 145). Overall, 'Office design might best be analyzed as symbols produced by organizational cultures' (Hatch, 1992: 143).

For instance, the change to open plan is argued by some to lead to greater bonding, teamwork, and communication (Ornstein, 1989). However, open plan offices can also lead many staff to feel resentment, as such offices produce increased noise and staff sometimes have concerns about loss of status and privacy (Tierney, 2012; and Frontczak et al., 2012).

Merchant banks present very different cultures. They often favour high-rise office blocks, which may be

Corporate status symbols.
**Source:** Shutterstock.

signs of status—for instance, the Burj Khalifa building is the tallest in the world. These images, it can be argued, express power and authority, with status linked to the highest offices. They present a highly formalized corporate culture stressing trustworthiness, wealth, and power.

# Mission statements

## Running case: changing the culture at Junction Hotel

It was Mark Wickham from changingculture.info.uk on the phone.

'Do your staff know your values?' asks Wickham inquisitively. 'No, not really,' reflects Chance. 'We have a mission statement, but never really communicate it.' 'Then I suggest that you teach your staff your mission statement,' Wickham replies. 'This is the best way to get across what your vision of Junction Hotel is. Without a clear vision, many firms fail.'

Thinking through this suggestion, Chance decides to make the mission statement the central focus of the Wednesday morning team meeting. He wants to make the hotel an upbeat, positive place where people feel good about coming to work and to provide a really high-quality service.

### Wednesday morning team meeting

The restaurant is packed, as every member of Junction Hotel had been called in to listen to what Chance has labelled 'mission day'.

'Junction Hotel is a great place to work. It is full of exceptional people with a passion for what they do,' Chance begins almost evangelically. 'We have a top-class chef, excellent front-of-house team, fantastic support staff, and quality cleaners. But we do not always work together and see the big picture. So, today I am unveiling our new mission—Gold Standard Service. This will make Junction Hotel stand out from the competition.' Standing in front of the flip chart, he unveils the mission statement and stands back to let the staff read it:

Junction Hotel aims to be the hotel of choice because we completely satisfy our guests.

Through a gold standard service we are committed to making your stay a pleasant experience by making a difference every day.

We aim to continually improve our service and go the extra mile for all our guests.

Covering the tables with big sheets of paper, Chance asks each department's team leader to facilitate a session to think about how they need to change how they work to meet the Gold Standard Service Mission. 'It is important,' Chance states, 'that everyone is on board with the mission and knows how they personally, and how Junction Hotel collectively, can meet it. These documents will be fed back to the group via the new monthly newsletter—Junction News.'

Chance ends the team meeting with everyone repeating the mission statement. He says that it will be put up on notice boards, and at the start of the next meeting he will pick one member of staff at random to repeat back the mission in front of everyone.

Josh

Just sat through a ridiculous meeting where Chance made us repeat our mission statement over and over again. I felt like we were braying donkeys.

2 seconds ago via Android Like Comment

Do you know the mission statement of your university or the place that you work? Have you ever been told it? How did you react to it?

Mission statements are often presented as one of the key tools for senior managers to change the 'espoused beliefs' of organizational members (level 2 on Schein's iceberg). They became popular during the latter half of the 1980s and are now an almost obligatory feature of most organizations.

Mission statements offer senior management an opportunity to define explicitly the purpose of the organization (Drucker, 1974) and create a vision that all stakeholders (shareholders, employees, customers, and the general public) can buy into. This vision should be uplifting and thus, it is claimed, provide an opportunity for the organization to improve its public image and increase the commitment of the employees, and for senior management to assert their authority over the organization. Finally, a mission statement provides a common language for the organization.

## Real life case: mission statements

Google's mission is 'to organize the world's information and make it universally accessible and useful' (Google, 2012).

Kronenbourg's is 'Building our business on an economic model that respects People and Nature, taking a long-term outlook' (Kronenbourg, 2013).

Starbucks' mission statement is 'to inspire and nurture the human spirit—one person, one cup, and one neighbourhood at a time' (Starbucks, 2012).

The Trades Union Congress (TUC)'s mission statement is to 'be a high-profile organisation which campaigns successfully for trade union aims and values, assists trade unions to increase membership and effectiveness, cuts out wasteful rivalry and promotes trade union solidarity' (TUC, 2008).

The Adidas group 'strives to be the global leader in the sporting goods industry with brands built on a passion for sports and a sporting lifestyle' (Adidas, 2010).

One of the important outcomes of developing mission statements is for the senior management to discuss and agree the core organizational objectives. This process forces them to step back from everyday activity and define the organization's purpose. At times, this involves settling differences between competing visions of the organization that the senior managers hold and debating the future direction of the organization. Mission statements often state not only business objectives (such as being number one in the field) but also the ethical stance of the organization including its contribution to society. As a consequence, mission statements are generally written in uplifting language aiming to inspire employees and customers.

While mission statements have been highly popular with senior management, they are not always accepted by employees. Sometimes many of the employees simply pay lip service to them or do not treat them seriously (Bart, 1997). While the following mission statements might sound inspiring, when we investigate what happens to the companies, they can sound rather hollow:

*Respect, Integrity, Communication and Excellence* (Enron—who went bankrupt after committing planned accounting fraud) (Seeger and Ulmer, 2003).

*Our mission is to build unrivalled partnerships with and value for our clients, through the knowledge, creativity, and dedication of our people, leading to superior results for our shareholders* (Lehman Brothers—who went bankrupt in 2008, sparking the worldwide financial crisis) (cited in Schmidt and Rosenberg, 2015: 31).

True mission statements, therefore, are not what is written down but what people actually do. As Tony Hsieh, CEO of the successful Zappos, says, 'Values are not what we put on paper; they're what people do and how they feel doing it' (cited in Michelli, 2012: 16).

## Review questions

| | |
|---|---|
| **Describe** | What are some of the key ways in which managers can try to control culture? |
| **Explain** | Why have mission statements become popular? |
| **Apply** | Look up a few mission statements on the Internet and explore what the most common themes are. Would these mission statements inspire you? |

# Rites, rituals, and ceremonies

## Running case: Chance welcomes the new recruit

Ending the meeting, Simon Chance looks across at Sue Marshall. 'Thank you everyone. As some of you will be aware, we have a new member of the Junction Hotel family with us today. I am sure you will join me in our customary greeting,' at which point they burst out clapping. 'We also can congratulate Sam, who has been here 25 years as one of our receptionists.' 'You get less for murder!' Effingham shouts out to some laughter. 'It is my pleasure,' continues Chance undeterred, 'to offer her our Junction Hotel commemorative plaque and a special meal for two at our expense.' Again, everyone claps.

Deeper aspects of the culture are expressed through rites, rituals, and ceremonies. These are formal events, such as the graduation ceremony to mark completion of your degree, or informal activities, such as initiation ceremonies that members of a team do to each other. Rites, rituals, and ceremonies all play an important role in creating and reinforcing an organization's culture.

A **rite**, according to Trice and Beyer, is a 'Relatively elaborate, dramatic, planned set of activities that consolidate various forms of cultural expressions into one event, which is carried out through social interactions, usually for the benefit of an audience' (1984: 655). In other words, rites are events which express important parts of the culture.

Trice and Beyer describe a number of rites which include *rites of passage*, which occur when someone passes from one life stage to another. For instance, they describe how new army recruits 'receive uniforms and severe haircuts, are taught to make their beds in a ritualized fashion, learn to salute and march, are repeatedly humiliated and told to behave differently than in the past, and are generally stripped of past identities and statuses' (1984: 658).

Another is the *rites of renewal*, which act to reinforce existing social order. For instance, a team-building day helps team members refocus and *renew* their commitment to each other.

The *rite of conflict reduction* exists to preserve harmony where there is potential conflict. For instance, union and management negotiate for a pay deal where, publicly, each side has tough negotiating stances but, privately, both sides know what the outcome will be. In this situation both 'sets of bargainers may know pretty well throughout the negotiations what the final settlement will be' (Trice and Beyer, 1984: 661–2), but they put on an act for their supporters to show that they are tough negotiators.

Our final example is *rites of integration*. These occur to make everyone feel part of the group. An example is the office Christmas party, where everyone eats and drinks together symbolizing togetherness and organizational members make a special effort to talk to people they normally avoid—and 'Otherwise deviant behaviors, such as the acting out of sexual and other attractions, are sanctioned. Such occasions thus provide a break from the strict codes of behavior normally enforced, and they tend to reassert the importance and rightness of these codes by the clearly temporary and exceptional basis on which the usual prohibitions have been lifted' (Trice and Beyer, 1984: 663). However, as Bell and King (2010) point out, some of these rites of integration can equally exclude certain individuals and groups, reinforcing existing power relations and masculine values. **Ceremonies** are a formal and symbolic way of celebrating the organizational key values and provide senior management with the opportunity to publicly support actions they think are positive.

Universities have many formal ceremonies, such as graduation, when students have finished their degree, inaugural lectures for a new professor, and annual dinners at academic conferences at which people give speeches. In companies, ceremonies are often held as retirement dinners, formal celebrations of promotion, and people winning employee of the month awards.

Unlike planned events, such as ceremonies, **rituals** are more like habits that most members do without thinking. As Ott states, rituals 'are the mundane, systematic, stylized, programmed routines of daily organizational life that tell an alert observer about an organizational culture' (1989: 36).

While they often start for particular purposes, '[f]requently, the meanings and purposes of powerful rites and rituals are forgotten and take on lives of their own' (Ott, 1989: 37) and

**Rite** A solemn act or procedure to observe an event or occasion.

**Ceremonies** A public act, often planned and formal, which celebrates a particular event, achievement, or anniversary, largely planned by senior management or part of the organization's established calendar. They often have symbolic meaning that emphasizes important aspects of the organization's culture.

**Rituals** Everyday habits that individuals do without thinking which once had meaning but have gradually become part of the everyday activities of the organization.

become solely of symbolic importance. They are ways for management to be socialized (i.e. taught to see the world), for employees to know how to behave, and for what is seen as important.

---

### Real life case: culture in the banking industry

Paul Moore, former head of group regulatory risk at HBOS, said that prior to the credit crunch of 2008 there was a huge focus on targets and a culture of fear if you did not hit them. There was an allegation that one manager created a cash or cabbage competition. If you hit your targets you would get cash put on your desk on a Saturday morning; if you missed them then he would put a cabbage on it—cash or cabbage, in public, every Saturday.

**Sources:** BBC (2009); Heffernan (2011); Goodley (2012).

The taste of failure?

---

How do you think you would feel if you received cash or a cabbage on your desk?

### Review questions

| | |
|---|---|
| **Describe** | What are rites and rituals? |
| **Explain** | How do rites and rituals contribute to an organization's culture? |
| **Analyse** | What does the cabbage symbolize to the bank traders in the real life case above? How might such practices, and the culture they supported, have contributed to the financial crash? |

---

Informal or unofficial culture  Culture that is often not known or supported by management but one that many of the employees share. It can be in opposition to official, management-led culture.

**Informal** or **unofficial** ceremonies, rites, and rituals are done largely between employees and are often tolerated, sometimes condemned, and regularly unknown to management. A regular informal rite of passage is the initiation ceremony that new recruits are expected to undergo to join an organization. They sometimes involve fairly extreme activities, such as drinking a lot of alcohol or doing something humiliating in front of the rest of the group. These initiation ceremonies are displays of strength and endurance, but can also be practices to humiliate the new recruit and, through this, stress the importance of belonging to the group. They often can be used as ways that workers can express their own culture in opposition to management. For instance, some of our students have told us that members of the university rugby team all go out in their 'speedos' on nights out.

**Real life case:** student initiation ceremonies

Over recent years a number of scandals about unofficial UK university student initiation ceremonies have hit the headlines. Stories have come out of students having to drink 30 units of alcohol within 3 hours as part of a university rugby team initiation; those joining the Ferretz, an inter-collegiate (Cambridge) drinking society, have to consume 80 units, beginning with a bottle of gin and finishing with a bottle of port, consumed through a condom; having to eat a 15-course meal with delicacies such as a pig's snout with wasabi sauce and a pint of water with a goldfish swimming inside; and playing vomiting games while saluting an older student dressed in what looks like a Nazi uniform.

As one former student, Natalie Sutton, recalls of her initiation: 'We were told to prepare "bucket juice"—an intoxicating mixture of beer, spirits, alcopops, and wine. We were given OXO cubes to suck as we were paraded, singing and chanting, around the neighbourhood' (BBC News, 2008). Elsewhere another student states that they had to 'eat their own vomit' (*Courier Online*, 2011).

Sporting clubs and societies often have quite challenging initiation ceremonies. For instance, the University of York hockey club initiation ceremony was reported to include having to 'down drinks mixed with dog food and goldfish' (York Vision, 2010). Northumbria University rugby union members have reported being 'systematically humiliated' in a 'team-building exercise'. They claim they had to 'drop their trousers and do press-ups' while 'a crowd of people watched from the Students' Union' (*Courier Online*, 2011). The University of Gloucestershire's hockey team members had 'raw fish... stuffed down our bras and we were told to eat a nausea-inducing mixture of cat food, eggs, and breakfast cereal topped with Bovril' (BBC News, 2008). What many participants describe as most troubling is that while they did not enjoy the process, they completed it without question.

Have you been involved in an initiation ceremony? If so, did you feel you had to take part? Did you feel more part of the group afterwards?

While writing this chapter, we have been told stories where a new recruit in a food processing factory was told to go to the chiller to look for a 'black pudding' and then received a 'good kicking' from Harry, a well-built member of the production team. A student told us about working in a kitchen and how each new waiter would 'get showered' (having a bucket of water poured over their head) by the head waiter. A former nuclear power worker at Sellafield has told us how new recruits used to have their clothes taken away when they went through the showers for the first time and had to walk home in their new uniform.

**Research insight:** Life in a slaughterhouse
Ackroyd, S., and Crowdy, P. 1990. Can culture be managed? Working with raw material: The case of the English slaughtermen. *Personnel Review* 19(5): 3–13.

In a fascinating, and at times graphic, account, Ackroyd and Crowdy (1990) describe the culture of an abattoir. They found the slaughtermen regularly performed practical jokes on each other, such as filling the boots of someone they considered to be working too hard with blood, at room temperature, so the worker did not notice until they had walked in them all day.

> ▶ The slaughtermen also sprayed blood on their clothes and refused to use the showers. This was in direct defiance of the instructions of management, who stressed the importance of health, safety, and good hygiene. As Ackroyd and Crowdy demonstrate, this was to create a subculture—or what we might see as a counter-culture (a culture in direct opposition to the management)—born out of a strong sense of togetherness and common identity as slaughtermen.
>
> Their case demonstrates the challenges of management in changing culture, a theme we will return to in the following section.

# Informal culture

## Only joking: the power of stories and jokes

**Running case:** Sue is warned about Effingham

The meeting ends and Sue goes for coffee with the other receptionist. 'Who was the guy who made the joke about getting longer for working here than murder?' she enquires. 'Oh, that will be Effingham,' pipes up Mandy. 'Watch out for him. I don't know if this is true, but he once killed a chicken with his bare hands.' 'Really?' Sue replies in a shocked tone. 'No, not really … but I wouldn't put it past him,' Mandy says with a smirk.

What hidden messages are in this story?

Have you ever heard someone say 'it's only a joke' when they have just said something that could be seen as an attack on someone else? While what they said before might have been interpreted as a 'dig' or even an attack on someone, claiming it to be 'just a joke' allows the speaker to pass off the seriousness of the comment or responsibility for the comment by saying that it was not meant in a negative way. Jokes, as with stories, can thus allow us to say many 'truths' that we would not be able to get away with directly (Martin, 2001: 92).

Hidden in jokes and stories are messages about how to behave and the values of the organization. Managers and leaders sometimes use them to put across explicit messages about how the company wants to be seen. These are often presented as organizational histories on company websites or stories that an organization's leaders tell about themselves.

More commonly, colleagues tell each other and new recruits stories. They can be seen as informal or non-official messages communicating the values of the workforce (which can be different to those of management).

Stories communicate many things. For instance, they can be about people that have done well—organizational heroes—demonstrating values that the employee should follow. They can also be about villains or scapegoats, which act as warnings to the employee about what is considered bad behaviour. Stories also communicate how the organization sees itself, such as being cautious or brave, steady or dynamic. They are also based on certain metaphors, such as the organization as a family, school, or prison (Morgan, 2006), that can express the deep assumptions of the organization (see Chapter 11 for other uses of metaphors). Again, these metaphors will not necessarily be explicit, but they can be powerful ways of capturing some of the underlying assumptions of the members of the organization. They are particularly useful for new members to learn the informal rules and expectations of an organization.

## Real life case: stories told by organizational leaders

One of the powerful ways in which stories are used involve an organization's leader. Often, these stories not only send messages about the character of the leader, but also emphasize particular values or behaviours that are valued within the organization. Sometimes these stories are told informally to new recruits within the first few weeks of joining the organization. On other occasions they are created by the leader specifically to send a message and told at set-piece events (e.g. in speeches), in company literature, or by the leader themselves in conversations. Here are two examples expressing quite different messages.

'A common story at Southwest Airlines describes the CEO working on the baggage line on holidays so that employees can take the day off, illustrating the value that customers are number two and employees are number one at Southwest and "positively outrageous service" applies first to fellow employees' (Cameron and Quinn, 2006: 97).

'At the Revlon Corporation the story is told about Charles Revlon, the head of the group, who insisted that employees arrived for work on time, but seldom arrived himself much before noon. One day Charles wandered in and began to look over the sign-in sheet, only to be interrupted by a receptionist who had strict orders that the list should not be removed. Both insisted that they were in the right until, finally, Charles said "Do you know who I am?" and she said, "No sir, I don't". "Well, when you pick up your final paycheck this afternoon, ask 'em to tell ya"... The message here is that rules should be strictly obeyed by most people, but do not apply to those of high status, and should not be enforced where they are concerned' (Brown, 1992: 5).

What messages do you feel are contained in these stories? If you heard them, how would you act if you worked for one of these organizations?

Jokes, like stories, are a powerful way to communicate culture. They are said to produce a positive, harmonious environment in which employees can freely share knowledge and ideas (Wilson, 1979). They can be used to teach employees the right way to behave, e.g. through subtle teasing to indicate when someone acts in the wrong way.

For example, in describing her experience working as a stockbroker, Venetia Thompson states 'Being given a nickname was a rite of passage; whether racist, sexist, homophobic or just insulting, nicknames were willingly accepted by the recipients and thrown around with little thought as to what was actually being said, or whether it was in violation of some code of conduct in the Company handbook' (2010: 51).

Jokes are, therefore, like stories but with the added advantage that they allow us to say things that we would not otherwise be allowed to, acting as a 'licence' for negative communication (Collinson, 1988). Consequently, through jokes certain home truths can be told or, for staff resistant to management, can weaken management's authority (Taylor and Bain, 2003).

**Research insight:** The impact of humour in the workplace
Collinson, D. 1988. Engineering humour: Masculinity, joking and
conflict in shop-floor relations. *Organization Studies* 9(2): 181–99.
Collinson, D. 2002. Managing humour. *Journal of Management Studies*
39(3): 269–88.

David Collinson has written widely on the role of humour in the workplace. In these two influential articles he shows how humour is connected to identity, power, control, and resistance. He describes how workers used humour to control each other, reinforcing particular masculine values and attitudes which virtually everyone went along with—even when they did not believe in those values. It was also used as a way of resisting management, for instance by satirizing authority. Collinson shows how difficult it is for management to break into, and change, these strong cultures.

# Breaking taboos—the hidden rules of culture

**Running case:** Sue breaks a cultural taboo

'Do you remember the time he chopped off all those rabbit's heads and put them on the top table?' recounts Mandy. 'Yep, and when he pulled the guts out of that duck and threw them across the room when Chance walked in,' recalls Sam. 'He's a player, isn't he,' Mandy declares. 'He seems that way with the waitresses as well,' Sue pipes up, trying to join in. 'I saw the way he looked at that blonde.' Suddenly, the room goes quiet and Sue goes red, knowing that she has said something wrong. Mandy quickly changes the subject.

'What did I say wrong?' Sue asks Mandy when everyone leaves. 'Oh, it's nothing, dear,' Mandy answers, clearly uncomfortable. 'Just be careful ... the "blonde" is Simon Chance's daughter.'

While stories and jokes can give access to the hidden culture, it is only by actually breaking the rules that employees often discover deeper rules. These rules are not actually written down and, indeed, many of the organizational members are not aware that they exist.

Harold Garfinkel has built much of his research on uncovering these rules. In what Garfinkel called 'breaching experiments' he looked at wider cultural rules (throughout society). He asked research participants to breach (step over or break) certain social norms and disrupt shared realities (i.e. the common ways that people think). This is one of Garfinkel's examples:

The victim waved his hand cheerily.
(S) How are you?
(E) How am I in regard to what? My health, my finances, my school work, my peace of mind, my . . . ?
(S) (Red in the face and suddenly out of control.) Look! I was just trying to be polite. Frankly, I don't give a damn how you are.

(Garfinkel, 1967: 42–4, cited in Feldman, 1995: 10)

Garfinkel's work demonstrates that there are numerous social norms that we often only learn by breaking them. They are important for understanding culture because they reveal the hidden, unspoken side of organizational life and the deep values that are unexpressed.

Culture is thus created continually and recreated through conversations, actions, and meanings expressed by all organizational members.

## Review questions

| | |
|---|---|
| **Describe** | What are the underlying values within an organizational culture? |
| **Explain** | How can underlying values be uncovered? |
| **Explain** | What role does humour play in organizational culture? |
| **Analyse** | Why are the underlying values within an organization hard to change? |

# The symbolic side of culture

**Running case:** Gold Standard Service

### Two weeks later.

'Eighty percent of your staff now knows your mission statement,' declares Wickham proudly, 'and the Gold Standard Service is ready to be rolled out. How do you feel it is going?' 'Good, I think we've cracked it,' Chance replies.

Most management interventions to change corporate culture focus on the physical surroundings, the espoused (spoken) organizational aims, and stories about the organization's history and actions of the leaders; they rarely go to the deeper parts of the organizational culture (the depths of Edgar Schein's iceberg). Mary Jo Hatch (1993) argues that while Schein's model is relevant and useful as it provides a guide for understanding culture, it would be more useful if it also focused on symbols and symbolic behaviour. While Schein (and other cultural typologies) describe culture based on observations of artefacts, beliefs and values, and basic assumptions, Hatch claims her model gives a more sophisticated understanding by presenting the dynamism of organizational culture, linking the values, artefacts, symbols, and assumptions more explicitly together (see Figure 7.2 and Table 7.7). The Hatch cultural dynamics framework demonstrates how cultural assumptions 'reveal themselves in the perceptions, cognitions, and emotions of organizational members' (Hatch, 1993: 662). Culture, in this sense, is continually constructed and reconstructed, where meaning is created and recreated.

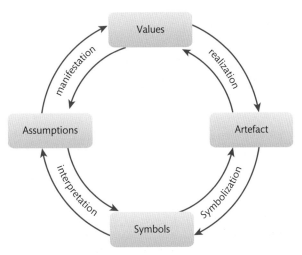

**Figure 7.2** The cultural dynamics model (Hatch, 1993).
**Source:** Hatch, 2013. Reproduced with permission of The Academy of Management.

**Table 7.7** The cultural dynamics model

| Feature | Description | Example | How to study it |
|---------|-------------|---------|-----------------|
| Manifestations | The process through which people become aware of their values without necessarily being aware of the underlying assumptions. | Assumption is people are hard working. This manifests itself in empowering practices that make members feel positive about the organization (values) | Explore how expectations 'come to be' within the organization. What emotions and perceptions are encouraged or constrained |
| Realization | The process of translating values into artefacts (rites, rituals, stories and humour) | Prize giving events (artefact) for best employees to celebrate hard work (values) | Observation—to see how artefacts are used in everyday practice and how values change |
| Symbols | Some artefacts are symbols because they come to mean something extra to organizational members. They represent consciously or unconsciously a more abstract meaning. i.e. a bunch of flowers symbolizing love | Receiving a certificate for the employee of the month (artefact) is seen as a sign of promotion potential (symbolic) as extra meaning is placed on the certificate | Observation—a researcher immersing themselves in the field to see how these artefacts are interpreted by the members |
| Interpretation | How organizational members use their assumptions to experience and give meaning to the symbols | The interpretation, thinking and feelings, that an organizational member goes through when receiving the employee of the month | How symbols are moulded by organizational members. Through observation, interviews and analysing the words people use (discourse analysis) |

**Research insight:** Rites, rituals, and ceremonies in practice
Rosen, M. 1985. Breakfast at Spiro's, dramaturgy and dominance. *Journal of Management* 11: 31–48.

In this influential article Michael Rosen (1985) provides an excellent account of how these rites of passage, rituals, and ceremonies are played out in practice. He provides a detailed description of the annual 'agency breakfast' for an advertising agency, Spiro's. It is held in a luxury hotel; all the 'associates' are formally dressed, eating off fine china, being served eggs Benedict by suited waiters—demonstrating an elite image. They listen to speeches which celebrate successes and explain away failure, and celebrate the awards they have won.

Rosen sees this breakfast not simply as an annual gathering, but as an opportunity for management to present certain messages and use symbols to put across key messages. These include being an elite (eating fine breakfasts at a quality hotel—the 'good life' that members aspire to); presenting members with a gift each time they reach five years' working for the company, symbolizing the importance of loyalty; and explicitly stating their values: 'laid-back people have no place in this agency. … Drive is what it takes to win. Get drive or get out of the kitchen. … I want people who want to win' (1985: 45). Rosen's case demonstrates the importance of being able to read these cultural clues.

To access the deeper parts of the culture requires reaching into areas outside the awareness of most organizational participants (including managers). This involves getting in touch with the symbolic side of organizations—the language, metaphors, and stories. However, culture is also changing constantly and is as much a product of the observer's perception as it is within the organization.

The deepest layer of the culture could be seen as the organization's subconscious. It shapes how organizational members experience the world, but they are not always aware of its existence. In order to get to this level of culture, techniques used in psychology and the therapeutic arts are used.

# Subcultures and professional cultures

As organizations grow, they develop their own subcultures. Subcultures are small groups within the organization that have their own distinctive cultural characteristics, including their own rites and rituals, language, norms, etc. They can develop informally (social networks) and formally (e.g. departments). In large multinational corporations they will be based on national differences (see Chapter 15) or different internal histories. Similarly, in chain stores different branches can develop their own distinct cultures based around regional cultures, branch histories, local practices, or the influence of a strong leader. Different departments can have distinct cultures, often produced because of the professions they represent (e.g. accounting might be more cautious than, say, marketing), as well as developing internal histories and cultures.

---

**Real life case:** organizational culture at Royal Bank of Scotland

Over the years prior to its near-collapse in 2008, the Royal Bank of Scotland (RBS) grew considerably through buying up other banks and financial institutions, not only in the UK but internationally. The group spanned different business lines (high street and investment banking), as well as different continents (such as Europe, North America, and Asia). They also represented different companies with their own backgrounds and histories.

In an exclusive interview for this book, RBS's then CEO Stephen Hester state 'the types of people we have serving customers in our branches in the UK might be completely different from traders sitting in a trading desk in Tokyo owing to the location, culture, and type of activity'. But, he concluded: 'I do not think it is desirable or possible to have a single culture across such a diverse set of inputs. So in the end what you really find is the majority of the culture is specific to the business unit and the geography and its history. Then you have some things that cross businesses and geographies that would be more shared by the senior management team.'

**Source:** Author interview with Stephen Hester, Royal Bank of Scotland, February 2012.

---

Visit the Online Resource Centre to read the full interview with Stephen Hester.

A key reason for subcultures developing is that employees are members of different occupations with their own values and outlooks. As Raelin has argued, many professionals are more loyal towards their profession than to the organization they are working for (Raelin, 1986). This can result in a professional being in conflict with the management as their professional objectives might conflict with the specific requirements of the firm. For instance, engineers might be interested in the advancing science, creating an elegant design, or their own pet project, rather than profit for the company. Similarly, in areas such as the National Health Service, doctors' aims are often reported to be in conflict with a management obsessed with targets (see Robinson, 2012). Indeed, management themselves can be considered a subculture with their own language and culture.

The professional or occupational culture is a product of many factors, including the skill, authority, work control, status, and 'education backgrounds, socialization, values, vocational interests, work habits and outlooks' that the employees hold (Raelin, 1986: xiv). The education and professional training that is undergone in order to be equipped to do a job instil certain norms and values that the professional is expected to follow. Newcomers are then informally socialized into the group through meeting with fellow professionals at conferences and networking events, through training, reading trade publications, and the collective identity that the members of these professions share.

Different subcultures can be a challenge for those managing organizations, as they have to work with a range of professionals with their distinct values and ways of looking at the world. In order to be successful the manager needs to understand these different perspectives and find ways to communicate with various subcultures.

# Can culture really be managed?

Throughout this chapter we have seen attempts by organizational managers and consultants to categorize, understand, and change culture in order to increase the performance of the organization. They have argued that a strong, i.e. unified, culture performs better, gives the employees a sense of purpose, and increases job satisfaction. However, this view has been heavily criticized.

A mere two years after Peters and Waterman (1982) published their book *In search of excellence*, which launched much business interest in culture, the magazine *Business Week* (1984) printed an article arguing that a third of all Peters and Waterman's 'excellent' companies were performing poorly. Similarly, many (e.g. Willmott, 1993) have criticized Peters and Waterman's work, arguing that it lacks conceptual development and did not really investigate the values and beliefs of the staff; rather, the authors took the management rhetoric as true and failed to investigate how it was interpreted by the staff.

Indeed, further questions have been raised recently about the research that underpinned *In search of excellence*. In an article for *Fast Company*, Tom Peters states they 'faked the data'. This is not to say they made it all up, but rather than developing a 'scientific' approach, it was developed by gut instinct (Peters, 2001).

Many academics (e.g. Meek, 1988) have argued that the way many of these management gurus have used the idea of culture trivializes it by exploring only the aspects that managers can control. They argue that organizational culture is far more complex and richer than simply a tool for management and as a result, the research reduces our understanding of organizations.

Led by Linda Smircich, these academics state that the underlying assumption of these mainstream management views is that culture is something the organization *has*, i.e. a possession (1983) that can be changed and controlled. This is from the structural-functionist perspective that aims for unity and consensus (see the Online Resource Centre). Culture is something owned and designed by the top management and available for manipulation (Meek, 1988: 455).

Furthermore, Lynn Meek (1988) has argued that this perspective, while borrowing the language of anthropology, has not used this theory appropriately, has drawn from a very limited range of the literature, and has mutated the theory by over-emphasizing the aspects of unity and control.

The alternative view is that culture is something the organization *is* (Smircich, 1983). This view does not see organizational culture as something separate from the organization available for one group (management) to control, but as part of the organization. Culture is thus a root metaphor, a way of looking at the world—everything can be seen as culture. For those of the *is* perspective, culture is not owned by the management: everyone is involved in creating it and no group has power to define it. Rather, it emerges over time and through negotiation (Table 7.8).

The problem of seeing culture as something the organization *has* is emphasized in an account by the academics and business consultants Deal and Kennedy (1984) (who developed the model we saw earlier in the chapter). They describe how after giving a presentation to the board about culture, the chairman claimed it to be the finest presentation he had heard in ten years and then turned to his Chief Executive Officer: '"George," he said forcefully, "I want a culture installed here next Monday". "With all due respect," we interrupted, "we believe you have a culture here now; that's one of our key points." "Bulls**t!" said the chairman. "We don't have one, and as you pointed out, that's the problem. George, I want a culture here and I want it now—by next week. Your butt is on the line." We left' (1984: 21).

**Table 7.8**  Culture as something the organization has or is? (Developed from Smircich, 1983)

| Organizational culture is something the organization … | … has | … is |
|---|---|---|
| Culture is | a property of management | a social process |
| Sees culture as | a controllable independent variable | everything that the organization is |
| Produced by | the leader | negotiation of the group |
| Culture produces | harmony and consensus | conflict |
| Researchers look for | a single organizational culture | multiple and contested realities |
| Culture is useful as | a management tool | a way of making sense of reality |
| Cultural change is produced | by the management | through interaction and shared meaning |

This story illustrates the difficulty of the managerialist perspective. The senior managers thought that culture is something they could simply 'have' and that could be ordered in by the following week, like buying a machine. They failed to see that they already had a culture and, furthermore, that it is not something that management can simply control, but is integral to the fabric of the organization.

# Control and resistance

**Running case:** is it really Gold Standard?

'Well, that was a waste of time,' Josh states to Toby on their way out of another Wednesday morning meeting. 'I mean they keep going on about this Gold Standard Service, but I don't see anything different.' 'More than that,' says Toby in agreement, 'they keep cutting back on the things that would make a difference to us, like giving more time before serving to get everything ready rather than quizzing us on the mission statement'. Josh smiles at him. 'Well, I pretty much ignore the whole thing anyway. It's just a fad. It will be a new thing in a couple of weeks—mark my words.'

Hugh Willmott argues that organizational culture is a form of control. By getting employees to believe in the values of the organization and winning their 'hearts and minds', corporate culture, he argues, is 'governance of the employee's soul' (Willmott, 1993: 517) and a way of the employees disciplining themselves. According to Willmott, because they believe in the organization's mission, employees lose their critical faculties and will accept things that are not in their best interests. Willmott argues that corporate culture is therefore a way for management to extend their control. Instead of controlling employees' bodies (as in Taylorism—see Chapter 3), corporate culture controls people's hearts, minds, and souls.

Therefore, while organizational culture is presented by its supporters as progressive and more humane (as previously discussed), from this critical perspective it is controlling. The unified culture, presented by those such as Peters and Waterman, 'systematically suppresses ideas and practices that might problematize the authority of core corporate values' (Willmott, 1993: 531). Willmott goes on and compares the practices of these strong cultures to totalitarian regimes where alternative perspectives are not tolerated. 'Those who kick against the monoculture [single standardized culture] are "moved sideways" or they are expelled.' As Peters and Waterman put it bluntly: 'The excellent companies are marked by very strong cultures, so strong that you either buy into their norms or get out. There's no halfway house for most people in the excellent companies' (1982: 77).

However, other critical researchers have stressed the ways that employees can resist the overtures of the management and how many do not believe in it. For instance, David Collinson (1992) presents a case study of an engineering firm in the north of England, which was originally a family-run business. The American-run company that has taken over the firm wants to bring about a culture change, from a grimy, complacent, and oppositional culture to one which is more dynamic and based on greater trust and harmony between workers and management. As part of this, they paint the factory walls in a bright white and institute a newsletter. The first newsletter has the headline 'Call Me Barney'—a reference to the new boss's attempt to engender an informal, first-name culture. However, following its publication, a doctored version of the newsletter appeared on the union notice board with the headline 'Bulls**t from Barney' (Collinson, 1992: 13).

Other commentators have also questioned the extent to which employees internalize the culture. They argue that many employees pay lip service to the cultural change programmes but sometimes actively, and often passively, resist the official organizational culture. In other words, they question if employees really believe in these cultural programmes. Professionals, in particular, often believe they have a calling and are thus less likely to tolerate management constraints.

## Review questions

| | |
|---|---|
| **Describe** | What is a subculture? |
| **Explain** | What is the difference between seeing culture as something the organization is and seeing culture as something it has? |
| **Analyse** | Consider the view that culture is something the organization *is*. How does this view challenge mainstream management thinking? |
| **Apply** | What do cases like 'Call me Barney' tell us about how employees can resist cultural control? |

# Chapter summary

Organizational culture is presented by many consultants and management academics as a tool that can be used to increase a sense of belonging and commitment to the organization. Its supporters present it as an alternative approach to managing organizations because it moves beyond simply controlling people by telling them what to do, and engages their hearts and minds. Organizational founders, leaders, and managers are seen as central in defining and communicating these values and shaping the way that employees feel and think about the organization. This perspective also stresses the importance of organizational culture as a way of binding together all the members of the organization for a common purpose. Culture is thus something the organization *has* and it *can be managed*.

The opposite perspective argues that culture is something beyond any one individual and is more a product of the group. This perspective emphasizes the collective, shared, and negotiated way in which culture develops. Culture, instead of being something fixed and controlled by managers, is constantly in flux and is interpreted by individual members of the organization. Culture is thus something the organization *is* and *cannot be managed*.

Finally, critical researchers have questioned the social consequences of cultural change programmes on the well-being of employees. Some see culture as something that controls and conditions employees to the extent that any who resist are excluded. Others have sought to emphasize the way that employees can resist these cultural programmes.

Whichever perspective you take, it is widely accepted that culture shapes much of what we say and do, often in ways that we are not conscious of. What an examination of organizational culture does demonstrate is that there is much more going on in organizations than we often see on the surface.

## Further reading

**Schein, E. 2010. *Organizational culture and leadership.* Jossey Bass: San Francisco.**
Popular management writer and consultant, Schein provides a good overview of organizational culture from a management viewpoint. He offers ways to understand culture and practical tools to change it.

**Peters, T.J., and Waterman, R.H., Jr. 1982. *In search of excellence: Lessons from America's best run companies.* Harper Row: London.**
An early, influential book in management circles on the role of culture. Needs to be read with a degree of scepticism given that it has been subject to substantial criticism for both its methodology and its findings.

**Smircich, L. 1983. Concepts of culture and organizational analysis. *Administrative Science Quarterly* 28(3): 339–58.**
This highly influential article provides a rigorous critique of the underlying assumptions of the notion that culture is something that managers can control. Smircich introduces notions from anthropology to offer a richer way of understanding culture.

**Willmott, H. 1993. Strength is ignorance; slavery is freedom: Managing culture in modern organizations. *Journal of Management Studies* 30(4): 515–52.**
Provides a fascinating critical reading of the corporate culture literature. Willmott argues there is a dark side of organizational culture, as it results in employees disciplining themselves.

## References

Ackroyd, S., and Crowdy, P. 1990. Can culture be managed? Working with raw material: The case of the English slaughtermen. *Personnel Review* 19(5): 3–13.

Adidas 2010. Corporate mission statement. Available at: http://adidas-group.corporate-publications. com/2010/gb/en/group-management-report-our-group/corporate-mission-statement.html(last accessed 24 November 2012).

Bandler, J., and Burke, D. 2012. How Hewlett-Packard lost its way. *CNN Money.* Available at: http://tech. fortune.cnn.com/2012/05/08/500-hp-apotheker/.

Bart, C. 1997. Sex, lies and mission statements. *Business Horizons*, November–December: 9–18.

Bass, B.M., and Avolio, B.J. 1993. Transformational leadership: A response to critiques. In: Chemers, M.M. (ed.) *Leadership theory and research: Perspectives and directions.* Academic Press: New York.

BBC 2009. The choice. BBC Radio 4, 3 November [radio programme].

BBC News 2008. Initiations: Why I took part in one. Available at: http://news.bbc.co.uk/1/hi/7646891. stm (last accessed 27 June 2012).

Bell, E., and King, D. 2010. The elephant in the room: Critical management studies conferences as a site of body pedagogics. *Management Learning* 41(4): 429–42.

Bock, L. 2015. *Work rules! Insights from inside Google that will transform how you live and lead.* John Murray: London.

Boyce, A.S., Nieminen, L.R., Gillespie, M.A., Ryan, A.M., and Denison, D.R. (2015). Which comes first, organizational culture or performance? A longitudinal study of causal priority with automobile dealerships. *Journal of Organizational Behavior* 36(3): 339–59.

Brown, A. 1992. Organizational culture: The key to effective leadership and organizational development. *Leadership and Organization Development Journal* 13(2): 3–6.

Burrows, P. 2003. *Backfire: Carly Fiorina's high-stakes battle for the soul of Hewlett-Packard.* John Wiley and Sons: Hoboken, NJ.

*Business Week* 1984. Oops! Who's excellent now? 2867(5 November): 76–88.

Cameron, K., and Quinn, R.E. 2006. *Diagnosing and changing organizational culture*. Jossey Bass: London.

Christie, A. 2015. Lend lease values. Personal communication with Daniel King.

Clark, L. 2002. *Finding a common interest*. Cambridge University Press: Cambridge.

Collins, J.C., and Porras, J.I. 1994. *Built to last: Successful habits of visionary companies*. Harper Collins: New York.

Collinson, D. 1988. Engineering humour: Masculinity, joking and conflict in shop-floor relations. *Organization Studies* 9(2): 181–99.

Collinson, D. 1992. *Managing the shopfloor: Subjectivity, masculinity and workplace culture*. De Gruyter: Berlin.

Collinson, D. 2002. Managing humour. *Journal of Management Studies* 39(3): 269–88.

*Courier Online* 2011. Northumbria freshers left intimidated by initiation. Available at: http://thecourieronline.co.uk/2011/10/northumbria-freshers-left-intimidated-by-initation/ (last accessed 13 December 2012).

Deal, T.E., and Kennedy, A.A. 1982. *Corporate cultures: The rites and rituals of corporate life*. Penguin Books: Harmondsworth.

Deal, T.E., and Kennedy, A.A. 1984. Tales for the trails: A journey into the existential underbelly of American business. *Hospital Forum* May–June: 16–26.

Dewatripont, M., and Xavier, F. (eds) 2012. *The crisis aftermath: New regulatory paradigms*. Centre for Economic Policy Research: London.

Drucker, P. 1974. *Management: Tasks, responsibilities and practices*. Harper and Row: New York.

EgonZehnder 2015. Interview with Kazuo Furukawa, Hitachi Corporation. Available at: http://www.egonzehnder.com/us/the-focus-magazine/leaders-dialogue/other/business-leaders/interview-with-kazuo-furukawa-hitachi-corporation.html (last accessed 22 June 2015).

Fast Company 2015. Google London. Available at: http://www.fastcodesign.com/3028909/8-of-googles-craziest-offices (last accessed 22 June 2015).

Feldman, M. 1995. *Strategies for interpreting qualitative data*. Sage: London.

*Fortune* 2015. 100 best companies to work for 2015. Available at http://fortune.com/best-companies/ (last accessed 12 August 2015).

Frontczak, M., Schiavon, S., Goins, J., Arens, E., Zhang, H., and Wargocki, P. 2012. Quantitative relationships between occupant satisfaction and satisfaction aspects of indoor environmental quality and building design. *Indoor Air* 22(2): 119–31.

Frost, P.J., Moore, L.F., Louis, M.R., Lundberg, C.C., and Martin, J. (eds) 1991. *Reframing organizational culture*. Sage: London.

Goodley, S. 2012. HBOS executives 'threatened' colleagues who questioned risk-taking. *The Guardian*, 30 October.

Google 2012. Google's mission is to organize the world's information and make it universally accessible and useful. Available at: http://www.google.com/about/company/ (last accessed 26 November 2012).

Handy, C. 2009. *Gods of Management: The changing work of organisations*. Arrow Books: London.

Hatch, M. 1992. The symbolics of office design: An empirical exploration. In: Gagliardi, P. (ed.) *Symbolics of corporate artifacts*. De Gruyter: Berlin, pp. 129–43.

Hatch, M.J. 1993. The dynamics of organizational culture. *Academy of management review* 18(4): 657–93.

Heffernan, M. 2011. *Willful blindness: Why we ignore the obvious at our peril*. Walker & Company: London.

Hitachi 2015. Basic credo. Available at: http://www.hitachi.com/corporate/about/philosophy/ (last accessed 22 June 2015).

Hofstede, G. 1991. *Cultures and organizations: Software of the mind*. McGraw-Hill: New York.

Hsieh, T. 2010. *Delivering Happiness: A path to profits, passion, and purpose*. Business Plus: New York.

Jeffery, R. 2014. What you can learn from Hitachi. *People Management*, 25 May.

Kahle, L.R. and Gurel-Atay, E. 2013. *Communicating sustainability for the green economy*. ME Sharpe: Armonk, NY.

Kotrba, L.M., Gillespie, M.A., Schmidt, A.M., Smerek, R.E., Ritchie, S.A., and Denison, D.R. 2012. Do consistent corporate cultures have better business performance? Exploring the interaction effects. *Human relations* 65(2): 241–62.

Kronenbourg 2013. Respecting people and nature: Sustainable development report. Available at: http://www.kronenbourg.com/1er-brasseur-France/actualites/responsabilite-solidaire/Documents/CSR-Report_KRONENBOURG_ENG.pdf (last accessed 26 June 2015).

Lewis, M. 1989. *Liar's poker*. Hodder: London.

Malone, M.S. 2007. *Bill and Dave: How Hewlett and Packard built the world's greatest company*. Penguin Books: London.

Martin, J. 2001. *Organizational culture: Mapping the terrain*. Sage: London.

Meek, L. 1988. Organizational culture: Origins and weaknesses. *Organization Studies* 9(4): 453–73.

Michelli, J.A. 2012. *The Zappos experience: 5 Principles to inspire, engage, and WOW*. McGraw Hill: New York.

Morgan, G. 2006. *Images of organization*. Sage Publications: Thousand Oaks, CA.

Ornstein, S. 1989. The hidden influences of office design. *Academy of Management Executive* 3(2): 144–7.

Ott, J. 1989. *The organizational culture perspective*. Brooks/Cole Publishing Company: Pacific Grove, CA.

Ouchi, W. 1981. *Theory Z: How American business can meet the Japanese challenge*. Addison-Wesley: New York.

Packard, D. 1995. *The HP way: How Bill Hewlett and I built our company*. Collins: New York.

Peters, T. 2001. Tom Peters's true confessions. Available at: http://www.fastcompany.com/magazine/53/peters.html?page=0%2C3 (last accessed 17 June 2012).

Peters, T.J., and Waterman, R.H., Jr. 1982. *In search of excellence: Lessons from America's best run companies*. Harper Row: London.

Pettigrew, A. 1979. On studying organizational cultures. *Administrative Science Quarterly* 24(4): 570–81.

Posner, B.Z., Kouzes, J.M., and Schmidt, W.H. 1985. Shared values make a difference: An empirical test of corporate culture. *Human Resource Management* 24(3): 293–309.

Raelin, J. 1986. *Clash of cultures: Managers and professionals*. Harvard Business School Press: Boston.

Robinson, S. 2012. GPC warns of 'target culture' as GP commissioning framework revealed. GP Online. Available at: http://www.gponline.com/News/article/1115181/GPC-warns-target-culture-GP-commissioning-framework-revealed/.

Roper, J. 2015a. Company culture should come from leaders. *HR Magazine*, 26 May.

Roper, J. 2015b. Leaders still don't understand culture. *HR Magazine*, 4 June.

Rosen, M. 1985. Breakfast at Spiro's, dramaturgy and dominance. *Journal of Management* 11: 31–48.

Schein, E. 2010. *Organizational culture and leadership*. Jossey Bass: San Francisco.

Schmidt, E. and Rosenberg, J. 2015. *How Google works*. John Murray: London.

Seeger, M.W. and Ulmer, R.R. 2003. Explaining Enron communication and responsible leadership. *Management Communication Quarterly* 17(1): 58–84.

Sewell, G. 1998. The discipline of teams: The control of team-based industrial work through electronic and peer surveillance. *Administrative Science Quarterly* 43(2): 397–428.

Smircich, L. 1983. Concepts of culture and organizational analysis. *Administrative Science Quarterly* 28(3): 339–58.

Smircich, L., and Morgan, G. 1982. Leadership: The management of meaning. *Journal of Applied Behavioural Studies* 18: 257–73.

Starbucks 2012. *Starbucks: Our mission statement*. Available at: http://www.starbucks.ie/about-us/company-information/mission-statement (last accessed 24 November 2012).

Taylor, B. 2014. Why Amazon is copying Zappos and paying employees to quit. *Harvard Business Review*, 15 April.

Taylor, P., and Bain, P. 2003. Subterranean worksick blues: Humour as subversion in two call centres. *Organization Studies* 24(9): 1487–509.

Thompson, V. 2010. *Gross misconduct: My year of excess in the city*. Pocket Books: London.

Tichy, N.M. 1982. Managing change strategically: The technical, political, and cultural keys. *Organizational Dynamics* 11: 59–80.

Tierney, J. 2012. From cubicles, cry for quiet pierces office buzz. *New York Times*, 20 May.

Trice, H., and Beyer, J. 1984. Studying organizational cultures through rites and ceremonials. *Academy of Management Review* 9(4): 653–69.

TUC 2008. General Council report to Congress 2008. Available at: http://www.tuc.org.uk/the_tuc/tuc-15225-f0.cfm (last accessed 26 November 2012).

Turner, G., and Myerson, J. 1998. *New workspace, new culture: Office design as a catalyst for change*. Gower Publishing Ltd: Aldershot.

Wei, W. 2010. Amazon is paying Zappos CEO Tony Hsieh only $36,000. *Business Insider*, 22 October.

Willmott, H. 1993. Strength is ignorance; slavery is freedom: Managing culture in modern organizations. *Journal of Management Studies* 30(4): 515–52.

Wilson, C. 1979. *Jokes: Form, content, use and function*. Academic Press: New York.

Wilson, H. 2012. EU plans curbs on bank risk-taking. *Daily Telegraph*, 2 October.

Yarrow, J. 2011. HP CEO Leo Apotheker: 'HP has lost its soul'. Available at: http://www.businessinsider.com/hp-leo-apotheker-2011-3#ixzz2D9tVzlNU.

York Vision 2010. York Sport slams hockey initiation. Available at http://www.yorkvision.co.uk/sport/york-sport-slams-hockey-initiation/ (last accessed 13 December 2012).

Zappos 2015. About Zappos culture. Available at: http://www.zappos.com/d/about-zappos-culture (last accessed 23 June 2015).

Zappos Insights 2015. Zappos culture book. Available at: http://www.zapposinsights.com/culture-book (last accessed 25 June 2015).

# Part 3
## Managing the individual

# Personality and individual differences

## Chapter overview and learning outcomes

By the end of this chapter you should be able to:

- describe the main features of the nomothetic, ideographic, and social-radical approaches to personality

- describe a variety of models of personality

- explain how personality is measured in organizational settings

- analyse the effectiveness of different selection methods in assessing the personality of candidates for a job.

## Key theorists

| | |
|---|---|
| Carl Gustav Jung | Swiss psychoanalyst who noted the distinction between introverted and extraverted personalities |
| Katharine Cook Briggs and Isobel Briggs Myers | American psychologists who applied Jung's theory to create the Myers-Briggs Type Indicator personality test |
| Hans Eysenck | German psychologist who noted the role of emotional stability and instability in personality formation |
| Raymond Cattell | British psychologist who devised the 16 personality factor model of personality used in workplace selection |
| Sigmund Freud | Austrian psychoanalyst who outlined ways in which personalities change and develop |

## Key terms

| | |
|---|---|
| Nomothetic approach | Views personality as a set of measurable traits or types which can be represented on a static framework or model |
| Personality testing | The use of questionnaires to measure personality, often used in recruitment and selection in organizations |
| Ideographic approach | Views personality as complex and unique to each individual, and as something which changes through influences from the world around us |
| Social-radical approach | Recognizes that rather than just being able to measure personality, organizations have an effect upon the personalities of their members |

# Introduction

**Running case:** finding new staff

Junction Hotel

Fitness Centre Duty Manager
Full-time, fixed-term (12 months initially)
Salary negotiable

We are looking for an individual with a big personality to join the team of duty managers at our fitness centre.

Reporting to the Fitness Centre Manager and, on occasions, deputizing, you will be responsible for the day-to-day line management of a team of five full-time fitness centre staff and the recruitment of new staff when necessary.

Working with customers, including delivering personal training sessions, you will also have management and administration responsibilities, including preparation of staff rotas and associated paperwork.

Holding a degree in sports or leisure management, or a related area, you will have at least five years of experience in the leisure and fitness industry, at least two of which should be at management level.

We need an individual who is self-motivated and dynamic, and who can motivate both staff and customers.

Please send CVs and a covering letter to:

Simon Chance
General Manager
Junction Hotel

What do you think would be the ideal personality characteristics for the successful candidate in this job?

To what extent do we go into organizations as individuals with our own distinct personalities? So far in this book, theories of management and organization have paid little attention to the perspective of the individual.

- In the rational organization (Chapters 2, 3, 4), the individual is seen as useful only for the precise part they can play on an assembly line, as if they were a cog in the machine. When dealing with a large bureaucracy, such as our bank or even our university, we may feel like the organization sees us as a record on a computer rather than an individual—a feeling summed up in the phrase 'I am a name, not a number'.

- With the social organization (Chapters 5, 6, 7), a human aspect of the organization is recognized, but only as a part of a larger group or team. Group dynamics have a powerful influence over individual behaviour and perceptions. Anyone who has played sport may well know the mantra 'there is no "I" in team'—the idea that you put the team before your individuality.

In both of these cases the individual is, in one way or another, reduced to being part of a greater entity. However, as we will see in this and the following two chapters, organizations do have an interest in managing people at the level of the individual. Theories of motivation and learning, for example, use psychological knowledge to try to understand how the individual mind works.

In this chapter, we use psychological insights to examine the set of characteristics that mark us out as an individual and therefore as different from other people. It is common to speak of ourselves and others as having a **personality** that identifies us as an individual.

> **Personality** A set of characteristics of behaviour displayed by any individual.

Think about yourself compared with your friends and family. What differences in personality can you describe?

We examine three approaches to the study of personality:

- the nomothetic approach sees personality as a set of measurable traits or characteristics, and sorts people into particular **personality types** or scales. Such an approach is most familiar in the workplace in the form of personality tests.

> **Personality types** Broad personality groupings which are associated with a set of particular traits.

- the ideographic approach rejects as too simplistic the idea of personality as a set of traits and, instead, sees personality as something much more dynamic which develops as a result of our experiences and interactions. As such, it sees people as having rich, complex personalities, rather than as fitting into a certain personality type.

- a third approach, we suggest, is a social–radical approach that sees personality and its definition entirely as a product of society and its organizational and power structures. For example, rather than the workplace simply measuring an individual's personality, as in the nomothetic approach, the workplace is a part of an individual's environment which actively shapes their personality.

Throughout the chapter we will see how individual personalities are assessed by organizations when filling a vacancy, i.e. finding someone with the personality characteristics that are felt suitable for that job. It is with this link between personality and the recruitment and selection process that we begin.

# Personality in the recruitment and selection process

## Running case: whittling down

Chance is met by a deluge of paperwork. Over 200 CVs have been sent in for the job of duty manager and just over half of them seem to be suitable candidates.

Looking at the covering letters and CVs, Chance realizes that he can't use these alone to create a shortlist. Many of the letters simply parrot standard phrases, such as 'I am self-motivated', 'I am dedicated to the task', and 'I work well with other people', but what proof is there to back up these statements?

Chance starts to think about how to whittle down the shortlist and draws up a list of characteristics that a successful candidate will need:

- appropriate qualifications and experience
- well organized to manage rotas and similar paperwork
- calm demeanour in a fast-moving work environment
- good leadership—the candidate needs to motivate and enthuse the team during the course of a shift
- flexibility—needs to be prepared to do different tasks at short notice
- upbeat, motivating personality—especially when greeting customers at reception or engaging them in a personal training session
- able to communicate instructions clearly in a fast-paced atmosphere.

The various qualities are drawn up into a person specification which will be put in an application pack and sent to candidates.

When employers advertise a vacancy, they specify the characteristics that an ideal candidate should have—the degree grades required, the amount of experience in a similar job, the skills that they can offer to the organization, etc. Among these might be characteristics which relate to an aspect of personality—'dynamic', 'conscientious', 'pleasant manner', etc.

**Research insight:** 'We recruit attitude'
Callaghan, G., and Thompson, P. 2002. 'We recruit attitude': The selection and shaping of routine call centre labour. *Journal of Management Studies* 39(2): 233–54.

In a study of recruitment and selection in a call centre, Callaghan and Thompson (2002) note that while technical skills, such as numeracy and using a keyboard, are assessed, the greatest priority in the process is given to personality. In particular, a positive, energetic can-do attitude and an ability to use humour during calls are seen as aspects of good customer service. This is important, as it is the customer service that may differentiate the company from others which offer similar products (see also the discussion of emotional labour in service industries in Chapter 16).

Such characteristics are seen as being innate rather than something that can be learned. As one manager states:

[W]e recruit attitude. You can tell by talking to someone during interview whether they smile, whether their eyes smile. If you smile during your interview and you are enthusiastic, you'll be OK.

(Callaghan and Thompson, 2002: 240)

In this section we present an initial overview of how personality characteristics are considered in the recruitment and selection process. While often used together as a phrase, recruitment and selection refers to two distinct phases of the process of filling a vacancy (French and Rumbles, 2010):

- **Recruitment** is where the vacancy is publicized in order to generate a pool of applicants, and involves the advertising of jobs and the creation of relevant documentation. The desired personality characteristics are formalized as documents, such as a person specification.

**Recruitment** The process of attracting a pool of candidates for a particular job vacancy.

- **Selection** is where the choice is made of who to employ from the field of candidates and, as such, includes such techniques as interviewing, reviewing CVs, and—central to concerns in this chapter—personality tests.

Selection  The process of selecting the most appropriate candidate from a pool of applicants for a particular vacancy.

# Personality and recruitment

When recruiting for a vacancy, for example in a job advert or on a website, employers will demonstrate the characteristics that they desire in a successful applicant. This might include explicit reference to particular personality characteristics, such as 'outgoing', or might refer to behaviours that imply particular characteristics: for example, 'good with customers' implies personality characteristics such as patience and friendliness.

---

**Real life case:** recruiting personality at Pret a Manger

British sandwich chain Pret a Manger is notable for recruiting staff for their personalities and behaviours rather than for specific skills that they can demonstrate on their CV (Moore, 2015; Jacobs, 2015). Within their store, they aim to create a particular 'Pret buzz' (Moore, 2015) whereby staff constantly display personalities that are genuinely happy, sociable, cheerful and tactile (Rawlinson, 2013; Myerscough, 2013). Employees are issued with a book of desired 'Pret behaviours' (Preston, 2012), and potential employees are assessed against these.

The behaviours are grouped into three categories: passion, clear talking, and teamworking (Jacobs, 2015). Within these categories are listed behaviours that Pret a Manger 'don't want to see', 'want to see', and 'Pret perfect'. For example, they want to see people with a great sense of fun and who are genuinely friendly; they don't want to see moody and bad-tempered individuals who become easily flustered. A 'Pret perfect' personality will 'have presence' (Rawlinson, 2013).

---

Visit the Online Resource Centre for more background and discussion on these behaviours.

What sort of personality characteristics do you think an ideal candidate for Pret a Manger would have?

A further stage in the recruitment process where personality characteristics may be stated is in the documentation that is sent to interested candidates (or available to download in some instances). Such an application pack usually consists of two documents:

- the **job description** is a description of exactly what task and duties would be performed as part of the job
- the **person specification** is a list of knowledge, skills, experience, qualifications, and competencies that a successful candidate would be expected to hold. This might be split into 'essential' characteristics (the bare minimum that a candidate requires) and 'desirable' characteristics (those which might work in a person's favour when making a decision between candidates).

Job description  A document which outlines the formal duties and activities that the holder of a particular office will be expected to perform, and their place within the overall organizational structure.

Person specification  A formal list of the main requirements for a successful candidate for a particular job.

Again, in these documents there may be references to characteristics, either essential or desired, which relate to aspects of personality. A person specification will also outline the ways in which different characteristics will be assessed, that is to say the selection processes that will be used to match candidates to those characteristics.

Visit the Online Resource Centre to see examples of these documents.

## Personality and selection

A number of techniques might be used in a selection process. A CV can be used to assess whether the relevant qualifications are held; references can be used to check up on relevant experience, and aptitude tests can measure specific skills such as numeracy. But what about personality characteristics? How would a recruiter assess the personality of a candidate to see that it matches that which is desired and measure their 'enthusiasm' or 'friendliness?'

When you first started at university you will have met many new people and made judgements about their personality upon first meeting them. But how long, with friends, does it take to really get to know every facet of their personality?

Getting to know someone's personality is a lengthy process. We get to know a person and their personality over time. Even with our closest friends we sometimes find aspects of their personality that are new or which surprise us. For recruiters trying to get an idea of a candidate's personality, this length of time is not a luxury that is available.

Assessing large numbers of people can be problematic.
**Source:** Shutterstock.

With a large field of candidates, it's simply not possible to get to know each of them well enough to know every aspect of their personality. Even a short interview, where at least candidates are seen in person, gives only a superficial view of personality, and the time available for interviews is limited—only a small fraction of the field of candidates will be shortlisted for interview.

In this chapter we will see how techniques such as personality tests and questionnaires are used in the selection process. This is an efficient way of getting a measure of the personality of a large number of candidates, but it comes at the expense of the type of data that is produced—rather than the rich knowledge of a personality that we get from knowing somebody personally, it is presented, instead, as an abstract set of numbers and measurements.

The measurement of personality in the selection process thus involves a trade-off between the time available and the richness of the data about a candidate's personality that can be gleaned (see Figure 8.1).

This trade-off relates to the nomothetic and ideographic approaches to personality introduced previously.

- The nomothetic approach suggests that personalities can be represented as a set of standard characteristics and can thus be measured efficiently using instruments such as personality questionnaires

- The ideographic approach sees personalities as rich and complex. Representing personalities though efficient means, such as a personality test, comes at the expense of the richness of personality data gained—the complexity and insight into an individual personality is lost.

In this chapter we will relate a number of methods used in recruitment and selection to the nomothetic and ideographic approaches. Taken in isolation, any one technique of recruitment and selection fares badly in its predictive validity, that is to say how well it predicts performance in the job or gets an accurate picture of personality. Yet given the costs and time associated with recruitment and selection, it is important for organizations to get it right, i.e. to fit the right person to the vacancy.

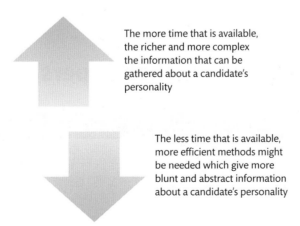

The more time that is available, the richer and more complex the information that can be gathered about a candidate's personality

The less time that is available, more efficient methods might be needed which give more blunt and abstract information about a candidate's personality

**Figure 8.1**
The personality measurement trade-off.

**Employability skills:** the recruitment and selection process

This chapter relates personality to the recruitment and selection process and will, therefore, be a valuable insight into the processes used when you apply for employment—whether for temporary or vacation work, for a placement, or when you graduate and begin your career.

While this chapter concentrates on personality, it is useful to do research and reading into all aspects of recruitment and selection ahead of applying for jobs. Understanding what recruiters are looking for, the ways in which they match applicants to jobs, and, importantly, the reasons why they reject candidates are all things which will give you a head start. Your university careers service will also have literature on the subject and will be able to offer advice.

 Visit the Online Resource Centre for suggestions on further research into the recruitment process.

On the other side of the fence, when you are in work, you may, at times, be involved in recruiting and selecting candidates to fill a job vacancy. You may do this as a fully-trained human resources professional; however, in many cases, managers with no formal training are called upon to sit on an interview panel or play a role in the recruitment and selection process. While issues around the accuracy of different selection techniques are important points to note as an employer, this chapter also highlights important issues and legal requirements around unfair discrimination in the recruitment and selection process.

**Review questions**

| | |
|---|---|
| **Describe** | What is meant by recruitment and selection? |
| **Explain** | What are the main differences in the nomothetic and ideographic approaches to personality? |
| **Analyse** | Why is the evaluation of the personality characteristics of a candidate a trade-off between efficiency and the richness of personality data gained? |
| **Apply** | Have a look at a variety of job advertisements, either in print or online. For each advert, consider what personality characteristics are required of the successful candidate. |

# Nomothetic approaches to personality

**Running case:** personality test

Having compiled the person specification, Chance realizes that most aspects would be easy to screen—qualifications and experience can be evidenced from a CV, certificates, and references, for example. But what of the personality characteristics?

What Chance needs to know is which one of the applicants can really cut the mustard. Who has the personality to manage staff and keep them motivated in a fast-moving environment?

Business manager Phil Weaver advises Chance to get them to undertake a personality test. Using the services of a personality testing firm, a link would be sent to the candidates to fill out a questionnaire over the Internet. The software would then produce personality profiles for all candidates.

'I've used them before. They save a lot of time and effort,' says Weaver. 'For a start, they screen out anyone unsuitable—any shy, retiring types will be shown up by the test and we can reject them straight away. We don't even need to look at their profiles—the software will just give a list of people with unsuitable personalities. And for those still in the running, we can use their profiles as extra information to draw up the final shortlist.'

Chance likes this idea—it is an efficient way to deal with the 200-odd applications quickly, leaving him just the most suitable personalities to deal with.

Have you ever undertaken a personality test, either for work purposes or otherwise? What did you think of the results?

Many of us, when younger, will have read the Mr Men and Little Miss books. Each book in this series focuses on a different cartoon character whose characteristics match their name—Mr Grumpy, Little Miss Shy, Mr Happy, etc. The characters' personalities can be summed up by one particular personality characteristic, or as it is also known, a personality **trait**.

While our personalities are hopefully not so one-dimensional that we can sum them up with one word, the idea that personality can be described as a set of traits is one with which we are familiar. Indeed, often if asked what a person 'is like' we will respond with a set of adjectives which relate to particular personality traits—friendly, sullen, outgoing, shy, etc.

**Trait** A characteristic of the person, often considered the behaviour, thoughts, and emotions that the person exhibits considered stable, over time.

Think of a friend or relative—could you produce a list of words to describe their personality? And could you produce a similar list for yourself?

The **nomothetic** approach also sees personality as a set of traits, which are organized into a model or framework. In this section we examine two particular approaches to nomothetic theories of personality:

**Nomothetic** An approach which views personality as a set of measurable traits or types.

- some theories classify people into broad personality *types*; associated with each type is a set of personality traits that people belonging to that type are likely to display
- some theories don't group traits into personality types; instead, they start from the traits themselves, usually plotting people on a number of scales between two opposite ends of a particular trait (for example between reserved and outgoing).

In both cases, the nomothetic approach suggests that personality is measurable, using instruments such as personality questionnaires. The personality types and scales are the frameworks on which an individual's personality can be represented and categorized. We will see that such personality tests are used in workplaces for training, for development, and, relevant to this chapter, for selecting candidates for a job.

# Theories of personality type

Theories of personality type bring together different traits in broad groupings, seeing the traits as being representative characteristics of the broader personality types. As we will see, the idea of personality types is used today in the workplace in the popular **Myers–Briggs Type Indicator** (MBTI); however, the idea of categorizing personalities into different types stretches back into antiquity.

## Theory in context: Hippocrates and the four humours

In Ancient Greece, around 400 BC, Hippocrates drew out four main personality types from his medical theory of the **four humours**. Blood, phlegm, yellow bile, and black bile were four basic substances, or humours, which Hippocrates believed made up the human body and were associated with certain characteristics and personality types. See Table 8.1 for a description of these. An imbalance in the presence of one of the humours would have effects both on physical health and also on the type of personality type displayed by an individual.

Table 8.1  Hippocrates' four humours and associated personality types

| Humour | Personality type | Description |
| --- | --- | --- |
| Blood | Sanguine | Warm and outgoing, a person who thrives in social environments—lively, with few concerns and cares in the world |
| Phlegm | Phlegmatic | Cool and rational—a controlled, thoughtful, and calm personality |
| Yellow bile | Choleric | The most volatile of the four personality types, impulsive, excitable, perhaps touchy and bad-tempered |
| Black bile | Melancholic | Reserved and withdrawn—quiet and socially the opposite to sanguine; an anxious temperament, governed by worries, concerns, and even despondency |

While much of Hippocrates' work has been disproven or superseded, he is seen as being the founder of medicine for his attempt to analyse and classify the workings of the human body. The four temperaments, or personality types, that he outlines give us words that we still use to describe people's personalities today—melancholic, sanguine, phlegmatic, choleric—and which we will see reflected in more recent personality-type classifications.

Can you think of jobs which are particularly suited to the four personality types described? Do you think of personality in such terms today, or are there other words that you might use for such personality types?

## Carl Jung: introverts and extraverts

While Hippocrates introduces the notion of personality types, it is with the work of psychoanalyst Carl Jung that we see the origins of the personality scales and type theories that are more commonly applied in the contemporary workplace. Jung's (1923) Psychological *types* outlines a distinction between **introversion** and **extraversion** (this is the way it is spelled in psychological theory), which is mirrored in many of the personality types and scales that we will see in this chapter.

Our common-sense understanding of these terms perhaps differs from the depth of Jung's analysis. We tend to think of an extravert as someone who is sociable and outgoing, able to 'work a room' and start up a conversation with people, engaging in small talk. The introvert is more reserved, possibly uncomfortable in social situations, and might seem unsociable and withdrawn.

Certainly these common-sense understandings ring true, but they need to be understood in the context of the specific meanings of Jung's terminology. The basis of Jung's (1923) work is in the relationship between our inner selves and the external world. In effect, there are two particular worlds to which we relate, and we may do so to different degrees:

- the external world is the rational, day-to-day, everyday reality that goes on around us
- the inner world is the world of our own thoughts, dreams, fantasies, etc.

Jung's (1923) theory of introversion and extraversion is about the balance we maintain between these inner and external worlds, and particularly from which of these we gain our energy.

- An extravert thrives on action and being engaged with people—if inactive, an extravert can feel restless. *An extravert gets little energy from within, instead getting their energy from others in a social situation.*
- An introvert is capable of, and indeed thrives on, working alone, perhaps doing work that needs consideration or contemplation rather than needing to be a part of a crowd or a team. *An introvert gets their energy from within—social situations drain them of that energy.*

With the example of a person 'working a room', it's not that an introvert is incapable of this; however, they would find that it drains them of energy, while an extravert would get their energy from such a situation. Cain (2012) argues that contemporary workplaces tend to favour the personality characteristics of extraverts more, with working environments, such as open plan offices, and job adverts calling for 'team players' and upbeat personalities. This doesn't mean that an extravert personality is better, but simply that working environments suit that side of the scale more; indeed, Cain suggests that such environments could miss out on valuable ideas that are generated by more contemplative introverts.

Looking back to the Pret behaviours case, do you think an introvert or extravert personality would best suit those behaviours?

**Study skills:** lectures and seminars

Cain (2012) suggests that it's not just the workplace that favours extraverts over introverts, but that this is found in schools and universities too. There is a pressure to speak up in class as a way of demonstrating your knowledge and your commitment to the course, and this 'speaking up' is something to which extraverts are more inclined. Does this mean, then, that introverts get nothing out of seminars and are thus at a disadvantage? Let's think about the role that seminars play in your university education. ▶

▶ Lectures give a broad introduction to a topic, highlighting the main areas of importance, but often there is not enough time to go into depth beyond that—they are an invitation to further explore the subject. Furthermore, in a lecture you are usually passive, sitting quietly and taking notes while the lecturer speaks to you, but not engaging any further with the subject matter.

In seminars, you are able to address the lecture topic in more depth, discussing it and relating it to relevant readings and case studies. You are much more active in a seminar and are not just receiving knowledge, but engaging with that knowledge. A seminar tutor should not need to speak very often, only to keep discussion going and to respond to, and clarify, any points that participants make.

Some people may feel more comfortable than others in speaking up in seminars, but perhaps something to consider—whether you are more extravert or introvert in nature—is that it is the quality of contribution that is important, not the length of time that any one individual speaks. The quality of contribution comes from being prepared—doing the reading and thinking about the ideas presented in the lecture.

Being actively engaged doesn't necessarily mean speaking up all the time as an extravert may do. A person can be engaged by listening and comparing what is being said with their own ideas. However, seminars do need people to speak and contribute in order to work. Just one carefully considered point or observation can make a big contribution. And Cain suggests that such considered contributions are where introverts excel.

It is not a simple either/or distinction between an individual being either introverted or extraverted: they are two important and complimentary aspects of personality as opposed to mutually exclusive opposites. However, an individual may lean more towards one end or the other on this scale. Jung's (1923) work suggested a complex relationship between an individual's position on the introversion/extraversion scale on the one hand, and two psychological functions on the other: how we perceive the world (sensing or intuition) and how we make judgements about the world (thinking or feeling). These relationships form the basis for one of the most familiar workplace personality instruments—the Myers–Briggs Type Indicator (MBTI).

## Myers–Briggs and the application of Jung

While it is now one of the most popular personality profiling instruments in the workplace, the MBTI was developed from an amateur interest in personality types held by Katharine Cook Briggs and her daughter Isabel Briggs Myers. They were heavily influenced by Jung's work on personality types and they used these as a basis for their own classification of personality types, eventually published as the MBTI (Myers, 1962).

The MBTI uses a questionnaire to work out where an individual lies between a set of four personality indices:

- *extraversion/introversion (E/I)*—as outlined by Jung, to which orientation are we more inclined when directing our actions and energies: the world around us or our inner selves?
- *sensing/intuition (S/I)*—how do we perceive and gather information about the world around us?
- *thinking/feeling (T/F)*—once we have information, how do we analyse and act upon it, using it to make judgements and decisions?
- *judgement/perception (J/P)*—how do we deal with, and act upon, the world around us? Do we plan in advance or act in the moment?

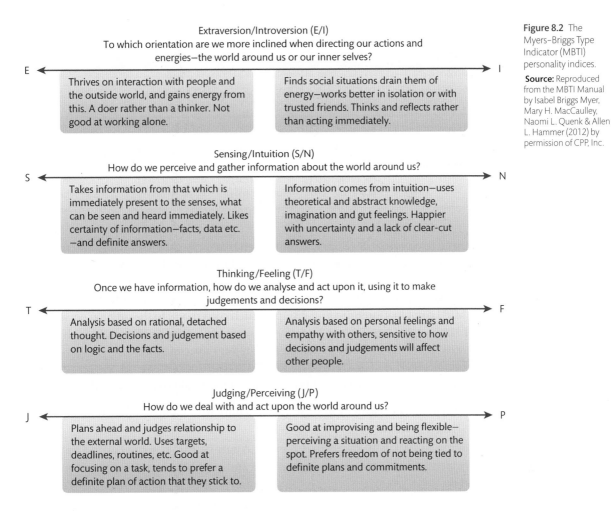

Extraversion/Introversion (E/I)
To which orientation are we more inclined when directing our actions and energies—the world around us or our inner selves?

E ← | I

Thrives on interaction with people and the outside world, and gains energy from this. A doer rather than a thinker. Not good at working alone.

Finds social situations drain them of energy—works better in isolation or with trusted friends. Thinks and reflects rather than acting immediately.

Sensing/Intuition (S/N)
How do we perceive and gather information about the world around us?

S ← | N

Takes information from that which is immediately present to the senses, what can be seen and heard immediately. Likes certainty of information—facts, data etc. —and definite answers.

Information comes from intuition—uses theoretical and abstract knowledge, imagination and gut feelings. Happier with uncertainty and a lack of clear-cut answers.

Thinking/Feeling (T/F)
Once we have information, how do we analyse and act upon it, using it to make judgements and decisions?

T ← | F

Analysis based on rational, detached thought. Decisions and judgement based on logic and the facts.

Analysis based on personal feelings and empathy with others, sensitive to how decisions and judgements will affect other people.

Judging/Perceiving (J/P)
How do we deal with and act upon the world around us?

J ← | P

Plans ahead and judges relationship to the external world. Uses targets, deadlines, routines, etc. Good at focusing on a task, tends to prefer a definite plan of action that they stick to.

Good at improvising and being flexible—perceiving a situation and reacting on the spot. Prefers freedom of not being tied to definite plans and commitments.

**Figure 8.2** The Myers–Briggs Type Indicator (MBTI) personality indices.

**Source:** Reproduced from the MBTI Manual by Isabel Briggs Myer, Mary H. MacCaulley, Naomi L. Quenk & Allen L. Hammer (2012) by permission of CPP, Inc.

Figure 8.2 shows these four indices, with examples of the types of behaviour and personality that might be expected at either end.

While people can lie at points along this scale (e.g. a medium preference for sensing, a strong preference for feeling, etc.) the results tend to be presented as a four-letter personality type according to which end of each index an individual is more inclined towards. A person might be an ENTP (Extravert–Intuition–Thinking–Perceiving) personality type, or an ISTP, or an ESTP—or any of the sixteen possible combinations of the letters.

Where do you think you lie on each of the MBTI indices shown in Figure 8.2?

The MBTI instrument is not used as a recruitment and selection tool, but it does suggest aptitudes for particular jobs; indeed, one of its earliest uses was during World War II in matching women's personalities to wartime jobs that would best suit them (Myers and Myers, 1995: xiii). As such, it tends to be used more as a developmental tool for individuals. For example, in staff development and training it is used to help people understand their own personality and how they relate to their external world, to their work, and to their colleagues.

**Table 8.2** Keirsey's (1988) temperament sorter

| Grouping | Artisan | Guardian | Rational | Idealist |
|----------|---------|----------|----------|----------|
| Common characteristics from MBTI | SP (Sensing–Perceiving) | SJ (Sensing–Judging) | NT (Intuition–Thinking) | NF (Intuition–Feeling) |
| Related Hippocratic group | Sanguine | Melancholic | Phlegmatic | Choleric |
| Personality types and related occupations | Promoter (ESTP) Crafter (ISTP) Performer (ESFP) Composer (ISFP) | Supervisor (ESTJ) Inspector (ISTJ) Provider (ESFJ) Protector (ISFJ) | Fieldmarshal (ENTJ) Mastermind (INTJ) Inventor (ENTP) Architect (INTP) | Teacher (ENFJ) Counsellor (INFJ) Champion (ENFP) Healer (INFP) |

It is also used for personal development and, given that it matches personality and aptitude for jobs, is a tool used in career development—matching personalities to suitable careers.

A specific link between personality 'temperaments' and specific occupational areas was made by David Keirsey (1998). Keirsey was influenced by the MBTI instrument, sorting the sixteen MBTI combinations into four groups, which correspond to the original personality types of Hippocrates (see Table 8.2). **Keirsey's temperament sorter** then links each of the sixteen MBTI combinations to a particular type of role or occupation.

For example, ENFJ is characterized by Keirsey as 'the teacher'. We can see how the different characteristics that make up this personality type would contribute to this role:

> **Keirsey's temperament sorter** A personality-testing instrument which relates personality types to suggested occupational roles.

- (E)xtraversion—the teacher will be working mainly with groups of people rather than in isolation

- I(N)tuition—Chapter 10 shows that learning comes best from going beyond learning simple facts and instead recognizing patterns and associations, as an intuitive person would do

- (F)eeling—the teacher has a degree of empathy with, and can respond to, students

- (J)udgement—the teacher is able to plan lessons methodically rather than making things up on the hoof.

Interestingly, just one change of letter—from Extraversion to Intraversion—gives INFJ, suggested as 'the counsellor'. Similar teaching skills are required, but here it is in a much more private, individual situation than teaching.

As with the MBTI, Keirsey has an associated personality questionnaire which is used to place people in the relevant groupings (www.keirsey.com has more about the groupings and a test questionnaire).

 Visit the Online Resource Centre for more discussion of occupations and the Keirsey groupings.

# Trait theories of personality

> **Trait theories** Nomothetic theories of personality which see individual traits rather than broad personality groups as the foundations of personality.

While type theories sort people's personalities into broad types from which particular traits emerge, **trait theories** see personality traits as the main building blocks of a personality. Usually, traits are arranged in pairs of opposites (e.g. sociable–unsociable) with people scored at some point in between each pairing so as to build up a personality profile. As with type theories, some form of questionnaire is used as the instrument by which these scales are measured. In this section we examine two of the more popular trait theory testing instruments used in the workplace: the **16 personality factor** and the big five personality scale.

> **16 personality factor** A personality test which measures personality on a set of 16 scales of opposing character traits.

> ### Research insight: Eysenck—from types to traits
> Eysenck, H.J., and Eysenck, M.W. 1985. *Personality and individual differences: A natural science approach*. Plenum Publishing Corporation: New York.

Similarly to Keirsey, Hans Eysenck (in Eysenck and Eysenck, 1985) made groupings of personality types which mapped on to the ancient groupings of Hippocrates and, similarly to all the modern-day theories of personality examined so far, he made a distinction between extraversion and introversion.

However, Eysenk added another dimension between emotional stability and emotional instability (the latter sometimes called **neuroticism**). Eysenck's two scales were plotted on to a matrix giving four personality types, the quadrants of which map on to Hippocrates' original four humours (see Figure 8.2). Again, this is a classification of personality types that has an associated questionnaire.

> **Neuroticism** Emotional instability.

Eysenck's work, while still dividing personalities into types, moves us towards trait theories. Firstly, it outlines a set of specific traits within each quadrant (e.g. a stable extraverted person is sociable, outgoing, talkative, etc., in Figure 8.3). Secondly, Eysenck's dimension of emotional stability and instability features alongside the extraversion–introversion scale in many trait theories.

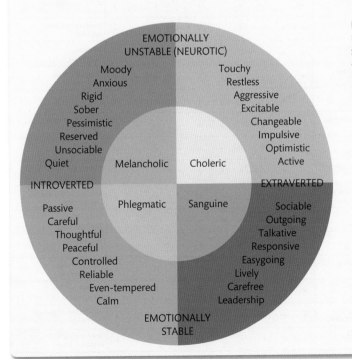

**Figure 8.3** Eysenck's model of personality.

**Source:** Eysenck, H.J. and Eysenck, M.W. *Personality and Individual Differences*. Plenum Publishing, 1985.

## Cattell's 16 PF traits

Cattell's (1966) 16 personality factor (16 PF) theory is one of the most popular personality questionnaires used in selection processes (e.g. Dakin et al., 1994). Cattell analysed questionnaires and the words within them that people used to describe personality (Newell and Rice, 1999: 140), and by grouping similar ideas together, suggested that a personality boils down to sixteen core factors (see Figure 8.4).

These factors are arranged in opposites: for example, the 'Dominance' scale ranges between deferential and avoiding conflict at one end to being dominant and forceful at the other. The scale is normally distributed: that is to say that on any of the scales, approximately a third of the population should be located in the middle band, with numbers tailing off towards the extremities.

Both Jung's extraversion and introversion aspects can be seen in the scale (e.g. factor H—social boldness), as can Eysenck's emotional stability (factor C).

**Big five personality scale** A personality test which measures personality according to a set of five traits: openness, conscientiousness, extraversion, agreeableness, and neuroticism.

## The big five personality factors

The **big five personality scale** (McCrae and Costa, 1990, 1996), another of the well-known trait theories used in the workplace, suggests that the number of factors whereby a

**Figure 8.4** Cattell's sixteen personality factors.

**Source:** Reproduced by permission of the Institute for Perso nality and Ability Testing, Inc. (IPAT), Champaign, Illinois, USA.

## Primary Factors

| Factor | | Standard Ten Score (STEN) | | | | | | | | | | |
|---|---|---|---|---|---|---|---|---|---|---|---|---|
| | | 1 | 2 | 3 | 4 | 5 | 6 | 7 | 8 | 9 | 10 | |
| A: Warmth | Emotionally distant from people | + | + | + | + | + | + | + | + | + | + | Attentive and warm towards others |
| B: Reasoning | Fewer reasoning items correct | + | + | + | + | + | + | + | + | + | + | More reasoning items correct |
| C: Emotional Stability | Reactive, Emotionally changeable | + | + | + | + | + | + | + | + | + | + | Emotionally stable, Adaptive |
| E: Dominance | Deferential, Cooperative, Avoids conflict | + | + | + | + | + | + | + | + | + | + | Dominant, Forceful |
| F: Liveliness | Serious, Cautious, Careful | + | + | + | + | + | + | + | + | + | + | Lively, Animated, Spontaneous |
| G: Rule-Consciousness | Expedient, Non-Conforming | + | + | + | + | + | + | + | + | + | + | Rule-Conscious, Dutiful |
| H: Social Boldness | Shy, Threat-Sensitive, Timid | + | + | + | + | + | + | + | + | + | + | Socially bold, Adventurous, Thick-Skinned |
| I: Sensitivity | Objective, Unsentimental | + | + | + | + | + | + | + | + | + | + | Subjective, Sentimental |
| L: Vigilance | Trusting, Unsuspecting, Accepting | + | + | + | + | + | + | + | + | + | + | Vigilant, Suspicious, Sceptical, Wary |
| M: Abstractedness | Grounded, Practical, Solution-Oriented | + | + | + | + | + | + | + | + | + | + | Abstracted, Theoretical, Idea-Oriented |
| N: Privateness | Forthright, Straightforward | + | + | + | + | + | + | + | + | + | + | Private, Discreet, Non-Disclosing |
| O: Apprehension | Self-Assured, Unworried | + | + | + | + | + | + | + | + | + | + | Apprehensive, Self-Doubting, Worried |
| Q1: Openness to Change | Traditional, Values the familiar | + | + | + | + | + | + | + | + | + | + | Open to change, Experimenting |
| Q2: Self-Reliance | Group-Oriented, Affiliative | + | + | + | + | + | + | + | + | + | + | Self-Reliant, Individualistic |
| Q3: Perfectionism | Tolerates disorder, Unexacting, Flexible | + | + | + | + | + | + | + | + | + | + | Perfectionist, Organised, Self-Disciplined |
| Q4: Tension | Relaxed, Placid, Patient | + | + | + | + | + | + | + | + | + | + | Tense, High energy, Impatient, Driven |

personality can be adequately represented boils down to five. The big five is also known as the OCEAN scale, OCEAN being an acronym for its five personality dimensions:

- *openness to experience*—the degree to which people are open to new ideas, questioning and imaginative, or prefer existing ways of doing things
- *conscientiousness*—the degree to which people are good, orderly, diligent workers
- *extraversion/introversion*—as with the MBTI, the degree to which a person is outgoing and gregarious, their energies directed externally rather than internally
- *agreeableness*—the degree to which someone is a 'good person', trustworthy and cooperative, and will get along with others in the organization
- *neuroticism (emotional stability)*—as with Eysenck, the degree to which somebody is calm and emotionally stable, or more prone to anxiety and anger.

The main questionnaire for the big five personality test (Costa and McCrae, 1992) runs to 240 questions and takes approximately 45 minutes to complete; however, Gosling et al. (2003) note that a number of shorter questionnaires have been based around the framework, some as short as ten, or even five, questions. The results of big five tests can thus be presented with a range of precision, from detailed percentages which break each factor down into sub-elements, to broad results such as 'mid-agreeableness', 'high conscientiousness', etc.

Visit the Online Resource Centre for information about a UK-wide experiment to test personality against the big-five personality scale.

# Nomothetic approaches in recruitment and selection

**Running case:** the personality test

Chance chooses a personality test based on the 'big five' characteristics. He is asked to think about the ideal candidate for the job, and, in consultation with the testing company that he had employed, an ideal range in each scale is drawn up:

Openness to experience—Mid
Some flexibility needed, but in many respects this is a routine job. Someone too creative might be too disruptive, but someone completely reliant on routine would not be flexible enough when the need arises.

Conscientiousness—High
Needs to be well-organized, for example in putting together rotas and managing the paperwork, and being able to take charge of a shift from start to finish with no one else above them to refer to.

Extraversion—High
Needs to have a very outgoing personality, both in leadership of the team and in being able to motivate them for a shift, and in dealing with, and motivating, customers in the gym.

Agreeableness—High

Needs to be warm and friendly in dealing with customers—most of the time will be spent on the gym floor.

Neuroticism—Mid-to-Low

A bit of nervous energy would be good, but, overall, the gym is a fast-paced atmosphere and the person in charge needs to maintain a sense of calm. This is especially the case as injuries and medical emergencies sometimes need to be dealt with.

The tests are administered. Candidates who are nowhere near the ideal profile are rejected instantly. A list of 20 candidates who match the desired profile, or are fairly close to it, is sent to Chance. Chance looks at the list alongside the original application forms and CVs, and draws up a shortlist of five candidates.

How would you feel if you had been rejected from the shortlist by the method just outlined?

Nomothetic approaches to personality suggest that personality is an objective entity which can be measured and either categorized or plotted out on some form of personality scale as a combination of different strengths of different traits. In the process of recruitment and selection, this suggests that, if a desired personality profile can be outlined for a particular role, in a person specification for example, then personality tests can be used as an instrument to find the most appropriate candidate to match that personality profile.

**Personality test** A written test whereby the responses to a set of questions are said to provide a measure of personality.

The **personality test** is usually a questionnaire where a candidate selects one of a number of different options for a set of different questions. Some questionnaires will ask candidates to locate themselves on a scale, as in Table 8.3.

Such a question would be part of the calculation of a candidate's position on the extraversion/introversion scale—the more strongly a candidate agrees with this proposition, the more likely they are to be extravert in nature. The scale allows neutral responses, and there might be some subjectivity in answering: for example, how easy is it to tell the difference between agreeing and agreeing strongly?

Other questionnaires might try to force an opinion one way or another, thus the question might be a more simple:

I enjoy parties and social gatherings: YES/NO

or:

Do you tend to prefer:

A quiet night in, or

Parties and social gatherings

**Table 8.3**  A typical personality test scale question

|  | Strongly agree | Agree | Neutral | Disagree | Strongly disagree |
|---|---|---|---|---|---|
| I enjoy parties and social gatherings |  |  |  |  |  |

This means that neutral answers are avoided, leading to a more definite position on a personality scale. However, this does not allow for subtleties in a personality to be expressed—a person might enjoy parties occasionally, for example, but be equally happy with quiet nights in.

The questionnaires are usually trademarked commercial products for which a company wishing to recruit will pay for the right to use.

Visit the Online Resource Centre for links to these and to some similar tests that you can try for free.

## Personality testing assessed

Personality tests provide an efficient means of screening candidates and are thus often used for pre-screening, especially when there is a large volume of applications for a job which need to be whittled down quickly. Thus a personality test is sometimes administered at the same time as the application, especially in online applications. In other instances a personality test may be used further down the selection process, possibly alongside other selection tools such as the interview or references.

However, the efficacy of personality tests is a matter of great debate, particularly around their **predictive validity**—the degree to which the result of a personality test accurately predicts the performance of a candidate in the job itself. The results for personality tests suggest that their predictive validity is low, at the most between 30% and 40% (Pilbeam and Corbridge, 2006: 173), and as low as 15% for some self-administered tests (Reilly and Chao, 1982: 32). More positive results emerged from the 1990s onwards, leading to renewed interest in personality testing; however, Morgeson et al. (2007) suggest that the better results come from tests which are customized and specific to a particular job, and that generic, off-the shelf personality tests remain poor in their predictive validity. Faragher (2014) further notes that while such tests can produce a personality profile, they need to be interpreted within the specific context of the organization, the job, and the person to which they are being applied—the danger comes from relying solely upon the test result.

> **Predictive validity** The ability for a test to predict a candidate's job performance.

There are a number of issues which potentially diminish the predictive validity and usefulness of personality tests, including:

- candidates may fake the answers to a test, giving answers that they think will improve their scores, rather than giving an honest answer (Furnham, 1997; Morgeson et al., 2007)
- the language and assumptions of tests may lead them to have a particular bias; for example, Thompson and McHugh (2009: 283) suggest that personality tests are good at finding managers who are '"male, middle-class and middle-aged," and in the West, white'
- Passer et al. (2003) question the extent to which the different traits are independent variables that can be measured, or do they have an effect upon each other?

This final point invites us to question just how realistic personality profiles are as a representation of personalities. They can be seen as reductionist, that is to say they reduce a complex, human phenomenon such as a personality down to a few figures on a set of scales.

Do you feel that human characteristics and emotions can be represented on a numerical scale? How would you feel if you received a Valentine's card stating 'On a scale between love and hate, my feelings for you measure 78.3%'?

This is part of the trade-off in recruitment and selection that we encountered earlier (see Figure 8.1). Personality tests give a snapshot of a personality, but they don't give the full picture of the richness of an individual's personality. In this respect, personality tests are often used alongside other techniques that will give further information, especially, as we shall see, in an assessment-centre approach.

An ideographic approach, which we encounter in the next section, would suggest that using more and more techniques, rather than relying on the reductionist personality test alone, would help build up more of a picture of the complexities and richness of individual personalities.

## Review questions

| | |
|---|---|
| **Describe** | What is meant by a nomothetic approach to personality? |
| **Explain** | How are personality tests used to measure personality in type and trait theories? |
| **Analyse** | Why do personality tests have a low predictive validity? |
| **Apply** | Referring back to the Pret a Manger case, what do you think would be an ideal personality profile for one of their recruits? Use scales such as MBTI, OCEAN, Eysenck, or Cattell to formulate your recommendations. |

# The ideographic approach to personality

## Running case: the whites of their eyes

The five candidates had been called in for interview. The panel, made up of Simon Chance, Meg Mortimer, Linda Wilkinson, and the current fitness centre manager, Carl Jones, have a discussion beforehand to work out their lines of questioning. They have the candidates' CVs, application forms, and personality test results before them.

Briefing the panel, Chance suggests that the interview would be an opportunity to get a more accurate view of the candidates' personalities, i.e. to see whether it matched with the results of the personality test.

'These personality tests are just figures on a piece of paper. They may give us an overview of what they are like, but we need to confirm that they are accurate. Not only that, there is much more to what people are—what makes them tick—than a few points plotted out on a scale. We need to dig behind that to get a much more rounded picture of what these people are like.'

'A piece of paper isn't enough. We need to see the whites of their eyes.'

For many people, the singer Michael Jackson had an unusual personality. During his life, stories would appear daily in the media alleging the seemingly bizarre goings on in his life. Without passing judgement on Jackson, it is perhaps not too controversial to say that his personality was unique and there will probably never be anyone like him ever again.

To consider a personality like Jackson perhaps brings to the fore some failings of the nomothetic approach:

Michael Jackson.

- Firstly, could any personality test and its associated personality scale really put across the true complexity and individuality of Jackson's personality? Do the results on paper get anywhere close to the reality of the person in the flesh?

- Secondly, with methods such as MBTI, there are only sixteen possible combinations of personality type (ENTJ, ISFP, etc.). On such a reading, one sixteenth of the world's population would share a personality type with Michael Jackson.

Now, while Michael Jackson might be a particularly far-fetched yardstick by which to measure our personalities, the argument of the **ideographic approach** is that, while our own personalities might be a little more mundane, they are, nevertheless, equally unique. We are all far richer and complex as individuals than nomothetic, trait theories would suggest.

**Ideographic approach**
An approach which sees personality as complex, unique to each individual, and dynamic.

Do you think that, following MBTI, you share a personality type with one sixteenth of the world's population?

# The personality as dynamic

In the previous section, we encountered a number of theories that saw personalities in static terms, that is to say they were something that could be plotted out on a set of scales or a framework. The ideographic approach suggests that our personality is not so static: that, instead, it is developed and moulded through social interaction. Our personality is adaptable and open to being changed by new experiences.

**Real life case:** the UK riots

In August 2011, London and other areas of the UK experienced a brief, but intense, period of rioting. While the riots were triggered as a protest against the police killing of a suspect, it seemed, as they spread, that people were taking part in looting seemingly out of enjoyment with no other goal.

In the aftermath and seeking to explain the riots, a distinction came to be drawn in people's efforts to explain what had happened.

On the one hand, it was suggested that the acts of violence were the result of sheer criminality—the suggestion being that this was an innate characteristic of the people involved.

On the other hand, other commentators argued that the rioting came about because of factors such as social deprivation and the influence of gangs. In other words, the behaviour came about as the product of people's immediate environment.

See *The Guardian*'s (2011) set of reports, 'Reading the riots', for more background and analysis of the 2011 riots.

**Nature versus nurture** The debate between whether our personalities are something natural, i.e. that we are born with, or are nurtured and develop over time.

**Processual** Always in a process of changing and developing.

The case of the riots, and the discussion here, is an example of the **nature versus nurture** debate. Are our personalities something that we are born with, or do they change over time? In the previous section, the type and trait theories see personalities, to different extents, as a fixed and measurable phenomenon. Eysenck even suggested that personality is so predetermined that it has genetic and biological elements.

The ideographic approach, however, suggests that our personalities are **processual**—this means that they are not static in the sense that a framework of traits would suggest, but, rather, they are in a continual process of being changed and influenced. Our personalities are always a work in progress rather than being a finished article.

---

### Theory in context: Sigmund Freud

The ideographic approach has its roots in the psychoanalytic tradition of Sigmund Freud. Freud is, perhaps, most associated with the stereotypical view of the psychoanalyst, with a patient lying on the couch, speaking to the therapist, talking about their dreams and desires and their past—the analyst analysing this and using what is said by the patient to uncover hidden truths about their state of mind.

Certainly, Freud's psychology is based in a prominent role for our unconscious, inner self, and the role of this in determining personality and behaviour. However, equally important is that personalities develop in an individual way, from childhood onwards. Personalities are not reducible to broad types; rather, each personality is unique and a result of development through environmental factors, i.e. the experience to which we are exposed throughout our lives.

Freud (1927) thus outlines three aspects of the mind that are in battle (or in balance) and which lead to different stages of development and to problems if unbalanced.

- At the most unconscious level is the *id*—the most basic human drive. This is the irrational and impulsive side of our nature, one which craves instant gratification (and thus is wont to engage in what might be inappropriate behaviour socially).

- At the level of consciousness is the *superego*—this is the environment around us (family, etc.). From this we learn the rules and values of society—it tells us what is appropriate or inappropriate behaviour. The superego is thus about things like upbringing and the influence of societal factors on our development.

- Mediating between the id and superego is the *ego*. For Freud, the ego is absent at birth, but takes shape—at first venturing into the outside world in service of gratifying the needs of the id, but later becoming a balancing factor between the two.

Thus, for Freud, the ego is a vital factor. People function normally when the ego manages its balancing role, but it causes personality abnormalities when this role fails to be fulfilled.

---

## Influences on the self

**Psychodynamic** A description of Freud's approach to personality which sees personality as continually being developed and changed by various influences.

The approach of Freud (1927) is sometimes described as a **psychodynamic** approach—it is rooted in psychology and suggests that personality is dynamic rather than static. Our sense of self and our personality are the product of influences over time—social influences, even unconscious influences.

Rather than a standard set of traits on a framework which can be measured, individual differences are a result of our interactions and experiences in society. While this will be a unique personality development for each individual, it can be seen that there are a number of particular areas of society that will, at different times in our lives, have an influence on our personality—albeit differently for each individual. Examples of such influences include:

- *Family and upbringing*—a key focus in Freud's work is the early effects that our family and upbringing have on our personality development. This is where we learn rules, values, etc. from a baby onwards and is thus a very important early formative stage in our personalities.

- *School*—going to school brings in more influences: rules, teachers, things learned, and also peer pressure and group dynamics from other pupils.

- *University*—for many readers of this book, university will be a major influence on personality at the moment. Some of you will be starting your very first term at university. It's common when returning home after a first few weeks at university to hear people back home say 'you've changed'. The implication is that the new influences and experiences at university have, in some way, changed personality and behaviour.

- *Organizations and the workplace*—in our careers we will work in several organizations. Like schools and universities, the workplace is a social phenomenon in which we will interact with people and have new experiences, and so organizations themselves are an influence on personality (we examine this later in this chapter under the social–radical approach).

- *Social categories*—it's not just specific organizations that have an influence on the development of ourselves as individuals. Categorizations in society also give us a sense of self—possibly with pressures to conform to certain types of behaviour—while at the same time acting as markers of our identity within society. For example, gender not only marks our identity in society, but also produces pressures for certain types of behaviour (e.g. 'boys don't cry'), which carries over into expected workplace behaviours (see, for example, the discussion of women and emotional labour in Chapter 16). Other social categories, such as race, religion, and social class, also have an impact on identity and personality in terms of how we develop as individuals, but also how others see us.

Visit the Online Resource Centre to read more on social categories and the individual.

The list is potentially infinite. If our personality develops from our experiences and interactions, then any aspect of society can, potentially, have an influence on us. In that we all have unique histories of social interaction and influence (we all come from different families, schools, etc.), so the ideographic approach sees every personality as unique, rather than conforming to a standard set of traits.

What organizations, individuals, or societal phenomena could you add to the list just given? How do you think they have influenced your personality?

## Problems with the ideographic approach

While the ideographic approach recognizes the individuality of personalities over and above broad personality types or scales, we suggest that this approach does bring some important drawbacks.

- Freud's work has not been used in mainstream management theory to the same extent as we saw with his contemporary, Jung. Its origins are in a clinical setting—the therapist's couch—and it is more concerned with identifying personality problems and focusing on 'abnormal' personalities, rather than identifying general personality types.
- The ideographic approach doesn't solve the problem of the time taken to get to understand a personality. Understanding comes from lengthy therapy sessions. Again, is this practical and efficient enough for a workplace recruitment setting? It brings us back to the problem personality tests were meant to solve—the need for efficiency.
- Where the nomothetic approach can be seen to be too scientific—reducing a personality to something that can be calculated—the ideographic approach is without any form of standardization. Given that personalities are unique and open-ended, our understanding of them is open to interpretation. Different people may perceive the same personality differently and, as we will see in the next section with interviewing, there are many factors that can alter and cause bias in that perception and interpretation.

In many respects, the ideographic approach raises questions, albeit valid questions, about the measurement of personality, rather than offering solutions. It recognizes that nomothetic approaches do not give a measurement of the entirety of an individual's personality, but rather than offering an alternative way of measuring personality it highlights the difficulties in getting such a full measurement. The ideographic approach lays out the complexity of personality rather than offering any hope of measuring that full complexity.

Nevertheless, the ideographic approach does allow us to appreciate the limited nature of information gained about personality in different selection processes. Furthermore, as we will see, it allows us to view the ideal selection process as one of building up information about personality from different sources rather than relying on any one single, limited source.

## The ideographic approach and selection

### Running case: interview thoughts

As the interviews progress, different panel members react differently to different candidates. Although they won't record it officially in their notes, each has their own reasons for liking or disliking particular candidates.

- Meg Mortimer dislikes one candidate who she felt came across as 'too common' for the hotel.
- Linda Wilkinson looks favourably upon a candidate who comes from her home town.
- Simon Chance takes a dislike to the accent of one of the candidates, which he feels sounds arrogant.
- Carl Jones dislikes a candidate because he had worked at a chain of gyms that he has had a major dispute with.
- Linda Wilkinson is not keen on a candidate who calls her 'Leslie Wilkinson' by accident when they are first introduced.
- Simon Chance is drawn to a candidate who supports the football club of which he is chair.
- Carl Jones feels that a young mother will be unable to juggle parenting responsibilities with commitment to the fitness centre.

The job interview would seem to be a way to make up for the deficiencies of nomothetic approaches, such as a personality test. If a personality test gives just a snapshot of a personality, presented as a few numbers and percentages, then the interview at least allows the selection panel the chance to see people in the flesh and get a better measure of their personality.

The bad news is that the predictive validity of interviews is even worse than that of personality tests (Pilbeam and Corbridge, 2006: 173; Reilly and Chao, 1982: 15). Why should it be that being able to meet and speak to the candidate in person produces even worse results?

Think of a time when you have had a job interview—how well did you think the panel were able to judge your personality?

Newell and Rice (1999: 159) suggest that many of the problems are due to **interpersonal perception** in the interview process. That is to say, the interpretation of the personality of a candidate can be biased by certain factors.

- The **halo/horns effect** suggests that a positive or negative trait that is picked up early in an interview can then bias the way in which an interviewer perceives an interviewee from then onwards. So, a good initial impression can lead to a **confirmation bias**—other perceptions confirming that initial impression, and vice versa for a bad first impression (Chartered Institute of Personnel and Development, 2015).

- Similarly, interviewers can be drawn to candidates with characteristics similar to themselves—a sort of halo effect generated by seeing aspects of themselves in the candidate (Chartered Institute of Personnel and Development, 2015).

- The interview can also be subject to **stereotypes** and **discrimination**. In the previous section we saw that race, gender, class, and religion are all aspects of society that feed into the development of our personality and social identity. They can also be factors which bias people's interpretation in an interview. For example, Reilly and Chao (1982) suggest that both race and gender are aspects where negative stereotypes and discriminatory views can affect women and black candidates negatively.

Which perceptual biases do you think are taking place in the running case?

In the latter case such discrimination would not only be unfair, but also illegal if discovered to be the basis for making an appointment. The UK Government's Department for Business and Industry provides guidance on avoiding the perceptual biases listed previously.

Visit the Online Resource Centre to read more on avoiding these biases.

The type of interview described earlier is an **unstructured interview**. Much greater predictive validity comes from **structured interviews** (Pilbeam and Corbridge, 2006: 173), which focus on behaviours relevant to the actual job. Interviewers might ask hypothetical questions, such as 'what would you do in this particular situation?', or questions which draw upon actual working experience, such as 'describe what you did in a particular situation when . . .?'.

**Interpersonal perception** The way in which one individual perceives the personality of another.

**Halo/horns effect** The tendency for people to continually reaffirm their initial impressions of a person, whether good or bad.

**Confirmation bias** A form of selective perception where people only tend to take note of information which confirms their already held perceptions.

**Stereotype** Where a characteristic is attributed to a person because of their membership of a particular social group, e.g. because of race or gender.

**Discrimination** Where a person is treated negatively and unfairly because of their membership of a particular social group, e.g. because of race or gender.

**Unstructured interview** An interview with no preset formal structure.

**Structured interview** An interview with a set format and standard questions, based around job-specific questions.

The structure, formality, and focus of a structured interview minimizes the opportunities for perceptual biases to creep in on the part of interviewers; however, it also minimizes the extent to which interviewers are able to get a picture of the personality of the candidate. Newell and Rice (1999: 160) suggest that, while the structured interview is more valid, the unstructured interview still remains the most popular form of interview that is carried out.

## Informal measures

### Running case: informal measures

During a break in interview proceedings, Chance peruses his list of five candidates and decides to undertake a bit of his own detective work.

First, he tries to find them on social networking sites. Many of the candidates have, sensibly, set their privacy settings high. However, one candidate has left all of their information visible. This was unfortunate, as their most recent status update reads: 'Pulled a sickie today—good times, afternoon in pub for me. Hope I can get out of this job soon, interview tomorrow, fingers crossed!' Chance finds this bizarre as the candidate had scored well on the 'conscientiousness' aspect of the scale and seemed very sincere in the interview.

Chance also realizes that one of the candidates had previously worked in a gym owned by a former colleague. Chance gives his friend a call and asks about the candidate. 'I was glad to be rid of him,' says the friend. 'He had no warmth with customers—he was cold and aloof. I wouldn't employ him if I were you—you'll have the customers leaving in droves.'

Again, Chance finds this strange, as the personality test had scored the candidate high on 'agreeableness' and he had presented himself well in the interview.

Chance feels that his informal enquiries have provided some useful information to add to the selection process, but is left unable to ask the candidates about what he had found out—it wouldn't look good to tell them he'd been snooping around on their Facebook profiles and talking to their ex-bosses.

Perhaps the extent to which managers crave for as much personality data as possibly over and above that which can be provided by formal recruitment methods is shown by the informal measures that managers will engage in. It would be a naïve applicant who thought that informal measures did not take place—phone calls to previous employers and, more recently, checks of social networking sites should be expected.

### Real life case: Facebook as a selection tool

A recent controversy in selection has been the use of Facebook or of online searches by employers trying to find out information about candidates. A survey by US online recruitment consultants Jobvite (2014) showed that 93% of recruiters review candidate's online social profiles. Postings that refer to sex, drugs, alcohol, and guns, or which are littered with profanities and spelling errors, have a strong chance of making recruiters reconsider their decisions in a more negative light. A candidate who describes themselves as 'serious and hardworking' on an application form might find this declaration undermined by numerous and regular postings of photographs of themselves falling out of nightclubs on their social networking profile, for example.

Of course, people have become wise to this and any sensible candidate will ensure that their privacy settings make this information private. However, a more recent trend has been for employers to demand Facebook passwords during an interview so that they can then see the full range of information on the profile for themselves, regardless of the privacy settings that the candidate has set.

**Sources:** *Boston Globe* (2012); Barnett (2012); *Time Magazine* (2012); Jobvite (2014).

What information about you is freely available online and potentially available for current and potential employers to see?

From an ideographic perspective, we can see how social networks and online information provide an insight into personalities that leaves any formal assessment methods lacking. All aspects of a person's life are laid bare—their interests, the comments they have made, and the photographs that they are tagged in.

While people can choose to make this information private, employers requesting passwords is something that Facebook (2012) has described as 'distressing', and they suggest that passwords should not be handed over as it is a violation of the terms of service and compromises the privacy of the information of the candidate's linked friends on Facebook.

Alongside privacy and ethical issues is a consideration of the nature of the data that might be gathered from Facebook and similar social networks. In a study of social networking sites being used as a part of the selection process, Kluemper and Rosen (2009) make two points about the nature of the personality data provided.

- Compared to an instrument like a personality test, social networking sites give a rich and wide-ranging insight into a person's lifestyle. Kluemper and Rosen (2009) found that such sites could be used to get a good estimation of a personality on the big five scale.

- However, Kluemper and Rosen also caution about the nature of information that is available on such sites. Recruiters are able to find out information about aspects of a person's life which might feed into discrimination and stereotyping: marital status, sexual orientation, religion, etc. This raises legal issues—employers have access, through social networking sites, to information that cannot be used legally as the basis for selection decisions.

Visit the Online Resource Centre for more on the use of social networking sites in selection and personality assessment.

We can understand the desire of employers to access the wealth of information available online so as to get a greater insight into a candidate's personality, but it is an area that has possible legal issues, with a lot of information irrelevant to the selection decision being made available. A more formal way to increase the amount of information about a candidate for the selection process is through the assessment centre approach.

## Getting an overall picture: assessment centres and triangulation

**Running case:** the new duty manager

The interviews prove inconclusive, with different members of the panel having wildly differing perceptions of the candidates. It becomes apparent that few of the opinions have anything to do with people's aptitudes for the job and, in some cases, they are illegal and discriminatory.

'Only one way to settle this,' says Chance, 'let's get them down on the gym floor and see them actually doing the job'.

Each of the candidates is asked to meet with an actual gym member, speak to them, and devise and deliver a workout plan.

Following this the candidates are given an 'in-tray' exercise. Each is placed in front of a computer and given a number of tasks to address: timetabling classes, staff rotas, etc.

Finally, a second interview is offered to the candidates. In this instance, questions are worked out in advance, with each being of relevance to the job or reflecting on the exercise that had taken place.

One candidate above all others shines through. Although his personality test wasn't the best fit, he has done well on the extraversion and agreeableness aspects. The interview and his work with the customers brings this out, and the in-tray exercise shows that he can also apply himself to individual administrative tasks.

The job of duty manager is offered to David Smith, who accepts.

Pilbeam and Corbridge (2006) summarize research into different methods and their predictive validities (Table 8.4). Taken by themselves, any of the formal assessment methods that we have so far encountered in this chapter score woefully low in predictive validity.

However, by blending methods into an assessment centre approach, a greater predictive validity can be achieved. An **assessment centre** approach doesn't necessarily mean that the selection activity takes place within a specific building of that name. It refers to the fact that no one method is used in isolation, but is blended alongside other methods. The more methods used, the more complete a picture of the candidate is gained.

While methods such as personality testing and interviews may still be

> **Assessment centre** A recruitment strategy where different selection techniques are blended in a selection process.

Table 8.4 Predictive validities of different selection methods (adapted from Pilbeam and Corbridge, 2006: 173)

| Value | Method |
|---|---|
| 1.0 | Certain prediction |
| 0.9 | |
| 0.8 | |
| 0.7 | Assessment centres for development |
| 0.6 | Skilful and structured interviews |
| 0.5 | Work sampling / Ability tests |
| 0.4 | Assessment centres for job performance / Biodata / Personality assessment |
| 0.3 | Unstructured interview |
| 0.2 | |
| 0.1 | References |
| 0.0 | Graphology / Astrology |

© *People Resourcing: Contemporary HRM in Practice*, Pilbeam, S., and Corbridge, M., Pearson Education Limited, 2006.

used, methods that have found to be effective additions to an assessment centre blend include those which are related to the work itself, for example so called 'in-tray exercises', where a candidate actually works through some of the tasks that might be expected of them. For example, in the earlier example of Pret a Manger, one of the techniques used to assess whether or not a person demonstrates the Pret 'behaviours' is to get an applicant to actually spend a day working in one of their stores.

---

**Real life case:** multiple selection methods at Santander

The Spanish bank Santander outline the various stages of selection process for their graduate recruitment scheme in the UK. At each stage, a number of different methods are used. The four stages are:

Online application. This includes completing an application form, submitting a CV, and undertaking a situational judgment test which is similar to an in-tray exercise in that it describes hypothetical situations that may occur in the workplace and asks candidates to select how they would respond.

Additional testing. If the online application is successful, there are further online tests which Santander say may be verbal, numerical, or competency based.

Telephone interview. This stage is a 30-minute interview where aspects of the candidate's personality and skills are assessed. Candidates are asked to prepare examples of where they have previously displayed desirable behaviours.

Assessment centre. This includes a variety of activities such as groupwork and presentations to test interpersonal skills, and also includes a face-to-face interview with a senior manager.

**Source:** Santander (2015).

---

While an assessment centre approach doesn't give an understanding of personality in its full ideographic form, it does draw upon more sources of information than a personality test or an interview alone. Furthermore, its formal nature can avoid the assessors being party to some of the legally problematic information that more informal methods, while giving a fuller picture of personality, might provide.

---

### Review questions

| | |
|---|---|
| **Describe** | What social factors have an effect on our personality? |
| **Explain** | What is meant when the ideographic approach describes personalities as 'dynamic'? |
| **Analyse** | What differences are there between the assumptions about the nature of personality made by the ideographic and the nomothetic approaches? |
| **Apply** | Look again at the stages of the selection process at Santander. What useful information about a candidate do you think each stage adds to the selection process? |

# Towards a social-radical approach

**Running case:** the spark is extinguished

Six months after his appointment, David Smith is seeing out the last of the evening's guests and is about to lock up. Simon Chance catches a glimpse of him looking sullen, barely raising his voice to say goodbye to the remaining guests, then slamming the door shut and lamely throwing the keys on to his desk.

This confirms what Chance had been hearing—the bubbly, outgoing, motivated personality that Chance had recruited six months ago has become withdrawn, barely raising a smile during the day. It isn't the best image to project to customers.

Chance is puzzled as to what has happened. All of the recruitment stages—the personality test, the interviews, the situational assessments—had marked Smith out as having the exact personality that they had wanted. And to begin with, he had been just that—it was as if his personality had changed.

Chance calls Smith over to find out what has happened.

'It's the work here,' replies Smith. 'I have to fill in so many forms—rotas, pay sheets, class timetables, and accident reports. I feel like I'm suffocating in paperwork. It's all just me and a computer. I need to be around people, that's how I get my buzz. I have to just pass on orders to the other guys in the team—they see me as someone who gives them work, not works with them. And it's rubbing off on them, too. We have to go out there and motivate customers, but with this kind of work the spark is just extinguished.'

The nomothetic approach saw personality as something which can be measured and sorted into particular types and categories. The ideographic approach saw personalities as more unique and complex, developing as a result of social interaction and experiences. In both cases, however, they see personality as a 'thing', which the organization, in some way, observes and tries to understand.

Both of these approaches also suggest, largely, that personality is a property of the individual, independent of the organization. However, we saw with the ideographic approach that organizations themselves are one of the many societal influences on the self which change and develop our personalities. The workplace thus has a direct effect on the very thing it is trying to measure—personality.

> **Social-radical approach** The view that organizations have an effect on the personality of their members.

The **social-radical** view that we suggest in this final section brings about a shift in perception of the relationship between organizations and personality. It suggests that the idea of personality as an objective 'thing,' independent of the organization, is problematic. Instead, the organization has a part to play in creating and shaping personalities.

- Firstly, we see personality categorizations as a tool of organizations which come to take on lives of their own and actually have an effect on personalities, rather than simply measuring them. This is symptomatic of how Michel Foucault (1977) saw power operating in society, and so we term this the social part of the social–radical approach.

- Secondly, organizations directly affect personalities and this can be in a negative, as much as positive, way. This negative effect was observed by radical psychiatrist Félix Guattari (e.g. Guattari and Negri, 1990). We see this as the radical aspect of the social–radical approach.

# Foucault's critique of categorization

In Chapters 4 and 13 we encounter the work of Michel Foucault, who examined ways in which power operates throughout society. One of Foucault's (1977) interests, as we saw in Chapter 4, is how power is exercised by categorizing, calculating, and ordering the world around us. We are categorized and labelled as a means of convenience, i.e. it is a simple way of understanding and managing the world. What is important for Foucault is that although such categorizations are shortcuts, they come to take on lives of their own and people identify themselves by these labels.

Think of the results of personality tests—categories like INTJ, ENFP, etc.—these are frameworks that have been created specifically as a way of categorizing personalities in order to simplify them and make measuring them more efficient. But once such tests are administered, it is common that people come to wear them as labels and come to identify with them—people say 'I am an ENTP', etc. (compare this with the manager in Chapter 6, who takes a Belbin test and then starts to live up to the result—the label starts to define not only how the person identifies themselves, but how they actually act). Rather than simply reflecting a personality, the test and its associated label starts to affect and change that personality.

Deleuze and Guattari (1983) build on Foucault's work to examine how psychoanalytical traditions place labels upon people in both nomothetic and ideographic approaches. They would criticize Jung for ordering the personality into certain types and, equally, criticize Freud for his 'ordering role' (Deleuze and Parnet, 2002: 14) in interpreting people's unique personalities.

Félix Guattari worked as a radical psychiatrist in France. He was interested in trying new and different means of treating patients rather than traditional methods. Guattari treated patients not by labelling them as a particular personality type, as Jung would, nor by labelling them as having some sort of abnormality, as Freud would. Instead, Guattari saw people as having the potential to become something else, striving for new experiences and interactions so that their personality can constantly develop.

# The radical critique of the effects of organization on personality

The problem for Deleuze and Guattari, and in particular for Guattari, is that the potential of people to strive for new experiences and interactions is often stifled—none more so than by the effects of what organizations actually do and the way in which people are organized.

This is something that we saw in Chapters 2 and 3. Recall the Diego Rivera murals and Chaplin's *Modern Times*. In both cases people were shown as dehumanized, their personalities deadened by boring and monotonous factory work. Weber, too, noted how bureaucracy, with its repetitive routines, led to disenchantment—a loss of the magical elements of life.

Rational modes of organization are thus seen as having a stifling effect upon the personalities of workers. For Guattari, however, there is an alternative, and organizations could operate in such a way as to allow individual potential to be realized. Work which is focused on promoting individual potential and creativity is thus suggested as:

> [A]ctivities in which people can develop themselves as they produce, organizations in which the individual is valuable rather than functional… And redefining work as creative activity can only happen as individuals emerge from stifled, emotionally blocked rhythms of constraint.
>
> (Guattari and Negri, 1990: 15)

The social–radical view is a complex and critical view of personality which shifts the attention from most of what we have examined in the chapter, i.e. rather than organizations measuring personalities we now see organizations having a direct effect upon people's personalities, more often than not constraining what those personalities could have the potential to be.

The suggestion of the social–radical approach—that organizations should operate in a way that frees individual personalities to reach their potential—may sound idealistic. However, in the following chapters, where we see motivation theories that suggest people should 'self-actualize' and maximize their potential (Chapter 9), and where we see theories of learning that promote the reflective self-development of individuals (Chapter 10), we see people working towards achieving their potential rather than being stifled by the organization.

## Review questions

| | |
|---|---|
| **Describe** | What is meant by a 'social–radical' approach to personality? |
| **Explain** | How can personality types be viewed as putting 'labels' upon us? |
| **Analyse** | How can organizations stifle the potential for personalities to develop? What could they do to prevent this? |
| **Apply** | In the running case, what has been the main influence in changing Smith's personality? Is this a fault of the selection process assessing his personality incorrectly or of Junction Hotel in changing his personality? |

# Chapter summary

This chapter has examined two major perspectives on personality and their implications for the assessment of personality in the recruitment and selection process.

The nomothetic approach sees personality as something which is measurable and which can be outlined in terms of models of personality types and/or traits. Such models are the basis for personality testing in organizations, and some of these models are used in the recruitment and selection process.

The ideographic approach sees personality as complex and unique to each individual, and as something which is changed constantly by our interactions with society. It criticizes the nomothetic approach for giving too simplistic a view of personality.

Personality testing in organizations is seen to be of limited use, but, equally, many methods of selection fare badly in their predictive validity. While the use of social networks and other informal methods can gain more insight into personality, the practice is ethically dubious. An assessment centre approach blends selection methods in a more formal setting, and can gain more accurate and valid results in the selection process.

Finally, a social–radial approach takes account of the effect that organizations themselves have upon personality, both in categorizing it in personality tests and in their role as an aspect of society that shapes people's personalities.

## Further reading

**Chartered Institute of Personnel Development 2015. A head for hiring: the behavioural science of recruitment and selection. Available at http://www.cipd.co.uk/binaries/a-head-for-hiring_2015-behavioural-science-of-recruitment-and-selection.pdf**
This research report gives an overview of recruitment and selection techniques, how they link to psychological perspectives on personality, and how bias is found in the process and can be minimized.

**Bratton, J. 2010. *Work and organizational behaviour*, 2nd edn. Palgrave Macmillan: Basingstoke.**
Many textbooks cover theories of personality, for example see Chapter 4 of Bratton.

**Cain, S. 2012. *Quiet: The power of introverts in a world that can't stop talking*. Viking: London.**
An overview of Jung's introversion and extraversion from the perspective of the introvert.

**Kluemper, D.H., and Rosen, P.A. 2009. Future employment selection methods: Evaluating social networking web sites. *Journal of Managerial Psychology* 24(6): 567–80.**
A case study of the use of social networking sites in the selection process.

## References

Barnett, E. 2012. Facebook passwords 'fair game in job interviews'. *Daily Telegraph*, 23 March.

*Boston Globe* 2012. Job seekers getting asked for Facebook passwords, 20 March.

Cain, S. 2012. *Quiet: The power of introverts in a world that can't stop talking*. Viking: London.

Callaghan, G., and Thompson, P. 2002. 'We recruit attitude': The selection and shaping of routine call centre labour. *Journal of Management Studies* 39(2): 233–54.

Cattell, R.B. 1966. *The scientific analysis of personality*. Aldine: Chicago.

Chartered Institute of Personnel and Development 2015. A head for hiring: The behavioural science of recruitment and selection. Available at http://www.cipd.co.uk/binaries/a-head-for-hiring_2015-behavioural-science-of-recruitment-and-selection.pdf.

Costa, P.T., Jr., and McCrae, R.R. 1992. *Revised NEO Personality Inventory (NEO-PI-R) and NEO Five-Factor Inventory (NEO-FFI) manual*. Psychological Assessment Resources: Odessa, FL.

Dakin, S., Nilakant, V., and Jensen, R. 1994. The role of personality testing in managerial selection. *Journal of Managerial Psychology* 9(5): 3–11.

Deleuze, G., and Guattari, F. 1983. *Anti-Oedipus: Capitalism and schizophrenia*. University of Minnesota Press: Minneapolis.

Deleuze, G., and Parnet, C. 2002. *Dialogues II*. Continuum: New York.

Eysenck, H.J., and Eysenck, M.W. 1985. *Personality and individual differences: A natural science approach*. Plenum Publishing Corporation: New York.

Facebook 2012. Protecting your passwords and your privacy, 23 March. Available at: https://www.facebook.com/notes/facebookand-privacy/protecting-your-passwords-and-your-privacy/326598317390057C (last accessed 20 August 2015).

Faragher, J. 2014. Psychometric testing: The stark truth. *People Management*, June.

Foucault, M. 1977. *Discipline and punish: The birth of the prison*. Pantheon Books: New York.

French, R., and Rumbles, S. 2010. Recruitment and selection. In: Rees, G., and French, R. (eds) *Leading, managing and developing people*, 3rd edn. Chartered Institute of Personnel Development: London, pp. 169–90.

Freud, S. 1927. *The ego and the id authorized* (transl. J. Riviere). Hogarth Press: London.

Furnham, A.F. 1997. Knowing and faking one's five-factor personality score. *Journal of Personality Assessment* 69(1): 229–43.

Gosling, S.D., Rentfrow, P.J., and Swann, W.B., Jr. 2003. A very brief measure of the big-five personality domains. *Journal of Research in Personality* 37: 504–28.

Guattari, F., and Negri, A. 1990. *Communists like us: New spaces of liberty, new lines of alliance*. Semiotext(e): New York.

Jacobs, K. 2015. Pret's people management secrets. *HR Magazine*, 23 January.

Jobvite. 2014. Social recruiting survey 2014. Available at https://www.jobvite.com/wp-content/uploads/2014/10/Jobvite_SocialRecruiting_Survey2014.pdf.

Jung, C.G. 1923. *Psychological types: or, The psychology of individuation* (transl H. Godwyn Baynes). Harcourt Brace: New York.

Keirsey, D. 1998. *Please understand me II: Temperament, character, intelligence*. Prometheus Nemesis: Del Mar, CA.

Kluemper, D.H., and Rosen, P.A. 2009. Future employment selection methods: Evaluating social networking web sites. *Journal of Managerial Psychology* 24(6): 567–80.

McCrae, R.R., and Costa, P.T., Jr. 1990. *Personality in adulthood*. Guilford Press: New York.

McCrae, R.R., and Costa, P.T., Jr. 1996. Toward a new generation of personality theories: Theoretical contexts for the five-factor model. In: Wiggins, J.S. (ed.) *The five-factor model of personality: Theoretical perspectives*. Guilford Press: New York, pp. 51–87.

Moore, P. 2015. Pret a Manger—behind the scenes at the 'Happy Factory'. *The Guardian*, 14 April.

Morgeson, F.P., Campion, M.A., Dipboye, R.L., Hollenbeck, J.R., Murphy, K., and Schmitt, N. 2007. Reconsidering the use of personality tests in personnel selection contexts. *Personnel Psychology* 60(3): 683–729.

Myers, I.B. 1962. *Manual: The Myers-Briggs type indicator*. Consulting Psychologist Press: Palo Alto, CA.

Myers, I.B., and Myers, P.B. 1995. *Gifts differing: Understanding personality type*. Davies-Black: Palo Alto, CA.

Myerscough, P. 2013. Short cuts. *London Review of Books*, 3 January.

Newell, S., and Rice, C. 1999. Assessment, selection and evaluation: Problems and pitfalls. In: Leopold, J., Harris, L., and Watson, T. (eds) *Strategic human resourcing: Principles, perspectives and practices*. Financial Times/Pitman: London, pp. 129–65.

Passer, M.W., Smith, R., Atkinson, M., Mitchell, J., and Muir, D. 2003. *Psychology: Frontiers and applications*. McGraw-Hill Ryerson: Toronto.

Pilbeam, S., and Corbridge, M. 2006. *People resourcing: Contemporary HRM in practice*. Financial Times/Prentice Hall: Harlow.

Preston, R. 2012. Smiley culture: Pret a Manger's secret ingredients. *Daily Telegraph*, 9 March.

Rawlinson, K. 2013. Pret workers want more for their smile: Enough pay and hours to live on. *The Independent*, 4 January.

Reilly, R.R., and Chao, G.T. 1982. Validity and fairness of some alternative employee selection procedures 1. *Personnel Psychology* 35(1): 1–62.

Santander 2015. Apply. Available at: http://www.santanderearlyincareer.co.uk/apply (last accessed 13 August 2015).

*The Guardian* 2011. Reading the riots: Investigating England's summer of disorder. Available at: http://www.guardian.co.uk/uk/series/reading-the-riots.

Thompson, P., and McHugh, D. 2009. *Work organisations: A critical approach*. Palgrave Macmillan: Basingstoke.

*Time Magazine* 2012. Job seekers getting asked for Facebook passwords, 20 March.

# Motivation and the meaning of work

## Chapter overview and learning outcomes

By the end of this chapter you should be able to:

- describe the differences between extrinsic, intrinsic, and social factors of motivation

- explain the role and extent of pay in motivating workers

- analyse the role of psychology in understanding motivation, explaining the main contributions of

behaviourist, content, and process approaches

- explain how social factors, such as identity and orientations to work, contribute to our understanding of what motivates people to work.

## Key theorists

| | |
|---|---|
| Burrhus Frederic (B.F.) Skinner | Pioneered operant conditioning, which is used in workplace behavioural modification techniques |
| Abraham Maslow | Developed the hierarchy of needs, which was then used as a theory of workplace motivation |
| Frederick Herzberg | Suggested that only some job characteristics motivate people in the workplace, while other hygiene factors can only cause dissatisfaction |
| John Stacey Adams | Developed equity theory, which suggests that people are motivated by comparing their workplace rewards with others |
| Victor Vroom | Developed expectancy theory, which suggests that people are motivated by actions which help them achieve their desired goals |
| John Goldthorpe | Suggested that people had different predispositions, or orientations, to work, which influence the meaning and identity people derive from their work |

## Key terms

| | |
|---|---|
| Extrinsic motivators | Motivating factors that come from factors external to an activity, e.g. pay, praise, or prestige |
| Intrinsic motivators | Motivating factors that come from the activity itself |
| Behavioural theories of motivation | A use of stimulus and response techniques whereby behaviour is altered by a planned provision of rewards and punishments |

| Content theories of motivation | Theories of motivation which suggest that the content of work be designed so as best to meet the needs which motivate workers; examples include Maslow's hierarchy of needs and Herzberg's motivators and hygiene theory |
| --- | --- |
| Process theories of motivation | Theories of motivation which suggest that motivation is a result of individual processes of perception, comparison, and calculation; examples include equity theory and expectancy theory |
| Social theories of motivation | Theories of motivation which see motivation as part of the role of work in creating meaning and identity for people within society |

# Introduction

**Running case:** a sense of lethargy

Meg Mortimer senses something wrong in reception. Not massively wrong—well, at least not yet—but there just seems to be a sense of lethargy: people are sluggish in performing their tasks, with nobody wanting to go the extra mile. Smiles seem forced, and the performance of jobs is perfunctory—the job is done but with no great enthusiasm.

Mortimer looks at the reception team on duty today and makes some notes:

- David Morrison—a young porter who, in his spare time, is training to do a triathlon
- Jane Foster—a receptionist who is also undertaking a hospitality course and is tipped for great things within the hotel
- Sue Ridgewell—another receptionist who Mortimer considers to be good, but not as ambitious as Jane
- Steve Long and John McAuley—two students who work part time either as porters or sometimes behind reception, and Ellerby Peters, a student on work experience.

The reception area is quiet and all that Mortimer sees are the sullen faces of the reception team. What can she possibly do to make these people more motivated towards their work?

How do you feel at the start of a day's work? Do you look forward to the work, being with your colleagues, and getting stuck into the days challenges? Or do you feel dread, sensing hours of drudgery and boredom in front of you, with only the thought of the pay packet to get you through your shift? In other words, how much are you motivated by your work?

Why are you reading this chapter? What is keeping you reading the book rather than playing computer games, hanging out with friends, or going to sleep? It is because you have a test, essay, or seminar soon and you need to know about the topic, or is it that you are genuinely interested in motivation and want to know more? Without some motivation, unless you are forced to read this chapter in class, you will quickly stop reading and put the book away.

**Motivation** is vital at work. Nearly all work is, at least in part, shaped by motivation, and therefore motivation is central to organizational success. Without well-motivated (and skilled) employees most organizations will not succeed. This leads us to the questions: What motivates employees? How do managers increase their motivation? How much comes from within the person and how much can be shaped by the environment around them? Do motivation and higher levels of job satisfaction actually increase job performance (Judge et al. 2001)?

Motivation is a complex topic that is difficult to define. It is also difficult to capture. We cannot see motivation. It is invisible and can only be inferred from what people do. Motivation also varies between individuals and even within them (Dalal and Hulin 2008). This had led to a variety of different explanations, largely informed by psychology:

- Pay might seem like the obvious workplace motivator, but we see it as one of many possible workplace rewards. In particular, we distinguish between **extrinsic rewards** that are given by the organization, of which pay is an example; **intrinsic rewards**, such as a sense of achievement, which come more from within the individual worker; and **social rewards** that come from colleagues and co-workers.

- From a behaviourist perspective, **rewards** and **punishments** are used to motivate workers towards some behaviours and away from others. While this may have results, it can be viewed as **coercion** and manipulation, rather than as genuine motivation of behaviour.

- Extrinsic, intrinsic, and social rewards have been integrated into content theories of motivation, which show how individuals are motivated differently. Such content theories include the well-known motivation theories of Maslow (1943) and Herzberg (1966).

- Process theories of motivation see motivation as much more individual, subjective, and changeable. With equity theory and expectancy theory, individuals make their own comparisons and calculations which feed into their levels of motivation.

We suggest that these psychological perspectives, while commonplace in motivation literature, have their shortcomings and do not fully explain workplace motivation. An alternative view of motivation, which we consider at the end of the chapter, comes from looking at the wider social significance of work—the meanings that people attach to work and how this feeds into their identity in society.

**Motivation** The will and desire that a person has to engage in a particular behaviour or perform a particular task.

**Extrinsic reward** A reward that a person receives which is provided by somebody else.

**Intrinsic reward** A reward that a person senses for themselves, rather than it being provided by someone else.

**Social reward** A reward that comes from the feeling of being part of a group or team.

**Reward** In behaviourism, a positive response that is received for performing a particular behaviour.

**Punishment** In behaviourism, a negative response that is received for performing a particular behaviour.

**Coercion** Behaviour that arises from being forced in some way into performing that behaviour.

## Employability skills: find something that you are passionate about

Job adverts often call for 'self-motivated' candidates, but what do employers mean by this? In our interview, Joe Greenwell, the chairman of Ford in Britain, suggests that a big part of success in a job comes from passion for the work and curiosity about that work.

If you are going to be successful at anything you need to be genuinely enthusiastic about what you are doing. If you are not enthusiastic about it you are not going to be able to lead people…If you want to engender passion in the people you lead you'd better be passionate yourself…

> ▶ If you are passionate you are also curious. Curiosity is very valuable. If you want to get better at something you need to ask questions, roll your sleeves up and learn and be prepared to get told off and make mistakes.
>
> **Source:** Author interview with Joe Greenwell, Ford in Britain, 2012. (Visit the Online Resource Centre for full interview.)

 How can you demonstrate passion and curiosity about a job to an employer? What have you done at university or before that you could tell a prospective employer about to demonstrate passion and curiosity? What is it that you are passionate about? Could you make that part of your future job?

# Extrinsic, intrinsic, and social rewards—all about the money?

## Running case: triathlon man

David Morrison is a young porter at Junction Hotel. Much of the day is spent standing around reception, following a repetitive routine of opening doors and taking bags up to rooms. He has to do what he is told, when he is told, and he rarely feels challenged at work.

In his spare time he is training for a triathlon, with sessions morning, noon, and night.

In the morning, before work begins, David is in the pool of the fitness centre churning up the lengths towards his target. As he completes the final length, exhausted and gasping for breath from his effort, he looks up to his trainer, who is at the side of the pool: 'good job, 30 seconds less than yesterday'. Morrison smacks the surface of the water with his fist and lets out an almost primal cry of 'Yeeeeesss!' To say he is pleased with his achievement is an understatement.

All of this effort was done free of charge, of course. Indeed, he had to pay quite a lot of his own money for equipment, entry fees, and sports club memberships. And the sponsorship money for the triathlon will all be going to his charity—again, a feeling which makes him proud.

As he emerges from the changing rooms in his porter's outfit, David walks towards reception to perform the one element of the day for which he will actually be rewarded with a wage. His response to starting this part of the day is that he lets out a sigh, feeling all of his enthusiasm drain away. He stands in the corner of reception waiting for another day of opening doors and carrying suitcases. He looks up at the clock, 'I can't wait for lunchtime, when I'll be back in the pool,' he thinks.

What motivates you at work? Pay is often our first answer. We surely go to work to get paid rather than for enjoyment. Certainly, this is the case for many students who have part-time jobs in order to get through university. Working in bars, shops, or, occasionally, factories, many of our students say the pay is the only thing that keeps them turning up for work.

For Frederick Taylor and Henry Ford (see Chapter 3), pay was used as a motivator to get people to do otherwise monotonous and boring factory work.

- Taylor believed that workers had a 'natural laziness' (1911: 20)—they were inherently demotivated and thus piece rates (payment for the actual amount of work done) were used to motivate people to work.

- Rather than piece rates, Ford introduced the $5 day. While this was a massive increase from the previous $2.40 per day (Raff and Summers, 1987: 69), it was accompanied by wholesale mechanization and rationalization of the work process, and highly controlled working conditions (Beynon, 1984: 34). Workers disliked the conditions intensely, but the high wage motivated many job-seekers to want to work in Ford's factories.

Both Taylor and Ford had a simple, coercive view of motivation based on the assumption of *homo economicus*—that people are motivated by pay and economic reasons alone (see Chapter 5). In this section we examine the link between pay and motivation, but also between other workplace rewards and motivation. In particular, we note two types of rewards:

- extrinsic rewards, such as pay. They are external to the individual and used to motivate them to perform a particular action or behaviour. Other examples of extrinsic motivators might be promotion, working conditions, perks of the job (such as a company car), etc.
- intrinsic rewards which are internal to the individual. Examples include a sense of achievement or a feeling of job satisfaction. Lawler (1973) suggested that intrinsic rewards could, in fact, be much more powerful motivators than extrinsic rewards, such as pay and promotion.

## Motivation and pay—an unclear relationship

The link between motivation and pay is far from clear. It is certainly a major mechanism in the motivation of people in the workplace, but, as Handy (1993: 51) notes, little is known about how it actually works as a motivator. Furthermore, it is far from clear cut that it is the prime motivator in the workplace.

**Real life case:** how to get your employees to work for free

Pandora is a US-based popular music streaming service that is rivalling Spotify and iTunes, now worth a reported $3.6bn (Harrison 2015). It works by analysing music and connecting it together through a 'music genome', to enable users to discover new music.

However, the service's early days were a struggle. It was founded in 2000 with $2 million start-up, but just one year later, amid the bursting of the dot-com bubble, it went bankrupt. To get round this, CEO Tim Westergren convinced the employees to work for an ever smaller share of their salary, and by the end of 2001 they were not getting paid at all, getting stock options (on a company that was losing money) rather than salaries. Ultimately 50 employees worked for two years for free, the company owed $2m in back salaries (which they since have learnt is illegal), and Tim Westergren had personal debts of $500,000. Eventually they held out long enough for an investor, which meant that everyone could be paid.

How did he motivate these 50 employees to work for free? Westergren, a former musician, led by example, being the first to take a salary deferral. He also said he had a clear sense of purpose that everyone believed in. Additionally, they pulled together, Westergren states, because everyone ▶

▶ involved was passionate about music and believed the site would help artists. Westergren gave great speeches, stressing how unique, important, and life-changing the product they were making was. He stressed that what they were doing was magical. Westergren said that Pandora was changing culture, and he asked his employees 'How many times in your life do you have a chance to do that?' (Executive Grapevine 2015a).

**Sources:** Executive Grapevine (2015a); Harrison (2015).

Visit the Online Resource Centre to view Tim Westergren's full speech.

How would you feel working for free for two years? Why do you think that the employees stayed?

Tim Westergren's ability to get his employees working for free for over two years might be an extreme example, but it does show that pay is not the only factor affecting motivation. Studies into the relationship between motivation, pay, and other types of reward have shown a similar mixed picture.

- Between 1946 and 1992, a series of surveys of US workers showed that praise from managers, interesting work, and good wages are the main workplace motivators, with each of these taking the top position at different times (Wiley, 1997).

- The 2014 Global Workforce Study of 32,000 employees worldwide stated that the number one top attraction to an employer was the basic pay, with the number two reason being job security (Towers Watson, 2014).

- In a global survey of executives, managers, and employees (Dewhurst et al., 2009), financial rewards, such as bonuses and an increase in base pay, played an important part in motivating workers; however, non-financial incentives, such as praise from a manager, attention from managers, and being given responsibility, were shown as being slightly more effective motivating factors.

From the various results, it would seem that pay has an important role in motivation, but that a word of encouragement or praise from the boss can motivate employees just as much.

Rewards such as praise or interesting work are not as tangible as pay, but they are still extrinsic motivators and management have a role in providing these motivating factors within the workplace. However, such rewards may also contribute to workers gaining intrinsic rewards, such as a sense of achievement or a sense of pride in their work.

## Intrinsic motivation—the lottery question

**Real life case:** lottery millionaires

In November 2014 a syndicate of five paper mill workers shared a £2.9 million lottery jackpot, giving them around £600,000 each. Yet, rather than instantly quiting their jobs, they were straight back to work 'due to the workload'. Gary, one of the winners, said the company were 'quite short staffed' ▶

▶ so they didn't want to walk away because of their win. Because it was a family business, they felt a loyalty to the company (Flanagan, 2014). On the other hand, in March 2012, a syndicate of twelve UK bus drivers won a £38 million lottery jackpot. They quit their jobs instantly, leaving their boss with the headache of replacing a quarter of the workforce (Walker and Jones, 2012).

What would you do if you won enough money on the lottery to never have to work again? Would you give up university and any plans for a career?

For many of us, our first act on winning the lottery would be to quit our current job—no more of the 9 to 5 routine and answering to the boss. It is certainly an understandable response if people are in a boring, monotonous job or are unhappy in their work. If the only motivation for work is the pay, then there is no reason to carry on if money is no longer an issue.

However, a different picture emerges if the consideration is whether or not people would give up work *completely*. People might give up their current job but, once a new house and car have been purchased, and multiple holidays have been taken, they might seek out some form of work, or challenge, to occupy them.

The **lottery question** has been posed in numerous surveys and, repeatedly, the answer is that a majority of people would continue to work, either in the same or a different job. In an inter-national comparison, Harpaz (1989) reported that between 68.8% of respondents (in the UK) and 93.4% of respondents (in Japan) said they would continue to work in some form, even if they no longer needed the pay.

A life of leisure?
**Source:** Cathy Yeulet /123RF

**Lottery question**  A question which asks whether people would give up work if they had enough money to live without having to work.

### Real life case: Tony Hsieh, the billionaire who lives in a trailer

In July 2009, the American Internet entrepreneur Tony Hsieh sold Zappos.com, the online shoes retailer, to Amazon for $1.2 billion, leaving Hsieh with a net worth of a reported $820 million (Executive Grapevine, 2015b). Rather than retiring, the then 36-year-old carried on working for Zappos as its CEO for only $36,000 per annum (Holley, 2015). Even before he joined Zappos, Hsieh was already a multi-millionaire, having sold his first company LinkExchange to Microsoft for $265 million. Having this money, though, was not enough for Hsieh. "'I realized that, for me, investing was actually pretty boring," Hsieh told [Business Insider]. "I felt like I was sitting on the sidelines, and I really missed being part of building something'" (Wei, 2010). Since selling Zappos, Hsieh has now started social projects and a hotel to revitalize a poor area of Las Vegas and is living in a trailer worth $48,000. Erik Moore, an early investor in Zappos, states 'He would be just as happy with a dollar in the bank and being around people he cares about and care about him' (cited in Holley, 2015).

In the world of business we see billionaires who have earned amounts akin to a lottery win, but who continue to work. Why do the likes of Tony Hsieh, Bill Gates, Richard Branson, and Mark Zuckerberg still work when they have enough money to retire on extremely comfortably? Even if the money is no longer important, there is still intrinsic motivation—from the success of launching new products, perhaps, or a sense of achievement and pride in the company that they have built.

Intrinsic motivation, however, is not just something that motivates the rich. It can be seen to motivate workers who receive a more modest wage packet and, indeed, those who exert effort for no financial reward.

- It is often suggested (e.g. de Gieter et al., 2006) that workers in caring and public-service occupations, such as nursing and teaching, are motivated by intrinsic rewards. Rewards come from an intrinsic sense of satisfaction from caring or doing good for society.

- When people perform voluntary work for free, the lack of pay does not mean that people are demotivated in that work—intrinsic rewards can come from satisfaction or pride in doing good deeds.

 What activities do you do in your spare time? What motivates you to put in the effort to do them?

## Motivation from social factors

### Real life case: on the night shift

One of our students, who did a typical student part-time job primarily for the pay, told us of his experiences working as part of a team that stacked shelves in a major supermarket overnight.

The team of shelf-stackers would talk, and laugh, and joke with each other throughout the night shift. Management, adopting a somewhat Taylorist approach, thought that this wasted time and was ill-disciplined. Workers were instructed to stack their own individual shelves and to do so in silence—the only time that they should speak or interact with each other would be during breaks and away from the shop floor.

The result of this new disciplined regime was that productivity went down and workers stacked fewer items during their shift.

While participation in a sports team or a voluntary group might bring intrinsic rewards, for many it is also a social activity, and motivation may, indeed, come from social rewards, such as team spirit or a sense of belonging.

This seems to be the issue in the above case. Management's direct control had the opposite effect to what one might expect—productivity actually reduced. In this case it was the social side of the organization that actually motivated the workers in that it helped them through a monotonous overnight shift—social factors actually increased their motivation to work.

Studies of groups in factory environments (e.g. Collinson, 1988; Ackroyd and Crowdy, 1990) have shown similar evidence of joking and banter, which might seem to be at odds with management's desire for control and efficient work. However, in both cases, the motivation and control within the social group itself led to the amount of work required by management being completed by the group.

These cases illustrate a perspective on motivation which we saw reflected in Chapters 5 and 6, where the importance of the social side of the organization was highlighted. For example, in the Hawthorne studies (see Chapter 5) Mayo suggested that it was the social side of the organization which motivated workers, and in examining groups and teams (Chapter 6), it was demonstrated that group loyalty rather than management control can motivate people immediately.

Extrinsic, intrinsic, and social rewards are all factors which can motivate an individual. In the remainder of the chapter, we examine differing theories and perspectives on how these rewards might be deployed in the workplace by managers wishing to motivate their workforce.

## Review questions

| Describe | What is meant by extrinsic, intrinsic, and social rewards? |
|---|---|
| Explain | How does the lottery question help us to understand motivation? |
| Analyse | What is the role of pay in motivating people to work? |
| Apply | In the running case, what examples of extrinsic and intrinsic rewards motivate David Morrison? |

# Behavioural theories and motivation

## Running case: the smile card

Concerned that the reception staff do not seem motivated, Meg Mortimer approaches business manager Phil Weaver to help her increase morale. 'Easy,' he responds confidently, 'just reward them for smiling at customers, and punish them if they don't. That'll get the grins back on their faces. All you have to do is measure it, then you can manage them. How about a smile card?' Weaver suggests (Figure 9.1).

Weaver takes out a pen and quickly starts drawing out a card. 'All staff will carry the card with them and get ticks for desirable behaviours—like smiling at a customer, or offering information about the local area. They will get a black mark for those things that we don't want them to do like being unpleasant to a customer or not offering to help with baggage,' Weaver tells Mortimer.

'Once a month we will gather in the cards. Black marks will be subtracted from ticks and the winning total will get a pay bonus for that month.'

Name: _John McAuley_                                    Month: _May_

Desirable behaviours:                                   Black marks:

| Date | Behaviour observed | Manager initials | Tick | Date | Behaviour observed | Manager initials | Cross |
|------|--------------------|------------------|------|------|--------------------|------------------|-------|
| 1/5 | Helpful to customer with heavy suitcases | MM | ✓ | 2/5 | Passed through reception – ignored guest waiting at desk | SC | ✗ |
| 3/5 | Helped guest with airport taxi | MM | ✓ | | | | |
| 4/5 | Very cheerful with group of tourists | SC | ✓ | | | | |
| | | | | | | | |
| | | | | | | | |
| | | | | | | | |
| | | | | | | | |

**Figure 9.1** Junction Hotel's smile card.

How well do you think the smile card will tackle issues of morale and motivation among the reception staff?

If someone were pointing a gun at you, would you do what they said? Probably yes, for fear of being shot. But, deep down, would you be genuinely *motivated* by that gun to the head or *coerced* into doing what you were told? What if, instead, they offered you money? Would this motivate you to do anything at any time?

In this section we examine an approach to motivation which derived from the psychological tradition of **behaviourism**. Behaviourism is sometimes referred to as a 'carrot and stick' approach. It tries to motivate people's behaviour by providing a reward or incentive for good behaviours (the carrot) and, conversely, a punishment for bad behaviours (the stick).

**Behaviourism** An area of psychology which suggests that behaviour can be changed through the planned use of rewards and punishments.

Do you ever use rewards to motivate yourself? For example, if you have an essay to complete you might give yourself a reward, like a night out or a shopping trip, when you have completed it.

An effective motivator?

Behaviourism is also known as **stimulus–response** psychology. A stimulus, be it a punishment or reward, is provided as a means to encourage some form of behaviour or response.

In the workplace such stimuli might be the extrinsic motivators examined in the previous section. For example, pay may be the reward for people turning up to work, no matter how monotonous or dehumanizing that work may be. Pay can also be used as a reward in the form of bonus payments for particular behaviours that management wish to encourage.

Pay can also be the basis of punishment, for example withholding bonuses or, ultimately, firing a worker. While we may not work at gunpoint, many people may feel a metaphorical gun is pointed at their head as they need to work to pay bills and survive.

> **Stimulus–response**
> The underlying relationship of behaviourism, whereby a particular response, or behaviour, is the result of a particular stimulus—either a reward or punishment.

---

**Real life case:** punishment and reward in football

It is often the case that professional footballers receive rewards for playing well—a pay bonus for a team that wins the league, for example, or a new, improved contract for a player who impresses during a season.

However, there have also been reports of the stick rather than a carrot being used to punish players for poor performances. For example, Ukrainian football club Dynamo Kiev have a policy of withholding pay from players if the team fails to win a game (Okeleji, 2011). In the late 1990s, the manager of English club Wimbledon issued a threat of taking players to an opera or making them eat a meal of offal if they ever lost by five goals—the threat seemed to work, as they never lost by that margin (Ashdown and Smyth, 2009).

More drastic and disturbing punishments have also been used: for example, the Ivory Coast team were sent to a military camp after being knocked out of the early stages of a tournament and were humiliated on television by being shown performing military manoeuvres. The Iraq football team, under the management of the son of Saddam Hussein, were reported to suffer outright torture, such as beatings, scaldings, or being forced to bathe in raw sewage (Ashdown and Smyth, 2009; BBC News, 2010).

---

In this section we examine how pay and other extrinsic motivators are used as stimuli in behavioural motivation techniques, and to what extent such techniques genuinely motivate workers rather than simply coercing them into performing particular behaviours.

## Pavlov and classical conditioning

**Running case:** grinning like an idiot

**From:** John McAuley
Been grinning like an idiot all day—not a manager here to see me. Then, one frown and Chance suddenly appears putting a black cross on the card.

**From:** Steve Long
Haha, bad luck mate.

**From:** John McAuley
I mean, what an idiot Chance is. Feels like he's writing my school report or something.

Imagine you wanted to stop a particular bad behaviour such as biting your nails. One method could be to use a foul-tasting nail varnish. The motivation comes from the negative association that develops between the behaviour, nail-biting, and the immediate punishment for that behaviour, the unpleasant taste. Behaviour is said to be **conditioned**—the association between stimulus and response leads to a change in behaviour.

This association, and the subsequent modification of behaviour in response to a particular stimulus, is termed **classical conditioning**. While the **aversion therapy** described previously might aim to condition people into stopping a particular behaviour, similar associations can also be used to promote or encourage particular behaviours.

The original experiments in classical conditioning were undertaken by Russian psychologist Ivan Pavlov (Pavlov and Anrep, 1927), who, while investigating the digestive systems of dogs, noticed an unintended result. A dog's natural response is to salivate when faced with the stimulus of a bowl of food. Pavlov began to ring a bell whenever the food was presented. When this had been repeated often enough, Pavlov rang the bell alone with no food present. The dogs would still salivate just at the stimulus of the bell.

In Pavlov's experiments, this conditioned response of drooling would stop if the bell rang and there was no actual food provided. The association between the bell and food became weaker until, eventually, the conditioned response became **extinct**. To maintain the conditioned behaviour, a continuous **reinforcement** of the association between the stimulus and response was needed—the bell had to be rung every time that food appeared.

While classical conditioning might be applicable to humans in clinical settings, such as aversion therapies, its workplace use is limited.

- Punishment needs to be immediate and happen every time a behaviour occurs. In a workplace setting, every example of a negative behaviour would have to be spotted and punished immediately for classical conditioning of that behaviour to take place. In fact, in a workplace setting, punishments can have the by-product of causing anxiety and resentment towards managers and lowering morale (Villere and Hartman, 1991: 28).

- To motivate workers towards a particular behaviour, management would need to supply rewards continually so as to avoid extinction of that behaviour. Villere and Hartman (1991: 29) suggest that even something as simple as a boss smiling at an employee every morning needs to be maintained—a morning where the smile doesn't occur stands out and can be demotivating.

## Skinner and operant conditioning

**Running case:** automatically, all the time

**From:** meg_mortimer@junctionhotel.co.uk
**To:** phil_weaver@junctionhotel.co.uk

**Subject:** Smile cards

Phil,

Not sure about these smile cards—I feel like I have to be in reception all the time to be able to give out ticks on the card. They'll only smile when I'm around.

---

**Conditioning** A change in behaviour brought about using stimulus–response techniques typical of behavioural psychology.

**Classical conditioning** A type of conditioning of behaviour where a reward or punishment accompanies and reinforces every instance of the behaviour to be conditioned.

**Aversion therapy** A type of classical conditioning whereby a particular behaviour is continually accompanied by a punishment so as to discourage that behaviour.

**Extinction** Where a conditioned behaviour dies out because the reward or punishment is no longer provided.

**Reinforcement** In behavioural psychology, the continued encouragement of a behaviour by the provision of a particular reward.

**From:** phil_weaver@junctionhotel.co.uk
**To:** meg_mortimer@junctionhotel.co.uk

**Subject:** RE: Smile cards

Meg,

No—don't worry about being there 100% of the time. Just make sure you pass through there a few times a day. Reward them every so often and they'll smile automatically all the time.

When we are at work, we don't expect that after every customer served, after every call from a customer handled, or after every pint pulled, the boss will hand us a part of our wages as motivation for us to continue doing that work. Rather than the reward being instant and occurring after every desirable action, as is the case with classical conditioning, we know that a wage comes along at regular intervals—weekly or monthly, for example.

American psychologist B.F. Skinner (1969) developed the ideas of classical conditioning into **operant conditioning**. While Pavlov experimented with dogs, Skinner experimented with animals in an observation box. In one such experiment, if a rat pressed a lever in the box it received a reward in the form of a piece of food.

Skinner discovered that the reward did not need to be provided continuously, but could be intermittent, for example after every fourth press of the lever. Furthermore, he found that rewards that were *variable* rather than *fixed* (i.e. not after every fourth press of the lever, but after 2, then 5, then 4, then 6 presses, for example) were more effective motivators.

In human behaviour, the most effective forms of reinforcement have also been found

Variable rewards.
**Source:** Shutterstock.

> Operant conditioning A conditioning of behaviour which recognizes that rewards and punishments do not need to be continuous, but can be scheduled in a way to still condition behaviour.

to be variable, i.e. with an element of surprise and unpredictability. This explains how gambling can become such a powerfully addictive behaviour: 'The potential of winning on the next race keeps gamblers coming back again and again' (Villere and Hartman, 1991: 29). However, if you won every time it would become less addictive. If you knew that a fruit machine would pay out on every tenth press, there would be no incentive to play the first to ninth spins. But, because the payout ratio is random and variable, there is always the incentive to put more money in the machine and hope that the next spin will be the winner. This is why Twitter, Instagram, Pinterest, and email are so addictive, not because we know we will be rewarded each time we use them, but because we believe we might be. A Oliver Burkeman states 'If slot machines delivered £1 every time you inserted 50p, you might use them, but you'd never get addicted' (Burkeman 2011).

Skinner's work has been applied in the workplace by Luthans and Kreitner (1985) as **organizational behaviour modification** (OB Mod). They suggest that fixed and variable

> Organizational behaviour modification The use of operant conditioning techniques in a workplace setting.

**Schedules of reinforcement** A blend of fixed and variable reinforcements designed so as best to reinforce desired behaviours.

**schedules of reinforcement** have different effects in terms of motivating employees into particular types of desired behaviours. For example (Villere and Hartman, 1991: 29):

- a regular salary, paid weekly or monthly, is an example of a fixed-interval reward—it is provided regularly at a set time. While this might motivate us to turn up and work, it doesn't necessarily motivate us into putting in any extra effort in the workplace from day to day.
- variable rewards—such as a bonus, an award, a promotion, or even a pat on the back from the boss—tend to have a higher success rate in motivating workers into specific behaviours that managers wish to encourage, over and above what is done simply in order to collect the monthly pay cheque.

 Visit the Online Resource Centre for more on variable and fixed schedules of reinforcement in the workplace.

Operant conditioning thus demonstrates the motivational value of blending different types of reward and reinforcement. The regular salary is important—without it people would not turn up for work; however, blending this with variable forms of reward has a greater effect in motivating specific day-to-day behaviours.

 How could you apply Skinner's concepts to your own studies?

## Behaviourism: advantages and disadvantages

> **Running case:** target behaviours
>
> Steve Long is on portering duty, delivering room service to an elderly guest. While engaging her in pleasant chat, he notices through the window that Chance is walking into the crowded reception area.
>
> Steve instantly cuts off the guest mid-sentence and runs out of the room, slamming the door behind him. Leaving the customer upset and bemused in his wake, he rushes down to reception and starts engaging a group of waiting guests in conversation, showing them some tourist information leaflets, even though they have shown little interest in visiting the local attractions.
>
> As reception empties, Chance walks over with his pen. 'Well done, young man,' says Chance, placing a tick on Steve's smile card.

Organizational behaviour modification works on a seemingly common-sense principle that 'if a particular pattern of behaviour is rewarded, it will occur more often' (Makin and Sutherland, 1994: 6). However, behind this seemingly simple idea lies a pitfall—exactly what behaviour is being rewarded?

If a reward is given, for example, for reaching a particular target, it is behaviours which reach that target which might be motivated rather than the underlying behaviour that the organization is trying to promote. People can often find creative ways to meet those targets that don't necessarily correspond to the initial behaviours desired by management.

For example, Makin and Sutherland (1994) suggest that a way to promote safety-conscious behaviour in organizations could be to reward a lack of accidents. However, rather than motivating people into more safety-conscious behaviours, for example wearing safety goggles, a response can be simply not to report any accidents, so as to meet the actual target set. The underlying behaviour change—being more safety-conscious—is not addressed; people just engage in behaviours that they think will help them meet the target and get the reward.

> **Research insight:** The target becomes the behaviour
> Wray-Bliss, E., and Willmott, H. 1999. Battling with the gods: Workers, management and the deities of post-industrial management culture. In: Goodman, R. (ed.) *Modern organization and emerging conundrums: Exploring the post-industrial sub-culture of the third millennium.* New Lexington Press: San Francisco, pp. 377–89.
>
> An example of targets not achieving their original aim is seen in Wray-Bliss and Willmott's study of targets in a call centre. A number of calls per hour were required to be handled, which was monitored through the computer system (see Chapter 4 for more on this). The system was meant to bring about efficient handling of calls. However, with a target of nine calls per hour, call-centre agents who were struggling to meet this as the end of an hour approached would make up the shortfall by picking up a ringing phone and hanging up immediately. It would register as a call to help meet the target, but is slamming the phone down on customers a behaviour that the organization would wish to encourage?

At the start of this section, we asked if coercive behaviour, through punishment, genuinely motivates people within or simply alters their behaviour in response to the imminent threat. Even where rewards rather than punishments are used, we can question the ability of behavioural techniques to genuinely motivate deeply rather than simply influence people into particular behaviours for the reward that they bring.

A critique of behavioural techniques is that it sees people in simplistic, mechanistic terms (Martinko and Fadil, 1994: 16). No account is taken of cognitive processes whereby people think for themselves (ibid.)—people are seen almost like robots who respond unquestioningly to various stimuli or rewards. Perhaps this lack of depth of motivation is linked to the fact that behavioural techniques rely on extrinsic rewards and thus simply act at a surface level, ignoring the power of intrinsic and internal rewards.

Nevertheless, behavioural techniques, when applied to the workplace, may have demonstrable effects in some instances: that is to say, there are instances where they can be seen to bring about changes in behaviour as seen with Makin and Sutherland's (1994) previous example of accident reduction. Also, behaviour theories are often applied in a simple way whereas the original concepts are often more subtle, recognizing the internal cognition (thinking) of the individual (McGee and Johnson, 2015). While this section has examined behavioural techniques for their contribution to theories of motivation, they have had widespread use in management and organization theory, including in areas relevant to the following chapters:

- in knowledge and learning—behavioural techniques are used to understand how people learn new behaviours (see Chapter 10)
- in change management—behavioural techniques are one of many techniques that can be used to change the behaviours of workers (see Chapter 11)
- in leadership theories—behaviourism is used to understand how leaders can shape and condition the behaviour of followers (see Chapter 12).

Overall, behavioural theories provide a 'one size fits all' approach to motivation. For example, if pay is the basis of a reward system, it assumes that everyone will respond in the same way to pay as a motivator. In the next section we see motivation theory taking account of individual differences in what motivates people.

## Review questions

| | |
|---|---|
| **Describe** | What are the main features of classical and operant conditioning? |
| **Explain** | How can variable reinforcement have a strong motivational effect on people? |
| **Analyse** | Why might Skinner's work be seen as controlling? |
| **Apply** | How is the smile card at Junction Hotel an example of organizational behaviour modification? How well do you think it motivates the staff into appearing more lively and engaged with guests in the reception area? |

# Content theories of motivation

## Running case: differences in motivation

Jane Foster has been working at Junction Hotel as a receptionist for five years. She and her partner have not yet had children, and they are easily covering their mortgage payments and other outgoings.

Foster receives constant praise for the quality of her work from her boss, Meg Mortimer, and when Mortimer is away, Foster is the first choice to deputize as the front-of-house manager. She has been singled out as potential managerial material for the future and, because of this, the company are sponsoring her to do a part-time degree in hospitality management at the local university on day release.

Mortimer is surprised that Jane has barely participated in the smile card scheme, even not handing in her card on occasions. 'I know when I'm working well and that gives me pride,' says Jane. 'I don't need ticks in a box to tell me that.'

Steve Long is a student and is working next to Foster today. His circumstances, however, are different. He is studying full-time for a degree in accountancy. He works part-time in the reception area as a means of supplementing his income—he is finding rent payments hard to meet and needs the money. Mortimer thinks his work is also good, but is surprised that he refuses when she asks him if he would like managerial responsibility. Nevertheless, he has thrown himself head first into the smile card scheme and has twice been the winner, pocketing the bonus cheque.

What motivates you in the workplace may be different to what motivates your colleagues. While one worker might be there for the pay, another might wish for career progression and status. **Content theories** of motivation suggest that managers need to consider that different people are motivated by different things.

    Behaviourist theories discussed in the previous section used extrinsic motivators to design motivation techniques that were applied equally to all workers in one organization. Content theories recognize that a range of different motivators—extrinsic, intrinsic, and social—may exert a different level of motivation on different people.

    Content theories assume that individuals have a set of needs and that the content of work can be designed to meet those needs and thus motivate the individual. In this section we examine two widely used content theories—Maslow's **hierarchy of needs**, and Herzberg's motivators and hygiene theory.

> **Content theories**
> Theories of motivation which suggest that the content of work should be designed so as best to meet the needs which motivate workers.

## Maslow's hierarchy of needs

For many management students and practitioners, Maslow's hierarchy of needs is overwhelmingly the most familiar model of motivation; indeed, some former business students say that it is one of the few theories that they remember from the entirety of their studies. His ubiquitous triangle (see Figure 9.2) pops up in lectures, training courses, and textbooks such as this.

    The allure of this triangle is that it promises a simple framework to understand what motivates people at work. Unfortunately is often applied too simplistically, with Maslow's original insights either misrepresented or simply removed. Indeed, Maslow did not intend it to be a theory of workplace motivation and suggested that he had not seen proof that it worked in a workplace context (Dye et al., 2005: 1380).

    So why are we examining Maslow's hierarchy if it is largely discredited as a model of workplace motivation, even by its own creator?

> **Hierarchy of needs**
> Maslow's theory which shows that individuals have a set of needs in hierarchical order, whereby people are motivated by the most immediate unsatisfied need.

- Firstly, although his model's efficacy in the workplace is largely disputed, it is something that you will still encounter in studies and in your management career so it is important that you understand the model, its background, and its flaws.

- Secondly, while the way in which Maslow has been used in the workplace might be problematic, this is not to say that Maslow's work is without merit. For instance, he recognizes aspects of workplace motivation that simplistic views, such as the Fordist/Taylorist *homo economicus* or the behaviourist stimulus–response approaches, ignore.

### Elements of the hierarchy

In this section, we present Maslow's hierarchy in the important context of his wider psychological interests before examining how it is applied to workplace motivation.

**Figure 9.2** Maslow's hierarchy of needs.

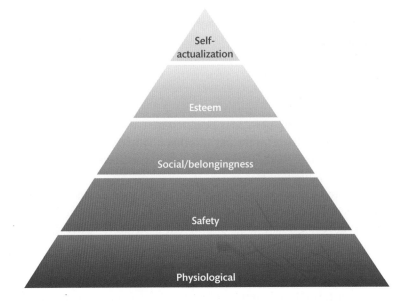

Maslow (1943) suggested that people have five basic needs:

• physiological needs—basic physical needs for survival, such as food and water

• safety needs—a need for safety, physical health, and security

• love and belongingness—social needs, such as being part of a group, interacting with others, and a need for affection

• esteem needs—a need for status, recognition, and self-respect

• self-actualization—a form of ultimate self-fulfilment, the achievement of our ultimate potential and creativity and what we, according to Maslow, are 'fitted for'.

**Prepotency** One characteristic having dominance over others.

For Maslow, these needs are arranged in a hierarchy of **prepotency** (see Figure 9.2). The most dominant need that will motivate an individual is the most basic need of which they are deprived. Once needs at one level have been satisfied, an individual will go on to be motivated by the next level of needs. So, if an individual is starving (rather than simply having an appetite), they will be motivated by the most basic need for food. When this need is satisfied they will be motivated by safety needs, and so on, moving up the hierarchy. The needs do not have to be 100% satisfied before the next level emerges. Indeed for Maslow 'most members of our society, who are normal, are partially satisfied in all their basic needs and partially unsatisfied in all their basic needs at the same time' (1987: 69–70).

**Theory in context:** Abraham Maslow

An aspect of Maslow's work that is often missing from management accounts is that his research interests began far away from workplace motivation. He was a primatologist, interested in behaviour among monkeys, and much of his research was about patterns of dominance within monkey populations (Cullen, 1997; Dye et al., 2005).

> ▶ These interests then transferred into an interest in dominance in sexual behaviour in humans. His particular focus was based on interviewing women in their twenties about their sexual desires (Cullen and Gotell, 2002). It is from these streams of research that he developed his hierarchy of needs. In its original form it was not a theory of workplace motivation, but a theory of needs that humans needed to fulfil in order to attain psychological health and well-being.
>
> His interest in dominance both in primates and in sexual behaviour is important here—the hierarchy of needs is essentially a theory of how any one unsatisfied need dominates over others in its motivational effects at any one time.

The hierarchy of needs was not first applied to workplace settings by Maslow, but by Davis (1957) drawing upon Maslow's work. In this reading, different workers will be motivated by different factors, depending on their position in the hierarchy of needs. For example:

- a worker with not enough money to feed themselves will probably take on any work—they will be motivated by the immediate need to eat (physiological needs)
- a worker who has money for food but is just about managing to cover bills and rent might be motivated by job security to meet these safety needs (shelter, warmth, etc.)
- a worker who is meeting their bills easily will be motivated more by the social/belongingness aspects of the organization—group and team dynamics, and the culture of the organization become important
- as people fulfil their social needs, workers are motivated by esteem needs, such as a desire for promotion within an organization, or recognition of their work, for example by an appreciative word from a manager
- the final aspect of motivation is self-actualization—fulfilment of potential and achievement within the workplace.

## Insights from Maslow

Maslow's hierarchy provides valuable insights into human motivation which have relevance to the workplace. In particular, he goes beyond behavioural psychology, which he viewed as too simplistic, deterministic, and having 'no earthly use in any complex human situation' (Maslow, 2000: 7), towards a more multifaceted view of what motivates behaviour:

- it shows that individuals are motivated differently—what works for one worker may not for another. This provides an important counter-argument to the likes of Taylor, who saw pay as a universal motivator. In Maslow's hierarchy, pay is one of a number of motivators—it may work at certain lower levels of the hierarchy, but other motivating forces take over as an individual moves upwards. People are often motivated by a number of the basic needs at any one time.
- the hierarchy integrates different types of motivating factors within its framework. Extrinsic rewards, such as pay, are important, particularly at lower levels; social rewards are important motivators at the belongingness level; and at higher levels, intrinsic rewards such as achievement and self-respect become important.
- the hierarchy shows that an individual's motivation is not fixed—it is dynamic and people can progress over time. Thus, a student might be motivated by pay in order to

meet safety needs of paying rent and bills, but, later in life, a professional might be motivated by esteem needs, such as promotion.

- A person's background and previous experiences might shape what needs are dominant for them. For instance, Maslow argues that a person who had a more unstable childhood might be dominated by 'belonging needs'. For other people, self-esteem needs might be more important than love (Maslow, 1943).

- People do not necessarily start from the bottom of the hierarchy and work their way up. For the average American, Maslow considered, they do not experience hunger (which for Maslow was more akin to starvation) and therefore might strive for higher needs (self-esteem or self-actualization) and in doing so risk their lower needs not being fulfilled. For instance, someone might give up their job rather than lose self-respect, even if they might be in danger of going hungry over a six-month period (Maslow, 1943).

- Some people, particularly with strong characters, might even give everything up for the sake of their values.

Maslow provides a much more positive view of motivation than the simple carrot and stick or, ultimately, coercive methods. Indeed, in his original work, Maslow placed a strong emphasis on human values, showing that people might be motivated by factors other than pay and promotion, such as growth and creativity. Furthermore, his insights are more significant than are often represented. For instance, preconditions include autonomy, freedom of inquiry and expression, and freedom to defend yourself and seek justice (Maslow, 1987).

> **Self-actualization** For Maslow, a realization, or actualization, of an individual's ultimate human and creative potential.

Indeed, the aspect of his hierarchy that Maslow emphasized most was **self-actualization**. He had views about the nature of personality similar to the social–radical approach from Chapter 8 (personality), namely that people had unrealized potential and that it was the role of society, and organizations within society, to help them to achieve this potential (Dye et al., 2005: 1383). This humanistic view looks at motivation from the viewpoint of the individual and stresses the uniqueness of each individual. Self-actualization is a concept of people reaching their creativity and a sense of self-fulfilment and achievement, in the same way as an artist or musician might do. For Maslow, this could also be achieved in the workplace.

## Critique of Maslow and the use of Maslow

The critique that we present of Maslow's work is in many ways a critique of the way it has been frequently applied, or misapplied, by others in the study of management and organizations.

---

**Real life case:** Maslow at Tesco

A case study presented by a leading UK newspaper, along with classroom teaching materials, maps the work practices of UK supermarket Tesco on to Maslow's hierarchy.

Examples provided are:

- physiological needs are met by providing regular monthly pay, a restaurant, and lockers for belongings
- formal contracts of employment and health and safety procedures meet security needs

- social needs are met by team and group working

- esteem comes from praise for hard work, ensured through the appraisal system

- self-actualization (here renamed self-fulfilment) comes from promotion opportunities, a personal development plan, and fast-track management schemes.

At first sight, this case seems to apply Maslow to Tesco's work practices well—a restaurant surely meets the physiological need for food, for example. But it is a very simplistic application, categorizing a number of practices under Maslow's headings without understanding how people are really motivated by these drives in Maslow's work.

- It ignores the dynamic nature of Maslow's model—it would seem that all motivating forces are acting at once and Tesco is seen to provide for those needs, whereas in Maslow's model it is only the most immediate unsatisfied need that motivates individuals.

- A physiological need for food comes from being deprived of food—a very basic urge. It does not describe people popping casually into the staff canteen for lunch. We assume that Tesco already pay enough for workers to afford food, so this more basic need would not be acting as a motivator—it is one which is already satisfied and so the model has been misapplied.

- This application of Maslow underplays the role of self-actualization, even renaming it as self-fulfilment. In Maslow's original work, self-actualization is an ultimate realization of creativity and potential as a human being, not simply being on a fast-track promotion scheme.

**Source:** http://businesscasestudies.co.uk/tesco/motivational-theory-in-practice-at-tesco/

The argument that can be made against the use of Maslow's theory in the Tesco case is that it has been applied too simplistically and at a surface level, without understanding the deeper insights of his work. This is symptomatic of many of the uses of Maslow's work in management theory.

For instance, in Maslow's work, self-actualization is a healthy state—being at any level below shows that not all basic human needs are met and thus a person is psychologically unhealthy. In management theory, self-actualization seems to become a vague target to aim towards in a career, with workers in the meantime occupying any number of steps along the way. In any of these instances, according to Maslow, the individual would be unhealthy (Dye et al., 2005). Management theory misunderstands the significance of self-actualization.

A further problem with the use of Maslow's theory is that, while it is often presented in management theory as an exact depiction of human motivation or a guideline on how to motivate, in fact it lacks empirical evidence. That is to say, the applicability of the theory in workplace reality has not been proven.

Have you ever walked into a workplace at the start of the day thinking about what is motivating you in terms of physiological, safety, belonging needs, etc.? Do you think it is realistic that a worker goes into work thinking along the lines of 'Yesterday I met my esteem needs, so today I want to self-actualize'?

Wahba and Bridwell (1976) review a number of studies into Maslow's hierarchy, showing that not even the existence of the five levels of the hierarchy as distinct and separate categories have been proven empirically in the workplace, let alone the idea that people move up from one level to the next. As we saw earlier, Maslow himself stated that he had not seen proof of his theory working in organizational settings.

Furthermore, while there are problems with the application of Maslow's hierarchy in workplace settings, it is also often applied without any consideration of critiques of Maslow's original theory itself.

For example, looking back to Maslow's original studies on domination, Cullen and Gotell (2002: 538) argue that his work is highly gendered in nature. 'Implicit in Maslow's portrayal is an assertion of the naturalness of female submission and the eroticization of male dominance and this assertion, in turn, forms the gendered foundation of the needs hierarchy' (2002: 538). Dye et al. (2005: 1389) note that Maslow is also dismissive of gay men and of black people.

The concept of self-actualization, in Maslow's terms, is thus founded on particular assumptions which privilege white, male, heterosexual ways of being and, furthermore, the concept of self-actualization can be seen as elitist. Maslow suggests throughout his work that not everyone is capable or seems to want to be able to self-actualize (see the collected works in Maslow, 2000). Dye et al. (2005) suggest that maybe this is why the model is so popular in the management context—it suggests management to be an elite capable of self-actualization and, at the same time, dismisses other workers as being motivated by basic, ultimately unhealthy needs.

These critiques both of the misapplication of Maslow and of Maslow's original theory show that while his triangle may have widespread and popular use in management theory, it should be *handled with care*. Certainly, it should not be seen as the one and only model of motivation in itself—many other theories of motivation are discussed in this chapter.

## Study skills: models and heuristics

The simple nature of models such as Maslow's hierarchy gives them an appeal to students and managers alike—it is a nice idea to think that motivation can be plotted out in such a simple framework. Indeed, some students write very poor essays on motivation which see motivation as nothing more than Maslow's hierarchy, ignoring all other theories on the subject.

Models exist as a simple way to present complex ideas. A model is what is known as a heuristic—a way of presenting information or theories in an accessible, easily understandable manner.

The danger is that people rely on these simplified versions rather than looking at the topic in depth. A model is also just one viewpoint on a topic—there may be other models which present the same area of study in a different way and from a different viewpoint.

If using a model such as Maslow in an essay, don't simply repeat it. Think about approaching it in more depth, for example:

- what is the model actually trying to say about the nature of motivation? Don't just draw the triangle—say what each level means and what it implies about how people are motivated.

- what assumptions underpin the model? For example, we have seen how Maslow's hierarchy derives from his earlier research about domination and we have noted the importance he places on self-actualization.

- what alternative views are there? What other models exist and what do they say that is different or that challenges Maslow's model?

- does it hold up to empirical scrutiny? We have seen how Maslow's hierarchy has not been proven in a workplace setting. Have other models been applied successfully or unsuccessfully in the workplace? (See Chapter 1 for more discussion on critical thinking.)

# Herzberg: motivators and hygiene factors

## Running case: a sense of responsibility

Steve Long has now won three of the smile card bonuses on the trot, and is starting to see the bonus as a part of the regular pay he expects to receive. He has already allocated this month's bonus towards a trip to London to see his friends. He is, therefore, shocked when his friend John McAuley is announced as this month's winner. Having to cancel his trip, Long is unhappy, feeling like he's had a pay cut.

The contrast with Jane Foster can't be greater. With her degree studies progressing, she is now being given the responsibility of managing shifts in the reception from start to finish, even if Mortimer is around. And, where usually she leaves paperwork in Mortimer's pigeon hole to be signed off, Mortimer has said 'sign it yourself—if you're in charge you have the responsibility'. Foster does all of this, willingly and happily, for the same level of pay as Long.

While Maslow's hierarchy is based in the needs of individuals and then looks at how they might be satisfied in the workplace, Herzberg's motivators and hygiene framework starts with the actual characteristics of the job itself. For Herzberg (1966, 2003), these characteristics of the job can be divided into two distinct groups:

- **motivating factors** are factors that have the potential to increase the satisfaction of a worker. They include achievement, recognition for that achievement, the work itself, having responsibility, and the potential for personal growth (Herzberg, 1987: 9). These are largely intrinsic factors and are factors that are likely to satisfy the higher levels of Maslow's hierarchy.

- **hygiene factors** cannot, in themselves, do anything to increase satisfaction; however, this does not mean that they can be ignored. If they are not provided or addressed sufficiently they have the potential to cause dissatisfaction. Such factors are extrinsic factors, such as company policy, supervision, interpersonal relationships, working conditions, job status, job security, and pay (Herzberg, 1987: 9), and are more likely to satisfy lower level needs on Maslow's hierarchy.

Herzberg's research was carried out originally with engineers and accountants, and consisted of asking them to name an event at work that had caused them extreme satisfaction or extreme dissatisfaction. The results, shown in Figure 9.3, show the motivating factors at the top of the diagram, providing more instances of satisfaction than dissatisfaction, and hygiene factors at the bottom, showing greater instances of dissatisfaction.

Herzberg's view of pay as a hygiene factor seems to go against our common-sense view of pay—surely a pay rise motivates people? Herzberg (1987: 6) suggests, however, that while a pay rise might motivate in the short term, it only motivates people as far as seeking the next rise. In other words, a pay rise soon comes to be seen as a 'normal' level of pay, which doesn't motivate in its own right. While it provides no extra motivation, if the pay were to be reduced back to its old level it would then demotivate. All that happens, for Herzberg, is that pay levels spiral while adding no additional motivation to workers.

**Motivating factors** For Herzberg, characteristics of a job which can bring about increases in the job satisfaction and motivation of workers.

**Hygiene factors** For Herzberg, characteristics of a job which cannot bring about increases in the job satisfaction and motivation of workers, but which can cause demotivation if they are not addressed sufficiently.

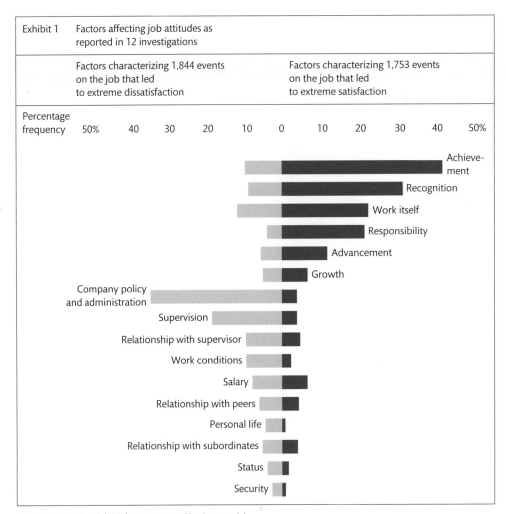

**Figure 9.3** Herzberg's (1987) motivators and hygiene model.

**Source:** based on Herzberg (2003: 87–96). Reproduced by permission of Harvard Business Publishing.

## Herzberg and job enrichment

**Job simplification**
Where a job is broken down into simple tasks, as with Taylorism or Fordism.

**Horizontal loading**
Increasing the scope of a job by adding elements of work of a similar nature and at the same level of hierarchical responsibility.

**Job rotation** Where workers alternate between different tasks of a similar nature.

For Herzberg, increased satisfaction comes from the design of work itself in a way that minimizes hygiene factors and maximizes motivators. This suggests a move away from **job simplification**, as seen with rational work design (see Chapter 3) where work is broken down into simple tasks, and towards increasing the intrinsic motivation that workers derive from jobs.

Herzberg (1987) first discusses two forms of job redesign which emphasize the **horizontal loading** of the task. Rather than performing one repetitive task, the worker is given an expanded variety of tasks:

- **job rotation** is where a worker moves between different tasks in the work process rather than sticking to one repetitive task. For example, a worker in a fast-food restaurant does not generally spend the whole of their working life at one task; instead, they will rotate between working on the till, making burgers, and cleaning tables, etc.

- **job enlargement** is where a worker is given several tasks at the same level of difficulty: for example, a fast-food worker assembles all elements of the burger rather than just adding the relish.

Would you be any more motivated if you went from one monotonous job to being rotated between four or five monotonous jobs?

For Herzberg (1987: 10), such forms of work do not increase motivation. If two forms of work have zero motivation, then adding them together still makes zero. Instead, he suggests that intrinsic motivators, and thus job satisfaction, will be increased through **job enrichment**. Enrichment comes from **vertical loading**, where more authority and autonomy over tasks are given to workers, for example through increasing individual responsibility or complexity of tasks, and allowing self-directed teams rather than tightly-controlled individuals.

The aim of job enrichment is to increase not just the number and variety of tasks, but also their quality and ability to provide intrinsic forms of motivation. Vertical loading suggests that workers have a part in much more of the work process from start to finish, rather than being just one small 'cog in a machine'.

**Job enlargement**
Where more tasks are added to increase the challenge and variety of the job.

**Job enrichment**
Where the quality of work is increased through the provision of increased responsibility, autonomy, and variety of tasks.

**Vertical loading**
Where a job is enriched by adding tasks which would normally be associated with elements of responsibility linked to positions higher in an organization's hierarchy.

---

### Real life case: job enrichment at Volvo

A classic case of job enrichment is the development of Volvo's car manufacturing plant at Uddevalla, Sweden, in the 1980s. The factory floor and organization could not stand in greater contrast to that of the Fordist assembly line. Rehder (1994) states that:

- rather than working individually on a line, workers were divided into six autonomous work groups. Each occupied an area of the factory that was designed to feel as self-contained as possible. The teams would work on four cars at a time, with each car in a different state of progress

- workers were trained in all the skills necessary to build a car and knew how their tasks fitted into the overall production process

- teams had a lot of independence, setting their own work schedules, and even having a say in recruitment when new members of a team were appointed. They also had a say in higher management decisions.

Overall, job enrichment seemed to motivate workers much more than a traditional assembly line—there was a strong team work ethic reported at Volvo.

**Source:** Rehder (1994).

---

While job enrichment at Volvo had an effect of increasing motivation and satisfaction of workers, it is something which came at a cost—the production process was around 11% more costly than a traditional car assembly process (Gibson, 1973: 65). While Gibson suggests this can be made up for by the increased productivity and motivation of the workforce, Rehder (1994: 13) notes that following financial pressures and falling sales, the Uddevalla plant was closed by Volvo in 1993.

It's not just cost that management need to invest if they want to bring about job enrichment; there is time spent training and, ultimately, management have to give away a lot of control—something that would be anathema to managers of a Taylorist persuasion (see Chapter 3). Indeed, for Herzberg, it is a long-term undertaking rather than a quick fix for motivation (1987: 13).

Furthermore, Herzberg's model can be seen to bring about motivation at the equivalent of higher levels of Maslow's hierarchy, designing work to bring about intrinsic rewards. A bias towards these factors could come about owing to his original research featuring white-collar workers. The insight from Goldthorpe later in this chapter shows that some people will work for instrumental reasons—the pay—rather than for any sense of growth or intrinsic reward.

In such an instance, job enrichment (or rotation or enlargement) could, potentially, be seen as a form of intensification of work. For example, workers may not want extra responsibility, especially if there is no extra pay attached to this. Workers would be having to learn and perform extra tasks as part of their work for potentially the same wage.

Again, Herzberg (1987: 13) noted that not all people want job enrichment, nor can all jobs be enriched. We get an idea of how motivation can be increased in some instances by job enrichment, but not a recommendation that this should be applied in all cases.

### Review questions

| | |
|---|---|
| **Describe** | What are the main features of Maslow's and Herzberg's models? |
| **Explain** | What is the role of intrinsic motivators in both of the models? |
| **Analyse** | What are the problems in the way Maslow's original theory has been used as a theory of workplace motivation? |
| **Apply** | Can you use Maslow and Herzberg's models to explain the differences in motivation between Long and Foster in the running case? |

# Process theories of motivation

**Process theories**
Theories of motivation which suggest that motivation is a result of individual processes of perception, comparison, and calculation.

We all enter the workplace with different prior life experiences, different feelings, and different interpretations of the world. As we saw in Chapter 8, we are all individuals. **Process theories** focus on motivation as a function of individual thought processes, moving from the content of work and static frameworks, as seen in the previous section, to motivation as a far more individual, fluid, and subjective process.

Motivation is based on people's past experiences and the meanings that people attach to those experiences. While content theories might try to explain *how* people act in relation to different motivating factors, with process theories the unique and individual ways in which people *feel and interpret* these factors are also considered.

In this section we examine two examples of process theories—equity theory, where people compare their rewards to those of others, and expectancy theory, where people evaluate different actions to judge how they will achieve their desired goals.

# Adams—equity theory

## Running case: it's not fair

Sue Ridgewell, working on reception, has long suspected that her co-receptionist, Jane Foster, got favourable treatment from Meg Mortimer. It was the little snide comments and put downs from Mortimer that did it—nothing serious, but Foster, the blue-eyed girl who was taking the hospitality course, seems to get far more positive comments.

At first, Ridgewell tries to do better, thinking she must be in the wrong and that maybe if she tries harder she, too, will get praise from the boss, but after a while, she realizes that whatever she does there is no praise or reward, and she seems to get fewer ticks on her smile card, even though she feels she is putting in much more effort with the customers.

The result is that Ridgewell stops trying as she sees no point, and feels further demotivated by the overall sense of unfairness of the treatment that she receives relative to Foster.

This feeling is compounded when Ridgewell accidentally overhears a conversation behind the reception between Mortimer and Foster. It seems Foster will get more paid time off to do the coursework for her course and other staff will be asked to cover.

How would you feel if your heard one of your colleagues was getting paid more than you for the same job, or if they got time off whenever they requested it (and you cannot), or if a less skilled colleague was promoted over you? We like to think that the treatment we receive is always fair. Adams (1963), based on his research at General Electric, argues that when we see something as unequal or unfair, we are likely to be less motivated.

Adam's concept of **equity theory** is based on our perceptions of fairness and justice—do we feel that we are getting what we deserve based on the efforts we put in (**inputs**) and the rewards that we get compared with others (**outcomes**)? It is very much an individual, subjective level of motivation compared with content theories, for two reasons:

- it is motivation that comes not from the total amount of a reward (e.g. the amount of a pay rise) but from how fairly individuals feel that reward has been distributed

- it is based on individual perceptions of fairness—what one person feels to be fair may be perceived as unfair by another.

As students you are often asked to engage in group work as part of your degree. This can often bring up issues based around fairness and equity when there is a feeling that one group member has not put in the same effort as others—should that member get the same mark as other group members? Are there any instances where you have felt aggrieved at someone receiving the same grade as you for what you perceived to be less effort?

Adams (1963) suggests a number of reactions that individuals might have if they perceive an inequity between inputs and rewards:

- if people feel they are being under-rewarded compared with others, they will feel anger and try to redress the balance, either by negotiating a pay rise, decreasing their level of effort, or engaging in some form of workplace resistance

- if people feel over-rewarded compared with others, they will feel guilt and work harder and, although Adams realizes this is unlikely, take a pay cut.

**Equity theory** A process theory of motivation which suggests that people are either motivated or demotivated depending on how they are rewarded in the workplace compared with others.

**Inputs** In equity theory, efforts and contributions made by an individual to their work.

**Outcomes** In equity theory, the rewards and results of a person's inputs.

In both cases, individuals attempt to change either inputs or outcomes to redress the inequity. Adams suggest that other actions may be taken, such as changing the point of comparison (comparing with different people); trying to find reasons and explanations for the inequity; or, ultimately, leaving the job.

How realistic this is is open to debate. There is little evidence, for example, in support of the idea that guilt for over-reward will make people work harder. Huseman et al. (1987) suggest that not all people fit into the equity theory model of comparative behaviour.

However, equity theory does indicate that when organizations are designing pay and reward systems they need to be seen to be fair. People are thus judging the fairness of the system and how they are treated as much as what they personally will get out of it. If they believe they are treated unfairly, then this can have a negative effect on their motivation.

It is very difficult for managers to control something as subjective as individual perceptions of fairness. Tyler and Bies (1990) suggest that such perceptions can, to some degree, be managed through discussion and explanation by management of changes to pay systems, and by making certain that reward criteria are applied consistently and without personal bias.

For example, Greenberg (1990a) studied levels of theft in a US manufacturing plant following a 15% pay cut due to a drop in orders. The theft can be seen as resistance due to a perceived inequity following the pay cut. However, Greenberg found that theft levels were much lower among workers who had been given a detailed explanation for the cut from management than those who had been given a short, inadequate explanation. The discussion and explanation had helped lower the amount of perceived inequity.

More recently, research attention has moved from equity theory to the concept of **organizational justice**, which states that not only does the outcome matter but, building on equity theory, the processes through which a decision is reached needs to be seen as fair as well (Colquitt et al., 2001). Organizational justice separates the final decision, what researchers call distributive justice (as in equity theory), with how it is implemented, what researchers call procedural justice (Greenberg, 1990b). What is interesting from the research is that the negative effects of receiving a negative outcome can be mitigated when the process is seen to be fair (Skarlicki and Folger 1997). In recent research, who makes the decision is also seen as important. Kouchaki et al. argue that if a decision is made by a group it is seen as less fair than if it is made by an individual (Kouchaki et al., 2015).

> **Organizational justice** A concept that stresses the importance of the process as well as the outcome for the perceived fairness of a decision.

## Vroom–expectancy theory

> **Expectancy theory** A process theory of motivation which suggests that people will be motivated into actions and behaviours that they can link with them achieving goals and rewards that they desire.

While equity theory is based on individual perceptions of fairness, Vroom's (1964) **expectancy theory** examines how individuals link specific actions to how they perceive they will help them achieve specific goals. People will seek out positive rewards or outcomes for themselves and will pursue behaviours that they *expect* will lead them to that reward.

Expectancy theory suggests three elements which form the calculation of what will motivate people towards a particular behaviour and away from other potential behaviours.

- (E)xpectancy is the belief that a particular effort or action will lead to a particular outcome.

- (I)nstrumentality is the belief that that outcome will attract a particular reward.

- (V)alence is the value that an individual attaches to that reward.

For Vroom, the motivational force (MF) of a particular action boils down to a calculation, $MF = V \times I \times E$. Expectancy theory suggests people will be motivated to perform efforts that they believe will be instrumental in them achieving goals and rewards that they value. Similarly, if an effort cannot be linked to a goal they value, or if it is linked to a goal they do not value highly, the motivation to perform that effort will diminish.

Say a person highly desires a pay rise (V). They believe that increased sales figures will be instrumental in them getting that pay rise (I). From experience, they have found that door-step selling generates most sales (E), so the effort to which they are motivated is to go out selling from door to door. Likewise, an effort which doesn't contribute to increased sales, for example helping a colleague to write a report, is something they will not be motivated to perform.

However, a colleague who values good working relationships (V) may find that the respect of colleagues is instrumental in achieving this (I) and would thus be more motivated to the effort of helping a colleague with a report if they believed it would gain them respect from that colleague (E).

Why are you reading this chapter now? Can you link it to a particular reward that you desire at some point in the future (e.g. getting a degree, passing a module)?

## Goal setting theory

### Running case: where do I start?

Ellerby Peters has his head in his hands. He was excited to get the work experience placement at Junction Hotel and wanted to do well so that he could get a reference for his CV, but now only one day into his placement he felt despondent—I don't know what to do, he thinks to himself. In his briefing meeting with Meg Mortimer he was told his job was to sort out the back office behind the reception desk. 'Just do your best,' Mortimer told him as she headed off for a meeting. But what did that mean? It felt just so overwhelming. 'Where do I start?' he thought, 'Why did I ever take this placement?'

As he sat there Jane Foster walked in and spied the upset looking student. 'Are you alright, Ellerby?' she enquired attentively. 'I just don't know what to do,' Peters replied honestly. 'I was told to sort this room out, and all Mrs Mortimer said was "good luck". I've no idea how to do this'. Jane Foster smiled sympathetically. 'Don't worry, let's start. What is it we want to achieve?'

**Goal setting theory** is one of the most widely researched and supported process models of work motivation. It underpins many work practices, from appraisal systems to funding in the voluntary sector. It works on the principle that we respond much better to specific, clear, stretching goals with good feedback rather than vague phrases such as 'do your best' (Locke and Latham, 1990a). Goals need to be measurable and are often captured in the acronym SMART (specific, measurable, achievable, realistic and time-related). Providing the person is committed to the goals, does not have other conflicting goals, and has the skills to achieve the goals, then this approach has a positive impact on performance (Locke and Latham, 1990b). The person puts their energy into achieving their goals.

Goal setting theory
An approach that argues that motivation is influenced by the difficulty, specificity, and feedback of reaching your goals.

The concept is based on the principles that hard goals are more satisfying when they are achieved and therefore can make work feel more meaningful (Locke and Latham, 2006), that having clear outcomes helps give focus, and that getting feedback means that people can judge their progress. Often this approach works best with short- and medium-term goals, because they are easier to set clearly and have feedback; long-term goals, while useful, are often less specific and harder to measure.

One of the dangers of the goal setting approach is that it results in 'tunnel vision', where employees only focus on their goals and lose sight of wider objectives. This can be seen in many areas like the National Health Service, which has been criticized for being too focused on hitting targets and not enough on caring for patients. Goal setting can also be seen as encouraging unethical behaviour, such as at Enron where they received large bonuses for posting large revenues. The appeal of the bonuses, Ordóñez et al. argue (2009), meant Enron employees focused on increasing revenues even at the expense of making real profits (ultimately leading to the company going bankrupt). Goal setting can also mean employees only focus on things that are measureable and therefore ignore less tangible parts of the job which might be important. They might even demotivate, because motivation becomes extrinsic (a focus on the goals) rather than being the intrinsic satisfaction with the task itself. Therefore, having goals can be useful but they should be used carefully.

**Study skills:** Setting your own goals

One of the challenges of being a student is that many of the goals that you might set yourself (getting a good degree and a good job) are often quite distant, a long time in the future, and therefore not good to motivate yourself consistently. Similarly, they are not that specific and therefore may actually lose you motivation. Using goal setting theory, you can break these goals down into more concrete and immediate goals. Some systems, such as David Allen's *Getting things done*, offer practical ways of managing yourself and motivating yourself for short-term goals (Allen, 2015). To gain a broader perspective on what is useful in your life, Steven Covey's *The seven habits of highly effective people* encourages you to reflect on the wider goals that you want in your life and how to get there (Covey, 1989). Covey encourages a 'character ethic' rather than narrow goal setting (see Chapter 17 for a wider discussion). Understanding what your goals are can give you a greater sense of focus, so long as you do not lose sight of the possibilities of learning new things that you had not planned to.

These process theories of motivation certainly offer some common-sense insights such as the idea that we manage our behaviours to concentrate on those which bring us a reward. They offer organizations guidelines on designing pay and reward systems (to make sure that they not only are fair but also appear to be fair to everyone) and also some practical suggestions for individual motivation (such as goal setting theory). However, questions remain as to whether they bear up to empirical scrutiny—do they really match up to the reality of how people are motivated? In particular, do we calculate our inputs and outputs in quite the precise, mathematical way suggested by expectancy theory?

## Review questions

| Describe | What are the main features of equity theory and expectancy theory? |
| --- | --- |
| Explain | How do process theories see motivation from the point of view of the individual? |
| Analyse | Why might goal setting theory produce unintended consequences that might produce ethically questionable outcomes? |
| Apply | What examples can you see of expectancy theory, where people match actions to expected rewards, throughout the running case in the chapter? |

# Social approaches to motivation: the meaning of work

## Running case: the meaning of work

Meg is confused by how differently everyone in the reception area seems to be motivated. Some workers respond well to the smile card scheme; others ignore it but are still good workers. She can't put her finger on exactly what she needs to do to motivate her staff.

Rather than taking a manager's viewpoint, as Weaver had done with the smile card, she decides to find out what the employees feel and hands out an anonymous questionnaire to all employees. One of the questions, 'What does your work mean to you?', gives some differing yet revealing answers:

- 'Work is a means to an end—I come in, do my shift, take the cheque. Other than that it has no other meaning.'
- 'I get a lot out of work and it is really helping me get on in life. I'm really proud to tell people about what I do and the responsibility I have here.'
- 'My work is nothing but constant drudgery. I only express myself and get any meaning in life through my sports.'
- 'I'm here because my parents told me they were ashamed of me being on the dole—they have been constantly nagging me to get a job'.

Watch any quiz or game show on television—when a contestant is introduced to the audience, more often than not their occupation will be stated alongside their name, age, and where they live. As one of just four facts given in a brief introduction, their work is presented as a key aspect of that person's identity.

This is not just on television—think about when you are introduced to people, at a party for example. One of the first questions asked is about work. Indeed—the centrality of work to life is perhaps encapsulated in the question 'what do you do for a living?'

For Hughes (1951) work is one of the 'most significant' things by which we are judged in society, and the name of our occupation is both a combination of 'price tag and calling card'. By this, Hughes suggests that the work we do is a significant indication of our value and position within society.

What, if any, judgements or assumptions do you make about people when you hear what job they do?

The approaches to motivation we have discuss so far have taken a psychological approach—motivation is determined by a number of stimuli, needs, perceptions, etc. These concepts suggest that if management understand all these factors then they can design work which will increase workers' motivation. Taken overall, we suggest that these psychological approaches have a number of problems:

- It is difficult to find empirical evidence for many of these theories—they may appear plausible, but do they reflect the reality of workplace motivation?

- Can broad frameworks of motivation, such as Maslow's hierarchy, ever appreciate the complex, individual nature of personalities, as discussed with the ideographic approach in Chapter 8?

- Often when applied to work these complex theories of motivation are boiled down to a simplistic and narrow framework (e.g. Maslow) or even an equation (expectancy theory).

- Motivation theories tends to focus on just one aspect of the job—reward, satisfaction, etc.—rather than having an overall view of both the job and how it links to the outside world.

In this final section we suggest that the motivation also comes from work being an indicator of our identity to the rest of society. Motivation, and the meanings we attach to work, are as much a social phenomenon as they are a psychological one. What, for example, does it mean to be a doctor within society? Or a cleaner? Or to be without work?

## Why do we work?

Why do we work at all? Is it out of economic necessity or to gain a sense of identity within society? Part of the reason is the imperative from society to work—it is something that we are expected to do; furthermore, not working is almost seen as a form of deviant behaviour, against the norms of society.

### Theory in context: the parable of the talents

The English word 'talent', meaning aptitude or skill, originates in an ancient biblical currency used in the 'parable of the talents' in the Gospel of St Matthew. A master entrusts his servants with a number of talents. On his return, two of the servants have put their talents to work, doubling their value, and they are duly rewarded. The third has buried his talents in a hole in the ground, gaining nothing, and is punished for laziness. The parable of the talents, from the Christian bible, is about money, but the use of the word 'talent' in English to mean aptitudes suggests an obligation to work and be productive—not to let our abilities and skills go to waste.

Indeed, a duty to work can be seen in the teachings of many major religions. Max Weber (1930) is noted for the notion of the Protestant work ethic, whereby religious salvation comes about as a result of hard work throughout life. Noon and Blyton (2007) note similar work ethics in Islamic, Buddhist, and Catholic faiths. A similar message is given by each—work is good and a religious duty, while not working is seen as lazy and contrary to religious teachings.

Although the influence of religious teaching may have diminished in the UK in recent years, such work ethics still remain. This is seen in the tabloid media screaming headlines about 'Dole scroungers' and 'Benefit cheats', or television programmes like *Benefits Street*—it is as if one were not playing a rightful role in society unless economically productive.

Furthermore, for those excluded from work, especially at a time of recession, stories in the papers are of pity and of their own frustration, again as if they are barred from a fundamental aspect of existence and expression within society—the right to work. For example, Kingsley et al. (2011) interviewed young, long-term unemployed people in the UK. While they spoke about the financial problems of being unemployed, they also explained how a lack of work hits at their sense of self-identity within society, giving them less self-belief.

Visit the Online Resource Centre for more insights about the effects of unemployment on self-identity.

For Michel Foucault, who believed that power shapes our view of the world (see Chapter 13), society overall creates the idea that our bodies are working bodies and that it is abnormal if one's inclination is not to work: 'the body becomes a useful force only if it is a productive body' (Foucault and Rabinow, 1984: 173).

It is not just in religion and the media that a normal working life is presented. In school and university we are taught and guided towards our ultimate goal of work—even this textbook includes 'employability skills'. From many social and institutional angles, work becomes an obligation or duty. Rather than something for which we are motivated by some form of reward, work has a much more central part in our sense of self and identity, fuelled by a societal sense of obligation.

From a young age, we are also socialized into the expectation that we will work and that work will be a central aspect of our identity. Young children are often asked 'What will you be when you grow up?', implying that work is central to the child's identity, and older children are asked 'When are you going to get a job?' Such expectations therefore shape our sense of the importance of employment, with government policy-makers expressing concern that some children grow up with no positive role models and therefore do not aspire to work (Gregg and Wadsworth, 2011). Research shows that from an early age our expectations are shaped not only by what we aspire to but also by what we think we can achieve. Due to their background and previous experiences, many people 'simply eliminate from consideration occupations they believe to be beyond their capabilities, however attractive the occupations may be' (Bandura et al. 2001: 188). Socioeconomic, family, academic, and self-perception all therefore shape what types of careers people chose and what they consider valuable and important in life. These can be considered vital, deep-seated sources of motivation.

How influential has your upbringing been in your choosing to go to university and planning what sort of job you would like in the future?

## Orientations to work

The extent to which our working life links with our life in general and gives us a sense of identity within society was investigated by Goldthorpe (1968). In his study of workers in a Luton car factory, he noted a particular paradox. On one hand, workers did not seem to be deriving an intrinsic or social satisfaction from their work. On the other hand, workers were not expressing any dissatisfaction with their work, even though they disliked some aspects of it.

Goldthorpe (1968) concluded that such workers had an 'instrumental orientation to work'. They saw their work merely as a means to an end. They had no desire for intrinsic satisfaction from the work—they would simply keep their head down, do their shift, and then pick up the pay packet at the end of the week.

Goldthorpe brings a different perspective to motivation. It is not simply a workplace phenomenon with managers manipulating certain rewards; instead, orientations to work have more of a link with our working identity in society. Goldthorpe (1968) suggests three particular **orientations to work**:

- The instrumental orientation to work suggests a strong separation between working life and non-working life. The only aspect of working life that is carried into the outside world is the pay packet. It is this which—following an instrumental calculation—allows the worker to enjoy the life that they do in the outside world, and they desire nothing more from work.

- A bureaucratic orientation to work suggests more of a loyalty to the organization— service in return for progress. Meaning and social identity are carried into the outside world—a promotion within the organization is seen as a marker of status and identity in the outside world.

- A solidaristic orientation to work is one where meaning, again, is carried outwards into society, but it is a meaning that derives from membership of a group rather than individual status. There is, thus, solidarity between the workers. While there are economic benefits which derive from the organization, loyalty and moral leaning is to the group rather than the organization itself.

Goldthorpe's work shows that professional status contributes to our working identity in the outside world, but that elements in society, such as class, also contribute to that identity. Many accounts of solidaristic group loyalty, for example, link group loyalty in industrial environments to an element of working-class identity (see, for example, Collinson, 1988; Ackroyd and Crowdy, 1990).

A more recent workplace issue is that of **work–life balance**, a desire to achieve a sensible balance between work commitments and private life. The degree to which people achieve this has also been analysed in terms of professional identity (Caven, 2004) and the links with social factors, such as class and gender (Hakim, 2000; Özbilgin et al., 2011).

> **Orientations to work** A perspective which suggests that people have a predisposition to work that is influenced by our lives outside work and the meaning that we attach to work.

> **Work–life balance** A balance between work and career on one hand, and wider aspects of life, such as family and leisure time, on the other.

@ Visit the Online Resource Centre to read more about the effects of class and gender on personal identity.

## Work and innate creativity

For a final word on motivation and society, we turn to Karl Marx (1867/1990) who, as we saw in Chapter 3, suggested that people are inherently creative—they have a desire to transform the world around them. In a Marxist sense, motivation is thus innate—a very different view of motivation from that of Taylor and Ford seen earlier in this chapter, who saw people as innately lazy.

A similar view of natural human creativity was seen in Chapter 8 with the social–radical approach. People have unlimited potential; it is the nature of work which demotivates them from achieving this rather than workers being disinclined to work.

Ironically, this is the view of people that Maslow held with his self-actualization concept, but it has been written out of the interpretation of Maslow used in management theory. Perhaps if management were able to tap into this aspect of human motivation or design work to enable people to fulfil it, then the whole area of motivation theory, with its associated models and theories, would be rendered obsolete—an important part of management (motivating people to work) would be covered by the innate motivation of people themselves.

## Review questions

| **Describe** | What are the three orientations to work suggested by Goldthorpe? |
| **Explain** | How does work provide us with an identity and meaning within society? |
| **Analyse** | Are motivational techniques just another way of getting staff to do things that they would otherwise not do? What would work be like if it were designed to produce the maximum level of self-actualization rather than productivity? |
| **Apply** | What orientations to work do you see in the Junction Hotel staff? |

# Chapter summary

In this chapter we have seen a number of perspectives on motivation: behavioural reward and punishment techniques; content theories which suggest that workers have needs which motivate them and for which appropriate job characteristics can be designed; process theories which suggest that motivation is a result of subjective individual calculations; and social theories which link work motivation with the wider significance of work as a facet of our identity within society.

It seems that any one motivation theory seen in isolation is inadequate—neither Maslow, nor expectancy theory, nor any other theory alone, can explain motivation. However, taken together, theories of motivation outline different facets of what motivates us in the workplace. Perhaps the problem with motivation theory has been that, rather than illuminating different facets of motivation in the workplace, theories have been applied as absolute descriptions and even as 'how-to' lists.

The chapter began by examining the role of pay in workplace motivation, suggesting that this is an important motivating factor in the workforce, but is far from being the only motivating factor. As a summary, we present how different theories of motivation would view pay as a motivator (Table 9.1). While this shows different perspectives on pay, it also gives an insight into the different ways that the theories view motivation overall.

Table 9.1  Motivation theories and different perspectives on pay as a motivator

| | |
|---|---|
| Taylorism/Fordism | Pay is the sole motivator for otherwise lazy and unmotivated workers |
| Behaviourism | Pay is a stimulus—it can be used as a reward or its withdrawal as a punishment to condition people's behaviour |
| Maslow—hierarchy of needs | Pay motivates differently in different parts of the hierarchy: at lower levels pay is needed to survive; at higher levels intrinsic motivators have more of an effect, although pay could be an indicator of status/esteem |
| Herzberg—motivators and hygiene factors | Pay is an element that has to be provided in sufficient amounts, otherwise it will cause dissatisfaction; however, pay does not in itself cause any increased motivation |
| Adams—equity theory | Pay is one basis on which workers will compare themselves against the inputs and rewards received by others |
| Vroom—expectancy theory | Pay is a reward; however, the degree to which it motivates depends on how much an individual values pay as a reward and how much workers link particular behaviours to receiving that reward |
| Social theories | Pay may be an indicator of status and working identity in society, but we are also motivated to work because being a working, economically-productive individual is seen as normal and an obligation by society |
| Goldthorpe—orientations to work | The role of pay depends on an individual's orientation to work; an instrumental orientation might make pay more of a motivating factor, but other orientations, such as bureaucratic and solidaristic, also exist |

## Further reading

Herzberg, F. 2003. One more time: How do you motivate employees? *Harvard Business Review* 81(1): 87–96.
Herzberg's explanation of his motivators and hygiene theory.

Hughes, E.C. 1951. Work and the self. In: Rohrer, J.H., and Sherif, M. (eds) *Social psychology at the crossroads: The University of Oklahoma lectures in social psychology*. Harper: Oxford, pp. 313–23.
An examination of the role of work in providing identity within society.

Villere, M.F., and Hartman, S.S. 1991. Reinforcement theory: A practical tool. *Leadership and Organization Development Journal* 12(2): 27–31.
An overview of the use of operant conditioning techniques in the workplace.

McGee, H.M., and Johnson, D.A. 2015. Performance motivation as the behaviorist views it. *Performance Improvement* 54(4): 15–21.
This article provides an overview of behavioural theories of workplace motivation.

## References

Ackroyd, S., and Crowdy, P.A. 1990. Can culture be managed? Working with 'raw' material: the case of the English slaughtermen. *Personnel Review* 19(5): 3–13.

Adams, J.S. 1963. Towards an understanding of inequity. *Journal of Abnormal and Social Psychology* 67(5): 422.

Allen, D. 2015. *Getting things done: The art of stress-free productivity*. London: Penguin.

Ashdown, J., and Smyth, R. 2009. Which teams have been punished for defeats? *The Guardian*, 30 September.

Bandura, A., Barbaranelli, C., Caprara, G.V., and Pastorelli, C. 2001. Self-efficacy beliefs as shapers of children's aspirations and career trajectories. *Child Development* 72(1): 187–206.

BBC News 2010. How do you punish a football team? Available at:http://www.bbc.co.uk/news/10402967 (last accessed 29 June 2012).

Beynon, H. 1984. *Working for Ford*. Penguin: Harmondsworth.

Burkeman, O. 2011. This column will change your life: Get into the habit of random rewards, *The Guardian*, 23 April.

Caven, V. 2004. Constructing a career: Women architects at work. *Career Development International* 9(5): 518–31.

Collinson, D.L. 1988. 'Engineering humour': Masculinity, joking and conflict in shop-floor relations. *Organization Studies* 9(2): 181–99.

Colquitt, J.A., Conlon, D.E., Wesson, M.J., Porter, C.O., and Ng, K.Y. 2001. Justice at the millennium: A meta-analytic review of 25 years of organizational justice research. *Journal of Applied Psychology* 86(3): 425–45.

Covey, S. 1989. *The seven habits of highly effective people*. Simon & Schuster: London.

Cullen, D. 1997. Maslow, monkeys and motivation theory. *Organization* 4(3): 355–73.

Cullen, D., and Gotell, L. 2002. From orgasms to organizations: Maslow, women's sexuality and the gendered foundations of the needs hierarchy. *Gender, Work and Organization* 9(5): 537–55.

Dalal, R.S. and Hulin, C.L. 2008. 'Motivation for what? A multivariate dynamic perspective of the criterion', in Kanfer, R., Chen, G., and Pritchard, R.D. (eds) *Work motivation: Past, present, and future*. Taylor and Francis: New York, pp. 63–100.

Davis, K. 1957. *Human relations in business*. McGraw-Hill: New York.

De Gieter, S., De Cooman, R., Pepermans, R., Caers, R., Du Bois, C., and Jegers, M. 2006. Identifying nurses' rewards: A qualitative categorization study in Belgium. *Human Resources for Health* 4: 15.

Dewhurst, M., Guthridge, M., and Mohr, E. 2009. Motivating people: Getting beyond money. *McKinsey Quarterly*, November. Available at: http://www.mckinseyquarterly.com/Motivating_people_Getting_beyond_money_2460 (last accessed 29 June 2012).

Dye, K., Mills, A.J., and Weatherbee, T. 2005. Maslow: man interrupted: Reading management theory in context. *Management Decision* 43(10): 1375–95.

Executive Grapevine 2015a VIDEO: CEO's inspirational speech that got employees working for free. Available at: http://www.executive-grapevine.com/board-leadership/article/2015-06-18-video-ceos-inspirational-speech-that-got-employees-working-for-free?utm_source= eshot&utm_medium = email&utm_campaign = BL%20-%2024/06/2015 (last accessed 18 July 2015).

Executive Grapevine 2015b Zappos billionaire CEO lives in a trailer, *Executive Grapevine*. Available at: http://www.hrgrapevine.com/markets/hr/article/2015-07-22-zappos-billionaire-ceo-lives-in-a-trailer (last accessed18 July 2015).

Flanagan, E. 2014. Stalybridge lottery syndicate win £2.9m jackpot—but say they will stay on at work. *Manchester Evening News*, 4 November.

Foucault, M., and Rabinow, P. 1984. *The Foucault reader*. Pantheon Books: New York.

Gibson, C.H. 1973. Volvo increases productivity through job enrichment. *California Management Review* 15(4): 64–6.

Goldthorpe, J.H. 1968. *The affluent worker: Industrial attitudes and behaviour*. Cambridge University Press: London.

Greenberg, J. 1990a. Employee theft as a reaction to underpayment inequity: The hidden cost of pay cuts. *Journal of Applied Psychology* 75(5): 561.

Greenberg, J. 1990b. Organizational justice: Yesterday, today, and tomorrow. *Journal of Management* 16(2): 399–432.

Gregg, P. and Wadsworth, J. 2011. Workless households. In: Gregg, P., and Wadsworth, J. (eds) *The labour market in winter: The state of working Britain*. Oxford University Press: Oxford, pp. 72–83.

Hakim, C. 2000. *Work-lifestyle choices in the 21st century*. Oxford University Press: Oxford.

Handy, C.B. 1993. *Understanding organizations*. Penguin Books: London, New York.

Harpaz, I. 1989. Non-financial employment commitment: A cross-national comparison. *Journal of Occupational Psychology* 62(2): 147–50.

Harrison, J. D. 2015. When we were small: Pandora. *Washington Post*, 6 February.

Herzberg, F. 1966. *Workand the nature of man*. World Pub. Co.: Cleveland, OH.

Herzberg, F. 1987. One more time: How do you motivate employees? *Harvard Business Review* September-October: 88-L 99.

Herzberg, F. 2003. One more time: How do you motivate employees? *Harvard Business Review* 81(1): 87–96.

Holley, P. 2015. Why this CEO is worth almost $1 billion but lives in a trailer park, *Washington Post*, 21 July.

Hughes, E.C. 1951. Work and the self. In: Rohrer, J.H., and Sherif, M. (eds) *Social psychology at the crossroads: The University of Oklahoma lectures in social psychology*. Harper: Oxford, pp. 313–23.

Huseman, R.C., Hatfield, J.D., and Miles, E.W. 1987. A new perspective on equity theory: The equity sensitivity construct. *Academy of Management Review* 12(2): 222–34.

Judge, T.A., Thoresen, C.J., Bono, J.E., and Patton, G.K. 2001. The job satisfaction–job performance relationship: A qualitative and quantitative review. *Psychological Bulletin* 127(3): 376–407.

Kingsley, P., Hickman, L., and Saner, E. 2011. What's it like to be young and looking for work in Britain? *The Guardian*, 1 November.

Kouchaki, M., Smith, I.H., and Netchaeva, E. 2015. Not all fairness is created equal: Fairness perceptions of group vs. individual decision makers. *Organization Science* 26(5): 1301–15.

Lawler, E.E., III, 1973. *Motivation in work organizations*. Brookes/Cole Pub. Co.: Monterey, CA.

Locke, E.A., and Latham, G.P. 1990a. *A theory of goal setting and task performance*. Prentice Hall: Harlow.

Locke, E.A. and Latham, G.P. 1990b. Work motivation and satisfaction: Light at the end of the tunnel. *Psychological Science* 1(4): 240–6.

Locke, E.A. and Latham, G.P. 2006. New directions in goal-setting theory. *Current Directions In Psychological Science* 15(5): 265–8.

Luthans, F., and Kreitner, R. 1985. *Organizational behaviour modification and beyond*. Scott Foresman: Glenview, IL.

Makin, P.J., and Sutherland, V.J. 1994. Reducing accidents using a behavioural approach. *Leadership and Organization Development Journal* 15(5): 5–10.

Martinko, M.J., and Fadil, P. 1994. Operant technologies: A theoretical foundation for organizational change and development. *Leadership and Organization Development Journal* 15(5): 16–20.

Marx, K. 1867/1990. *Capital*, vol. 1 (transl. Fowkes, B.). Penguin Books: London.

Maslow, A.H. 1943. A theory of human motivation. *Psychological Review* 50(4): 370–96.

Maslow, A.H. 1987. *Motivation and personality*. Harper and Row: New York.

Maslow, A.H. 2000. *The Maslow business reader*. John Wiley: New York, Toronto.

McGee, H.M. and Johnson, D.A. 2015. Performance motivation as the behaviorist views it. *Performance Improvement* 54(4): 15–21.

Noon, M., and Blyton, P. 2007. *The realities of work: Experiencing work and employment in contemporary society*. Palgrave: Basingstoke, New York.

Okeleji, O. 2011. Dynamo Kiev players pay for losing. Available at: http://www.bbc.co.uk/sport/0/football/13775725 (last accessed 29 June 2012).

Ordóñez, L., Schweitzer, M.E., Galinsky, A., and Bazerman, M. 2009. Goals gone wild: How goals systematically harm individuals and organizations. *Academy of Management Perspectives* 23(1): 6–16.

Özbilgin, M.F., Beauregard, T.A., Tatli, A., and Bell, M.P. 2011. Work-life, diversity and intersectionality: A critical review and research agenda. *International Journal of Management Reviews* 13(2): 177–98.

Pavlov, I.P., and Anrep, G.V. 1927. *Conditioned reflexes: An investigation of the physiological activity of the cerebral cortex*. Oxford University Press: London.

Raff, D., and Summers, L. 1987. Did Henry Ford pay efficiency wages? *Journal of Labour Economics* 5(4): 557–86.

Rehder, R.R. 1994. Saturn, Uddevalla and the Japanese lean systems: Paradoxical prototypes for the twenty-first century. *International Journal of Human Resource Management* 5(1): 1–31.

Skarlicki, D. P., and Folger, R. 1997. Retaliation in the workplace: The roles of distributive, procedural, and interactional justice. *Journal of Applied Psychology* 82(3): 434–43.

Skinner, B.F. 1969. *Contingencies of reinforcement: A theoretical analysis*. Appleton-Century-Crofts: New York.

Taylor, F.W. 1911. *The principles of scientific management*. Harper: New York.

Towers Watson 2014. The 2014 global workforce study. Towers Watson: London.

Tyler, T.R., and Bies, R.J. 1990. Beyond formal procedures: The interpersonal context of procedural justice. In: Carroll, J. (ed.) *Applied social psychology and organizational settings*. Erlbaum: Hillsdale, NJ, pp. 77–98.

Villere, M.F., and Hartman, S.S. 1991. Reinforcement theory: A practical tool. *Leadership and Organization Development Journal* 12(2): 27–31.

Vroom, V.H. 1964. *Work and motivation*. Wiley: New York.

Wahba, M.A., and Bridwell, L.G. 1976. Maslow reconsidered: A review of research on the need hierarchy theory. *Organizational Behavior and Human Performance* 15(2): 212–L 40.

Walker, P., and Jones, S. 2012. EuroMillions lottery win buys Corby bus drivers ticket to retirement. *The Guardian*, 19 March.

Weber, M. 1930. *The Protestant ethicand the spirit of capitalism* (transl. Parsons, T.). G. Allen & Unwin: London.

Wei, W. 2010. Amazon is paying Zappos CEO Tony Hsieh only $36,000. *Business Insider*, 22 October.

Wiley, C. 1997. What motivates employees according to over 40 years of motivation surveys. *International Journal of Manpower* 18(3): 263–80.

Wray-Bliss, E., and Willmott, H. 1999. Battling with the gods: Workers, management and the deities of post industrial management culture. In: Goodman, R. (ed.) *Modern organization and emerging conundrums: Exploring the post-industrial sub-culture of the third millennium*. New Lexington Press: San Francisco, pp. 377–89.

# 10
# Knowledge and learning
*Developing the individual, developing the organization*

## Chapter overview and learning outcomes

By the end of this chapter you should be able to:

- describe a variety of theories of individual knowledge and learning

- explain the importance of deep learning, where knowledge is learned from experience and from 'learning to learn'

- describe the importance of knowledge and learning at organizational levels

- explain and analyse the concept of the 'learning organization'.

## Key theorists

| | |
|---|---|
| Michael Polanyi | Recognized the importance of the 'tacit' dimension of knowledge which comes from personal experience, rather than explicit knowledge such as facts and figures |
| David Kolb | Devised a learning cycle which demonstrated how knowledge is gained through a cycle of experience and reflection |
| Howard Gardner | Outlined a theory of multiple intelligences, whereby individuals exhibit different types of intelligence, such as logical, musical, or spatial |
| Ikujiro Nonaka | Suggested that a successful 'knowledge creating company' is adept at transforming tacit and explicit knowledge within its workforce |
| Chris Argyris and Donald Schön | Suggested that successful organizational learning is that which goes beyond 'single loop' to become 'double-loop' learning |
| Peter Senge | Outlined a model of the key characteristics of the learning organization |
| Jean Lave and Etienne Wenger | Noted the existence of communities of practice, and that social groups engage in learning a common area of knowledge and practice |

## Key terms

| | |
|---|---|
| Explicit knowledge | Knowledge which can be expressed to other people as a set of words, facts, diagrams, or instructions |
| Tacit knowledge | Knowledge which is personal, a form of second nature or knowing things 'off by heart', and which is difficult to explain to others |
| Experiential learning | Learning which comes from experiences and reflecting on those experiences |
| Learning styles | Ways in which different individuals approach learning and learn more effectively |
| Reflective practice | A form of professional development and training where workers reflect on actual workplace experiences and events |
| Organizational knowledge | Knowledge which is a collective property of an organization rather than belonging to an individual |
| Organizational learning | Sharing and transferring knowledge so that it becomes a collective property of the organization |
| Learning organization | An organization which is set up so as to facilitate continual learning at individual and organizational levels |
| Communities of practice | Social groupings that are based around a common occupational practice and set of knowledge and that develop and share that knowledge among themselves |

# Introduction

### Running case: an alarming experience

Simon Chance has had a busy morning dealing with a full-scale evacuation of the hotel. One of the heat detectors in the restaurant became faulty, setting fire alarms ringing, and all of the guests and staff had to go outside into the car park and wait until the all-clear was given.

Inside the hotel, the maintenance team are having problems. Bob Smith is their expert on the fire alarm system—he knows it inside out and can fix any problems in minutes. Unfortunately, today he is off work sick and nobody else in the team knows how to deal with the problem. Chance sees the remaining engineers standing around the alarm's control panel, flicking through manuals and scratching their heads, but none of them really know what to do—they hadn't had to deal with a problem in the alarm system before.

At great cost, Chance has to bring in an outside engineer, who takes a couple of hours to arrive and a further two hours to fix the problem. In the meantime, he has to deal with a crowd of unhappy guests who are waiting outside with growing impatience.

If you were in charge of training and development of the maintenance team, what would you do to avoid a repeat of this problem?

Do you see the workplace as somewhere to simply pick up a wage or do you see it as more than that, maybe somewhere where you go to develop as an individual? Certainly in the previous two chapters there has been a suggestion that the workplace is somewhere where our personalities develop (Chapter 8) and even where we engage in our highest creative achievements through self-actualization (Chapter 9).

In this chapter we examine how people in organizations develop as individuals and become better at their work by learning and gaining new knowledge from their workplace experience. Knowledgeable workers also benefit the organization. In recent years it has been suggested that knowledge can give organizations a competitive advantage within the economy, especially in certain sectors, such as technology, where constant development and innovation are important.

The chapter thus examines both knowledge (what people know) and learning (how people gain that knowledge).

- Firstly, we look at knowledge and learning at an individual level, drawing a distinction between explicit knowledge, which can be learned off by heart as a set of facts, and a deeper tacit knowledge, which is learned from experience and reflection upon that experience. We also look specifically at management knowledge—what knowledge is needed to be a manager and how do people gain that knowledge?

- Secondly, we move to the level of the organization. The management of knowledge is concerned with how individuals learn, but also with how knowledge, both explicit and tacit, is transferred between people in and across the organization. Knowledge becomes an organization-wide property rather than something belonging to any one individual. We see how organizations that promote the sharing of knowledge become learning organizations, and how this equips them to deal with change and uncertainty.

To conclude, we examine organizational knowledge in a contemporary context, where it can be shared and developed through computer networks and across organizational boundaries.

# Individual learning: knowledge, experience, and styles

## Running case: training and development

Later in the day, Chance ponders upon the problem with the fire alarm. While there is a lot of knowledge and expertise in the maintenance team, it isn't shared—each person has their own specialist area.

The morning's events have demonstrated how reliant they are on specific individuals who seem to be the only ones who know how to do key tasks. If that person is absent, the task can't be performed.

Chance decides that the maintenance staff need to learn more about each other's specialisms—to have a broader knowledge of maintenance tasks and equipment across the hotel. He sets to work on a training and development programme that will increase knowledge and learning across the maintenance team.

**Experiential learning**
Learning which comes from experiences and reflecting on those experiences.

**Surface learning**
Learning a set of facts in themselves, possibly for the purposes of a test or exam, rather than with any additional depth.

**Deep learning**
Learning that tries to achieve a deeper understanding of, and engagement with, the material being learned.

**Learning styles** The different ways in which different individuals approach learning.

We have all engaged in learning at some point in our lives, whether it is formulas for a maths exam, lines for a play, or new techniques for a sport. By reading this book you are engaged in a learning process. But what does it really mean to have learned something? Is knowledge something as simple as remembering lists off by heart, or is there more to it?

In this section we examine individual learning and how we learn. In particular, we examine how **experiential learning** takes us from **surface learning**, where we simply learn a set of facts, to **deep learning**, a richer form of learning where we understand knowledge in its *context* and from our own *experience*, and where we begin to think about the ways in which we learn best and develop our own preferred **learning styles**.

# From lists to patterns

**Running case:** learning rewards

Chance does an audit of the qualifications currently held within the maintenance team, and then offers incentives for people to add to their knowledge and gain more qualifications. Courses in plumbing, gas, and electricity, as well as workshops for particular pieces of equipment, will be offered to the maintenance team, with a bonus paid for each qualification gained. Chance calls this scheme 'learning rewards'.

One of the maintenance staff, Mike Bridges, throws himself into the scheme and gains several certificates from a local college. He is the first person to be called upon when the refrigeration unit in the hotel bar breaks down, as he has undertaken a day's workshop with the manufacturers of the refrigeration equipment.

Unfortunately, that knowledge doesn't seem to help him when he is faced with the task of getting the refrigeration unit working again. 'I passed that test six months ago,' explains Bridges to bar manager John Vintner. 'Took my bonus and haven't looked at the manual since. I've never actually touched one of these things before, let alone repaired one.'

What sort of learning do you think the learning rewards scheme promoted? Is it of any use to the hotel?

To help understand the nature of individual learning, we are going to engage in a process of learning ourselves. The Finnish language is a language unlike most other languages and one with which you will probably not be familiar. Have a look at the list of five Finnish words in Table 10.1, and their English translations, and learn them—you will be tested on these later.

How did you go about trying to learn the words? Did you simply read them and commit them to memory, or did you devise some form of system for learning the words? Did you stop and think about how you have learned a language before or did you dive straight in?

The Finnish flag.

The particular strategy you adopt says a lot about not only how you go about learning, but also reveals some of the key learning theories.

## A behaviourist view of learning

If you were offered a £10 reward for each word you remembered correctly, would you be more likely to have learned them by the end of the chapter than without it? Such an approach is underpinned by ideas from **behavioural psychology**. As we saw in Chapter 9, behavioural psychologists argue that people are motivated by rewards and punishments. Learning theorists have adopted these ideas to provide our first learning perspective. Vocabulary tests from school language lessons follow this type of pattern—learn the words and you are rewarded with a good grade; fail to learn them and you may receive a punishment, for example a detention or failing a language module.

How much of your learning is motivated by the grade that you will earn?

As we saw in Chapter 9, however, for behaviourist theories to work, the reward needs to be maintained. This suggests that, after gaining the initial £10, people will no longer be motivated to retain the words in their memory. Unless further rewards come along, they will eventually forget what they have learned.

With no reward on offer for the Finnish language test other than your own satisfaction at learning the words, let's see how well your learning of the words has gone so far. Without referring back to the original list, can you say the Finnish words for the following English words listed?—no cheating and looking back!

- Market.
- Town.
- River.
- Out.
- University.

Whenever we have tried this exercise in a class situation, people have generally remembered very few of the words. The odd person may remember one or two words, but very few people learn and remember all five of the words.

## Knowledge as forms and patterns

Perhaps we need to approach the way in which we learn the words differently. Read the descriptions given and, with no need for any form of reward or punishment, we suggest that there is a good chance that you will remember these words not just for the next time you are tested in this chapter, but for days, weeks, months—even years—afterwards:

- the word for market is 'tori'. Margaret Thatcher was a well-known Tory prime minister. Imagine Margaret Thatcher in her blue dress, perfectly styled hair and carrying her

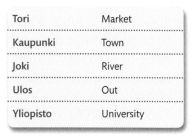

Table 10.1  Some words in Finnish, part 1

| Tori | Market |
| --- | --- |
| Kaupunki | Town |
| Joki | River |
| Ulos | Out |
| Yliopisto | University |

Behavioural psychology/behaviourism An area of psychology which suggests that learning can be managed through the use of rewards and punishments.

handbag, walking around a market looking at all the stalls. A famous Tory is in the market, the word for which is 'tori'.

- the word for town is 'kaupunki' pronounced cow-punk-ee. Imagine a cow with a Mohican haircut and a safety pin through its nose—a cow-punk—and it is walking down the main street in your home town. Town is cow-punk-ee.

- the word for river is 'joki', pronouced yok-ee, but let's keep it at the English pronunciation for now—jokey. Imagine you are on a boat cruising along the river, having drinks and everyone is having a good laugh—it's quite a 'jokey' atmosphere on the river. 'Joki' means river.

- the word for out is 'ulos' or 'you-loss'. Imagine your team is out of a tournament. Why would the team be out? Because 'you-lost'.

- the Finnish word for university is 'yliopisto'—pronounced 'ill-ee-oh-pist-oh'. Imagine waking up at university one morning and you feel ill. Why are you feeling ill? Because last night you had a bit too much to drink. You are at university and you feel ill-ee-oh-pist-oh (by now you should be able to work this one out for yourself!).

Go back to Table 10.1 and test yourself again on the words in Finnish. Did you do better this time? What do you think it is about the way you learned the words this time round that helped you to remember them better?

**Gestalt psychology**
An area of psychology which suggests that we perceive things as forms, patterns, and connections rather than as a set of discrete individual items.

The type of learning this time is different—it is learning through creating associations and patterns. The importance of associations and patterns is a part of **Gestalt psychology**, a branch of psychology which developed in Germany in the early 1900s. Kurt Lewin, who we encounter in Chapters 6, 11, and 12, was associated with the Gestalt school. His interest was in how individual behaviour was affected by the way people perceive the world around them. Gestalt psychologists as a whole were interested in human perception, and their work has been applied to studies of learning and behaviour.

The German word 'Gestalt' translates as 'form', 'pattern', or 'configuration'. Gestalt psychology is thus concerned with how we structure perceptions in memory into particular patterns or forms. Gestalt psychology gives us the familiar saying that 'the whole is different than the sum of its parts' (Koffka, 1955: 176). Think of how we perceive a melody, for example. We don't think about it note by note—a B flat followed by a C; instead, we perceive the song as a whole. It's the same with recognizing a familiar face. We don't think of a friend's face in terms of each individual part—the eyes, nose, etc.; we simply recognize the overall pattern without breaking it down into its constituent parts. The whole is different to the sum of its parts.

Our methods for learning the Finnish words are based on a similar idea and is a method which is used in real life language learning programmes, such as Linkword (see www.link-wordlanguages. com for an example). Rather than take a set of individual words, devoid of any context or familiarity, we have woven them into a pattern of connections that then helps us to recall the words. It is as if we are making the word that we are learning part of an overall story, or part of a 'Gestalt'.

You may use similar methods when trying to memorize a list of names or items, perhaps as revision for an exam. Some people use 'mind-maps'—diagrams which show how different ideas connect rather than just trying to learn a list of words. Another trick for memorizing items is where the learner mentally traces out a familiar journey, placing the items to be remembered in locations along the way.

Visit the Online Resource Centre for further examples of learning techniques.

Contextualizing knowledge in this way—as part of a pattern—is an effective way to learn, certainly more effective than learning a simple list of words off by heart. However, in the next section we ask an important question about the quality of the knowledge that has been learned—you may *know* some words in Finnish, but do you *know* how to speak Finnish?

## From explicit to tacit knowledge

### Running case: a feel for the task

Another of the maintenance staff, Gerry Dawson, walks up to the bar to see the younger Mike Bridges staring blankly at the faulty refrigeration unit.

'Let me have a go,' says Dawson, rolling up his sleeves and prodding inside the unit instinctively. 'You might have all your qualifications in there,' he says, pointing at Mike Bridges's head, 'but I spent years working in a pub. I used to have to fix these all the time.'

'It's second nature to me. My knowledge of these machines is here,' continues Dawson, raising his hands and pointing to his fingers. 'I just have a feel for these things.'

Whether learning a list off by heart or using a more Gestaltist way to remember the list of words, we have, as yet, only learned a list of words. Can you use the words in a phrase or hold a conversation in the language, for example? We do not *know* every aspect of the language because, as yet, we have no *experience* of speaking the language.

The type and quality of knowledge learned is an issue that has been addressed by a number of philosophers of knowledge (e.g. Russell, 1912; Ryle, 1949; Polanyi, 1958). Based on these insights, we suggest three types of knowledge which relate to the example of learning words in a language.

- *Knowledge that* is knowing a fact: for example, that the Finnish word for market is 'tori'.

- *Knowledge how* is where there is a deeper understanding of how that fact can be used in context. For example, I not only know that the Finnish word for market is 'tori', I know how to use it in a sentence and how to construct the grammar in that sentence.

- *Knowledge of*, sometimes known as acquaintance knowledge (Russell, 1912), comes from a familiarity with something—the way in which we know a friend rather than the way in which we know a fact. This distinction is not captured well in English, where the same verb 'to know' covers both of these ideas. In French (and many other languages) there are two verbs which translate as 'to know'—*savoir*, meaning to know a fact, and *connaître*, meaning familiarity. Thus, the phrase 'I KNOW Paris is the capital of France'—a fact—is translated as 'Je *sais* que Paris est la capitale de la France'. However, the phrase 'I KNOW Paris well', indicating familiarity with, and experience of, the city, is translated as 'Je *connais* bien Paris'. In terms of knowing Finnish, knowledge *of* would suggest being a regular speaker of the language: for example, being so well acquainted with the language that you know the slang and sayings that people use.

Moving from knowledge *that* towards knowledge *how* and knowledge *of* requires people to actually practise speaking the language, finding out what people really say, making mistakes and being laughed at, and learning from those mistakes. Michael Polanyi (1967) recognizes such a 'tacit dimension' of knowledge—where knowledge is more than just words on a page, it is something which people pick up from experience. Following Polanyi, there is thus a distinction between two types of knowledge:

**Explicit knowledge**
Knowledge which can be expressed to other people as a set of words, facts, diagrams, or instructions.

**Tacit knowledge**
Knowledge which is personal, a form of second nature or knowing things 'off by heart', and which is difficult to explain to others.

- **explicit knowledge** is that which can be codified or written down, and then communicated clearly to other people, for example a set of instructions, a diagram, a reference manual, a list of words, etc.

- **tacit knowledge** is knowledge which comes from experience—from doing and practising something. It is thus much more of a personal form of knowledge that we carry within us.

We can see how explicit knowledge would relate to knowledge *that* in that it is a simple set of facts that can be stated. We can also see how tacit knowledge relates to knowledge *of*—it is knowledge that can by gained only from doing and experiencing something. Knowledge *how*, the ability to do something, perhaps bridges the two. We can learn how to do something from a set of instructions on a page, but it is through practising and experiencing that action that we really come to know how to perform it—when rather than having to think about it, it becomes 'second nature'.

## Real life case: learning to drive

A major learning experience for many people is learning to drive. It is a learning process which has both explicit and tacit dimensions.

Drivers have to take a theory test before they are allowed to get behind the wheel of a car. This involves learning many aspects of driving theory—what road signs mean, stopping distances at different speeds, how to indicate at a roundabout, etc. This knowledge is learned as explicit knowledge from books, the Highway code, and on websites, etc., following which the learner driver takes the theory test.

Learning to drive has both explicit and tacit dimensions.

But passing a test based on explicit knowledge does not mean a learner then *knows* how to drive—there is another part of learning to drive which involves getting behind the wheel with an instructor and gaining knowledge through the experience of driving. At first a driver will be unsure, driving slowly, and possibly stalling the car often. With practice and experience, driving becomes easier.

A particular development in learning to drive is when tasks that have to be thought about become second nature. Rather than thinking about each gear change in advance, it is done almost without actually thinking about it.

It is this ability and knowledge—knowing how to drive in practice rather than reciting facts from a theory manual—that is tested in the actual driving test.

Think about other common learning experiences in life, for example learning to ride a bicycle or learning to swim. To what extent can these be split into explicit and tacit knowledge? How could you teach someone else to do these activities?

Polanyi (1967: 4) sums up the nature of tacit knowledge when he says that 'we know more than we can tell'. While explicit knowledge can be written down, tacit knowledge is much harder to share because it is so personal and comes only from doing and experiencing something.

This is summed up in the example of learning to drive a car. There is only so much about knowing how to drive a car that an instructor can impart as tacit knowledge—as theory and as a set of instructions, for example. There is a tacit element of knowledge of driving a car, however, that simply cannot be told to other people—they have to learn it from their own experience.

How did you learn to speak your own native language? And how much of that language could you teach to others?

Tacit and explicit knowledge present two aspects of language learning. The vocabulary lists and grammar tables are the explicit knowledge, the building blocks upon which our learning takes place—the knowledge *that*. The knowledge *how* to speak the language and the intimate knowledge *of* the language come from tacit knowledge that we develop personally the more we practise speaking the language—learning comes from experience.

# Experiential learning

## Real life case: 'Googling' symptoms

Many doctors complain about patients who look up their symptoms on a search engine and enter the surgery already having made a self-diagnosis. It is as if the medical knowledge of a doctor is unimportant given that so much medical knowledge can now be found on the Internet.

However, what the patient is lacking is experience. They may know some medical facts, but the doctor will have trained and been in practice for years. They will have seen patients with similar symptoms; they will have learned from the diagnoses they have made previously and from the occasions when they have made a misdiagnosis. They will have experience of which drugs work best for which patients, and which are less effective.

A recent study from Harvard Medical School (Semigran et al., 2015) found that, where patients used more specialized online symptom checkers that use data and other explicit knowledge to create a diagnosis based upon symptoms that are input, the correct diagnosis was only listed first on 34% of occasions. Triage recommendations tended to be risk averse, with patients often recommended to seek further medical advice where self-care would have been sufficient.

The explicit knowledge—data stored online and used to inform symptom checkers—is similar to that which doctors will have learned during medical training, but an important further part of a doctor's expert knowledge comes from their experience as much as it does from facts and figures about how a body works.

**Sources:** Tang and Ng (2006); Alexander (2012); Paddock (2012); Semigran et al. (2015).

The example of medical knowledge shows how knowledge relevant for a particular job can be seen as a blend between facts, or explicit knowledge, and the tacit knowledge that comes from experience—using that explicit knowledge in practice and learning from what works and what doesn't work.

It is often said that we learn from our mistakes. If we do something wrong, we learn from that experience so as not to repeat that mistake in future. However, in this section we see how all experiences—whether a mistake is made or whether we do things well—are a basis for learning when we *reflect* on those experiences.

## Kolb's learning cycle

**Experiential learning**
Learning which comes from experiences and reflecting on those experiences.

**Kolb's learning cycle**
A model of experiential learning which suggests that people learn through different stages of experience and reflection, and which suggests that people have particular learning style preferences for different parts of that cycle.

David Kolb's (1984) learning cycle is a model of **experiential learning**. It suggests that learning moves through a continuous cycle between acting, i.e. having an experience, and reflecting on that action (see Figure 10.1).

**Kolb's learning cycle** suggests that learning passes through four stages of experience and reflection:

- *concrete experience* is where we do or have an experience—an action is performed.
- *reflective observation* is where we review and reflect on the experience. What went well? What went badly? What could be done better? etc.
- *abstract conceptualization* is where we conclude and learn from our reflections on the experience. After reflection, the actor makes links with theory and explicit knowledge—given what went wrong, what theory might help explain this? What explicit knowledge or theory might help to rectify this next time?
- *active experimentation* is planning and trying out what has been learned from the experience. Different options are tried out for next time until the cycle goes back to the next concrete experience and then begins again.

Kolb's cycle shows how tacit and explicit aspects of knowledge link together in the process of learning. This blending together of tacit and explicit knowledge within Kolb's cycle can

**Figure 10.1** Kolb's learning cycle.

**Source:** based on Kolb (1984).

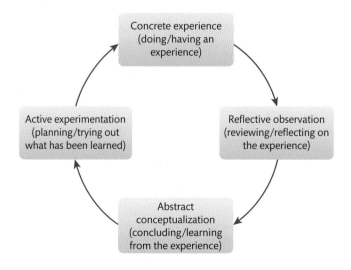

be demonstrated if we apply it to a specific learning experience. For example, a golf player learning to play and improve their game might go through the stages of Kolb's cycle as follows:

Applying tacit and explicit knowledge.
**Source:** Shutterstock.

- *Concrete experience*: the golfer plays a round of golf and is not happy with her score.

- *Reflective observation*: the golfer thinks back over the round and why it didn't go well. She thinks about different aspects of the game, and identifies her golf swing as the main problem.

- *Abstract conceptualization*: the golfer refers to some explicit knowledge—maybe a golf manual written by an expert, maybe a golf coaching DVD, maybe even a golf class. From this theory and instruction she begins to identify what is wrong with the swing and what could be changed next time.

- *Active experimentation*: the golfer goes to a driving range to put what she has learned about her swing into practice—putting different ideas into action to see which works best with her golf swing.

- *Concrete experience*: the golfer is back on the course and plays another round of golf. The score is a slight improvement from last time . . .

- . . . and so the cycle goes on, and each time round the golfer improves her swing more and more.

## Study skills: the role of feedback

How do you use feedback? Do you just read the grade and if it is acceptable put it in your bag and forget about it? Or do you read the feedback and try to learn from it, and apply that learning to your next assignment?

Feedback identifies what you have done well and what you can improve for next time. However, it can only help if you both read it and act upon it. If referencing is identified as a problem, for example, then you can consult referencing guides for next time round or ask a tutor for help. You could even go back to the essay and redo the referencing in the light of the feedback and what you have learned subsequently from referencing guides. This will all help when you come to write your next piece of coursework.

In some respects, the way you use feedback as part of a process of learning as a student has similarities with Kolb's learning cycle. There is the experience—doing the coursework; the reflection—looking at and thinking about the feedback; the conceptualization—looking at guides or asking the advice of a tutor; and the experimentation—trying out things before the next piece of work is attempted.

The feedback plays a vital role in this cycle of development as a student. If you only look at the grade, then you miss out on an important developmental opportunity that will improve your future work.

# Learning styles

Simon Chance walks into the bar where, by now, the whole maintenance team are standing around looking at the faulty refrigeration unit. Standing back and watching them approach the task, he notes that each of them takes a different approach to the problem.

Some jump straight in and start fiddling with different components to see what will happen. Others stand back for a while, thinking about the problem before actually doing anything with the refrigeration unit.

Furthermore, people consult different sources for information. Some look at instructions in a manual, others look at a circuit diagram of the refrigeration unit, while yet others discuss the problem within the team, asking people about their previous experiences with similar equipment.

Chance realizes that, while he could send his maintenance staff on training courses, when it comes to actually engaging with the actual job there are many differences between how each individual actually learns.

While all stages of Kolb's cycle are an important part of the learning process, he suggests that people prefer certain parts of the cycle to others. People have distinct learning preferences or learning styles. Using the example of our golfer, some golfers may prefer to spend time reflecting on the round of golf, while others may want to get straight to the driving range to start practising and experimenting.

Visit the Online Resource Centre to read more on learning styles.

This section examines different ways in which the different learning styles of individuals have been modelled. In a similar way to personality tests in Chapter 8, many of these frameworks of learning styles also have associated questionnaires through which individuals can measure their preferred learning styles.

## Honey and Mumford's learning styles

**Learning styles questionnaire** Based on Honey and Mumford's development of Kolb, a questionnaire which ascertains people's preferred learning styles.

Kolb's work was developed by Honey and Mumford (1992, 2006) into their **learning styles questionnaire** (LSQ). Figure 10.2 shows the four stages of the cycle of learning, which are similar to Kolb's model (although, unlike Kolb, they have an 'escape route' which recognizes that people sometimes change focus to concentrate on learning something different: for instance, someone may stop learning to play the piano and take up the guitar instead).

Each of the stages is linked with one of four particular learning styles:

- *activists* prefer the actual experience itself—they are doers rather than thinkers. They like action and are prepared to try new things.

- *reflectors* spend time thinking over what they have done. Rather than being in the thick of the action they prefer to stand back and watch and review, seeing a situation from a number of different perspectives.

- *theorists* are rational and logical thinkers who work best with abstract knowledge such as models and theories.

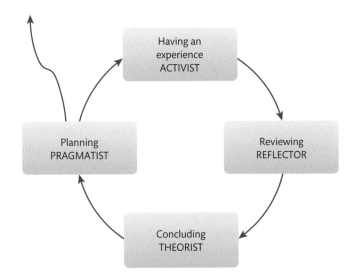

**Figure 10.2**  Honey and Mumford's learning styles.

**Source:** based on Honey and Mumford (2006)

- *pragmatists* will try out new ideas to see how they work. Rather than trying to theorize, they prefer practical actions.

Can you make any connections between these learning styles and the personality scales in Chapter 8?

The Honey and Mumford learning styles questionnaire is, similarly to personality tests, a set of questions which help locate an individual within these four learning styles. Given that learning is seen as a cycle which needs to pass through all of the stages, it might help an individual to recognize whether they have a tendency to get caught up in one area; for example, a reflector might spend too much time thinking about what has happened without progressing further in the cycle and taking practical steps.

The LSQ also allows an organization to see the variety of learning styles that people might have, which can help with training and development in understanding that people learn in different ways. In a similar way to Belbin (see Chapter 6) it also recognizes that in a team, people will have different ways of approaching learning that they can contribute to a project or task—some will jump in and get on with the task, while others will sit back and reflect, etc.

## Learning styles and multiple intelligences

While Honey and Mumford, like Kolb, deal with the link between doing and reflecting or knowledge and experience, other models of learning styles have pinpointed particular types of intelligence which lead to particular learning preferences.

Howard Gardner (1983) suggested that people exhibit a number of different types of intelligence:

- *verbal/linguistic intelligence*—the ability to understand and use language to express oneself.
- *musical intelligence*—performing music and understanding musical composition and pitch.
- *spatial intelligence*—an awareness of space and patterns around us.

- *bodily/kinesthetic intelligence*—the ability to do things with the body: sports, arts, etc.
- *logical/mathematical intelligence*—the ability to perform analytical, scientific tasks.
- *interpersonal intelligence*—the ability to understand, empathize, and work with others.
- *intrapersonal intelligence*—being able to understand ourselves and our feelings.

**Multiple intelligences** Gardner's theory that there are different types of intelligence that people possess in different combinations.

For Gardner, individuals exhibit these types of **multiple intelligence** in different combinations. Different intelligences predispose us to different tasks or jobs—interpersonal intelligence is good for dealing with people, for example. We can see that some of these intelligences are also more tacit in nature, coming from experience and actually doing things.

The model also highlights areas of ability that we might not initially consider to be types of intelligence. For example, while playing football may not require intelligence in the traditional, academic sense of the word, you may often hear a footballer described as an 'intelligent' player. In knowing how to 'read' a pass, swerve a ball, or get into the right position, a football player draws upon kinesthetic intelligence—bodily abilities and movements learned from experience of playing the game—and visual-spatial intelligence, which provides an awareness of the other players on the field and the formation that they fit into.

**VARK model** A model and questionnaire which places individuals into one of four preferred learning styles—visual, auditory, reading and writing, or kinesthetic.

Gardner's multiple intelligences model does not have an associated questionnaire like so many similar models; however, it does suggest that people are more predisposed to learn tasks and knowledge in different ways. The **VARK model** (Fleming, 2001) (Table 10.2) places the emphasis on how we learn and is tested by an associated questionnaire. It suggests four preferences for how we learn.

Visit the Online Resource Centre for links to the associated questionnaire for the VARK model.

Can you link the learning styles in the VARK model with Gardner's multiple intelligences?

With VARK, we see how different material will appeal more to the learning abilities of different learners. For example, when fixing a car a visual learner might use a diagram of the engine, a reader/writer might look for instructions in a book or on the Internet, and a kinesthetic learner might jump in and see what happens when they touch and play about with different components.

Such intelligences might also be applied to our language example. An auditory learner might learn better from listening to language lessons on a tape, while a reader and writer might prefer to read the language from a book.

The implication of VARK is that people who are teaching and training people need to take account of the fact that people respond differently to different methods and materials

Table 10.2 The VARK model (based on Fleming, 2001)

| Type of learner | Description |
| --- | --- |
| Visual | Learns best from visual clues, e.g. from diagrams, pictures, signs, and symbols |
| Auditory | Learns best from listening to descriptions and explanations |
| Reading/writing | Learns best from reading texts and using written notes to organize that knowledge |
| Kinesthetic (tactile) | Learns best by doing things—actually touching and manipulating objects |

of teaching and training. However, the model, and its associated questionnaire, also helps individuals to appreciate for themselves their own learning styles. Many of the models examined in this section, whether VARK or Honey and Mumford, feed into individual development processes of learning to learn.

Some management theorists (e.g. Hassard and Holliday, 1998; Bell, 2008) suggest that visual media such as art and fictional media such as film and television can teach us aspects of management and organization that are not conveyed by theory as delivered in lectures and textbooks. In other words, these visual media appeal to a different set of learning styles from those which are written and spoken.

Visit the Online Resource Centre for more on the use of fictional and artistic media in teaching management and organization.

# Learning to learn: from surface to deep learning and beyond

We have so far seen two broad approaches to knowledge. On the one hand, knowledge is a set of simple, explicit facts that we commit to memory. On the other hand, knowledge is learned in context and through experience and action, so that it becomes a deeper, more personal form of tacit knowledge.

The distinction is echoed in a number of approaches which distinguish between the quality of learning that people undertake (Marton and Säljö, 1976; Pask, 1976). Here, we present a commonly-used distinction between surface learning and deep learning:

- surface learning is simply learning a set of facts off by heart. The learner has no real interest in the knowledge itself; instead, it is a means to an end—to pass a test, for example.

- deep learning is where a learner gains a deeper level of knowledge and understanding—not just learning facts, but engaging with the knowledge, making links and comparisons with other knowledge that the learner already has. This might be through using that knowledge in experience, as discussed previously in the chapter, so that it becomes a deeper, personal form of tacit knowledge.

Which of the two styles do you think you use in your university work?

Surface and deep learning can thus be compared in terms of the knowledge that is acquired from each, as in Table 10.3.

Table 10.3  Deep learning and surface learning compared

| Surface learning | Deep learning |
| --- | --- |
| Facts and figures, learning by rote, out of context | Learning as part of a pattern or in context |
| Knowledge that | Knowledge how/knowledge of |
| *Savoir* | *Connaître* |
| Explicit knowledge only | Explicit knowledge developing into tacit knowledge through experience (e.g. Kolb's learning cycle) |

The difference between surface learning and deep learning can be applied to the earlier example of learning the Finnish language. A surface learner would simply learn the words for the sake of passing an assessment. A deep learner might learn the words, but also try putting them into a sentence, relating them to words already learned, practising them in conversation with others, and even relating them to the culture of the country.

# Learning to learn

Models of learning styles have shown us not just how deeper levels of knowledge are acquired, but how people also have preferences for particular learning styles. Gregory Bateson (1973) used the term **deutero learning** to describe levels of learning with greater depth, where the individual not only gains deeper knowledge but engages in a form of self-awareness whereby they learn how to learn.

Again, this can be explained with reference to the Finnish learning example. Earlier in the chapter we learned some words by associating them with particular images and patterns. Learning to learn is where a learner realizes that the system works well for them and applies that same system to another learning situation—learning German, for example, or memorizing a shopping list. Learning to learn involves comparing this with other learning methods to develop an appreciation of what works best for each individual learner.

In a similar vein, Freire (1970) criticizes what he terms **banking education**, where learners are seen as being like an empty bank account, there to be filled passively with 'deposits' of knowledge. Such a type of education does not move beyond explicit knowledge and surface learning. Again, such theorists call for a type of learning that goes beyond the surface and engenders a greater depth of knowledge and creativity in students.

**Deutero learning**
Bateson's conception of a higher level of learning whereby people are aware of how they 'learn to learn'.

**Banking education**
Freire's critique of learning and teaching styles which see learners as being like bank accounts to be 'deposited' with amounts of knowledge.

Visit the Online Resource Centre to read more about Freire's theories.

The importance of Bateson's and Freire's contributions is not to dismiss explicit knowledge and surface learning completely, but to see that for individuals to achieve creativity and reach their potential (as mentioned at the start of this chapter) this needs to form part of a process of deeper learning and learning to learn.

## Deep learning and learning to learn in the workplace: reflective practice

So far in the chapter we have examined learning at an individual level. In the remainder of this chapter we will see it applied within the workplace. Donald Schön (1983) suggested that professionals in industries such as education, health, and architecture would develop their knowledge and practice of their work better—indeed, into a form of artistry—if they worked as reflective practitioners. **Reflective practice** means that a worker doesn't simply do their job, but, as with Kolb and with Honey and Mumford in this chapter, they see their work as an ongoing cycle of continuous learning, whereby they reflect upon their experiences in the workplace.

**Reflective practice**
A form of professional development and training where workers reflect on actual workplace experiences and events.

In the next two sections of this chapter, we place ideas of reflective practice, deep knowledge, and learning to learn into management and organizational settings.

- Firstly, we examine the job of management itself. How as a management student might you 'learn' to be an effective manager, and what part does reflective practice play in management knowledge?

- Secondly, we look at how knowledge relevant to particular organizations, such as technical knowledge, is not only learned by individuals within an organization but also shared across the organization. Schön, along with Chris Argyris (Argyris and Schön, 1978), was a pioneer of organizational learning, whereby organizations themselves 'learn' how to learn and to 'reflect' on that process of learning.

### Review questions

| | |
|---|---|
| **Describe** | What is meant by explicit and tacit knowledge? |
| **Explain** | How does learning develop through a cycle of experiential learning? |
| **Analyse** | How do the levels and quality of learning and knowledge increase as a learner moves from surface learning to deep learning to deutero learning? |
| **Apply** | How would you take account of different learning styles in developing a training programme for the maintenance staff at Junction Hotel? |

# Reflective practice and management knowledge

What are your expectations of a management degree? It would be a reasonable assumption that, in undertaking a management degree or a similar course, a student would learn and accumulate a certain amount of management *knowledge* that can then be taken into a management career.

In this section we examine what it means to 'know' how to manage; that is to say, what is management knowledge? Is it an explicit set of facts and theories, or is it a tacit form of knowledge that comes from experience? Furthermore, if we can pinpoint what is meant by management knowledge, how does someone, for example a student of management, learn this knowledge—how does one learn how to manage?

This short section of the chapter brings a **reflexive** approach to your study of knowledge and learning in organizations. Reflexive means that the chapter is not just describing a set of ideas and theories; rather, it invites you as both a current student and a potential future manager to locate yourself personally within the subject matter of the chapter.

- For you as a student, the topic of this chapter—knowledge and learning—is relevant to how you engage in study. Some material in this chapter may be familiar from 'study skills' or 'personal development' sessions at university. For example, you may have taken

**Reflexivity** Where an individual is connected in some way to a text they are reading about or writing, rather than simply looking at a text to which they are completely disconnected.

the VARK questionnaire as a way of understanding your preferred means of learning. The aim of such techniques is to improve your quality of learning as a student, taking you from surface learning to deep learning and deutero learning styles. You are not simply approaching each learning task in isolation, to pass a test for example; rather, you think more widely about how you learn best.

• For you as a student of management and, potentially, a future manager, theories of knowledge and learning are relevant to the quality of knowledge of 'how to' manage that you will take with you into a managerial career. In this section we see how this links with management knowledge as being tacit and coming from experience, and how students may learn such tacit knowledge in addition to the explicit knowledge gained during their studies.

## What is management knowledge?

It is not uncommon for graduate trainees to arrive as newcomers in managerial positions to much suspicion, even sneering, at their graduate status. The insinuation is that these wet-behind-the-ears university types may have all of the knowledge from a degree, but they lack the experience of actually doing management in the 'real world'.

This mirrors the distinction between explicit and tacit knowledge. An amount of management knowledge comes from experience rather than from learning from books.

So, on the one hand, we can see that a management degree outlines a terrain of explicit management knowledge. In defining such management knowledge, we might look at particular theories that are learned—examples in this book might be theories of motivation, rational organizational design, management of groups and teams, and management of change, etc. In other words, there is a list of theories, ideas, and models which, together, make up management knowledge.

To see management knowledge just in these terms would, perhaps, follow Freire's (1970) 'banking education' model (Figure 10.3). A student arrives at the start of the degree as an empty vessel and, through lectures, textbooks (such as this), and other sources, is eventually filled with items of knowledge that will equip them to manage. The degree to which you, as a student, have assimilated such knowledge is tested by means such as essays, examinations, presentations, and other assessments. Ultimately, a degree certificate is awarded to prove the amount of management knowledge that a student holds and which they can then go on to apply in the workplace.

But does this accumulation of management knowledge mean that a student *knows* how to manage? Has a student *learned* to be a manager during the course of their degree, with the degree certificate as proof of this? Amanda Hay (2015: 409) suggests that management knowledge can present a 'sanitised' view of how to manage 'which avoids the complexities of the lived experiences of managers'. Rather than being a label that something like a degree certificate allows us to wear, the identity of a 'manager' is, for Hay, something that is always ongoing and developing. With management knowledge, as with the knowledge of driving a car or learning a language, there is an amount of tacit knowledge that is only learned from experience.

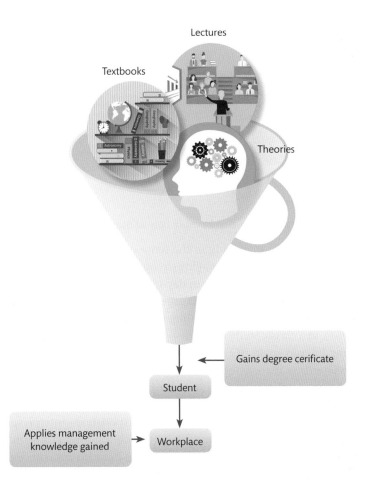

**Figure 10.3** Freire's (1970) banking model applied to management education.

---

## Theory in context: origins of 'management'

A tacit dimension to management knowledge is embedded in the origins of the word 'management' as described by Holden and Tansley (2008). It may surprise you to learn that 'management' as a word derives from the training of horses—something which requires skill, but also experience. The word can be traced back to around 1555–65 to an early Italian word *maneggiare*: to handle, train (horses). In turn, this derives from the Latin word *manus*, meaning hand. The implication is that training horses, while a skilled job that one gets a feel for, is learned by experience and doing. As such, there is a tacit dimension to such knowledge.

The origins of management?

The balance between management as explicit knowledge and management as a more tacit knowledge that comes from experience is also reflected in contemporary definitions of the word *management*. From several dictionaries, the following definitions of 'management' are presented:

- to direct or conduct business affairs
- be successful; achieve a goal
- be in charge of, act on, or dispose of
- to watch and direct
- to dominate or influence
- to continue to get along; carry on: *learning how to manage on my own.*

There is a contrast between managing in the sense of a planned, controlled activity and managing in the sense of coping—managing to cope and get along. This has been reflected in studies of what managers actually do in day-to-day work. Hales (1986) notes a contrast between formal and informal aspects of managerial work—the latter often involving interpersonal skills such as negotiation and dealing with conflict.

Carlson (1951), in a classic study of Swedish executives, further found that the majority of their working life was spent in conversations—on the phone, in person, etc. This suggests that the majority of management work involves something not necessarily taught on a management degree—it requires interpersonal and communication skills.

As we look into management as both a concept and an activity, we begin to see areas of management knowledge that are learned through experience—interpersonal skills and dealing with the 'messy' side of the organization (the politics, conflict, and negotiation that takes place; see Chapters 12 and 13). While these can be found as content of a management degree, the extent to which they can be taught as explicit knowledge rather than through experience is debatable.

### Employability skills: placements and work experience

Many of our students who have done placements in a workplace say that it is only through the experience of the workplace that they have come to fully understand the 'messy' and interpersonal side of the organization.

While a degree programme provides an important amount of theory and skills for management, employers are also interested in 'real world' experience. This is partly the reason why some degree programmes have work placements as a means to locate the explicit knowledge gained at university into a workplace context where students can add to that learning through experience.

Even if you have not undertaken a placement, employers will be interested in what else you have done at university other than the degree itself. Work experience, such as vacation jobs, involvement in running societies or sports clubs, and voluntary work, shows evidence of management learning through experience.

This is not to say that your degree work is not important. Remember that Kolb's learning cycle recognizes the importance of both experiential and theoretical knowledge—it is the combination of both which contribute to the learning cycle.

# Management as reflective practice

The idea that management learning comes from experience feeds into a lot of training and development programmes. In many management courses, managers are encouraged to become reflective practitioners. Assessment in such courses consists of keeping journals and records of work undertaken, and reflecting on this experience in the light of explicit management theory. Management knowledge is thus seen, as with Kolb's cycle, as a combination of both explicit and tacit elements, and is a knowledge which develops through experience and reflection on that experience.

Such management education aims to equip managers not only with a store of management knowledge, but also with the ability to manage in practice—where managers need to react to events, drawing upon both explicit knowledge and knowledge gained through experience when doing so.

In the next section, we see how knowledge and learning at an organizational level also help organizations to both develop knowledge and be able to use that knowledge to change and react where necessary.

## Review questions

| | |
|---|---|
| **Describe** | What are the explicit and tacit aspects of management knowledge? |
| **Explain** | What does it mean when management is described as a reflective practice? |
| **Analyse** | To what extent does a management degree equip a student with the knowledge of how to manage? What further knowledge or experience is required? |
| **Apply** | Do you think that you approach your studies as a deep or a surface learner? |

# Organizational knowledge and learning: the learning organization

So far in the chapter we have seen learning as a process whereby an *individual* adds to their knowledge. In this section we examine knowledge and learning as something that also exists at the level of the *organization*.

- Firstly, we examine the concept of **organizational knowledge**, the possession of which gives success and competitive advantage to organizations, and even to national and regional economies. We see where knowledge resides and how, as with individual knowledge, it can exist in explicit and tacit forms.

- Secondly, we examine how knowledge is transferred within the organization, a process known as **organizational learning**. For knowledge to be organization-wide, it needs to be transferred between individuals. We examine how this happens, particularly with tacit knowledge, which individuals develop through experience and may find difficult to articulate to others.

**Organizational knowledge** Knowledge which is a collective property of an organization rather than belonging to an individual.

**Organizational learning** Sharing and transfer of individual knowledge so that it becomes a collective property of the organization.

- Finally, we examine how organizations that implement and are adept at organizational learning are known as **learning organizations**. Learning organizations not only increase their store of organizational knowledge, but are also seen to be more adept at coping with and responding to a need for change and innovation.

## Organizational knowledge

**Learning organization**
An organization which is set up so as to facilitate continual learning at individual and organizational levels.

**Knowledge-intensive firms** Organizations whose main business involves the development and innovation of knowledge.

**Knowledge workers** Workers employed for their specific knowledge and their ability to use this knowledge to innovate and develop new ideas and products.

There are sectors of the economy where knowledge and the development of that knowledge are vital for the competitive advantage, and even the survival, of an organization. Think about the mobile phone industry, for example. Consumers eagerly wait to upgrade to the newest smartphones with the latest technical innovations. It is important for companies to stay ahead of the game by developing this knowledge and innovating—those that get left behind can find their market share falling rapidly.

A similar premium on knowledge can be found in industries such as pharmaceuticals, technology, and microelectronics, etc. Companies in such sectors are said to be **knowledge-intensive firms**—a key part of their strategy is the development of leading-edge knowledge. Workers who contribute to this and are valued for their particular knowledge and skills are described as **knowledge workers** (Alvesson, 2004).

Can you think of any other sectors of the economy that could be described as 'knowledge-intensive' or professions where workers could be described as 'knowledge workers'?

Visit the Online Resource Centre for some suggestions.

## From organizational knowledge to knowing in organizations

Knowledge, however, can be located in all organizations—not just those that are involved in cutting-edge technical innovation. Knowledge of an organization's culture or day-to-day routines is as much a part of organizational knowledge as specialist skills and expert knowledge.

Furthermore, organizational knowledge is multifaceted—there are different aspects of what, collectively, makes up organizational knowledge. Two dimensions which make up this multifaceted nature are:

1. Is the knowledge located in individuals within the organization or is it more of a collective property of the organization that is shared between people?

2. As with individual knowledge, is the knowledge explicit or tacit?

Blackler (1995) outlines five particular facets of knowledge or, as he describes them, 'images' of knowledge, which we have located along these scales of individual/collective and tacit/explicit in Figure 10.4 (Blackler, 1995: 1023–6).

These five images of knowledge are described in Table 10.4, where we place them in an organizational setting with an example of the types of knowledge that might be found in a restaurant kitchen.

We tend to privilege embrained knowledge, for example, the specialist knowledge of a head chef in a kitchen—they are seen as the valued worker upon whose knowledge the organization depends. However, Table 10.4 shows the variety of embodied, encultured, and embedded knowledge that is found within all staff within a kitchen—there are many types and locations of organizational knowledge.

**Figure 10.4** Blackler's (1995) five images of organizational knowledge.

Table 10.4  Facets of organizational knowledge (based on Blackler, 1995)

| Type of knowledge | Description | Example |
|---|---|---|
| Embrained knowledge (explicit and individual) | The individual knowledge that we hold in our brains which is explicit in nature, equating to 'knowledge that'. It is reflected in an employee's qualifications, for example. | *A chef may hold a qualification from catering school and may know a set of recipes or facts about food.* |
| Embodied knowledge (individual and tacit) | The knowledge that comes from actually doing and experiencing a task. This is tacit knowledge that an individual develops—'knowledge how'. | *A chef who has made a dish many times will be able to prepare it as if it were second nature.* |
| Encultured knowledge (organizational with tacit and explicit dimensions) | Shared understandings in the organization—the stories, traditions, values, etc. that make up an organizational culture (see Chapter 7). Often it is unwritten and tacit—described simply as 'the way things are done around here', although organizations may try to make cultures explicit by describing them in documents (see the Sloan Becker case in Chapter 14). | *Different kitchens have different cultures—expected behaviours and ways of doing things. Some may be noisy and brash, some may be quieter.* |
| Embedded knowledge (organizational with tacit and explicit dimensions) | Knowledge embedded in the routines of an organization. Routines may be formalized and explicit, but also have informal tacit elements. Think of a university timetable—at first you have to consult it regularly; it is an explicit piece of printed knowledge. After a while you get used to your timetable to the point where you automatically go to rooms at the right time—it has become tacit knowledge. | *Kitchens have many rigid routines that have to be followed—prepping food before the restaurant opens for business, procedures for taking orders, etc.* |
| Encoded knowledge (organizational and explicit) | Explicit knowledge found in books, manuals, computer databases, and sets of instructions, in the form of words, signs, symbols, lists, etc. It is also collective, as it is knowledge that can be shared and accessed by the whole organization. | *A kitchen may have a library of recipe books which have step-by-step instructions for dishes, knowledge which all members of the organization may access.* |

Indeed, for Blackler (1995), to talk of knowledge as a 'thing' misses its dynamic and social nature—it is always changing and is located within, and among, people. Learning and developing knowledge becomes a constant part of organizational activity.

# Organizational learning

## Running case: learning at the pub

Simon Chance calls in the maintenance manager, George Andrews, to review the training programme.

Chance has taken account of different learning styles among the workforce and realizes how difficult it is to accommodate all of these styles.

He has issued each member of the maintenance staff with a tablet computer which has access to a vast array of documentation—manuals for every piece of machinery in the building, diagrams of circuitry, and even videos from the manufacturers. Staff can access whatever material they feel helps them most.

Furthermore, the tablets give the maintenance engineers access to online forums where they can post their experiences of dealing with different problems for others to read, learn from, and search when they, too, encounter similar problems.

'It's all great,' says George Andrews. 'The tablets are really useful and put a lot of information at their fingertips.'

'But, in terms of learning, I think they learn most at the pub on a Friday evening—that's when they really talk among themselves and share experiences of what they've been doing during the week. And, in comparison to providing training and tablet computers, that doesn't cost us a penny.'

Organizational learning is a process whereby an organization increases the amount of knowledge that it holds collectively. Knowledge is *shared*, or *transferred*, between people in the organization and, furthermore, is transferred between people and the organization itself.

For Nonaka and Takeuchi (1995: 6), the ability for an organization to create knowledge and innovate continually is something which brings competitive advantage. This is noted by Nonaka, in particular, in successful Japanese firms where workers are striving continually to improve the task that they do (see Chapter 7). There is a recognition that workers know their task best—they develop tacit knowledge the more they perform it, and thus they know all the shortcuts and tricks that help them to perform the task better.

The problem for Nonaka is that such tacit knowledge is personal and comes from experience—it is difficult to put it into words in order to share that knowledge with others. As Brown and Duguid (2000: 76) state: 'Actual work practices are full of tacit improvisations that the employees who carry them out would have trouble articulating.' This is similar to earlier examples of individual knowledge—we may know from experience how to ride a bike, but it is difficult to put that tacit knowledge into words in order to share and transfer that knowledge.

Nonaka's model of the *knowledge-creating company* (Nonaka and Takeuchi, 1995, 2007) focuses on the ways in which particular types of knowledge are transferred. For Nonaka, it is the interaction between different types of knowledge—explicit and tacit—that creates knowledge within the organization. Such knowledge can be transferred between explicit and tacit knowledge in four ways (see Table 10.5), which we again illustrate with reference to an example of a restaurant kitchen.

At the heart of Nonaka's model is the assumption that the richest form of knowledge is the tacit knowledge that exists within individuals who perform a particular job. However, for the organization to benefit fully from that knowledge it cannot just reside as tacit knowledge within one individual—what if the individual were ill or left the organization, for example? How are other members of the organization meant to learn and develop if the only expert keeps their knowledge to themselves?

**Table 10.5** Knowledge transfer in Nonaka's knowledge-creating company (based on Nonaka and Takeuchi, 1995)

| Type of knowledge transfer | Description | Example |
| --- | --- | --- |
| From explicit to explicit: combination | Sources of encoded knowledge—manuals, databases, etc.—are added to, combined, sorted, and categorized. A library combines a number of different forms of explicit knowledge, sorting and categorizing it in a library catalogue, for example. Such a databank of explicit knowledge, however, does not mean that people necessarily read and learn from it. | *A chef has a set of recipe books on a shelf with Indian, Chinese, and French cuisine within. More books are added, covering Italian and vegetarian cuisine. The amount of explicit knowledge has been increased, but this does not necessarily mean that the chef has tried and experimented with any of the recipes in the books.* |
| From explicit to tacit: internalization | As in learning to drive, a learner begins with explicit instructions but continues to practise and reflect on that practice (cf. Kolb's learning cycle) until they have internalized the knowledge—it has become tacit. | *A chef takes a recipe—a set of explicit instructions—and makes a dish. She continues to experiment and repeat this until she knows the dish 'off by heart'.* |
| From tacit to explicit: externalization, articulation | An expert or person who is well-experienced in a task attempts to make their tacit knowledge explicit by writing it down as a set of instructions, diagrams, or similar encoded knowledge. The expert is trying to articulate their tacit knowledge to an external audience. | *A top chef writes a recipe book featuring instructions on how to make various dishes.* |
| From tacit to tacit: socialization | Perhaps the least controllable form of knowledge transfer, as the knowledge remains unspoken—it is never made explicit. Knowledge is acquired through observation and imitation. This might be how cultures are learned—they are absorbed from observation and experimentation rather than being told to people explicitly. | *A trainee chef learns from observation under the tutelage of a kitchen's head chef.* |

The key aspect of knowledge transfer, for Nonaka, is thus how tacit knowledge is made explicit—expressed in words or diagrams or in some form that other people can take on board, practise, and convert to tacit knowledge of their own. Nonaka's model suggests a form of training and knowledge transfer that is still run by the organization itself; however, the transfer of tacit, experiential knowledge has also been observed as more of a social phenomenon which takes place informally among workers.

### Real life case: 'war stories'

A classic study by Orr (1996) observed the work of photocopier engineers at Xerox in the United States. These are the people who are called out to various clients when photocopiers break down (as they often do).

Using tacit knowledge.

The engineers had knowledge from their training and, furthermore, had encoded, explicit knowledge about each model of photocopier in the form of manuals and diagrams. This, however, was not enough—machines have their own idiosyncracies, and complex problems can emerge that are beyond the instructions in the manual.

Orr discovered that a great deal of the knowledge that workers had was learned from conversations. Engineers developed tacit knowledge from their experience with machines, which they shared in social situations, such as over lunch. Orr described the sharing of 'war stories', where one engineer would tell how they dealt with a particular problem on a particular machine—a knowledge that other engineers could take and apply to similar situations.

Unlike the Xerox engineers, who are based at a head office before being sent out to jobs, some maintenance engineers are based at home and are emailed a set of jobs at the start of the day. What learning opportunities might an engineer in this situation miss out on?

Orr's study shows that explicit knowledge of photocopiers—knowledge from training and the manuals—was enhanced by the sharing, in a social situation, of more individual, tacit knowledge that other workers could then go away and apply. Rather than organizational knowledge, it was a form of knowledge that existed at the level of the group, where they learned from 'war stories' of each others' experiences (Orr, 1996).

Xerox recognized the value of this sharing of knowledge and set up a suggestions database where such knowledge could be tapped into and shared across the whole organization (Orr, 1996; Duguid, 2006). (See Chapter 14 for more on information sharing through computer networks.) Such a sharing of knowledge might be familiar to people who have searched online forums if, for example, their car has broken down or if their computer has a virus. The idea is to learn from the descriptions that others have posted of how they have dealt with similar situations.

The idea of pooling such knowledge in an organization so that others may use it to enhance their own knowledge and be equipped to deal with particular situations as and when they arise can be seen as part of a strategy of becoming a learning organization.

# The learning organization

While organizational learning highlights issues of how knowledge is shared and acquired, the learning organization is concerned with the organizational characteristics which promote and facilitate such learning and knowledge transfer. Organizational learning is thus a feature of the learning organization rather than—as sometimes happens—the two terms being used interchangeably.

By being able to share learning and knowledge, an organization and its members have more abilities at their collective disposal. This goes beyond work-specific knowledge, such as how to fix a photocopier or make a particular recipe, and relates to an organization's capacity to adapt and transform when needed. Competitive advantage comes not just from knowledge as applied to product development but also from the knowledge that enables an organization to be more flexible and adaptable in the face of changing environmental conditions. The organization is seen in biological, evolutionary terms as a 'complex organism' (Senge, 1990: 85) that constantly adjusts in response to its changing environment.

Such an ability to change and adapt is examined elsewhere in the book by two observations about the nature of the contemporary environment facing organizations.

- In Chapter 4 we examined post-bureaucratic organizations, where structures and communication lines are flexible rather than rigid, and where the organization can easily adapt to changes and bring together different configurations of people and knowledge so as to develop further knowledge. The Googleplex was given as an example of a post-bureaucratic organization. We can also see Google as typical of the organizations discussed in this chapter, which place a premium on continually developing knowledge for competitive advantage.

- In Chapter 11, we see an emergent approach to change which suggests that, rather than being able to plan change for the future, organizations have to react to events as they happen, as if riding along on the rapids of a river.

Proponents of the learning organization thus emphasize a focus both on the development of individual and organizational learning within organizations, and furthermore on seeing the organization as being in a continuous process of change and transformation (Senge, 1990; Pedler et al., 1997).

## Single- and double-loop learning

Such a level of learning and transformation at the organizational level is addressed by Argyris and Schön (1978). Their concept of single- and double-loop learning has similarities with the difference between surface learning and deep learning at an individual level and is influenced by Bateson's (1973) levels of learning, which suggested that increased individual creativity derives from learning to learn or deutero learning.

At an organizational level, a move from surface learning to a more creative and deep form of learning is where an organization as a whole moves from single- to double-loop learning.

**Single-loop learning**
Learning in organizations which merely adapts to achieving a particular goal.

**Double-loop learning**
Learning in organizations that goes beyond achieving a goal to question assumptions behind the goal being set, and that questions assumptions, values, and strategies more widely in the organization.

- **Single-loop learning** is where an organization tries repeatedly to solve the same problem or achieve the same goal—a simple form of 'error correction' to ensure that the goal continues to be achieved. For example, an organization might have a sales target for a particular product each year. If it fails to achieve it then it takes steps the following year to correct the problem—hiring new sales staff, for example, or looking at the bonus system. The sales target itself is not questioned.

- **Double-loop learning** questions the goal itself and the underlying assumptions behind it. It wouldn't just ask how to achieve the target sales; it would ask whether the sales of that product contribute enough to profits to warrant pursuing that goal, whether the market for that product has any future, and even whether targets are a good way to motivate sales staff. In other words, rather than the simple sales target itself, just about everything is up for discussion—an organization's values, policies, and objectives (Argyris and Schön, 1978).

## Characteristics of a learning organization

Double-loop learning is thus a more thorough and deep questioning of what an organization does, which goes beneath the surface of solving one isolated problem, a questioning which readies an organization for the type of change and adaptability required of a learning organization. For Senge (1990), such a form of learning is part of five characteristics which make up a successful learning organization (see Table 10.6).

The learning organization paints a picture of an organization where there is harmony, trust, and an openness of communication between co-workers, and between workers and management, with all members of the organization unified behind the vision of the organization. To what extent this is realistic or achievable forms the basis for assessing the learning organization.

**Table 10.6** Senge's five characteristics of the learning organization (adapted from Senge, 1990: 6–11)

| | |
|---|---|
| **Personal mastery** | The organization encourages the personal development and learning of individuals in the organization so that they can reach their potential |
| **Mental models** | People are not stuck in old ways of thinking and old routines, and are open to new ideas; people engage in higher levels of learning where goals and assumptions are questioned constantly (as with double-loop learning) |
| **Shared vision** | All organizational members have a shared, mutually-agreed vision, which is reinforced through strong and inspiring leadership (see Chapter 12 on leadership) |
| **Team learning** | People work and learn together in teams with the importance of dialogue and discussion between people being highlighted, in a similar manner to the case of the Xerox photocopier engineers |
| **Systems thinking** | People think about the organization in terms of relationships and connections (see Chapter 11), with all actions having consequences both inside and outside of the organization; systems thinking is about seeing how they fit into 'the bigger picture' |

## Learning organizations assessed

The development of knowledge and learning in organizations has, so far, been presented as a good thing. It gives organizations a competitive advantage in an increasingly knowledge-based economy, and it allows individual workers to develop their potential and creativity, perhaps even moving them towards 'self-actualizing' in their work (see Chapter 9).

The learning organization perspective is a far cry from the Taylorist view of individual and organizational learning presented in Chapter 2. Rather than encouraging learning, Taylor saw individual knowledge as a source of power for workers and a threat to his authority. Taylor's strategy was the absolute opposite of a learning organization—he removed knowledge from workers, placing it all in the hands of management, with individual learning reduced to learning a simple, repetitive task.

However, the view of the learning organization is not without critics; indeed, its vision of harmony in the organization, shared visions, and unhindered individual learning and development is seen by critics as an unrealistic, naïve, or 'utopian' (Coopey, 1998; Driver, 2002) view of how organizations operate. Among many critiques of the learning organization we suggest three broad areas that may prevent the learning organization from being an ideal or achievable form of operating in organizations (see Driver, 2002, for more).

- The assumption of trust, open communication, and a sharing of knowledge ignores the influence of organizational politics (see Chapter 13) where people may choose to retain or restrict access to knowledge as a source of power for their own personal advantage.

- It assumes that people have the ability and desire to engage in constant learning and development. As seen with orientations to work (Chapter 9), some people prefer to do repetitive and unchallenging work as a means of simply getting a wage.

- While a learning organization may not employ the forms of rationalized control that characterize Taylorism, its shared vision relies on a strong shared culture, which itself can be seen as a form of control (see Chapter 7). The idea of a shared vision also means that there is an element of control that prevents dissent against that vision (see Driver, 2002).

Visit the Online Resource Centre to consider some more critiques of the learning organization.

While the concept of the learning organization is thus open to critique, in the final section we outline how knowledge and learning are still important to the contemporary economy and organizations.

# Learning beyond the organization

**Real life case:** standing on the shoulders of GIANTs

Grenoble Innovation for Advanced New Technologies (GIANT) is an 'innovation campus' located amongst the mountains of the French Alps. It brings together 30,000 people from a number of university science and management departments, French government scientific agencies, and technology companies. Research is undertaken in areas such as new energy sources, nanotechnology, and life sciences. While new ▶

> ▶ scientific knowledge is created, the aim of GIANT is also to develop this knowledge into commercial products, such as batteries and fuel cells, and to benefit society, for example by using this knowledge and product innovation to tackle social issues such as affordable housing and renewable energy.
>
> The campus was developed not as a new organization, but as a means for existing organizations to collaborate and share knowledge. There was a recognition that, while the participating organizations all excelled in their fields, they were not making the most of their knowledge and expertise by working alone. Thierry Grange, Dean of Grenoble Management School, suggested that a symptom of this was that ideas were created, but these were not translated into jobs. GIANT addresses this by having existing technology companies working alongside scientific researchers to translate ideas into new products and innovations, and the campus also encourages start-up businesses to develop specific new products and ideas. The sharing of knowledge and expertise between the different organizations is intended to create synergies that otherwise would not exist if the organizations were to act in isolation.
>
> **Sources:** Prest (2010); Reisz (2010); GIANT (2015a, b).

 Visit the Online Resource Centre for more about GIANT and similar innovation campuses.

To conclude this chapter we look at knowledge which is shared across, and between, organizations, rather than residing within the bounds of any one organization. Of course, knowledge does transfer between organizations—when a person leaves an organization and joins another, for example, and takes their particular knowledge with them. The concept of the learning organization recognizes, in fact, the importance of suppliers and other stakeholders that an organization deals with (Pedler et al., 1997).

Here, we briefly suggest three contemporary areas where work-related knowledge is shared across organizational boundaries.

- **Professional knowledge.** Professions such as medicine, architecture, and law have a knowledge base which is common to all practitioners, regardless of which organization they are based in—knowledge which they need to constantly update. A doctor, for example, needs to know about the latest medical discoveries and opinions, and about the latest drugs and treatments. Thus, there are journals, conferences, email lists, and similar networks through which professional knowledge is shared, potentially on a global scale.

- **Knowledge clusters.** Knowledge clusters occur where a number of organizations engaged in the same industry are located in close geographical proximity. They are able to collaborate with each other, share resources, and benefit from each others' particular knowledge (see Coughlan, 2011). For example, Mediacity in Salford, UK, is a concentration of media-related organizations, bringing together large broadcasters, such as the BBC and ITV, but also smaller, knowledge-intensive companies, for example manufacturers of specialist broadcast equipment or graphic design companies. Another example of a knowledge cluster is where universities set up, or are associated with, nearby 'science parks'. Academics can collaborate and share knowledge with companies and organizations engaged in the same field. The previous case study of GIANT is an example of this; similarly, computer firm Microsoft has a research facility in conjunction with Cambridge University in the UK (Microsoft Research, 2015).

**Professional knowledge** A common body of knowledge relevant to a particular profession or occupation.

**Knowledge clusters** Geographical areas where a number of knowledge-intensive organizations in a particular industry are congregated in close proximity.

- **Open source and online collaboration**. In Chapter 14 we examine the effects of computer networks on organizations, including the ability for organizations to share knowledge as data through networks. Open source software is computer code which is made freely available so that anyone can apply their knowledge to it and develop it. If you use operating systems such as Linux, many people have applied their knowledge collaboratively to developing such systems—in some cases for free as a hobby, in other cases as part of their work. A similar type of online collaboration can be seen with Wikipedia, where people have contributed their knowledge collaboratively in an open forum to create an encyclopaedia (Mulgan et al., 1995). (See Chapter 14 for more on this.)

Open source and online collaboration A form of knowledge sharing and collaboration where computer code is made publicly available and developed collaboratively.

Visit the Online Resource Centre for more on materials that deal with learning beyond the organization.

## Communities of practice

A concept which we can use to unite the three examples is that of **communities of practice**. Lave and Wenger (1991) first used this concept to note the learning of specific areas of knowledge, especially occupational knowledge, in social contexts. The example of the photocopier engineers earlier in this chapter is an example of a community of practice within an organization—they are engaged in the same area of work, their work is based on a common set of knowledge, and they develop and share that knowledge as a form of social practice.

Communities of practice Social groupings based around a common occupational practice and set of knowledge, who develop and share that knowledge among themselves.

An organization may consist of many communities of practice within it: not just the photocopier engineers, but also the accountants, the legal staff, and the gardeners, etc. who all learn and develop their knowledge within their social groups.

To what extent is the 'community of practice' perspective relevant to the maintenance engineers in the Junction Hotel running case?

The three examples given are examples of where communities of practice exist across organizational boundaries. For example, with medical knowledge, there may be a community of practice of people involved in treating a particular illness. Although they may all work in different institutions, and even different countries, they are involved in a common practice based on a common body of knowledge which they share and develop in social situations such as conferences.

Collaborators in specific open-source applications can also be seen as a community of practice. Even if some of the collaborators are individuals involved as part of a hobby, it is a shared practice with a common body of knowledge, with knowledge shared and developed often through online social forums, such as discussion boards.

## Knowledge as a public or private commodity

Back in 1984, French philosopher Jean-François Lyotard noted the increased storage of knowledge in computer systems and networks, something which is examined further in Chapter 14. Lyotard (1984) warned of the dangers of organizations being able to privately monopolize and hoard knowledge. He suggested 'freeing up' the data banks of knowledge to make them publicly available.

While open-source applications can be seen as a 'freeing up' of data banks, for many organizations, knowledge is seen as a valuable possession and is often protected by legal instruments, such as patents and copyrights. A number of debates about the nature of organizational knowledge and its public availability are ongoing.

- The mobile phone and computer industries are often engaged in court battles and disputes over patents; for example, there has been an ongoing series of patent disputes between Apple and Samsung over the intellectual properties of touch-screen features such as 'double-tap' and 'pinch to zoom' (Gibbs, 2015).

- The amount of personal knowledge and data held by companies such as Google and Facebook, and how such data may be used commercially, is an ongoing debate, with concern expressed even at governmental levels. At the time of writing, the music streaming service Spotify was facing a backlash from its users over plans to gain access to user data such as contacts and photographs. In response, Spotify said that this data would be used to improve individual user experiences of the service (Hern and Rankin, 2015).

- A study of peer-reviewed medical and scientific papers suggested that only 13% were freely available; the rest were behind subscription paywalls (Dunn et al., 2014). Harvard University suggested that knowledge in the form of scientific research is a public commodity and that researchers should publish in online sources that do not require payment (Sample, 2012). A debate amongst the scientific community in Australia further suggests that the public have a right to free access to scientific knowledge that is often funded by government grants from taxpayer's money, rather than this knowledge being restricted and used to increase publishers' profits (Davey, 2015).

We introduce these current debates here briefly at the conclusion of the chapter in order to indicate the ongoing importance of knowledge to organizations and its position as a topic of contemporary debate.

 Visit the Online Resource Centre for more on these issues and their subsequent developments.

## Review questions

| | |
|---|---|
| **Describe** | What are the different types of organizational knowledge? |
| **Explain** | What does it mean for an organization to 'learn'? |
| **Analyse** | What is the importance of converting tacit to explicit knowledge as a part of organizational learning? |
| **Apply** | How would Junction Hotel benefit from being a learning organization? What steps have already been taken towards this with the maintenance department? Would there be any negative effects of being a learning organization? |

# Chapter summary

This chapter has examined knowledge and learning at both individual and organizational levels and across organizational boundaries. A distinction is made between knowledge being viewed simply as a 'thing' which people and organizations accumulate, and knowledge as more of a dynamic and social process—something which exists through action. It is the latter that is generally viewed as being a better-quality and more enduring form of knowledge, a knowledge with depth rather than simply being at the surface level.

For individuals this means developing knowledge from an explicit set of facts to a more personal, tacit knowledge which comes from experience, reflecting upon that experience, and, ultimately, recognizing one's own preferences for learning styles.

For organizations this means working out how to tap into the deep, tacit knowledge of individuals and sharing that knowledge throughout the organization. Concepts such as organizational learning and the learning organization suggest that organizations which excel at this sharing of knowledge and which also undertake deeper, double-loop learning will gain a competitive advantage, not just through innovation in their particular sector of the economy, but also by being more capable of responding to change and adjusting their operations when required.

The concept of change, and how organizations plan for and react to change, is considered in Chapter 11.

## Further reading

**Brown, J.S., and Duguid, P. 2000. Balancing act: Capturing knowledge without killing it.** *Harvard Business Review* 78(3):73–80.
A good introduction to the Xerox photocopier case and how Xerox subsequently tried to tap into the tacit knowledge of their engineers.

**Honey, P., and Mumford, A. 2006.** *The learning styles helper's guide.* **Peter Honey Publications Ltd: Maidenhead.**
Introduces the theory of learning styles.

**Mulgan, G. , Steinberg , Y. , and Salem , O. 1995. Wide open: Open source methods and their future potential.** *Demos.* **Available at: http://www.demos.co.uk/publications/wideopen (last accessed 3 July 2012).**
A report into open source methods, including case studies of Linux and Wikipedia.

**Nonaka, I., and Takeuchi, H. 2007. The knowledge-creating company.** *Harvard Business Review* 85(7/8): 162.
Nonaka's overview of knowledge creation and transfer in organizations.

## References

Alexander, B. 2012. Consulting Dr. Google is rarely a good idea. Here's why. *NBC News*, 20 July.

Alvesson, M. 2004. *Knowledge work and knowledge-intensive firms.* Oxford University Press: Oxford.

Argyris, C., and Schön, D.A. 1978. *Organizational learning.* Addison-Wesley Pub. Co.: Reading, MA.

Bateson, G. 1973. *Steps to an ecology of mind.* Ballantine Books: New York.

Bell, E. 2008. *Reading management and organization in film.* Palgrave Macmillan: Basingstoke.

Blackler, F. 1995. Knowledge, knowledge work and organizations: An overview and interpretation. *Organization Studies* 16(6): 1021–46.

Brown, J.S., and Duguid, P. 2000. Balancing act: Capturing knowledge without killing it. *Harvard Business Review* 78(3): 73–80.

Carlson, S. 1951. *Executive behaviour*. Arno Press: New York.

Coopey, J. 1998. Learning to trust and trusting to learn: A role for radical theatre. *Management Learning* 29(3): 365–82.

Coughlan, S. 2011. Battle of the knowledge superpowers. *BBC News Online*, 28 September.

Davey, M. 2015. Australian academics seek to challenge 'web of avarice' in scientific publishing. *The Guardian*, 14 August.

Driver, M. 2002. The learning organization: Foucauldian gloom or utopian sunshine? *Human Relations* 55(1): 33–53.

Duguid, P. 2006. What talking about machines tells us. *Organization Studies* 27(12): 1794–804.

Dunn, A., Coiera, E., and Mandl, K. 2014. Is biblioleaks inevitable? *Journal of Medical Internet Research* 16(4).

Fleming, N.D. 2001. *Teaching and learning styles: VARK strategies*. Neil Fleming: Christchurch, NZ.

Freire, P. 1970. *Pedagogy of the oppressed* (transl. M. B. Ramos). Seabury Press: New York.

Gardner, H. 1983. *Frames of mind: The theory of multiple intelligences*. Basic Books: New York.

GIANT 2015a About GIANT. Available at: http://www. giant-grenoble.org/en/about-giant (last accessed 14 August 2015).

GIANTGIANT 2015b Presentation. Available at: http:// www.giant-grenoble.org/images/giant_stv_uk_bd. pdf.

Gibbs, S. 2015. Facebook, Google, Dell, HP, eBay back Samsung in patent war with Apple. *The Guardian*, 21 July.

Hales, C.P. 1986. What do managers do? A critical review of the evidence. *Journal of Management Studies* 23(1): 88–115.

Hassard, J., and Holliday, R. 1998. Introduction. *Organization-representation: Work and organization in popular culture*. London: Sage, pp. 1–16.

Hay, A. 2015. 'I don't know what I am doing!' Surfacing struggles of managerial identity work. *Management Learning* 45(5): 509–24.

Hern, A. and Rankin, J. 2015. Spotify's chief executive apologises after user backlash over new privacy policy. *The Guardian*, 21 August.

Holden, N., and Tansley, C. 2008. Management in other languages: How a philological approach opens up new cross-cultural vistas. In: Tietze, S. (ed.) *International management and language*. Routledge: London, New York.

Honey, P., and Mumford, A. 1992. *The manual of learning styles*. Peter Honey Publications Ltd: Maidenhead.

Honey, P., and Mumford, A. 2006. *The learning styles helper's guide*. Peter Honey Publications Ltd: Maidenhead.

Koffka, K. 1955. *Principles of Gestalt psychology*. Routledge & Kegan Paul: London.

Kolb, D.A. 1984. *Experiential learning: Experience as the source of learning and development*. Prentice Hall: Englewood Cliffs, NJ.

Lave, J., and Wenger, E. 1991. *Situated learning: Legitimate peripheral participation*. Cambridge University Press: Cambridge, New York.

Lyotard, J.F. 1984. *The postmodern condition: A report on knowledge*. Manchester University Press: Manchester.

Marton, F., and Säljö, R. 1976. On qualitative differences in learning. I—Outcome and Process. *British Journal of Educational Psychology* 46: 4–11.

Microsoft Research 2015. Microsoft Research Cambridge. Available at: http://research.microsoft. com/en-us/labs/cambridge/ (last accessed 14 August 2015).

Mulgan, G., Steinberg, Y., and Salem, O. 1995. Wide open: Open source methods and their future potential. *Demos*. Available at: http://www.demos. co.uk/publications/wideopen (last accessed 20 August 2015).

Nonaka, I., and Takeuchi, H. 1995. *The knowledge-creating company: How Japanese companies create the dynamics of innovation*. Oxford University Press: New York.

Nonaka, I., and Takeuchi, H. 2007. The knowledge-creating company. *Harvard Business Review* 85(7/8): 162–71.

Orr, J.E. 1996. *Talking about machines: An ethnography of a modern job*. ILR Press: Ithaca, NY.

Paddock, C. 2012. Dr Google and the unwise practice of self-diagnosis. *Medical News Today*, 23 July.

Pask, G. 1976. Styles and strategies of learning. *British Journal of Educational Psychology* 46: 128–48.

Pedler, M., Burgoyne, J., and Boydell, T. 1997. *The learning company: A strategy for sustainable development*, 2nd edn. McGraw-Hill: London.

Polanyi, M. 1958. *Personal knowledge: Towards a post-critical philosophy*. University of Chicago Press: Chicago.

Polanyi, M. 1967. *The tacit dimension*. Routledge & Kegan Paul: London.

Prest, M. 2010. A technological powerhouse to rival MIT and Oxbridge. *The Independent*, 19 January.

Reisz, M. 2010. Grenoble takes Giant steps towards collaboration. *Times Higher Education*, 11 March.

Russell, B. 1912. *The problems of philosophy*. Oxford University Press: London, New York.

Ryle, G. 1949. *The concept of mind*. Hutchinson: London.

Sample, I 2012. Harvard University says it can't afford journal publishers' prices. *The Guardian*, 24 April 2012.

Schön, D.A. 1983. *The reflective practitioner: How professionals think in action*. Basic Books: New York.

Semigran, H.L., Linder, J.A., Gidengil, C., and Mehrotra, A. 2015. Evaluation of symptom checkers for self diagnosis and triage: Audit study. *British Medical Journal* 351: h3480.

Senge, P.M. 1990. *The fifth discipline: The art and practice of the learning organization*. Doubleday/Currency: New York.

Tang, H., and Ng, J.H.K. 2006. Googling for a diagnosis—use of Google as a diagnostic aid: Internet based study. *British Medical Journal* 333: 1143–5.

# Part 4
## Managing the organization

# Changing the organization
## Planning and emergence

## Chapter overview and learning outcomes

By the end of this chapter you should be able to:

- describe a range of triggers to change and factors which resist against change

- explain how change can be messy, causing conflict and resistance

- describe three approaches to the management of change: the naïve, planned, and emergent approaches

- analyse the different perspectives that these three approaches give of the nature of an organization and how it might be changed.

## Key theorists

| | |
|---|---|
| Kurt Lewin | Psychologist whose work on group dynamics has been applied to many areas of planned change, including force-field analysis, the three-step model of change, and organization development |
| Ralph Stacey | Has applied chaos and complexity theories to organizational change |
| Rosabeth Moss Kanter | Has written prolifically about change management, focusing on the attributes of companies that have undergone successful change programmes |
| Bernard Burnes | Has analysed the work of Lewin and advocates its relevance to contemporary organizational change |
| Thomas Cummings and Christopher Worley | Have outlined the wide variety of change management techniques which are used in organizational settings |

## Key terms

| | |
|---|---|
| Naïve change | An approach to change which sees the organization in simplistic terms, as if it were a set of building blocks which can be rearranged easily |
| Planned change | An approach which sees change as planned over a long-term series of steps; pays attention to human and social aspects of change, which are seen as 'hidden aspects' below the surface, as if the organization were an iceberg |
| Emergent change | An approach to change which sees the organization as being like a river, in constant flow, and suggests that in such an environment change emerges rather than being planned in advance |

| Force-field analysis | A technique whereby triggers for, and resistance against, change are plotted on a diagram in order to identify areas on which to focus a change-management programme |
| Three-step model | Lewin's model whereby a process of change goes through three stages of unfreezing, movement, and freezing |
| Complexity theory | An emergent approach to organizational change, suggesting that small changes can have unpredictable and potentially limitless consequences |

# Introduction

## Running case: successful change at 'Coral Reef?'

Six months after taking over at the fitness centre, manager Carl Jones is sipping champagne with the hotel's management team in the boardroom. The toast—to the success of the fitness centre. Jones had been brought in as a 'new broom' to turn around the ailing fortunes of the fitness centre. Six months on, the results speak for themselves.

- The centre has been refurbished and rebranded as Coral Reef, with the image and ambience of a warm, beach environment.
- Turnover has trebled, and the fitness centre is beginning to make profits and a financial contribution to the hotel.
- The percentage of hotel guests using the centre has doubled from 20% to 40%.
- Full-time membership of the club, from the local area, has doubled.
- A new range of beauty and health services is offered.
- Many more female guests are using the centre where previously the clientele was 95% male.

These achievements, especially the profit figures, are seen as outstanding by Simon Chance. Leading the toast to Jones, he praises his 'authoritative, decisive, and, ultimately, successful programme of change'.

Has Carl Jones been a successful manager of change?

We all encounter change in our lives, whether it is a major decision—to move house or change job, for example—or something as minor as a change of hairstyle. Change might be forced upon us by particular circumstances or something that we do of our own volition.

In organizations, **change management** is any form of effort or initiative undertaken to alter a particular aspect of the organization. This might be to improve the current situation of the organization or, as we have seen with recent economic turmoil, to respond to particular events that necessitate some form of change for the survival of the organization.

We begin the chapter by viewing change from two conflicting perspectives. On the one hand, change might be seen by managers as a reasonable action to take in response

Change management
An effort or initiative undertaken to alter a particular aspect of the organization.

to certain triggers or pressures—moving to larger premises, for example, if the current premises are crowded. On the other hand, change can cause anxiety, fear, and upset among the workforce that it affects—the new premises might necessitate a longer commute for the workforce, even resulting in some having to give up their jobs. Rather than being a smooth process, change can be messy and can meet with conflict and resistance.

We present three broad approaches which examine the implementation of change against the backdrop of such conflicting perspectives. These approaches are derived from three particular metaphors or ways of seeing the organization, which we suggest offer different insights into the subject.

- Firstly, we examine a **naïve approach to change** which stems from viewing the organization in simplistic terms, as a set of building blocks. This approach, where managers can change the organization by rearranging elements of the organization at will, is one that we suggest is misguided and misses out on many aspects of the organization that are important to the change process.

- Secondly, we suggest that viewing the organization as an iceberg shows that it has hidden depths which affect the implementation of change. Such hidden depths are the human and social aspects of the organization, within which resistance and anxiety can develop. The **planned approach to change** suggests that, using knowledge from behavioural psychology, change can be implemented in a set of steps using techniques which overcome that resistance and bring about attitude change.

- Finally, an **emergent approach to change** sees the organization as a river, constantly in flow. The organization is never still for long enough for change to be a planned process; change is what emerges in the course of events.

The three approaches take us from managers being in absolute control *of* change, to managers almost being controlled *by* change, having to react to events as they happen.

**Naïve approach to change** An approach to change which sees the organization in simplistic terms, as if it were a set of building blocks which can be rearranged easily.

**Planned approach to change** An approach to change which sees change as planned over a series of long-term steps. Pays attention to human and social aspects of change, which are seen as 'hidden aspects' below the surface, as if the organization were an iceberg. Closely linked with organization development.

**Emergent approach to change** An approach to change which sees the organization as being like a river, in constant flow, and suggests that in such an environment change emerges in the course of events rather than being planned in advance.

# Conflicting perspectives of change: triggers and resistance

**Running case:** Coral 'grief'

The boardroom celebrations do not extend down to the Coral Reef fitness centre. The long-standing staff have seen their jobs and workplace change out of all recognition in the past six months—changes which have made them unhappy.

Egged on by his colleagues, one of the trainers walks up to the grinning photograph in the fitness centre entrance, underneath which reads 'Carl Jones, Fitness Centre Manager.' He draws on a moustache and spectacles; then, applying his marker pen to the fitness centre entrance sign, 'Coral Reef' is rechristened as 'Coral Grief.'

Later, with the staff having long left the building, Meg Mortimer goes down from the party to check that the fitness suite is locked up. Noticing the doctored photograph and sign she smiles to herself. Of course, she cleans it up before it can be discovered, but after the six months she's had coping with the fallout from Jones's changes, she isn't going to pursue the culprits any further.

When a change takes place, it can be a messy process. People may have different, even conflicting, views and opinions of the change. What might seem like a perfectly rational and necessary change to a senior manager may upset other workers who are happy as they are, or leave them anxious about their job security and working conditions.

In this section we see change as a process that takes place amidst conflicting perspectives across the organization. On the one hand, there are a number of **triggers** which provide an impetus for managers to make a change. On the other hand, reaction to that change might be manifested in different forms of **resistance**.

**Triggers** Factors which push towards a change taking place.

**Resistance** Factors which prevent or hinder a change taking place.

---

## Real life case: alternative perceptions of change

A case study of change in a financial services institution (King, 2001) was undertaken by getting employees and managers to draw their perceptions of the change process.

Before the change, the organization was perceived as traditional, secure, and averse to risk, with a 'family' culture that was collective, sharing, and supportive. This safe, but conservative, organization was seen by management as old-fashioned and uncompetitive, so stuck in its ways that it could, potentially, go out of business. The financial services sector was characterized by market deregulation, increased automation and Internet banking, and an increase in the amount and intensity of competition within the market.

A change was undertaken—towards a more dynamic, risk-taking, and sales-driven culture. Targets and charts permeated the organization, with graphs showing sales of mortgages and financial products placed on the wall of the staff room. Management were more visible, with one manager sitting opposite the clock-in machine as people arrived for work.

The change was 'officially' a success. Targets were met and the move to a new sales culture completed. However, many staff left and were replaced with new recruits. Away from the official success story, different perspectives within the organization emerged. The research involved both managers and workers drawing their perceptions of the change process. Away from the official success story, the drawings showed that some employees had a different perception of the change process.

### The management perception

A common theme linked management illustrations of the change process—a journey towards a brighter future. One senior manager highlighted the 'baggage' of the organization's past culture dragging it back as it climbed towards its future. It could still go backwards, but if the organization reached the top of the hill it faced a bright future. A branch manager envisaged the organization crossing a bridge towards riches and rewards. Taking that journey would require the right attitude; however, the bridge could be cut and the change prevented by negative attitudes from employees, such as fear and ignorance. Those that complied with the change were portrayed as 'angels', while those that contributed to its failure—through their fear and ignorance—were presented as 'devils'.

### The employee perception

Employee drawings suggested a different perception of the change. A long-standing employee of the organization drew small workers on an assembly line, whipped to work harder by an overbearing management and with the targets looming large over the whole organization. A newer employee illustrated herself swamped by the amount of paperwork and a constantly ringing telephone—happy only when the ▶

▶ end of the working day came along. In the most dramatic image, an employee, who eventually left, drew a worker shedding tears of money, pushed to this by a ruthless manager depicted as a Nazi.

The drawings illustrated conflicting perceptions of the change. For management, the past was bad and the future good. The change was about the organization growing and developing, and was a rational and purely technical response to environmental pressures within the financial services sector. Management should control the change—any resistance or obstruction of the change was problematic and to the detriment of the organization's future. *They perceived employees that obstruct or resist change as devils.*

For employees, the concern was more with the present situation. They took the change personally, visualizing themselves shrinking in the face of management targets and intensified work regimes. They felt pain and powerlessness, and that they had little choice in what was happening. To them the change was destructive and they felt like victims. *They perceived management implementing the change as Nazis.*

**Source:** King (2001).

The conflicting perspectives on the change can be shown as a number of triggers exerting a force for the change to take place (increased competition in the sector, technology, deregulation, etc.), but equally an amount of resistance among the workforce against that change. A swastika to depict a manager is an incredibly powerful and, indeed, offensive image to use, but it demonstrates how clearly the workers were upset by the change and how angry they were with the management. *Change can provoke very strong emotions and resistance.*

# Triggers for change

## Running case: flashback—embarking on change

Six months before the celebrations in the boardroom, Carl Jones had started his first day as the new fitness centre director. His brief: the centre was a loss-maker—it needed to not only hold its own, but to start making money for the hotel. Jones saw two main areas of potential for income growth:

1. External memberships—Junction Hotel offered fitness centre membership to non-residents; however, take-up was low. The fitness industry was highly competitive and dominated by a number of large-scale branded chains. Junction Hotel needed its own, smaller-scale gym to trade on its more personal atmosphere, while matching the offerings of its larger competitors.

2. Income from hotel guests—hotel guests could use the gym facilities for free and Jones was not allowed to change this. However, he thought that the fitness centre could provide paid extras for the guests—classes, beauty treatments, etc. Indeed, the fitness centre could become a reason for people to stay at the hotel *per se*, with spa weekend packages being offered.

Jones had started by listing the current features of the gym.

- The fitness centre had no separate identity or brand of its own—it was not marketed within the hotel or externally to the local population.

- The décor was somewhat basic (cold, plain walls); the gym had basic equipment (none of the electronic machinery found in competitors' gyms); showers were provided, but no sauna or spa facilities, as found in competitors' gyms.
- Opening hours: the fitness centre was open from 7 am until 7 pm, and was only fully staffed between 9 am and 5 pm; competitors were open earlier and later.
- There was a reception desk at the entrance, which was largely unstaffed, and extras, such as towels, were not provided; staff would be on hand to give advice if asked, although, in practice, this was given mainly to a number of regular members who had devised workout programmes with the staff.
- Unlike competitors, no exercise classes or lessons were offered. There were two treatment rooms—some of the staff had physiotherapy qualifications and would provide treatments, charging separately for this and pocketing the money themselves. For much of the time, the treatment rooms lay unused—with one of them even being used as an informal staff room.
- The five fitness centre staff worked as a team, all working a 9–5 shift, Monday–Saturday, with the centre being unstaffed on Sundays. Work tasks were arranged informally. Tasks included the maintenance and cleaning of gym equipment, pool life-guarding duties, general monitoring of the gym floor and the safety of users, and checking membership cards when people entered—this was the closest there was to any form of reception duties. All staff had a sports science qualification, which they were proud of. No staff uniforms were worn.
- The basic nature of the gym floor gave it a 'spit and sawdust' feel. Regular members tended to be male and heavily into weight training. Casual users, such as hotel guests, and people considering gym membership, particularly women, said that they found it intimidating. The staff found no problem with the culture and enjoyed working with the regular members. The fewer new members the better, otherwise it might disrupt the way that things were run.

Jones had started to think of what changes he could make to turn around the fitness centre. At the time, he was working within two financial parameters.

1. There was a healthy budget for investment—equipment, building works, etc. Whatever needed to be done, should be done.

2. While the investment budget was plentiful, Jones had to keep increases in running costs to a minimum. Day to day, the fitness centre had to be making a profit. In particular, there was little room to increase staff costs.

What changes would you make if you were in Carl Jones's position?

Triggers for change are forces which give an impetus for a change to occur, whether they are external triggers from outside the organization, or internal triggers from within. Potentially, the number of triggers for change in an organization is limitless.

Senior and Swailes (2010) suggest that external triggers for change can be identified using the PEST (political, economic, socio-cultural, and technological) model, as introduced in Chapter 4, to think more broadly about the sectors of the organization's external environment from which these triggers might originate (Figure 11.1).

**Figure 11.1** The PEST model and external triggers for change.

Some, or indeed all, of these sectors of the environment may be acting on an organization at any one time. For example, in UK universities, triggers from all four sectors of the external environment have, perhaps, pushed universities towards a more commercial and student-focused way of operating, and away from more traditional, academic 'ivory tower' cultures (Figure 11.2).

The impetus for change can also come from internal triggers—a reorganization or restructuring, for example, may come from a recognition of problems within the organization itself, such as poor communication or coordination between departments. Based on Senior and Swailes (2010: 22), we suggest a number of potential internal triggers to change:

- new senior staff may bring in their own ideas and vision for how the organization should be run—a new broom sweeps clean
- managerial aspirations, whims, and decisions may lead to change
- unions within the organization may bring their own pressure and action for changes
- the politics and power of particular groups, individuals, and coalitions within an organization (see Chapter 13) may be a force towards change

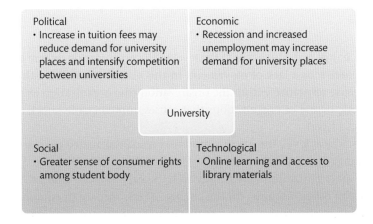

**Figure 11.2** Aspects of the external environment acting as triggers for change in UK universities.

- changes may be required as an organization grows in size: for instance, new premises to cope with the increased capacity

- a redesign of technology, jobs, or even the physical layout of the organization may bring with it a need for further changes.

 Visit the Online Resource Centre for further examples of potential internal triggers to change.

# Resistance to change

While triggers and forces for change may exist, change is often resisted strongly by individuals, by groups of individuals, or, indeed, by organizational forces as a whole.

As seen in the financial services institution case, change can arouse very strong and powerful human emotions and feelings, which are displayed as resistance to change. Based on Drafke (2009: 431–437), examples of why people resist change might include the following:

- generally, people are not predisposed to change from their everyday routines with which they become comfortable—disruption to routines is not liked

- people may worry about job security or pay issues, i.e. they perceive that they will lose out in some way as a result of the change

- change may disrupt social and informal ties, e.g. being moved from an office with people they enjoy to one where they dislike the people

- people may not recognize or understand the need for the change which is being proposed and which may have a considerable effect upon them

- the change may go against the values held by individuals, e.g. a clash of professional and commercial values

- taking all of the points mentioned, change can create anxiety when people are unsure of what is about to happen.

 Visit the Online Resource Centre for further reasons why people resist change.

**Inertia** A tendency for an organization as a whole to resist change or lack the impetus for change.

Resistance to change may also occur at the level of the organization, where organizational factors cause **inertia**, or a lack of movement. In this chapter we will see that groups and cultures can cause resistance within the organization (the organization as an iceberg), as can the systemic nature of organizations that causes unpredictable knock-on effects (the organization as a river).

At a more practical level, the organization may also be shackled against undergoing a particular change, for example owing to contractual obligations or fixed investments. Furthermore, an organization may simply lack the capability to change. This may be a lack of finance or other resources for the change, a lack of space or equipment, or a lack of capability or skills within the organization's workforce (Senior and Fleming, 2006: 286).

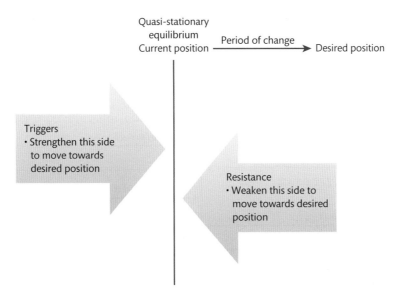

**Figure 11.3**
Force-field analysis.

# Force-field analysis

The multitude of triggers and resisting factors show that there are a number of different factors at work in any change situation. The whole situation in any one organization can become very complicated to understand.

**Force-field analysis** (Lewin, 1943) is a technique which provides a snapshot or overall view of a change situation. The triggers and resistance factors are shown on a diagram (Figure 11.3) as arrows converging on one point—the current position. At this point the organization is in a 'quasi-stationary equilibrium'. To move to a desired situation, i.e. to change, the organization needs to strengthen the triggers to change and weaken the resisting forces.

In the earlier case of the financial services institution, it is possible to plot out the triggers for change and the resistance factors on a force-field analysis diagram (Figure 11.4). In this instance, the triggers, such as deregulation, competition, and senior staff initiatives, are pushing the organization in the direction of a sales-oriented culture. However, these triggers are met by resisting in terms of staff fears, the strength of the current culture, and a dislike of the new working methods, etc.

Force-field analysis derives from the psychology of Kurt Lewin. In Chapter 6 we saw how Lewin analysed the influence of group dynamics, or peer pressure, upon individual behaviour. For Lewin (1943), group dynamics is one of many forces in an individual's **life field** which influence their behaviour. While consisting mainly of psychological forces, this life field may also contain factors from the physical and social world that a person encounters. Such forces can be plotted on a force-field analysis diagram for an individual.

Take, for example, an individual who wishes to give up smoking. A similar diagram can be drawn (Figure 11.5) which shows the triggers pushing the individual towards that change (e.g. family pressure, health concerns, the cost, the unpleasant nature of smoking)

Force-field analysis  A technique whereby triggers and resistance to change are plotted on a diagram in order to identify areas on which to focus a change-management programme.

Life field  A set of forces, both psychological and material, which influence the behaviour of an individual.

**Figure 11.4** Force-field analysis of the financial services institution case.

pitted against forces resistant to giving up smoking (e.g. its addictive nature, peer pressure in social situations, stress in work and life in general).

There are more triggers than there are resisting factors, so will the change happen inevitably? Possibly not, as the addictive nature of smoking is a major factor and a considerable weight in preventing the change to being a non-smoker. Another aspect of force-field

**Figure 11.5** Force-field analysis for an individual giving up smoking.

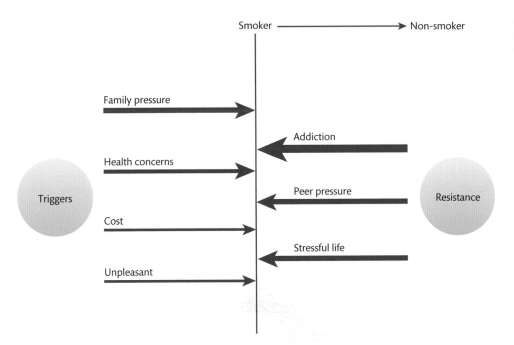

**Figure 11.6** Weighted forces in a force-field analysis diagram.

analysis is that different forces can be given different strengths—as in Figure 11.6—by showing the different arrows with different weights.

The change to being a non-smoker might come about by attention to reducing the resisting factors, for example by avoiding socializing with the people who smoke or by taking some form of treatment for the nicotine addiction. Viewing this situation from the point of view of a government wanting to implement a national programme to stop people from smoking, they might also pay attention to strengthening some of the triggers—increasing the cost of cigarettes, for example, or placing diagrams of diseased lungs on cigarette packets to prompt health concerns (compare these tactics with behaviour modification as discussed in Chapter 10).

Can you construct force-field analysis diagrams for a personal change that you have experienced? How would the diagram help you to plan and implement the change?

Although derived from Lewin's work in individual psychology and behaviour, force-field analysis can be used in individual, group, organizational—even societal—situations of potential, or desired, change. In that 'any event is the resultant of a multitude of factors' (Lewin, 1943: 293), the value of the force-field analysis diagram is that it provides a snapshot of those factors. It highlights the conflicting factors and perspectives in a change situation, and suggests areas where the implementation of a change management process might focus.

Visit the Online Resource Centre for further examples of force-field analysis diagrams.

## Review questions

| | |
|---|---|
| **Describe** | What is meant by triggers for change and resistance against change? |
| **Explain** | How does a force-field analysis diagram plot out the forces at work in a change situation? |
| **Apply** | Using the information in Figures 11.5 and 11.6, what actions might you take when designing a programme to persuade people to stop smoking? |
| **Apply** | Using the information about the change in the fitness centre, draw a similar force-field analysis diagram for the situation facing Carl Jones (see the Online Resource Centre for a suggested answer). |

# Types of change and the nature of the organization

**Running case:** Jones's action plan

### Fitness centre action plan

**1.** Identity and marketing

- rebrand as Coral Reef—extensive marketing campaign to accompany this

**2.** Décor and equipment

- décor in coral reef style—redesign pool area with tropical island theme and develop part of changing area into health spa
- redecorate gym and replace equipment—I suggest electronic card-controlled equipment and the card can double up as the entrance key at reception
- build extension to create a studio for classes

**3.** Customer service

- extend opening: 6 am to 11 pm daily, with centre, including reception desk, staffed at all times; towels to be provided at the reception desk, and customers greeted and handed towel on arrival
- staff to maintain presence on the gym floor and pool for safety purposes, but should also welcome and encourage guests

**4.** Classes and treatments

- provide beauty and health treatments in the treatment rooms
    - no recruitment allowed, so slots within the treatment rooms to be rented to local practitioners—hairdressers, beauticians, etc.
    - classes, e.g. pilates in the new studio; pool to offer swimming lessons and aqua aerobics—existing staff to do this, but bring in local expertise on a freelance basis as and when needed

**5.** Staff

- expected to work flexibly within the 6 am to 11 pm working day, including weekends, according to a rota; staff to always present an upbeat, friendly image

- will promote the paid treatments and classes—some sort of bonus incentive for this

- one qualified member of staff should be on duty at all times; as this will stretch existing staff across the new opening hours, employ local students to work along alongside qualified staff as and when needed

**6.** Culture and atmosphere

- *must* change from spit and sawdust to upmarket, tropical luxury—changes to décor will help

- staff to get new uniforms; they are expected to be the embodiment of this culture—motivating people to exercise but, at the same time, creating a relaxing atmosphere

- culture *must* be less aggressively masculine and less intimidating to potential members and hotel guests

When we speak about 'change' we could be speaking about a whole variety of activities where something is done differently—from a small change in one worker's rota, to a department relocating to a different office, to an overall corporate rebranding. All are examples of change in an organization. Cummings and Worley (2009) suggest four main areas of change management, focusing on different aspects of organizational life.

- *Strategic interventions* are major shifts in the overall focus and direction of the organization. Areas of focus might be corporate strategy, products and services offered, culture change, rebranding, or organizational learning.

- *Technostructural interventions* look at areas of technology and the organization's structure. Examples include the design and division of work, downsizing, bringing in new technology, and redesigning the organization's bureaucratic structure.

- *Human process interventions* are concerned with human social issues in the organization—how people relate to each other, communication, decision making, and leadership. They are based around group dynamics and team-building activities.

- *Human resource issues* are focused on people at a more individual level. Examples include performance management, recruitment, appraisal, reward management, motivation, and managing diversity.

This list touches on many topics covered in other chapters in this book, and it shows that the focus of change is wide and far-reaching; indeed, change is potentially infinite in its scope.

Further categorization can be made in terms of the scale of change from small to large: from fine-tuning to tuning, and from adjustment to departmental or corporate transformation (Senior and Swailes, 2010: 39–41). Senior and Swailes also suggest that the degree of change that an organization faces may be predictable or a complete surprise, depending on the turbulence of the environment (see Chapter 4) that the organization faces.

Taking into account the variety of both types and scale of change, and the differences in the environmental turbulence encountered by the organization, change-management theories tend to divide into two camps: a *planned approach*, which sees change managed through a series of steps from one point to another (as with force-field analysis), and an *emergent approach*, which sees change as more unpredictable, likely to be carried along by the flow of events within the organization and unpredictable influences from the environment.

# Change and the nature of organization

What is an organization? This might seem like an obvious question to ask, but we suggest that to understand the nature of change and its implementation, a step back needs to be taken to see the nature of what is actually being changed—the organization itself. Whether change can be planned or whether change is emergent, for example, depends very much on the nature of the organization itself.

In this section we introduce three **metaphors** which provide three different ways of answering the question 'what is an organization?' These metaphors see the organization as either a set of building blocks, an iceberg, or a river.

**Metaphor** A figure of speech whereby we try to understand something by suggesting a resemblance to the characteristics of something else.

> ### Study skills: the use of metaphors
>
> Metaphors are ways of visualizing or imagining the world around us in order to gain new insights. For example, Morgan (2006) constructs his whole book *Images of organization* around different metaphors to understand different aspects of organizational life and theory. One chapter sees 'organizations as machines' as a means of visualizing the rational, Taylorist organization (which we examine in Chapter 2), while 'organizations as brains' is the metaphor used to envisage learning organizations (which we examine in Chapter 10).
>
> The three metaphors used in this chapter—building blocks, iceberg, and river—are different ways in which we can view the nature of what an organization is which lead to different ways of approaching the change process.
>
> The metaphors are not necessarily mutually exclusive—there is no need to choose one as being better or more truthful than the other two. Instead, each uncovers different aspects of an organization's nature—each tells us something different and new about what an organization is. They provide a set of lenses to view and understand the nature of an organization, each of which may inform our knowledge about implementing change over an organization in different ways.

**Change agent** A manager, consultant, or other person who instigates and manages change.

The metaphors help us to put ourselves in the place of a manager or consultant who has the job of implementing change within an organization, a so-called **change agent**. They help us to ask four questions about the nature of an organization that inform the nature and implementation of change in that organization:

- Is the *structure* of the organization stable or is the organization constantly changing?
- How does a change agent gain *knowledge* about what is going on in the organization, e.g. when trying to identify and understand the triggers and resisting forces that might be shown in a force-field analysis diagram?

**Table 11.1**  Metaphors of change and the nature of organization

| Metaphor | Description | Related approach to change |
|---|---|---|
| The organization as a set of building blocks | The organization has a solid *structure* that management have complete *power* to control and change at will. Managing change is as easy as rearranging a set of children's building blocks. This takes a very mechanical view of how we gain *knowledge* of the organization, and there is little account taken of human elements. *Resistance* to change and to management power is seen as being alien to the organization. | Naïve approach to change |
| The organization as an iceberg | Like an iceberg, the *structure* of the organization has hidden depths lurking beneath the surface—the human and social aspects of the organization. *Knowledge* of these hidden, human depths is harder to uncover and the change agent relies on human sciences, such as psychology, to understand the organization. *Resistance* is an understandable human reaction to change, but, ultimately, psychologically-informed techniques, which are planned and implemented over a period of time, give management *power* to bring about change. | Planned approach to change |
| The organization as a river | The organization is in a constant state of flux and flow, like a set of rapids on a river. As such, it is never still long enough to have a stable *structure*. Management has little *power* over an organization that is changing constantly and evading its grasp. *Resistance* is continual—think of trying to paddle against the rapids. *Knowledge* is something that comes from experience and action, from jumping in and riding the rapids. | Emergent approach to change |

- How does *power* operate in the organization, e.g. what ability does a change agent have to control and bring about change in an organization?
- To what extent is *resistance* a challenge to power in the organization, and how might that resistance be overcome?

Using the metaphors to address these questions leads us to three approaches to change that we examine in the remainder of this chapter (Table 11.1). To the familiar planned and emergent approaches to change, which we equate to the organization as an iceberg and a river, respectively, we add a naïve approach to change which sees the organization in simplistic terms as a set of building blocks.

## Review questions

| | |
|---|---|
| **Describe** | What are the categories of change outlined by Cummings and Worley? |
| **Explain** | How do metaphors help us to understand the nature of an organization? |
| **Analyse** | How are structure, knowledge, power, and resistance key features of the organization which influence different approaches to change? |
| **Apply** | Using Cummings and Worley's categories, what types of change are being attempted in the fitness centre? (Visit the Online Resource Centre for a suggested answer.) |

# The organization as a set of building blocks: a naïve approach to change?

### Running case: letter to employees

Dear Fitness Staff,

As loyal employees of the fitness centre, I'm sure you will be as excited as me by the changes that will transform our centre into a leading gym and health spa facility. From this week the fitness centre will be known as Coral Reef. To match the name change we are undertaking a massive refurbishment programme.

It's not just the buildings and equipment that will change, however. We aim to attract new customers and hotel guests with a set of activities and treatments with our new unique selling point of 'tropical luxury'. To make this work we need to change the culture of Coral Reef and this can only be done through you—the staff.

For this, we are introducing our 'simply the best' culture change programme. You, as staff, will become 'simply the best' at carrying our new culture in the following ways:

- you will give 'simply the best' customer service, greeting customers when they arrive, smiling at all times, and making conversation with customers on the gym floor

- you will encourage customers to be 'simply the best' by motivating them to achieve their fitness goals and providing encouragement to all customers on the gym floor

- you will become 'simply the best' at generating revenue for Coral Reef by promoting our new courses and treatments—each month there will be a bonus for the best at selling.

There will be some changes to working arrangements, with flexible rostering during an extended working day. To cover extra hours, new part-time staff will be brought in along with freelance instructors and treatment practitioners. I'm sure you will welcome them all in due course and help them to also be 'simply the best'.

Best wishes
Carl

How do you think the fitness centre staff will react to receiving this letter?

Imagine yourself as a manager implementing a change. The ideal situation, with the least amount of hassle, would be if you could simply rearrange the elements of the organization as if you were playing with a set of children's building blocks. Our first way of seeing the nature of an organization is that it is like a set of building blocks that fit together and can be rearranged at will.

The organization as a set of building blocks.

Perhaps any change that focuses purely on structural or technological features of the organization (see Cummings and Worley's (2009) technostructural interventions in the previous section) can be seen as taking this building block view of the organization. It is not, however, difficult to criticize this as a naïve view, based on a number of simplistic assumptions that it makes about the nature of an organization:

- the *structure* is simple and solid, where every conceivable element is visible—there are no hidden aspects to the organization

- *knowledge* is simply what can be measured, calculated, or represented as some form of model, equation, or diagram; it is a view of the organization almost as if it were a machine (think of similarities here with Taylor and Ford from Chapter 3)

- management have total *power* over the organization from the top down

- *resistance* has no place in the organization; change is thus a matter of simply issuing orders and commands which will then be followed.

It is a very clean and simple view of what an organization is, but we know that organizational life is not this simple—it can be complex, messy, and unpredictable. This view fails to note that change is often perceived differently by workers and management, and thus often meets resistance. By paying attention to just the building blocks aspects of the change, management are blinkered to other human and social issues which ensue as a result, and which may make an important difference between the success and failure of that change.

This is not to say that change involving technostructural elements is naïve and simplistic *per se*—there are times when technology needs to be changed or an organization restructured. What is naïve is the assumption that this is all that needs to be changed while ignoring all human processes and interactions. We could say that it concentrates only on the triggers to change and remains ignorant of any potential resisting forces, such as the fears and anxieties that often accompany change.

And yet how many managers see their organization in these terms, for example by restructuring a bureaucracy without thinking about how people will fit into the new system? Or, perhaps, by making changes to technology or the buildings without thinking about how people will actually use them or interact within them? Or even announcing a new culture without understanding that the culture has to work through people?

## Real life case: Wimbledon FC/AFC Wimbledon

Wimbledon FC, known as the Dons, had a rapid rise to success from being a small, non-league side in 1977 to reaching the top flight of English football by 1985 and winning the FA Cup in 1988. However, the club remained small in terms of its fan base. Along with this, the club retained a special culture, termed the 'crazy gang', typified by on-field 'hard men' such as Vinnie Jones.

The special culture was part of the experience of Wimbledon for players and fans alike, but the businessmen who ran the club saw other opportunities when Wimbledon reached the big time. Their logic was that there were areas of the country without Premiership football where fans would attend in their droves if they had a nearby club to support, meaning more money in the bank and greater profits. The plan was to move Wimbledon FC to Milton Keynes, a town 70 miles away without its own league football club.

At first sight the move was successful—the club moved to Milton Keynes, renaming itself the Milton Keynes Dons and eventually building its own stadium. What it couldn't take to Milton Keynes, however, were the existing fans and the special culture.

Wimbledon FC supporters were angry about the prospect of their club being uprooted and taken to another location. Rather than travel to Milton Keynes, the fans set up a trust within days to create their own alternative football club in Wimbledon, known as AFC Wimbledon:

> Wimbledon supporters set about creating a replacement, a football club which would continue the history and identity of OUR club. Through the hard work and determination of WISA and The Dons Trust, AFC Wimbledon was born, and will continue to live the dream of football in our local community.
>
> (Source: Reproduced by permission of Wimbledon Independent Supporters' Association)

AFC Wimbledon had to start from scratch in terms of finding a team, a ground, players and staff, and also in terms of dropping back several divisions to play non-league football. Where it didn't have to start from scratch, however, was in terms of fans and the Wimbledon culture. AFC Wimbledon kept most of the Wimbledon fan-base and regularly attracted larger crowds than the 'official' Wimbledon, now based in Milton Keynes. This was despite the fact that the Milton Keynes side was a professional club in the second tier of English football and AFC Wimbledon was a non-league side several divisions short of league football.

In 2011, AFC Wimbledon gained promotion to League 2, the fourth tier of English football's profes-sional league structure—meaning that a situation could occur in future where the two clubs are playing in the same league!

The move to Milton Keynes could be seen as a perfectly rational business decision to take advantage of potentially larger crowds and gain more income. However, it can also be interpreted as an example of a building blocks approach to change. The change involves simply the visible, structural elements of the organization—the buildings, league position, name, etc. It is ignorant or blinkered to other more intangible aspects—the culture, ties with the community, and traditions, etc. Yet it is these with which the fans identified as being the essence of the club, not the building blocks, such as the ground. It is this aspect over which the management had no power—they could move the building blocks to a new location, but they couldn't get that culture to follow them in the same direction.

**Sources:** White (2003); Mumford (2004); *The Guardian* (2004); Hutchins et al. (2009); Nakrani (2011); Hognestad (2012); Tynan (2012); Wimbledon Independent Supporters' Association (2012).

Visit the Online Resource Centre to read other examples of naïve approaches to change.

## Review questions

| | |
|---|---|
| **Describe** | What is meant by a naïve approach to change? |
| **Explain** | What important aspects of organizational life are ignored by a naïve approach to change? |
| **Apply** | In what ways could the management of the original Wimbledon be seen to have taken a 'naïve' approach to change? (Visit the Online Resource Centre for more on this question.) |

# The organization as an iceberg: the planned approach to change

## Running case: culture clashes

The new culture was at odds with the spit and sawdust culture that the original staff were used to. They wanted nothing to do with the 'simply the best' culture, and they felt that the constant smiling and upbeat small-talk trivialized their professional qualifications and commitment to fitness. As much as possible they tried to avoid the new culture, making perfunctory smiles only when in view of the boss. The fact that the new rota had disrupted their personal lives, meaning they couldn't work together as a group, didn't help.

Conversely, the new staff—part-timers and freelance instructors—were inducted into the culture from the start and identified with it a lot more. This irritated the older staff, who started to refer to the new staff as the 'grinners'. Two groups emerged who would lunch, socialize, and chat separately. The grinners began to refer to the original staff as the 'oldies'. Contact between them was minimal.

The divisions were more than obvious at a launch night for the new fitness centre. With staff seated (in their oldies and grinners groups) Carl Jones stormed on to a makeshift stage with 'Simply the Best' blaring out over a loudspeaker. After some speeches about the new culture, Jones brought on some staff to model the new uniform. Based around the tropical theme, it consisted of a Coral Reef plain top with garish patterned beach shorts.

The oldies looked aghast and their hearts sank—it went against every professional and cultural value that they held. The grinners, however, were jumping up and down and whooping at their 'cool' new uniforms and swarmed Carl Jones to get their hands on their own uniforms to try on.

Think of the trouble that an iceberg can cause for a passing ship. It's not the part of the iceberg that is visible above the surface that causes the problems—it's the vast bulk of the iceberg that is hidden from view beneath the surface of the water that can cause a ship to run aground.

The metaphor of an iceberg sees the organization as having 'hidden depths' that lie 'beneath the surface'. The technical and structural features which make up the building blocks of an organization are merely the tip of the iceberg—the part that is easily visible and perhaps easiest, on first glance, to manage and over which to exert power. Hidden

The organization as an iceberg.

**Figure 11.7** Aspects of the organization above and below the surface.

The building blocks of the organization, e.g. buildings, technology, structure, rules, procedures

Social aspects, e.g. cultures, group dynamics

Human aspects, e.g. attitudes, anxieties, values, feelings, emotions

below the surface, in the bulk of the iceberg, are the more intangible aspects of the organization (Figure 11.7).

These hidden aspects include human aspects, such as anxieties, attitudes, values, and emotions; and social aspects, such as cultures and group dynamics. In a similar manner, Edgar Schein used an iceberg to describe layers and depths of organizational culture (see Chapter 7).

## The planned approach to change

While hard to uncover at first, human and social aspects are an important part of the organization and, if ignored, could potentially cause a change management initiative to be met with resistance and potentially run aground. Thus the iceberg metaphor highlights the following aspects of an organization relevant to the change process, which make up the key assumptions behind the planned approach to change.

- As with the building blocks approach, the *structure* is solid, but it also has hidden depths consisting of the human and social elements, which make up a considerable part of the organization 'beneath the surface'.

- Gaining *knowledge* of the organization means getting 'beneath the surface' to the hidden depths. Psychologically-based techniques are used to get to know and understand these human and social aspects of the organization.

- A manager, or change agent, using a set of psychologically-informed techniques, ultimately has *power* to bring about top-down change in the organization. It is not as instant, simple, and neat as the building blocks approach would suggest, but is a wide-ranging and long-term process.

- *Resistance* is understandable—it is a natural human and social reaction to change. Part of the job of overcoming resistance to change is to understand why it occurs in the first place before implementing a plan to overcome that resistance.

Unlike the naïve approach, the planned approach recognizes that change is not a simple and straightforward process, and that resistance to change can be expected. Given that such resistance resides in human and social aspects of the organization, psychological knowledge and techniques are used to overcome that resistance. To manage change requires a series of carefully planned and managed steps to take an organization, or a part of the organization, from point A to point B.

## The three-step model of change

Implementing planned change through a series of managed steps is most famously outlined in Kurt Lewin's (1947) **three-step model of change**. For Lewin, the implementation of organizational change follows three broad steps of unfreezing, movement, and freezing.

**Three-step model of change** Lewin's model whereby a process of change goes through three stages of unfreezing, movement, and freezing

- Unfreezing is where the current situation is first outlined, perhaps using a force-field analysis diagram, and the organization is shaken out of its current state and prepared for the need for change.

- Movement is where the organization moves and changes slowly towards the desired state.

- Freezing occurs once the change has been achieved—it is reinforced so as to avoid slipping back into the previous way of doing things.

**Research insight:** Three-step model at British Airways
Goodstein, L.D., and Warner Burke, W. 1991. Creating successful organization change. *Organizational Dynamics* 19(4): 5–17.

During the 1980s, British Airways underwent a major change from being a nationalized, loss-making airline to becoming a private, commercial, profit-making operation. Accompanying this was a change in culture and emphasis, from a bureaucratic, militaristic style to one focused on customer service.

Goodstein and Burke (1991) suggest that the change was achieved by following a three-step pattern. Examples of each of the steps include the following:

- unfreezing from the current state was achieved through downsizing, bringing in a new top management team, and redefining the purpose of the company as service and not transportation

- movement was brought about through attention to communications, peer support groups, a new training centre, and off-site, team-building activities

- freezing, or reinforcement of the change, came from promoting staff who demonstrated the new values, new reward and appraisal systems, and continued development and training.

As with force-field analysis, the three-step model derives from Lewin's psychological background and, in particular, his work on group dynamics. Movement is not as simple as rearranging a set of building blocks; instead, it requires psychological techniques to uncover all of the human emotions and dynamics that are going on beneath the surface and to then begin to change people slowly towards adopting new behaviours.

One of the main techniques developed from Lewin is the **T-group** (or sensitivity training group). A small group of participants learns, with a facilitator, about its own group dynamics and interpersonal processes. Just as the forces at work in an individual's psychology can be plotted out in a force-field analysis, so the intangible values and attitudes that guide group behaviour, and possibly cause resistance, can be identified. By understanding how the group works, it can thus be strengthened and negative behaviours can be changed.

> **T-group (training group)** An activity which aims to get a group to understand and change its dynamics and attitudes.

## Organization development

### Theory in context: Kurt Lewin and attitude change

Nowadays, Kurt Lewin's work is associated with change in an organizational context; indeed, it is often presented as a set of tools by which management can exert power over an organization. In fact, very little of Lewin's work took place in organizations and, indeed, his political leanings were to the left and to Marxism, rather than towards capitalism and the quest for effective management (Cooke, 1999).

Lewin's background was in social change. As a Jewish refugee from the Nazi regime, his interests were in removing discrimination and promoting harmonious relations within society. His work in America was in attitude change with respect to relations between different ethnic groups. It was from this work that T-groups emerged, leading to his foundation of the National Training Laboratories (NTL), a behavioural science institute (Burnes, 2004).

Lewin died in 1947 shortly after the foundation of the NTL. The NTL continued to develop his theories, especially with respect to applying his ideas of social attitude change in organizational contexts.

Lewin's work on group dynamics in society was developed in the context of group dynamics in organizations—a key area of resistance to change and thus an area where management might intervene in change. The group level is the key to successful organizational change; indeed, the T-group is the forerunner of many of the group- and team-building activities commonplace in contemporary organizations, as discussed in Chapter 6.

Lewin's work laid the foundation for an all-encompassing approach to change known as **organization development** (OD). While it draws upon the behavioural science knowledge and techniques developed by Lewin, it is combined with other, potentially limitless techniques (see the list from Cummings and Worley earlier in this chapter) to address change at an organization-wide level:

> **Organization development** A wide-ranging set of change management techniques, including techniques which derive from behavioural and Gestalt psychology.

> Organization Development is an effort (1) planned, (2) organization-wide and (3) managed from the top to (4) increase organization effectiveness and health through (5) planned interventions in the organization's processes using behavioural science knowledge. (Beckhard, 1969: 9)

OD doesn't rule out the type of technostructural interventions addressed in the building-blocks approach, but blends them alongside more psychologically-informed techniques aimed at the aspects of the organization below the surface of the iceberg.

## Real life case: the police, institutional racism, and change

UK police forces have recently undergone large-scale, organization-wide attitude and cultural change in response to a problem identified as 'institutional racism'. The term was used in the Macpherson Report (1999), which investigated the handling of the murder of black teenager Stephen Lawrence in London in 1993 and a series of failures by the Metropolitan Police in bringing a prosecution. The report concluded that the police force was not explicitly racist, but institutional racism could be detected at the level of cultures and individual attitudes, defined as:

> The collective failure of an organisation to provide an appropriate and professional service to people because of colour, culture or ethnic origin. It can be seen or detected in processes, attitudes and behaviour which amount to discrimination through unwitting prejudice, ignorance, thoughtlessness and racist stereotyping. (Macpherson, 1999)

Overall, change-management initiatives within the police to counter institutional racism seemed to follow OD lines. On the one hand, there were structural interventions, such as basing the results of police exams on displaying the right attitudes, with failure for displaying discriminatory attitudes. On the other hand, group dynamics were seen as a key area of attention. It was not the case that all individuals were racist, but the prevailing culture at group level allowed racist attitudes to prevail. Police training thus includes diversity training in a situation similar to Lewin's T-groups. Such training highlights individuals' own language and attitudes, and also brings trainees into contact with members of other community groups so as to be aware of their cultures and attitudes (*National Police Training Magazine*, 2000, 2001).

The similarities to an OD approach, covering both organization-wide and group-level issues, are evidenced in a recent Association of Chief Police Officers (2010) document which outlines the main 'strategic themes' for police equality, diversity, and human rights strategy:

- Operational delivery: delivering services that are easy to access and that respond to and meet the needs of all communities

- People and culture: building a working environment that includes everyone and encourages all staff to develop and make progress

- Organizational processes: building equality into the organization's processes and how the service manages its performance

(Association of Chief Police Officers, 2010: 19)

10 years after the Macpherson Report, the success of change can be evidenced by 67 of the original 70 Macpherson recommendations having been implemented (House of Commons, 2009). There has been a shift in the culture of the police force since the Macpherson report in 1999, and diversity management is now seen as a critical aspect of managing the organization. Nevertheless, problems still exist, and incidents of racism are still reported (House of Commons, 2009). Furthermore, it remains the case that ethnic minorities are under-represented in police recruitment and over-represented in police stop-and-search statistics (Morris, 2015; Andrews, 2015). Over fifteen years since the MacPherson report, change in the police force is still an ongoing process.

Visit the Online Resource Centre for links to more case material on police force change, and also a wider discussion of links between change management and culture change.

The attitude and culture change brought about in the police force would seem to have been ideal for the concerns of Lewin, based, as they were, in race relations and social attitude change. However, the case also highlights one of the critiques of Lewin's work and the planned approach to change. Attitude change, such as that witnessed in the police force, does not happen overnight—attitudes and cultures take time to change, in some cases generations.

Do you think that the police force, described in the case above, has reached a point of 'refreezing'?

Thus a critique of the planned approach is that it is too long-term and slow-moving, a drawn-out process which requires consensus amongst groups (Burnes, 2004). In Chapter 4 we saw that the environment faced by contemporary organizations is one which is much more volatile and unpredictable. The idea, posited by the three-step model, that an organization can exist in static 'frozen' states is described by Kanter et al. (1992: 10) as a 'quaintly linear and static' notion, one which bears no relation to the complex and fast-moving nature of organizational life, where organizations need to be nimble and react quickly to change. Such an environment, where the organization is seen as if it were a river, is examined in the following section.

## Review questions

| | |
|---|---|
| **Describe** | What are the main features of the planned approach to change? |
| **Explain** | How does the planned approach to change address features of the organization 'below the surface'? |
| **Analyse** | How can an organization development approach help to bring about attitude and culture change? |
| **Apply** | How might the three-step model have been used to implement the change in the fitness centre at Junction Hotel? |

# The organization as a river: the emergent approach to change

## Running case: unintended consequences

A number of unintended and unpredicted consequences emerged as a result of the change, which had knock-on effects on the hotel and beyond.

- The information technology system at the fitness reception was unable to handle bookings for the freelance treatment providers and for the fitness classes. Eventually, this function was handed over to the main hotel reception, who were not happy with the additional work. Indeed, as bookings became more popular, it got in the way of checking in hotel guests, who started to complain about the waiting times.

- It became increasingly difficult to coordinate the times of freelance treatment providers, as they started to outnumber the two treatment rooms available. Some refused to use one of the rooms as the 'oldies' were still using it as their unofficial room for lunch breaks. As a result, Chance decided to block out three of the guests rooms and use them as treatment rooms—with a loss in revenue for the hotel.

- Reception staff were having to deal with irate fitness customers as the freelancers became unreliable, cancelling bookings at the last minute. Meg Mortimer became more and more exasperated with the situation, especially as when one member of staff went off ill with stress she then had to cover her work.

- The new health spa and showers were installed hurriedly. It turned out that they put a strain on the hotel boiler, which broke down on a number of occasions, meaning that there was no hot water for the hotel rooms. As well as bringing more complaints to the already overworked reception, it also meant that laundry had to be outsourced temporarily, at an extra cost.

- As memberships grew, so did the demand for hotel car park spaces. Residents complained (at reception again) about the lack of spaces. More concerned, however, were the local council, who received complaints from residents about overspill car parking on their streets.

Simon Chance had known there were problems and had had to play a mediating role between Meg Mortimer, who seemed to bear the brunt of things, and Carl Jones. Mortimer constantly plotted and briefed against Jones with other managers, but Chance wanted this project to work; he therefore supported Jones, and he eventually issued an informal warning to Mortimer that her job would be at risk if she didn't go along with the events. Chance had also had a meeting with the council's residential services division to deal with the parking issues.

If you were going white-water rafting on a river, of course you would plan ahead—working out your route and making sure you had the appropriate safety equipment, etc. But the precise, step-by-step details of the journey are impossible to plan—part of the skill of rafting is reacting *on the spot* to the twists and turns of the water beneath you. No two journeys will be the same; the ever-moving and ever-changing nature of the river is unpredictable:

> You cannot step twice into the same river, for other waters are continually flowing on . . . Everything flows and nothing abides; everything gives way and nothing stays fixed.
>
> (Heraclitus, *c*.500 BC, quoted in Morgan, 2006: 241)

The river metaphor suggests something which is in constant *flow*, never the same from one moment to the next. As such, it emphasizes the dynamic, complex, and ever-changing nature of organization, with *change as the constant natural state of the organization*. The organization is not a stable entity that is occasionally 'moved around' by management, as with the planned approach—the organization never stays still long enough to be 'unfrozen' and 'frozen'. This gives a radically different view of the nature of the organization from that of the building blocks or the iceberg.

- An organization never stays still for long enough to be described as a *structure*, such as an iceberg or a set of building blocks. Complex, hidden depths exist, but their dynamic nature makes them difficult to even begin to grasp.

The organization as a river.

- It is never possible to have complete *knowledge* of every aspect of the organization to use as a basis for planning owing to the continually-changing nature of the organization—it is always beyond our grasp.

- Without complete knowledge of the organization, *power* is much more difficult for management to exert. Power is not top-down and in the hands of management, but exists within the movement of the organization itself. You may be in charge of the raft, but you are very much controlled by the movement of the river beneath it.

- Wherever management tries to exert power over an organization it will always meet with natural *resistance*, just as trying to exert power over the course of a river by setting up a dam, for example, will always meet with resistance from the flow of the water. The resistance within the river is always there as a challenge to those who seek to exert power over it.

## The emergent approach to change

The metaphor of the river suggests a complex and messy situation for management to deal with, one that is both fast-flowing and with complex murky depths—potentially beyond management knowledge and power. Change is not a discrete period of upheaval planned in advance to take an organization from point A to B; instead, change is the norm and is always present. With the emergent approach, change is managed in a much more ad hoc fashion, reacting to events as and when they occur. Change is what *emerges* along with the flow of the river.

The emergent approach to change is not one specific approach to change, but a number of approaches which recognize the complex and interconnected nature of organizations. Two particular approaches are the processual approach and the systemic approach.

# The processual approach to change—political consequences

The **processual approach to change** paints change as an 'untidy cocktail' (Burnes, 2004: 989) of individual perceptions and political struggles. This reflects change as a political process. It also emphasizes that there may be no single, individual cause of change and that in the change process there is an interconnectedness and inter-relatedness of individuals, groups, organizations, and society.

Earlier in the chapter we discussed how change causes anxiety and upset. The planned approach would see this as elements of resistance 'beneath the iceberg' to be overcome by psychological means. In a processual approach, human and social elements, such as fear, anxiety, and the power of different groups and subcultures within the organization, become the basis for political battles—rather than being overcome there is active resistance to change (see Chapter 13 for more on these political aspects of the organization).

> Processual approach to change  An approach to change which emphasizes the messy and political nature of change.

# The systemic approach to change—knock-on effects

The processual approach recognizes the interconnectedness of different aspects of an organization. A similar approach comes from an understanding of an organization as a system (**systemic approach to change**), defined by Evered (1980) as 'a set of different parts which combine and work together as an organized whole'.

The different parts are interdependent—if one part of the system breaks down then it can affect the functioning of the system as a whole. Think, for example, of a car. It is a system in that different parts and components function together as a whole. If one of the components fails, the interdependency of the parts of the system means that the system as a whole—the car—can stop functioning.

The organization can be seen as a system—it has a number of different parts (people, technology, departments, etc.) which are interdependent and which function together as a whole. A change in one part of the organization may have knock-on effects in other parts of the system.

A simple example of this systemic interdependence can be seen within a rail network. You may well have been standing on a station platform and heard that your service is late because of a signal failure elsewhere in the country. A rail network is a system with a number of inter-related parts—tracks, points, signals, trains, and drivers—all elements that work together to make the rail network function. Rather than being a problem in isolation, the broken signal causes trains to block the track, affecting any services behind them. These knock-on effects can carry on down the line—the effects can be felt throughout the network (Meek, 2001).

> Systemic approach to change  An approach to change which recognizes the organization as an interconnected system whereby change in one area can have consequences and knock-on effects in other areas.

# Changing a system

If we see the organization as an interconnected system, it follows that making a change will have knock-on effects and consequences, but to what extent can such consequences be managed? The emergent approach would suggest that, rather than managers being in control of the consequences of a change, such consequences are unpredictable and uncontrollable, as if the managers were being carried along by the flow of the river.

## The watchmaker and the surgeon

Collins (1998: 148) highlights the degree to which we can change one part of a system without affecting its overall functioning. We can consider whether the organizational change manager is more like a 'watchmaker' or a 'surgeon'—whether change is a simple mechanical job, or whether the systemic interdependencies make it a much more complex and emergent phenomenon.

- The watchmaker can identify a component which is not working and simply replace it—the system will then begin working again. There is no problem in shutting down the system for a while, making some changes and then restarting it.

- For the surgeon, however, this luxury is not available. Say a heart needs replacing—it's not possible to shut down the body temporarily to do this. The interdependencies it has with the rest of the system means that it must maintain its action for the rest of the system to survive. The knock-on effects of changing one part of the system have to be considered. Therefore, the surgeon has to make arrangements to ensure that the heart's role within the system (i.e. circulating blood) is somehow maintained while attending to that one component.

While organizational change managers are not surgeons, they have to think about the effects that making a change might have. To return to the rail example, there are often planned engineering works on railways. Unlike a watch, the railway system cannot simply be shut down. The railway manager has to maintain a flow of passengers by providing, for example, alternative bus services or timetabling alternative rail routes.

Imagine if your university library building closed for six months for refurbishment. What effects would it have on the rest of the university and how might the university deal with those effects to keep the university running?

Visit the Online Resource Centre for further discussion on this topic.

## Open and closed systems

A further distinction in the nature of a system is between an open and a closed system (Jackson and Carter, 2007: 211).

- A closed system has a distinct boundary around it and operates fully within it—there is no movement across the boundary.
- An open system interacts with its environment—there is movement across the boundary.

As we have seen, and as common sense might suggest, organizations are open systems. They are affected by activity from their environment (think of the PEST model earlier in this chapter and in Chapter 4). In the opposite direction, organizations can affect their own environment. Think of the effects of pollution or an organization creating extra traffic on the streets around it and thus causing those streets to be congested. Many people are affected by, and have an interest in, the activities of particular organizations.

The **Gaia hypothesis** (see Jackson and Carter, 2007: 214) or a 'systems view of the world' (Capra, 1992) sees *all aspects of the world* being potentially interconnected. The nature of organizations as both dynamic and open systems means that the 'ripples and knock-on effects' (Collins, 1998: 149) or 'waves of consequences' (Darwin et al., 2002: 177) of any change or intervention within the system have to be considered. The interdependencies of parts of a system, both inside and out, mean that the consequences of a particular change could, potentially, be limitless. Thus, in Chapter 17, the concept of corporate social responsibility suggests that organizations have a responsibility for the effects of their actions on the world around them—if their activities cause harm to the environment, for example.

> **Gaia hypothesis** A theory popular in environmental movements where the whole world is seen as an interconnected system.

## Chaos and complexity theory—the butterfly effect

The idea of knock-on effects and consequences is mirrored in studies of scientific and natural systems. **Chaos theory** emphasizes the unpredictable and interconnected nature of many scientific systems. Small changes in a natural system can have unpredictable knock-on effects of a disproportionate magnitude.

Lorenz (1972) noted this with his famous question: 'Does the flap of a butterfly's wings in Brazil set off a tornado in Texas?' A minute change in the natural ecosystem—the air disturbances of a butterfly's wings—has the potential to set up a series of knock-on effects such that it might actually alter weather patterns. Lorenz's **butterfly effect** is perhaps one of the best-known aspects of chaos theory.

> **Chaos theory** A branch of science which sees natural systems as both ordered and, at the same time, unpredictable.
>
> **The butterfly effect** The suggestion in chaos theory that a small action can have unpredictable knock-on effects of a greater magnitude.

### Theory in context: the 'butterfly effect'

Many films use the idea of the butterfly effect as the basis for their plot: i.e. how would things be different now had a small change happened in the past?

- In *Back to the Future* (Zemeckis, 1985), the lead character must ensure that his parents meet in the past, otherwise he will cease to exist in the present day.

- *Sliding Doors* (Howitt, 1998) outlines two very different sets of events that emerge from the simple act of either getting on the tube or taking a taxi.

- In a film that uses Lorenz's terminology, *The Butterfly Effect* (Bress and Gruber, 2004), the lead character played by Ashton Kutcher goes back in time several times to try to change past events for the better. Small changes in the past are found to have amplified into major consequences in the present day, with the character finding himself a prisoner, a college student, and an amputee as a result of small actions he has changed.

> **Complexity theory** The application of chaos theory to social systems, such as organizations, suggesting that small changes can have unpredictable and potentially limitless consequences.

**Complexity theory** has extended the ideas of chaos theory beyond purely scientific systems into systems in general. The recent financial crisis, as examined in Chapter 15 on globalization, is an example of such interconnectedness where a change in one small area—the collapse of one bank—had knock-on effects that led to the near-collapse of the world's financial systems. In a similar manner, complexity theory would suggest that, in that an organization is a system, small changes in one area of an organization can have disproportionate effects.

---

**Real life case:** 'Sachsgate'

In October 2008, UK news was dominated by a seemingly trivial affair—a prank call made on a late-night BBC radio show by presenters Jonathan Ross and Russell Brand. During the call, a series of insulting messages were left on the voicemail of *Fawlty Towers* actor Andrew Sachs.

The original broadcast attracted little attention, but was picked up in the press a few days later, eventually developing into a storm of complaints and further media coverage that eventually claimed the jobs of Ross and Brand and of the head of BBC Radio 2, Lesley Douglas. Further down the line, comedians now complain that, as a result of compliance regulations brought in since the scandal, their acts are suffering from restrictive regulations in terms of what they can and cannot say.

The original broadcast had not been live and had been referred to Douglas for clearance before transmission. She had not heard the broadcast. Trusting the advice of other staff, she sanctioned the broadcast with a single word, 'Yes', sent from her mobile phone.

**Sources:** Gibson et al. (2008); Holmwood (2008); *The Guardian* (2008); Holmwood (2009);  Lawson (2009).

---

 If Douglas's text message had said 'No', how different would the consequences be today?

An implication of chaos theory is that long-term predictions in systems are impossible to make (Tsoukas, 1998). Take a system like the weather. We know that weather forecasting is not a precise science. Meteorologists can model the system and have a good stab at predicting the weather for the next few days, but, beyond that, the system is so complex and open to any number of knock-on effects and changes that prediction is impossible, and, indeed, very few forecasters now provide long-range forecasts.

In Stacey's (1992) terms, it is not that the future is *unknown*, it is the fact that the future is inherently *unknowable*. There are no equations or models that can tell us precisely what the long-term weather will be—it is something that will emerge in the future.

Stacey suggests that the idea of the future being 'unknowable' applies to organizations. As such, this emergent approach to change dismisses the idea that change is a 'planned' activity where the change manager can work towards a particular desired outcome—the consequences of a change intervention are yet to emerge when action is taken. Rather than being planned, change is unpredictable—its knock-on effects and ultimate outcomes are unknowable.

## Managing with emergence

Using the river metaphor, we see the organization as an emergent phenomenon. This presents a picture of knock-on effects of action which become uncontrollable and unplannable, and a murky world of political processes and power struggles lie within this. To plan change precisely becomes impossible, just as it is impossible to predict the weather beyond the very short term.

Does this mean that we can do without management and leadership if they are so evidently powerless to control change? For Jenner (1994), managers still have a role in guiding the system; rather than managing change, managers are, in effect, managing *with* change—they are carried along by the flow of the river as much as the rest of the organization.

One value of the emergent approach is simply for management to appreciate the systemic nature of an organization (Stacey, 1992) and the fact that a change will have knock-on effects—an appreciation beyond the simplistic view of change that is arranging a set of building blocks.

Furthermore, the emergent approach suggests ways in which management can create opportunities for creativity and innovation among their workforce. Rather than the river being something to be feared and coped with, it is something to be embraced for the potential that it offers.

## Real life case: the Googleplex

Google is a massive multinational organization which also relies on technological innovation. Its headquarters in California, the Googleplex, and similar buildings worldwide, resemble playgrounds in many respects. There are slides linking floors, table football and similar games on offer, and free food in the various canteens around the building. Rules about such things as set office hours are relaxed (imagine how Frederick Taylor, in Chapter 3, with his time and motion study would react to this!). Fixed work spaces, such as offices, are rare. Workers have laptops and are encouraged to roam the building, having impromptu, chance meetings and conversations with co-workers.

**Sources:** *Time Magazine* (2006); Google (2009); *National Geographic* (2012); Waber et al. (2014).

The Googleplex creates an environment almost like a river, with workers free to roam the building as they please. In a creative and innovative industry we can see how this might benefit Google. Rather than being stuck in offices behind walls and divided from other workers, the staff can meet and share ideas—even random connections and meetings can occur. In Chapter 10 we saw how learning organizations have an interest in sharing knowledge across the organization so as to promote innovation and the development of new products. The post-bureaucratic (see Chapter 4), river-like form of organization at Google is designed to allow more space and more opportunity for knowledge and new ideas to emerge from chance meetings (Waber et al., 2014), rather than being planned from above.

Visit the Online Resource Centre for other examples of companies that use such emergent approaches to promote innovation.

The emergent approach is one which seemingly makes management over an organization a more difficult task to achieve; however, it brings with it opportunities for more creative and innovative approaches to management and organization.

## Employability skills: emergent careers and transferable skills

The distinction between planning and emergence is one that is reflected in the nature of contemporary careers. Van Buren (2003) suggests that a 'boundaryless career' is becoming the norm for many workers. Where previously it was possible to plan for a career path within one organization, now many workers move from one job to another on short-term contracts.

> For Van Buren, employability is a key issue in such a boundaryless career. A CV needs to demonstrate transferable skills—skills which might have been gained in one job, but which can transfer from one organization to another. An important part of writing a CV is to show how skills and experience gained in one organizational setting are transferable and of value to the organization to which you are applying for a job.
>
> Transferable skills can also enhance employability when applying for your first job. Think about things you do at university and whether they demonstrate skills that would be of value to an employer. Playing in a sports team may demonstrate teamwork. Being the treasurer of that sports team is evidence of managing a budget.
>
> Often, your careers service will be able to help you in teasing out such transferable skills to place on your CV.

## Review questions

| | |
|---|---|
| **Describe** | What are the main features of the emergent approach to change? |
| **Explain** | What does it mean to take a systemic view of an organization? |
| **Analyse** | How can the butterfly effect be used to analyse the ways in which small changes in an organization lead to unpredictable consequences? |
| **Apply** | Would the form of organization at the Googleplex be suitable for all organizations? Would it work in a fast-food restaurant, for example? |

# Chapter summary

**Running case:** denouement

Back in the present day, Meg Mortimer returns to the boardroom where the party is in full swing and Carl Jones is the man of the moment. He is being fêted as a great manager and implementer of change. 'Easy to say once it's all been done and dusted,' thinks Meg, 'but if it weren't for me coping with the fall-out it would never have happened.'

Meanwhile, the five 'oldies' have moved away from defacing the picture of Carl Jones. They are in a pub, meeting a representative of an upmarket residential development with gym facilities. They sign on the dotted line to go into partnership to run the facilities themselves as a gym and personal-training business. They too raise their glasses to toast change—and the change they are looking forward to most is going into work the next day to hand in their notices to Carl Jones.

Knowing the full story, how well do you think Carl Jones managed change at the fitness centre? Do you think the change can be described as the naïve, planned, or emergent approach (or any combination thereof?)

Once the upheaval of a period of change is out of the way and a change has been achieved, it can often be presented as having been successful. This, however, might mask a lot of upset, resistance, and unintended consequences that have happened along the way.

In this chapter we have seen how change can be a messy process. What might seem like perfectly rational triggers to change from one perspective may cause fear and anxiety from another, leading to resistance to that change.

We have seen that a naïve view of change would ignore this resistance, seeing the organization simply as a set of building blocks that can be rearranged at will. A planned approach to change recognizes this resistance as existing in the 'hidden depths' of the organization, beneath its surface, and would use techniques based in psychology to overcome that resistance. An emergent approach—the organization as a river—views resistance as part and parcel of the dynamic, interconnected, and political nature of the organization, part of the course of events that managers have to deal with.

While it is argued that the emergent approach is more in tune with the dynamic, changeable nature of our contemporary world, all three approaches contribute to our understanding of the nature of change. The planned approach, for example, is suited to changing deeply-held attitudes and cultures, as found in the police force, and even a building-blocks approach might be appropriate when quick and drastic action is required. All three approaches uncover, and make us aware of, different characteristics of the organization which are important when engaging in change.

## Further reading

**Burnes, B. 2004. Kurt Lewin and complexity theories: Back to the future?** *Journal of Change Management* 4(4): 309–25.
An introduction to the work of Lewin, which is then related to complexity approaches.

**Cummings, T.G., and Worley, C.G. 2009.** *Organization development and change.* **South-Western/Cengage Learning, Mason, OH.**
A practical overview of a wide range of change management techniques and interventions.

**Grugulis, I. , and Wilkinson, A. 2002. Managing culture at British Airways: Hype, hope and reality.** *Long Range Planning* 35(2):179–94.
A critical study of change over time at British Airways.

**Senior, B., and Swailes, S. 2010.** *Organizational change.* **Pearson Education: Harlow.**
An accessible introduction and overview of the wide field of change management.

## References

Andrews, K. 2015. Black Britons face a double whammy—failed race relations law, now budget cuts. *The Guardian*, 28 July.

Association of Chief Police Officers (ACPO) 2010. *Equality, diversity and human rights strategy for the police service.* ACPO, ISBN: 978-1-84987-031-3.

Beckhard, R. 1969. *Organization development: Strategies and models.* Addison-Wesley: Reading, MA.

Bress, E., and Gruber, J. 2004. *The butterfly effect.* Katalyst Films.

Burnes, B. 2004. Kurt Lewin and the planned approach to change: A re-appraisal. *Journal of Management Studies* 41(6): 977–1002.

Capra, F. 1992. A systems view of the world. *Resurgence Magazine* 151: 34–37.

Collins, D. 1998. *Organizational change: Sociological perspectives.* Routledge: London.

Cooke, B. 1999. Writing the left out of management theory: The historiography of the management of change. *Organization* 6(1): 81–105.

Cummings, T.G., and Worley, C.G. 2009. *Organization development and change.* South-Western/Cengage Learning: Mason, OH.

Darwin, J., Johnson, P., and McAuley, J. 2002. *Developing strategies for change.* Financial Times/Prentice Hall: Harlow.

Drafke, M.W. 2009. *The human side of organizations*. Pearson/Prentice Hall: Upper Saddle River, NJ.

Evered, R. 1980. Consequences of and prospects for systems thinking in organizational change. In:Cummings, T.G. (ed.) *Systems theory for organization development*. John Wiley and Sons: New York, pp. 5–13.

Gibson, J., Gibson, O., and Conlan, T. 2008. Puerile prank that left BBC stars and executives on the ropes. *The Guardian*, 30 October.

Goodstein, L.D., and Warner Burke, W. 1991. Creating successful organization change. *Organizational Dynamics* 19(4): 5–17.

Google 2009. Life at the Googleplex. Available at: http://www.youtube.com/watch?v=eFeLKXbnxxg (last accessed 24 August 2015).

Hognestad, H. 2012. Split loyalties: Football is a community business. *Soccer and Society* 13 (3): 377–91.

Holmwood, L. 2008. Countdown to a PR calamity: How the BBC bungled its way into 'Sachsgate'. *The Guardian*, 21 November.

Holmwood, L. 2009. Chris Moyles criticises 'weird state' BBC is in following Sachsgate. *The Guardian*, 14 July.

House of Commons 2009. *The Macpherson report: Ten years on*. Her Majesty's Stationery Office: London. Available at: http://www.publications.parliament.,uk/pa/cm200809/cmselect/cmhaff/427/427.pdf.

Howitt, P. 1998. *Sliding doors*. Paramount.

Hutchins, B., Rowe, D., and Ruddock, A. 2009. 'It's fantasy football made real': Networked media sport, the Internet, and the hybrid reality of MyFootballClub. *Sociology of Sport Journal* 26: 89–106.

Jackson, N., and Carter, P. 2007. *Rethinking organisational behaviour*. Financial Times/Prentice Hall: Harlow.

Jenner, R. 1994. Changing patterns of power: Chaotic dynamics and the emergence of a post-modern organizational paradigm. *Journal of Organizational Change Management* 7(3): 8–21.

Kanter, R.M., Stein, B., and Jick, T. 1992. *The challenge of organizational change: How companies experience it and leaders guide it*. Free Press: New York.

King, D. 2001. *Devils and Nazis: Representations of change through postmodern research*. British Academy of Management, University of Edinburgh: Edinburgh.

Lawson, M. 2009. Is censorship taking over the BBC? *The Guardian*, 18 November. Available at: http://www.guardian.co.uk/tv-and-radio/2009/nov/18/bbc-trust-censorship.

Lewin, K. 1943. Defining the 'field at a given time'. *Psychological Review* 50(3): 292.

Lewin, K. 1947. Frontiers in group dynamics. *Human Relations* 1(2): 143–53.

Lorenz, E. 1972. *Does the flap of a butterfly's wings in Brazil set off a tornado in Texas?* Speech before the American Academy for the Advancement of Science, December, 1972.

Macpherson, W. 1999. *The Stephen Lawrence Inquiry: Report of an inquiry*. The Stationery Office: London.

Meek, J. 2001. 'Things fall apart'. *The Guardian*, 1 March.

Morgan, G. 2006. *Images of organization*. Sage Publications: Thousand Oaks, CA.

Morris, N. 2015. Black people still far more likely to be stopped and searched by police than other ethnic groups. *The Independent*, 6 August.

Mumford, S. 2004. Allegiance and identity. *Journal of the Philosophy of Sport* 31: 184–95.

Nakrani, S. 2011. AFC Wimbledon celebrate 'phenomenal' rise to League Two. *The Guardian*, 22 May.

*National Geographic* 2012. Inside Google. Available at: https://www.youtube.com/watch?v=eC_DvRd-NMs (last accessed 28 November 2012).

*National Police Training Magazine* 2000. On your marks—watch your language, July.

*National Police Training Magazine* 2001. Temple is thanked, August.

Senior, B., and Fleming, J.D 2006. *Organizational change*, 3rd edn. Pearson Education: Harlow.

Senior, B., and Swailes, S. 2010. *Organizational change*, 4th edn. Pearson Education: Harlow.

Stacey, R.D. 1992. *Managing chaos: Dynamic business strategies in an unpredictable world*. Kogan Page: London.

*The Guardian* 2004. Wimbledon become MK Dons FC, 21 June.

*The Guardian* 2008. Sachsgate emails. 'I would say take it out but it . . . is VERY funny', 21 November.

*Time Magazine* 2006. Life in the Googleplex. Available at: http://www.time.com/time/photogallery/0,29307,1947844,00.html (last accessed 28 November 2012).

Tsoukas, H. 1998. Introduction: Chaos, complexity and organization theory. *Organization* 5(3): 291–313.

Tynan, G. 2012. FA Cup: MK Dons book grudge tie against AFC Wimbledon. *The Independent*, 14 November.

Van Buren, H.J., III, 2003. Boundaryless careers and employability obligations. *Business Ethics Quarterly* 13(2): 131–49.

Waber, B., Magnolfi, J., and Lindsay, G. 2014. Workspaces that move people. *Harvard Business Review* 92(10): 68–77.

White, J. 2003. Pitch battle. *The Guardian*, 11 January.

Wimbledon Independent Supporters' Association 2012. WISA—A brief history. Available at: http://www.wisa.org.uk/history/index.html (last accessed 28 November 2012).

Zemeckis, R. 1985. *Back to the future*. Universal.

# 12

# Leadership

*Life at the top*

## Chapter overview and learning outcomes

By the end of this chapter you should be able to:

- describe the key leadership theories
- explain why contingency theory argues that there is no best leadership style
- explain the differences between leadership and management
- analyse whether there is too much emphasis on the individual leader
- explain the key principles of distributive leadership.

## Key theorists

| | |
|---|---|
| Fred Fielder | One of the founders of contingency theory, he developed the Least Preferred Co-worker model, which assesses an individual's leadership style |
| Paul Hersey and Ken Blanchard | Key writers who developed situational leadership—a perspective which argues that the appropriate leadership style depends on the situation |
| James Meindl | A key critic of the heroic leadership perspective, Meindl argues that there is a romanticism of leadership |
| Rosabeth Moss Kanter | A Harvard Business School professor who specializes in leadership for change; has written widely and is considered to be a highly influential writer |

## Key terms

| | |
|---|---|
| Behaviourism | Drawn from psychology, behaviourism is the study of human behaviour |
| Contingency theory | States that the type of leadership style adopted is dependent (contingent) on the situation |
| Trait | A characteristic of the person, often considered the behaviour, thoughts, and emotions that the person exhibits considered stable over time |
| Post-heroic | A perspective which argues that we need to move beyond seeing the leader as hero |
| Followership | A theoretical perspective which stresses the importance of followers |
| Glass ceiling | A barrier that a particular group (e.g. women) cannot move beyond |

# Introduction

**Running case:** Simon Chance prepares for the day

Sitting in his office Chance gathers together his notes for the day. It's Wednesday and he is due to lead the staff meeting. As Chief Executive Officer (CEO) of the Second-Chance Consortium he feels that it is important—indeed his duty—to give a clear sense of direction to his followers and therefore likes to take the weekly meeting at least once a month. After the meeting he has a one-to-one session with Linda Wilkinson and then Graham Effingham—two interesting and different characters. He is then hosting a small lunch for the local chamber of commerce before spending the afternoon preparing for a big evening meal with potential investors. He looks at his bookshelf, which includes the biographies of Nelson Mandela, Winston Churchill, and Gandhi. 'I wonder what they would do with Junction Hotel?' Chance thinks to himself.

## Leaders as heroes and villains

Who do you admire as a great leader? Popular answers often include Gandhi, Martin Luther King, Julius Caesar, Winston Churchill, Nelson Mandela, Mother Teresa, and John F. Kennedy. They are regularly presented as visionaries: courageous, heroic, and principled individuals who lead their people to better futures; extraordinary people that do extraordinary things.

In the business world, leaders are also presented as having extraordinary powers. Howard Schultz is widely credited with reinvigorating Starbucks by refocusing the company on its core values (Groth, 2011; BBC, 2011). Anne Mulcahy is credited with turning round the struggling Xerox, making it profitable through increasing efficiency. Jim Sinegal is praised with inspiring Costco to continued success due to his down-to-earth manner (his name badge simply says 'Jim') and restricted earnings ($350,000 per annum), result in his followers loving him (Goldberg and Ritter, 2006). Mark Zuckerberg has become the 'poster boy' for social media. His role in founding and leading Facebook has won him plaudits around the world. Finally, Steve Jobs, the co-founder and CEO of Apple, was widely praised not only for being the inventor of the iPhone, iPod, and iMac, but for rescuing Apple from near bankruptcy in 1997 and taking it on to become the world's most valuable company by 2011. The announcement of his death in October 2011 was greeted by an outpouring of grief worldwide. Customers and employees laid flowers, tributes, and part eaten apples outside their stores, and tweeted and updated their Facebook statuses with details of their affection for the former Apple CEO. Jobs's importance was underscored by the drop in share price of 5% when his death was announced (Kollewe, 2011), although, under new CEO Tim Cook, Apple continue to go from strength to strength.

Yet leaders can also be the villain. Reverend Paul Flowers, the former chairman of Co-operative Bank, oversaw a disastrous merger with the Britannia which led to the bank facing significant financial trouble. He then appeared out of his depth when facing questions in a government select committee, saying he thought the bank had assets of around £3 billion when the true total was around ten times that; the committee chairman accused Flowers of not knowing 'very basic' figures about the bank. He then was caught on camera buying drugs (Harris, 2014).

In October 2010, Tony Haywood resigned from his position as CEO of British Petroleum (BP) facing continued criticism in the US press and by the US president for his handling of the Deepwater Horizon oil spill. It was not only the scale of the disaster (which some claim will cost BP approximately $90 billion), or numerous failed attempts to block the leak, but also his handling of the media, encapsulated in the widely quoted comment: 'There's no one who wants this thing over more than I do, I'd like my life back' (*The Guardian*, 2010; Durando, 2010). Haywood was seen as out of touch and not sympathetic to the lives of those the oil spill had affected.

Guido Barilla, CEO of Italian Pasta firm Barilla, sparked a social media storm and boycotts by gay rights activists after saying that he would only portray a 'classic family' in adverts for his products (Davies, 2013).

Mikael Hed, CEO and cofounder of the Finnish company Rovio, the creator of Angry Birds, left the company after profits halved and Angry Birds dropped out of the top 100 free downloaded apps, with insiders claiming 'He was in way over his head' (Adams, 2014).

In June 2015, just days after being comfortably elected FIFA Chairman for the fifth time, Sepp Blatter resigned amid accusations of bribery within FIFA and questions over his leadership.

## Real life case: the rise and fall of Twitter's CEO

Leaders can be celebrated as heroes and villains, as the story of former CEO of Twitter reveals.

In 2013, *Business Insider* hailed Dick Costolo, the CEO of Internet giant Twitter, as one of the most impressive CEOs in Silicon Valley (Shontell, 2013), and he had been number 78 in Time magazine's top 100 most influential people in the world (*Time Magazine*, 2011). Yet by the end of 2014, analysts and investors were calling for his resignation. How did Costolo go from being the darling of Wall Street to being seen as a failure?

Costolo was seen as a success largely because of his role in the public floatation of Twitter in 2010. At the time Twitter was heralded as offering a new way of doing business. While it had yet to make money, the speed of Twitter's growth in users was seen as vital for long-term dominance of the industry. Costolo won praises in the media for the way he ran Twitter. He had numerous articles written about him, his personal style, and even how being a professional comedian helped him in being a better leader (Manjoo, 2015). Hs management practices were presented as innovative. In an article praising his leadership style, Costolo was described as holding 12–15 engaging, inspiring meetings a day. They were unusual because everyone stood, they were open, and he did not allow PowerPoint. Costolo was also praised for focusing on the big picture, arguing it was a better use of his time. He even trained new managers with a six-hour management course as part of their induction (Bercovici, 2015).

Yet while being lauded as a great leader he was also heavily, and publicly, criticized. American business news channel CNBC's Jim Cramer stated Costolo's conference call with analysts was 'incoherent,' and Robert Peck, an analyst for American bank SunTrust, is cited predicting 'Costolo probably wouldn't last another year' (Sun, 2015). Why? One issue is the limited growth in user numbers. In 2013 Costolo claimed Twitter would have 400 million users, whereas at the time of writing its website says it has 302 million active monthly users (Twitter, 2015). Secondly, technological issues including the new iOS 8 meant that many users were inactive. Thirdly, analysts argued that the way Twitter presents information to its users using the timeline makes it inefficient to discover new material. Fourthly, users were leaving because of abuse and trolls. Finally, there were also problems within the boardroom. Top executives including the vice president (VP) of product, the creative director, the chief operating officer, the head of news, the senior VP, and many other senior executives have recently left. Most troubling for investors is that since being listed as a public company, Twitter has failed to make a profit. Costolo has taken responsibility for what has happened at Twitter, stating that many of the problems were 'nobody's fault but mine' (Thielman, 2015), and resigned from Twitter in June 2015 without any pay-off.

Costolo's story illustrates how business leaders can, in a short time-frame, move from being hero to villain, widely praised leader to outcast. Whatever you think of Costolo, it is clear from the media coverage that we are fascinated with business leaders.

Do you think Dick Costolo become a 'bad leader' between 2013 and 2015? Why do you think the media placed so much emphasis on Dick Costolo in examining Twitter's difficulties?

## The importance of leadership

What makes a great leader and how can you become one? Leadership is one of the most popular topics in the business press, in airport lounge bookshops, and within academia. There are numerous books on the lives of great leaders and advice on how to develop your leadership skills. Since the 1990s within academia, an average of 10 articles focusing on leadership have been published daily (Grint 2000). As we will see in this chapter, many leadership theorists have created models trying to capture the essence of what makes great leaders or effective leadership behaviour. This is used in understanding leadership, organizational effectiveness and strategy, and leadership development. If you apply for a graduate scheme, you may come across these theories as your organization seeks to train you as a future leader. Yet, as we will also see in this chapter, there are those who think there is an over-emphasis on the importance of leaders and are calling for more distributive or democratic forms of organizing. These debates are set to continue and shape the future for our organizations.

## Beyond the popular image of leadership: an overview

**Behavioural theory** A psychological perspective which seeks to understand and change the behaviour of individuals.

**Situational leadership** A theory which stresses the importance of adapting the leadership style to meet the situation.

Thus business leaders are regularly presented as heroes or villains. The business press focuses heavily on the 'man at the top' (and often it is a man), as though they, virtually single-handedly, are the difference between a company's success and its failure. For instance, the debate over Stephen Hester's bonus (see Chapter 17) was conducted through the lens that *he* alone is responsible for transforming RBS (and therefore should receive his bonus depending on RBS's success or failure). Faith, it seems, is directed firmly at the leader as the one who can transform the organization.

This has led to substantial interest in investigating the background, leadership style, and personality traits of these *individual great leaders* to understand what makes them excel. Yet, while the individual leader is important, as Stephen Hester states in our interview, leaders need to be humble about how much they personally can achieve. Indeed, as is clear in his interview, in large organizations a leader can only succeed through impacting many other people—Hester states he spends a third of his time with staff. We therefore need to broaden our focus to how leaders can impact their staff, which leads us to **behavioural theory**.

Visit the Online Resource Centre to read the full interview with Stephen Hester.

Not all leaders can be effective in all situations. Winston Churchill, so highly praised for leading Britain through World War II, was not seen to be appropriate in peacetime and did not get re-elected. **Situational leadership** therefore draws attention to the importance of the context for the type of leadership approach used.

Leadership, though, is seen as not just choosing the right style but also transforming the organization. **Transformational leadership** therefore provides the image that leadership involves more than doing deals: it can inspire followers and offer a vision of a better future.

This view, though, still provides the heroic vision of the leader, one which **post-heroic** leadership theory seeks to challenge. These views argue that there is too much emphasis on a single individual at the top and draw our attention to the process of leading that occurs throughout the organization. Some of these theories, such as Greenleaf's servant leadership, argue for a more bottom-up rather than top-down leadership style. **Social identity theory**, discussed later, also sees the leader less as standing at the front and more as helping the group to form a collective identity (for a review see Haslam et al., 2011).

More recently, theories such as **transformative theory, followership theory**, and **servant leadership theory** have focused on the *impact* the leader has on their *followers*. They all see that in order to get things done leaders have to build alliances, persuade or encourage, or use coercive tactics in order to get their way. In traditional theories, leadership has been about visionary leaders, inspiring others through force of personality or political might in order to get things done. More recent theories have begun to see leadership as more of a *social practice* of bringing others in the organizations with the leader. Rather than the individualized, heroic model, these theories look to the social processes involved in leading, emphasizing the collaborative nature of leadership and the importance of social relations. However, despite these theoretical moves, much of leadership practice and popular media portrayals retain the **command and control** approach, where the leader sets the direction of the organization and determines how things are done, and the employees are followers.

Finally, we will turn our attention to **alternative models of organization** which emphasizes alternative modes of decision making which can occur without a leader. While not that common, these approaches offer possibilities to increase engagement, participation, and ideas from throughout the organization.

## Employability skills: developing your leadership skills—insights from prominent business leaders

Stephen Hester, CEO of RSA Insurance Group and former CEO of the Royal Bank of Scotland, states that he worked on developing his skills over the course of his career. In his interview exclusive for this book be states that he realized early in his career that his 'strongest skills were analytical skills and communication skills, my weaker skills were dealing nicely with people or managing people well. And I got a long way with just analytical and communication skills, but I did not get as far as I wanted to get. So, I needed to spend a point in the middle bit of my career working really hard to improve my ability to manage people.' So how did he go about this? 'Concentrating on it, thinking about it; I actually took on an external coach for a couple of years to help work with me on those things, getting feedback from other people, the same way anyone would learn about anything.'

Joe Greenwell, the former Chairman of Ford in Britain, echoes many of these sentiments, stating you need the capacity to 'learn all

Stephen Hester, former CEO of the Royal Bank of Scotland
**Source:** Oli Scarff/Getty Images.

---

**Transformational leadership** A leadership which stresses the leader's ability to transform the organization by offering a better vision for the future.

**Post-heroic** A collection of theories that argue that traditional leadership over-emphasizes the importance of leaders and under-emphasizes followers.

**Social identity theory** Drawing from psychological theory, how an individual's identity is derived from being part of a group.

**Followership theory** Stresses the importance of followers and seeks to emphasize their importance in theory and practice.

**Servant leadership theory** A bottom-up perspective which sees the leader being the most effective when they support followers to enable them to do their jobs.

**Command and control** A top-down leadership style that emphasizes the importance of the leader who tells others what to do.

**Alternative models of organization** Workers' cooperatives and mutual organizations which seek for non-hierarchical modes of organizing and not-for-profit objectivities, often to bring about benefits to the members and society.

the time', to use data well, and to understand the marketplace and the customer. Fundamentally, you need to have energy and enthusiasm, a passion for what you do, an acute awareness of your strengths and weaknesses, and an ability to overcome your weaknesses. Listen and learn from others, particularly good leaders. Above all you need to focus on the essentials of the business—revenue costs and profit.

**Sources:** Author interview with Stephen Hester, February 2012; author interview with Joe Greenwell, 2012.

Visit the Online Resource Centre to read the full interviews with Stephen Hester and Joe Greenwell.

 What skills and experience do you have of leadership and what areas do you need to improve? Identify one or two areas that you want to work on and spend some time considering how you can develop.

# Definitions of leadership

The following are some popular definitions of leadership:

> Leadership has traditionally been seen as the ability and capacity to influence others.
>
> (Bass, 1985)

> The ability of an individual to influence, motivate, and enable others to contribute towards the effectiveness and success of the organisations of which they are members.
>
> (House et al., 2004: 56)

> Managers are people who do things right and leaders are people who do the right thing.
>
> (Bennis and Nanus, 1985: 21)

## Differences between leadership and management

**Management** The everyday practices of running the organization in a smooth fashion.

**Leadership** The process of leading or influencing the behaviour of others. In the broadest definition, it can be carried out by anyone in the organization.

So what are leadership and management? While some commentators use the titles 'leadership' and 'management' interchangeably, Grint and Holt (2011) argue that they are different. **Management** is concerned with organizations running smoothly, creating stability, and following the rules; **leadership** focuses on the vision of the future of the organization and creating new rules. Management is, therefore, business-as-usual, or as Bennis and Nanus have it 'do[ing] things right', whereas leadership is concerned with the future of the business, or in Bennis and Nanus's terms 'do[ing] the right thing' (1985). These differences are summarized in Table 12.1.

This definition impacts not just particular organizations but whole sectors. Grint and Holt cite the US car industry, which they say focused on the efficiency of sports utility vehicles (SUVs), which is a tame problem, rather than questioning whether these are appropriate vehicles for the twenty-first century (Grint and Holt, 2011: 90). Thus leadership is about asking the right questions, acting with vision, and rethinking the status quo. Leadership does not necessarily coincide with a formal position in the organization, but is more a way of thinking about how to solve organizational problems.

Table 12.1 The differences between leadership and management (based on Grint and Holt, 2011)

|  | Leadership | Management |
|---|---|---|
| Type of problem | Uncertain | Certain, knowable problems |
|  | Vu jàdé (never seen this before) | Déjà vu (seen this before) |
|  | Wicked problems (complex problem, not a simple cause and effect) | Tame problems (complicated, but it is resolvable through unilinear acts and it is likely to have occurred before) |
| Response | Ask right questions | Give correct answers |
|  | Innovative response to the novel problem | Same process or standard operating procedure that resolved the problem the last time it emerged |
| Outlook | Art | Science |
|  | Vision | Operational |
| Example | Creating a transport strategy | Timetabling the railways |

© Grint & Holt, *Followership in the NHS*, 2011. Available at http://www.kingsfund.org.uk/publications/articles/leadership_papers/nhs_followership.html

# Individualistic leader: great man theory and trait theory

**Running case:** Chance looks for inspiration

Chance rises up to begin his speech to the staff at Junction Hotel. He loves these moments—laying out the vision and mission of the hotel, reminding the staff of the direction that they are going in, and rallying the troops. At times like this he imagines what other leaders would do. He loves the innovation of Steve Jobs and his drive and determination, and the passionate outlook of Howard Schultz, but he is happiest and feels most leader-like when he imagines himself as Winston Churchill. As he concludes his speech about how the hotel will overcome adversity and move into a brighter future, particularly if the investors' meal goes well, Chance declares with gusto, in Churchillian tones, that Junction Hotel will never be defeated.

Make a list of who you think are great leaders—what makes them great? Are there any common characteristics that made them great?

What makes a leader outstanding? A visit to the business section of high-street bookshops quickly reveals our fascination with *great* business leaders. Their shelves are often full of the biographies and autobiographies of some of our most successful leaders, including *Elon Musk: How the billionaire ECO of SpaceX and Tesla is shaping our future* (Vance, 2015); *Lean in: Women, work, and the will to lead* by Sheryl Sandberg (2015) of Facebook; Richard Branson's *Losing my virginity* (2009) and *Business stripped bare* (2009); Walter Isaacson's *Steve Jobs: The exclusive biography* (2012); Alan Sugar's *What you see is what you get* (2011), and Duncan

Bannatyne's *Anyone can do it* (2007). These books tantalize the reader with the promise that these leaders will reveal the secrets of leadership.

This interest in what makes leaders great stems back to **great man** theory, founded by historian Thomas Carlyle. Using biographies of great leaders to examine their background, character, key actions, and philosophy, it aims to learn what makes certain leaders great. As a result, great man theory often provides hagiographies: heroic accounts of leaders, emphasizing their wisdom, charm, intelligence, insight, or political savvy.

> **Great man** A theory that certain individuals are born great and can lead organizations and societies.

---

**Real life case:** Winston Churchill—the exemplar of a great man

Winston Churchill is often said to be the UK's greatest statesman of the twentieth century, leading the country in a time of crisis when it 'stood alone' against Nazi Germany. Centres, such as Winston Churchill Leadership, and numerous biographies aim to study the personality, background, and skills of Churchill to uncover his greatness and unique character.

Churchill is widely presented (e.g. Roberts, 2003) as having a 'sense of destiny' and superior insight into the potential danger that Hitler posed. He is described as a visionary: inspirational, courageous, and an innovative leader with good people-management and listening skills. A good public orator, he also impacted those he met, leaving them feeling braver after the meeting.

Winston Churchill.

Some accounts of Churchill (e.g. Roberts, 2003; Longstaffe, 2005) try to uncover his key leadership principles and learn from them for today's leaders. They suggest that his listening and communication skills, coupled with his courage and passion, offer an example for modern-day leaders. 'Churchill's leadership principles have proved both timeless and to be a continual source of inspiration to modern-day leaders, in both politics and business at a time when effective leadership has never been more essential' (Longstaffe, 2005: 83).

**Sources:** Roberts (2003); Longstaffe (2005); www.winston-churchill-leadership.com

---

What makes great leaders stand out? Focusing on their leadership abilities, personal characteristics, and even physical appearance, **trait theory** aims to provide a list of key characteristics or **traits** that make great leaders great. In his book *On leadership*, John Gardner listed the key traits that make for a successful leader; these include:

> **Trait theories** Nomothetic theories of personality which see individual traits rather than broad personality groups as the foundations of personality.
>
> **Trait** A characteristic of the person, often considered the behaviour, thoughts, and emotions that the person exhibits, considered stable over time.

- Physical vitality and stamina
- Intelligence and action-oriented judgement
- Eagerness to accept responsibility
- Task competence
- Understanding of followers and their needs
- Skill in dealing with people
- Need for achievement

- Capacity to motivate people
- Courage and resolution
- Trustworthiness
- Decisiveness
- Self-confidence
- Assertiveness
- Adaptability/flexibility                    (Source: Gardner, 1989)

Visit the Online Resource Centre to read some leader profiles. What do you think are their most important traits?

Interest in trait theory can be traced to Sir Francis Galton's book *Hereditary genius*, published in 1869. Galton believed leadership traits were genetic and that certain people, largely members of the aristocracy, were *born* good leaders. This view is now largely dismissed as being elitist and leading to discrimination (particularly as eugenics is associated with Nazi Germany). However, leadership traits continue to fascinate (Antonakis et al., 2012; Bono et al., 2014). Even today, trait theory presents leaders as superior, with characteristics such as greater intelligence, self-confidence, determination, integrity, and sociability above ordinary people. In Kirkpatrick and Locke's statement: 'it is unequivocally clear that leaders are not like other people' (1991: 59). Indeed, these special qualities are cited to provide the justification for business leaders earning substantially more than most people (see Chapter 17 for a discussion). The big five personality traits (see Chapter 8) have been linked to leadership, with leaders seen to be more extravert, more conscientious in terms of the emergence of leaders (but not their effectiveness), and more open to experience because they are more analytical. Agreeableness was more mixed, and leaders were less neurotic (Bono et al 2014: 201–4). More recently, trait theorists have argued that individuals can cultivate certain traits and therefore develop their leadership skills by learning from successful people.

## The individualistic (heroic) leader assessed

The focus on individual leaders continues to be popular, with top business leaders celebrated regularly and presented as people to learn from and who are critical to organizational success.

However, the assumptions that individualistic leadership theories are based upon are problematic. They have tendencies towards elitism, particularly in early versions which saw great leaders coming, almost exclusively, from the aristocracy and being a result of 'breeding'. While few hold such views today, the assumption still persists that certain people are born *natural* leaders and stand apart from *ordinary* people.

Individualistic models also suffer from difficulty in defining what makes a great leader. It is hard to imagine one person having all the traits a great leader should possess. Indeed, as far back as 1948, Stogdill concluded that there was no universal list of traits that could be defined for all leaders, making the concept inconclusive at best and, arguably, meaningless.

Moreover, leadership traits that are successful in one situation might prove counter-productive in another. For instance, Winston Churchill was widely seen as one of the greatest wartime leaders, with approval ratings of over 78%; however, after the war he led the Conservative Party to one of its heaviest defeats (Addison, 2011). His traits, as a strong and determined personality that everyone could rally round, may have worked in wartime, but in peacetime, without a clear common enemy or collective vision for the country, his strong-willed personality was unsuited for the more political environment.

Many researchers have also questioned whether these traits are objective and measurable. Complex personalities, they argue, cannot be simply reduced down to a list of definable characteristics (see Chapter 8 on personality). These traits do not actually exist in an objective sense but are a result of researchers interpreting the actions of the leaders.

Many of the key traits such as individualism, assertiveness, and control are often associated with a masculine personality (Calás and Smircich, 1993). Individualistic theory reinforces dominant, masculine images of the heroic leader (Bryman et al., 1988) and, as Badaracco (2001) argues, downplays the quiet, less heroic, but often more effective, aspects of leadership (Table 12.2).

## Review questions

| | |
|---|---|
| **Describe** | What are the key principles behind great man and trait theories? |
| **Explain** | What are the differences between leadership and management? |
| **Analyse** | What are the strengths and weaknesses of the great man theory? |

Table 12.2 Strengths and weaknesses of individualistic leadership theories

| Strengths | Weaknesses |
|---|---|
| Focused research on leadership | Lacks empirical evidence |
| Some evidence, as there are a number of great leaders throughout history | Lacks explanatory value |
| Still popular with some | Masculine and Western bias |
| | Stogdill (1948) points out that there is no universal list—inconclusive |
| | Class bias—breeding |
| | Not necessarily applicable to work organization |
| | Post-hoc rationalization |
| | Dated |

# Behavioural theory

In the kitchen, Effingham is pacing up and down barking orders like a sergeant major: he knows this meal is critical to the hotel's success. 'Right, everyone, we have a big dinner tonight, with members of the board, potential investors, and the press. I don't want anyone to put a foot wrong. Mike, start peeling the potatoes and then cut them into chips like I showed you last week; Josh, corkscrew the carrots—I want 100 of them by 4 pm; and, Toby, start dicing the onions. We have to be on the case tonight lads. Mike, come over here and I'll show you how I want the meat prepared.'

As a response to the criticisms of the individualistic perspective, academic research began to focus on what leaders actually do. Behavioural theories drawing on **behaviourism**, particularly behavioural psychology (see Chapters 9 and 10), focus on how a leader's behaviour shapes their followers. Behaviour theories begin with the premise that all behaviour is a result of what they call *conditioning* (Figure 12.1). How we behave is thus a result of learned reacting to positive signs (rewards) or negative ones (punishment), and then adjusting our behaviour accordingly (see Chapter 9). Consequently, the actions of followers emerge from how the leader responds to their behaviour and the signals that they exhibit.

One of the earliest focuses of the impact of a leader's behaviour was developed in the late 1940s by the **Michigan studies**, and in the 1950s and early 1960s by the **Ohio State studies**. They stated that leaders are either employee- or task-focused, as shown in Table 12.3.

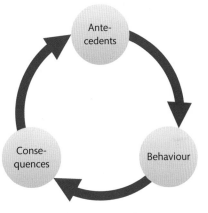

**Behaviourism**
Drawn from psychology, it looks at behaviours.

**Michigan studies**
Early leadership studies which stressed the benefit of being employee-orientated rather than task-orientated to improve output.

**Figure 12.1**
Skinner's A–B–C of behaviourism conditioning.

**Table 12.3** Differences between employee-centred and task-centred leadership (based on the Ohio State leadership studies)

| Overall focus | Employee-centred | Task-centred |
|---|---|---|
| Leadership style | Listens to the subordinates, encourages participation, has a friendly manner that aims to enhance self-esteem, and builds an environment of trust, warmth, and concern; social sensitivity | Focuses on the task, provides clear expectations, instructions, and deadlines, focusing on maintaining standards |
| Leader's focus | Towards satisfying emotional and social needs of employees | Towards goals |
| Inspired by | Human relations theory | Taylorism |
| McGregor's Theory X or Y (see the Online Resource Centre for a discussion) | Theory Y | Theory X |
| Leader's primary aim | Increased satisfaction | Higher production |
| Potential problems | Lower production | Increased turnover absenteeism and grievances of employees |

**Ohio State studies**
Conducted at a similar time to the Michigan studies and also considered leaders to be people- or task-orientated.

The Ohio studies have led to the conclusion that the most effective leaders combine task- and employee-focused approaches.

This approach was developed in 1964 by Robert Blake and Jane Mouton, who developed the Leadership Grid®. They argued that the team management style, which combines a high concern for both people and production, was most effective, whereas the worst style is the impoverished management style, which has low concern for both (Blake and Mouton, 1964).

# Autocratic, democratic, and laissez-faire leadership styles

A related approach to leaders' behaviour was developed in the late 1930s by Kurt Lewin and colleagues. They claimed there were three key styles of leadership: **autocratic**, **democratic**, and **laissez-faire**. See Table 12.4 for a summary.

The autocratic style emphasizes *command and control*. All decisions are made by the leader, one step at a time, with little input from the group, so that the followers never know for certain what the next step will be. The leader is personal in his praise and criticism of the followers, but aloof from the group unless demonstrating what the next step is.

While this approach is good for rapid decision making, it tends to be dysfunctional, creating discontentment, hostility, scapegoating, and aggression within the group, and blocking creativity. Such groups tended to 'develop a pattern of aggressive domination towards one another, and their relation to the leader was one of submission or of persistent demands for attention' (Lewin et al., 1939: 277).

In many senses, the laissez-faire approach offers the complete opposite perspective. The group has *complete freedom to act without any participation of the leader*. The leader provides the resources and information but does not participate or interfere outside of this. Lewin et al. (1939) state that the laissez-faire approach is highly inefficient and unproductive, resulting in discontent, hostility, scapegoating, and aggression as the groups feel they lack direction.

The democratic approach makes *all policy matters a subject for group discussion*. The leader facilitates group discussions but does not dominate. The aim is to involve all the group

**Autocratic** A command and control leadership style.

**Democratic** A leadership style which encourages the involvement of the group, but the leader ultimately makes the decisions.

**Laissez-faire** A leadership style which leaves all decisions to the group.

Table 12.4  Lewin's three leadership styles (Lewin et al., 1939)

| Name | Decision making | Role of group | Advantages | Disadvantages |
|------|-----------------|---------------|------------|---------------|
| Autocratic | Centralized | Followers | Quick decision making | Can hinder creativity |
| Participative | With group, leader overall | Participating and involved | Involvement and originality | Can be slow in time of crisis |
| Laissez-faire | Left to the group | Have full autonomy | Freedom of group members | Slow decision making and often unproductive |

members and allow them to make decisions, as they will implement them and be impacted by them. The democratic approach, Lewin et al. claim, is the most effective. There is less aggression, change is more easily accepted, relations between the group members are friendlier, and the group is more creative. It creates a sense of belonging and participation within the group.

What is your leadership style? Visit the Online Resource Centre to take the Lewin quiz and find out.

### Theory in context: Lewin's leadership styles

Like many of the theories that we use in organizational behaviour, Lewin's did not start out as business and management theories. Lewin's three leadership styles actually started life as Lewin assessed the reactions of 10-year-old children to a group leader in 'theatrical mask-making for a period of three months' (Lewin et al., 1939: 271). Therefore, it is questionable if this research can be applied easily to understanding management practice, as the context is quite different.

Bill Cooke, an expert on Kurt Lewin's work, argues that the styles were also part of Lewin's left-wing political project. Lewin, he claims, saw these three leadership styles as representing three different political systems.

- Autocratic style: Fascism, dictatorship, and control
- Participative style: social democracy, a left-wing reform movement embracing socialism and government intervention for the good of society
- Laissez-faire: free-market capitalism.

Lewin, a German Jew who left Germany when Hitler came to power, had an obvious opposition to autocratic leadership styles. As a socialist he was also opposed to the laissez-faire approaches, as he thought that the capitalist market should not be left to itself because the poor and weak suffer in such systems. Lewin wanted to demonstrate that it was 'right, proper and possible to intervene to effect social change on behalf of the disadvantaged' (Cooke, 1999: 92). Therefore, the superiority of the democratic model was, for Lewin, support for the social democratic model of government (Thelen, 1992). This model of leadership, therefore, could be read as a political project to further a more democratic and fairer society rather than simply as three categories of leadership.

## Behavioural approaches assessed

These behavioural approaches have focused attention on how the leaders' actions impact followers, bringing in followers to research for the first time. They also offer the potential for leadership skills to be learned and developed over time.

However, they still search for a 'one best way'—an ideal form of leadership that should be used by all leaders in all situations. Behaviourism also offers a simplistic and mechanical understanding of followers' behaviour, as simply a reaction to stimulus with little free will. See Table 12.5 for a summary.

Table 12.5  Strengths and weaknesses of behaviourism

| Strengths | Weaknesses |
| --- | --- |
| More subtle than many previous theories | Hard to measure |
| Examines the interaction of the leader and follower and the impact the leader has on the group | Presents a 'one best way' approach and does not take into account the situation |
| Practice of leadership | Male and Western bias |
| Possibility of training | Questionable validity of research |
| | Overemphasis on taxonomies |
| | Simplistic |
| | Examines only behaviour, not its impact |

## Review questions

| | |
| --- | --- |
| **Describe** | What are behavioural theories of leadership? |
| **Explain** | Why do behaviourists believe the leader's behaviour impacts the followers? |
| **Analyse** | Why is it important that Lewin's original study was about mask-making by 10-year-old children rather than about practicing managers? How might knowing this background be useful in your essay/exam? What are the implications that Lewin's political leanings might have on his theory of leadership? |
| **Apply** | How would you describe Effingham's leadership style? Do you think it is appropriate for working in the kitchen at Junction Hotel? |

# Contingency leadership theory

**Running case:** Chance prepares for his one-to-one meetings

Returning to his office, Chance gathers his notes for his one-to-one sessions. First, he is meeting Linda Wilkinson, his keen, committed, but sometimes anxious domestic manager. Although she is experienced, Chance sometimes feels he has to be careful what he says to her as she has a habit of taking things the wrong way. They have to have a tricky discussion over why the maintenance staff are not fixing rooms up to the standard that some customers require. Wilkinson, though, can be defensive of her team, and Chance wonders quite how to put it.

Being direct with Effingham, though, is never a problem. The boisterous and outspoken chef is the complete opposite and obsessed with the restaurant. However, Chance wonders if this style always works well with others in the hotel, as Effingham has a reputation for falling out with other members of staff. It is this issue that Chance needs to raise with Effingham. He wonders if he should just come out and say it.

How do you think Chance treats these two? Visit the Online Resource Centre to read our online profiles of them and make up your own mind.

Why are some leaders more effective in some situations than others? **Contingency theory** argues that the appropriate leadership style depends on a combination of the situation, the skills and experience of the followers, the complexity of tasks, the speed of decision making required, and the type of organization. The leader's approach, therefore, needs to adjust to the context they are facing (Figure 12.2).

Contingency theory argues that a leader's success is dependent on two factors: (1) the leader's *preferred leadership style*—their typical way of interacting with followers; (2) *situational control*—the degree of control the leader has over the situation. Effective leadership depends on getting the perfect match between the situation *and* the personality.

> **Contingency theory**
> Suggests that the best structure for an organization is determined by factors such as environmental uncertainty, the organization's size, and the technology that the organization uses.

## The Least Preferred Co-worker scale

One of the most famous proponents of the contingency approach was Fred Fiedler. Fiedler argued that everyone has a preferred leadership style which is more suited to certain situations. To understand when you are more likely to succeed, he argued, you need to understand your preferred leadership style.

To diagnose leadership style Fiedler developed the Least Preferred Co-worker scale (LPC). This works by asking the user to think of the *one person in their life* they find hardest to work with and rate their characteristics (Fiedler and Chemers, 1984). The test is not about the Least Preferred Co-worker themselves, but the motivation and personality of the person filling in the form. The model works on the assumption that the LPC is, on average, equally unpleasant—what varies is the perception of the LPC. Fiedler (1967) argued people are either task- or relationship-orientated. He believed task-orientated people tend to see their LPC in more negative terms, whereas people-orientated individuals see the positive factors in the LPC.

While the LPC model mirrors behavioural theories, it does not suggest that one style is superior. Rather, Fiedler argued, the most effective leadership style depends on the situation, which is a result of three factors: the quality of the relationship the leader has with the followers; the nature of the task; and the degree of formal authority the leader has (see Table 12.6).

Fiedler argued that it is easier to be a leader when the group accepts and trusts its leader, when tasks are highly structured, and when the leader has formal authority than it is when the group distrusts the leader, tasks are vague, and the leader has little formal authority.

Visit the Online Resource Centre to see the LPC diagram, take the LPC questionnaire, and discover what your leadership style is.

**Figure 12.2**
Leadership style to match the situation.

Situation — Matching leadership style

Wrong leadership style

**Table 12.6** Key factors in Fiedler's (1967) Least Preferred Co-worker scale

| Leader–member relations | Good—the group tends to trust the leader and accept them |
| | Poor—the group tends to distrust the leader and does not accept the leader's position |
| Task structure | Structured—with clear goals; highly standardized and predictable, with only a few ways to carry it out |
| | Unstructured—ambiguous goals, many ways of undertaking the task, and unclear criteria to judge success |
| Leader position power | Strong—the leader has considerable formal authority and has the power to influence the group |
| | Weak—the leader has little formal authority and little power to influence the group |

### Real life case: Formula 4 Leadership

One of the stated benefits for contingency theory is that it offers practical guidance for leaders to adjust their leadership style to meet the circumstance they face. However, how do you diagnose what state the group is in? One solution offered to businesses is the computer application 'Coach on the desktop.' Designed by Formula 4 Leadership, this application asks the user a series of questions about the situation that they face. Based on the answers, the program offers a diagnosis of the situation and an analysis of the correct response a leader should make.

**Source:** http://www.formula4leadership.com

 Visit the Online Resource Centre for an interview with the owners of Formula 4 Leadership.

## Situational leadership

A more flexible contingency leadership theory is offered by Hersey and Blanchard (1988), who state that leaders can adapt their style to the situation rather than simply having a fixed style that needs to be matched to the appropriate situation. They call this situational leadership.

Hersey and Blanchard present their model as a four-square matrix. The horizontal axis is the complexity of the task (either low or high) and the amount of direction the leader gives to the group. On the vertical axis is the relationship focus: how supportive the leader needs to be. Their model (see Table 12.7) argues that groups go through stages as they mature, and the leader needs to adjust their behaviour to match the situation of the group.

- Stage 1: *telling or directing*. High task- and low relationship-focused. In this stage the group are new, they are committed (they want to be seen as doing well), but they have low levels of competency (do not have many skills). The leader is highly directive, telling the subordinates what to do and how to do it. The leader has very little relationship with the followers.

Table 12.7  Situational leadership model (based on Hersey and Blanchard, 1988)

| | Title | Leader's focus | | Followers | | Appropriate communication style | Appropriate leadership style |
|---|---|---|---|---|---|---|---|
| | | Task | Relationship | Commitment | Competency | | |
| S1 | Telling/ directing | High | Low | High | Low D1 | Top-down Announced as the followers are after certainty | Goal focused Clear well-defined task: what is to be done, how to do it, and who is responsible Closely supervised |
| S2 | Selling/ coaching/ explaining | High | High | Lack (lost initial motivation) Aim to build self-esteem | Some competent D2 | Two-way to involve and motivate the employees and develop their competency | Leader provides some direction as followers are still relatively inexperienced |
| S3 | Participating/ supporting/ asking | Low | High | Lack (as unsure of their skill) | Moderate to high D3 | Facilitation model | Day-to-day decision making by followers as they have experience, but involvement by leader to bolster confidence and motivation |
| S4 | Delegating/ empowering | Low | Low | High | High D4 | Little support or facilitation needed | Leaders are still involved in decisions and problem solving, but control is with the followers |

- Stage 2: *selling or coaching*. High task and high relationship. At this stage the group increases their competency (they have started learning to do things), but, as a result, they begin to lose confidence and their motivation drops as they become aware of what they cannot do. In this situation the leader remains quite directive, telling them what to do, but is more encouraging and therefore focused on building up personal relationships.

- Stage 3: *participating or encouraging*. Low task and high relationship. As the group develops, it increases its level of skill and confidence and the commitment levels begin to rise again. To support this stage the leader becomes less focused on the task and more on helping to support and encourage the group through adopting a facilitation style.

- Stage 4: *delegating and empowering*. Low task and low relationship. At this final stage the group have matured and have high levels of skill and confidence. As a result, the leader can allow them to run things on a daily basis and is only really involved in problem solving and key decisions.

Visit the Online Resource Centre for a link to the diagram.

## How it works

The leader diagnoses the commitment and competency of the followers and then shapes their leadership style accordingly. For instance, faced with an inexperienced but highly motivated group (D1), the leader needs to adopt a direct and goal-focused approach, providing clear tasks with clear instructions (S1). The followers with low skill levels will appreciate clear tasks as this removes ambiguity.

As the group learns new skills (D2), they become increasingly uncertain and can thus lose motivation. The leader therefore needs to develop the group's confidence by focusing on relationship and commitment, using two-way dialogue to increase involvement. As their skills increase (S3) the group needs less direction but more encouragement, as they tend to be uncertain of their skills (D3).

An experienced, motivated, and confident group (D4) works best with more autonomy, with the leader only involved in problem solving and key decisions (S4).

More recently, Hersey and Blanchard have argued the leader also needs to explain to the group why they are changing style; otherwise the group can be left feeling isolated, believing that the leader does not care (compare this model to Tuckman's group formation on pp. 177–82).

> **Study skills:** leadership in group work
>
> During your time at university, you will probably spend time working in groups. While it is unlikely your group will officially appoint a 'leader', you will, at times, take on leadership roles, both in terms of organizing your group and by supporting and encouraging other group members. As you read through this chapter, consider your own leadership style and how it can be adjusted to meet different situations.

# Path–goal and congruence model

One of the primary problems of early contingency theory is that it sees leadership style as simply matching the leader's focus on task and/or relationships to the followers' commitment and competency, ignoring wider factors such as culture, power and politics, and identity.

To overcome this narrow perspective, House (1996) developed **path–goal theory**, and Nadler and Tushman (1997) developed the congruence model. These theories broaden the analysis to include factors such as the organization's environment, the resources available to the leader, and the organization's history (see the Online Resource Centre for more details). By taking into account more variables, they offer a more subtle and far-reaching understanding of the environment the leader faces. However, they also become more complicated and mathematical as they try to deal with almost every factor the organization faces.

**Path–goal theory**
Developed by Robert House, argues the leader's effectiveness is dependent on the motivation, satisfaction, and performance of her subordinates.

## Situational and contingency leadership theories assessed

Situational and contingency theories have been used regularly in training programmes for future leaders because they offer practical guidelines and tools to help leaders assess and adapt their leadership styles to meet the situations they face. They offer a more subtle understanding than individualistic and behavioural approaches, as they increase attention on leaders' impact on followers, but they do little to explain how leaders move from low to high development levels (Northouse, 2010). There is also a lack of empirical evidence to support them (Bryman, 1986).

One underlying problem is that all contingency theories work on the assumption that the context of the group, including the skill levels, motivation, leader–follower relations, organizational history, etc., is an objective reality which the leader can know 'transparent[ly] through scientific analysis' (Grint, 2005: 1470). However, human behaviour is far more unpredictable and complex than these models suggest.

Also, although these perspectives challenge the notion there is one best leadership style, they still assume that each situation demands a particular leadership style, thus moving from the *one best way* to *one best response*. Table 12.8 summarizes the 'pros' and 'cons'.

Visit the Online Resource Centre for more details on these models.

Table 12.8  'Pros' and 'cons' of contingency theory

| Pros | Cons |
| --- | --- |
| Understand situation | Neat models, but applicable to real life? |
| No ideal leader | Still limited view on the group |
| Variety of leadership styles | Potentially normative |
| More flexible models | North-American and gender bias |
| Impact on followers | Limited look at structure, politics, etc. |

### Review questions

**Describe**    What is meant by contingency leadership theory?

**Explain**    Why does contingency theory offer a more flexible approach to leadership?

**Analyse**    How could contingency theory be criticized as still representing a 'one best way'?

## Contemporary views of leadership

### Running case: Linda Wilkinson's one-to-one

As their meeting progresses Simon Chance realizes that Linda Wilkinson is struggling a little with managing the maintenance team. 'They just ignore some of my requests,' she says honestly. 'You know, I ask them to do things, try to offer them incentives to fix the rooms, but they just don't seem to make it a priority. I've even tried just pulling rank on them and telling them—it works OK for a day or so and then they go back to their old ways.' Chance listens intently and then leans forward. 'You need to inspire them—they need to want to do a good job.' 'Easier said than done,' thinks Wilkinson.

Table 12.9 Transactional and transformational leadership styles (based on Burns, 1978)

| Transactional | Transformational |
| --- | --- |
| Cut deals with employees | Transform institutions |
| Exchange with workers | Offer a vision of the future that people want to buy into |
| Monitor and control workers | Let workers feel part of the solution |
| Extrinsic motivation | Intrinsic motivation |
| Short-term self-interest | Long-term substantive goals |
| Works best with inexperienced followers | Works best with experienced followers |
| Contingency theory | Charismatic leadership |
| Manager | Leader |
| Tame problems | Wicked problems |
| Preserver/trustee | Insurgent entrepreneur |
| Organizational man | Maverick |

One of the problems with the leadership styles presented so far is there is little that is uplifting in these models. They tend either to focus on heroic leaders who are born that way or to present leadership as a mundane, mechanical model. This concern led Burns (1978) to form his transformative leadership model. Burns argues there are two styles of leadership: transactional and transformative. Transactional leadership operates by trying to control followers and cut deals with them. Transformative, however, is more uplifting. Table 12.9 sums up the main differences between these two approaches.

Transformational leaders lead by inspiring, causing a change in the followers, creating a shared mission, and encouraging followers to take ownership of their work. Drawing from Maslow's hierarchy of needs (see Chapter 9), Burns argued that great leaders focus attention away from low-level needs (such as pay) towards loftier goals, such as self-esteem and self-actualization. They help followers achieve their goals and motivate them along the way (Bass and Riggio, 2006). According to Tichy and Davanna, transformative leaders are visionary change agents (see Chapter 11) who are courageous, are driven by values, have a strong belief in people, can cope with complexity, and are life-long learners. Similarly, Bass (1985) identified the following characteristics of transformational leaders:

- *idealized influence*—high moral and ethical standards, and therefore respected by the followers which creates loyalty
- *inspirational motivation*—strong vision for future based on values and ideals, which builds confidence and inspires followers
- *intellectual stimulation*—challenges organizational norms and encourages alternative thinking
- *individual consideration*—recognizes unique growth and developmental needs of followers.

> ### Real life case: Howard Schultz's transformation of Starbucks
>
> In 2007 Howard Schultz, then the chairman and former CEO of Starbucks, wrote a highly critical memo to the board. In it he argued that Starbucks was chasing growth for its own sake and felt invincible—it had lost its soul. A year later he seemed correct. Starbucks was closing stores, and campaigners, and even their employees who they call partners, were turning against them. Starbucks seemed to have lost its way (Schultz, 2011: 41).
>
> Schultz then shocked everyone by returning as CEO. He aimed to transform Starbucks by returning to its core values—a focus on people. Schultz enacted many of the key traits of a transformational leader; he offered an inspiring vision for the future. Starbucks, he claimed, not only has to make money, but also has to create value for the employees and the wider community. To this end he changed part of the mission statement to 'We want to be invited in wherever we do business. We can be a force for positive action' (Starbucks, 2012).
>
> **Sources:** BBC Radio 4 (2011); Schultz (2011); Starbucks (2012).

Visit the Online Resource Centre to read more about Starbucks.

What can a leader do to create passion and zeal in their followers? What would give you passion and zeal for your work?

**Transactional leaders** believe their followers are motivated by rewards and punishment, so they lead through offering exchanges or transactions (promises of higher pay, promotion, or status) for increased effort. The primary focus of transactional leaders is to plan, organize tasks, monitor progress, and fix problems as they arise. According to Bass (1985), the following characteristics define transactional leaders:

- *contingent reward*—tangible or intangible support or resources for effort and support
- *management by exception: active*—monitor performance and take corrective action when necessary
- *management by exception: passive*—monitor performance and only take action when really serious
- *laissez-faire*—avoidance of leadership responsibility.

Transformational leaders, therefore, are best at dealing with wicked problems, whereas transactional leaders are similar to managers as they focus on finding answers to everyday, tame problems. As Kanter (1992) states, for an organization to be successful it needs a mix of both of these types. Too many questioners and everything gets confused; too many people who follow the same old patterns and organizations get stuck in dead ends.

## Transformative theory assessed

The transformative theory reignites the idea of the heroic leader, often using masculine traits to describe their personality, presenting them as having almost superhuman

> **Transactional leaders** Leaders who do deals with employees in order to get the task done. Seen in opposition to transformational leaders who offer a better vision of the world that employees can buy into.

characteristics. However, they are not operating in a top-down, command and control manner but aim to inspire their followers with passion to go the extra mile.

From a critical perspective, though, this could be seen as a form of control, manipulating the workers' desires and interests (see Lukes as discussed in Chapter 13) or inspiring them with a vision to get them to work harder against their real interests (see Chapter 7).

## The dark side of leadership and its responses

### Real life case: Deutsche Bank

Just a month after Deutsche Bank were fined $2.5bn and ordered to fire seven employees for their involvement in rigging the Libor rate (see Chapter 17 for a discussion), the two joint CEOs of Deutsche Bank stepped down. While they have not been implicated in the rate fixing themselves, they were seen as responsible for the actions of their employees. Prior to their departure it was reported that a flyer was being distributed that stated 'A radical new start would restore our credibility and could produce a real boost to morale' (Channel News Asia, 2015).

Paul Achleitner, chairman of the supervisory board, praised them, saying: 'Their decision to step down early demonstrates impressively their attitude of putting the bank's interests ahead of their own' (cited in Goodley 2015).

How responsible do you think the actions of the two CEOs are in the actions of their company?

In response to this concern about the 'dark side' of charismatic and transformational leaders and to the spate of corporate scandals that have been in the news (see Chapter 17 for more details) is **authentic leadership**. Authentic leadership is seen as a valuable alternative to leaders who emphasize profit over people, prioritizing ethics and people as it emphasizes the legitimacy that leaders gain through having honest relationships with their followers. Avolio and Gardner argue that this concept of leadership is a more positive version of leadership (2005) that can guide leaders' behaviour towards more ethical ends (Gardner et al., 2011), giving leadership a moral foundation. Authentic leadership involves using your personal experiences, emotions, needs, and beliefs as you lead. This means being self-aware and acting in line with your core beliefs, rather than using followers to further your own personal ends. However, in response to this emphasis on authentic leadership, Ford and Harding argue that such a position is impossible and that it is a more subtle way of controlling people (2011). An authentic leader, Ford and Harding state, would be so absorbed into the organization that they would lack subjectivity (consciousness).

While a focus on transformational leaders has been popular in recent years, a more balanced approach is offered by the C-I-P model (Table 12.10). This model suggests that charismatic, ideological and pragmatic leadership styles all offer pathways to outstanding leadership with related strengths and weaknesses.

> **Authentic leadership**
> An approach which emphasizes leadership through use of personal experiences, emotions, needs and beliefs.

Table 12.10  The C-I-P Model

| Style | Charismatic | Ideological | Pragmatic |
|---|---|---|---|
| Orientation | Vision of future | Idealizing the past | Problem solving in the present |
| Outlook | Constantly positive outlook | Rigid worldview reliant on personal values | Shaped by the environment |
| Use of emotions | Constantly positive | React with negative emotions, perceived injustice | Largely does not attempt to influence large groups, focuses on small group of trusted elite |
| Example | Herbert Hoover or Jack Welch | Steve Jobs or Donald Trump | Larry Page or Rupert Murdoch |

Table drawn from Griffith et al. (2015)

### Review questions

| **Describe** | What is the difference between transactional and transformational leadership? |
|---|---|
| **Explain** | How does the C-I-P model strike a balance between transactional and transformational leadership? |
| **Analyse** | To what extent is a transformational leader a reincarnation of the heroic leader? |

# Challenging the leader-centric view: the post-heroic perspective and the importance of followers

**Running case:** crisis in the kitchen

As Effingham goes in for his one-to-one, a call comes through to the kitchen. It's the mayor; he is a vegetarian, and they didn't know. With only 40 minutes until they arrive and Effingham in his meeting, there is panic in the kitchen as there is nothing prepared and there are no ingredients for vegetarians. Suddenly, Josh springs into action. 'We could do risotto,' he declares. 'We could use the veg from the roast.' Sensing Josh's idea, Toby chips in, 'Yes, and we could add the finely chopped onion on top—that would make it really nice.' Excited by their decisions, taken without Effingham there, they get to work.

All the theories we have present so far are leader-centric. They are based on the assumption that the leader is central to an organization's success: a superman (or, occasionally, superwoman), with extraordinary powers to transform the organization virtually single-handedly. They achieve this either through force of character (great man, trait, and transformational theory) or through skill in working with the group (in contingency theory). This leader-centric lens portrays leaders as powerful, whereas the followers are simply passive, merely responding to leaders' actions. However, is such a picture accurate? Some leadership scholars argue not: the leaders' significance is overstated, producing what Meindl et al. (1985) call a 'romanticism of leadership'.

---

**Research insight:** The romantic view of leadership

Meindl, J.R., Ehrlich, S.B., and Dukerich, J.M. 1985. The romance of leadership. *Administrative Science Quarterly* 30(1): 78–102.

Pillai, R., and Meindl, J.R. 1991. The impact of a performance crisis on attributions of charismatic leadership: A preliminary study. In: *Proceedings of the 1991 Eastern Academy of Management Meetings*, Hartford, CT.

In a series of influential studies, Meindl and colleagues have argued that we overestimate the power and control of leaders. Using attribution theory (how people look for causes for events), they argue that often we over-attribute the success (or failure) of an organization to the leadership.

An early study (Meindl et al., 1985) found when reading 33,248 press articles there was a significant correlation between references to the organizational leader in the article title and strong company performance. They found that in the years that the firms did well these articles emphasized the leader more.

In a later study, Pillai and Meindl (1991) gave a group of people an identical CV of a male CEO but different information about the company's success. In the scenario, when there was a sudden increase in performance, the CEO was considered charismatic, but when performance declined, they stated he lacked charisma. In other words, the performance of the firm changed the way the leader's personality was viewed.

The implication is that leaders get credit (or the blame) even when there is little evidence that they have done anything remarkable. The perception of the 'great leader's' personality is thus constructed based on organizational performance and not the cause of it.

---

Why do you feel the 'romanticism of leadership' has been such an enduring concept?

This romanticism presents leaders as saviours of the organization, solely responsible for its fate, justifying the often incredibly large salaries (and bonuses) and high status which leaders receive (as discussed in Chapter 17). Indeed, followers often collude in this image, looking to leaders and investing hopes and fears in the leader to be saviours or scapegoats if things go wrong (see Grint, 2010).

This infatuation with great leaders means that we have lost sight of followers (Uhl-Bien et al., 2014), what Bjerke calls **followership** (1999). Followership theory argues that followers are essential to leadership. Moreover, followers are not passive, simply re-sponding to the behaviour of the leader, but have their own ways of thinking and acting.

**Followership** In leadership theory: (a) the importance of looking at followers and (b) the ability to follow a leader.

**Real life case:** followers care about their work but are not engaged

*The 2014 Global Workforce Study* (Towers Watson, 2014) canvassed over 32,000 followers from around the world. They found that workers wanted to be engaged in their work and have a passion for what they did: 40% were highly engaged and would 'go the extra mile' for their job, up from only 21% in 2007; 24% felt were actually disengaged because they did not have an emotional connection with the company, and a further 36% felt unsupported or detached, meaning 60% did not feel fully engaged (Figure 12.3).

This 'engagement gap', the researchers stated, happens because organizations are not tapping into the full potential of their staff or creating an energized workforce. The top driver to increased worker engagement was senior management being seen as effective.
**Source:** Towers Watson (2014).

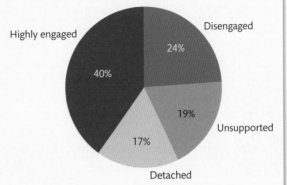

**Figure 12.3**  Worker engagement as found by the *2014 Global Workforce Study*.
**Source:** © Global Workforce Study 2014, reproduced by permission of Towers Watson.

## Social constructionist theory of leadership

The social constructionist perspective (see the Online Resource Centre for more details) challenges the leader-centric view. It argues that what counts as good leadership is determined by the followers' perceptions as well as by the intentions of the leader.

For a leader to be considered successful (or at least accepted), they need to live up to (or potentially redefine) the followers' beliefs or expectations of them. For instance, all professions have social and cultural expectations of how they should be treated and led. Doctors tend not to respond well to just being told what to do, because part of their identity and training is tied up in being autonomous (Dent, 2003). Consequently, a leader needs to respond to these expectations in order to be accepted. The followers have to actually want to follow the leader.

## Leadership as a practice

When we discuss leadership, we often think of a single leader at the top of the organization. Instead, leadership should be thought of as an act that can be done by anyone throughout the organization. Many engage in acts of leadership—like an administrative assistant 'showing the ropes' to a new employee (Raelin, 2005), a shop worker solving a customer's problem, or an engineer designing a new tool to solve a problem. Everyone has the capacity to take a lead at certain points, which Raelin calls being **leaderful** (2005). This perspective shifts the focus to the act of leading instead of the personal characteristics of a leader.

Leadership is as an activity that takes place throughout the organization. This is particularly important in knowledge-intensive, creative, or customer-service-focused industries where traditional command and control leadership styles are less effective.

**Leaderful** Where everyone has the capacity to be a leader or take a lead through doing activities.

**Theory in context:** the changing nature of society needing alternative forms of leadership

Over the last 50 years there have been dramatic changes, particularly in the West, in the nature of society and the economy, which challenge traditional leadership theories. Firstly, since the 1960s there has been a gradual loss of faith in authority figures to solve our problems. Secondly, the shift from manufacturing to the information or knowledge economy has meant that the nature of jobs has changed. Thirdly, these better-educated 'knowledge workers' desire more autonomy and use of their skills. Fourthly, there is a change in organizational structure, with flatter organizations based more around teamwork.

The 'knowledge worker' thus holds specialized skills, meaning their ideas and input are essential for organizational success. They are employed to think rather than be told what to do. As Niall FitzGerald, deputy chairman of Thomson Reuters, puts it: 'the way in which the world has developed means authority is no longer to be given. It must be earned. People will only give their loyalty to those they respect—they will not give it to the position . . . You have to engage people' (Thomson and Lloyd, 2011: 31).

Such shifts require different approaches to leadership. Instead of top-down, command and control leadership, this new economy requires involving the workers by getting their ideas and input. Organizational success is based on building upon the experience and knowledge of the workforce.

The question therefore emerges of how to create the right conditions to encourage and enhance the actions of organizational members. Rather than the leader standing at the front of the organization directing and controlling the passive followers, the leader's role is to create the environment in which followers can flourish.

**Real life case:** Vineet Nayar

Vineet Nayar is the former CEO of HCL Technologies, one of India's largest IT companies. During his time at HCLT, the company's revenue almost tripled. But it was also praised for being highly democratic. Nayar argues that while traditional command and control structures might be the easiest, they are often not the most effective. The aim should be to decentralize power, responsibility, and accountability. This resulted in HCLT being voted the Number One Best Employer in India and the Best Employer in Asia and the United Kingdom.

At the heart of Nayar's approach was a challenge to conventional business wisdom. He called it 'Employees First, Customers Second'. This is not designed to be nice to employees, but rather a way of being more effective. Traditional hierarchy, Nayar argued, often got in the way of teams that were trying to work together. 'The senior managers, sitting at their lofty remove from the real action, are the ones who can exercise the Hand of God decision that often puts at risk everything that is happening in the value zone' (Nayar, 2010: 96). Nayar also reversed accountability, so that if an issue came up or they wanted more information, an employee could open a 'ticket', meaning that the managers became responsible for solving the problem. Managers were also subject to 360-degree appraisal: they were appraised not only by their managers but also by their employees. HCLT also had opinion polls on the company strategy and online forums so that employees could talk directly to Nayar.

**Sources:** *USA Today* (2007); Nayar (2010); Frauenheim (2014).

**Servant leadership** (Greenleaf, 1970), also known as 'leading up' and 'connective', argues for a more bottom-up, equal, and supportive leadership style. The leader should give priority to the needs of their followers and colleagues, aiming to serve rather than to be served. Drawing on the example of Jesus Christ, servant leadership sees the leader more as a steward of the organization than the person leading from the front. The leader takes on a more supportive role, listening to the staff and building community and trust within the organization.

This is a dramatic change in the model of leadership. The leader is humble and acts to bring the best out of the employees:

> The difference manifests itself in the care taken by the servant—first to make sure that other people's highest priority needs are being served. The best test, and difficult to administer, is: Do those served grow as persons? Do they, while being served, become healthier, wiser, freer, more autonomous, more likely themselves to become servants? And, what is the effect on the least privileged in society? Will they benefit or at least not be further deprived?
>
> (Greenleaf, 1970: 7)

In a recent review of 39 studies, Parris and Peachey argue that servant leadership is a viable leadership theory as it helps organizations improve *and* increase the well-being of the followers (2013). Similarly, **environmental leadership** aims to cultivate a self-sustaining group where employees find gratification through the group and task. These perspectives aim to create a more egalitarian and less hierarchical culture where the relationship between the leader and follower are more collaborative in nature.

Other post-heroic leadership theories have questioned the distinction between leaders and followers as somewhat artificial (Collinson, 2005). This view sees leadership as a social practice, a *process* rather than individual characteristics. Leadership is about creating shared meaning and understanding by using symbols, forming shared language, and shaping values (see, for instance, Smircich and Morgan, 1982). The followers are seen not simply as accepting this reality but as active participants in its construction.

Another key post-heroic leadership style is **distributive leadership**. This view argues that leadership does not simply follow a formal position in the hierarchy but can be seen throughout the organization. Teamworking, empowerment, and more participatory approaches are encouraged as they create a more inclusive, motivated, and involved workforce, utilizing everyone's skills and abilities within the organization.

Proponents of this perspective argue that top-down leadership can be a source of frustration, particularly for professionals who generally desire autonomy and input into decision making processes. Not engaging followers or using their passion, ideas, and knowledge can be experienced as demotivating, particularly when the followers feel decisions are being imposed on them.

Rather than being tied to the formal role or position, distributive leadership works on the premise that different people can take on leadership responsibilities at different points, largely linked to their knowledge and expertise. Leadership therefore works on a rotational basis with members of the group stepping forward and leading the group when their specialism or skills demand it and then acting as normal members of the group the rest of the time. This is particularly effective in situations where other members of the group

**Servant leadership** A bottom-up perspective which sees the leader being the most effective when they support followers to enable them to do their jobs.

**Environmental leadership** A self-sustaining group where employees find gratification through the group and task.

**Distributive leadership** An approach which emphasizes that leadership can occur throughout the organization by a wide variety of organizational members.

recognize that a particular individual has the knowledge to respond to that particular situation.

**Real life case:** Springest using holacracy

The Dutch-based independent comparison website company Springest announced in 2013 that they were using the holacracy system. Rather than having conventional top-down management, they are seeking to us the self-management system (Robertson, 2015) in conjunction with the time-management system 'Getting Things Done' (Allen, 2015). Springest state that they feel holacracy helps develop learning, increases responsibility, and increases motivation as it gives people more space for their own development (Timmerman, 2014).

An even more radical version of this is holacracy. This perspective offers an alternative to hierarchical organizations by suggesting the possibility of self-organizing systems. It seeks to remove power from management and redistribute it throughout the organization without having the problems of completely 'flat management', where there can be a lack of responsibility (Robertson, 2015). To make this happen, rather than having fixed job descriptions tasks are decided around the work and then people service these tasks. Decisions, authority, and responsibilities are within the team, and clear, transparent rules are made for everyone to follow. (See also the discussion of post-bureaucratic, structureless organizations in Chapter 4.)

**Real life case:** distributing the power and getting results

Ricardo Semler was Latin American Businessman of the Year in 1990. He is widely heralded as leading one of the most innovative and democratic organizations in the world. Semler argues he treats Semco's 800 employees as responsible adults. Workers can set their own hours, chose their own information technology, share all information, and even set their own salary. Semco has three core values: democracy, profit-sharing, and information. Twice a year subordinates evaluate their managers and they even interview their future managers. Key decisions are made collectively via a vote. Letting people participate in decisions that affect their lives has positive effects on their motivation and morale, Semler claims (Semler, 1999).

## Post-heroic leadership assessed

The post-heroic leadership theory has therefore sought to redress the balance that has over-emphasized the role of individual leaders at the top of the organization's hierarchy by drawing attention to the everyday practices of leadership which occur throughout it. However, such theory often ignores issues of gender and race and does little to really transform the power relations within organizations.

# What do leaders actually do? Practice-based theories

What do leaders actually do in practice? Our common-sense views, which are derived from such writers as Henri Fayol (see Chapter 2) and emphasized in mainstream leadership theory, present leadership and management as a rational activity conducted by heroic characters—reflecting and having creative visions and strategies. However, as Alvesson and Sveningsson (2003) argue, much of what managers and leaders actually do in practice is mundane and involves everyday activities, such as listening and chatting.

One of the first writers to bring this to the attention of management theory was Henry Mintzberg. In a famous article in 1975, he compared the folklore (the stories of myths about managers and leaders) to what he called the fact (the actual practices). His theory is summarized in Table 12.11.

Mintzberg discovered that practice is more messy, confusing, and disjointed than the idealized image presented in leadership theories. Much of leadership and management work is political (see Chapter 13 of this book) and involves dealing with competing priorities. Mintzberg also found that, far from being the work of an idealized reflective planner, the average day of managers he studied was characterized by brevity and discontinuity. Most of the managers surveyed 'worked without interruption for [only] a half hour or more only about once every two days'. He concluded the current system of 'managing does not breed reflective planners; managers respond to stimuli'.

Table 12.11  What managers really do—folklore and fact (based on Mintzberg, 1975)

| Folklore | Fact |
| --- | --- |
| Systematic, reflective planner | Brevity, discontinuous activity, orientation to action |
| No regular duties, but is a coordinator and then sits back | Regular duties, such as presiding over rituals, ceremonies, and negotiations |
| Uses formal management information system | Does not use them but prefers verbal communication instead of documents |
| Management is a science | Little has really changed over the last 100 years but has become a little more scientific |

More recently, a number of researchers have discovered that the overwhelming majority of decisions are taken 'on the hoof' (Chia and Holt, 2006: 643) and therefore leaders need to be 'skilled, [at] improvised in-situ coping' (Chia, 2004: 33). Holmberg and Tyrstrup (2010) argued recently that more of management and leadership activity is event-driven—responding to situations rather than planning for the future. Classic leadership theory of the reflective planner or heroic visionary could therefore be seen as a romanticized fantasy, as reality is far more messy and confusing (Sveningsson and Larsson, 2006).

While this might come as a disappointment in comparison to the classic fantasy view of leaders and managers, the revelation that reality is more messy and confusing can be comforting. Reflecting on Mintzberg's article some 15 years later, one manager stated that it was a relief to discover that most managers do not spend their time planning and coordinating as in the idealized image, but rather were 'keeping a lid on the chaos'.

## Review questions

| | |
|---|---|
| **Describe** | What are the key principles behind post-heroic leadership? |
| **Explain** | Why do post-heroic leadership theorists argue that it is important to focus attention on followership? |
| **Analyse** | Why do post-heroic leadership theorists argue that shifting from command and control to distributive leadership could increase productivity in the organization? |
| **Analyse** | Why is the idealized view of leadership challenged by seeing what managers actually do in practice? |

# Breaking the glass ceiling: leadership and gender

**Real life case:** the CEO of an American firm is more likely to be called John than be a woman

From 'great man theory' onwards, most leadership theory of the last century tended to assume that leaders need to be men. Most of the leaders studied were men, and the researchers were men. However, things are changing, albeit slowly. In 2011, a UK government-commissioned report, *Women on Boards* (Davies, 2011), called for higher representation of women in the boardroom, with a target of 25% of women serving on the boards of FTSE 100 companies by 2015 and all chairmen of FTSE 250 companies setting out the percentage of women that they aim to have on their boards by 2013 and 2015. In May 2015 the figure for FTSE 100 companies was 23.5%, still short of the target, but it has risen significantly from 15% in 2012. FTSE 250 companies increased from 7.8% in 2011 to 18% in 2015 (Vinnicombe et al., 2015). Some companies such as Diageo and Intercontinental Hotels Group have led the way with 45.45% of women on their boards, whereas Coca Cola Hellenic Bottling Company was bottom of the list with only one female board member. Some of the major US firms have progressed better, with General Motors, IBM, PerpsiCo, Lockheed Martin, and DuPont all having women CEOs (*The Economist*, 2015).

▶ The problems run deeper than simply not enough women at board level. In a survey by O2 that was widely publicized in the Human Resource Management trade press, nearly half of women believe all the decision makers in their organizations are men and 17% felt it was 'impossible' for a woman to reach a senior management position (Newbery, 2015). An O2 HR director states: 'While the diversity debate has moved on outside of the office, not enough women are actually seeing this progress at work. If we're to achieve sustainable and long-lasting change, we can't just look at women already at the top; we need to focus our efforts on women at every level, creating a strong pipeline of female talent across British businesses' (cited in Newbery, 2015).

Why does this matter? In February 2012, David Cameron, the UK Prime Minister, claimed there is a 'positive link between women in leadership and business performance, so if we fail to unlock the potential of women in the labour market, we're not only failing those individuals, we're failing our whole economy'. He argued that this was not only to increase equality but that there is clear evidence it would lead to improved performance and maximizing of the pool of talent. He cited Scandinavian countries as examples that the UK could learn from, where representation of females is higher (Hope, 2012).

Cameron is not the first to raise such concerns. In 2008, 17 leading businessmen wrote a letter published in the *Daily Telegraph* stating 'Women contribute to properly balanced boards . . . their participation has a beneficial impact on the character and culture of the board' (cited in Thomson and Lloyd, 2011: 25). The *Women on Boards* report claimed: 'Evidence suggests that companies with a strong female representation at board and top management level perform better than those without and that gender-diverse boards have a positive impact on performance' (2011: 3). Some of their key claims include:

- women 'take non-executive roles more seriously, preparing more consciously for meetings . . . ask the more awkward questions'
- more diverse boards are less likely to produce 'groupthink'
- having at least one female director reduces the chances of going bust by 20%
- more gender-balanced boards are more likely to follow guidelines when making decisions
- increasing female representation increases the talent pool.

The report cited Norway as the prime example—it has over 44% of positions occupied by women. It was not always like this. In 2002 only 6.8% of posts were filled by women, rising to 18% by 2005. Concerned by this, the Norwegian government drafted legislation giving companies until 2008 to meet their quota, with the threat of fines, and even liquidation, if they missed them. Norway has a training programme for women, as well as well-supported childcare, a welfare state, and maternity and paternity leave. With the right pressure, things can change.

Visit the Online Resource Centre for more statistics on the representation of women in companies.

Internationally, the UK is in a weak position when it comes to appointing women, with countries including Sweden, France, and Norway being far more successful (Figure 12.4).

As a result, the number of women, and therefore the talent available, to lead large organizations is diminished.

The lack of women in senior positions has long been identified as a problem and has been labelled the **glass ceiling** effect (Kanter, 1977; Davidson and Cooper, 1992), describing how most women are unable to comfortably progress beyond middle management.

**Glass ceiling** An invisible barrier that minority groups (particularly women) cannot pass through to get to senior positions in the organization.

**Figure 12.4**
International comparison of percentage of female new appointees.
**Source:** © Vinnicombe, Doldor, Sealy, Pryce, Turner, Cranfield University 2015.

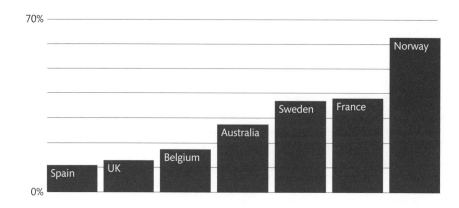

Furthermore, men are able to accelerate their careers in female-dominated occupations through the **glass escalator** (Williams, 1992). Female managers, Wood and Newton (2006) have argued, have to work twice as hard to reach the top as they face many challenges within organizations and owing to their position in society, which can limit their capacity to rise up the career ladder. Men, therefore, despite considerable advances by women in junior and middle management, continue to monopolize senior positions of power and authority (Wajcman, 1998), and the women who reach senior positions exist in a male-dominated world.

> Glass escalator Occurs when men enter female-dominated professions and glide past women to more senior positions.

The *Women on Boards* (Davies, 2011) report identifies reasons for the glass ceiling, including:

- problems with maintaining work/life balance
- masculine culture and poor networks for women
- maternity issues/leave
- traditional bias
- lack of opportunities
- tendency to recruit men.

To deal with this situation, the *Women on Boards* report put forward a number of proposals to equalize opportunities for women, including:

- mentoring and support that helps overcome some of the gender issues
- changing corporate and societal attitudes
- challenging stereotypes about male and female roles (particularly those which suggest women cannot lead)
- childcare, flexible work arrangements, career breaks, and sabbaticals
- affirmative action, creating informal support and providing senior management sponsorship
- working with head-hunters to make women more visible in the recruitment process.

**Real life case:** improving gender balance on French boards

Diafora are a French company that train and coach young female French managers to develop their 'power, influence, visibility and impact' to rise to the top of large organizations. With only 8% of top management positions occupied by women, Diafora believe that 'companies are better served by diverse leadership and management teams—and that mixity [a French word that means gender balance] is a proven contributor to better corporate performance, better corporate governance and more human workplaces for all'.

They help female managers better understand themselves and the political (see Chapter 13) and cultural (see Chapter 7) environment in which they work. They aim to reveal the 'hidden rules of the game and how to make women's unique qualities visible and valued. They discover a new vocabulary and behavioral style that conveys authentic leadership'.

**Source:** http://www.diafora-leadership.com/

# Alternatives to leadership

**Running case:** Effingham returns to the kitchen

'OK, everyone, I've just heard we have the mayor tonight, and he's vegetarian. I want you, Toby, to start preparing another main course and Josh another starter.' Looking up he notices none of them move. 'Come on, everyone!' Effingham shouts in exasperation. 'It's OK,' Josh smiles, 'we knew about this one as Saffron overheard Hunter on the phone—we've already got it sorted.' Effingham looks confused. 'What's this?' he says pointing at the starter. 'It's meant to be pork.' 'But we knew the mayor is vegetarian,' Toby declares proudly. Josh pipes up confidently: 'Look, we have it all under control.' Looking round the kitchen, Effingham is forced to agree.

**Real life case:** the problem with top-down leadership at Toshiba

In July 2015 the president and CEO of Japanese company Toshiba, Hisao Tanaka, stepped down amid accusations that the company had inflated profits by $1.2 billion (Farrell, 2015). One of the fundamental problems was that the company had a top-down culture where followers did not question their superiors. As one report stated: 'Within Toshiba, there was a corporate culture in which one could not go against the wishes of superiors'. It went on to state: 'Therefore, when top management presented "challenges", division presidents, line managers and employees below them continually carried out inappropriate accounting practices to meet targets in line with the wishes of their superiors' (cited by Ando, 2015). It was clear that senior managers had too much power and not enough accountability. As a response, Toshiba will hire more independent directors, lawyers, and accountants (Executive Grapevine, 2015).

All the theories mentioned thus far have presented organizational leadership, and with it existing hierarchies and power structures, as inevitable, and, to a certain extent, essential to the success of organizations. As our real life case with Toshiba illustrates, top-down, hierarchical companies can produce significant problems. Theories deriving from anarchist literature, cooperative movements, and Scandinavian social theory, however, question these assumptions and argue that alternative, non-hierarchical, and non-leader-centred ways of organizing are not only possible but preferable. They state that worker-owned and worker-run organizations can not only produce benefits for society but also be more effective, creative, and motivational than traditional top-down organizations (e.g. Brown and Hosking, 1986; Reedy et al., 2012; Land and King, 2014).

Such approaches are not new. The Rochdale Pioneers, founded in 1844, were one of the first cooperative organizations, and many building societies started as mutual societies. In the UK, the coalition government (2010–15) called for mutual societies to run public services. However, these organizations still retain the traditional command and control structures.

More radical worker-run organizations do away with formal hierarchy altogether, in the belief that all members of the organization should be involved in decision making as it is more democratic, increases involvement, and results in better, more representative decision making. They are self-managed, built around consensus decision making, and conducted in the interests of the workers and wider society. All members of the organization have their say in how things are run and all have a share of the profits (Schwabenland, 2006; Parker et al., 2007).

This view goes beyond the participative approach of post-heroic leadership (and empowerment, which we will examine in the next chapter) as all the power resides with the members, who, on an equal basis, decide how the organization is run and receive the benefits. Generally, these organizations have a social purpose and seek to make products or sell services that people need. They work on a completely different value structure, as shown in Table 12.12.

Table 12.12  Differences between worker-run and shareholder-run organizations

| Worker-run organizations | Shareholder management-run organizations |
| --- | --- |
| Cooperation | Competition |
| Collective decision making | Senior management make decisions |
| Bottom-up decision making | Top-down decision making |
| Individual freedom | Economic freedom |
| Network | Command and control |
| Consensus decision making | Leader decides |
| Self-governing | Leader-governed |
| Workers' democracy | Share-owning democracy |
| Self-management | Hierarchical management |
| Vertical | Horizontal |
| Socially-driven | Shareholder-driven |
| Profit-sharing | Profit-driven |
| Self-help | Economic benefit |

While small in number, there are many examples of this approach, from manufacturing and housing cooperatives through to youth groups. For example, Suma is a wholefoods cooperative that has a democratic management structure. The cooperative is jointly owned by all the members and everyone within the organization gets paid the same. They are committed to being ethical, ecological, and vegetarian (Suma, 2015).

One of the key aims for these groups is to change the way that organizations are run based on more democratic, participatory lines with the purpose of social progress.

One group which aims to develop such an approach is called Radical Routes. They state:

> We want to see a world based on equality and co-operation, where people give according to their ability and receive according to their needs, where work is fulfilling and useful and creativity is encouraged, where decision making is open to everyone with no hierarchies, where the environment is valued and respected in its own right rather than exploited.

(http://www.radicalroutes.org.uk/aims-and-principles.html)

Workers take control of the means of production, organize themselves, and decide the aims and purposes of the organization. By getting rid of the organization's leader, who makes decisions, they work in a more cooperative, consensus-driven, and democratic manner.

**Real life case:** Unicorn Grocery Manchester—a food cooperative

Unicorn Grocery offers an alternative form of supermarket based in Manchester. It is run as a workers' cooperative, which means that everyone takes equal responsibility for all the decisions that impact their business, from big strategic plans to the everyday practices. To work like this they need to be able to communicate well, and therefore they hold regular meetings so that everyone can know what is going on and have their say.

One of the key features of how it is run is that it is non-hierarchical, which means that there is no top management, but everyone has an equal say. Everyone gets equal pay and input in decision making. This requires them to manage themselves and each other, and requires, as they state, 'initiative, hard work, and trust!'

They operate through consensus-based decision making. They admit this is not the quickest or most straightforward way, but it does result in learning from everyone and enabling them to make 'strong, well-founded decisions upheld by a unified and active membership' that everyone feels they have a sense of ownership over.

**Source:** http://www.unicorn-grocery.co.uk/co-op.php

Consensus-based approaches offer alternatives to hierarchical, management-led approaches, aiming towards a shared solution. Consensus-based approaches build on the group's knowledge and insight, founded on learning from each other, and creating a shared understanding of the problem and the solution. The aim is to get overwhelming agreement and informed consensus, striving for everyone to say yes, but, where this is not possible, getting support from most of the group. The aim is for informed consent—they can live with the proposed settlement.

There is an obvious challenge in getting more people involved—many reject the potential for large-scale group discussions. However, techniques like World Café (Brown et al.,

2005) and Open Space Technology (Owen, 2008) can be used to hold meetings between only a handful or a few thousand people. They allow members of the organization to propose subjects to discuss, focus on the topics that matter to them, and build consensus through conversations. They have been used for cultural change programmes, business planning, and international conferences in for-profit organizations, social enterprises, and government agencies. Supporters of these systems argue that they are more democratic and participative and that they create better decisions that everyone can buy into by engaging with a much wider range of decision making.

Visit the Online Resource Centre for further discussion of these systems.

### Review questions

| | |
|---|---|
| **Describe** | What are worker-run organizations? |
| **Explain** | Why do worker-run organizations require different leadership styles and decision-making processes? |
| **Analyse** | Why would alternative organizational structures require a different attitude for everyone in the organization? |
| **Apply** | What type of leadership takes place at Unicorn Grocery (see the real life case above)? What are the advantages and disadvantages of this? |

# Chapter summary

### Running case: the evening meal

'Well, I must say,' declares the mayor, 'that is one of the finest meals I have had in a long time. To have produced that at such short notice you must have a wonderful chef.' 'I agree,' declares Steph, one of the potential investors, 'it was an individual meal, full of character and style.' Chance feels chuffed to lead Junction Hotel and is pleased to see the team pulling together.

Over the last 100 years, leadership theory has become more advanced, from considering that certain individuals are born with innate natural ability to lead organizations through their charisma or strength of personality. The context the leader faces, their behaviour, and, most significantly, the impact they have on their staff has become an increasing focus of research as academics and practitioners try to understand how to lead more effectively and to motivate and inspire followers. More recently, a few business leaders have been praised for handing over responsibility to their workers and creating cultures where people can put forward their own ideas.

However, in practice, despite these advances, command and control leadership style is highly prevalent; leaders are still paid substantially more than their subordinates and often presented as heroes. Women and ethnic minorities are still under-represented at senior level, and this is a trend that does not seem to be changing very quickly.

For leaders to really succeed they need to use power—this is the subject of the next chapter.

## Further reading

**Bass, B.M. 1985. *Leadership and performance beyond expectation*. Free Press: New York.**
This is one of the most influential mainstream leadership texts; it explores why certain leaders outperform others. This book was central in the establishment of the transformational view of leadership.

**Grint, K. 2005. Problems, problems, problems: The social construction of 'leadership'. *Human Relations* 58(11): 1467–94.**
A prominent writer on leadership argues that leaders actively construct the situation that they face, proving a fascinating challenge to conventional situational leadership.

**Meindl, J.R., Ehrlich, S.B., and Dukerich, J. M. 1985. The romance of leadership. *Administrative Science Quarterly* 30(1): 78–102.**
This highly influential article provides a telling critique of the heroic leadership model and provides the opening to the post-heroic.

**Pettigrew, A., and McNulty, T. 1995. Power and influence in and around the boardroom. *Human Relations* 48(8): 845–73.**
This article examines the power and influence of board members of some of the top 200 companies and asks some interesting critical questions about the influence that this elite group have.

**Griffith, J., et al. 2015. How outstanding leaders lead with affect: An examination of charismatic, ideological, and pragmatic leaders. *Leadership Quarterly*, http://dx.doi.org/10.1016/j.leaqua.2015.03.004**
This article provides an interesting overview of charismatic, ideological, and pragmatic leadership styles.

**Uhl-Bien, M., Riggio, R.E., Lowe, K.B., and Carsten, M.K. 2014. Followership theory: A review and research agenda. *Leadership Quarterly* 25(1):83–104.**
This article provides a good overview of leadership theory and the importance of followership. It argues for the importance of followership and the need for more research in this area.

## References

Adams, S. 2014. The worst CEO screw-ups of 2014. *Forbes*, 17 December.

Addison, P. 2011. Why Churchill lost in 1945. BBC Online. Available at: http://www.bbc.co.uk/history/worldwars/wwtwo/election_01.shtml (last accessed 30 November 2012).

Allen, D. 2015. *Getting things done: The art of stress-free productivity*. London: Penguin.

Alvesson, M., and Sveningsson, S. 2003. Good visions, bad micro-management and ugly ambiguity: Contradictions of (non-) leadership in a knowledge-intensive organization. *Organization Studies* 24(6): 961–88.

Ando, R. 2015. UPDATE 2-Toshiba inflated profits by $1.2 bln with top execs' knowledge—investigation. *Reuters*, 20 July.

Antonakis, J., Day, D.V., and Schyns, B. 2012. Leadership and individual differences: At the cusp of a renaissance. *Leadership Quarterly* 23(4): 643–50.

Avolio, B.J., and Gardner, W.L., 2005. Authentic leadership development: Getting to the root of positive forms of leadership. *Leadership Quarterly* 16(3): 315–38.

Badaracco, J.L. 2001. We don't need another hero. *Harvard Business Review* 79(8): 120–6.

Bass, B.M. 1985. *Leadership and performance beyond expectation*. Free Press: New York.

Bass, B., and Riggio, R. 2006. *Transformational leadership*, 2nd edn. Lawrence Erlbaum Associates: London. S

BBC 2011. Howard Schultz—CEO of Starbucks, BBC Radio 4, 12 May [radio interview]. Available at:

http://www.bbc.co.uk/programmes/p00gwwkb (last accessed 5 July 2012).

Bennis, W., and Nanus, B. 1985. *Leaders: The strategies for taking charge.* Harper Collins: New York.

Bercovici, J. 2015. Twitter's CEO: How I stay focused under fire. *Inc*, March.

Bjerke, B. 1999. *Business leadership and culture: National management styles in the global economy.* Edward Elgar: Northampton, MA.

Blake, R., and Mouton, J. 1964. *The managerial grid.* Gulf: Houston, TX.

Bono, J.E., Shen, W., and Yoon, D.J. 2014. Personality and leadership: Looking back, looking ahead. In: David Day (ed.) *The Oxford Handbook of Leadership and Organizations.* Oxford: Oxford Handbooks, 199–220.

Brown, J., and Isaacs, D. 2005. *World Café: Shaping our futures through conversations that matter.* Berrett-Koehler Publishers Inc.: San Francisco.

Brown, M.H., and Hosking, D.M. 1986. Distributed leadership and skilled performance as successful organization in social movements. *Human Relations* 39(1): 65–79.

Bryman, A. 1986. *Leadership and organizations.* Routledge: London.

Bryman, A., Bresnen, M., Beardworth, A., and Keil, T.T. 1988. Qualitative research and the study of leadership. *Human Relations* 41(1): 13–30.

Burns, J.M. 1978. *Leadership.* Harper & Row: New York.

Calás, M., and Smircich, L. 1993. Dangerous liaisons: The feminine-in-management meets globalization. *Business Horizons* 36(2): 71–81.

Channel News Asia 2015. Workers at Deutsche Bank HQ call for Jain to quit as job cuts loom. Available at: http://www.channelnewsasia.com/news/business/workers-at-deutsche-bank/1879102.html (last accessed 19 June 2015).

Chia, R. 2004. Strategy-as-practice: Reflections on the research agenda. *European Management Review* 1(1): 29–34.

Chia, R., and Holt, R. 2006. Strategy as practical coping: A Heideggerian perspective. *Organization Studies* 27(5): 635–55.

Collinson, D. 2005. Questions of distance. *Leadership* 1(2): 235–50.

Cooke, B. 1999. Writing the left out of management theory: The historiography of the management of change. *Organization* 6(1): 81–105.

Davidson, M., and Cooper, C. 1992. *Shattering the glass ceiling: The woman manager.* Paul Chapman Publishing: London.

Davies, E. 2011. Women on boards. Department for Business Innovation and Skills. Available at: http://www.bis.gov.uk/assets/biscore/business-law/docs/w/11-745-women-on-boards

Davies, L. 2013. Pasta firm Barilla boycotted over 'classic family' remarks. *The Guardian*, 26 September.

Dent, M. 2003. Managing doctors and saving a hospital: Irony, rhetoric and actor-networks. *Organization* 10(1): 107–27.

Durando, J. 2010. BP's Tony Hayward: 'I'd like my life back'. *USA Today*, 1 June. Available at: http://content.usatoday.com/communities/greenhouse/post/2010/06/bp-tony-hayward-apology/1#.UJzn14beckR

Executive Grapevine 2015. Toshiba to cut interim CEOs' pay by 90%. *Executive Grapevine*, 20 July.

Farrell, S. 2015. Toshiba boss quits over £780m accounting scandal. *The Guardian*, 21 July.

Fiedler, F. 1967. *A theory of leadership effectiveness.* McGraw-Hill: New York.

Fiedler, F., and Chemers, M. 1984. *Improving leadership effectiveness: The leader match concept.* John Wiley and Sons: Chichester.

Ford, J., and Harding, N. 2011. The impossibility of the 'true self' of authentic leadership. *Leadership* 7(4): 463–79.

Frauenheim, E. 2014. Vineet Nayar's happy feet. Available at: http://www.workforce.com/articles/20311-vineet-nayars-happy-feet (last accessed 18 June 2015).

Gardner, J. 1989. *On leadership.* Free Press: New York.

Gardner, W.L., Cogliser, C.C., Davis, K.M., and Dickens, M.P. 2011. Authentic leadership: A review of the literature and research agenda. *Leadership Quarterly* 22(6): 1120–45.

Goldberg, A., and Ritter, B. 2006. Costco CEO finds pro-worker means profitability. *ABC News.* Available at: http://abcnews.go.com/2020/Business/story?id=1362779#.ULJqJYYsL3V (last accessed 23 August 2015).

Goodley, S. 2015. Deutsche Bank bosses resign following Libor manipulation scandal. *The Guardian*, 7 June.

Greenleaf, R.K. 1970. *The servant as leader.* Robert K. Greenleaf Center: Newton Center, MA.

Grint, K. 2000. *The arts of leadership.* Oxford University Press: Oxford.

Grint, K. 2005. Problems, problems, problems: The social construction of 'leadership'. *Human Relations* 58(11): 1467–94.

Grint, K. 2010. The sacred in leadership: Separation, sacrifice and silence. *Organization Studies* 31(1): 89–107.

Grint, K., and Holt, C. 2011. Leading questions: If 'Total Place', 'Big Society' and local leadership are the answers, what's the question? *Leadership* 7(1): 85–98.

Groth, A. 2011. 19 amazing ways CEO Howard Schultz saved Starbucks. *Business Insider*, 19 June. Available at: http://www.businessinsider.com/howard-schultz-turned-starbucks-around-2011-6?op=1

Harris, J. 2014. The Rochdale Pioneers to Paul Flowers: How the Co-operative dream died. *The Guardian*, 23 April.

Haslam, A., Reicher, S., and Platow, M. 2011. *The new psychology of leadership: Identity, influence and power*. Psychology Press: Hove.

Hersey, P., and Blanchard, K.H. 1988. *Management of organizational behaviour: Utilizing human resources*. Prentice Hall: Englewood Cliffs, NJ.

Holmberg, I., and Tyrstrup, M. 2010. Well then—what now? An everyday approach to managerial leadership. *Leadership* 6(4): 353–72.

Hope, C. 2012. Plans for women's quotas on company boards dropped. *Daily Telegraph*, 28 May.

House, R. 1996. Path-goal theory of leadership: Lessons, legacy, and a reformulated theory. *Leadership Quarterly* 7(3): 323–52.

House, R.J., Hanges, P.W., Javidan, M., Dorfman, P., and Gupta, V. (eds) 2004. *Culture, leadership, and organizations: The GLOBE study of 62 societies*. Sage: London.

Kanter, R. 1977. *Men and women of the corporation*. Basic Books: London.

Kanter, R.M. 1992. *The change masters: Corporate entrepreneurs at work*. Cengage Learning: London.

Kirkpatrick, S.A., and Locke, E.A. 1991. Leadership: Do traits matter? *Academy of Management Executive* 5(2): 48–60.

Kollewe, J. 2011. Apple stock price falls on news of Steve Jobs's death. *The Guardian*, 6 October. Available at: http://www.guardian.co.uk/technology/2011/oct/06/apple-stock-steve-jobs

Land, C., and King, D. 2014, Organizing otherwise: Translating anarchism in a voluntary sector organization. *Ephemera* 14(4): 923–50.

Lewin, K., Lippitt, R., and White, R. 1939. Patterns of aggressive behavior in experimentally created social climates. *Journal of Social Psychology* 10: 271–301.

Longstaffe, C. 2005. Winston Churchill, a leader from history or an inspiration for the future? *Leadership; Management Skills; Communication Skills; Modern History* 37(2): 80–83.

Manjoo, F. 2015. Dick Costolo thinks it's o.k. to never tweet. *New York Times*, 25 February.

Meindl, J.R., Ehrlich, S.B., and Dukerich, J.M. 1985. The romance of leadership. *Administrative Science Quarterly* 30(1): 78–102.

Mintzberg, H. 1975. The manager's job: Folklore and fact. *Harvard Business Review* 53(4): 29–61.

Nadler, D.A., and Tushman, M.L. 1997. *Competing by design: The power of organizational architecture*. Oxford University Press: Oxford.

Nayar, V. 2010. *Employees first, customers second: Turning conventional management upside down*. Harvard Business Press: Boston.

Newbery, C. 2015. A fifth of women believe it's 'impossible' to attain a top job. *People Management*, 20 January.

Northouse, P. 2010. *Leadership: Theory and practice*. Sage: London.

Owen, H. 2008. *Open space technology: A user's guide*. Berrett-Koehler Publishers Inc.: San Francisco.

Parker, M., Fournier, V., and Reedy, P. 2007. *The dictionary of alternatives*. Zed Books: London.

Parris, D.L., and Peachey, J.W. 2013. A systematic literature review of servant leadership theory in organizational contexts. *Journal of Business Ethics* 113(3): 377–93.

Pillai, R., and Meindl, J.R. 1991. The impact of a performance crisis on attributions of charismatic leadership: A preliminary study. In: *Proceedings of the 1991 Eastern Academy of Management Meetings*, Hartford, CT.

Raelin, J. 2005. We the leaders: In order to form a leaderful organization. *Journal of Leadership and Organizational Studies* 12(2): 18–31.

Reedy, P., Coupland, C., and King, D. 2012. Freedom is an endless meeting: The role of alternative organizations in resisting dominant contemporary discourses of the self. 10th International Conference Discourse and Organization: Amsterdam.

Roberts, A. 2003. *Hitler and Churchill: Secrets of leadership*. Weidenfeld & Nicolson: London.

Robertson, B.J. 2015. *Holacracy: The new management system for a rapidly changing world*. Henry Holt and Company: New York.

Schultz, H. 2011. *Onward: How Starbucks fought for its life without losing its soul*. John Wiley and Sons: Chichester.

Schwabenland, C. 2006. *Stories, visions and values in voluntary organisations*. Ashgate: Farnham.

Semler, R. 1999. *Maverick! The success story behind the world's most unusual workplace*. Random House: London.

Shontell, A. 2013. 4 of Silicon Valley's most impressive CEOs just ate dinner together. *Business Insider*, 1 May.

Smircich, L., and Morgan, G. 1982. Leadership: The management of meaning. *Journal of Applied Behavioral Science* 18(3): 257–73.

Starbucks 2012. *Our Starbucks Mission Statement*. Available at: http://www.starbucks.com/about-us/company-information/mission-statement (last accessed 25 November 2012).

Stogdill, R.M. 1948. Personal factors associated with leadership: A survey of the literature. *Journal of Psychology* 25: 35–71.

Suma 2015. About Suma. Available at: http://www.suma.coop/about/ (last accessed 23 August 2015).

Sun, L. 2015. Does Twitter Inc. need a new CEO? Available at: http://www.fool.com/investing/general/2015/05/06/does-twitter-inc-need-a-new-ceo.aspx (last accessed 19 June 2015).

Sveningsson, S., and Larsson, M. 2006. Fantasies of leadership: Identity work. *Leadership* 2(2): 203–24.

*The Economist* 2015. Sex in the boardroom, 6 June.

*The Guardian*, 2010. BP's Tony Hayward: Resignation statement, 27 July.

Thelen, H. 1992. *Research with Bion's concepts*. In: Pines, M. (ed.) *Bion and group psychotherapy*. Tavistock/Routledge: London.

Thielman, S. 2015. Twitter's Dick Costolo to step down amid stalled growth and troll troubles. *The Guardian*, 12 June.

Thomson, P., and Lloyd, T. 2011. *Women and the new business leadership*. Palgrave Macmillan: Basingstoke.

*Time Magazine* 2011. The 2011 TIME 100 Poll, 21 April.

Timmerman, R. 2014. Why we're adopting Holacracy as our organisational operating system at Springest. Available at: https://medium.com/@rubzie/why-were-adopting-holacracy-as-our-organisational-operating-system-at-springest-436c946c2b69 (last accessed 3 August 2015).

Towers Watson 2014. *The 2014 Global Workforce Study*. Towers Watson: London.

Twitter 2015. About Twitter. Available at: https://about.,twitter.,com/company (last accessed 19 June 2015).

Uhl-Bien, M., Riggio, R.E., Lowe, K.B., and Carsten, M.K. (2014). Followership theory: A review and research agenda. *Leadership Quarterly* 25(1): 83–104.

*USA Today* 2007. CEO's bold experiment: Management by democracy. Available at: http://usatoday30.usatoday.com/money/companies/management/2007-12-16-workplace-democracy_N.htm (last accessed 18 June 2015).

Vinnicombe, S., Doldor, E., Sealy, R., Pryce, P., and Turner, C. 2015. The female FTSE board report 2015. Cranfield School of Management: Cranfield.

Wajcman, J. 1998. *Managing like a man: Women and men in corporate management*. Polity Press: Cambridge.

Williams, C. 1992. The glass escalator: Hidden advantages for men in the 'female' professions. *Social Problems* 39(3): 253–67.

Wood, G., and Newton, J. 2006. Childnessness and women managers: 'Choice' context and discourses. *Gender, Work and Organization* 13(4): 338–58.

# Power and politics in organizations

*The murky world of organizational life*

## Chapter overview and learning outcomes

By the end of this chapter you should be able to:

- describe the 'power as property' view
- explain why power and politics exist within organizations
- explain why power and politics challenge the image of organizations as rational places
- explain why Lukes and Foucault believe that power shapes how people see the world
- analyse the different underlying assumptions of 'power as property', 'structure as power', and 'power as productive'.

## Key theorists

| | |
|---|---|
| Stephen Lukes | A Marxist theorist who argues that power works in often invisible ways, defining the choices that people make in ways they are often not aware of |
| Jeffrey Pfeffer | US management theorist who has investigated power in organizations and is a leading proponent of the 'power as property' view |
| John French and Bertam Raven | US social psychologists who argue that individuals can have certain sources of power |
| Michel Foucault | A French historian and philosopher who presents a challenging interpretation of how power operates, seeing it as productive rather than repressive |
| Max Weber | A German sociologist who argued there are three categories of authority |

## Key terms

| | |
|---|---|
| Power | A highly contested term, but can be seen as the capacity to get things done or to influence others |
| Office politics | Often seen as game-playing or manipulation, but can also be seen as an essential part of organizational life |
| Influence | The capacity to impact others, directly or indirectly |
| Emancipation | Literally—freedom from slavery; freedom from (often onerous) levels of control |
| False consciousness | A Marxist term—false beliefs held by the proletariat (workers) who do not know their true position in society as the revolutionary force to overthrow capitalism; instead, they see the current structure of society as unchangeable and largely fair |
| Empowerment | To be delegated power or authority to make (some) decisions |

# Introduction: politics at work

**Running case:** Linda Wilkinson's new idea

Linda Wilkinson is excited, but nervous, about her idea of introducing a new wedding service for Junction Hotel—a new, comprehensive wedding planner, an upgrade to the bridal suite, and new themed weddings.

She has been working on the idea for weeks, building up the argument by writing a 20-page document with evidence from other hotels, and including a survey of potential clients and information that she gathered at the UK hoteliers' wedding fair.

She is sure that this will be a success and has put together what she thinks will be a convincing case that will bring Junction Hotel into the twenty-first century. All she needs to do now is convince the board.

We like to think of organizations as rational places where decisions are made based on merit, follow rational and logical procedures, and are taken in the long-term interest of the organization. Everyone involved in decision making, we hope, leaves aside personal interest and works for the common good. We also tend to believe that as individual employees we are judged on our merits, based on our hard work and performance, and that we get promoted or praised accordingly. In our idealized view organizations are meritocracies, free of power and politics.

Jeffery Pfeffer (2010) claims this view is a fantasy. 'Power and politics is an essential feature of organizational life. It takes more than good performance to do well in organizations', he states; 'being politically savvy and seeking power are related to career success and even managerial performance' (Pfeffer, 2010: 4). Pfeffer argues that as organizations have only one chief executive officer (CEO), and other senior positions are limited, competition to get to the top can be ferocious and highly politically charged. The result can be that 'Some of the individuals competing for advancement bend the rules of fair play or ignore them completely. Don't complain about this or wish the world were different', Pfeffer (2010: 4–5) counsels. 'You can compete and even triumph if you understand the principles of power and are willing to use them' (ibid.: 5).

While most managers do not want to admit to being involved in political activity, their regular activities demonstrate a different reality. They include 'showing up opponents at meetings, getting access to some critical information, making a point with the boss ... forming alliances' (Pfeffer, 1981: 369). Getting resources—such as budgets, staff members, the go-ahead for projects—or being judged as successful are politically charged. Power and politics are also involved further down the organization, impacting details such as who gets to choose shifts through to big issues such as increased pay and promotion.

This chapter argues that power and politics are a central feature of organizational life. Like organizational culture, power and politics are subterranean, below the surface, often invisible, but impact upon everything. This observation reveals a shadow organization where decisions are made for alternative reasons than those officially stated. If you want to get on in organizations or understand how they work, then you need to understand power and politics.

Consider an organization that you know well, somewhere you have worked, a club or society you have been involved in, or even your family. Are there any features that you would class as political? How did you feel about this?

Often power and politics are portrayed in negative terms, as actions by manipulative individuals for personal financial or status gain. Yet power and politics could also be seen as essential to the functioning of organizations. Take a charity worker who needs to get food to starving people in a war-torn area. She/he would need to use political skills to negotiate a safe passage for the lorries between the warring factions. It takes power to get things done.

# Chapter outline

This chapter starts with defining power and politics before moving on to explore office politics in everyday situations. We will then explore three key theoretical perspectives to understand power: *power as property* (which sees power as the possession of an individual or group), *structure as power* (which sees how the social structure shapes the way people think), and *power as productive* (which examines how power operates within everyday relations between people and organizations). Finally, we will explore how some writers and managers have sought to produce more equal and balanced management practices.

While power and politics are important to organizational life, until relatively recently these subjects did not receive much attention from organizational researchers, who preferred to view organizations as rational and bureaucratic (see Chapters 2–4) (Clegg and Haugaard, 2012). Consequently, many of the following theories did not arise from studying management, but rather came from political and social science, and, therefore, ask slightly broader questions about the way that power works in influencing society.

**Real life case: FIFA in crisis**

By any standards, 2015 was a turbulent year for FIFA (the Fédération Internationale de Football Association). Following the highly controversial decisions to award the 2018 and 2022 World Cups to Russia and Qatar, questions began to be raised over vote rigging and corruption. In June 2015 the FBI and Swiss prosecutors charged 18 senior officials with corruption, money laundering, tax evasion, and racketeering (Gibson, 2015). Sepp Blatter, who in May had been re-elected as president for the fifth term, resigned and the organization seemed in crisis.

This was hardly the first time that accusations of corruption and political game-playing had been made (Jennings, 2006). But it also increased the spotlight on the political skills of Blatter.

The former Swiss wedding singer's rise to become the most powerful man in world football is well documented. He knew the organization and its processes inside out, and he has been labelled a brilliant politician and Machiavellian (Kuper, 2015). Speaking to BBC Radio, Gabriele Marcotti stated that Blatter was very clever at building his power base. Before he became president, FIFA was predominately run in the interests of Europe and South America, whereas Blatter reached out to the countries previously excluded and offered them things that FIFA previously hadn't. By developing FIFA's commercial income he was able to distribute that money to help support football in less developed ▶

▶ nations and, through this, gain their loyalty (BBC, 2015b). Mark Palios, the former Football Association CEO, stated 'Everyone acknowledges that he is a great politician ... he is very empathetic, he understands what drives people' (BBC, 2015b).

According to columnist Craig Foster, Blatter is '[t]he consummate political operator ... shifting blame and manoeuvring himself in the geopolitical landscape [and managing to] eliminate any obstacles that stand in the way of each successive term' (2014). Former UEFA general secretary Gerhard Aigner states: 'He wants to appear like a king ... He can be terribly ruthless . . . when his power is at stake—he will do almost anything to defend it' (cited in BBC, 2015b).

He does have his supporters, with Russian president Vladimir Putin saying he deserves a Nobel prize for how he has run FIFA (Hunderson, 2015). Kushal Das, from the All India Football Federation, stated: 'What's being reported about FIFA and Blatter from Europe is not something that we in Indian football recognise' (cited in Chaudhary, 2015). They accuse Blatter's critics of not seeing the good he has done for world football and trying to regain power back for Europe and South America.

What political skills did Sepp Blatter demonstrate? What is the dividing line between building alliances and acting for political gain?

# What is power?

While what has allegedly happened at FIFA might be fairly extreme, small-scale political activity is at the heart of much of organizational life.

As with many of the subjects that we cover in this book, there is no single definition for power and politics. Some define **politics** as illegitimate, unofficial, or unsanctioned behaviour by those who manipulate or control decisions for their own (selfish) interest (Ferris et al., 2005), against formal authority or accepted ideology.

For other researchers, **power** is actually used to overcome resistance in order to achieve the desired results (e.g. Pfeffer, 1981). According to this view, power is therefore 'the ability to get things done, to mobilize resources, to get and use whatever it is that a person needs for the goals he or she is attempting to meet' (Kanter, 1977: 166). According to this view, power is therefore *legitimate* and can be 'defined as the capacity to effect (or affect) organizational outcomes' (Mintzberg, 1983). A central question, therefore, is whether power is an enabling force, allowing things to be done, or if it is negative and creates restrictions (Lawrence et al., 2012). This tension leaves Burns to ask: 'can we subdue the voracious, crafty, and inescapable beast of power?' (Burns, 1978).

Another question is: does power actually need to be used to exist? Robert Dahl believes that power exists only when it is actually used. For him, power only exists through actual actions and observable behaviour. As Henry Mintzberg has argued, 'having a basis for power is not enough. The individual must act' (1983: 25). Others, though, argue that it is merely having the potential to use power that counts. For instance, a manager might only threaten to fire someone; they do not actually use their power, but the threat alone makes the employee work harder.

What is the boundary between power and influence (Figure 13.1)? Some scholars use these terms interchangeably, whereas others see influence as the legitimate activity of managers and power as the illegitimate use to gain personal ends or play the system.

**Politics** A process of game-playing and tactics that occurs within organizations where different individuals jostle with each other to gain personal advantage.

**Power** The capacity to get things done or to influence others.

Official sanctioned        Unofficial unsanctioned

Power

Influence        Politics

**Figure 13.1** Three views of power.

# Definitions of power

- 'A has power over B to the extent that he can get B to do something that B would not otherwise do' (Dahl, 1957)

- 'Power is the capacity of individuals to overcome resistance on the part of others, to exert their will and to produce results consistent with their interests and objectives' (Huczynski and Buchanan, 2004)

- 'the probability that one actor within a social relationship will be in a position to carry out his own will despite resistance, regardless of the basis on which this probability rests' (Weber, 1978: 53)

- 'Power is a property of the system at rest; politics is the study of power in action' (Pfeffer, 1981: 7).

Therefore, there is no single definition of 'power' or of 'politics'; the terms in the debate are used in different ways by different authors. Care should be taken when assessing the different theoretical viewpoints presented.

How would you define power?

# Why are there power and politics in organizations?

**Running case:** Effingham and Mortimer meet to discuss rumours of Linda Wilkinson's wedding plan

'Have you heard about Linda's plans for her new wedding package?' Effingham asks Mortimer. 'Yes, it's a good idea, isn't it? I can really see it taking off for the hotel,' Mortimer replies positively. 'You think?' scoffs Effingham. 'It's going to be bad news for the hotel. Wedding food is always dire *and* really dull to make—I don't want to be lumbered with stuffing hundreds of tuna *vol-au-vents*. And have you thought about the hassle it will be for the rest of the hotel—discos until 1 am, drunken uncles setting off fire extinguishers, and the like.' 'Oh,' replies Mortimer thoughtfully, 'I see what you mean.' 'Yep,' Effingham responds confidently, 'we need to stop this.'

Why are there power and politics in organizations? The answer to this question depends on the theoretical assumptions you take (Figure 13.2).

Those from the **regulation** perspective (functionalist and interpretivist) ultimately believe that conflict is the breakdown of consensus.

The **functionalist** perspective privileges order, consensus, and harmony as it suggests that organizations share collective goals (visit the Online Resource Centre for more on this). Social scientists such as Talcott Parsons see power only tied to legitimate authority and therefore argue 'the threat of coercive measures, or of compulsion, without legitimation or justification, should not properly be called the use of power at all' (Lukes, 2005: 331). They believe that everyone in the organization shares the same interests and therefore see politics as the breakdown of this harmony.

The **interpretivist** perspective sees organizational members hold different views but, ultimately, still seek harmony. For these theorists, most actions within the organization are bureaucratic or rational and, therefore, not political. Political activity is reserved for overcoming resistance: 'the conscious effort to muster and use force to overcome opposition in a choice situation' (Pfeffer, 1981: 7). This perspective would suggest that although members of an organization have different interests, ultimately they can achieve harmony by understanding each other and seeing where their common interests reside.

From the opposite perspective, those that see things through the **radical change** perspective argue that conflict is inevitable because members of the organization share different, often competing interests. While power and politics arise, in part, through personal ambition they are also about seeking to take control and shaping the future direction of the organization. Power and politics are inevitable as, in order to get anything done, organizational members have to use scarce resources (time, money, equipment, etc.) and be reliant on other people (who might have different views, belief systems, or priorities). In short, this scarcity and divergent perspectives mean that in order to get things done, power and politics are essential. The radical change perspective suggests that the workers and management have different objective interests and use power to further their own interests.

Those from the **radical structuralist** perspective, such as that held by Steven Lukes (see the section on 'Power as structure' later in this chapter), argue that power works because the broader

**Figure 13.2** Burrell and Morgan's sociological paradigms framework.

**Source:** © Sociological Paradigms and Organizational Analysis: Elements of the Sociology of Corporate Life, Burrell, G., and Morgan, G. (1979), Ashgate Publishing.

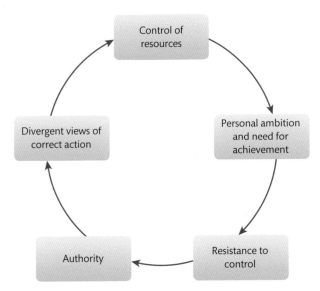

**Figure 13.3**  Power as a product of competing interests.

capitalist society hides employees' *true* interests from them. The **radical humanist** perspective takes this argument one step further by arguing that individuals do not have *true* interests. Like the interpretivists, they believe that people have different interests, but they do not see that this should produce consensus. Instead, they think that power works by shaping the individual's sense of identity and producing what they believe are their interests (Figure 13.3).

A number of authors from a psychological and philosophical perspective have argued that the need for power is a core part of human identity. Friedrich Nietzsche (1990) called this drive 'the will to power', arguing that the need to expand one's power is the ultimate driver of human actions. David McClelland argued that this drive is an essential motivating force, alongside the need for achievement and belonging (1975). According to this view, the need for power is seen as an essential human trait.

> **Radical humanist** A radical change perspective which emphasizes the 'subjective' contradictions capitalism has on the consciousness of people, often outside their awareness, producing alienation and oppression.

# The individual's power

## Running case: Linda seeks help

*Dear Sarah*

*As you know, I have been working on this new wedding project for Junction Hotel, which I am very excited about. However, while it makes perfect sense on paper and is the right thing to do to make Junction Hotel more profitable, all I'm getting are negative reactions and people telling me why it won't work. Meg Mortimer says that it is going to put off our regular clients, Effingham says that he'll need a new kitchen to make it work, and David Hunter thinks that the bridal suite is going to cost too much money and thinks it will only be used at weekends.*

*On top of all this, I seem to really have peeved Graham off, as he is now spreading lies about me being incompetent when all I've tried to do is help him. Graham was the one that pushed me into this and now he's deserted me.*

I'm really worried that it's going to go horribly wrong at the board meeting next week. I think I'm being stitched up and there is nothing that I can do.

Any advice? I'm feeling desperate and want to give the whole thing up.

Yours, as always

Linda

What advice would you give to Linda?

# Office politics–political skills

When we think of power and politics in organizations we often think of manipulation, treacherous personalities, sucking up to the boss, and personal feuds. Stories of managers putting unrealistic pressures on the workers, people with less talent getting promoted over more worthy peers, and favouritism shown by the boss regularly fill the advice pages of the business press as employees try to grapple with a complex political landscape. The common term for this is *office politics*.

## Real life case: examples of office politics in the news

- In April 2015 Ferdinand Piëch, the chairman of German car company Volkswagen, resigned after criticizing the company's CEO, Martin Winterkorn, in an interview with *Der Spiegel*. A statement from the board said: 'The members of the steering committee came to a consensus that, in the light of the past weeks, the mutual trust necessary for successful cooperation was no longer there' (BBC, 2015a). The 2011 Automobile Man of the Year had a long history of political skirmishes and stated that all it takes to fall out with him is 'to make the same mistake twice' (*Automobile*, 2011). It was reported that the board was concerned about his activities in corporate governance (for instance installing his wife on the board) and that his 'Machiavellian ways have spread paranoia among those below him' (Milne, 2015).

- In 2010, Michael Geoghegan stepped down as CEO of HSBC holdings after a reported 'unprecedented bout of boardroom back-stabbing, when it became clear that he stood no chance of replacing the departing Stephen Green as HSBC chairman—a role won by the finance director, Douglas Flint' (Moore, 2010).

- In October 2014 Chris Viehbacher resigned after receiving a payoff of, reportedly, approximately €3m and €250,000 per month (Ward, 2015) from the French pharmaceutical company Sanofi. The German-Canadian had clashed with Serge Weinberg, the chairman, 'over his management style and alleged communications problems with the board' (Ward, 2015). Mr Weinberg had told the *Financial Times*: 'We had some worries about management style, about execution, focus and also about the nature of the relationship with the board' (Thomson, 2014). Furthermore, the *Financial Times* reported, 'Mr Viehbacher's decisive character and quick decision-making had irritated some board members, and its chairman, in particular' (Thomson, 2014). ▶

- Australian oil and gas company Tap Oil have been subject to continued speculation about the relationship between the CEO and the principal Thai shareholder (Macdonald-Smith, 2015), with rumours that the company may be split and some of the directors replaced with the Thai owners' own directors (Tap Oil, 2015).

Can you think of any examples of office politics either that are in the news or that you have seen at work?

Office politics, although often presented as rife within organizations, rarely makes it into the public arena, as companies and the individuals involved do not want to discuss it or even admit that there is a problem.

Office politics can take many forms, including being humiliated by one's boss, being subject to gossip, and being offered support that never materializes. Popular management advice books present tips about how to succeed, negotiate, or just survive office politics. These include learning the unspoken rules of the game, standing up for oneself, being seen in a positive light, being associated with a successful project, and ingratiating oneself to key people—all seen to be essential for office politics. Many claim that office politics is at least as important as being good at your job for career progression. Table 13.1 lists some examples of issues arising from office politics and suggested solutions.

Visit the Online Resource Centre to see more examples of office politics.

# Niccoló Machiavelli's *The Prince*

**Running case:** Linda gets her answer

Dear Linda

Many thanks for your letter. Your wedding plan seems a really good idea—well done for coming up with such a good initiative. It seems, though, that office politics are getting in the way of your plans. You need to accept that office politics exists and you cannot go it alone.

It sounds to me that you need to start working with the other senior members of Junction Hotel. Have a think about what is in it for them and why they would want to back your wedding scheme. Even if it is good for the hotel, you need to show how it is good for them. What are the buttons you need to press to convince them that it's a good idea? Don't forget the rest of your staff as well—you will need them on board if it is going to work.

I enclose a book on dealing with office politics at work. It has some good exercises in it and advice as to how to increase your power base and personal style at work. It might be worth having a read.

Good luck and keep in touch

Sarah

Table 13.1 Examples of situations in office politics and suggested solutions

| Situations in office politics | Suggested solutions |
|---|---|
| Regularly falling out of favour with the boss or with colleagues | Think about how you present yourself at work and how others might interpret your comments |
| Being the scapegoat for decisions | Build alliances with others and get a mentor |
| Swamped with work while a colleague slacks | Be more assertive at work and ask your colleague politely, but firmly, to take on some tasks |
| Having a boss that does not solve problems in a team and instead follows the line of least resistance | Do not expect the boss to be the saviour and try to tackle the problem yourself |

Those involved in office politics are often accused of being manipulative, dishonest, controlling, cunning, and duplicitous. Such people are often la- belled 'Machiavellian', meaning that they manipulate others for personal gain (Wilson et al., 1996). Based on Ital- ian philosopher Niccolò Machiavelli's work *The Prince* (1532/1984), someone who is Machiavellian is seen as an un- scrupulous character who stops at nothing to gain, and retain, power and influence.

Machiavellian office politics.

Machiavelli, however, is subtler than his popular portrayal. He provided one of the earliest accounts of how power actually works in organizations. Rather than taking an idealized view (what we would like to happen) of leaders as good people anointed by God or born with authority, Machiavelli took a real- ist view (a description of what really happens) by examining how power was actually gained (and lost) by the elite. He therefore challenged the view that leaders are necessarily good simply because of their position (a dominant view at that time). Rather, he argued, to get to the top and maintain their power, leaders need to perform sometimes ethically questionable acts.

A key question for Machiavelli (1532/1984) is: Is it better to be loved or feared? He replied:

> The answer is that one would like to be both the one and the other; but because it is difficult to combine them, it is far safer to be feared than loved if you cannot be both.

He argued that people obey because they fear the consequences of not doing so. Therefore, the leader should use coercive power and be prepared to do evil; to produce good, some- times the leader has to do evil. For Machiavelli, the end justifies the means.

**Real life case:** Jack Welch

Between 1981 and 2001 Jack Welch was the CEO of General Electric, one of the world's largest companies. He was highly successful and named CEO of the year on numerous occasions, taking GE to the top of most of the markets it competed in. He had a relentless drive to improve shareholder value.

To achieve this outcome Welch sacked the worst-performing 10% of his staff every year. He was thus nicknamed 'Neutron Jack' because the people disappeared but the buildings were left standing.

> Welch was considered a demanding boss and was prominently listed on Fortune's list of the most difficult bosses to work for. He certainly appeared to use subordinates, if not solely as a means for his own end, then solely as a means to increase the wealth of GE shareholders.          (Bowie, 2000: 186)

**Sources:** Tichy and Stratford (1993); O'Boyle (1998); Bowie (2000).

Have you met someone who you would describe as Machiavellian? How would you describe them? Did they get what they want?

What do you think of Machiavelli's question—is it better to be loved or feared? Are there times when you have to do things that you think are wrong in order to get the right outcome?

**Research insight:** Machiavellian leaders using ethical leadership
Den Hartog, D.N., and Belschak, F.D. 2012. Work engagement and Machiavellianism in the ethical leadership process. *Journal of business ethics* 107(1): 35–47.

As we have seen in Chapter 12 and will see in Chapter 17, as a response to criticism of various corporate scandals, in recent years there has been greater emphasis on business leaders acting in more ethical ways. Ethical and authentic leadership should 'send clear messages about ethical values' and model good behaviour (Den Hartog and Belschak, 2012: 36). This is seen to have benefits for the firm, as having a strong set of values makes the work feel more meaningful to the followers, increasing their motivation. However, Den Hartog and Belschak argue 'that highly manipulative Machiavellians may try to enact an ethical image if they feel this benefits them' (Den Hartog and Belschak, 2012: 39). In other words, they *act* publicly in a way that appears ethical but privately they continue with a 'deceitful and unethical value system' (ibid.: 39). They state that it is 'likely that Machiavellian leaders will increasingly see maintaining their ethical image at work as important for their success in the organization' (ibid.: 44). However, they also found that 'followers do seem to distinguish between authentic and inauthentic displays of ethical leadership' (ibid.: 45): this surface acting (see Chapter 16) does not always convenience followers, which may, the authors suggest, 'make their leadership less impactful' (ibid.: 45).

**Employability skills:** enhance your political skills

Even if you do not want to be Machiavellian, political skills are very important to success within organizations. Consequently, it is necessary to understand what skills an individual might need in order to survive. Political skill has been defined as 'the ability to effectively understand others at work, ▶

> ▶ and to use such knowledge to influence others to act in ways that enhance one's personal and/or organizational objectives' (Ferris et al., 2005: 127).
>
> Academic articles (see Ferris et al., 2007), popular business books, newspaper columns (for instance *The Guardian*'s 'Work' section), and websites offer advice as to how to be a good political operator or just how to survive at work. Some of the overall advice is included in Table 13.2.

Table 13.2  Ways to build your political skills (adapted from Ferris et al., 2007, www.office-politics.com and Yeung, 2009)

| Political skill | Description | Example |
| --- | --- | --- |
| Accept that office politics exists | Accept and understand that organizations are not meritocracies, but office politics exists and is vital for survival (and career) | Understand the political landscape and informal rules of your organization |
| Develop social skills | Listen to, and be sensitive to, others and adapt your ideas to fit their worldview | Have a convincing personal style that influences others and elicits the desired response from others |
| Networking ability | Develop diverse contacts within, and outside, the organization that are useful for personal and organizational purposes | Attach yourself to potential high-flyers and get a mentor to support your development; go to lunch with people and for a drink after work |
| Appearing sincere | Appear authentic, sincere, genuine, and as though you have no ulterior motives | Make sure that you do not appear to have political motives for your actions |
| Political nous | Learn how things really work | Watch what is deemed acceptable and unacceptable behaviour, and the unwritten rules of what is a success |
| Personal characteristics | Self-confidence, self-awareness, with a strong locus of control and an outgoing and likeable personality | Have the type of personality that others want to be with and charm people |
| Self-promotion | Demonstrate how accomplished you are, presenting yourself, and your successes, in the best possible light | Get on flagship projects that the boss pays attention to; appear in company newsletters, etc. |
| Building coalitions | Build power bases either with peers (alliances) or subordinates (empire-building) | Bring a range of people on to your side and make them feel they will benefit from your projects |

Are you skilled in any of these areas and are there some that you would like to improve? From what you have read, what advice would you offer Linda Wilkinson in dealing with her situation?

## Implications of office politics at work

**Running case:** Linda Wilkinson decides what to do

Reading Sarah's letter, Linda Wilkinson feels a little despondent. Surely she should have her ideas judged on their merits alone. But she has noticed that some members of Junction Hotel seem to get their own way far more than they should. Are they better at playing the politics, she wonders?

Certainly, she will need to get Simon Chance and the board to like the idea. This should be possible, as the figures add up and it will generate good public relations for the hotel. However, she will also need the senior management team to like it. Effingham seems to have the ear of Meg Mortimer and Phil Weaver, and he seems to be against the idea. She will also need to show that she will be able to get her team to back it, otherwise it will not run smoothly. 'How do I go about this?' she wonders.

'Hi, Graham, can we have a chat?' asks Wilkinson. 'Not really,' responds Effingham, 'I'm busy.' 'OK,' continues Wilkinson uncertainly, 'I wanted to talk to you about the menu plans for the wedding proposal.' Effingham does not respond. 'Well, I think this is a great opportunity to really develop the restaurant and get us lots of new customers,' continues Wilkinson, undeterred. 'You do a great job and I think the wedding service could really be the making of the restaurant.' 'Serving *vol-au-vents*,' mutters Effingham. 'Not at all,' replies Wilkinson, grabbing her chance. 'I think that we—well, you actually—could invent a really exciting new way of doing wedding food.' Effingham looks up. 'I mean,' Wilkinson continues, 'the new wedding service is about redefining what Junction Hotel is about and the type of service we can offer. If it goes through, we will all get the chance to be genuinely innovative and creative,' Wilkinson continues positively, thinking about Effingham's trigger words, 'putting Junction Hotel above the rest. Look, I know you're busy now, but when you have some time I would be ever so grateful if you could give me an hour of your time to put forward some menu ideas that will make Junction Hotel really stand out.' Effingham looks up again. 'Oh, on another note,' states Wilkinson, pretending it to be an afterthought, 'you know that we are meeting next week about the kitchen upgrade. A better kitchen will help make the business case for this.'

The existence of office politics demonstrates that work is not always meritocratic but decisions are sometimes made on political grounds. This impacts on the way people feel about work. Research by Zivnuska et al. suggests that organizational politics is often disliked by employees because it means that rewards such as increased pay or promotion are not simply produced through effort, merit, and contribution, but through other factors—particularly politics (Zivnuska et al., 2004). However, more recently Kane-Frieder et al. have argued that engaged employees often see organizational politics not as a hindrance but a challenge to be worked through: it offers a strategic advantages because employees less engaged with work are less willing to play political games whereas more engaged employees do (Kane-Frieder et al., 2014). What the study of organizational politics does reveal is that organizations are sites where individuals (and groups) with different interests, goals, and visions of the future of the organization compete. Individuals and groups also have a need for power and desire to control their own futures. In short, power and politics are essential parts of organizational life.

However, the Machiavellian image of office politics tends to present political activity as a result of individual manipulation, selfishness, careerist focus, or incompetency. In particular, this view of power sees it as a result of the activity and mindset of particular individuals. This view sees politics as something to be downplayed or, ideally, eliminated. Within this perspective, politics only occurs when there is a breakdown of normal relations, something that happens when Machiavellian individuals seek to manipulate the system. This view ignores the idea that power is a normal part of everyday practice. It is to this topic that we now turn.

### Review questions

| | |
|---|---|
| **Describe** | What is meant by politics in organizations? |
| **Explain** | Why do theories suggest office politics is common in organizations? |
| **Explain** | What are some of the key strategies for dealing with office politics? |
| **Analyse** | Machiavelli wrote about politics at a governmental level, so why is his analysis also relevant to politics in organizations? |

## Levels of power in organizations

When we think of power in organizations, often our first impression is of organizational leaders making decisions, controlling the resources, and setting the organization's strategic direction. Yet if we look closer, we can see it is not this clear-cut. Organizational leaders are reliant on workers to make their plans happen. Workers therefore have some power, and power, therefore, can be seen as distributed across the organization rather just being in the hands of the leaders (see Table 13.3).

For instance, studies that explore the implementation of strategy 'illustrate that despite senior management's apparent authority to speak and enact strategy, other groups of

Table 13.3  Levels of power

| Executive power | Management power | Worker power |
|---|---|---|
| Set wider operational goals | Operational decisions | Specialist knowledge that managers or co-workers do not have |
| Strategic direction of the company | Individual career progression | Specialist skills that make the employee valuable |
| Set key overall policies | Appraisals | Implement management requests |
| Hire and fire key management | Work allocation | Work-to-rule and go-slow, do the job poorly |
| Open and close key stores/factories | Set targets/pace of the machine | Withholding information |
| Agree major purchasing decisions (e.g. a new IT system) | Rewards and punishment | Resist management control |

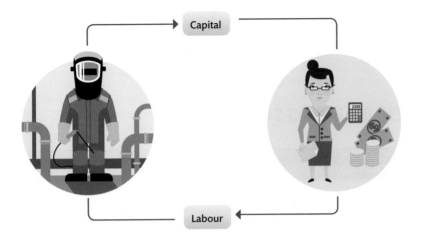

**Figure 13.4** The capitalist wage–labour relationship.

employees are [often] critical to how it actually plays out in an organization, providing a much better understanding of why some strategies ... work while others fail' (Dick and Collings, 2014: 1517).

However, while employees potentially have substantial power (e.g. to withhold their labour, quit, withhold information) in comparison with managers' power (e.g. to give or withhold rewards), except in times of dispute (e.g. in strikes), it could be said that they rarely use it. As Jeffery Pfeffer argues, 'most of the time in most work settings the authority of the manager to direct the work activities is so legitimated and taken for granted, that issues of relative power and sanctions seldom become consciously considered' (1981: 5–6).

Equally, it could be argued that managers rarely use their power to fire employees or impact their promotion opportunities. Most of the time managerial authority is taken for granted. Therefore, while power is operating in organizations, the dynamics of the labour–capital relationship (see Chapter 3) are often not visible to the participants (Figure 13.4).

Organizations therefore can be seen as more complicated than the formal organizational chart indicates. As Whittle et al. state, 'Formal structures, then, do not determine organizational processes or outcomes, and organizational behaviour cannot be "read off" from the formal structure chart' (Whittle et al., 2015: 381). To understand why this is the case and how power operates in organizations, we need to explore deeper theoretical perspectives.

# Theoretical interpretations of power

In the following section we will discuss the three main ways of looking at power:

- *power as possession*—sees power as something that is owned or possessed by individuals or groups
- *power through structure*—sees power as something that is a product of the social structure
- *power as productive*—sees power as something that produces new ways of thinking and acting, rather than a negative force which prevents action.

They each present alternative views of what power is and how it impacts organizational members. They come from different ideological viewpoints and therefore provide not only different views of power but also beliefs about how society should work.

# Power as a possession

**Running case:** Linda Wilkinson tries convincing Effingham

'You need me,' thinks Effingham as he listens to Linda Wilkinson's suggestion. 'I am the only one who can come up with ideas for the menu that will rescue your wedding service. However, I'm liking the idea of in-venting a new wedding menu—this could my chance to try out things I've always wanted to. This could be good for me, though I'm not telling her yet. And, if the restaurant is busier then maybe I could use it to help boost the kitchen and get the new refit we want?'

Who has power in this situation and why?

Visit the Online Resource Centre to read an analysis of the situation.

When we think about power our common-sense reaction is to think that power is some-thing that belongs to an individual, a position (e.g. the CEO), or a group (e.g. the human resources department) who use their power to further their own interests.

The underlying metaphor for this view of power is as a possession, something that be-longs to or is held by an individual or group. Steven Lukes states that this view leads people to 'discuss its location and its extent, who has more and who less, how to gain, resist, seize, harness, secure, tame, share, spread, distribute, equalize or maximize it, how to render it more effective and how to limit or avoid its effects' (2005: 61).

So how do individuals acquire power? Jeffery Pfeffer argues it is by 'having something that someone else wants or needs, and being in control of the performance or resources so that there are few alternative sources, or no alternative sources, for obtaining what is de-sired' (1981: 99). This can include doing *jobs important to the organization* and having the skill to do them properly, particularly if it is a rare skill; *controlling resources*, however small, in a strategic way, to get others *dependent* on you; being good at *solving importantproblems* to the organization or reducing uncertainty (McNulty et al., 2011); controlling information that others need; and having the ability to *control the information about alternatives* and the premise upon which decisions are made. The key underlying principle of Pfeffer's view is that power is created by having something that others need without a suitable alternative and being able to withdraw this at any given point.

Personal characteristics such as *energy and endurance*, an understanding of the political dynamics within the organization, and a willingness to use this insight all further someone's power. This is easier for those higher up, as those 'with relatively more power are better able to get their perception of the problem and the environment accepted' (Pfeffer, 1981: 141).

# French and Raven: bases of power

**Running case:** David Hunter's office

'Damn,' exclaims Hunter, 'blasted printer has run out of ink again. Does anyone know where the toner is? The cupboard seems to be locked.' 'You have to call out Frank, the maintenance guy, now,' Meg Mortimer responds wearily. 'Effingham put a new toner in a month ago and a bit leaked out, so Frank says none of us are to be trusted to do it.' 'But that's silly,' Hunter responds crossly. 'We've always been able to do it before.' 'Well, you can phone him and ask,' responds Mortimer.

'Why should I phone him? He's only maintenance,' huffs Hunter. However, compliantly, he picks up the phone. 'Hi, Frank, it's David here. The printer has run out of ink and we really need it replacing.' 'Oh,' responds Frank gruffly, 'no can do. I've got this shower to mend in room 17 and then there is that toilet in room 12. After that I have the curtain rail in room 10.' 'Can't they wait?' Hunter replies exasperatedly, 'I've got to print this to give to Chance in an hour! Can't you just give me the key?' 'Look, we can't afford for another error with the printer again,' Frank responds. 'I've had the training, and the engineer said I am the only one who can change the printer toner or it will invalidate the warranty.'

Who has the power in this situation? Is that power reflected in their positions in the hierarchy?

Another theory that adopts the 'power as possession' perspective was developed by John French and Bertram Raven (1958), who examined the sources or, as they put it, the 'bases of power' that individuals can hold. Although they say that there are many, they name six common sources that are seen across most organizations (Raven, 1965, 1993), which are described in Table 13.4.

These forms of power are also divided between hard power, which constrains the individual because they have to comply with the leaders' demands, and soft power, which provides followers with more freedom and autonomy (Pierro et al., 2013).

While in this model the power is possessed by particular individuals, for it to be effective what really matters is if the powerless person perceives that the powerful person has power. For instance, it does not matter if the leader actually has the power to withhold promotion, so long as the follower believes they do. The strength of the power base is also dependent on how much the follower desires the item offered. For instance, a threat to sack someone will hold far less sway over an employee who does not really want the job and believes that they will have better job prospects elsewhere.

The follower's perception is produced primarily by two things. Firstly, the follower's upbringing and socialization shape how they perceive the power base. For instance, some followers will believe that the management have an automatic right to lead and will accept their authority unquestioningly, whereas others will believe that the leaders need to earn this right or will even be hostile towards leaders. This perception is a product of socialization, such as the follower's schooling, previous experiences (i.e. of authority), and the wider culture they are a part of. For instance, in the 1950s, when French and Raven were writing, authority was accepted more readily than it is today. Secondly, this perception is dynamic and changes over time based on experience of the actions of an individual. Therefore, if a

Table 13.4  French and Raven's six bases of power (based on French and Raven, 1958; extended in Raven 1965, 1993)

| | Type | Description | Example | |
|---|---|---|---|---|
| **Hierarchical** | Legitimate | The extent to which an individual is socialized and has internalized the belief that certain groups (e.g. managers) have a legitimate right to command. This belief is set by cultural values and acceptance of current social structure. | You respond to a request because it is a manager telling you rather than because you think it is a good idea. | **Hard power** |
| | Reward | Extent to which an individual can use rewards from the organization. The employee must desire the reward in order for it to work. If they do not want the reward it will have no sway over them. | You take on a task because you believe that you will get a promotion out of it. | |
| | Coercive | Perception that one's boss has the power to punish. This can be strong punishments, such as sacking, through to more symbolic forms such as withdrawing positive interaction. The more legitimate this approach, the more it will be accepted. | You aim to hit your sales targets because they are part of your appraisal and you do not want to fail. | |
| **Personal** | Expert | Knowledge that another person needs but does not have: for instance, a lawyer's advice as to whether an advertising campaign is legal. What is essential for it to be valid is that the recipient trusts the advice of the giver. | You require an IT specialist in order to fix your computer. | **Soft power** |
| | Referent | To be the type of person that others want to emulate. Being friendly/supportive towards others. | A colleague you want to emulate asks you to take on a task which you do not want to do but, because you want to emulate them, you do it anyway. | |
| | Informational | Changes in perspective as a result of being given information. | You hold information that others want and can present it in such a way that they change how they see a situation. | |

person uses expert power but is proved to be wrong on a number of occasions, this basis of power will diminish over time.

The basis of power can also be divided up into that which is hierarchical, derived from the leader's position in the organization, and that which is more influenced by the perception of personal skills and characteristics. Therefore, while someone can be senior in the organization, if they lack the skill or knowledge that an expert holds then they can be beholden to that expert.

## Weber's three ideal types of authority

Our final individualistic view on power is developed by Max Weber (2004) (whose views on bureaucracy we saw in Chapter 3). He argued there are three ideal types of authority.

- *Charismatic*—based on a heroic leader, where people unquestioningly follow the leader. One of the problems with this type is that it relies on a single leader for its survival. The followers also become subservient.

- *Traditional*—based on tradition or custom. The leader holds their authority based on the status they are given or inherited (such as the monarchy).

- *Rational–legal*—based on formalized laws and regulation, akin to bureaucracy. Weber saw this form as superior, as it does not rely on the charisma of a single leader or the unquestioning following of tradition.

Therefore, while bureaucracy sometimes has a bad reputation, Weber considered that well-constructed rules can produce the best form of authority.

## 'Power is property' assessed

While the perspective that power is the property of an individual or group is intuitively appealing, it does suffer from some key problems. Firstly, it tends to individualize power—seeing it as something that is solely the possession of an individual or group. Power is therefore considered a zero-sum game, where some people have power (often the managers) and others do not. In reality, power is not something that an individual holds, nor is there a fixed quantity of it. Secondly, this perspective ignores more societal reasons for why people think how they do. Although French and Raven describe how individuals are socialized into seeing the world in a particular way, this view of power downplays issues such as gender and the labour–capital divide, which others, such as Steven Lukes, feel are essential. It is to this perspective that we now turn.

| Review questions | |
| --- | --- |
| **Describe** | What are French and Raven's five bases of power? |
| **Explain** | What are the key principles of the 'power as possession' perspective? |
| **Apply** | Which of the five bases of power does Effingham hold in the case study? |

## Power as structure: Steven Lukes's three dimensions of power

In 1974 Steven Lukes, a Marxist political scientist, wrote a highly influential account of power (republished and updated in a second edition in 2005). He aimed to offer a more comprehensive view of how power operates—offering three dimensions or what he called faces of power. Drawing on Marxist theory (see Chapter 3 for a discussion of Karl Marx's theory), Lukes asked: why do the powerful, i.e. managers or leaders, achieve compliance by the less powerful, i.e. the workers, particularly when followers act against their own best interests? The first two dimensions, he concluded, were inadequate in answering this question and, therefore, the third dimension offered a deeper understanding of how power operates in practice.

*Dimension 1* is direct observable conflict and still sees power as a possession. This perspective draws from the political theorist Robert Dahl, who defined power as: 'A has power over B to the extent that he can get B to do something that B would not otherwise do.' Dahl (1957: 202–3) focused on decision making by the US political elite and provided one of the first rigorous explorations of how power works in practice. For Dahl 'who[ever] prevails in decision making [provides] the best way to determine which individuals and groups have more power' (1958: 4, cited in Lukes, 2005: 18). Dahl, who had a pluralist outlook, saw different groups having preferences which can lead to conflict when they clash. Dahl argued that the one who comes out on top has the power. While Dahl believed power can be present even when no opposition appears, his methods and assumptions focus only on overt, observable behaviour and, therefore, when there is actual, visible conflict.

*Dimension 1 assessed:* the advantage of dimension 1 is that it focuses on the actual processes involved in decision making. However, according to Lukes, this perspective is too narrow as it only focuses on observable aspects of power and ignores many covert, less observable aspects. This aspect is examined by dimension 2.

*Dimension 2* sees power as the ability to determine what can or cannot be spoken about—what Lukes calls behind-the-scenes agenda setting. Those with power can limit the range of topics that can be discussed and, by doing so, can keep certain controversial issues 'off limits'. Consequently certain things, such as employees pay rises, managerial incompetence, or a proposal by a competing group, are not spoken about, and therefore cannot be decided upon. Leading supporters of this view, Bachrach and Baratz, state a person or group has power to the extent he or she—'consciously or unconsciously—creates or reinforces barriers to the public airing of policy conflicts' (1970: 8, cited in Lukes, 2005: 6). Dimension 2 thus broadens the definition of power away from purely observable conflict to non-decision processes where the powerful can ignore the grievances of the less powerful.

## Real life case: limiting the agenda—the Hutton Inquiry

After the second Iraq war, Tony Blair's government set up the Hutton Inquiry into the death of the government scientist Dr David Kelly. Many criticized this inquiry, arguing that they limited the scope of decision making to a far too narrow remit and therefore did not examine fairly the real reasons behind the war or Dr Kelly's death. This could be seen as a classic example of keeping certain controversial issues off the agenda.

**Sources:** *Daily Telegraph* (2003); Runciman (2004); Wheeler (2006).

How did the government keep certain issues off the agenda? Can you think of any examples you have seen in organizations where someone more powerful has kept issues off the agenda?

*Dimension 2 assessed:* This view of power is more subtle and demonstrates a deeper understanding of how power actually operates in practice. Power can be covert (concealed), allowing the powerful to maintain their position through establishing the 'rules of the game' that privilege certain groups at the expense of others. However, it still assumes that if there is no conflict or grievance then there is consensus and therefore no use of power. According to Bachrach and Baratz 'if there is no conflict, overt or covert, the presumption must be that there is consensus on the prevailing allocation of values, in which case nondecision-making is impossible' (1970: 49, cited in Lukes, 2005: 23).

*Dimension 3* states that power shapes not only our behaviours, but also our desires and beliefs. Therefore, while it might appear that there is consensus or that certain individuals and groups have no grievances, dimension 3 argues that this gives a false perception of harmony. Workers, owing to their position in the capitalist working relationship, are often not conscious of their *true* interests and therefore this conflict between labour and capital (the workers and managers) rarely materializes. It remains latent—present but rarely visible.

*Dimension 3 assessed:* this dimension goes beyond behaviouralism (Lukes, 2005), as it argues that just because you cannot observe the conflict it does not mean it does not exist. Rather, the powerful (i.e. management) influence, shape, or determine the very wants and desires of the less powerful (i.e. workers), distracting them from their true interests. Conflict, therefore, does not materialize (become visible) because the workers have been socialized (taught) to believe that they do not have different interests from management. This is achieved through processes of socialization, such as schooling, company induction programmes, and wider culture, where the worker is taught to see their interests as being the same as the organization's. To quote Karl Marx (1859/2012: 11–12): 'It is not the consciousness of men that determines their existence, but, on the contrary, their social existence determines their consciousness'. In other words, how people see the world (their consciousness) is shaped by the society in which they live and its values, a process influenced by economic interests of the powerful. Consequently, according to Lukes (2005), not only do workers not know that they are oppressed, but they enthusiastically participate in their own oppression.

For further information on Lukes' three dimensions, visit the Online Resource Centre.

## Running case: Linda Wilkinson meets her team in the dining room

Having spoken to Effingham, Linda Wilkinson decides that she needs to get her team on board.

'As you know, we are developing this exciting new wedding package which will provide lots of great opportunities for Junction Hotel with more weddings, the new bridal suite, and a new exciting menu with the big, sit-down meal in the evening. Now, as you might have heard, some of the board are sceptical about this and I need to be able to convince them at next week's board meeting. I want to know that I have your backing. We are all in this together. If it goes well then we will all benefit. It will really put Junction Hotel on the map. There will be a lot more shifts, working 12–3 pm to prepare for the wedding and then 5–11 pm for the evening function. We will have new uniforms and will be doing silver service. I think we can make Junction Hotel a really special place for people's special day, but I need your support.'

Are the *true* interests of the workers being served by this deal?

## Power as structure assessed

**False consciousness** A Marxist term—false beliefs held by the proletariat (workers) who do not know their true position in society as the revolutionary force to overthrow capitalism. Instead, they see the current structure of society as unchangeable and largely fair.

Lukes's theory is helpful because he alerts us to the often invisible processes of power within organizations, providing a compelling explanation of how the more powerful can gain compliance over the less powerful (Figure 13.5). He thus moves power beyond individualistic power to explore the wider structural aspects.

As with any Marxist (radical structuralist) analysis of its type, Lukes believes employees suffer from **false consciousness**. This creates a state of mind where workers do not recognize their 'true' interests or their oppression and exploitation because they get distracted by everyday issues. Workers are thus unable to think of alternative ways of doing things (i.e. self-management) because they are socialized into believing that the current way society runs is fixed and is the only way things can be (i.e. that we must have management-led organizations).

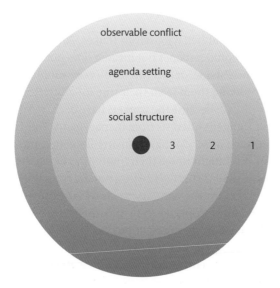

**Figure 13.5** Lukes's (2005) three levels of power.

This view is based on the assumption that employees, collectively, have 'true' interests which they are not aware of, but the Marxist theoretician is. However, many, particularly from the post-structuralist viewpoint, have argued that there is no universal interest that all employees share and the Marxist theorist is not necessarily better placed to identify what these interests are. As a response in the more recent edition, Lukes recognizes that he implied that everyone of a particular class has the same interest, whereas he now argues that workers have multiple, and sometimes contradictory, interests and needs.

Have you ever considered the alternatives to capitalism in depth?

### Review questions

| | |
|---|---|
| **Explain** | What are the three dimensions of power as outlined by Lukes? |
| **Explain** | Why Lukes considers the first two dimensions inadequate? Why does he consider the third dimension to capture the true nature of power? |
| **Analyse** | Do workers really know their true interests? Is it possible to really know your true interests? How do different theories of power answer this question? |
| **Apply** | From Lukes' perspective, do the workers at Junction Hotel really know their true interests? If not, how might they act differently if they did? |

# Power as productive: French philosopher Michel Foucault

**Running case:** Linda Wilkinson plans her next steps

Linda Wilkinson sits down to read the book Sarah sent her on gaining power at work. She completes the self-diagnostic test and decides that she needs to be more confident and assertive. She is excited that by being more assertive she might be able to get the outcome she wants, but she still feels scared of tackling Effingham. That will be a real test of the new, confident Linda.

She finds an assertiveness quiz online and starts to work through the programme. Her results show that she is quite assertive, but not as much as she could be. Looking at these results she starts to read more on assertiveness training. Breathe deeply, relax, don't apologize for having an opinion ... 'This is going to be good,' she thinks to herself.

Visit the Online Resource Centre to try the assertiveness quiz. How do you feel about completing it?

In his most recent edition of *Power: A radical view*, Lukes argues that Michel Foucault's work explores the fourth dimension of power (Lukes, 2005). Foucault was a French philosopher and historian who aimed at rethinking our assumptions about how power operates, providing a radical departure from the previously discussed theorists. His views on power, however, are complex and he never came up with a full theory of power; therefore we present a summary in Table 13.5.

Foucault (1977) asks us to think differently from traditional perspectives about how power operates. Power is not something that one group possesses and which forces the powerless to do things against their own interests. Rather, for Foucault, power is a creative, positive force that brings certain ways of thinking and behaving into being and, through that, introduces a new reality. He offers this view as a result of three key theoretical perspectives.

- *Power/knowledge*—for Foucault, knowledge is intertwined with power. He argued the 'human sciences', like sociology and psychology (which feature heavily as the underpinnings of many of the theories in this book—see Chapter 1), produce new techniques of power. For instance, psychology creates personality tests used in recruitment and selection, and Belbin's teamwork framework (see Chapter 6). These techniques are powerful, not only by helping management, but also by claiming to enable us to discover the truth about ourselves. Knowledge, for instance in work psychology, offers to reveal how we really think in a way that allows us to change how we act (Rose, 1998). For Foucault, this knowledge cannot be thought of as neutral, but is linked fundamentally to power because it is created and is used to transform how we understand ourselves. This extends the investigation of power to the role that knowledge plays in how we understand ourselves at work.

- *Power relations*—for Foucault (1981), power exists in relations between people and occur when power is exercised (used). Foucault sees power as a relationship where both sides have some power and each person has some choice in what they do. Therefore, for Foucault, there must always be the opportunity for **resistance**, otherwise it is domination.

**Resistance** Drawn from critical theory, where marginalized and oppressed groups (such as workers and minorities) resist the aims and requests of more powerful groups, such as management.

Table 13.5 Foucault's reconceptualization of power (drawn from Foucault 1981 and 1971)

| Classic view | Foucault's view |
|---|---|
| Power is a repressive, coercive, controlling, authoritarian force | Power is also productive and creative; it produces new knowledge and behaviours and, through this, new realities |
| Power forces people to do things that they do not want to do | Power also works in a positive fashion by guiding individuals, giving them choices, and shaping how they see things and their identity |
| Power is a property, a thing that certain groups possess | Power has no essence—it is not a thing that one group possesses and other (weaker) groups do not possess; rather, power is relational—it exists in the relationship between people and only when it is exercised (i.e. used) |
| Power is top-down, possessed by an elite and held over the powerless (such as the workers) | Power also is bottom-up; rather than being possessed by a small elite, power is everywhere—it is like a net, a system of relations spread throughout society; it is also constantly shifting; one group does not always hold it—it changes over time |
| Power crushes resistance | Where there is power there is resistance, which is the production of alternative discourses; if there is no possibility of resistance then there is no power, as this is domination |
| Control through direct repression | Control through invisible strategies of normalization |
| Knowledge is seen as either objective and disinterested—it does not take sides (mainstream view)—or emancipatory (critical view), freeing people from power | Knowledge is linked fundamentally to power; new knowledge (such as sociology) produces new techniques of power (Foucault used the phrase power/knowledge to indicate this link) |
| Individuals or groups have true interests that exist outside of power | Who we think we are—our identity—is a product of knowledge and of power; power is everywhere and in all relations with people |
| Asks who has power and how they gain and maintain their position and use or abuse power | Investigates specific techniques and practices through which power operates |

For example, a manager might ask one of their team to write a report which is additional to their existing workload. The employee has a number of options, including completely ignoring the request, doing it very slowly, or not writing it in the way the manager would like. The important point here is that both the employee and the manager have a range of options available to them and therefore power is more a relationship than a one-way process. The employee can always resist the manager's request.

- *Disciplinary power and normalization* provides the third area where Foucault (1977) rethought power. Disciplinary power operates through hierarchical observation, normalizing judgement, and examination—observing people and judging them against a series of norms, standards and values, which separates the normal from abnormal. These norms provide the standards by which we learn to judge ourselves. We do this in many areas of life, from testing ourselves against what 'level' we are at—for instance we judge ourselves at school and compare averages for height and weight using the Body Mass Index (BMI)—through to sales targets that workers judge themselves by. Power through normalization is often not conducted in a domineering or controlling manner. Rather, it can be experienced as positive in that we decide how to engage with it. For instance, the 'five-a-day' campaign to get people eating more fruit and vegetables encourages people to eat more healthily, while failing to eat healthy is seen as a moral failure for which the individual is blamed. This form of power is invisible, as we tend to treat these norms as unquestionable facts, designed by experts for our own good. Foucault's view reveals how power shapes seemingly neutral everyday practices that are missed by other approaches.

We can see all three of these accounts of power at work in Foucault's most famous book, *Discipline and punish* (1977). This book examines the history of prison and starts with a graphic scene of the botched torture and execution of 'Damiens the regicide'. Foucault describes how this criminal was placed on a scaffold, his 'flesh torn from his breasts, arms, thighs and calves with red-hot pincers ... [and] his body drawn and quartered by four horses and his limbs and body consumed by fire' (1977: 3). Ultimately, six horses were needed to pull Damiens apart and still the executioner struggled to tear his limbs off him, requiring the executioner to cut his limbs off.

Foucault then presents a description of a criminal who is being reformed, which takes place a mere eight years later. His day includes getting up at 6 am, working for 9 hours, and receiving 2 hours of schooling (reading, writing, drawing and arithmetic, and then listening to an instructional text). The aim of this style of punishment is to reform the prisoner, i.e. to make them a better person.

When thinking about the form of power in the two accounts of the prisoners our initial reaction is that the first one is brutal and the second is more humane. These cases provided not only two different styles of punishment, but also two types of power—the public execution (physical force) and the timetable (reform). However, Foucault questions the assumption that the second, reforming the prisoner, is necessarily better. He argues that while the first prisoner had violence (and power) directed on the body, the second has this power internalized within him, with the one doing the punishment seeking to control the values and the beliefs of the prisoner; in short, in changing who they are. The second form of power is a key example of what Foucault called disciplinary power, which was most evident in his discussion of the Panopticon.

Visit the Online Resource Centre for pictures of the Panopticon.

The Panopticon (which literally means all-seeing-eye) was a prison devised by English philosopher and social theorist Jeremy Bentham (see Chapter 4) for the purposes of reforming the prisoner in a cost-effective manner. It could achieve a high level of efficiency, as in the centre of the prison stood the prison guard who could see into every prison cell at all times. In theory, therefore, it only required one prison guard who could watch all the prisoners at one time. This was achieved because the prisoner was unable to tell if they were being watched and therefore had to always assume that they were. There are two key implications for this.

First, this image of the Panopticon has been used to make the claim that a key area of modern power is through **surveillance**. The power of the Panopticon was that the prisoner never knew if they were being watched and therefore they had to act in the right way at all times. It is therefore used to render (make) visible key aspects of someone's behaviour. A modern example of this is the call centre, where all of the call-centre operatives are monitored constantly for things like their call length and success rates, as well as the time taken between calls and even toilet breaks. They can also be listened to at any stage of their call, meaning that they

**Surveillance** The observation, either overt or covert, of people to gain information about them or to exert order and control over them.

always need to perform because they never know when they might be being heard. Similarly, shop workers can be investigated by mystery shoppers who judge whether they are smiling at the right point. Even university lecturers are now increasingly subject to surveillance practices like student feedback and evaluation surveys, or fellow staff members watching a lecture or seminar. This is then fed into lecturers' performance appraisals and can impact their careers.

The second key development of this form of power is how it is used to reform the prisoner through a series of routines and practices in order to make them a better person. Seemingly everyday practices, such as timetables, filling in forms, or types of training, are used to change the prisoner in how they understand themselves and the way that they act. This form of power is at its strongest when it is internalized by the prisoner as a form of **self-discipline**. A series of experts (social workers, probation officers, mentors, etc.) work with the prisoner to help them transform themselves. Rather than forcing them to change through coercive force, reform and self-discipline are used to train the prisoner to change their behaviour and become a better person. It works best where the prisoner wants to become a better person. The prisoner thus internalizes the power and monitors themselves against these particular standards. In this sense, discipline does not just mean punishment, but comes from the Latin and means training to produce a specific character or pattern of behaviour, particularly a form of training that produces moral or mental improvement.

This form of self-discipline is often seen as essential for those who want to be successful. For instance, a successful boxer needs to follow a strict timetable with set times for exercise and rest, eat particular types of food, and avoid certain activities. They will follow the advice of experts (trainers, nutritionists, psychologists) and work on particular areas of physical and mental development (power/knowledge). By following this regime and being self-disciplined (discipline and normalization) the boxer is able to develop certain capabilities and skills and is moulded into becoming a particular type of person. However, they are also limiting the development of other skills and outlooks. By going through this training the boxer is transformed and could, arguably, become a different person. Power therefore works in a positive way—creating a new type of person—but it also stops other possibilities into which the individual could develop.

**Self-discipline** The process by which an individual trains and controls themselves, usually for the purposes of self-improvement.

## Study skills: the power of university

Going to university to gain your degree is another example of this form of self-discipline. By going to university, studying the subjects, and meeting new people, many claim that university changes who they are—that they come out as someone different to the person that went in. Part of this will involve reading certain texts and debating particular ideas that might change how you think. You might train yourself to go to the library regularly, turn up to 9 am lectures, read around the subject, plan your assignments, and do your work on time. It is unlikely that you will have someone watching over you telling you what to do; rather, you will have internalized the power and become self-disciplined. This form of power should not necessarily be seen as something oppressive—forcing you to do work against your will. Rather, you may begin to identify yourself as a different person who studies hard to get good grades.

How self-disciplined are you?
**Source:** Wavebreak Media Ltd /123RF.

At work, this form of power operates on us through techniques like training, appraisal, and management development. The power of normalization is most evident in appraisal systems where employees are asked to 'confess' their strengths and weaknesses and judge themselves against a series of categories of what is considered normal behaviour. In particular, they are asked to define areas they do well in and those that require development. They are then made responsible for their own improvement by writing things like self-development plans. In this sense employees engage in their own self-surveillance, judging themselves against these set categories (power/knowledge) with the view to self-improvement. Employees, therefore, act as their own supervisors by monitoring and judging themselves against particular norms (Townley, 1994). (Compare with how people internalize the labels bestowed by personality tests, as described in Chapter 7.)

The same argument could be made about management. We might find some of the techniques used by Taylorism controlling, oppressive, at times brutal, and often dehumanizing (see Chapter 3). However, under Taylorism workers are not expected to actually believe in the cause of the organization. In contrast, the so-called more humane developments of the human relations school (see Chapter 5) appear more sympathetic to the interests of the staff, as people feel that they belong. However, through Foucault's reading of power these workers are actually more controlled. Through processes such as teamwork, motivation, and culture, workers are expected to act as though they believe in the purpose of the organization and want to progress and develop themselves into better forms of employees. Employees are more controlled because they believe in the organization and therefore have no possibility to resist it (for a very interesting discussion of this topic see Cederström and Fleming, 2012).

Therefore, like Lukes, Foucault argued that people actively participate in practices which involve invisible power. However, unlike Lukes, Foucault does not necessarily see this form of power as coercion—forcing people into changes against their will. Rather, they participate actively in practices which result in them being new types of people. The question is: Do we like the people that we have become?

## The power as productive view assessed

**Running case:** Linda Wilkinson reviews her progress with Sarah

Linda Wilkinson decides to phone Sarah. 'Hi, Sarah, it's Linda. Is now a good time to talk?' 'Sure,' Sarah replies. 'I have ten minutes before my next appointment, but, until then, I'm all yours. How was the book?' 'Brilliant,' enthuses Linda, 'amazing. It really made me think—I feel like a new me!' 'That's great,' replies Sarah. 'It works, doesn't it?' 'Yes,' acknowledges Linda. 'I did the assertiveness quiz you recommended and I came out OK, but not that strong, so I started work on those exercises and have changed the way that I speak to people. I'm much more direct, but not aggressive. I learned those phrases and I'm using them all the time.' 'How have people reacted to you?' asks Sarah. 'I'm amazed ... really differently. Effingham . . . ' replies Linda. 'The bully guy?' Sarah interjects. 'Yes, him,' answers Linda, 'well, I stood up to him yesterday and asked, I mean I requested, him to deliver the new menu for the weddings by midday. And guess what? He did it!' 'Fantastic!' exclaims Sarah. 'Yes, it is,' continues Linda. 'I feel like a different person. I've still got work to do and I'm working through the exercises, but I feel transformed.'

According to Foucault, how might power/knowledge, power relations, and normalization be occurring in this case?

**Agency** The capacity individuals have to act independently of the social structures and make free choices.

**Structure** Social life is largely determined by the social structure, the reoccurring patterns which influence the choices available. Structures are difficult to change.

While Foucault has produced a powerful re-reading of power, his theories have been criticized for a number of reasons. Firstly, because Foucault sees power everywhere, his critics argue that Foucault presents a world of complete domination without hope for a better world. This, his critics state, creates despair as there is no escape from power (McNay, 1994; Thompson and Ackroyd, 1995). Secondly, they claim Foucault's theory seems to discount human **agency** (i.e. the capacity of individuals to exist independently of the social **structure**). There is little account in Foucault's theory of those that can resist power. Finally, because Foucault does not offer a set of values by which to judge the use of power, many have questioned the political benefits of his work. Without a clear set of values to judge power, Foucault's critics argue that he does not give us the capacity to resist (e.g. Callaghan and Thompson, 2001).

## Review questions

| | |
|---|---|
| **Describe** | What is meant, for Foucault, by the term Panopticon? |
| **Explain** | What are Foucault's key views on power? |
| **Analyse** | Why does Foucault see power as productive rather than repressive? |
| **Apply** | What type of power is the assertiveness quiz exerting on Linda Wilkinson? Do you see this as being repressive or productive for Wilkinson? |

# Obedience to authority

Would you electrically shock someone just because a scientist told you to? The infamous experiment by Stanley Milgram (1974) predicts that you probably would. Conducted in 1961, in what remains one of the most controversial experiments in history, Milgram devised a scientific study of obedience to authority. He wanted to find out whether normal, law-abiding citizens would give a lethal electric shock because they were following authority. He discovered that almost two-thirds of people would.

The participants were university students who thought they were taking part in a study of memory and learning, and they received a small payment for their participation. When they joined they were met by a scientist and another 'volunteer' (who actually worked for the experiment), and were told they were studying the effects of punishment on learning (a behaviourist approach). They drew lots, with one person acting as the learner who would receive shocks and the other as the teacher who applied the shocks. While it appeared random, it was actually a fix so that the person who had the experiment done to them ended up as a teacher.

The teacher then saw the learner strapped to an electric shock device and the generator, which had power up to 450 volts. They were then told that the learner had been given a list of word-pairs to memorize. Whenever the learner got it wrong the teacher had to administer electric shocks, which were small at first, starting at 15 V. Every time the learner made a mistake they were increased, all the way up to 450 V (which is twice the household level). When they administered the shock they could hear what they thought was the learner (but what was actually a tape recording) shouting things like 'I cannot go on'. Two-thirds of the subjects continued to do this past the switch marked 'fatal'.

The results shocked Milgram. Indeed, before the experiment all the psychiatrists that Milgram questioned stated that most people would stop early. The results were disturbing, as most people gave an electric shock of 450 V. Why did they do it? The answer, for Milgram, lay in their acceptance of authority. After a while the screams became very loud and the teacher would often voice their concerns that they were harming the learner, but, usually, the scientist would reassure them that they were not doing any real harm or simply say 'the experiment requires it'. It was not that they were uncaring; indeed, many of the experi-menters voiced concerns, but they were willing to obey the commands of the scientist over their own judgement.

Another experiment which revealed how people respond to authority was Zimbardo's prison experiment. Zimbardo wanted to test good people versus an evil situation. Unfortu-nately, he found that the unpleasant situation won (Zimbardo, 2007).

Zimbardo set up a mock jail and selected twenty-one normal, healthy, and emotionally stable men and placed them into two groups: ten as prisoners and eleven as guards. The guards wore uniforms, including special glasses to prevent eye contact. Unexpectedly, the prisoners were picked up from home, put in a police car, finger-printed, blindfolded, placed in prison uniforms, and had nylons put on their head to give the appearance of baldness. They were also given identification numbers instead of names.

After only six days into the fourteen-day experiment, it was abandoned. The relationship between the guards and the prisoners was vicious, with three of the guards using their power in sadistic ways, developing techniques to break the prisoners, and making them feel worthless. They wanted to show their power over the prisoners. The prisoners felt dehu-manized and some even had breakdowns. They also accepted their roles. When their ap-peals for parole were turned down they merely returned to their cells, seemingly accepting their role and identity as prisoners.

Zimbardo's experiment further questioned the impact of power and authority. He ar-gued that merely being given the label prisoner or guard shaped the way individuals be-haved, demonstrating the power of the social environment (in this case the prison) on individual behaviour, and even on Zimbardo himself, as running the experiment pushed his power too far by allowing the experiment to continue beyond what was acceptable (2007).

The two studies ask us fundamental questions about ourselves (would we be a sadistic guard or electrocute someone if we were participant in the study?) and also wider society (are bad events not a product of bad people but of the type of society that we have?). The results show the uncomfortable reality that 'we ourselves could be perpetrators' (Reicher et al., 2014: 397). Both these experiments show (as do the insights of Zygmunt Bauman, 1989) the potentially dangerous effects of people following authority unquestioningly. Instead of using their own judgement, people regularly defer to authority figures (Milgram, 1974), who, when in this position, can abuse their power (Zimbardo, 2007) or simply say they are following the rules (Bauman, 1989). Critical theorists therefore look for less hierarchical and more empowering organizations.

## Study skills: dealing with controversial research

Both Milgram's and Zimbardo's studies have been very controversial not only for the results but for the way that they were carried out. Some of the key criticisms of the two experiments include:

- The studies have not been replicated (Lovibond and Adams, 1979; Reicher and Haslam, 2006), which critics argue means that the results are less valid.

- Both pieces of research have been criticized as being unethical in the way that the participants were treated, and it is highly unlikely that such research would be allowed to take place today (Reicher et al., 2014).

- Alternative explanations for the results can be found that stress the importance of personality, group processes, or the cultural context (see Reicher et al., 2014, for a review).

- In the prison experiment, the researchers selected quite a homogenized group (a group of people with similar characteristics and backgrounds), and thus it is little surprise that they acted in similar ways (Bartels, 2015).

- Some critics also claim that those that want to take part in a study on 'prison life' are more likely to be predisposed to aggression, authoritarianism, Machiavellianism, narcissism, and social dominance (Carnahan and McFarland, 2007). Some of the prisoners, it has been claimed, also may have anticipated the purpose of the study as being 'anti-prisons' and therefore acted in a way that would help the researchers (Bartels, 2015). Zimbardo also encouraged his guards to behave in a tyrannical fashion.

It is not only the research but also the way that the research is reported that has been criticized. Two recent studies of how the study has been reported in psychology textbooks found that nearly all the accounts reported that all the guards were sadistic (Griggs, 2014; Bartels, 2015), whereas in fact the original study reported that only three of the eleven guards acted with excessive abuse (Zimbardo, 2007). In a reply to his critics, Zimbardo argues that the dismissal of his research is more ideological, ignoring his evidence and explaining it in trait-based terms rather than as a result of the situation. He states that 'blaming other people for the bad acts in which they have engaged seems to absolve the rest of us of any responsibility for ignoring these pernicious and destructive environments, or failing to take steps to ameliorate them' (Haney and Zimbardo, 2009: 807–8). In other words, it is easier, and more comforting, to blame a few individuals rather than to investigate how any of us might, given the right circumstance, act in bad ways.

Thus the way that academic research is conducted, analysed, and interpreted can be as much a result of the beliefs and theoretical position of the researcher as the result of the 'evidence' that is presented. Therefore, as you read academic research, it is very valuable to look at the assumptions that the researchers have and how they use them to interpret research findings.

# Empowering workers

## Running case: numbers are short for the bar

Mark, the bar supervisor, needs to find someone to work tonight's shift as the other staff are unavailable. Mark knows that Carole never wants to work on Tuesday evenings, as it is her salsa dancing night and she is training for a competition; however, he gives her a call.

'Hi, Carole, it's Mark. Look, I know it is short notice but I really need you to come in tonight. Sue has just phoned in sick and Jim is away at the moment.' 'But Mark,' Carole huffs, 'you know I can never work Tuesdays, it's my one night out to enjoy myself.' 'Yes, I know,' Mark butts in anxiously, 'but I really need you this once. Please do this for me.' 'Go on then,' Carole relents, 'as it's you, but you can't let this happen again.'

How could Mark be more empowered in this situation? What do you think will be the consequences of this?

So far in this chapter we have focused on how people gain and use power in organizations. However, many workers feel powerless and unable to make key decisions that impact their work. Heavily bureaucratic organizations create systems and cultures in which workers must follow prescriptive rules over which they have little say (see Chapter 4). Heroic leadership styles (see Chapter 12) concentrate power in the leaders' hands. They then dictate decisions, resulting in many employees having little authority or control, and, consequently, they feel powerless. This can be frustrating—not only do they feel dehumanized (see Braverman's critique of Taylorism in Chapter 3) but also this situation can be counterproductive, as it could be argued that workers often have better ideas of how to complete a task than their managers.

Supervisors, in particular, suffer from this position. As Kanter states, supervisors are 'caught in the middle' between the managers that demand their targets to be met and the workers who 'have the power to slack, to slouch, to take too much time' (a supervisor quoted in Kanter, 1977: 187). The supervisor in this position has little power to actually influence the work because they do not have access to rewards or punishment that can influence the employees' behaviour or the processes that shape how the activities occur.

Kanter argues that this feeling of powerlessness significantly impacts the mindset of workers. Drawing on psychoanalysis by Karen Horney, Kanter claims that powerless people tend to become 'critical, bossy, and controlling' (1977: 189) and neurotic (excessively anxious about everything), and therefore attempt to dominate (control) everything around them. This behaviour, Kanter argues, despite appearances, is rational because acting in this controlling and neurotic way is the only power available to them. Such behaviour, though, can result in more controlling leadership behaviour, creating a 'vicious cycle: powerless authority figures who use coercive tactics, provoke resistance and aggression, which prompts them to become even more coercive, controlling, and behaviourally restrictive' (1977: 190).

Powerlessness can make people overly focused on rules. As we saw in Chapter 2, highly bureaucratic organizations can lead people to remove themselves from taking personal responsibility and to follow the rules regardless of the effect on customers or clients. They do only the minimum they need in order to get things done. Finally, those with less power guard their territory more jealously as they seek to protect their domain. This can result, Kanter argues, in competitiveness, sectarianism, and hostility between sections, resulting in the powerless being less effective and feeling less satisfied with their work.

To tackle this situation she argues that workers should be empowered. Empowerment distributes power away from being solely in the hands of managers to the people actually doing the job. They get to define how to achieve their tasks and, in negotiation with their manager, what overall goals are. Consequently, 'when more people are empowered—that is, allowed to have control over the conditions that make their actions possible—then more is accomplished' (Kanter, 1977: 166).

Empowerment is a post-bureaucratic form of management as it aims to move away from command and control to more participatory forms of management and decision making (see Chapters 12 and 17). Empowered workers have the capacity to make on-the-spot decisions that can satisfy customers rather than having to refer to managers or the rule book, have more opportunities to participate in decision making, and can be more self-determined. This frees people up to do their jobs in response to customer needs, which is particularly important in the service sector (see Chapter 16).

Empowerment is said to increase engagement and commitment: employees feel they have more control over their work because they are implementing their own ideas. Proponents of this approach say that empowered employees quickly take responsibility, have increased motivation, commitment, and skills, and move away from a blame culture, all of which results in a more positive outlook. Employees can become less cynical, and this can improve their relationships with their leaders (Lorinkova and Perry, 2014).

In order for empowerment to work, three key factors are often considered important. Firstly, it requires employees to understand the production process or how things currently operate (with a view to changing them); secondly, it requires trust from management to give over key information; and, thirdly, it requires a high level of teamwork and cooperation among the members.

Quality circles provide an example of empowerment in action. They started in the Japanese car industry, where they began as a grass-roots movement of workers who wanted to take more responsibility for their work. A quality circle often has around ten volunteers who come together to solve a problem of mutual concern, such as how to improve their products, the production process, or other related aspects. The members aim to identify the root of the problem, devise solutions, and disseminate the results to the relevant people in the organization. Rather than seeking to produce large-scale changes, these are often incremental (step-by-step) changes designed by the same people that will implement them (see Chapter 11). Workers in these situations have been very successful not only in empowering themselves but also in improving the production line.

However, they have been less successful in the UK. Some have put this down to cultural differences between Japan (which is more collectivist) and the UK (which is more individualistic; see Chapter 15 for more details on national cultural differences). Often, empowerment programmes are said to fail because senior management fail to let go of control or to trust the workers to make decisions (Jensen and Raver, 2012). Similarly, employees can be resistant to change as they do not want to take on the extra responsibility that the empowerment programme produces. As a result, empowerment programmes sound very good in principle, but in many cases they do not live up to their supporters' hopes (Cunningham and Hyman, 1999).

## Critique of empowerment

Writers from the critical management studies perspective have argued that while empowerment sounds positive in principle, rather than workers having more autonomy they could, in fact, be seen as being under more subtle forms of control (Alvesson and Willmott, 1992a). Such critics argue that most empowerment programmes increase workers' responsibility but do not give wider power to set organizational aims and objectives. Therefore, workers are made responsible for all aspects of the implementation, which results in workers internalizing the blame, believing that if they do not achieve the task it is their fault. Empowerment, critical theorists argue, gives the illusion of autonomy, but it actually elicits a more subtle form of control as employees become their own supervisors (think back to the image of the Panopticon earlier in the chapter).

# Emancipation

For Rosabeth Moss Kanter, empowerment was important not simply in giving the powerless more discretion and influence, but also as a step towards changing the 'fabric of job relationships' (1977: 11). She argued that real change requires a more substantial overturning of the way organizations and society operate in order to produce a truly equal and fair workplace.

Marxists, such as Lukes, would agree. Within their perspective they argue that capitalist working relationships always produce power dynamics which act in the favour of management. Therefore, while systems such as empowerment might produce changes that can benefit workers, they ultimately will always favour management. Marxists argue that the entire basis of capitalism needs to be overthrown and a new society with a new economic system created. It is only when this change happens and power is truly in the hands of workers who can determine their own ends that a more equal, fair, and effective distribution of power can occur.

Those of the critical management studies perspective are generally not optimistic that the whole of capitalism will be overthrown. Alvesson and Willmott (1992b) argue that a more realistic objective is what they call 'microemancipation'. Microemancipation involves small-scale changes that help the individual or group to take control of their own destiny. For these writers 'emancipation is not a gift bestowed upon employees; rather it necessitates the (often painful) resistance to, and overcoming of, socially unnecessary restrictions' (1992b: 433). In other words, power cannot be given by managers (because it always comes with strings attached); rather, it needs to be fought for actively to produce a fairer system.

According to this view, workers therefore need to try to achieve microemancipation by working on small-scale changes that they choose themselves. Workers (and indeed management) can thus temporarily escape from domination and control through small changes in how they work. 'Inherent in the concept of microemancipation is an emphasis on partial, temporary movements that break away from diverse forms of oppression, rather than successive moves toward a predetermined state of liberation' (1992b: 447). Microemancipation therefore aims for little breaks with the normal ways of doing things in order to think and act differently.

Microemancipation, however, does not come without a cost. It might mean a reduction in productivity; workers might be less work-focused and, therefore, might not get promotions or might even lose their jobs. Microemancipation has its costs as well as benefits. Furthermore, as King and Learmonth argue, in practice it is challenging to practice microemancipation: even small changes are hard to achieve or think of when one is a manager (King and Learmonth, 2015). More recent critical work therefore explores the possibilities of non-domination (Griffin et al., 2015) or of *creating* emancipation through actualizing equality and through dissent to transform society and organizations now, rather than in a distant future (Huault et al., 2014).

## Review questions

| **Describe** | How would you define empowerment? |
|---|---|
| **Explain** | What negative reactions can feeling powerless produce? |
| **Analyse** | Why do some critical theorists argue that empowerment increases control over workers? |

# Chapter summary

**Running case:** Wilkinson enters the boardroom

Linda presents to the board. She feels more confident about the proposal and feels that she has the backing of her team. As she looks up, she sees Effingham give her a smile. Or is it a smirk? 'I can do this,' she thinks to herself. 'Breathe deeply, believe in yourself, be confident ... '

While we often do not like to think about it, power and politics are central parts of everyday organizational practice. They impacts individuals' careers, decision making processes, and organizational effectiveness. Power can be seen as one of the drivers of organizational life, propelling people's actions, thinking processes, and even belief systems. While for some people power and politics are just on the surface, seen in decision making and conflict, such writers as Lukes and Foucault offer a deeper view of power that shapes our fundamental ways of thinking and acting in the world.

It might be nice to think of a world where power does not exist, but as theorists as diverse as Jeffery Pfeffer and Michel Foucault have demonstrated, such a view is impossible. Power is with us in all situations in our lives. The real question that power raises is: How do we use it in ways that are positive and productive?

## Further reading

Clegg, S.R., and Haugaard, M. (eds) 2012. *Power and Organizations*, vols 1–4. SAGE Publications Ltd: London.
This comprehensive introduction provides many of the key articles from the last 50 years about power and organizations. This book is a useful resource if you want to find influential articles to get an in-depth understanding of the topic.

McNay, L. 1994. *Foucault: A critical introduction*. Blackwell: Cambridge.
A very readable introduction to Foucault's work which provides a good explanation of his views on power.

Lukes, S. 2005. *Power: A radical view*. Palgrave Macmillan: Basingstoke.
This gives a good overview of the issues of power and politics—particularly the three faces of power. It presents an interesting Marxist view of power that demonstrates how it is structural and often invisible.

Pfeffer, J. 1992. *Managing with power: Politics and influence in organizations*. Harvard Business School Press: Boston.
Pfeffer is in the 'power as a possession' camp, and this book is his key text on the subject. It explores how managers can use power and politics in organizations.

Townley, B. 1994. *Reframing human resource management: Power, ethics and the subject at work.* **Sage: London.**

A challenging, but very interesting, account of how Michel Foucault's work can be applied to real life organizations. It gives good examples, such as the role of appraisal systems as a form of power.

## References

Alvesson, M., and Willmott, H. 1992a. *Making sense of management.* Sage: London.

Alvesson, M., and Willmott, H. 1992b. On the idea of emancipation in management and organization studies. *Academy of Management Review* 17(3): 432–64.

*Automobile* 2011. 2011 Man of the Year: Ferdinand Piech. Available at: http://www.automobilemag.com/features/awards/1101_2011_man_of_the_year_ferdinand_piech/.

Bartels, J.M. 2015. The Stanford prison experiment in introductory psychology textbooks: A content analysis. *Psychology Learning and Teaching* 14(1): 36–50.

Bauman, Z. 1989. *Modernity and the holocaust.* Polity Press: Cambridge.

BBC 2015a Volkswagen chairman Ferdinand Piech quits in power struggle. Available at: http://www.bbc.co.uk/news/business-32468360 (last accessed 29 June 2015).

BBC 2015b There's only one Sepp Blatter. BBC Radio Five Live, 27 May.

Bowie, N. 2000. A Kantian theory of leadership. *Leadership and Organization Development Journal* 21(4): 185–93.

Burns, J. 1978. *Leadership.* Harper & Row: New York.

Callaghan, G., and Thompson, P. 2001. Edwards revisited: Technical control and call centres. *Economic and Industrial Democracy* 22(1): 13–37.

Carnahan, T., and McFarland, S. 2007. Revisiting the Stanford Prison Experiment: Could participant self-selection have led to the cruelty? *Personality and Social Psychology Bulletin* 33: 603–14.

Cederström, C., and Fleming, P. 2012. *Dead man working.* Zer0 Books: Winchester.

Chaudhary, V. 2015. Yes, FIFA has problems—but Sepp Blatter is a champion of world football. *The Guardian,* 31 May.

Clegg, S., and Haugaard, M. (eds.) 2012. *Power and organizations,* vols 1–4. SAGE Publications Ltd: London.

Cunningham, I., and Hyman, J. 1999. The poverty of empowerment? A critical case study. *Personnel Review* 28(3): 192–207.

Dahl, R. 1957. The concept of power. *Behavioral Science* 2: 201–25.

Dahl, R. 1958. A critique of the ruling elite model. *American Political Science Review* 52: 463–9.

*Daily Telegraph* 2003. The truth about Dr Kelly, 22 July.

Den Hartog, D.N., and Belschak, F.D. 2012. Work engagement and Machiavellianism in the ethical leadership process. *Journal of Business Ethics* 107(1): 35–47.

Dick, P., and Collings, D.G. 2014. Discipline and punish? Strategy discourse, senior manager subjectivity and contradictory power effects. *Human Relations* 67(12): 1513–36.

Ferris, G., Treadway, D., Kolodinsky, R., Hochwarter, W., Kacmar, C., Douglas, C., and Frink, D. 2005. Development and validation of the political skill inventory. *Journal of Management* 31: 126–52.

Ferris, G., Treadway, D., Perrewé, P., Brouer, R., Douglas, C., and Lux, S. 2007. Political skill in organizations. *Journal of Management* 33(3): 290–320.

Foster, C. 2014. Sepp Blatter's Qatar admission reveals a Machiavellian master at work. *Sydney Morning Herald,* 17 May.

Foucault, M. 1977. *Discipline and punish: The birth of the prison* (transl. A. Sheridan). Penguin Books: London.

Foucault, M. 1981. *The history of sexuality: The will to knowledge,* vol. 1. Penguin: London.

French, J., and Raven, B. 1958. *The bases of social power.* In: Cartwright, D. (ed.) *Introducing social psychology.* Institute for Social Research, University of Michigan Press: Ann Arbor, MI, pp. 150–67.

Gibson, O. 2015. Sepp Blatter to resign as FIFA president after 17 years in role. *The Guardian,* 2 June.

Griffin, M., Learmonth, M., and Elliott, C. 2015. Non-domination, contestation and freedom: The contribution of Philip Pettit to learning and democracy in organisations. *Management Learning* 46(3): 317–36.

Griggs, R.A. 2014. Coverage of the Stanford Prison Experiment in introductory psychology textbooks. *Teaching of Psychology* 41(3): 195–203.

Haney, C., and Zimbardo, P.G. 2009. Persistent dispositionalism in interactionist clothing: Fundamental attribution error in explaining prison abuse. *Personality and Social Psychology Bulletin* 35(6): 807–14.

Huault, I., Perret, V., and Spicer, A. 2014. Beyond macro- and micro-emancipation: Rethinking emancipation in organization studies. *Organization* 21(1): 22–49.

Huczynski, A., and Buchanan, D. 2004. *Organizational behaviour*. Pearson Education Ltd: Harlow.

Hunderson, B. 2015. Vladimir Putin says Sepp Blatter deserves Nobel Prize. *The Telegraph*, 27 July.

Jennings, A. 2006. *Foul! The secret world of FIFA: Bribes, vote rigging and ticket scandals*. HarperSport: London.

Jensen, J.M., and Raver, J.L. 2012. When self-management and surveillance collide: Consequences for employees' organizational citizenship and counterproductive work behaviors. *Group and Organization Management* 37(3): 308–46.

Kane-Frieder, R.E., Hochwarter, W.A., and Ferris, G.R. 2014. Terms of engagement: Political boundaries of work engagement-work outcomes relationships. *Human Relations* 67(3): 357–82.

Kanter, R. 1977. *Men and women of the corporation*. Basic Books: London.

King, D., and Learmonth, M. 2015. Can critical management studies ever be 'practical'? A case study in engaged scholarship. *Human Relations* 68(3): 353–75.

Kuper, S. 2015. FIFA president Sepp Blatter plays a long game. *Financial Times*, 27 May.

Lawrence, T.B., Malhotra, N., and Morris, T. 2012. Episodic and systemic power in the transformation of professional service firms. *Journal of Management Studies* 49(1): 102–43.

Lorinkova, N.M., and Perry, S.J. 2014. When is empowerment effective? The role of leader-leader exchange in empowering leadership, cynicism, and time theft. *Journal of Management*, 26 November, doi: 10.1177/0149206314560411

Lovibond, S., and Adams, W. 1979. The effects of three experimental prison environments on the behaviour of non–convict volunteer subjects. *Australian Psychologist* 14(3): 273–87.

Lukes, S. 2005. *Power: A radical view*. Palgrave Macmillan: Basingstoke.

Macdonald-Smith, A. 2015. Tap Oil CEO seeks deals in bid to ward off Thai shareholder; assets for sale. *Sydney Morning Herald*, 15 March.

Machiavelli, N. 1532/1984. *The prince*. Oxford University Press: Oxford.

Marx, K. 1859/2012. *A contribution to the critique of political economy*. Forgotten Books: London.

McClelland, D. 1975. *Power: The inner experience*. John Wiley & Sons Inc. Chichester.

McNay, L. 1994. *Foucault: A critical introduction*. Polity Press: Cambridge.

McNulty, T., Pettigrew, A., Jobome, G., and Morris, C. 2011. The role, power and influence of company chairs. *Journal of Management and Governance* 15(1): 91–121.

Milgram, S. 1974. *Obedience to authority: An experimental view*. Travistock: London.

Milne, R. 2015. Piëch is a specialist in corporate defenestration at Volkswagen. *Financial Times*, 13 April.

Mintzberg, H. 1983. *Power in and around organizations*. Prentice Hall: Englewood Cliffs, NJ.

Moore, J. 2010. HSBC still out of Africa after walking away from Nedbank takeover. *The Independent*, 16 October.

Nietzsche, F. 1990. *Beyond good and evil*. Penguin Books: London.

O'Boyle, T. 1998. *At any cost: Jack Welch, General Electric, and the pursuit of profit*. Knopf: New York.

Pfeffer, J. 1981. *Power in organizations*. Harper Collins: New York.

Pfeffer, J. 2010. *Power: Why some people have it—and others don't*. Harper Collins: New York.

Pierro, A., Raven, B.H., Amato, C., and Bélanger, J.J. 2013. Bases of social power, leadership styles, and organizational commitment. *International Journal of Psychology* 48(6): 1122–34.

Raven, B.H. 1965. Social influence and power. In: Steiner, D., and Fishbein, M. (eds) *Current studies in social psychology*. Holt, Rinehart, Winston: New York.

Raven, B.H. 1993. The bases of power: Origins and recent developments. *Journal of Social Issues* 49(4): 227–51.

Reicher, S.D., and Haslam, S.A. 2006. Rethinking the psychology of tyranny: The BBC prison study. *British Journal of Social Psychology* 45(1): 1.

Reicher, S.D., Haslam, S.A., and Miller, A.G. 2014. What makes a person a perpetrator? The intellectual, moral, and methodological arguments for revisiting Milgram's research on the influence of authority. *Journal of Social Issues* 70(3): 393–408.

Rose, N. 1998. *Inventing our selves: Psychology, power, and personhood*. Cambridge University Press: Cambridge.

Runciman, W. 2004. *Hutton and Butler: Lifting the lid on the workings of power*. Oxford University Press: Oxford.

Tap Oil 2015. Letter to shareholders. Available at: http://www.tapoil.com.au/IRM/Company/ShowPage.aspx/PDFs/2027-10000000/LettertoShareholders (last accessed 29 June 2015).

Thompson, P., and Ackroyd, S. 1995. All quiet on the workplace front? A critique of recent trends in british industrial sociology. *Sociology* 29: 615–33.

Thomson, A. 2014. Sanofi board ousts chief executive Chris Viehbacher. *Financial Times*, 29 October.

Tichy, N., and Stratford, S. 1993. *Control your destiny or someone else will: How Jack Welch is making General Electric the world's most competitive company*. Doubleday: New York.

Townley, B. 1994. *Reframing human resource management: Power, ethics and the subject at work*. Sage: London.

Ward, A. 2015. Sanofi's ousted CEO Viehbacher received €3m pay-off. *Financial Times*, 22 January.

Weber, M. 1978. *Economy and society*. University of California Press: Berkeley.

Weber, M. 2004. *The essential Weber* (ed S. Whimster). Routledge: London.

Wheeler, B. 2006. MP investigates Dr Kelly's death. *BBC News*. Available at: http://news.bbc.co.uk/1/hi/uk_politics/4995076.stm (last accessed 24 November 2012).

Whittle, A., Housley, W., Gilchrist, A., Mueller, F., and Lenney, P. 2015. Category predication work, discursive leadership and strategic sensemaking. *Human Relations* 68(3): 377–407.

Wilson, D.S., Near, D., and Miller, R.R. 1996. Machiavellianism: A synthesis of the evolutionary and psychological literatures. *Psychological Bulletin* 119(2): 285.

Yeung, R. 2009. *Office politics: The new rules*. Marshall Cavendish: London.

Zimbardo, P. 2007. Revisiting the Stanford Prison experiment: A lesson in the power of situation. *Chronicle of Higher Education* 53(30): B6–B7.

Zivnuska, S., Kacmar, K.M., Witt, L., Carlson, D.S., and Bratton, V.K. 2004. Interactive effects of impression management and organizational politics on job performance. *Journal of Organizational Behavior* 25(5): 627–40.

# Part 5
## Contemporary trends

# Information, communication, and technology

## Chapter overview and learning outcomes

By the end of this chapter you should be able to:

- describe theories and processes of communication in organizations

- explain how technology mediates communication, producing a trade-off between efficiency and richness of communication

- explain how technology produces information within the organization, especially when it is used to perform bureaucratic tasks

- analyse the effects of the Internet and computer networks upon organizations.

## Key theorists

| | |
|---|---|
| Albert Mehrabian | Noted the important role of non-verbal communication in organizational settings |
| Richard Daft and Robert Lengel | Devised media richness theory, which examines the abilities of different media to communicate rich information and meaning |
| Shoshana Zuboff | Wrote about the 'informated' organization, which generates a large amount of computerized activity about its own activities |
| Frank Blackler | Noted the simultaneous nature of organizations 'imploding' into computer code and 'exploding' into computer networks |
| Gilles Deleuze and Félix Guattari | Philosophers who devised the concept of the rhizome, which has been used to describe organizations which operate through computer networks |
| Saskia Sassen | Noted how the control of the Internet and of organizations within the Internet mirrors wider control structures in society |

## Key terms

| | |
|---|---|
| Communication | The transfer of meaning or information from one person, or several, to another |
| Noise | Anything which disrupts and distorts communication so that the meaning perceived by the recipient is different from the meaning intended by the sender |
| Information, communication, and technology (ICT) | A set of contemporary electronic technologies which facilitate communication between people and the sharing of information |
| Social presence | The degree to which the physical presence of the sender of a message can be felt in a particular communications medium |

| Media richness | The ability of different communications media to communicate rich, personal meanings rather than lean, impersonal information |
| --- | --- |
| Informating | Where a large amount of an organization's activity and knowledge is stored as computer code in a database |
| Network | Where organizations are linked by sharing data through computer networks or through the Internet |
| Rhizome | A mass of random, tangled connections which some people suggest is similar to the nature of the Internet and cyberspace |

# Introduction

**Running case:** 'Guests First'

**From:** simon_chance@junctionhotel.co.uk
**To:** senior_management_team@junctionhotel.co.uk

Dear colleagues

As you are aware we have been facing a tough time economically, leading to some efficiencies being made in work processes and staff numbers. At the same time, we face the challenge of maintaining our position as a luxury hotel.

It is my belief that we can achieve this balancing act if we recognize that the key factor which adds value and luxury status to the hotel is our people and the attention to customer service that they provide.

For this reason, I am introducing our new 'Guests First' initiative. It means that, for all of us, whatever our role in the organization, we need to perform our roles with the recognition that without our guests we have no income. It is through you putting the guests first that we can maintain our status as a luxury experience.

Could you all, as senior managers, please cascade this down to the people in your departments and we can all start putting the guests first as soon as possible!

Many thanks

Simon

'Information, communication, and technology' (ICT) refers to a raft of contemporary computer technologies which facilitate communication and the sharing of information. It is an ever-present part of our daily lives. Think of a commonly-used device, such as a smartphone. It is a form of communications technology, allowing us to communicate by phone, text, or email. It also allows us to manage information, such as our personal diaries, or access information through the Internet.

ICT is also an important part of organizational life, with whole departments devoted to running and maintaining the communication technologies that an organization uses. In this chapter we suggest not only that communication is an important process within organizations, but also that ICT has had a profound impact on the nature of what organizations do and, indeed, on what organizations *are*.

Familiar communications technology.
**Source:** Shutterstock.

- Firstly, we examine theories of communication within organizations—the ways in which information and meaning are transferred between people. Communication is an important managerial activity, but one which is prone to *mis*communication—what a person sending a message means may not be the same as how the person receiving that message understands it.

- Secondly, we examine how technology, such as email, facilitates communication. In particular, we see that while technology can make communication more efficient, different media convey different degrees of the rich meaning that comes from face-to-face communication.

- Thirdly, we examine how information is communicated *between* organizations, especially as more and more organizational activity takes place through computer code.

The final point brings us to the nature of organizations which operate through global, electronic networks, including the Internet. We see how this changes both the nature and activity of organizations but, at the same time, brings particular challenges of maintaining the boundary of the organization in order to keep its valuable data safe.

# Communication in organizations: getting the message through

Effective **communication** is an important part of organizational success. It means that the wishes, desires, and orders of those at the top have been successfully transmitted to, and understood by, all people within the organization who will then act upon them. Communication is therefore important for the exercise of managerial power, but is it something which always takes place flawlessly?

In this section we examine some of the main features of communication between people in organizations, but also the ways in which **miscommunication** can occur. We see how **noise** can interfere in the communication process, resulting in the original, intended meaning being distorted and, potentially, a completely different message being received. We question the amount of power that management actually have over the communication process and the degree to which communication allows managerial power to be exerted.

**Communication** A process whereby information is transferred from a sender (or senders) to a receiver (or receivers).

**Miscommunication** Where some of the meaning of a communication is distorted.

**Noise** Anything which distorts the transfer of a message from source to recipient so that the intended and perceived meanings differ.

# Features of communication

Message An item of communication sent from a sender to a recipient.

Rather than being a simple transfer of a **message** from a sender to a recipient, communication has many facets and features which mean that the nature of any one communication, or the way in which we pass on a message, will be different from another. We begin this section by examining four particular features which make up the nature of communication:

- Is it formal or informal?
- What channel does it take—is it spoken, written, symbolic, or expressed in the form of gestures?
- How long does it take to reach its intended recipient and for a reply to be received?
- Is it between individuals or among many people?

## Formal and informal channels of communication

### Running Case: at the Squash Club

Head chef Graham Effingham and maintenance manager George Andrews are having their weekly match at the squash club. While getting changed, Andrews brings up the subject of the 'Guests First' email.

'Have you seen that latest rubbish from Chance? Does he have nothing better to do with his time?' asks Andrews. 'Tell me about it,' replies Effingham. 'It's not as if we're not busy enough already. And doesn't he think my waiters are trained in customer service?'

'Why is he doing it—does he think it will make any difference?' asks Andrews.

'Well, word on the street is that Chance is coming under a lot of pressure from the consortium. They are seeing the hotel as a bit of a loss-making distraction and they want to concentrate money and efforts on the football club. This is Chance trying to show he's serious about the hotel,' replies Effingham. 'Interesting . . .,' replies Andrews, 'I heard Chance has been arguing with that business manager—Weaver. This should have been Weaver's initiative, but they disagreed, and now Chance has taken it on himself to launch the initiative.' 'Well, he probably needs the distraction,' replies Effingham. 'From what?' asks Andrews. 'Have you not heard? His wife walked out on him last week . . .'

Formal communication Official communication within an organization, following authorized pathways.

Organization chart A diagram of the structure of an organization.

Hierarchy The levels and ranks of an organization. Any one level reports to the level immediately above and commands the level immediately below.

Matrix structure An organizational structure that combines a traditional functional hierarchy with separately-managed project teams that draw people from different functional departments.

When you think about communication in organizations, do you think of it as something official, signed by the managing director and sent on company letter-headed paper, or do you think of the conversations and gossip between workers in the staff canteen? The first feature of communication that we examine is its formal and informal aspects.

**Formal communication** is the official communication from management downwards, such as memos and commands, that follow formalized channels. These channels can be represented by the **organization chart** (Figure 14.1), which was presented in Chapter 2 as a diagram of hierarchical structure which facilitated organizational control. However, the chart can also be seen as a map of organizational communication, showing who communicates with whom as orders and messages are passed up and down from one level to the next throughout the **hierarchy**.

As seen in Chapter 4, this form of hierarchical bureaucracy has been superseded in many organizations by more flexible structures, such as the **matrix structure** (Figure 14.2; see Chapter 4 for more explanation). Formal communication channels are thus not just

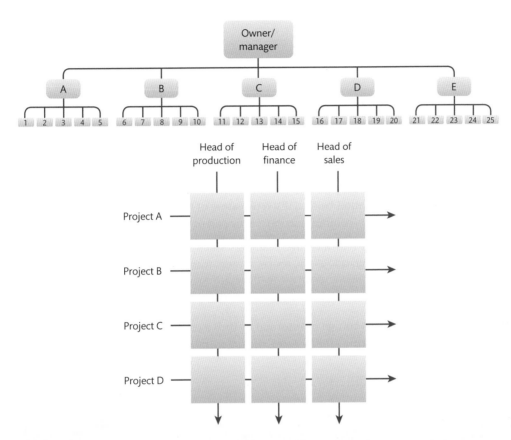

**Figure 14.1** An organizational hierarchy.

**Figure 14.2** A typical matrix structure.

vertical, as with the organizational hierarchy, but can also be horizontal—with communication flowing across the organization through formally-constituted project teams.

Alongside formal channels of communication, however, are the **informal communications** that take place: the 'water-cooler' conversations and quick chats at the photocopier, for example. Such communication is not part of the organization's authorized, formal communication, but information about the workplace is, nevertheless, shared.

For example, a workplace football team may bring together people from different parts of the organization—sales, accounting, production, etc.—and even from different levels in the hierarchy. Conversation in the bar after a match is likely, at some point, to turn to work-related issues. People get to learn about what is going on in other parts of the organization—information that they might not hear otherwise. And a football team is just one of potentially many informal social groups that may exist in an organization.

It is here that organizational issues might be discussed in ways that would not be mapped out by the formal organizational channels of the organization chart. There is a 'suppleness of communication' (Deleuze and Guattari, 1987: 214) that bypasses official bureaucratic structures and communication channels.

Such communication is sometimes linked with **gossip**, where people get to find out work-related information to which they would otherwise not be party. Gossip in organizations is an area of study in itself and has been analysed as not just a form of informal communication but also a source of power and a means of maintaining the cohesion of groups within organizations (e.g. Noon and Delbridge, 1993; Kurland and Pelled, 2000).

Visit the Online Resource Centre for more analysis of gossip in organizations.

**Informal communications** Communication in an organization not following official and formal guidelines.

**Gossip** Rumours and information communicated through informal means.

Management are able to control the content of formal communications, such as memos and emails. To what extent can they control both the content and the accuracy of informal communications, such as gossip?

**Post-bureaucratic organization** A trend away from rigid, bureaucratic rules and structures in organizations towards more flexible, less hierarchical and rule-driven organizations.

**Organizational learning** Sharing and transfer of individual knowledge so that it becomes a collective property of the organization.

In more recent theories of organization, the distinction between formal and informal communication can become blurred. For example, **post-bureaucratic organizations** (see Chapter 4) minimize structure and formal roles and, instead, emphasize dialogue between people as the main feature of an organization. Models of **organizational learning** also emphasize the importance of sharing work-related knowledge through conversations, as with the case of the Xerox photocopier engineers (see Chapter 10).

Rather than communication being a discrete feature of the organization, mapped out by the organization's structure, communication is a big part of what the organization actually *is*:

> It is through the telephone calls, meetings, planning sessions, sales talks and corridor conversations that people inform, update, gossip, review, reassess, reason, instruct, revise, argue, debate, contest and actually *constitute* the moments, myths and, through time, the very *structuring* of the organization.    (Boden, 1994: 8, original author's emphasis)

Communication, whether formal or informal, is thus a continual and ongoing process in organizations, or, as Broekstra (1998) states, the organization *is* a conversation.

## Channels of communication

**Running case:** raising the bar

With the evening bar shift about to begin, John Vintner, the bar manager, is making a few announcements in the staff room. 'Oh, and finally,' he announces with a sarcastic and mocking tone, 'we have an email from Mr Chance.'

'Ooh,' reply the bar staff in mock fascination, before descending into giggles.

'We have a new initiative for customer service,' announces Vintner, his voice both grandiose and mocking. Vintner continues to read out the email, strutting around the staff room, making grand sweeping gestures with his arms, his voice becoming more mocking in tone as he continues. Each mention of the phrase 'Guests First' is telegraphed with ever more exaggerated facial mugging and, as the announcement continues, the staff fall more and more into hysterical laughter.

Finally, Vintner returns to his normal tone of voice. 'Well, guys, as far as I'm concerned you've been putting guests first for years—so off you go and do the same as always.'

What is the bar manager communicating through his gestures and tone of voice over and above the words that he is reading out?

Have you ever found yourself giving directions to somebody while speaking on the telephone, only to realize that you are pointing and tracing out the directions with your free hand, even though the other person cannot see you? Such gestures show how communication involves factors beyond the words themselves—much of what we understand from a conversation comes from non-verbal body language.

> **Research insight:** Mehrabian's 55–38–7 ratio
> Mehrabian, A. 1971. *Silent messages*. Wadsworth: Belmont, CA.
>
> Albert Mehrabian (1971) studied communication among workers in a laboratory and was particularly interested in how people communicated emotions and attitudes. While we might think that the information conveyed in a conversation would be from words alone, Mehrabian's study discovered that much more is communicated through body language, such as hand gestures, comportment, and eye contact. The 55–38–7 ratio suggests that:
>
> - 55% of communication is from body language
> - 38% of communication comes from the tone of voice
> - just 7% of communication is from the actual words.
>
> Mehrabian's work has implications for communication that does not take place in a face-to-face setting—how much meaning is lost if 55% of communication is from bodily gestures?

**Channels of communication** are the means by which a communication is transferred or mediated from a sender to a recipient. As we will see later in the chapter, different channels are seen to have different degrees of richness, i.e. the amount of information that they can communicate. Four general types of channel through which communication in organizations takes place are:

- oral communication is through spoken words: conversations, meetings, briefings, negotiations, phone calls, etc.
- bodily, non-verbal communication is the gestures, facial expressions, and body language that convey meaning beyond the actual words spoken
- written communication takes place through words on paper, or on a computer or telephone screen; examples include letters, memos, emails, text messages, a newsletter, or a noticeboard
- symbolic communication uses signs and symbols, e.g. drivers understand that a symbol such as a red circle with a white horizontal line through the middle means 'no entry'.

Which examples of the four channels of communication have you engaged in today—either as a sender or receiver?

**Channels of communication** Ways in which a message is expressed, e.g. orally or in written words.

## Synchronicity and feedback

A conversation is generally a two-way process—we take it in turns to say something, listen to the response, and then respond accordingly. We also understand how a person feels about our words from the bodily, non-verbal reactions—the look on their face and their body language. This process of receiving a response to communication is **feedback**.

However, not all feedback is as instantaneous as it is with a conversation. Many of us may have experienced the frustration of sending an email or a letter only to be left waiting for a response. **Synchronicity** describes the amount of delay between sending a message and that message being received, and gives a further facet of communication.

- Synchronous communication is where transmission of the message by the sender and receipt of the message happen simultaneously, and there is thus the possibility for

**Feedback** Reaction or response to a message.

**Synchronicity** The degree to which something happens immediately or after a delay.

feedback to be instant. Examples include face-to-face conversations, phone calls, and video calls.

- Asynchronous communication is where there is a delay between the sending and receiving of the message. Thus, feedback is not instantaneous—the sender may have a long delay before getting a response to their communication. Examples include letters, emails, and text messages.

## Focus of communication

A final facet of communication is the focus of the message—whether is it directed to one person or is a more impersonal form of communication directed to many people, even the whole organization. Table 14.1 shows a number of different types of focus of communication that may take place in organizations.

Table 14.1  Different types of focus of communication

| Focus | Description | Examples |
|-------|-------------|----------|
| One-to-one | Personal communication between two individuals | Conversation, personal email, personal letter, phone call |
| One-to-many (broadcasting) | One person sends a communication to many people (even a whole organization) | Bulk email, speech at a staff meeting, memo |
| Many-to-many | A communication to many people that doesn't come from one personal, identifiable source (e.g. it might come from the board or a marketing department) | Newsletter (although there may be individual items within this, e.g. an address from the Chief Executive Officer) |
| Many-to-one | A group of people communicate to just one person | A project group might have a single email address and communicate their results collectively through this to one individual within the organization |

## Communication and miscommunication

**Running case:** misinterpretation

Chance's email is one of many in the inbox of fitness manager Carl Jones. With a busy workload to deal with, he only has time to glance at the email, picking up on the phrase 'Guests First.'

**From:** fitnessmanager@junctionhotel.co.uk
**To:** fitness_staff@junctionhotel.co.uk

Guys,

Quick message to pass on from Simon Chance—we now have to put guests first.

Carl

Duty manager David Smith picks up on the email. He knows that there are some peak times when the gym is quite crowded and takes this to mean that hotel guests should have priority over external members. He conveys this instruction to his team of fitness staff.

Come Monday evening at 6 pm, when the gym is usually busiest, the staff are asking paying gym members to make way on the equipment for hotel guests. This leads to arguments between staff and customers and between customers. This continues throughout the week, and ten members cancel their memberships.

Noticing this exodus, Chance makes his way to the fitness centre to confront the manager.

'What's the issue here? The members are leaving in their droves,' says a panicked Chance. 'I'm implementing just what you asked for—putting guests first. The members aren't happy being asked to make way for hotel guests, you know—what did you expect?' replies Smith.

'What?' asks a puzzled Chance, before realization dawns. 'No—that's not what I meant in the email. What I meant was . . . oh . . . tell you what, do you have five minutes for a quick chat?'

The four features of communication that we have examined all play a role in an overall model of the communication process. A simplified version of this model is shown in Figure 14.3.

Communication passes through the following stages, as illustrated in the model:

- the communication begins with the **source**, be this one or many people, who have a particular intended meaning that they wish to communicate to one or many people
- the source **encodes** the communication, i.e. they form a message using a verbal, bodily, written, or symbolic channel
- the message is sent, using either formal or informal means of communication
- the **recipient** (or recipients) receives and **decodes** the message, and perceives a particular meaning from it before providing feedback, either synchronously or asynchronously.

## Noise and miscommunication

Messages are open to misinterpretation. The intended meaning of the sender and the perceived meaning of the receiver can differ, sometimes vastly. Where there is more than one recipient, each recipient may have their own different perception of the meaning.

**Source** The sender or originator of a message.

**Encodes** Converts the intended meaning of a communication into a form that can be sent as a message.

**Recipient** The person or persons receiving a message.

**Decodes** Converts a received message into the meaning perceived by the recipient.

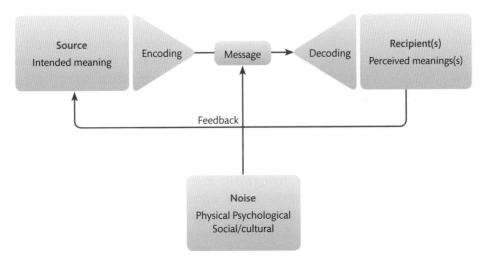

**Figure 14.3** A model of the communication process (based on Shannon et al., 1949).

Table 14.2 Examples of noise in the communication process

| Type of noise | Examples |
| --- | --- |
| Physical noise | Background noise getting in the way of a conversation<br>Interference on a phone line<br>Corruption of data in a computer file |
| Psychological noise | Semantics—people interpret words in different ways, attaching their own meanings to subjective ideas such as 'good', 'dedicated', etc.<br>Perception—people may attach different degrees of importance to different parts of a message<br>Attention—people may not give their full attention to a message, being distracted by other things |
| Social/cultural noise | People may speak a different language from the original communication, and thus mistranslations may occur<br>Different cultures may interpret messages differently (see Chapter 15 for examples of cultural misunderstandings and differences) |

Anything which intervenes in the communication process and alters the original intended meaning of a message is termed noise (Shannon et al., 1949). We think of noise in physical terms, perhaps such as someone shouting over a conversation so that it can't be heard, but, in the communication process, noise can take a number of forms. Examples of noise are shown in Table 14.2.

Noise exists as a barrier to communication and the effective transfer of meaning from the sender to the recipient. The model in this section shows noise intervening in a single communication. In the next section we see how the potential for noise increases as the number of stages of communication of a message increases.

Have you ever had a situation where something you have said or a message that you have sent has been misinterpreted? What do you think was the cause of that misinterpretation?

## Communication and power

Many of you will have played the party game where a message is whispered from person to person, often with a wildly different message from the original appearing at the end of the line. Noise interferes as the message is passed from one person to the next, and this can happen at any stage along the way. Now think about the power that the first person in the line has to control the final message that appears at the end of the line. They can say the message very clearly to the next person along, but, after that, they have no control over what miscommunication and noise may happen further down the line.

A similar problem faces a manager trying to communicate a message across an organization—it has to pass from person to person and, at any stage, there is the potential for noise and miscommunication. Nichols (1962) suggested that, from top management at board level down to operators on a factory floor, only 20% of the meaning of an original message remains. It would seem that management have very little **power** over how their communication is interpreted and acted upon.

Power The capacity to get things done or to influence others.

Visit the Online Resource Centre for an example of the power (or lack thereof) to communicate meaning in the lyrics of songs.

This lack of power over meaning and interpretation of communication is compared by Latour (1986) to a passing move in a rugby game. As players throw the ball to each other they each have to receive it and, with a new exertion of force, throw it to the next player. It is a fragile exercise which can fail if one player should drop the ball or throw it in the wrong direction. The power of the initial throw only lasts until the first person catches the ball—how it is then passed on is literally 'in the hands' of the next person along the line.

How is this view of power and communication similar to the whispering game described earlier?

Latour uses this rugby metaphor to understand the movement of power in social settings such as organizations. We generally think of power being held by managers at the top of an organization and being exerted across the organization (see Chapter 13 for a discussion of this). Latour's rugby ball metaphor suggests that, in fact, the successful exercise of power is 'in the hands' of others. Each person who receives a managerial command, order, or similar communication of power will, in some way, have to interpret it or decode it in their own mind. Management can never be certain just how their acts of power, their words, commands, and deeds will be interpreted and acted upon by individuals within the organization (Gergen, 1992).

Latour's rugby ball metaphor illustrates how noise can disrupt communication at many levels within an organization as messages are passed from person to person and department to department. The official, formal communications of the organization through which orders and power are carried out are open to being modified and disrupted in the day-to-day informal conversations and communications that take place throughout the organization.

In the next section, we see how such issues of miscommunication and noise affect an organization as it uses technology to communicate across the whole organization.

## Review questions

| | |
|---|---|
| **Describe** | What are the four main features of communication in organizations? |
| **Explain** | How can noise alter the intended meaning of a message? |
| **Analyse** | In what ways do management lack the power to ensure consistent communication of a message across an organization? |
| **Apply** | What examples of noise and miscommunication can you identify in the running case throughout the chapter so far? |

# Technology and communication: the medium is the message

## Running case: email exchange

**From:** lindawilkinson@junctionhotel.co.uk
**To:** reception_staff@junctionhotel.co.uk; porters@junctionhotel.co.uk

**Subject:** Guests First

Hi everyone

I hope you are all well. We have a new initiative beginning this week called 'Guests First'. The aim is to make guests feel like they are the most important part of our business and, as reception area staff, you will be at the front line of this.

It's vital that we do this to maintain our reputation for customer service in these difficult times. So, can we all make that extra effort from now on to put the guests first!

Many thanks

Linda

...........

**From:** suesmith@junctionhotel.co.uk
**To:** lindawilkinson@junctionhotel.co.uk
**cc:** reception_staff@junctionhotel.co.uk; porters@junctionhotel.co.uk

**Subject:** RE: Guests First

Dear Linda

I read with interest your email and I would be grateful if you could clarify what you mean by 'extra effort'. In particular, it implies that my effort in the job up until now has been insufficient—could you please point out the faults that you seem to think exist in my work.

Best wishes

Sue

...........

**From:** lindawilkinson@junctionhotel.co.uk
**To:** suesmith@junctionhotel.co.uk
**cc:** reception_staff@junctionhotel.co.uk; porters@junctionhotel.co.uk

**Subject:** RE: RE: Guests First

Dear Sue

I wasn't implying that there's anything wrong with your work, but, in times like these, we all need to go that little bit further . . . We really need to pull together in these difficult times rather than engaging in internecine discussions such as these.

Best

Linda

..........

**From:** suesmith@junctionhotel.co.uk
**To:** lindawilkinson@junctionhotel.co.uk
**cc:** reception_staff@junctionhotel.co.uk; porters@junctionhotel.co.uk

**Subject:** RE: RE: RE: Guests First

Linda

I see—so now I'm the problem then, and I can't even raise a point without being branded a troublemaker. Ten years I've been here with no one saying a bad thing about my work—now it seems I don't put in enough effort and I'm a troublemaker!

Sue

..........

**From:** janedavies@junctionhotel.co.uk
**To:** lindawilkinson@junctionhotel.co.uk
**cc:** reception_staff@junctionhotel.co.uk; porters@junctionhotel.co.uk

**Subject:** RE: RE: RE: RE: Guests First

Sue—come on, give Linda some slack. We need to try everything we can to keep afloat in this recession.

Jane

..........

**From:** bobjones@junctionhotel.co.uk
**To:** janedavies@junctionhotel.co.uk
**cc:** reception_staff@junctionhotel.co.uk; porters@junctionhotel.co.uk

**Subject:** RE: RE: RE: RE: RE: Guests First

Could you all have this discussion in private and not use reply all—I'm fed up of seeing this nonsense in my inbox!

Thanks

Bob.

...........

**From:** gailwilliams@junctionhotel.co.uk
**To:** bobjones@junctionhotel.co.uk
**cc:** reception_staff@junctionhotel.co.uk; porters@junctionhotel.co.uk

**Subject:** RE: RE: RE: RE: RE: RE: Guests First

Looks like a few people have gotten out of the wrong side of bed this morning :)

...........

**From:** suesmith@junctionhotel.co.uk
**To:** gailwilliams@junctionhotel.co.uk
**cc:** reception_staff@junctionhotel.co.uk; porters@junctionhotel.co.uk

**Subject:** RE: RE: RE: RE: RE: RE: RE: Guests First

OH SHUT UP. THIS ISN'T A JOKE

...........

**From:** lindawilkinson@junctionhotel.co.uk
**To:** suesmith@junctionhotel.co.uk
**cc:** reception_staff@junctionhotel.co.uk; porters@junctionhotel.co.uk

**Subject:** RE: RE: RE: RE: RE: RE: RE: RE: Guests First

Look everyone—we need to calm down a bit. This doesn't help anything at all. Maybe we need to sit down and have a face-to-face meeting about this. Let's say my office at 10.30 am.

Thanks

Linda

Imagine you are a chief executive wanting to communicate an important message to all 1,000 members of your organization. How would you go about doing this? You could speak to each worker individually—but that would take a long time, especially if the message was complex. **Communication technology** might help the chief executive to communicate their message more efficiently, for example:

- a simple technology, like a microphone, would allow the CEO to address all staff at once in one large auditorium

- printing/photocopying technology would allow a letter to be sent to all employees conveying the message

- even more efficiently, the message could be sent instantly as an email to all employees.

However, while each of these communications **media** allow the message to be delivered more efficiently (think of the difference in time between speaking to each employee individually, and composing and sending a mass email) this efficiency comes with a loss of **richness**—much of the information gained from the body language of a face-to-face conversation is lost, for example.

How many types of communications technology can you think of? Which do you use in your daily life? Do you use different technologies for different tasks?

**Research insight:** What is technology?

Cooper, R. 1993. Technologies of representation. In: Ahonen, P. (ed.) *Tracing the semiotic boundaries of politics.* Mouton de Gruyter: Berlin, pp. 279–312.

We tend to think of technology in terms of the latest gadgets—smartphones, games consoles, etc.—or perhaps in terms of heavy machines. Cooper (1993) however, suggests a wider view of technology—it is any form of tool that turns a human weakness into an advantage. In other words, it facilitates human action, opening up new possibilities and potential.

Think of a communication tool like a microphone. It is developed from the fact that the human voice is too weak to address a large crowd, but turns that weakness into an advantage whereby one speaker has the ability to communicate with many people at once. Technologies such as email allow a person to be able to communicate not only with many people, but also over a global geographical reach. Again, human potential is increased by technology.

In this section we first examine how communications technology enhances the abilities of people to communicate in organizations, both efficiently and over geographical distance. We then examine examples of how such technologies not only communicate information but in fact *create* information. The organization is **informated** (Zuboff, 1988)—in effect becoming a giant computer database.

**Communication technology** Technologies which facilitate communication between people and the sharing of information.

**Media** A specific form of technology or technologies which convey and carry information, e.g. telephone, letter, email.

**Richness** The amount and quality of information conveyed by any one message.

**Informated** The process whereby information about an organization's activities is created.

## Efficiency and richness: a trade-off

In recent years, email has come to dominate communications both within and outside organizations, replacing many forms of communication like telephone calls and things that previously might have been written on paper (e.g. a memo).

The convenience of email can be seen by the fact that it allows global communication without the expense of telephone conversations, or the delay and expense of postage. It also means that, unlike a telephone conversation, the recipient does not have to be there physically—they can pick up emails as and when they log on to their computer network.

When was the last time you wrote a letter?

In this section we use email as an example to examine the trade-off that communications technology brings between efficiency and richness. Email certainly allows for efficient communication—a message can be sent to an entire workforce across the whole globe with just one click of a button. Using **social presence theory** and **media richness theory**, we examine the extent to which this is at the expense of the richness of the message and the amount of information that it can convey.

## Social presence theory

**Social presence theory** Examines the degree to which the physical presence of the sender of a message can be felt in a particular communications medium.

**Media richness theory** Examines the ability of different communications media to communicate rich, personal meanings rather than lean, impersonal information.

Social presence theory is the degree of perceived immediacy of a person in a communication. What sense does a particular communications medium give of the person writing the message actually being there (physically present) in the room with you (Short et al., 1976; Rice, 1992)?

The most obvious form of social presence is a face-to-face conversation. As shown by Mehrabian's study, it is from this that important non-verbal aspects of communication, such as gestures and facial expressions, are gleaned. With an email, the sender is absent, and so the communication that comes from their physical presence—body language and tone of voice—is missing. In Mehrabian's analysis, this would leave just the words, which communicate a meagre 7% of intended meaning.

---

**Real life case:** the growth of emoji

Anyone who uses any form of mobile or online communication will be familiar with emoji, small pictograms which convey the meaning of an emotion (e.g. a smiling face), an object, an action (e.g. walking), or an idea. First developed in Japan in the late 1990s, the word emoji roughly translates from Japanese as 'pictograph' (Hern, 2015). In 2015, linguist Vyv Evans suggested that emoji was the fastest growing form of language in the UK, with 72% of 18–25-year-olds finding it an easier way than words to express emotions in online communications (Lough, 2015).

For communication coach Robin Kermode (2015), emoji add to written words the body language and tone of voice that give meaning to face-to-face communication, telling us whether a sentence is serious, or ironic, or meant as a joke, for example. Without these pictorial clues, words can be open to misinterpretation—a picture of a smiley face clears up whether a sentence is intended as a joke or as a serious comment. For Kermode; 'The reason emojis have become the fastest growing new language is that they are merely a depiction of the body language signals that humans have been reading for centuries'.

Many of you will use particular tactics in emails which increase social presence and give more communications clues. **Emoticons**—facial expressions created out of punctuation marks, such as :) being used to denote a smiley face—are often added to emails or similar text-based communication methods, such as text messages and Twitter. Emoticons, which have since developed into the more pictorial emoji described above, are a surrogate for the physical facial expression that would be seen if the person typing the email were actually present—they make up for some of the non-verbal meaning that has been lost (Lo, 2008).

The degree to which smiley faces can be used in professional workplace communication is debatable, but signatures on emails with links to web pages or that contain personal information are other examples of bringing social presence into this largely written form.

To what extent do profiles on social media sites, such as Facebook, increase social presence by including photos and other informal aspects of the person's life?

## Media richness theory

The amount of social presence desirable in a particular communication depends on what is being communicated. For instance, think about the following items of information that might need to be communicated at different times within an organization:

- a single piece of data: a figure
- a summary of data, e.g. a table or a chart
- a fact
- an instruction or order
- an item of tacit knowledge about how to perform a particular task (cf. knowledge transfer in Chapter 10)
- an emotion or feeling ('I'm trying to communicate my feelings about this deal').

In some cases, basic facts are all that need to be communicated. In others, a richer, more personal form of communication that puts across information, such as a person's feelings and attitudes, is required. Daft and Lengel's (1986) theory of media richness recognizes two particular contingencies of information which might make different communications media more or less appropriate at different times.

- **Uncertainty** relates to an absence of information. This uncertainty can be reduced by providing basic facts and data. For example, a head of sales looking to produce a sales forecast would reduce uncertainty by reading an email with sales figures for the past year. The lack of gestures and facial expressions does not alter the value of information in this email for someone who simply needs to know the basic facts.

- **Equivocality** is the amount to which a communication is open to interpretation. It involves attitudes, feelings, and items of disagreement, something which can't be resolved by the provision of basic facts alone. For example, an email to workers which outlines complaints about customer service might need to be carefully worded. Workers could misinterpret it: a member of staff who is working well might think it applies to them, for example, and take unnecessary offence. A manager may decide that email is not the best way to communicate such a complex message that might affect people emotionally and might instead have a quiet word with a few individuals.

Emoticon
Punctuation marks used in electronic communications, designed to simulate facial expressions.

Uncertainty A lack of knowledge about a particular factual issue.

Equivocality Situations where meanings are ambiguous and open to interpretation.

Can the emoticons and emoji described in the previous section be viewed in terms of reducing equivocality?

Daft and Lengel (1986) provide a continuum between rich and lean media (see Figure 14.4). Richer media are those which provide more of the personal, face-to-face qualities of communication, which might be needed in situations of equivocality where feelings and attitudes are being expressed, while leaner media provide more basic information and facts.

The amount of richness of a particular medium can be described in terms of the four features of communication explored in the previous section. Are verbal, bodily, or written channels used? Is the communication personal or addressed to many people? Is feedback immediate or is the communication synchronous? From Figure 14.4 we see the different levels of richness in different media, with aspects of richness lost as the diagram moves down towards leaner, more efficient modes of communication.

- Face-to-face communication is the richest form of communication. It is personal, contains bodily gestures and vocal tone clues, and provides immediate feedback.

- A telephone conversation is personal and may give rich communication information and feedback from the tone of voice, but it lacks the bodily gestures of a face-to-face conversation.

- An email addressed to a specific person is an example of a written personal document which lacks the richness of communications forms such as a conversation face to face or by telephone. The sender has to formulate the words in such a way as to best convey their intention, but it might be difficult to interpret by the reader, for example whether a comment is made as a joke or seriously. Furthermore, there is no opportunity to clarify the meaning of a communication through feedback, and thus misunderstandings, for which there is already more potential, may go uncorrected.

- Bulk emails, those sent to a group of recipients, are an example of a written, impersonal document. Richness is lost further as the communication moves from being personal to impersonal. Think about how many bulk or 'spam' emails you receive—do you even open all of them, let alone read the message contained within?

- Numerical documents, such as spreadsheets or a set of accounts, are the leanest and least rich medium, containing basic facts and information.

Think about specific communications technologies that you use—email, SMS, social media. Where would you place them on the media richness continuum in Figure 14.4?

**Figure 14.4**  Media richness theory.

**Source:**  Based on Daft and Lengel (1986).

We can see in this model the trade-off between efficiency and richness of communication: for example, while a bulk email may be an efficient form of communication, it lacks richness—and some people may not even open and read the email. Conversely, while a face-to-face conversation may provide rich communication, useful in situations of an equivocal nature, it is time-consuming and inefficient if communication needs to be over a wide scale.

The importance of media richness theory is not necessarily to choose the richest medium for all communication, but to choose the medium appropriate for what is being communicated.

## The medium is the message

> ### Real life case: fired by email
>
> In 2011 a number of British Army officers, some of whom were serving, or had recently served, in Afghanistan, were informed by email that they were being made redundant. They were informed that their contracts would end in a year and that they should begin to plan for their future careers.
>
> The case attracted a lot of press coverage, not only because of the redundancies themselves, but because of the manner in which the communication was made—by email rather than in person, which was seen to be insensitive for such potentially upsetting news.
>
> **Sources:** *The Independent* (2011); Quinn (2011); BBC News (2011).

The case of the army redundancies shows the importance of using the right medium of communication for the purpose. Furthermore, the choice of communication medium might in and of itself contribute to the message and how it is perceived, as Marshall McLuhan (1964) stated: 'The medium is the message'. Thus, a letter might seem too formal as a way to ask a friend out for a night out, when a text message might suffice. Likewise, an email might be too distant as a means to deliver bad news when a face-to-face conversation might communicate more sincerity and concern.

While face-to-face conversations might be the richest form of communication, it doesn't follow that it is the most appropriate form of communication in all cases. Think about getting driving directions—would you prefer someone to tell you every twist and turn of the journey face to face, or would you prefer to simply look at it on a map? The map might be a leaner form of communication—it is impersonal, with symbols, but it gets the message across concisely and efficiently.

Thus, on occasions leaner forms of communication might be more appropriate for communicating information in organizations—it is simpler to see a summary of sales figures as a table than have somebody recite them face to face.

What do you think would be the most appropriate ways to communicate the following within an organization?

- Facts about a project
- Figures, such as accounts
- Instructions for repairing a piece of machinery
- Directions to the head office
- Feedback to members of a project team
- Praise to an individual who has secured a new contract
- Anger at a colleague who is stirring up trouble
- An idea for a new product
- A new culture

**Research insight:** Communicating a culture

Gergen, K.J., and Whitney, D. 1996. Technologies of representation in the global corporation: Power and polyphony. In: Boje, D.M., Gephart, R.P., Jr., and Thatchenkery, T.J. (eds) *Postmodern management and organization theory*. Sage: Thousand Oaks, CA, pp. 331–57.

Gergen and Whitney's (1996) study of culture change in a recently merged multinational firm, Sloan Becker, highlights the relevance of media richness in communicating something as open to interpretation as an organizational culture.

In a bid to integrate the two newly-merged firms and their cultures, it was decided to implement a common set of principles or a common culture. This came under the slogan 'Simply Better', summing up the idea that workers should improve their 'performance' continually to reach the potential and promise within Sloan Becker. The new culture would be disseminated globally through a printed booklet.

However, as a relatively lean medium, lacking the richness of information that would come from the presence of the original authors, much of the culture was left open to the interpretation of the workers receiving and reading the booklet. Terms such as 'performance' are equivocal—they mean different things to different people; however, there was no opportunity for feedback for workers to ask about, and clarify, the meaning of terms and statements in the booklet.

The recipients were left to make their own interpretations of the culture, in discussion with familiar people around them. What emerged at Sloan Becker was not the one unified culture that management desired, but a whole patchwork of different cultures and meanings across the organization.

Gergen and Whitney's case highlights the problem of using a relatively lean medium, like text, to communicate richer, more equivocal ideas, such as culture and corporate values. The leaner medium cannot communicate every nuance of the culture, and it allows more possibility for noise to intervene in the communication process and for people's perceived meanings of the culture to be different to the original intended meaning. As with the lyrics of a song (see the Online Resource Centre), the original author lacks power over the interpretation that others will make—the meaning of the culture here is passed on by others and redirected in a manner similar to Latour's rugby ball metaphor.

**Employability skills:** communication

When advertising a vacancy, many employers call for good 'communication skills'. We might think of this as equating to good interpersonal skills—being able to engage in conversation, for example.

While this is a part of communication, effective communication skills are about putting a message across in the most appropriate manner for what is being communicated. It is about making the message as clear as possible and not leaving it open to misinterpretation and miscommunication. As we have seen in this section, on occasions the most appropriate communication might be a face-to-face conversation and at other times it might be sending figures in an email.

▷ Think about your own experience of communication and how you might be able to demonstrate skills to a potential employer. It might be from collaborating on a project with other students. What variety of communication methods did you use and which did you find most effective? How did you overcome any areas of confusion or miscommunication?

While emoticons and emoji might bring richer meaning to text-based communication, are they appropriate for workplace and professional communication?

## Review questions

| | |
|---|---|
| **Describe** | What are the main features of media richness theory? |
| **Explain** | How do different communications media convey the social presence of the sender of the message? |
| **Analyse** | How is communication a trade-off between efficiency and richness? |
| **Apply** | How can the miscommunication in the email chain at Junction Hotel be analysed in terms of media richness and social presence theories? |

# The informated organization

So far, in examining communication, we have seen information largely in terms of communications such as words, gestures, and diagrams, etc. Leaner communications media gain efficiency at the expense of richness. However, in this section we see how the creation of information by such lean media, often as a result of organizational techniques such as **bureaucracy**, is an important aspect of the nature of organizations which use information and communications technology.

Zuboff's (1988) concept of the informated organization suggests that more and more of what an organization actually does—its processes and the information that it holds—is stored as computerized information, to the extent that the organization becomes like a computer **database**.

The nature of such information, however, derives from technologies and tools that pre-date the use of information and communication technology in organizations.

## Bureaucracy and information technology

We may not think of something like a form as a piece of technology. However, think back to the analysis of the UCAS form for university admissions in Chapter 2. Using Cooper's (1993) earlier definition of technology, it emerges from a human inadequacy—people are unable to process the applications of thousands of university students in person. The form is the tool which makes this processing possible—it standardizes information in a manner which can then be processed more easily, and communicated and shared within the organization.

**Bureaucracy** From the French *bureau*, meaning office; bureaucracy covers official, formal elements of rational organizational design, such as the hierarchical organization structure, the rules and procedures, and the official paperwork, which exert impersonal control over the organization.

**Database** A computerized store of structured, organized data.

For Cooper and Burrell (1988), this at the heart of what bureaucracy does. It is not simply a structure—it is a technology of classifying and ordering people. Forms, records, and paperwork all are used for ordering organizational populations by not only storing information but also using that information to create further information. For example, with the UCAS form it is easy, given the standard nature of the form, to create information such as the average age of applicants, the number of people applying for business degrees, the average qualifications, etc.

Bureaucratic records thus not only store lean information—facts and figures about people—they go on to create further lean information from the analysis of data that is already stored. In Zuboff's terms, bureaucratic records are a basis for *informating* the organization.

## The organization as a database

Where bureaucratic records are stored in computer databases, the potential for information processing and sharing, and creating new information, is increased. Given the processing power of information technology and computers, a greater amount of information can be stored and processed. More and more of what the organization actually *is* comes to be stored within a computer system.

Think about how your bank knows you. Rather than the rich, face-to-face version of you, they will know you as a leaner entry on a database. It is a 'highly caricatured' (Poster, 1995: 91) version of you that boils you down to a few database fields, such as name, address, account number, etc.

What other 'highly caricatured' forms of you are held by other organizations?

It is not just you and all of the other customers that are held on a database by your bank; financial and account information will also be held in various computer systems. Indeed, the whole bank operates by updating various entries on the different databases. When you withdraw an amount of money it is deducted on the database field relevant to your account.

For Zuboff (1985: 10), it is not that banks simply use databases: banks are 'becoming more like databases'. So much of their activity is done through the computer data that they hold, it is as if the database is the equivalent of the bank itself.

Chapter 4 shows how information technology and computer records can be used to intensify control and surveillance over workers, as seen in call centres. Do you think such technology brings any advantage to workers?

Rather than being a second-class form of communication compared with richer communications media, leaner forms of communication are the means by which organizations are informated and through which database information is held. In other words, the organization becomes almost purely information. In Blackler's terms (1995: 1032) it has 'imploded' into code. The possibilities for communication using such code are enhanced when, as we see in the next section, organizations communicate through electronic networks such as the Internet.

# Organizations and networks

Much of our experience of contemporary organizations is mediated through the Internet. We manage our money through online banking, log on to our university emails, and order shopping from online retailers. While the previous section showed us how much of organizational activity is represented as computer code, in this section we see how this code is communicated through computer **networks**—between people and organizations, and between organizations.

When did you last access any data through a computer network or the Internet—either on a phone or a computer, or any other device? Or, alternatively, when was the last time you went for a day without accessing information in such a way?

The section begins by examining the nature of organizations as they operate more and more through global networks, which can be summarized by two potentially contradictory trends.

- On the one hand, organizations become more of a 'free-for-all', with boundaries between organizations becoming less obvious and organizations operating globally on an almost random basis. The concept of the **rhizome** is introduced as a means to understand this particular aspect of the contemporary organization.

- On the other hand, we see how structures of control exist within the Internet and how these structures both affect, and are used by, organizations.

## The 'implosion' and 'explosion' of organizations

Frank Blackler (1995: 1032) suggests that contemporary organizations have undergone two simultaneous processes. On the one hand organizations have imploded into computer code; on the other hand they have simultaneously exploded out into computer networks.

This implosion and explosion metaphor encapsulates two consequences of the informating of organizations as previously described by Zuboff. Much more of what an organization does is stored as electronic data—the organization becomes a database (implosion). At the same time, the very nature of that data means that it can be shared in global computer networks such as the Internet (explosion). Rather than ICT being a tool that facilitates communication in the organization, the technology becomes the very medium through which the organization operates and exists.

The implosion and explosion of contemporary organizations.

**Networks** The sharing of data through linked computer systems or through the Internet.

**Rhizome** A mass of random, tangled connections which some people suggest is similar to the nature of the Internet and cyberspace.

**Placelessness**
Where organizations exist in networks and seem to have no one fixed geographical location.

**Boundarylessness**
Where the extent of sharing and dispersal of an organization's computer data gives a sense that there is no boundary to the organization.

In this section we examine the implications of this. If technology is the very medium of organizing, what implication does this have for the nature of the organization itself? In a global, networked world, what exactly is an organization?

Blackler (1995: 1033) states that, through computer networks, organizations can 'operate relatively independently from geographical location, thereby blurring the boundaries between one organization and another'. We consider these ideas of **placelessness** and **boundarylessness** in turn, examining how contemporary organizations both increase their geographical reach and have blurred boundaries between each other.

## Organizations and geographical reach

### Real life case: the 'digitisation' of Lloyds Bank

In October 2014, the UK-based Lloyds Banking Group announced plans to close 200 branches, with a loss of 9,000 jobs, as part of a process of 'digitising' the business (Treanor, 2014). The move is a response to a trend for customers to use online and mobile technology to make banking transactions rather than going into physical branches (Arnold, 2014; Ahmed, 2014). One banking executive reflected this by stating that their busiest branch was the '7.20 commuter service to Waterloo' (Arnold, 2014): in other words, people are doing transactions on their mobile phones on the way in to work.

While digitization follows trends in customer behaviour, it also has cost savings for the bank. Arnold (2014) reports that the average costs of a transaction in a branch is $4, compared to just 4 cents online. It is easy to see why Lloyds wants more transactions to be handled online, including areas such as mortgage applications which still tend to be carried out in branches (Guthrie, 2014).

The digitization process doesn't mean the end of branches, however. Banks realize that many customers, including older, wealthier, and small-business customers, prefer to do their banking face to face (Arnold, 2014). Contact with staff in a branch also gives staff the opportunity to sell further financial products to customers (Ahmed, 2014). Lloyds and other branches are therefore refocusing the purpose of their branches, away from routine transactions that can be done online and towards selling more complex products and services (Arnold, 2014).

How could you view the case above in terms of Zuboff's and Blackler's theories? How might social presence theory be used to explain why physical branches are still needed?

Where are you when you interact with your university, performing actions such as emailing a tutor, submitting an essay, or renewing a library book, etc.? Do you do it on the premises or elsewhere, through a computer network? Much interaction with our universities is often done from home or from a device somewhere outside the university. We have even received emails from students on the other side of the planet while they have been on holiday.

For many tasks, it is not necessary to be within the physical boundaries of the organization geographically. It could be argued that the university has extended its geographical reach—if the organization is imploded into its database, that database is being interacted with in some way from a student's living room, from a cyber café, or from a hotel room in the Caribbean. *It becomes difficult to draw the boundary around the organization in geographical terms. Where exactly does the organization end?*

Similar interactions can be seen to take place with other organizations: for example, online banking, as described above, and ordering online shopping, etc. all take place in geographical locations beyond the organization itself.

For Latour (1997: 4), closeness is no longer defined in terms of geography, but in terms of how people are linked together through a network. Two people separated by a large geographical space are still close together in network terms if they are having an online conversation. In Chapter 15 we examine a similar idea with McLuhan's (1964) **global village**. While people may be far away geographically, communication technologies make people feel much closer together. Such technologies contribute to processes of globalization—even the smallest organization can now use the Internet to operate on a global basis.

> **Global village** A metaphor to describe a perception of the globe shrinking in size as a result of the speed and global reach of transport and communications technologies.

When you use the Internet, how many different global locations do you interact with?

## Teleworking and telecommuting

An example of where the increased geographical reach of organizations has an effect on working practices is with **teleworking** or **telecommuting** (Nilles, 1975). Computer technologies allow a worker to work from home, accessing organizational databases and their email through the Internet.

As such, the worker at home becomes a part of the organization's computer network—the home is connected directly to the organization. Where an organization's network may encompass geographically dispersed organizational premises, the worker's home effectively becomes one of such premises. With mobile and wireless technology, and the use of laptop or tablet computers, it's not just from home that a worker may telecommute, but also a café, waiting at a train station, or anywhere in reach of a wi-fi or mobile Internet signal.

> **Teleworking, telecommuting** Working away from a place of work by logging into a workplace's computer network.

Castells (1996: 394) suggests that it is only people who substitute work done at home for work done in the workplace who are true teleworkers. For example, a writer is not a teleworker—writers have always worked at home; the only difference is that now they can email work to a publisher rather than send it by post. However, a lawyer who is able to retrieve case notes from their firm's server, comment upon them, and circulate those comments to other members of the legal team—all from home—is doing work that would previously have to be done in the office. They are telecommuters in the true sense.

What do you think are the advantages and disadvantages for both workers and employers of teleworking?

Teleworking leads us to question when a worker is actually 'in' the organization for which they work. Is it when they are physically within its premises, or is it when they are connected to the organization through a network? Teleworking also blurs the distinction between home and work life. If working from home but logged into our organization's network, we are at once both at home and at work. This blurring of boundaries is further examined in the next section.

## Organizations and the blurring of boundaries

In addition to making organizations 'placeless' by extending their geographical reach beyond their physical boundaries, computer networks also blur the boundaries *between* organizations. While organizations hold data in computer systems about their own operations, this data is shared between organizations through networks.

Let us take two examples that we have used previously. In this chapter we have seen how banks are effectively databases of customer and financial data. In Chapter 4 we saw how supermarkets operate in a similar way—barcodes are the key to organizational databases of stock levels and the like.

Now, imagine a customer at the supermarket checkout pays for their goods using their debit card. This sets off a number of interactions between data across computer networks, and which blur the distinctions between the supermarket and the bank (based on Lawley, 2006: 105–6).

- The supermarket's computers link to those of the bank, which checks its own database to ensure that the card is valid and that there are sufficient funds in the customer's account.

- The customer may ask for 'cashback' with their transaction. The supermarket cashier hands the requested cash over to the customer. The cashier, although an employee of the supermarket, is also, in effect, playing the role of that customer's bank teller.

- The economy doesn't just have one supermarket and one bank—it has many retail outlets and many financial institutions. Many transactions similar to the one above will be carried out throughout the day. To minimize the number and complexity of transactions, the Bankers Automated Clearing Service (BACS) (Boddy and Gunson, 1996: 173) acts as an umbrella organization, mediating transactions between the different banks and settling indebtedness between them at the end of each day. The databases between banks and retail outlets are thus in constant communication and interacting from second to second.

The link between supermarkets and banks is just one example of interactions that blur the boundaries between organizations. Think, for example, of hotel booking sites, such as Expedia, which interrogate the computer networks of individual hotels and hotel chains in response to a customer enquiry, and make bookings on those networks on behalf of the customer.

Can you think of any other examples where computer networks blur the boundary between different organizations?

## Organizations as rhizomes

We usually think of an organization as some form of structure, but organizations that are mediated through computer networks perhaps challenge our traditional views of what an organization actually *is*. As we have seen, computer networks both remove the geographical boundaries of organization and blur the distinctions between organizations. It is as if an organization can pop up anywhere and at any time within a computer network. Organizations become a constant and unpredictable movement of data, making multiple

The root-tree and rhizome.

connections between networks which appear and disappear throughout the course of a day, and through which data is shared.

Deleuze and Guattari's (1987) concepts of the 'rhizome' and the 'root-tree' are a useful means of examining these two contrasting views of the organization. These are botanical metaphors which illustrate contrasting types of structure—as Jackson and Carter (2007: 306) suggest, they explore different ways that we might be 'rooted to the spot'.

- A tree always grows in relation to a central structure—its roots and trunk—from which other outgrowths 'branch out'. In this respect, it is similar to the more traditional view of an organizational structure, as represented by the organization chart (see Figure 14.1), where different parts of the organization 'branch out' from the level above.

- The rhizome, however, is an underground root system typified by the random movement of grass. It develops in a random fashion and is not constrained by any central structure or root system; it is ' . . . a tangled mass of randomly developing connections following no logical pattern. It is always connecting points to other points' (Jackson and Carter, 2007: 306).

Cooper (1998: 126) sees cyberspace as a rhizome, seeking to 'expand its possibilities of unconstrained freedom'. Data moves freely around the Internet, seemingly moving around networks and making infinite connections and combinations. Given that organizations use the electronic networks of cyberspace, the links between the organization and the rhizome become apparent. As Sean Cubitt notes:

> The new transnational companies are themselves placeless creatures. In Deleuze and Guattari's terms they are 'rhizomes' . . . The old companies were sedentary and rooted to a specific spot. But we can no longer picket the typical new company's headquarters, because there is none: only the shifting, headless rhizome of connections between its executives and their employees. (Cubitt, 2001: 129–30)

Cubitt suggests that the nature of organizations is thus a shifting random set of data connections. The rhizome certainly has some explanatory power in mapping the movement and communication of organizational data, and where people and other organizations interact with an organization in myriad different connections and combinations.

We have seen that Zuboff describes banks as being databases, but to what extent are they also rhizomes?

The rhizome is sometimes used to suggest that the Internet is completely unstructured—a free-for-all. Certainly, there are cases where the unrestricted nature of the Internet has had an impact upon organizations. For example, the Internet has made the illegal downloading of music possible; this has had an impact on recording companies, which have had to explore new ways of operating as a response, for example through legal downloads and music-streaming services such as Spotify (Kusek and Leonhard, 2005; Sweney, 2012).

It may be tempting to view cyberspace as a 'free-for-all'—an uncontrollable frontier whereby all manner of illegal activities take place, for example illegal downloading, pornography, and leaks of confidential information—and these are, perhaps, at the less murky end of what goes on. For some people, the Internet allows laws to be bypassed, but we should be careful about seeing it as a complete free-for-all. As Hardt and Negri (2000) note correctly, the Internet has both its rhizomatic and root-tree elements—there is a flow of data between networks within the Internet, but, at the same time, this is controlled and structured. In the next two sections we examine this control and structure in terms of the organization of the Internet and how organizations structure themselves within the Internet.

## The organization of the Internet

There is a great deal of *control* and *organization* within cyberspace and the Internet. While there are many hyperbolic and somewhat utopian views of cyberspace as being some entity separate to the real world, as Sassen (2000: 28) points out, 'digital space . . . is partly embedded in actual societal structures and power dynamics. Its topography weaves in and out of non-electronic space'. By this, Sassen means that cyberspace interacts with and is, indeed, controlled by existing structures within society, where 'recurrent attempts to control its data and steer its data flows have been made' (Röhle, 2005: 404). In other words, organizations exert control over the Internet.

Lawley (2006) suggests that the Internet, and the networks and technologies through which it operates, are controlled and organized at four particular levels (see Figure 14.5):

Internet service provider (ISP)  An organization which provides a link to the Internet.

- computer and network hardware
- Internet access and **Internet service providers (ISPs)**
- navigation within the Internet
- the use of the Internet through forums and communities.

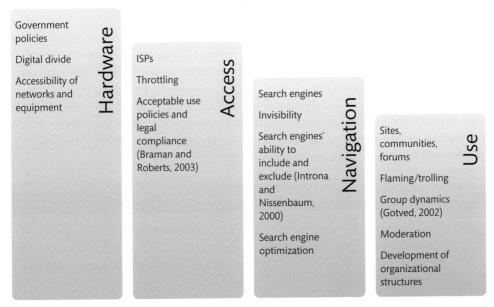

**Figure 14.5** Levels of Internet organization (based on Lawley, 2006).

## Internet hardware

### Real life case: cutting the cable

In 2011, a woman in Georgia who was scavenging for copper cut through an underground wire. Unfortunately, this was the wire which carried Internet data to the neighbouring country of Armenia. The whole of Armenia was cut off from the Internet for five hours while the cable was being repaired.

**Source:** Parfitt (2011).

The nature of the Internet is put into perspective when we realize that, rather than being a random free-for-all, it has to travel through cables and physical **hardware**. This can be seen when national regimes may wish to restrict their population's access to the Internet. Recent years have seen stories in the news of dictators in various countries under threat from revolution. One of their first responses is to cut off access to the Internet within those countries so that people are unable to access information about what is happening.

Access to networks and computer equipment to use them is pertinent to discussion of a so-called **digital divide** between an infrastructurally-rich developed world and a developing world which has little access to such technology (see e.g. Munro, 2000; Sassen, 2002). In the UK, there has been a debate recently about the widespread availability of broadband, with areas that do not have access to broadband being seen to be at a disadvantage in an information-rich economy (BBC News, 2012).

**Hardware**  Computer equipment and infrastructures through which computer networks operate.

**Digital divide**  A divide between people who have access to computer hardware and network infrastructures, such as the Internet, and those who do not.

## Internet access and Internet service providers (ISPs)

Given access to digital networks and hardware, a further level of Internet organization can be found in the way that people connect to the Internet. ISPs are companies which provide a service for users to connect to the Internet and, in doing so, are able to control and regulate how people use the Internet.

**Throttling** Where an ISP deliberately reduces the speed at which a client can download data.

For Braman and Roberts (2003) it is the 'terms of service' and 'acceptable use policies' of ISPs, to which users must sign up, which effectively become the law of the Internet. While people may wish to download masses of files, ISPs may engage in **throttling**—slowing down the rate of data transfer for those who they deem do it in excess.

### Real life case: copyright alert systems

Home downloading of copyrighted content has long been a problem that film, music, and media companies have wanted to tackle. The practice is illegal, but enforcing that law is difficult—it's much harder to detect a user downloading a film at home than it is to detect someone stealing a DVD from the shelf of a store.

Many governments have placed the onus for enforcing the law upon Internet service providers (ISPs). As the companies that connect domestic users to the Internet, ISPs are best placed to track what data individual users are downloading. In the USA in 2013, the Copyright Alert System was implemented by five leading ISPs, using a 'six strikes' rule. Users making copyrighted material available for download receive a series of letters which began with a friendly warning and eventually escalate to punishments such as slowing down the customer's Internet speed, restricting the sites that they can access, or directing them to 'educational videos.'

**Sources:** Peoples (2013); Warr (2013); Woolacott (2014).

In addition to applying their own terms of use, there is an ongoing debate about the degree to which ISPs should be used to enforce national laws. Few would argue with ISPs enforcing a child pornography blacklist—such sites are blocked by ISPs before they can be accessed (BBC News, 2010). However, the debate about ISPs enforcing copyright laws, as in the case above, is ongoing. For example, in the UK an experiment with a similar copyright alert system issues only warning rather than punishments, while also blocking access to known illegal downloading websites (Temperton, 2014).

See the Online Resource Centre for more information about copyright alert systems in different countries.

## Internet navigation and search

The previous section explored the rhizomatic nature of the Internet, but if the Internet were completely random and unstructured it would be unusable. How would you find relevant sites for example? It would just be a sea of unstructured data.

**Search engine** A website which allows users to search for items on the Internet.

**Search engines**, such as Google, organize the data on the Internet, making it navigable for users. However, this can affect organizations in different ways. An organization which appears at the top of search lists will be seen by many more people than one which is down on the fifth page. Through their ability to include and exclude, search engines have the power to make sites 'disappear' (Introna and Nissenbaum, 2000: 180).

As a result of this, the importance of **search engine optimization** (SEO) has become more apparent to organizations (Scott, 2015). An industry has emerged where consultants offer to examine clients' webpages and structure them in such a way that they will appear higher up on search engine results.

**Search engine optimization** Techniques to increase the rank of a website on search engine results.

---

### Study skills: literature searching

The organization of information which is available through computer networks is of direct relevance to your studies, for example when you search for literature for a piece of coursework or an exam. There is a vast number of potential sources available—books, journal articles, and databases, to name but a few—and knowing how to go about finding relevant information for your work can be confusing and daunting.

Many university librarians nowadays refer to their job as 'information management'. They know the best ways to search for, and find, information relevant to a particular academic subject, understanding how such information is organized, categorized, and catalogued. As part of your induction to university they will pass on some of this information to you, highlighting the databases and search facilities that will best help you to find information that you need.

Searching for information is a skill in itself—knowing the right databases and catalogues to use, and how to use the appropriate search terms within them. A further skill is knowing which are appropriate academic sources to use. A general search on a commonly-used search engine, such as Google or Bing, will give all manner of results, many of which are unsuitable for academic work. Knowing the right databases and search facilities to use, and how to use them, will help greatly in sourcing relevant academic material.

---

## Structuring Internet forums and communities

Many of you will use or read Internet forums and discussion boards, or be a member of **Internet communities** where people interact. You may be used to moderators who delete unsuitable posts and even ban members who engage in disruptive acts, such as **flaming** or **trolling**. A final level of organization of the Internet is at the level of individual sites and communities which develop their own rules and terms of usage.

We suggest that many online communities, in fact, take on structures that are familiar in other organizations. While they may begin as fairly unstructured, as they grow they need to maintain order so that they can continue to operate without unwelcome disruptions. Online communities thus take on bureaucratic forms (see Chapter 2), such as hierarchies (through various levels of moderators), rules, and procedures.

Further organizational characteristics can be seen in terms of the social interactions in such sites, linking with the dynamics of groups and teams and organizational cultures (see Chapters 6 and 7). Gotved (2002) suggests that online communities develop their own norms and values, just as with social groupings in the 'real world'.

With online communities becoming structured like their 'real-world' counterparts, we now turn to how real-world organizations structure themselves within the Internet.

**Internet community** A group whose main form of interaction is through the Internet.

**Flaming** Abusive messages sent to Internet forums and communities.

**Trolling** Messages sent to Internet forums and communities which deliberately aim to disrupt their normal functioning and norms of behaviour.

# Organizations within the Internet

**Real life case:** the Sony Pictures hack

The news often features stories of high profile companies being subject to a 'hack'—a well-planned and wide ranging attack on their computer systems whereby valuable data, such as customer credit card details, are stolen and sometimes made public.

In October 2014, such an attack on the US media firm Sony Pictures Entertainment received widespread attention, not least because some of the data released publicly included emails with unflattering discussions about famous film stars, and full digitized versions of yet-to-be released blockbuster movies. In addition to this, a large amount of confidential business information and personal details of employees, including salary and financial details, were released into the public domain (*The Guardian*, 2014; Peterson, 2014).

While this release of data caused embarrassment to many individuals, and potential harm to both commercial interests and individuals, it also had the effect of stopping Sony Pictures from operating as an organization. Not only had data been stolen and made public, the data on Sony's servers was wiped and many of the computers and servers left inoperable. As Sony Pictures CEO, Michael Lynton, stated: 'The bigger challenge was that the folks who did this didn't just steal practically everything from the house; they burned the house down' (cited in Ignatius, 2015). While there was a back-up of data, simple tasks like communicating with staff and managing the payroll could not happen without the hardware and networks to process that data. Until these were replaced, Sony either had to improvise with older equipment or otherwise were unable to carry out simple, everyday organizational tasks (Ignatius, 2015).

While the previous section has shown how the Internet is structured and organized at various levels, the final issue that we address is how organizations within the Internet are structured. If, as Blackler suggests, organizations are imploded and exploded into code simultaneously, then this computer code is a valuable asset of the organization—it is essentially what the organization *is* and the medium through which it operates.

The rhizomatic nature of the Internet means that, as we have seen, organizations can use this data to communicate through networks, expanding their geographical reach and interface with other organizations. However, it is this same rhizomatic nature that poses a threat to organizations and this valuable code. Organizations are vulnerable to their networks being accessed for a number of malicious purposes, for example:

- hacking—unauthorized people gaining access to a computer network to view confidential data, steal valuable data, or vandalize a company's data
- computer viruses—malicious programs that enter a computer network and destroy data within that network
- denial of service attacks—multiple and repeated attempts to access the network of a particular organization which overloads the network and makes it unusable.

Rather than being boundaryless in cyberspace, organizations need to engage in forms of electronic boundary maintenance in order to keep their data secure.

## The 'Janus face' of organizations

Janus is a figure from Roman mythology. His role was that of a gatekeeper—to maintain border and boundary controls within ancient Roman walled cities. Janus's two faces looked simultaneously inwards to protect what was within the walls and outwards to look out for any impending hostile threats from outside (Burchett, 1918).

In a similar manner, an organization looks inwards to protect the database that makes up so much of what it is—the valuable computer code into which it has imploded. At the same time, it looks outwards to the networks in which it operates so as to be alert to hostile threats from outside, such as hackers and viruses.

The Janus figure is used here as a metaphor for organizational 'gatekeeping' and boundary maintenance within cyberspace. However, unlike the entrance to an ancient Roman walled city, there is not one gateway, but a multitude of ways in which data can be shared across an organization's boundary. Organizations thus put in place a number of 'border controls' and security measures across their network boundaries. Examples include:

JANUS.

The Janus face.

- *passwords*—giving different levels of access to different people
- *firewalls*—a technology which screens data entering a network for potential threats, preventing hostile data from entering
- *filters*—either as part of a network or on an individual computer, filters can screen emails and similar communications for harmful viruses and can also be used to screen out bulk email, so called 'spam', or even content and language that an organization deems to be unacceptable.

The Janus face of organizations thus refers to the multiple levels of access and boundary maintenance—passwords, firewalls, etc., that regulate the data flow necessary for an organization to operate, while maintaining data security.

Have you ever found email difficult to use because the inbox is over-run with spam messages? Or, on the contrary, have you ever found perfectly reasonable emails being directed to a spam folder?

This is a tricky balance that organizations need to maintain. On the one hand they need to keep data moving so that business is actually taking place, but not have that movement so free that any malicious entry can be obtained. Make the barriers too tough, however, and genuine interactions will not be able to take place—throwing the baby out with the bath water.

For example, let us return to the example of the bank. While you might want access to your bank account from home, you would not want any other random person having that access. Indeed, if the bank did not maintain adequate levels of security then they would find all of their accounts emptying into the wrong hands pretty rapidly. However, if there was a password regime that took five minutes to gain access to online banking, many people would give up and the activity would simply not take place.

The communication of data between organizational networks, and how that communication is structured and regulated, is thus a major component of what makes up the structure and nature of contemporary, network-mediated organizations.

## Review questions

| | |
|---|---|
| **Describe** | What are the four ways in which Lawley suggests the Internet is structured? |
| **Explain** | What is meant by organizations 'imploding' into code and 'exploding' into global networks? |
| **Analyse** | Why do organizations need to maintain a balance between data security and data flow? |
| **Apply** | Can you think of examples of organizational 'border controls'—electronic or physical—that you have encountered? |

# Chapter summary

In this chapter we have examined the nature of communication in organizations and, in particular, how this is mediated by contemporary ICT. Technology can affect the richness and degree of social presence in communications within an organization, and can also affect the nature and structure of organizations as they communicate information through networks such as the Internet.

ICT is a contemporary topic and, as such, it is constantly changing in terms of the latest technologies available and the ways in which they affect, and are used by, organizations. Debates are ongoing about control over the Internet—either by governments limiting access to the Internet or private companies holding data within the Internet (*The Guardian*, 2012).

Visit the Online Resource Centre for further discussion of these ongoing debates.

This chapter has identified changes that ICT brings to the nature of organizations as more and more of their activities are codified and mediated through global networks. These technologies also play a major part in the subject of the next chapter—globalization.

## Further reading

Rollinson, D. 2008. *Organisational behaviour and analysis: An integrated approach.* Financial Times/Prentice Hall: Harlow.

Many textbooks have a chapter on communication; Chapter 15 is recommended in particular.

Rice, R.E. 1992. Task analyzability, use of new media, and effectiveness: A multi-site exploration of media richness. *Organization Science* 3(4): 475–500.

Introduces and critiques social presence theory and media richness theory.

Zuboff, S. 1985. Automate/informate: The two faces of intelligent technology. *Organizational Dynamics* 14(2): 5–18.

Although written in 1985 it still makes relevant points about the informated organization and the organization as a database.

*The Guardian.* 2012. Battle for the Internet. Available at: http://www.guardian.co.uk/technology/series/battle-for-the-internet (last accessed 16 August 2015).

A useful series of newspaper articles examining issues of control over the Internet.

## References

Ahmed, K. 2014. High street branches are still important for Lloyds. *BBC News Online*, 28 October.

Arnold, M. 2014. Banks must cut costs but remember what their customers want. *Financial Times*, 20 October.

BBC News. 2010. Internet porn block 'not possible' say ISPs, 20 December.

BBC News. 2011. Army job loss e-mails: Soldiers get apology. 17 July.

BBC News. 2012. Rural communities 'at risk' without broadband access. 24 September.

Blackler, F. 1995. Knowledge, knowledge work and organizations: An overview and interpretation. *Organization Studies* 16(6): 1021–46.

Boddy, D., and Gunson, N. 1996. *Organizations in the network age*. Routledge: London, New York.

Boden, D. 1994. *The business of talk: Organizations in action*. Polity Press: London, Cambridge, MA.

Braman, S., and Roberts, S. 2003. Advantage ISP: Terms of service as media law. *New Media and Society* 5(3): 422.

Broekstra, G. 1998. An organization is a conversation. *Discourse and Organization*. Sage: London, pp. 152–76.

Burchett, B. 1918. *Janus in Roman life and cult: A study in Roman religions*. George Banta Publishing Company: Menasha, WI.

Castells, M. 1996. *The rise of the network society*. Blackwell: Malden, MA.

Cooper, R. 1993. Technologies of representation. In: Ahonen, P. (ed.) *Tracing the semiotic boundaries of politics*. Mouton de Gruyter: Berlin, pp. 279–312.

Cooper, R. 1998. Assemblage notes. In:Chia, R. (ed.) *Organized worlds: Explorations in technology and organization with Robert Cooper*, vol. 2. Routledge: London.

Cooper, R., and Burrell, G. 1988. Modernism, postmodernism and organizational analysis: An introduction. *Organization Studies* 9(1): 91–112.

Cubitt, S. 2001. *Simulation and social theory*. Sage: London, Thousand Oaks, CA.

Daft, R.L., and Lengel, R.H. 1986. Organizational information requirements, media richness and structural design. *Management Science* 32(5): 554–71.

Deleuze, G., and Guattari, F. 1987. *A thousand plateaus: Capitalism and schizophrenia*. University of Minnesota Press: Minneapolis.

Gergen, K.J. 1992. Organization theory in the postmodern era. In: Reed, M., and Hughes, M.D. (eds) *Rethinking organisation: New directions in organization theory and analysis*. Sage: London, pp. 207–L 26.

Gergen, K., and Whitney, D. 1996. Technologies of representation in the global corporation: Power and polyphony. In: Boje, R., Gephart, R. Jr., and Thatchenkery, T. (eds) *Postmodern management and organization theory*. Sage: London, pp. 331–57.

Gotved, S. 2002. Spatial dimensions in online communities. *Space and Culture* 5(4): 405–14.

Guthrie, J. 2014. Lloyds: Mechanisation is never mechanistic. *Financial Times*, 28 October.

Hardt, M., and Negri, A. 2000. *Empire*. Harvard University Press: Cambridge, MA.

Hern, A. 2015. Don't know the difference between emoji and emoticons? Let me explain. *The Guardian*, 6 February.

Ignatius, A. 2015. 'They burned the house down': An interview with Michael Lynton. *Harvard Business Review*, July/August.

Introna, L.D., and Nissenbaum, H. 2000. Shaping the Web: Why the politics of search engines matters. *Information Society* 16(3): 169–85.

Jackson, N., and Carter, P. 2007. *Rethinking organisational behaviour*. Financial Times/Prentice Hall: Harlow.

Kermode, R. 2015. Emoji invasion: The end of language as we know it. *The Guardian*, 25 June.

Kurland, N.B., and Pelled, L.H. 2000. Passing the word: Toward a model of gossip and power in the workplace. *Academy of Management Review* 25(2): 428–38.

Kusek, D., and Leonhard, G. 2005. *The future of music: Manifesto for the digital revolution*. Berklee Press: Boston.

Latour, B. 1986. The powers of association. *Psychological Review* 32: 264–80.

Latour, B. 1997. On actor-network theory: A few clarifications. Working paper for Centre for Social Theory and Technology, University of Keele. Archived at http://www.nettime.org/Lists-Archives/nettime-l-9801/msg00019.html

Lawley, S. 2006. Accelerating organisations through representational infrastructures: The possibilities for power and resistance. *Advances in Organization Studies* 19: 91–118.

Lo, S.K. 2008. The nonverbal communication functions of emoticons in computer-mediated communication. *CyberPsychology and Behavior* 11(5): 595–7.

Lough, K. 2015. Emoji is the fastest growing new language ever—but the over 40s feel left behind. *Evening Standard*, 19 May.

McLuhan, M. 1964. *Understanding media: The extensions of man*. McGraw-Hill: New York.

Mehrabian, A. 1971. *Silent messages*. Wadsworth Pub. Co. Belmont, CA.

Munro, L. 2000. Non-disciplinary power and the network society. *Organization* 7(4): 679–95.

Nichols, R.G. 1962. Listening is good business. *Human Resource Management* 1(2): 1–10.

Nilles, J.M. 1975. Telecommunications and organizational decentralization. *IEEE Transactions on Communications* 23: 1142–7.

Noon, M., and Delbridge, R. 1993. News from behind my hand: Gossip in organizations. *Organization Studies* 14(1): 23–36.

Parfitt, T. 2011. Georgian woman cuts off web access to whole of Armenia. *The Guardian*, 6 April.

Peoples, G. 2013. Copyright alert system launches, US ISPs to get infringement notices this week. *Billboard*, 25 February.

Peterson, A. 2014. The Sony Pictures hack, explained. *Washington Post*, 18 December.

Poster, M. 1995. *The second media age*. Polity Press: Cambridge.

Quinn, B. 2011. MoD 'clerical error' results in soldiers being sacked by email. *The Guardian*, 15 February.

Rice, R.E. 1992. Task analyzability, use of new media, and effectiveness: A multi-site exploration of media richness. *Organization Science* 3(4): 475–500.

Röhle, T. 2005. Power, reason, closure: Critical perspectives on new media theory. *New Media and Society* 7(3): 403.

Sassen, S. 2000. Digital networks and the state. *Theory, Culture and Society* 17(4): 19–33.

Sassen, S. 2002. Towards a sociology of information technology. *Current Sociology* 50(3): 365–88.

Scott, N. 2015. SEO: 10 things every leader should know. *Director*, July/August.

Shannon, C.E., Weaver, W., and Blahut, R.E. 1949. *The mathematical theory of communication*, vol. 117. University of Illinois Press: Urbana.

Short, J., Williams, E., and Christie, B. 1976. *The social psychology of telecommunications*. Wiley: London, New York.

Sweney, M. 2012. Downloads, Spotify and Napster help offset UK CD sales slide. *The Guardian*, 16 February.

Temperton, J. 2014. UK ISPs are now blocking 93 piracy websites. *Wired*, 28 November.

*The Guardian*. 2012. Battle for the Internet. Available at: http://www.guardian.co.uk/technology/series/battle-for-the-internet

*The Guardian*. 2014. Sony Pictures denounces 'brazen' cyberattack but downplays North Korea role. *The Guardian*, 3 December.

*The Independent*. 2011. Soldiers' email sackings condemned. 15 February.

Treanor, J. 2014. Lloyds Banking Group to axe 9,000 jobs and 200 branches. *The Guardian*, 28 October.

Warr, P. 2013. ISP anti-piracy system reportedly ready for US launch. *Wired*, 23 February.

Woolacott, E. 2014. ISPs slap customers with 1.3m copyright alerts. *Forbes*, 29 May.

Zuboff, S. 1985. Automate/informate: The two faces of intelligent technology. *Organizational Dynamics* 14(2): 5–18.

Zuboff, S. 1988. *In the age of the smart machine: The future of work and power*. Heinemann Professional: Oxford.

# Globalization

## Managing between the global and the local

## Chapter overview and learning outcomes

By the end of this chapter you should be able to:

- describe the key features of globalization
- explain how contemporary globalization can be described as giving a sense of being in a 'global village'
- explain how organizations operate on a global scale
- explain how national and local cultures affect the ways in which organizations operate globally
- analyse how global inequalities are caused by globalization.

## Key theorists

| | |
|---|---|
| Marshall McLuhan | A theorist of media who first described the effects of globalization as a 'global village' |
| Roland Robertson | A sociologist who has analysed globalization from the perspective of global consciousness and the relationship between the global and the local |
| Geert Hofstede | Attempted to outline national managerial cultures on a set of four numerical scales |
| Naomi Klein | Author of 'No Logo', one of the earliest and most popular manifestos of the anti-globalization movement |

## Key terms

| | |
|---|---|
| Globalization | Activities, both organizational and in wider society, taking place on a global scale |
| Global village | A perceived shrinking of the globe and increased sense of global proximity due to the effects of transport and communications technologies |
| Global culture | A homogeneous, worldwide culture that emerges as a result of globalization and the activities of global organizations |
| National culture, local culture | Individual and distinct cultures as seen in individual nations or territories |
| Glocalization | Adapting global practices to local cultures and contexts |
| Anti-globalization movement | A collective term for protestors and critics of globalization and its perceived inequalities |

# Introduction

## Running case: 'Junction International'

Simon Chance is discussing Junction Hotel's global ambitions with his team of investors. The hotel has joined up with an online booking website; this means that it is showing up on global searches, resulting in an increase in the number of guests coming from across the globe.

In response to this, Chance has tried to give the hotel a more international feel. So far, it has all been fairly superficial—hanging welcome signs on the doors in different languages, displaying a set of clocks showing different world times behind reception, and a providing a selection of international newspapers in the hotel lobby.

Chance sees an opportunity in the global market and wants to take his international strategy further. As an independent hotel, Junction doesn't have the global presence of some of the big-name hotel chains, but nevertheless, Chance still wants the hotel to be an international player.

At the meeting, it is decided to work towards an internationalization plan, codenamed 'Junction International'.

You may often hear that we live in a 'globalized' society and that contemporary business takes place within global horizons. The global nature of our own existence, and the array of products and services that we consume, is, perhaps, summed up in the following popular statement circulating the Internet:

> Being British is about driving in a German car to an Irish pub for a Belgian beer, then travelling home, grabbing an Indian curry or a Turkish kebab on the way, to sit on Swedish furniture and watch American shows on a Japanese TV. And the most British thing of all? Suspicion of anything foreign.

(quoted in Race, 2015)

Although humorous in its intent, the quote highlights not only the global nature of the economy, but also how this global variety can be seen in the goods and services available within one particular country, in this case the UK.

Furthermore, as individuals we are more aware and in touch with the globe as a whole. Films, videos, and television programmes bring to life situations from other countries, and the Internet allows us to communicate directly with people in those countries.

In your day-to-day Internet and media activity, which countries do you come into contact with?

**Globalization**
Defined in many different ways, globalization is where activities take place on an increasingly global scale.

This chapter examines two broad issues related to **globalization**—which might be seen as complementary or contradictory—and how they relate to organization and management issues on a global scale, especially as it relates to individual national issues.

• On one hand, the world is organized into nation states, but it is suggested that these are becoming less relevant—globalization suggests that we are one globe and features of globalization make individual nations less relevant. We examine the move towards what McLuhan (1964) termed a 'global village' and the features of globalization that contribute to this trend, and the role of organizations in contributing to this.

- On the other hand, it is suggested that despite trends towards globalization, individual nations, and the differences between them, are still important—their laws, cultures, customs, etc., still exert an influence on how management is practised within their borders. We thus look at the implications of national and cultural differences for managing and organizing on a global basis.

Within the debates on globalization, we also see a number of perspectives that are critical of the effects of globalization, suggesting that it perpetuates inequalities on a global scale rather than being a uniformly global process.

Globalization is a complex and multifaceted process which commands full books in its own right. In this chapter we examine some of the key features of the process, beginning with its early development.

Do an inventory of all the goods that you own or have in your house—clothes, food, electronic goods, white goods, transport, etc. Where was each made? Think also about companies whose services you use—banks, insurance, utilities, etc. Who owns these companies and in what countries are they based?

# The development of globalization

## Running case: globally connected

Chance has been examining ways for Junction Hotel to have a presence on a global scale while remaining independent. A particular trade association—Global Luxury—catches his attention. Membership of Global Luxury is exclusive and subject to a number of stringent tests to earn the label of 'luxury hotel'.

While hotels in this association remain independent, their people meet regularly to discuss common issues. Furthermore, the hotels engage in cross-promotion, producing a joint brochure and a website from which bookings for any of the hotels can be made. Marketing and booking is thus pooled between the member hotels, while each individual hotel remains independent.

Regular meetings are held between the members of the chain, both at continental and, for top representatives, at global levels. For European meetings, Chance leaves on the 6 am flight to Amsterdam and is in a meeting room at the airport for 8.30 am. Representatives from other European hotels in the network will also be there. None of them will actually leave the airport during the day. Instead they will get on their return flights in the early evening and Chance will be back home in time for supper.

Global meetings are rare, at least in person, as there are greater distances to travel. Meetings tend to take place by phone or videoconferencing—even then the time has to be chosen carefully, as morning in the USA can be the middle of the night elsewhere.

Chance feels much more globally connected than he was in his previous life as a football club chairman. Looking at his email inbox, he used to have a list of clubs from various small-sized English towns. Now his inbox spans the globe, with messages from Australia, Germany, Brazil, and China, among others, sitting next to each other.

When globalization is mentioned, we tend to think of it as a relatively recent phenomenon, one which is a part of our modern era of international travel and instant global communication through the Internet. However, instances of individuals, organizations, and nations operating on an international or global stage can be witnessed throughout history.

- In the 1500s, European explorers, such as Francis Drake and Walter Raleigh, travelled the high seas, circumnavigating the globe to discover 'new' lands, such as the Americas.
- The discovery of new worlds made international trade possible, bringing newly-discovered goods to European markets. Founded in 1600, the East India Company is one of the earliest global companies which traded cotton, tea, and opium, moving goods between China, India, and the UK (Chaudhuri, 1965).
- Exploration and trade led to European countries developing global empires, **colonizing** countries in Africa, Asia, and the Caribbean, exploiting the natural resources of those countries, and reducing their inhabitants to slavery. As recently as the beginning of the twentieth century, Western colonial empires covered 84.6% of the global economy (Loomba, 1998).
- It is not just organizations that operate globally; workforces also move globally in search of work. In Chapter 2, we saw that Henry Ford's factory had a multinational workforce, many of whom did not speak English. This was typical of the **migration** to the USA of people in search of work opportunities in the early 1900s from countries such as Poland, Italy, and Ireland (LeMay, 1987).
- Major religions are another example of organizations which have operated globally for centuries, often with recognizable organizational structures that divide up the hierarchy by continent and country (see Chapter 2).
- Many sporting events are global in scale (see Maguire, 1999) and have been so for many decades. The modern Olympics were first held in 1896, for example, and the football World Cup was first held in 1930.

While these examples show that global organization and activity is not a new phenomenon, in this section we examine how the globalization that we experience today is qualitatively different: that is to say, we experience globalization differently now than in the past. In particular, there is a feeling that the world is a lot smaller and more immediate.

**Colonization** Invasion and conquering of land, and enslavement of people, in Africa, the Americas, and Asia from the 1500s to the 1900s by European countries, such as England, Spain, Belgium, Portugal, France, and the Netherlands.

**Migration** Leaving one country or area to move to another—possibly for reasons of finding work, or, alternatively, for avoiding oppressive regimes.

# The global village

**Real life case:** a cricket tour to Australia

Since 1882, England and Australia have regularly taken part in a cricket contest called the Ashes. When the Ashes began, there were no commercial aeroplanes; the only way to go to Australia was by a boat journey lasting six weeks. Now, a direct plane journey can take 24 hours. Where previously an English touring party (or anyone wishing to visit Australia for other reasons) would be cut off from home for the three months' journey time plus the time of the tour, now it is not uncommon for England players to return home, mid-tour, for family events such as childbirths (England and Wales Cricket Board, 2012).

▶ Similarly, communication has become much more immediate. If the only form of communication available is a letter, which has to be transported by boat, then the time between sending a message and receiving a reply would be a frustrating and impractical three months. Now, rather than waiting three months for a reply, telephones and the Internet can be used to communicate instantaneously in real time. So, when an England player returns to the tour from the birth of their child, they can still see the newborn in real time over the Internet using videoconferencing software such as Skype.

Compared with the time when a boat was the only means of transport, it is as if the distance between the UK and Australia had shrunk.

How might the changes in transport and communications described in the real life case facilitate trading and business between the UK and Australia? What types of business and organizational activity are possible now that would not have been when the Ashes began in 1882?

When people say that the world is becoming a smaller place, it does not mean that it is literally shrinking in size. Rather, it means that the world *feels to us* as if it is getting smaller. It takes less time to travel across the globe than it did even a few decades ago and we can communicate instantly with people on the other side of the planet.

Marshall McLuhan (1964) described the world as a **global village**. When he was writing in 1964, this related to the role of the media in particular. Films and television brought images from across the world to our attention—we could see other people and cultures as if they were our neighbours, as if the

The global village.

**Global village** A metaphor to describe a perception of the globe shrinking in size as a result of the speed and global reach of transport and communications technologies.

globe were a village. Thinking about the case of Australia, much of Australian life feels familiar to UK consciousness through soap operas, such as *Neighbours* and *Home and away*. And it is not just Australia that is brought to our consciousness—US life is familiar through its extensive film and television industry. Global problems, such as war and famine, and global issues and events are also made familiar through news broadcasts.

Perhaps the world is now, more than 50 years since McLuhan first used the term, even more of a global village. News broadcasts switch seamlessly between live images from different parts of the globe, budget airlines make international travel available to more of us, and the Internet allows us not just to communicate instantly across the globe, but to see the minutiae of everyday life across the planet through applications such as Google Street View and videos posted on YouTube.

How many people do you communicate with globally, either personally, through email and messaging services, or through online discussion boards and similar forums?

**Intensification of consciousness**
Alongside the idea of the global village, an increased awareness of events and people worldwide.

Robertson (1992: 8) describes globalization as 'the compression of the world and the **intensification of consciousness** of the world as a whole'. This captures the idea of the compression or shrinking of journey times, and times for communicating with people, alongside people having a greater awareness and perception of what goes on elsewhere within the globe (see Figure 15.1).

**Figure 15.1**
Robertson's (1992) 'intensification of consciousness'.
**Source:** Based on Robertson, *Globalization*, 1992.

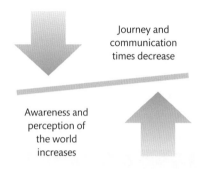

Journey and communication times decrease

Awareness and perception of the world increases

In a similar vein, Waters (2001: 5) defines globalization as 'a social process in which the constraints of geography on social and cultural arrangements recede and in which people become increasingly aware that they are receding'. Again, this encompasses the idea that geography (physical space) is less of an issue in separating people across the globe and that we are aware of the world feeling much more immediate to us. We live in a global village *and we are more than aware that we live in that global village.*

## Aspects of globalization

Waters's definition highlights globalization as a 'process' rather than a distinct 'thing'. Rather than being one single, distinct phenomenon, it is multifaceted and encompasses a number of different trends and phenomena. Furthermore, globalization is an evolving and interdisciplinary field of study: that is to say, it is ever-changing and combines insights from a number of different academic areas.

Parker and Clegg (2006) suggest six main aspects (see Figure 15.2) which together contribute to the multifaceted nature of globalization or, more specifically, 'global interconnectedness' (ibid.: 655).

Each of these in themselves do not constitute globalization; rather, they are interrelated aspects which together combine towards the processes of globalization that we experience today and within which organizations operate. We therefore use these headings as a basis to give an overview of aspects of globalization that affect contemporary organizations. In this section we examine how four of these—the economy, politics, technology, and the natural environment—contribute to globalization. Later in the chapter we examine the specific importance of global business and organizations and of global culture.

### The global economy

There is a saying that 'When America sneezes, Britain catches cold'. The USA is the world's largest economy and is also the largest purchaser of UK exports (see Table 15.1). A recession or other economic problem in the USA will thus affect the demand for UK exports and affect UK businesses that export to the USA. Many other countries will have a similar set of global dependencies for their export trade. Global economies are interconnected.

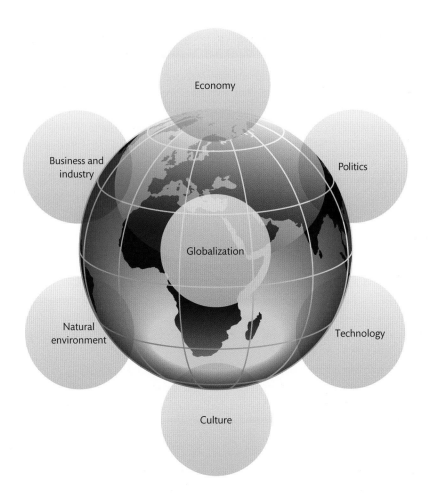

**Figure 15.2** Parker and Clegg's (2006) six aspects of global interconnectedness.
**Source:** Based on Parker and Clegg, 2006.

There are other influences on the global economy too. China is rapidly catching up with the USA as the world's largest economy and, at the time of writing, a stock-market collapse in China was having knock-on effects on stock markets across the globe (*The Guardian*, 2015). Furthermore, as Table 15.1 shows, the UK is dependent on the state of the economy not only in the USA but also in many other countries. Ireland accounts for almost half as much in exports as the far larger USA, for example.

Recent events in the global economy have demonstrated that interdependency is not just about trading and exports, but also about the global interconnectedness of financial institutions and financial products. The 2008 financial crisis was a global phenomenon which hit countries and continents across the globe.

**Table 15.1** UK exports 2014 (£ millions)

| | |
|---|---|
| USA | 38,858 |
| Germany | 31, 432 |
| Netherlands | 22,553 |
| Switzerland | 21,313 |
| France | 19,627 |
| Irish Republic | 18,124 |
| China | 15,934 |
| Belgium | 12,597 |
| Spain | 8,774 |
| Italy | 8,708 |

*Source:* HM Revenue and Customs (2015).

**Real life case:** the global financial crisis

This financial crisis began in the so-called subprime mortgage market in the USA. Lehman Brothers, one of the world's oldest financial institutions, collapsed, impacting its operations across the globe overnight (Osborne et al., 2009). The panic quickly spread to other banks, many of which had interests tied to the financial products of Lehman; many banks around the world had to be bailed out and nationalized (Cooper, 2010: 54), and the crisis also led to a global rise in food and other commodity prices.

World leaders came together in numerous emergency meetings at institutions such as the World Economic Forum to work out how to recapitalize the banks. As banks stopped lending to each other, the global economy faltered. Stock markets were extremely volatile, with crashes in one stock market affecting others internationally.

Some small economies were hit particularly hard. Iceland, whose economy was little over $10 billion a year, had an astronomical debt of around $100 billion, with the stock market crashing by 77% within three days; Ireland and Singapore both reported a fall in gross domestic product (GDP) of around 9%, and in China an estimated 10 million people lost their jobs through the slowdown in trade (Ferguson, 2011). The Euro suffered substantial problems, with whole countries needing to be bailed out and strong financial controls placed on them (Castle, 2012), notably Greece, which is still dealing with the profound consequences of the crisis.

The speed with which this crisis developed and the devastation that it caused show the interconnected nature of the economies and financial markets of the world, and the impact that a problem in a seemingly small area can make globally.

## Global politics

Politics is often seen as an activity which takes place at a national level—general elections, national prime ministers, presidents, etc. However, politics also increasingly takes place at international levels, partly because of the global nature of the economy and its importance to individual nations.

**Real life case:** the European Union

The European Union (EU) is a political entity made up 27 European nations. It began life as a free-trade area (the European Economic Community) before taking on its current title in 1993.

The activities of the EU have effects on businesses and organizations within its constituent nations—as a result of both economic activity and policy. While this is not an exhaustive list, examples of how the EU affects organizations in its member states include:

- the single currency (the Euro) means no exchange rate fluctuations—makes exporting and importing more stable and predictable
- removal of trade/labour barriers—companies can trade freely across borders and, likewise, there are no restrictions on where people may work within the EU

- employment law—harmonizes some conditions of employment, e.g. maximum working hours per week, legislation on workplace discrimination

- investment—regeneration or investment to particular areas, especially where unemployment might be a problem.

Many global political groupings and agencies have an effect upon the global economy and the conditions for individual organizations within that economy. For example, the World Trade Organization (WTO) in effect sets the rules and regulations for world trade (and, as we will see later in the chapter, comes under criticism for how it does this).

## Global technology

Global technology refers to those technologies which contribute to the aforementioned 'global village': that is to say, they allow barriers of geography to be overcome so that people can travel the globe or communicate globally with much more ease. Examples of such technologies include:

- transport—cars, planes, trains, etc. and their associated infrastructures, such as roads and railway lines

- communications technologies—e.g. the telephone and the infrastructure through which it works

- media technologies—television transmitters, satellites, etc. which allow the dissemination of words and images, such as news, film, and television shows

- computer networks—the Internet allows an instantaneous transmission and reception of images, words, data, communication, etc.

Such technologies obviously have an impact on what organizations can do on a global scale. The Internet and computer networks, and how they affect organizations, are examined in more detail in Chapter 14.

## Globalization of the natural environment

### Real life case: global oil production and water supply

The Druzhba pipeline is the one of the longest in the world, connecting Eastern Russia with much of Europe. Running through some of the most politically unstable countries in the world, it has been affected by numerous disputes, with countries such as Ukraine threatening to pull out (Parfitt, 2007).

Several wars, such as in Iraq and Libya, have been seen by some as wars over control of oil (Bignell, 2011). There are predictions that as a result of climate change in the future there will be wars over water (Pederson, 2012). Golan Heights, which borders Israel, Lebanon, and Jordan, is a cause of considerable political tension as it contributes a significant proportion of Israel's water supply (Asser, 2010).

A final aspect of globalization is that of the natural environment and its resources—the resources of the earth become commodities to be traded on a global basis. Such resources are of importance because of their value and, in many cases, their finite nature—think of the importance of fuel to the world economy, for example.

Depletion of natural resources and climate change are aspects of damage to the environment that are viewed as global problems. Workers, too, can be seen as natural resources that are now employed on a global scale. For example, a global division of labour has emerged because in the developing world, where manufacturing now tends to be concentrated, labour is cheaper—in some cases employed in sweatshop conditions. Such problematic issues have fuelled an anti-globalization movement, which is examined towards the end of this chapter, and issues of corporate social responsibility with respect to workers and the environment are further examined in Chapter 17.

## Physical and intangible spaces of globalization

Earlier in this section, it was suggested that there is a difference in the experience of globalization today compared to forms of globalization that went before—that we now experience a 'global village' where the world feels smaller and more immediate. We suggest that this difference comes about from the nature of globalization having shifted from a globalization primarily of physical space to one which is supplemented by a global, intangible space.

**Physical space**
Aspects of globalization that involve goods and people moving across land.

**Intangible space**
Aspects of globalization that take place through intangible means such as media transmissions, data in computer networks, and imagery.

- Globalization of **physical space** refers to the actual land of the globe itself—the *terra firma* on which we stand. Early globalization was thus about discovering new lands, physically moving products across the globe to trade them, and conquering land to create empires.

- Global **intangible space** is that which brings about some form of global connectedness without movement over actual land—data in computer networks and television signals, etc. It is these abstract elements which bring about global consciousness, the immediacy of communication, and global images that we are now afforded.

Visit the Online Resource Centre for a discussion of 'soft power', the global intangible influence that is wielded by some countries through, for example, their media and cultural activities.

Globalization has both physical and abstract elements, and these are reflected in Parker and Clegg's aspects of globalization that we have used in this section. For example:

- the global economy has physical aspects—the physical goods which are produced and then exported across land and sea; equally, it has intangible elements, the 'symbol economy' (Clegg and Gray, 1996: 303) of financial transactions and data flow between financial institutions

- global technology has physical aspects (transport which crosses land) and intangible aspects (the signals and data which are beamed through communications, computer, and media networks).

Among these various physical and intangible elements lie organizations. While organizations are affected by the aspects of globalization listed previously, Parker notes that they are not simply passive bystanders; rather, they play their part in making globalization happen:

> Organizations are not simply affected by globalization: the combined activities of all kinds of organizations stimulate, facilitate, sustain and extend globalization.
>
> (Parker, 1996: 484)

We now turn to organizations themselves—their role in both the global economy and global culture, noting how they contribute to physical and intangible elements of globalization.

## Review questions

| | |
|---|---|
| **Describe** | What early examples of globalization have existed throughout history? |
| **Describe** | What are the physical and intangible aspects of globalization? |
| **Explain** | What is meant by the phrase 'global village'? |
| **Analyse** | What is meant by globalization being experienced as an 'intensification of consciousness'? |
| **Apply** | Think of an organization that you know. How do Parker and Clegg's aspects of globalization affect this organization? |

# Global organizations

## Running case: part of a franchise?

Simon Chance is enjoying the new status of Junction Hotel being part of Global Luxury group, but he feels that while it has brought an undoubted cachet to the hotel, it is not paying off in terms of revenue. Indeed, it is creating extra cost and expense to keep up to the luxury standards required to stay within the group.

Chance wonders whether there are other ways to have a global reach but to also maintain the efficiency and cost-competitiveness necessary for the current economic conditions. Will it even be possible to survive as an independent hotel?

At his regular meeting with the board of investors, an option put on the table is to buy a similar hotel that is up for sale in France. While the board of investors like the sound of 'Junction Paris' and see it as a possible start for a whole chain of Junction Hotels, they soon realize that the costs for this form of expansion will be prohibitive.

Another option presented is to become a *franchise* of a global hotel chain. A number of such franchises exist; the one with the best reputation for quality is the US Luxonational chain.

Luxonational don't own their own hotels; instead, independent hotels apply to become franchise holders, which they would get subject to passing a set of standard requirements. The business belongs to the franchise holder in return for an annual fee, based on the size of the hotel, being paid to Luxonational in return for the right to run the franchise. The franchise has to be renewed annually, subject to maintaining the standard requirements.

Being part of the Luxonational franchise would certainly make the hotel part of a global chain, but at what cost to the hotel? Chance is asked to investigate and bring his findings to the next board meeting.

When we think of global organizations, we tend to think of huge companies with recognizable brands. Certainly, a glance (*Fortune*, 2015) at the world's top multinationals by their annual income shows some familiar names, which tend to be concentrated in a number of industries:

- energy companies, such as Royal Dutch Shell (Netherlands), Sinopec (China), and BP (UK)
- automobile companies, such as Toyota (Japan), Volkswagen (Germany), and Ford (USA)
- finance companies, such as AXA (France), Bank of China (China), and Banco Santander (Spain)
- telecommunications and electronics companies, such as AT&T (USA), Siemens (Germany), and Samsung (South Korea).

Is there anything in the nature of the products and services in the list here which makes them more likely to be traded on a global scale? Would they benefit from economies of scale?

Such organizations can be so huge as to be bigger than the economies of individual nations. For example, US retailer Walmart, the largest multinational by income, has an income larger than individual medium-sized nations such as Belgium and South Africa (*Fortune*, 2015; Nationmaster, 2015).

Visit the Online Resource Centre for a full list of the top multinational companies and a comparison of the largest with national economies.

It would seem, then, that being a global organization is about size. Such massive conglomerates, however, are just one example of how organizations may operate on a global scale. In this section we will see different ways in which organizations are able to grow their operations to become global players, including possibilities for small-scale organizations to use technology to operate globally.

Using the terminology of the previous section we see how global organizations move from being achieved through physical means, such as goods, people, and premises, to being achieved through more intangible means, such as brands, licences, and computer networks.

> **Employability skills:** international credentials
>
> Many organizations promote themselves as 'international' or 'global' organizations, the terms bringing a certain cachet, even glamour, to the organization. Demonstrating international credentials can enhance employability in such organizations. Overseas placement experiences, languages learned, experiences of travel, and evidence of working with people from different international backgrounds are all good additions to your CV to enhance the international aspects of your employability.

# The structure and spread of global organizations

Organizations are not born global but, instead, they extend and expand their activities through a number of different types of multinational activity. This section outlines examples of structures and activities that organizations use to increase their activity on an international scale.

## Exporting

This is perhaps the most basic form of international activity—selling a product to another country and shipping it to that country. In its simplest form, this would mean a company operating in just one country selling goods that it distributes to other countries while not having any premises or operations in those countries. In practice, **exporting** may be combined with some of the activities discussed next.

*Exporting  Selling and distributing a good to another country.*

## Overseas investment and expansion

If an organization exports frequently to a particular country or area, it may find a benefit in setting up premises in that area. For example, to generate exports a company may open sales offices in different countries or operate after-sales service centres for different national markets.

**Foreign direct investment** is an example of overseas investment where, rather than exporting goods, an organization sets up a production plant in an overseas territory directly. Examples of this might be car firms setting up production plants closer to different markets globally. This happened in the 1980s when a number of Japanese firms, such as Sony and Nissan, set up production plants in the UK.

*Foreign direct investment  Setting up a production or office facility in another country.*

## Mergers, acquisitions, and joint ventures

Rather than setting up brand new operations in overseas territories, another way of expanding operations globally is by buying or **acquiring** companies overseas. This might be by buying a similar organization so as to expand operations internationally (e.g. a supermarket chain buys a supermarket chain in another country) or it may involve buying an organization at another point in the production chain (e.g. a food manufacturer buys an overseas supplier or a film company buys an overseas distributor).

*Acquisition  The purchase of another company or business.*

**Merger** Two companies joining together to become one single entity.

In some cases, two companies may feel it in their best interests to **merge**, perhaps to gain economies of scale by pooling certain operations. In 2011 British Airways and Iberia merged to form International Airlines Group (*The Guardian*, 2010). This allows some ground operations to be merged, for example check-in desks, and also cooperation and efficiency in terms of scheduling the routes that the two airlines fly and removing flights that duplicate each other, thus gaining efficiencies.

**Joint venture** Cooperation between two or more companies on a particular project.

Sometimes organizations in different countries find it in their best interests to cooperate in some way without merging their own operations—a **joint venture**. US electronics retailer Best Buy expanded its brand into the UK, but the stores were managed and products supplied by existing UK company Carphone Warehouse (Rushton, 2012).

> **Real life case:** the overseas expansion of Tesco
>
> The UK supermarket Tesco has used a number of different methods to expand into international territories. In the USA it engaged (ultimately unsuccessfully) in direct investment, setting up a new 'Fresh & Easy' chain (*The Economist*, 2007). In Thailand it set up a joint venture with a local firm (BBC News, 2006), while in the Czech Republic (Thompson, 2010; Tesco plc, 2015) and Turkey (Treanor, 2003; Tesco plc, 2015) it acquired, or bought out, existing chains of stores. (For more information about Tesco's overseas businesses, see Tesco plc, 2015.)

## Franchising and licensing

**Franchising** Granting the right to another company to operate an outlet or branch of a particular organization, subject to adhering to standards and conditions of the franchising company.

A company might not want the upfront expense that direct investment or an acquisition might necessitate. **Franchising** is where a company allows another organization to operate its business on its behalf using its brand and products. This will be for some form of fee, and will come with specific conditions as to how the franchisee operates and uses the brand. McDonalds, for example, do not own their restaurants. Their global expansion has come from their restaurants being run independently by franchise holders, albeit franchise holders who have to adhere to numerous conditions. For example, a franchise holder could not, of their own volition, change the menu offered.

Sometimes in a McDonalds restaurant, the name of the actual business holder—the franchisee—will be on display in the restaurant.

**Licensing** Granting the right to another company to produce a particular branded good.

**Licensing** is similar to franchising; however, here, a company grants a licence to produce its good (and sell it under their brand) in another territory. For example, adverts for Fosters beer play very much on the Australian origin of the product, but a small caption at the bottom of the advert indicates it to have been 'brewed under licence in the UK'. The strategy makes sense—it would be impractical to brew beer in Australia and export it to the UK. Licensing is a means to expand the brand globally. This is how Coca-Cola operates on a global scale—by licensing its syrup to overseas plants who then produce and sell it in their local markets.

## Subcontracting

With **subcontracting**, an organization employs the services of another organization to conduct an aspect of its work. This has become a global activity whereby an organization not only subcontracts, but does so to an organization in a different country—often where the costs of this are cheaper. Clothing and manufacturing organizations subcontract production of their items to a factory in a different country, leading to criticism in instances where the cost of labour is so cheap that people are employed in 'sweatshop' conditions (see Chapter 17).

> **Subcontracting**
> Hiring another person or company to perform a particular process or service for an organization.

---

### Real life case: call centres in India

The Indian call centre industry is a well-known example of subcontracting on a global scale, handling calls for credit card companies, insurance companies, technical helplines—any organizations that use a call centre to handle enquiries. Organizations will exist purely as subcontractors—an organization could run contracts for firms across the globe (UK, USA, Australia) in one building, for example.

While global technology allows for such calls to be handled on the other side of the planet instantly, in India the call centres try to create an illusion of being in the same country. Training in accents, pronunciation, and culture is given, for example by teaching about UK food, sport, or television programmes.

While workers on the UK contract will be learning about UK culture and current events, workers in a neighbouring room working on a US contract can, similarly, be learning about US culture.

**Sources:** Harding (2001); Deb (2004); BBC News (2011).

---

Visit the Online Resource Centre for detailed commentary on this real life case.

Global technology has allowed for administration tasks, in addition to manufacturing, to be subcontracted globally. The operation of call-handling centres in India is one example of this; others include handling paperwork, such as the typing up of medical notes which are scanned and emailed to workers performing the task.

## Global industries and labour markets

Subcontracting shows that it is not just organizations that are globalized—labour markets, too, are global. In the case of manufacturing and call centres, cheaper labour elsewhere in the world is used by global organizations. Global labour markets could also refer to large multinationals hiring their top staff or valued knowledge workers with key skills (see Chapter 10) from a global pool of labour. A university department, for example, will often be made up of an international variety of leading professors.

Industries, too, can be seen as global, with different organizations within an industry contributing to that globalization in different ways. These forms of global activity show that both physical aspects (setting up premises, exporting goods, etc.) and more intangible aspects (e.g. licensing a brand) contribute to organizations and industries extending their activities globally.

**Real life case:** sport as a global industry

Sport is an industry which, when taken as a whole and by looking at some of its individual aspects, can be seen as a global industry, demonstrating some of the features examined thus far in this chapter.

- Global competitions and events take place between national teams, such as the Olympic Games and the football World Cup.

- Furthermore, events such as Formula One are a global travelling show, with rounds in different countries across the globe, and teams themselves made up of an international mix of drivers, engineers, and sponsors.

- Such events are also global in that they are viewed globally through the media.

- Sports are governed by global governing bodies, e.g. the International Olympic Commission or the Fédération Internationale de Football Association (FIFA).

- Such bodies bring an element of global politics to sport. Furthermore, bidding processes for global events can include contributions and influence from politicians.

- Individual sports teams can become global brands: e.g. clubs such as Manchester United are popular in East Asia. Such brands are extended through licensing and franchising deals.

- Global brands are involved in sport through sponsorship.

- Large multinational brands are also involved in the production of sporting goods and clothing, e.g. Nike, Adidas.

- The existence of global labour markets can be seen in some elite-level clubs, especially in football, where players on one team will be from a variety of countries and continents.

- Global labour markets are also in evidence, from a different perspective, in the production of sporting goods, many of which are produced on assembly lines in the developing world. (See Maguire, 1999, for more on sport as a global phenomenon.)

# Technology and the potential for globalization

While global organization tends to be associated with large-scale global expansion, as described in the previous section, another aspect of global organizational activity worthy of mention is the ability of small-scale organizations, even individuals, to have a global presence. This is made possible by global technology, in particular that provided by the Internet.

**Real life case:** *Angry Birds*

Many of you will have played the game *Angry Birds* on a smartphone or tablet computer. The game and its variants have had hundreds of millions of downloads worldwide—it is a global phenomenon.

The organization that produces the game, however, is small in scale. Rovio Entertainment, based in Finland, had just over 40 employees at the time of its initial global success in 2010 (Cheshire, 2011), although this has now expanded to over 800 (Rovio Entertainment, 2013). *Angry Birds* demonstrates how a small-scale organization can be global in its reach.

The example of *Angry Birds* shows how larger-scale organizations—in particular those which provide some form of global network infrastructure—facilitate the global spread of smaller organizations. The global scale of the downloading comes from the intangible global technologies of computer networks and, furthermore, from being available through existing organizations, such as mobile phone download stores. It is as if a form of 'piggy-back' is provided by the larger organization—itself global—to enable the smaller organization to also achieve a global presence (see Chapter 14 on 'Information, Communication, and Technology' for more on the merging of an organization's operations through computer networks).

At an individual level, a similar situation exists with a site such as eBay—itself a global organization which allows a variety of smaller organizations to piggy-back on its infrastructure to achieve a global presence. As a sole trader on eBay, you can reach a potentially global audience for the goods that you are selling. It's a situation similar to the simple exporter mentioned earlier in this chapter, but now an exporter who, no matter how small-scale, can export globally.

Global organizations tend to be large in scale, but they can, in some instances, have a global reach on a small scale. In the next section we see how organizations contribute to what is sometimes described as a global culture.

## Review questions

| | |
|---|---|
| **Describe** | What are the different ways in which organizations might extend their activities internationally? |
| **Explain** | How does global technology allow small-scale organizations to operate on a global scale? |
| **Analyse** | What are the advantages and disadvantages of the different types of international organizational activity, such as franchising or subcontracting? |
| **Apply** | Look at websites for a number of small and large organizations. In what ways do those specific organizations operate globally? |

# Organizations and global culture

## Running case: franchise requirements

**From:** simon_chance@junctionhotel.co.uk
**To:** board_members@junctionhotel.co.uk; senior_management_team@junctionhotel.co.uk

**Subject:** Re: Franchising

As requested, I've done some research into what becoming a franchise of Luxonational would entail. Here are the main points:

- *Branding.* Junction Hotel would lose much of its identity. Instead, it would be rebranded as 'Luxonational Nottingham'. All marketing and logos to be replaced by those of Luxonational.

- *Booking and marketing.* Common booking and marketing procedure with other franchises in the Luxonational chain. We would be marketed through the international Luxonational website and appear in their marketing materials—a much wider reach than before. We would do some local marketing, but this would have to adhere to a Luxonational 'template'. Information technology upgrade needed at reception to fit in with the standard booking procedure.

- *Hotel furnishings.* Standard Luxonational 'look'. Furniture in rooms, carpets, curtains, the reception layout—all fixtures and fittings would be those supplied by Luxonational. This will cost, but we are due for a refurbishment. Taking the standard Luxomania items will be cheaper owing to their bulk purchasing power.

- *Staff procedures.* Just like the furnishings, the staff will be branded as Luxonational staff, with new uniforms provided similar to the rest of the chain. Furthermore, certain staff procedures would be expected to be brought into line with the rest of the chain, including human resources issues, such as pay and holiday entitlements (not quite as generous as currently operating at Junction). Training provided by Luxonational manual or at a number of regional training centres that the head office run. Expectation of certain cultural behaviours and a brand 'look' that the workers will embody.

- *Purchasing.* Items such as towels, toiletries for rooms, toilet paper, pens, and many other consumables bought on a regular basis would have to be purchased from Luxonational. Restricts choice, but would bring economies of scale as such items are produced for the global range of hotels. Furthermore, the drinks in the bar, food supplies, and many other catering items would have to be sourced from Luxonational's preferred suppliers—this would give discount but dictates to the hotel what drinks and food they can serve.

**From:** meg_mortimer@junctionhotel.co.uk
**To:** simon_chance@junctionhotel.co.uk

**Subject:** Re: Re: Franchising

Simon, I've stayed at one of those Luxonational places before: identikit, sterile, characterless, bland—need I go on?

---

So far in the chapter we have seen how multinational companies are able to extend their reach across the globe, to dominate the globe in economic and business terms. In this section we examine claims that this dominance is also cultural, to the extent that there is a global culture that overrides cultures at a national and local level.

The media is seen as one aspect in this **cultural homogenization**. Across the globe we all watch the same films and television shows, listen to the same music, and play the same computer games. In many cases, these reflect a Western, predominantly US, culture. Such a global culture is shown by the following statement made in 1998 by Michael Eisner, then Chairman and Chief Executive of Disney:

> It doesn't matter whether it comes in by cable, telephone lines, computer, or satellite. Everyone's going to have to deal with Disney.

(quoted in New Internationalist, 1998)

Eisner is speaking here about the global prevalence of Disney films, media, and even imagery through merchandising. It is a global cultural presence, and the means by which this

**Cultural homogenization** A tendency for culture to become the same globally.

is achieved is not through physical globalization but intangibly through the satellites, television signals, and computer networks that he mentions.

Given that such media are usually presented in English, it is not surprising that a further element of global culture is the emergence of English as a global language (Bryson, 1990). While English is not the most widespread language by first speakers (indeed, it is not even second—the top three languages are Mandarin, Spanish, and then English) it, nevertheless, has a position of the second language of choice in many business and cultural areas. For example:

- The international language of air travel is English; in particular, all communications between pilots and air traffic controllers, wherever they may be in the world, are in English. This is even the case where the participants share a common language; thus a Spanish pilot will speak to a (Spanish-speaking) Argentinian air-traffic controller in English.

- International conferences, more often than not, choose English as their language of business. An example of this is academic conferences. Conferences set in a non-English-speaking country will transact their proceedings in English. Speeches, presentations, handouts, email communications, and websites are all in English, regardless of the native language of the host country.

## Global brands

### Real life case: I'd like to buy the world a Coke

Coca-Cola is a brand which enjoys a global reach and recognition; its brand was named the most valuable global brand of 2012 (Interbrand, 2012). Its global reach comes about, as we have seen, from licensing to licensees in different territories the right to use the Coca-Cola syrup to then produce, bottle, and sell the drink.

However, its global reach is also achieved by the power of the brand itself. Having been developed in the late 1800s, such was the global reach of the product by the 1970s that it embarked on the first ever global advertising campaign. A popular song of the time—'I'd like to teach the world to sing' by the New Seekers—was re-recorded as 'I'd like to buy the world a Coke'. People of different races and nationalities were shown in the advert, standing on a hillside, smiling and in harmony, all drinking Coca-Cola.

The implication of the advert is not just that Coca-Cola is a global product and a global brand, but that Coca-Cola unites the globe.

Visit the Online Resource Centre for a link to a video of the advert.

Beyond the media and the use of English, multinationals can be seen to contribute to global culture through their brand imagery. Brands are viewed as 'icons of culture and signifying devices' (Yakhlef, 2004: 238): that is to say, they give an identity to an organization and even create a meaning to people who consume them (as may be the case when people buy a particular pair of trainers for the brand).

Where brands create meaning and identity, they also contribute to global culture. Disney is, again, significant here. As we will see in Chapter 16, Bryman (2004) suggests that the Disney theme park, and the way it creates particular imagery that is experienced within that organization, is a model for other types of service and leisure organizations. Organizations want to create a particular feeling that reflects their brand through the decoration, the atmosphere, and even

The standardized airport.
**Source:** Shutterstock.

the behaviour of the staff within their premises (Witz et al., 2003; Yakhlef, 2004).

In Chapter 4 we saw how the 'McDonaldization of society' (Ritzer, 2015) brings about standardization on a global scale. The predictability element of McDonaldization is global predictability—there is a standard global product range (a Big Mac can be bought in McDonalds restaurants worldwide), and a standard brand and layout of the restaurants (the McDonalds arches have, in some surveys, been deemed to be a global symbol recognized more than the Christian cross). McDonaldization can also be seen in the worldwide spread of such places as shopping malls, multiplex cinemas, hotel chains, etc.

Taken together, McDonaldization and Disneyization are representative of organizations with a standard experience and atmosphere on a global scale. One hotel, fast-food restaurant, airport, or multiplex cinema feels the same wherever in the world you happen to be. It is as if, when in these organizational spaces, one could forget which country lies outside—such is their standardized nature that there is a global homogenous space created within organizations. Many of these spaces are branded, and thus global brands contribute to a standardized global culture not just through the ubiquitous presence of those brands but also through the organizational environments that they create.

Visit the Online Resource Centre for more on the homogeneous spaces of organizations such as airports.

## Review questions

| **Describe** | What is meant by global culture? |
| --- | --- |
| **Explain** | How do global organizations contribute to global culture? |
| **Analyse** | What roles do brands play in creating global culture? How do they help to create standardized organizational spaces? |
| **Apply** | What are the advantages and disadvantages that Junction Hotel should consider in thinking about becoming a franchise of Luxonation? |

# Globalization and national differences

## Running case: cultural misunderstandings

The franchise idea has been rejected—it was felt that it would create a bland space that would lose the distinctiveness of Junction Hotel. The international strategy continues, however, and even being on a few booking websites has brought in more international visitors to Junction Hotel.

This includes a group of Japanese tourists who had booked through the website and are trying to check in. They speak little English and the receptionists don't speak a word of Japanese between them. Even basic cultural niceties, such as greetings, are not understood between the two and gestures are being misunderstood. Flustered, the receptionist has asked the guests to sit in the bar and wait for a while. This leaves the reserved and polite guests feeling uncomfortable as another of Chance's rowdy football weekend parties also enters into the same area of the bar, chanting loudly.

Simon Chance goes into the bar to smooth over the situation, and thinks to himself that a bit of cross-cultural training for the staff might be needed. A global strategy will have to start much closer to home—within the hotel itself.

There is a saying that 'travel broadens the mind' and, certainly, any of you that have visited countries either near to, or far away from, home will have experienced different ways of life. It's not just the language that might be different—the food, mannerisms, and daily routines may also seem unfamiliar. It can take time to adjust to, and understand, the cultural differences between life at home and life in the new country. There might even be cultural misunderstandings—what is considered acceptable at home may offend people in other cultures or be seen as inappropriate behaviour.

Anyone experiencing such cultural differences might, understandably, be sceptical about the idea that we live in a globalized world with a standard, homogenized global culture. In this section we examine the extent to which national differences are still noticeable and still exert an influence on the way business is done, and the challenges of **cross-cultural management** that this creates for organizations operating in a global environment.

**Cross-cultural management**
Managing a workforce from different national and cultural backgrounds.

## Real life case: the order of the border?

In the European Union, the Schengen Agreement, signed in 1985, dismantled border controls between most of its member countries, allowing people to pass freely between countries. However, while the border might not contain and constrain the movement of people as it did previously, it can still be seen to demarcate differences between neighbouring countries.

This photo shows the border between Ahlbeck, Germany, and Świnoujście, Poland, on the Baltic coast, with the stone between the two poles marking the exact border. Given the history of World War II, this is a border that has been contested previously and was heavily secured. In the next photo, looking back from the beach, we see the remnants of a fence and a loop which held barbed wire to maintain the border along the beach, backed up by a watchtower in the distance. Now, it is possible to walk freely along the beach between the two Schengen countries. ▶

▶ However, the border still demar-
cates certain differences, not least *linguis-
tically*, with German and Polish being
spoken on either side. Crossing the
nearby road border further on, one is
faced with a long roadside market on the
Polish side with most stalls offering 'Billige
Zigaretten' (cheap cigarettes—note the
German language being used on the Polish side). This shows economic and political (e.g. levels of taxation) differences
between the two countries that result in
different prices being charged.

A border between Germany and Poland.

Furthermore, there are *cultural* differ-
ences that are still maintained. Sensitivities and values on the Polish side were offended by the tendency of German bathers towards naturist bathing. When the border was first opened up, this led to a
spat between representatives from the two towns, the Poles bemoaning German permissiveness and
the Germans amused by Polish 'puritanism' (France 24, 2008).

This example shows that, despite economic, political, and cultural globalization, there still
exist differences between nations. Policies, laws, and economic circumstances can exert an
influence; indeed, in Chapter 14 we saw how national laws could also have an influence on
how organizations use global technologies such as the Internet. Furthermore, linguistic
and cultural differences can begin to take effect, even just a few footsteps over the border. It
is to these linguistic and cultural differences, and their effects upon organization and management, that we now turn.

## From linguistic to cultural differences

A key aspect of national and cultural difference is that people speak different languages. As
explored earlier, English is widely used as a global *lingua franca* for business and organizations; however, linguistic differences—and the difficulties in translating between languages—are evident.

For example, while we have examined the presence of global brands and global advertising campaigns, their ability to convey a global message or identity can be undermined by
mistranslations.

- The French pronunciation of the Toyota MR2, 'MR Deux', sounds like a vulgar word
  in the French language (CNN Money, 2008).

- Coors' advertising slogan 'Turn it loose' was translated into Spanish as 'Get loose
  bowels' (CNN Money, 2008).

- KFC's slogan 'finger licking good' was translated into Chinese as 'eat your fingers off'
  (Adler, 2003).

Translation is a major issue in global organizations. For example, we suggested earlier that the European Union (EU) is part of global politics. Much of its energy is put into translation—both simultaneously through headphones at European Parliament meetings and in the reams of official documentation translated into all of its member languages. National differences through language are thus still important—English does not dominate as a language of the EU.

Furthermore, translation brings its own issues. Try using an online translation service or translation software. Put a paragraph in your own language, translate it into another language, then translate that back into your own language. The chances are that what you will have is clumsy—at times incomprehensible, at times amusing like the mistranslations listed earlier—but certainly not a perfect rendition of your original paragraph.

---

**Research insight:** Lost in translation

Blenkinsopp, J., and Pajouh, M.S. 2010. Lost in translation? Culture, language and the role of the translator in international business. *Critical Perspectives on International Business* 6(1): 38–52.

Blenkinsopp and Pajouh (2010) suggest that a 'mechanical perspective' on translation—translating word for word—often misses out on the cultural meaning of what was originally said.

For Blenkinsopp and Pajouh (ibid.), words can be embedded in the culture from which they come. This can lead to some 'untranslatable' words, for example the German word *schadenfreude*. This means a sense of pleasure in the misfortune of others; however, there is no equivalent word in English that conveys such an idea. As such, it is untranslatable; indeed, in English the original German word is used.

That words can be laden with untranslatable cultural values also has an effect in the business sphere. Blenkinsopp and Pajouh offer two 'untranslatable' words, *guanxi* in Chinese, often translated as 'relationship' into English, and a Farsi word *tarouf*, which refers to a form of superficial politeness. However, rather than simple translations, both words refer to particular types of behaviours, trust, politeness, and relationship-building that are particular to their own culture and impact how business relationships are carried out. The cultural and interpersonal behaviours suggested by these words in their original cultural context would be missed if one relied on a simple, mechanistic translation of the words.

---

Blenkinsopp and Pajouh's work on translation suggests that differences between nations are more than linguistic—there is a cultural element. What might work in business in one cultural context may not cross into other cultures.

For example, the opening of Euro Disney in Paris was seen to have been hampered by different cultural outlooks, from a view of Disney being an icon of US global culture, to a cynical viewpoint in France of its cultural inferiority—a 'cultural Chernobyl' (Hamnett, 1999). Such differences in cultural perspective could also be found among workers. Disneyland relies on a very American form of service culture, where workers are almost putting on an act in front of theme park guests (see Chapter 16). Curwen suggests that, again, a cultural mismatch led to high labour turnover at Disneyland Paris where 'French youth refused to see the need to cut their hair, dress uniformly and smile incessantly' (Curwen, 1995: 17).

Visit the Online Resource Centre for more about cultural differences as they relate to service.

Similar cultural mismatches have been suggested in the business world: for example, Al-Husan et al. (2009) examine cultural differences in transferring Western human resources management practices to the Middle East, and there are suggestions that Japanese management techniques do not function as effectively outside of the specific Japanese cultural context from which they emerge.

---

**Real life case:** cultural differences and teamwork

In the 1980s Japanese car manufacturers started to build factories in the UK (e.g. Nissan in Sunderland), introducing management practices such as *kaizen*, a system of continual improvement; *quality circles*, a small team dedicated to finding improvements where workers spend four hours a month looking at how to improve their work; *just-in-time production*, where parts arrive just when they are needed rather than being stockpiled in the factory; and more fluid boundaries so that people do not just work in one team but throughout the whole organization. All these approaches required strong levels of teamwork (Imai, 1986).

They found that practices that worked very well in Japan struggled in the UK context. UK workers liked to have more fixed teams and did not engage initially in the continuous improvement approach. The problem was trying to import practices that worked well in the collectivist Japanese culture—where the workers and management were extremely loyal to the organization rather than themselves or their immediate team—into the more individualistic UK—where workers saw themselves as individuals first rather than forming their identity as members of the organization and where they had more fixed views of their team.

So, instead, they developed a hybrid system, taking elements from both UK and Japanese culture. 'It is the accumulation of the little ideas that bring the big benefits in manufacturing', Mr Gibson (the plant deputy managing director) said. 'And here the changes have been made by the workers themselves. None of them came because some engineer was standing around with a stopwatch and a clipboard' (Lohr, 1987). In short, they developed systems that worked well by adapting UK notions of teamwork to Japanese styles.

---

# Can national cultures be measured?

Dutch researcher Geert Hofstede (1980) saw national cultures in a similar manner to organizational cultures (see Chapter 7) in that they demonstrated a set of values, attitudes, and sensitivities that amounted to the 'wiring of the brain' (Hofstede, 1980). As such, he suggested that differences between national cultures, and specifically national management cultures, could be measured and quantified.

Hofstede's study comes from a large-scale attitude survey of managers in the many national offices of computer firm IBM. From this, he devised a formal, numerical means of identifying and describing individual management cultures, which were plotted out on four **dimensions of culture** (adapted from Hofstede, 1980).

**Hofstede's dimensions of culture** Four numerical scales on which national management cultures can be located.

- Power distance concerns the mobility of people with regard to positions of power. Does power come from social status—who you are, who you were born to, and who you know—or is promotion more about merit, your proven abilities, and 'what you know'?

This also covers the way in which managers and subordinates interact—is a lot of deference shown to authority, or do management and workers interact more as equals?

- Uncertainty avoidance is the extent to which people are comfortable with risk and insecurity, or whether or not they tend to prefer stability and predictability.

- Masculinity/femininity concerns the level of assertiveness and aggressiveness within the organization, which Hofstede saw as a masculine trait, as opposed to a more feminine view of the organization based around concepts of welfare and nurture. It is also reflected in the level of equality between the genders.

- Individualism/collectivism is the extent to which the organization is seen as a community or a family to which a worker 'belongs' and has loyalty, or whether people work more as individuals, more interested in a sense of getting ahead than a sense of belonging.

Table 15.2 gives some examples of the results from Hofstede's survey. Some particular cultural features of different countries are highlighted by these scales (adapted from Hickson and Pugh, 1995).

- The UK and USA are seen to have very similar characteristics. The two countries have very highly individualistic approaches to work—workers are there for their own career rather than a sense of loyalty to an organization. Low power distance suggests that promotion on merit to the top of organizations is possible, perhaps reflected in the 'American dream' that anyone can become president. Both countries are also comfortable with risk and uncertainty. Overall, it suggests a forward-looking, individual-achievement-based culture.

- France has much higher power distance and uncertainty avoidance. A characteristic of the latter is a large amount of bureaucracy in French public and organizational life. Combined with high power distance, this brings about a more formal working environment with greater deference to seniority and perhaps explains the lack of willingness to engage in more informal service interactions, as highlighted earlier in the chapter.

**Table 15.2** Selected results of Hofstede's (1980) dimensions of national culture

| | Power distance | Uncertainty avoidance | Masculinity | Individualism |
|---|---|---|---|---|
| USA | 40 | 46 | 62 | 91 |
| UK | 35 | 35 | 66 | 89 |
| Japan | 54 | 92 | 95 | 46 |
| Sweden | 31 | 29 | 5 | 71 |
| France | 68 | 86 | 43 | 71 |
| India | 77 | 40 | 56 | 48 |
| Top-ranked | Malaysia | Greece | Japan | USA |
| Bottom-ranked | Austria | Singapore | Sweden | Guatemala |

Source: Based on Hickson and Pugh (1995: 33–5).

- A notable feature of Swedish management culture is its high femininity. Sweden is known for its egalitarian work legislation and practices between the genders; however, femininity also feeds into a management style that is less aggressive and abrasive, and more nurturing, cool-headed, and focused on practical outcomes.

- Japan is seen to have a unique set of characteristics, contributing to its very culturally-specific management style. There is very high uncertainty avoidance—decision making is time-consuming, conservative, and avoids risk (Kono, 1982). Individualism is low—Japanese workers have very high loyalty to the organization and will work long hours of unpaid overtime. Masculinity is also high—there are few women in senior management positions.

- Indian management has very high power distance and low individualism. It is characterized by 'paternalistic centralization'—managers will exert strong, centralized control in a way that shows concern for workers, too. There is loyalty to the workplace, but not the sense of devotion found in Japan.

Hofstede's findings have attracted considerable critique. We might question whether culture is something that can be reduced to numbers (cf. critiques of numerical personality scales in Chapter 8); whether surveys adequately measure rich and complex phenomena, such as cultures; and, indeed, whether a view of an overall national culture can be gained from a survey of just one organization—IBM. McSweeney (2002) gives a thorough critique of the methodology and conclusions of the work of Hofsetede, and his 'limited characterization' (2002: 112) of the concept of culture.

# Managing across the global and the local

While the rigid numerical calculation of Hofstede's scales should be treated with caution in terms of giving an absolute mapping of national managerial cultures, it suggests that national differences and cultures are important and exert an effect on how business and management operate. In the final part of this section we examine two particular ways in which organizations manage globally, but taking account of the local; namely managing people and cultures, and managing strategies.

## Managing people and cultures

The first implication of national cultural differences is that, in a multinational workforce, they might impact differently on how individuals are managed. For example, an assertive, ambitious, individualistic worker might be motivated differently to one whose culture suggests loyalty to the organization and belonging.

**Real life case:** managing across cultures in a football team

Top-level football teams are an example of a multinational workforce. Players will be from many different countries and continents. Sir Alex Ferguson, former manager of Manchester United, has noted how sensitivity to different cultural backgrounds is needed in managing across cultures within a team,  ▶

> where people not only have a different way of seeing the world, but also even basic things, like times for eating and sleeping, may be different (BBC Sport, 2011).
>
> Cultural differences can, however, have more serious consequences. A recent upheld case of alleged racist abuse in the English Premier League against Uruguayan player Luis Suárez hinged around his defence that there was a misunderstanding caused by cultural differences (Taylor, 2011).
>
> The Football Association (2011) investigation into the incident went into meticulous detail about the differing meanings and use of racially-sensitive words between the UK and South America. Suárez was fined and served a ban following the investigation; however, the report highlights a confused picture of cross-cultural differences that can revolve even around the meaning of a single word (see also Chapter 14 for more on cross-cultural issues in miscommunication).

These differences extend to the management of culture across organizations. Gergen and Whitney (1996) argue that the implementation of a global culture is simply impossible given the effects of different cultures in national context; instead, culture is seen through the lens of local cultures at a national level.

Furthermore, personal cultural differences extend beyond management over the organization, to relationships across organizations—dealing with clients, customers, and colleagues in different countries. Crace (2003) outlines the role of 'cultural consultants' in advising firms on cultural differences that might cause problems from seemingly innocuous behaviours: for example, a polite enquiry about somebody's family might be seen in Arab countries as planning an affair with a customer's wife; and putting a business card into a back pocket would cause offence in Japan.

### Study skills: working with students from other cultures

Universities are usually international, multicultural environments and, in project work, you may well find yourself working with people from other cultures. The cultural differences outlined in this section relate to the workplace, but apply equally to project teams and groups at university.

Crace (2003) outlines that even email communication, as is often used in project work, can lead to cultural differences. For example, some cultures tend to be very abrupt and curt in their use of email, which can upset people from other cultures not used to such directness.

What cultural differences do you notice between students at your university? Does this affect the way that you might work together on a project?

## Managing structure and strategies

### Real life case: the limits of McDonaldization

While McDonalds and its brand are globally ubiquitous and the company employs global standardized practices, it is not true to say that McDonalds, as it exists from country to country, is uniformly global; for example: >

- in France beer is served in restaurants, as local culture associates dining out with drinking (Audi, 2009)

- in parts of India, beef cannot be eaten because of religious laws, and so mutton is used in the burgers (Harding, 2000)

- in many Far Eastern countries, McDonalds is not viewed as a place to eat quickly; instead it is seen as place where people will sit and socialize for long periods of time (Watson, 1997).

**Glocalization**
Adapting global
practices and products
to local conditions.

**Glocalization** (Robertson, 1995) is a term which captures both the global activities of multinational firms and, at the same time, their adaptation of strategies for local markets as discussed in the previous section—at once acting globally and locally.

The highlighted case shows how an organization like McDonalds, while seemingly a contributor to a global, standardized culture, in fact adapts for local tastes, sensitivities, laws, and cultures. There are adaptations to McDonalds' menus in different national markets.

Similarly, in a set of adverts, the global bank HSBC describes itself as 'The world's local bank'. The suggestion is that, while it operates on a global scale, it understands and responds to different national markets. Indeed, many of the national subsidiaries operate independently, with a knowledge of their national market, while carrying the global HSBC branding.

Visit the Online Resource Centre for a link to these HSBC adverts.

Different degrees of glocalization are encompassed in Bartlett and Ghoshal's (1989) model of multinational structures and strategies, based around two particular dimensions:

- corporate integration—the extent to which the organization is standardized and controlled across its global operations. Is it an integrated, bureaucratic whole, or do individual, national units operate relatively independently?

- responsiveness to local markets—to what extent are the goods, services, and branding of an organization standardized globally, or are they adjusted to be more responsive to local needs and requirements?

Figure 15.3 shows different types of organization along the dimensions suggested by Bartlett and Ghoshal. This gives four particular types of global firm.

- Global firms benefit from high economies of scale through a globalized and highly standardized offering. There is a great deal of standardized control across the globe and little alteration of products to suit local markets. This is found in consumer electronics: for example, an iPad is the same standard product wherever it is sold. Look also at the international website of Swedish clothes retailer H&M—the websites for each national territory where it operates offer the exact same range of (mass-produced) clothing.

- Transnational firms have economies of scale, especially through standardized control mechanisms; however, there is some responsiveness to local markets, e.g. by adapting products, services, or marketing strategies. The organization is seen as a set of international subsidiaries with some independence, but also a sharing of learning across the global organization. The standardized bureaucratic control of McDonalds, coupled

**Figure 15.3** Bartlett and Ghoshal's (1989) model.

**Source:** Based on Bartlett and Ghoshal, *Managing Across Borders*, 1989.

with its responsiveness to local markets, as described previously, would be an example of this.

- A multinational or multidomestic firm is a global organization which runs more like a set of independent national subsidiaries. Different national subsidiaries may have different identities or product ranges: e.g. it is the national context which is important rather than standardized, global control. The example of Tesco would fit into this category—it runs a number of differently branded chains in different countries.

- An international firm uses knowledge from head office, but in a more autonomous way. People might be trained at head office, but they are then free to operate relatively autonomously once they have that knowledge.

In this section, we have seen that national and cultural difference do have an impact on the ways in which people and organizational strategies are managed. In the next section we see how these differences, on a global scale, can become global inequalities.

---

## Review questions

| | |
|---|---|
| **Describe** | What are Hofstede's four dimensions of national culture? |
| **Explain** | What is meant by cultural differences? |
| **Analyse** | How do organizations respond to national and cultural differences in the ways that they manage people and develop organizational strategies? |
| **Apply** | How would you advise Junction Hotel about dealing with cultural differences? |

# The inequalities of globalization

The previous section has shown that, rather than a uniform, standardized global culture, globalization still has to account for national differences. Differences within globalization can also be seen in its inequalities. Rather than being an even process, it can be seen as one which benefits some parts of the globe and not others; in particular, it is seen to benefit the developed, Western world at the expense of the developing world. In this respect, globalization has been the object of considerable protest and critique.

---

**Real life case:** the anti-globalization movement

Over the last two decades the so-called **anti-globalization movement** has become increasingly vocal, involved in often violent protests at meetings of global political and economic institutions such as the World Bank and the G8 group of eight leading world economies. The anti-globalization protestors have sought to challenge the 'Washington Consensus' of free-market capitalism that they argue is sweeping the world.

As the media often focus on the violence that can accompany these protests, their real message can get lost. For instance, in 2005 over 200,000 protestors, many of them families with young children, came together under the banner 'Make poverty history', campaigning for *trade justice*, to make trading laws fair for poor countries (Jeffery and Tempest, 2005); to *drop the debt*, to cancel unaffordable international debts for developing countries; and for *more and 'better' aid*, with rich countries giving a small percentage of their gross domestic product (GDP) to aid poor countries (Make Poverty History, 2012).

The central focus for much of the protests was the pro-capitalist policies of the World Bank, International Monetary Fund, and G8 which, the protesters claim, force poorer countries to privatize essential services, such as water, telecommunications, and energy production, to 'liberalize' their economies and make them more competitive. The protestors argue that, in reality, these moves serve the interests of global elites as they are often sold to rich multinationals who cream off the profits and move them out of these countries. They also argue that trade laws promote the free movement of capital but protect the interests of the richest nations.

They argue these polices have 'left a trail of destroyed economies, ruined nations and marginalized people' (Brahm, 2009: 16).

## Inequalities of the global economy

Inequalities in the world economy can be seen through a calculation of GDP per capita, i.e. national income per person.

Figure 15.4 shows that this income is unevenly distributed—the higher incomes per person are enjoyed mainly in North America, Western Europe, and other developed counties. There are much lower incomes, in some cases below the poverty line, in Africa, large parts of Asia, and South America.

The economic divide is further illustrated when looking at the distribution of headquarters of the top fifty multinational companies worldwide (see Figure 15.5). This mirrors the inequalities shown by GDP per capita distribution.

A central criticism made by anti-globalization protestors is that global politics reinforces and, indeed, creates inequalities within the global economy. Institutions such as the World Trade Organisation (WTO) and the World Bank are dominated largely by rich countries who can decide on policies which tend to suit their purposes. As Laurence Brahm puts it, 'the WTO has come to be seen as a forum for the G8 to extract trading conditions from

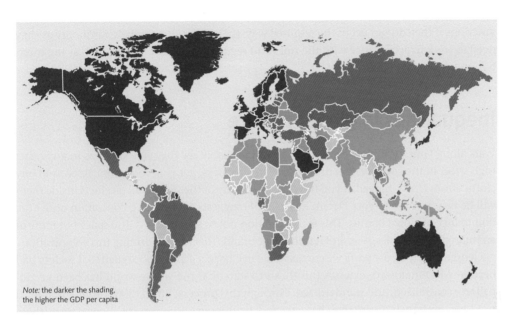

**Figure 15.4** Gross domestic product (GDP) per capita 2007–11.

**Source:** Based on data from the World Bank, http://data.worldbank.org

*Note:* the darker the shading, the higher the GDP per capita

**Figure 15.5** Location of headquarters of the top fifty multinational companies.

**Source:** Based on CNN Money, 2012.

less-developed nations' (2009: 71) for their own benefit. This view is even more strongly expressed by anti-globalization campaigner Walden Bello, who states the WTO is 'patently a method for the US and the EU to institutionalize their hegemony [leadership/power]' (cited in Brahm, 2009: 72).

Anti-globalization campaigners therefore state that these institutions promote and, indeed, force countries to adopt a free market model by, for instance, only lending money when an individual country promises to sell off formally nationalized industries. In doing so, not only are they promoting a particular form of capitalism, but they also erode the power of the nation state (i.e. an individual government's options and choices) by imposing sanctions if they do not act in the required way, therefore reducing their autonomy as they need to work in accordance with the rules and regulations of institutions such as the International Monetary Fund.

# Inequalities in global culture

Walk along your local high street and you will probably see the same shops as in any other high street in the country. You drink coffee in Starbucks, get your food from Tesco, and buy clothes from H&M. Indeed, if you travel abroad many of the shops and products inside them will be very familiar to you. Naomi Klein (2001) suggests a return to colonization under the dominance of global brands. This is colonization not so much of physical space but more of an intangible cultural space, and it is the large brands that are performing this colonization.

George Ritzer, whose work we encountered in Chapter 4 and who argued that society had become McDonaldized, extends this thesis to state that the whole world has become globalized, centralized, and standardized. Through this process, Ritzer (2007) argues that local products, with their distinctive character and qualities, have become swallowed up by these standardized global products. As a result, distinctiveness (*something* in Ritzer's language) becomes lost to standardization (which Ritzer calls *nothing*).

Klein (2001) uses Starbucks as an example of a firm that hastens this standardization by setting up their coffee shops in every community, squeezing out alternative, local providers. While their supporters argue that this is simply a result of offering something that people want—good coffee in a pleasant environment—their critics claim that they have developed tactics of flooding the market to drive local coffee shops out of business, and then reducing the number of their shops once they control the market. This criticism was recognized by Howard Schultz, who, when taking control of Starbucks as chief executive officer (CEO), stated that they should only work in communities that welcome them in (see discussion in Chapter 12) for fear that customers would reject them outright (Schultz, 2011).

# Inequality and global problems

Chapter 17 examines corporate social responsibility: an imperative for organizations to act in a way which is responsible to society, indeed to the globe. Part of the impetus for this has come from problems associated with globalization, such as:

- global warming and environmental problems, which are treated as global political issues
- sweatshop labour conditions, often arising from global brands subcontracting manufacturing labour to the third world
- global commodity chains, dominated by Western multinational firms, which pay below subsistence prices to third world suppliers.

These arguments are taken up in Chapter 17, alongside some potential global solutions to such problems, for example the Fairtrade movement, which aims to pay fair prices to suppliers in the third world.

An overall argument is that, as mentioned at the start of this chapter, a precursor of globalization was seen to be the colonization of and slavery in Africa, Asia, and South America. While such a level of colonization of physical territory no longer exists, the level of control that Western governments and multinationals have over both physical and intangible aspects of globalization amounts to a modern-day form of colonization. Indeed, it is not just Western countries that extend their reach in this way. More recently, China has placed considerable investment in Africa, and similar, albeit contested, suggestions of empire-building have been made (see *The Guardian*, 2012 for more discussion.)

## Review questions

| | |
|---|---|
| **Describe** | What inequalities exist within the global economy? |
| **Explain** | What are the main arguments of the anti-globalization movement? |
| **Analyse** | What problems do you think global politics and global culture might create in the global economy? |
| **Apply** | What can a small organization like Junction Hotel do to help minimize and overcome global inequalities? |

# Chapter summary

Globalization is a complex process, involving both physical and intangible spaces, and encompassing areas of society such as the economy, politics, culture, technology, and the natural environment. Organizations play a role in this, using a number of strategies to act globally, whether on a large or small scale.

On the one hand, there is an argument that globalization is a process that brings us together as a 'global village', leading to a homogeneous global culture with the differences between individual nations and their cultures becoming less and less pronounced. On the other hand, these national and cultural differences can be seen to still exist and, indeed, influence the global strategies that organizations undertake.

Furthermore, globalization can be seen to perpetuate inequalities between nations and problems on a global scale. Recent financial crises have highlighted not only the global nature of our society, and organizations within this, but also how problems, too, are global issues requiring a global response.

## Further reading

Hickson, D.J., and Pugh, D.S. 1995. *Management worldwide: Distinctive styles amid globalization*. Penguin Books Ltd: London.
A good introduction to Hofstede's scales, with examples of national cultures in a wide variety of countries worldwide.

Parker, B., and Clegg, S.R. 2006. Globalization. In: Clegg, S.R., Hardy, C., Lawrence, T., and Nord, W.R. (eds) *The SAGE handbook of organization studies*. Sage: London, pp. 651–74.
> An introduction and overview of globalization, including the six aspects of global interconnectedness outlined in this chapter.

Klein, N. 2001. *No logo: No space, no choice, no jobs*. Flamingo: London.
> An accessible introduction to the main arguments of the anti-globalization movement.

Waters, M. 2001. *Globalization*, 2nd edn. Routledge: London, New York.
> An introduction to globalization as it affects organizations and society more widely.

# References

Adler, C. 2003. Colonel Sanders' march on China. *Time Magazine*, 17 November.

Al-Husan, F.Z.B., Brennan, R., and James, P. 2009. Transferring Western HRM practices to developing countries: The case of a privatized utility in Jordan. *Personnel Review* 38 (2): 104–23.

Asser, M. 2010. Obstacles to Arab-Israeli peace: Water. BBC News, 2 September.

Audi, N. 2009. France, land of epicures, gets taste for McDonald's. *New York Times*, 25 October.

Bartlett, C.A., and Ghoshal, S. 1989. *Managing across borders: The transnational solution*. Harvard Business School Press: Boston.

BBC News. 2006. Tesco's Thai plans under threat. 27 September.

BBC News. 2011. India's call centre growth stalls. 27 September.

BBC Sport. 2011. In-depth interview—Sir Alex Ferguson on TV, youth policy, hairdryers and more. Available at: http://www.bbc.co.uk/sport/0/football/15064028 (last accessed 20 August 2015).

Bignell, P. 2011. Secret memos expose link between oil firms and invasion of Iraq. *The Independent*, 19 April.

Blenkinsopp, J., and Pajouh, M.S. 2010. Lost in translation? Culture, language and the role of the translator in international business. *Critical Perspectives on International Business* 6 (1): 38–52.

Brahm, L.J. 2009. *The anti-globalization breakfast club manifesto for a peaceful revolution*. John Wiley & Sons (Asia): Singapore.

Bryman, A. 2004. *The Disneyization of society*. Sage: London.

Bryson, B. 1990. *Mother tongue: The English language*. Penguin: London.

Castle, S. 2012. With details settled, a second Greek bailout is formally approved. *New York Times*, 14 March.

Chaudhuri, K.N. 1965. *The English East India Company: The study of an early joint-stock company, 1600–1640*. Cass: London.

Cheshire, T. 2011. In depth: How Rovio made Angry Birds a winner (and what's next). *Wired*, 7 March.

Clegg, S.R., and Gray, J.T. 1996. Metaphors of globalization. In:Boje, D., Gephart, R., and Thatchenkery, T. (eds) *Postmodern Management and Organization Theory*. Sage: Thousand Oaks, CA, pp. 293–307.

CNN Money. 2008. How not to sell abroad. Available at: http://money.cnn.com/galleries/2008/fsb/0807/gallery.bad_translations.fsb/index.html (last accessed 20 August 2015).

Cooper, J. 2010. *The origin of financial crises: Central banks, credit bubbles and the efficient market fallacy*. Harrman House: London.

Crace, J. 2003. Crossing cultures. *The Guardian*, 14 October.

Curwen, P. 1995. EuroDisney: The mouse that roared (not!). *European Business Review* 95 (5): 15–20.

Deb, S. 2004. Call me. *The Guardian*, 3 April.

England and Wales Cricket Board 2012. Smith celebrates birth of first child. Available at: http://www.ecb.co.uk/news/england/investec-tests/smith,318922,EN.html (last accessed 14 August 2015).

Ferguson, C. 2011. *Inside job*. Song Pictures: New York.

Football Association 2011. The Football Association and Luis Suarez: Reasons of the regulatory commissions. Available at: http://www.furd.org/resources/FA%20v%20Suarez%20Written%20Reasons%20of%20Regulatory%20Commission.pdf (last accessed 14 August 2015).

*Fortune* 2015. Global 500. Available at http://fortune.com/global500/ (last accessed 14 August 2015).

France 24 2008. German nudists versus Polish puritans, 6 August.

Gergen, K., and Whitney, D. 1996. Technologies of representation in the global corporation: Power and polyphony. In: Boje, D., Gephart, R.P., and Tatchenkery, T.J. (eds) *Postmodern management and organization theory*. Sage: London, pp. 331–57.

Hamnett, J.L. 1999. Euro Disney: A cross-cultural communications failure? In:Goodman, R.A., Atkin, I., Barry, J., and Pettersen, E. (eds) *Modern organizations and emerging conundrums: Exploring the postindustrial subculture of the third millennium*. Lexington Books: Lanham, MD, p. 240.

Harding, L. 2000. Give me a Big Mac—but hold the beef. *The Guardian*, 28 December.

Harding, L. 2001. Delhi calling. *The Guardian*, 9 March.

Hickson, D.J., and Pugh, D.S. 1995. *Management worldwide*. Penguin Books: Harmondsworth.

HM Revenue and Customs 2015. Annual trade. Available at: https://www.uktradeinfo.com/Statistics/Pages/Annual-Tables.aspx (last accessed 14 August 2015).

Hofstede, G.H. 1980. *Culture's consequences: International differences in work-related values*. Sage: Beverly Hills, CA.

Imai, M. 1986. *KAIZEN—the key to Japan's competitive success*. Random House: New York.

Interbrand 2012. Best global brands 2012. Available at: http://bestglobalbrands.com/previous-years/2012 (last accessed 14 August 2015).

Jefferey, S., and Tempest, S. 2005. 200,000 form Edinburgh human chain. *The Guardian*, 2 July.

Klein, N. 2001. *No logo: No space, no choice, no jobs*. Flamingo: London.

Kono, T. 1982. Japanese management philosophy: Can it be exported? *Long Range Planning* 15 (3): 90–102.

LeMay, M.C. 1987. *From open door to Dutch door: An analysis of US immigration policy since 1820*. Praeger Pub Text: Westport, CT.

Lohr, S. 1987. Nissan's revolution in Britain. *New York Times*, 2 June.

Loomba, A. 1998. *Colonialism-postcolonialism*. Routledge: London.

Maguire, J. 1999. *Global sport: Identities, societies, civilizations*. Polity Press: Cambridge.

Make Poverty History 2012. Available at: http://www.makepovertyhistory.org/takeaction/ (last accessed 14 August 2015).

McLuhan, M. 1964. *Understanding media: The extensions of man*. McGraw-Hill: New York.

McSweeney, B. 2002. Hofstede's model of national cultural differences and their consequences: A triumph of faith—a failure of analysis. *Human Relations* 55 (1): 89–118.

Nationmaster 2015. GDP: Countries compared. Available at: http://www.nationmaster.com/country-info/stats/Economy/GDP (last accessed 14 August 2015).

*New Internationalist* 1998. The mousetrap—Inside Disney's dream machine. 5 December.

Osborne, A., Aldrick, P., and Quinn, J. 2009. Lehman collapse: The drama of a mad 48 hours that will never fade. *Daily Telegraph*, 13 September.

Parfitt, T. 2007. Belarus cuts off Russian pipeline in bitter gas war. *The Guardian*, 9 January.

Parker, B. 1996. Evolution and revolution: From international business to globalization. In: Clegg, S.R., Hardy, C., and Nord, W.R. (eds) *Handbook of organization studies*. Sage: London, pp. 484–506.

Parker, B., and Clegg, S.R. 2006. Globalization. In: Clegg, S.R., Hardy, C., Lawrence, T., and Nord, W.R. (eds) *The Sage handbook of organization studies*. Sage: London, pp. 651–74.

Pederson, I. 2012. Central Asia could go to war over water. *Business Insider*, 15 September. Available at: http://www.businessinsider.com/central-asia-really-could-go-to-war-over-lack-of-water-2012-9#ixzz2DLumadrE (last accessed 20 August 2015).

Race, R. 2015. *Multiculturalism and education*, 2nd edn. Bloomsburg: London.

Ritzer, G. 2007. *The globalization of nothing 2*. Pine Forge Press: Thousand Oaks, CA.

Ritzer, G. 2015. *The McDonaldization of Society*, 8th edn. Pine Forge Press: Thousand Oaks, CA.

Robertson, R. 1992. *Globalization: Social theory and global culture*. Sage: London.

Robertson, R. 1995. Glocalization: Time-space and homogeneity-heterogeneity. In: Featherstone, M., Lash, S., and Robertson, R. (eds) *Global modernities*, Sage: London, pp. 25–44.

Rovio Entertainment 2013. Rovio Entertainment reports 2013 financial results. Available at http://www.rovio.com/en/news/press-releases/495/rovio-entertainment-reports-2013-financial-results (last accessed 14 August 2015).

Rushton, K. 2012. Carphone Warehouse likely to buy Best Buy out of European joint venture. *Daily Telegraph*, 14 November.

Schultz, H. 2011. *Onward: How Starbucks fought for its life without losing its soul*. John Wiley and Sons: Chichester.

Taylor, D. 2011. Luis Suárez-Patrice Evra racism case may hinge on cultural differences. *The Guardian*, 15 December.

Tesco plc 2015. Our business. Available at: https://www.tescoplc.com/index.asp?pageid=8 (last accessed 14 August 2015).

*The Economist* 2007. Fresh, but far from easy, 21 June.

*The Guardian* 2005. 200,000 form Edinburgh human chain, 2 July.

*The Guardian* 2015. China's 'Black Monday' sends markets reeling across the globe—as it happened, 24 August. Available at: http://www.theguardian.com/business/live/2015/aug/24/global-stocks-sell-off-deepens-as-panic-grips-markets-live

Thompson, J. 2010. Tesco bags stores in Czech Republic. *The Independent*, 24 December.

Treanor, J. 2003. Tesco's forays take it into Turkey. *The Guardian*, 12 November.

Waters, M. 2001. *Globalization*, 2nd edn. Routledge: London, New York.

Watson, J.L. 1997. Transnationalism, localization, and fast foods in East Asia. In: *Golden Arches East: McDonald's in East Asia*. Stanford University Press: Stanford, CA, pp. 1–38.

Witz, A., Warhurst, C., and Nickson, D. 2003. The labour of aesthetics and the aesthetics of organization. *Organization* 10 (1): pp. 33–54.

Yakhlef, A. 2004. Global brands as embodied 'generic spaces'. *Space and Culture* 7 (2): 237–48.

# The service and leisure economies

## Organizations as an experience, work as a performance

### Chapter overview and learning outcomes

By the end of this chapter you should be able to:

- describe the main features of 'Disneyized' organizations (Bryman, 2004) within the service sector and leisure industries

- explain how many service sector organizations create an 'experience' rather than a product which is consumed

- explain what is meant by 'performative labour' as an aspect of the service sector labour process

- describe the main features of emotional and aesthetic labour

- analyse how emotional and aesthetic labour impact workers differently depending upon their gender.

### Key theorists

| | |
|---|---|
| Alan Bryman | Developed the idea of the 'Disneyization of society' to suggest that characteristics of Disney theme parks are widespread in other service and leisure organizations |
| Arlie Hochschild | From research into the work of air hostesses, developed the term 'emotional labour' to show how workers are expected to manage their emotions in return for a wage |
| Pierre Bourdieu | Used the term 'habitus' to suggest that people have deeply-held dispositions which they demonstrate unwittingly in their behaviour and which are difficult to change |
| Erving Goffman | Used theatrical analogies in his 1959 book *The presentation of self in everyday life* to suggest that people put on different performances in different social contexts |
| Anne Witz, Chris Warhurst, and Dennis Nickson | Identified aesthetic labour in customer-facing service industries, where people manage their appearance and behavioural dispositions in return for a wage |

### Key terms

| | |
|---|---|
| Disneyization (of society) | As noted by Alan Bryman, the adoption of certain characteristics of the Disney theme park in a large number of service and leisure organizations, especially in organizations which are experienced by consumers as destinations in their own right |
| Performative labour | Cited by Bryman as an aspect of Disneyization whereby workers are on show in front of consumers and are required to put on some form of performance; such performance encompasses both emotional and aesthetic labour |
| Emotional labour | Workers managing the emotions that they display in front of customers and clients in return for the wage that they are paid |
| Aesthetic labour | Workers adhering to certain requirements of appearance and comportment in return for the wage that they are paid |

# Introduction

## Running case: a bar at the Junction Hotel

Jane Grimes, a local university student, has recently started part-time bar work at Junction Hotel. At the weekend, Grimes likes to go out around town with friends. This Friday, however, she is on the rota to work evenings.

At 7 pm, the bar is quiet. Grimes catches sight of the painting hanging on the wall—a reproduction of Édouard Manet's *A bar at the Folies-Bergère*. It has become a favourite of Grimes's, and after several weekend shifts in the bar, she realizes why. The facial expression on the painting sums up Grimes's feelings—she is bored. She would much rather be having a laugh with her friends than be stuck behind the bar.

Édouard Manet's *A bar at the Folies-Bergère*.
**Source:** © The Samuel Courtauld Trust, The Courtauld Gallery, London.

To compound matters, unlike the barmaid in the painting, she isn't allowed to look bored for too long. However she feels—bored, sad, angry . . . whatever—she has to put on a show—a smile, be pleasant, show interest in the customers. As the bar manager keeps reminding her, she is a part of the decoration in here and an unhappy face spoils things for customers.

Keeping a happy face becomes more and more of a test as the night wears on and the punters drink more.

The first man to arrive tells her 'how lovely' she looks. She smiles and says 'thank you,' but, inside, feels disgust. Her skin crawls at the thought that she is some sort of object for him to ogle at. Besides, she doesn't feel 'lovely' at all. The bar has a dress code, which includes a uniform that she hates, and rules on make-up and hair that she feels make her look like a doll rather than a real person.

As the night continues and customers drink more, they become ruder and the compliments on her looks become more suggestive. The regular bar-room bore sits at one end of the bar, unburdening his tales of marital woe to Grimes. She wants to tell him what a sad individual he is, but, instead, she has to smile and humour him. This is particularly difficult for her because his drawling, incoherent sentences are keeping her from serving others, and these gaps in service will show up on the printout from the till at the end of the shift.

Jane Grimes looks up again at the woman in the painting and the bored expression on her face. 'If only I could show my true feelings like she does; just drop the mask for a while,' she thinks. 'Instead, I have to keep up this performance for the rest of the shift.'

What aspects of this case do you recognize from your own experiences of work?

Service sector work will be familiar to many readers of this book. As a student you may well work part-time in a shop, bar, restaurant, or call centre. It is also likely that, upon graduating, you will also be employed in the service sector, which has replaced manufacturing as the dominant focus of many Western economies. In the UK, for example, service industries account for over three quarters of economic and employment activity (Office for National Statictics, 2015).

Many types of work are included in the measurement of the service sector used by the Office for National Statistics, including transport, communications, media, finance, and government services such as defence. In this chapter, we are particularly interested in aspects of service work defined variously as front-line, customer-facing, or **interactive service work**. This might include retail work or leisure work, such as bars and restaurants, but can include any job where work is performed in front of customers or clients.

# The service sector: from rationalization to performance

When rational management techniques, such as Taylorism, Fordism, and bureaucracy (see Chapters 2 and 3), were developed, manufacturing dominated the economy. An important issue in this chapter is whether the shift towards services and away from manufacturing diminishes the importance of rationalization to management and organization.

The organizations examined in Chapter 4 would suggest not. Call centres, supermarkets, budget hotels, and the fast-food restaurant are all contemporary examples of efficient, rationalized organizations, and all are located in the service sector. Indeed, Ritzer's (2015) McDonaldization not only examines service sector industries, but also shows explicitly how they employ bureaucratic, Taylorist, and Fordist techniques—the fast-food restaurant being compared with an assembly line for producing and serving food.

While service-sector organizations employ rationalized techniques, they also display their own particular characteristics, which we suggest are a result of work and the consumption of that work taking place *at the same time*. Think about a trip to a restaurant—it is not just the food that determines your enjoyment of the visit, but also the atmosphere, the décor, the attitude of the waiting staff, etc. We examine how it is the organization itself and the nature of the service work performed that are as much part of the experience for customers as the product and services offered.

- Service sector organizations, such as bars, restaurants, and shopping malls, often create their own particular theme, environment, or experience for the consumer in a similar way to the experience created by a Disney theme park. Bryman (2004) thus uses the term 'Disneyization' to describe characteristics of Disney theme parks which can be found in contemporary service and leisure organizations.

- If a theme or experience is part of what an organization is selling, then workers play a role in creating that experience. Unlike workers on a manufacturing assembly line, service workers are 'on show' to customers. Gabriel (2005) uses the metaphor of the 'glass cage' to at once invoke the McDonaldized, rationalized nature of much service work (alluding to Weber's iron cage of bureaucracy as discussed in Chapter 2) and, similarly, to highlight workers being constantly on display as if they were in a glass cabinet.

Organizations become almost like theatres, with workers putting on a performance in front of customers and clients. Indeed, Bryman (2004) suggests that workers are specifically paid to undertake **performative labour** in exchange for the wages they are paid. In this chapter we examine two particular aspects of how workers might be expected to engage in performative labour.

- **Emotional labour** (Hochschild, 1983) is concerned with expectations of how workers will behave and interact with customers and clients. In many cases this might be by

**Interactive service work** Jobs where the worker deals directly with a customer or client, found especially in the service and leisure industries.

**Performative labour** Paid interactive service work where the worker is engaging in some form of performance, as if on stage. Refers, in particular, to emotional and aesthetic labour.

**Emotional labour** Work where, in exchange for a wage, the worker is expected to manage their emotions to put on a particular emotional performance in front of customers or clients, especially in interactive service work.

smiling and being pleasant to customers, but we will see that other service work might demand different types of emotional display.

**Aesthetic labour**
Usually found in customer or client-facing service work where, in exchange for a wage, the worker is expected to manage their appearance and comportment in a manner directed by the organization.

- **Aesthetic labour** (Witz et al., 2003) is concerned with aspects of appearance, e.g. through dress codes, and how workers present and 'carry' themselves in front of customers.

While these aspects of performative labour can be found in many aspects of customer- facing service work, we conclude the chapter by suggesting that emotional and aesthetic labour are not gender neutral. The burden of peformative labour falls disproportionately upon women, to the point where women are seen to be objectified or sexually 'commodified' (Adkins, 1995) in service work.

## Review questions

| | |
|---|---|
| **Describe** | How is service sector work rationalized? (You may wish to look back to Chapter 4). |
| **Explain** | What is meant by 'putting on a performance' at work? |
| **Analyse** | What similarities and differences exist between manufacturing and service sector work? |
| **Apply** | What characteristics of customer-facing service work can you identify in the Junction Hotel case? |

# The organization as an experience

**Disneyization** Term coined by Bryman which describes characteristics of the Disney theme parks that can be seen in other service and leisure organizations.

**Theming** As with a theme park, this is where the image and identity of an organization, and the experience that it provides for consumers, is based around a particular theme.

We may think of the Disney theme parks as a place to visit on a special occasion—a land where we can experience spectacular images and sights before returning home to our more ordinary lives. Bryman (2004), however, suggests that the characteristics of Disney theme parks are more commonplace; indeed, they can be found in one form or another in many everyday service and leisure organizations. Bryman suggests four characteristics which make up this **Disneyization** of society.

Disneyland.

- As with theme parks, there are examples in service and leisure organizations of **theming**. Pubs are presented as sports bars or Irish pubs. Restaurants are themed around the food they serve (e.g. Chinese or Indian) or take on other themes, e.g. the Hard Rock Café themed around music (Beardsworth and Bryman, 1999). Even geographical areas are themed for the purposes of the tourist industry, e.g. 'Shakespeare country' around Stratford-upon-Avon in England, or Santa Claus Land in Finland (Pretes, 1995).

- A theme park encompasses a number of different types of consumption—shops, restaurants, leisure rides, etc. Such **hybrid consumption**, whereby a number of different types of consumption activity take place under the same roof, is also found in service and leisure organizations. Shopping malls are often combined with other leisure activities, such as bars, restaurants, and cinemas. New football stadia developments may encompass hotels and fast-food restaurants and may be built as part of a retail park.

- Goods are produced using the name or image of a particular organization. Disney **merchandising** (films, soft toys, etc.) is familiar and there may even be cross-promotion with, for example, a new Disney film being promoted at a fast-food restaurant. Top sports clubs also produce merchandizing—think of a Barcelona duvet or a Manchester United pencil case

- as we will see later in the chapter, workers are expected—through the management of emotion and appearance—to engage in performative labour as if they were on a stage.

**Hybrid consumption** Different types of consumption activity, which might otherwise take place in separate organizations, appearing together in one organization.

**Merchandising** The image or brand of one company or organization appearing on other products.

---

### Real life case: West Edmonton mall

The West Edmonton mall, in Alberta, Canada, is a giant shopping mall, but it encompasses many other attractions. Within its walls are a water park, cinemas, restaurants, an ice rink, a marine life centre, a miniature golf course, and even an indoor fairground with roller coasters. It has themed areas with attractions based around Chinese, European, and New Orleans themes.

The mall also has hotels and is so much of a destination in its own right that its website suggests taking a three-day stay at the hotel, with an itinerary for each day composed of activities to do purely within the mall itself.

**Source:** West Edmonton Mall (2015).

---

The example of the West Edmonton mall shows at least three examples of Disneyization. There is theming of some of the areas; there is hybrid consumption with different types of consumption in one place, such as retail, entertainment, and hotels; and with interactive service work in the various attractions within the mall, we can presume that performative labour takes place too. There is no merchandising of the mall as such—although a Disney store within the mall means that merchandising is not entirely absent!

Not all service and leisure organizations will exhibit all of the characteristics of Disneyization, and some will exhibit more than others; however, a common theme that we take forward is that these factors combine in different organizations in different ways as a means for the organization to create a particular **experience** for its consumers.

**Experience** Where consumption is of the organization itself rather than any product or service that it provides.

## From consuming products to consuming organizations: the organization as an experience

When we buy manufactured goods, such as a television, we don't actually see the work that has gone into making them. It is highly unlikely that we will have stood and watched the television being assembled in a factory—**production** took place in another place at another time, and our enjoyment of the product is none the worse for this.

**Production** The work done in an organization by the workers within that organization.

**Figure 16.1** The gap between production and consumption in manufacturing industries.

In manufacturing, production takes place in one particular place (the factory), whereas **consumption** of that product—using and enjoying the product—takes place elsewhere (the customer's home) and at a different time. There is a 'temporal and spatial buffer' (Korczynski and Ott, 2004: 576) between the labour performed in producing the item and the consumption of that item (see Figure 16.1).

**Consumption** The purchase and use by customers and clients of goods and services created by an organization.

At a Disney theme park, the product on offer is not a tangible good, such as a television; it is the experience of the time spent at the theme park which is consumed. The temporal and spatial buffer that existed with manufacturing has disappeared in service industries, such as Disney. The experience produced by the theme park *is consumed by the visitors at the same time and in the very same place*.

**Figure 16.2** Simultaneous production and consumption in the 'experience' of service and leisure organizations.

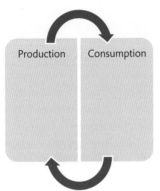

While there may be products sold in the theme park which were produced elsewhere, in terms of the experience that it provides, production and consumption are intertwined, both happening simultaneously (see Figure 16.2).

In that consumption takes place within the organization itself, a characteristic of many service and leisure organizations is that they are created as locations in their own right, to be experienced by consumers. As seen with the West Edmonton mall, shopping malls are destinations to be experienced for themselves rather than simply a place to shop. For Gottdiener (1998) the mall has to advertise itself as an attractive location or experience to compete with the town centre that it aims to replace and, increasingly, to compete with other shopping malls.

> As a result, almost every mall has an overarching motif that attempts to convey it as a unique and desirable location for its own sake.
>
> (Gottdiener, 1998: 80)

**Real life case:** the Black Country Living Museum

The Black Country Living Museum, in Dudley, England, is an outdoor museum where, brick-by-brick, buildings of historical significance from the surrounding area have been moved and set up—a church, a pub, a nailmaker, various shops, etc. The exhibits are working exhibits with which visitors can interact. So, visitors can have a drink in the pub, buy sweets from the confectionery shop, and ride on the working tram line within the museum. School parties can even experience Victorian-style teaching in the working classroom on the site.

**Source:** Black Country Living Museum (2015).

Museums are another type of organization that can be seen to be geared towards providing an experience. Featherstone (1991: 102) and Kirshenblatt-Gimblett (1998: 138) suggest that this is a shift in emphasis. Once museums concentrated on the product—think of dusty artefacts on shelves with 'do not touch' signs—but now they concentrate on the visitor 'experience'. People are encouraged to touch and interact with exhibits as part of that experience.

What organizations do you visit as a destination or experience in their own right?

## Controlling organizational realities

When we enter a theme park, museum, shopping mall, or similar organization, we are effectively leaving our everyday lives behind for a few hours and immersing ourselves in the experience that they create. It could be said that these organizations create their own particular 'realities', especially in a themed environment where that reality is meticulously created to match with the theme.

In fact, it is not just that organizations create their own realities: the experience that they create is so much *better* than the reality it is meant to imitate that it has been described as **hyper-reality** (Baudrillard, 1983; Eco, 1986). Referring to the painstaking recreation of a tropical rain forest at Disneyland, Eco states:

> A real crocodile can be found in the zoo, and as a rule it is dozing or hiding, but Disneyland tells us that faked nature corresponds much more to our daydream demands.        (Eco, 1986: 44)

We might expect something spectacular, better-than-reality, from a theme park, but the experience of something more mundane, such as a shopping centre, also aims to create something of a 'perfect world'. For example, in a town centre the weather can provide all manner of unpleasant surprises—rain, snow, and cold temperatures. In shopping centres, technology provides a constant perfect climate within its walls—much better than a 'real' climate outdoors (Ritzer, 2015: 87).

Technology and organizational control can also help to make the mall better than the world outside by reducing the instances of crime. Surveillance technology, such as closed circuit television (CCTV) cameras, along with private security forces are designed to ensure that the mall remains a safe space.

In such organizations, the environment is totally organized or 'climatized'—a 'total conditioning of actions and time' (Baudrillard, 1970: 23–4, author's translation). The better-than-perfect experience comes from very tight levels of organizational *control*:

> The shopping mall exerts great control over shops and shopkeepers. Before allowing shops to open, mall developers often must approve their design, logo, colours, and even names. Once open, mall managers proliferate rules and regulations and enforce them on shopkeepers. Security people inspect shops and take note of those that violate the rules (for example, opening or closing a few minutes early or late). Persistent violators may be expelled from the mall. Efforts are also made to exclude controversial groups.        (Ritzer, 1996: 116)

Bryman (1995: 181) notes how the themed experience and hyper-reality created by Disney theme parks also comes about as a result of tight levels of control over workers and over the organization itself. Many of the techniques used are familiar techniques of rational management, including manuals to control the work process, job roles delineated by different uniforms, and highly structured work routines. The magical experience of the theme park would seem to bear the rationalized hallmarks of Taylor and Ford.

**Hyper-reality**  An artificial reality which is better than anything that could be experienced in the reality that it aims to reproduce.

## Review questions

| | |
|---|---|
| **Describe** | What are the four main features of Disneyization? |
| **Explain** | How do organizations create 'hyper-real' environments? |
| **Analyse** | How does the nature of consumption differ between manufacturing and service sector products? |
| **Apply** | Think of a service organization that you use regularly—can you describe it in terms of the four features of Disneyization? |

# Work as a performance: the service sector labour process

### Real life case: the bar till

At one time in the UK, pubs tended to be small-scale 'locals', where the landlord and landlady would know most customers personally. Now many pubs are larger in size and part of national chains. The changing nature of pub work towards one that is more rationalized can be evidenced in the typical till found in such a busy establishment.

The till (or, as it is also known, EPoS, or electronic point of sale equipment) is very similar to that found in a fast-food restaurant (see Chapter 4). It has a button on the screen for each particular product, so there is no need to think about the prices for different items and add them up. The transaction becomes a matter of pushing three or four buttons for a round—the process of serving becomes much more efficient which is, of course, useful for a packed, busy bar.

The till also allows for control to be exerted over bar staff. A staff member swipes a card into the till before processing their transaction. This identifies the member of staff to the till (or, more precisely, to the computer system working behind the till); it may even inform the customer of this on the receipt—'you were served by X'. It also means that the number, time, and amount of transactions for each member of staff can be recorded and examined at a later date—just as in a call centre staff can be monitored by the data held on them in the computer system. So, even without a supervisor around, the data can reveal when people take breaks (which can be assumed by an absence of any transactions in that time period) and can also be used to compare the efficiency with which people work—the number of transactions they make per hour, for example. By recording the flow of drinks through the pumps, the system can even identify if staff are adding a free drink to a round for a friend.

**Sources:** Baker et al. (1998); Preece et al. (2002); ICRTouch (2015); Zonal Retail Data Systems (2015).

The bar till seems to be a perfect tool for the service sector manager wishing to bring elements of rationalization, as seen in Chapter 4, into their organization. It combines the efficiency of service of a fast-food restaurant with the surveillance and control of the call centre.

While rationalization is commonplace within the service and leisure sectors, the nature of work is much more than McDonaldization alone. Indeed, Korczynski and Ott (2004: 578) suggest that while rationalization is undoubtedly present in service work, there is little evidence of pure McDonaldization or Taylorism in practice; instead, rationalization is blended with customer-focused work.

It perhaps sounds obvious to say that service work should be customer-focused, but looking back at Figures 16.1 and 16.2 gives us an idea of why this is the case. In manufacturing work, the customer is distant from the worker on the assembly line: as long as the product is in good condition the customer has no interest in the worker's name, appearance, mannerisms, etc.

In a service organization, production and consumption take place at the same time. Workers in the service sector interact directly with customers—there is no distance in time or space between the work done and the consumption of that work. While a bar worker and a worker on an assembly line might both be subject to rationalization, a bar worker is also on show to the customers at the same time. Whether they are friendly, rude, well-groomed, or unkempt, they are a part of the customer's 'experience' of the organization.

Have you ever complained about the service you have received in an organization or maybe even not gone back to that organization because of bad service?

## Performative labour

In organizations such as the theme park, there is no tangible product to sell such as a television or a pint of beer; it is purely the experience that is consumed. Thus Disney views its staff as an important part of the experience that the organization creates, and exerts considerable control over their behaviour and appearance to ensure their 'performance' as a standardized 'product'.

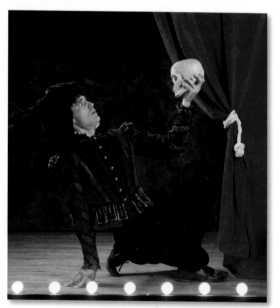

Performance time.

While rationalization exerts considerable control over workers at Disney, a further aspect of control over workers in service sector industries is shown in the final aspect of Disneyization—that of performative labour. This is where, in Disney and in other customer- and client-facing service industries, work is 'akin to a theatrical performance in which the workplace is construed as similar to a stage' Bryman (2004: 104). Work is a performance, and managers are the directors of that performance.

Performative labour draws together two strands of control over the service sector labour process, which we examine in the remainder of this chapter: emotional labour, where people control their behaviour and feelings in front of customers, and aesthetic labour, where workers adhere to particular requirements of dress, appearance, and comportment.

---

**Study skills: presentations**

Perhaps the closest thing to performance during a degree is when you have to give an assessed presentation, either individually or in a group. Of course, you need to be able to demonstrate your knowledge of the subject that you are presenting, but bear in mind that your presentation may be one of many that your tutor will have watched.

While you are not putting on a play or acting in the presentation, you can think about how you perform what you say as much as the words that you say. A student looking down into their notes and reading them out in a monotone will not engage the interest of the audience. A student who looks up, is confident, and speaks clearly will. If you can put across enthusiasm for the subject then it will be infectious.

Think about how your own lecturers present to you—what they do that engages you and that you can learn from (and likewise what they do that you should avoid!). And, as you read through the chapter, think about what lessons you can learn from emotional and aesthetic labour that you can use to further improve the impact of your presentation.

---

# The presentation of the self

Goffman (1959) applied metaphors of theatre and performance to analyse how people present themselves in different social situations, including the workplace. He noted how people put on different emotional and behavioural 'performances', including their use of dress, props, and appearance, depending on the situation.

For Goffman, a team refers to a set of individuals with a common interest—a group of workplace colleagues might be one such team. In life we are members of different teams at different times. Goffman suggested that in different teams we might offer a different 'presentation of the self', that is to say we may modify our behaviour and appearance accordingly.

Think about how you behave in different social circumstances—in a university seminar, in church, at work, at a rugby club social, etc. Do you act differently in these different situations? How do you *know* the appropriate performance to maintain in each?

Crucial to Goffman's (1959) work are three areas, which retain the theatrical metaphor:

- frontstage—where members of a team are involved in a performance and must maintain that performance
- backstage—where the team is out of view of the performance; the performance does not need to be maintained, but issues relating to the performance might be discussed among the team (similar to the wings or the rehearsal room in a theatre)
- outside—away from the situation completely.

It is not difficult to see how Goffman's theatrical metaphor resonates with the service industry; indeed, similar metaphors are even used in some service organizations. Disney, for example, refers to theme park workers as 'cast members' and speaks of **frontstage** areas as

**Frontstage** A theatrical metaphor to represent areas of the organization where workers are in contact with customers and clients.

being in front of theme park visitors and **backstage** areas being out of view of the visitors. Similarly, service organizations, such as cinemas or hotels, have 'front-of-house staff' who deal directly with customers and 'backroom staff' who work out of view of customers in offices or kitchens, for example.

We can thus make a direct link between Goffman's theatrical metaphors of society and the workplace, especially in the service sector:

- frontstage areas would be any areas where workers are facing and interacting with customers, and where some form of performance might be expected—at the counter, in the aeroplane cabin, on the gym floor, or on the phones in a call centre, for example

- backstage areas are in the workplace but out of view of customers—the offices, the staff room, the smoking area at the back of the building, or the galley in an aeroplane, for example

- outside areas would be away from work—at home, out with non-work friends; in other words, they represent private life rather than working life.

> **Backstage** A theatrical metaphor to represent areas of the organization where workers are out of view of customers and clients.

## Performance and the wage–labour relationship

It is worthwhile to outline here the specific meaning of labour as it applies to these performance aspects of work. Recall the following diagram from Chapter 3 which outlines the nature of the capitalist wage–labour relationship (Figure 16.3).

Workers receive a wage and, in return, provide their labour. So, labour has a specific meaning: it is that which is provided (or done) by workers in exchange for the wage paid to them. There are two types of labour with which we are familiar.

- Manual labour involves using physical abilities in return for the wage paid. It could be argued that Taylor and Ford's factory techniques relied on manual labour as they reduced work to simple, repetitive tasks.

- Intellectual labour is where a worker uses their knowledge, skill, or some other similar intellectual ability in order to carry out a task for which they are paid a wage.

While both of these types of labour might be required in service sector work, performative labour is where a particular emotional performance or standards of appearance are

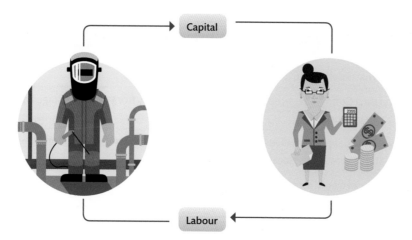

**Figure 16.3** The capitalist wage–labour relationship.

Capital

Labour

prescribed as part of what the worker does in return for their wage, or where there is an expectation that they will be performed as a part of the job.

So, while a member of bar staff may have to carry crates up from the cellar (physical labour) and operate till equipment (intellectual labour), they also have the additional burdens of smiling at customers (emotional labour) and adhering to a particular dress code (aesthetic labour). Performance is thus a further aspect of labour expected in exchange for the wage paid in service sector work.

## From the iron cage to the glass cage

Frontstage performances therefore become important to the organization—the service inter-action is a part of what the organization offers, and emotional and aesthetic performances of workers are a part of this. The emotional and aesthetic labour of the workers has a direct and immediate impact on the experience consumed by the customer *at the same time and in the same place*.

Gabriel (2005) adapts Weber's concept of the iron cage of society to take account of this immediate visibility of people's work. The iron cage (see Chapters 2 and 4) suggested that bureaucracy and rationalization were so commonplace that they trapped people in their monotonous routines. Ritzer (2015) later developed the iron cage metaphor to describe the prevalence of McDonaldization in contemporary society.

Gabriel's **glass cage** metaphor recognizes this iron cage aspect of rationalization in contemporary service work. The visibility of being behind glass equates to the visibility that rational forms of surveillance bring to the work that people do. The bar till, for example, records every transaction made by a worker and when it took place. The transparency of glass also refers to the further visibility of constantly being on show—doing service work in an organization is like being on display behind a glass cage.

On the one hand, this could be seen as a further level of control in the capitalist wage–labour relationship. Performative labour can be seen as an extra level of control, with emotional and aesthetic performances being demanded on top of rationalized efficiency as part of the wage–labour relationship.

However, as we will see with emotional labour, the nature of this part of the relationship, of performing a show front of stage, also creates spaces where resistance against that control may take place.

**Glass cage** Gabriel's metaphor to represent the visibility of workers in service sector organizations, both from the surveillance of rational organizational control and from the visibility of being 'on show' in front of customers and clients.

## Review questions

| **Describe** | What is performative labour? |
| **Explain** | Using Goffman's concepts, explain what is meant by front- and backstage areas of an organization |
| **Analyse** | How does performative labour affect the nature of the wage–labour relationship in the service sector labour process? |
| **Apply** | How can both aspects of the glass cage (rationalization and being on display) be seen in bar work? |

# Emotional labour

**Running case:** 'don't expect a tip'

'Get me a gin,' is the curt request from a customer later in the evening. When Jane Grimes has to change the optic, the customer, obviously at the end of a bad day, starts shouting: 'Come on, what type of amateurs are you? Get me my drink now.' Flustered, but trying not to show it, she serves the drink, smiles at the customer, and says: 'There you go, Sir, that will be £4.50 please.' The customer hands over the exact money and tells Grimes not to expect a tip. Her smile remains.

Anybody who has had to work in front of clients or customers will be familiar with the mantra that 'The customer is always right'. No matter how wrong, impatient, rude, or downright abusive the customer might be, you treat them as if they are right—the customer is king. You might want to shout or swear at the abusive customer, but these feelings and behaviours have to be suppressed—the expectation is that you will smile and remain pleasant.

You may have your own feelings that you have brought into work that particular day—personal events may have made you sad, upset, or angry. But, while in front of customers, you will again be expected to put these personal emotions into the background and perform the emotional display required by the organization.

Such a performance, where emotions are managed to project a particular set of feelings, potentially different to the feeling being held deeply within, is what Hochschild (1983) termed emotional labour, defining it as 'the management of feeling to create a publicly observable facial and bodily display [which] is sold for a wage' (Hochschild, 1983: 7).

**Research insight:** Emotional labour
Hochschild, A.R. 1983. *The managed heart: Commercialization of human feeling*. University of California Press: Berkeley.

Arlie Hochschild's concept of 'emotional labour' derived from her research into the work of air cabin crew. Hochschild noted how the smile of the air hostess was something that seemed to be 'bought' by the airline as part of the wages paid. Maintaining a particular emotional display—the smile—was a part of the wage–labour relationship as much as other aspects of the work of cabin crew, such as pushing trolleys and performing safety demonstrations.

Cabin crew are thus, when in front of passengers and throughout a flight, expected to maintain the appearance of a particular set of feelings—smiling and being pleasant to passengers, no matter how rude the passengers may be. This management of feeling and emotion as part and parcel of paid employment gives the title of Hochschild's (1983) text *The managed heart*.

The nature of cabin-crew work, where emotions and feelings have to be controlled in front of passengers as a part of the work done for wages, will be familiar to many people who have worked in customer-facing jobs. It is often characterized as retaining a smile in the face of the abusive customer, but there are a variety of ways in which workers might be expected to manage their emotions to give a particular form of emotional display (see Ward and McMurray, 2015, for some examples of the 'darker side' of emotional labour').

- *Smiling and being pleasant to customers.* This is the type of behaviour that people most associate with emotional labour—shop workers, bar staff, cabin crew, any job where workers maintain a smile and pleasant manner in front of customers, no matter how rude or abusive the customer may be.

- *Presenting an upbeat, motivational personality.* Gym instructors (Bryman, 2004: 120), tour reps (Guerrier and Adib, 2003), and teachers are all examples of workers who may have to put on an upbeat performance at work to motivate and interest others.

- *Presenting a respectful and sombre personality.* While emotional labour is often characterized as putting on a smile, in some work very different displays are needed. Nurses delivering bad news are discussed later in this chapter; funeral directors and social workers (Karabanow, 1999) are examples where, even if a worker is personally happy, they may need to manage emotions to put on a more serious display.

- *Remaining calm during tense situations.* Police officers and nightclub bouncers often have to deal with situations that could be inflamed easily. They may even be on the receiving end of verbal abuse or physical threats. Emotions have to be managed so as not to retaliate to such threats, but to stay calm and not let the situation get out of hand.

What other examples of work that requires emotional labour could you add to this list?

---

**Theory in context:** Fawlty Towers

To understand the concept of emotional labour, we could, perhaps, turn to an example of emotional labour *not* being performed. In the BBC hotel-based comedy *Fawlty Towers*, John Cleese plays hotel owner Basil Fawlty.

The comedy in the programme comes from a mis-match of our *expectations* and the actual *behaviours* within a hotel setting. We would *expect* a hotel owner to be pleasant and polite to guests, as these guests may bring repeat business or make recommendations to other people. If guests have a complaint, no matter how trivial or incorrect it may be, the management and hotel staff will deal with it politely and attempt to 'smooth over' the situation.

The actual *behaviour* in Fawlty Towers stands in marked contrast: Basil Fawlty is rude and will even shout at guests. It stands as an example of how not to perform emotional labour.

---

Visit the Online Resource Centre for a link to a clip of the show.

# Deep and surface acting

In that emotional labour involves putting on some form of act, it fits in with the performance and theatrical metaphors discussed earlier in this chapter. As customers, we may sometimes be well aware that an act is taking place. When we are encouraged to 'have a nice day' accompanied by a toothsome, sickly grin, it can feel fake and inauthentic.

In *The managed heart*, Hochschild (1983) noted that such a distinction between fake and authentic also exists in how emotional labourers themselves approach their work.

**Surface acting**
Emotional labour that is performed by workers conscious of the fact that they are engaged in an artificial performance.

- **Surface acting** is where the emotional display is fake and superficial—the smile and pleasantness are deliberately put on, like a mask. The worker is not acting as their 'authentic self' and, instead, is consciously acting and putting on a display in front of customers.

- **Deep acting** is, in Hochshild's words, where a worker is deceiving themselves as much as they are the customer. The feelings being displayed are much more authentic—the display is coming from within. This might mean that the worker is displaying their authentic feelings, or that they have taken on board the performance so much that it has become their authentic behaviour rather than a superficial performance.

Deep acting
Emotional labour
where the worker
internalizes and
believes in the
performance in which
they are engaged.

A distinction between the two is not necessarily clear cut—a receptionist might come across to customers as warm, genuine, and authentic but out of view in the back office they drop the mask and act as themselves. Being a better actor in front of customers does not necessarily mean that deep acting is being undertaken.

Furthermore, think of a situation where a nurse has to deliver bad news. On the one hand, if the nurse appeared superficial and artificial in delivering the news (i.e. surface acting), it could come across as crass and insensitive. A nurse would be expected to display genuine sensitivity and empathy in delivering such news, i.e. there is an expectation of acting with much more depth.

But this in itself is fraught with difficulties—if a nurse were to get emotionally involved at a deep level in all cases that they handled, it would have a detrimental effect on their own ability to cope with the job: the emotion would overwhelm them. There is thus a delicate balance between displaying deep emotional sensitivity but keeping this at such a surface level that it allows the nurse to remain unaffected while not appearing artificial.

Such difficulties in maintaining a balance of appropriate emotional performances, while maintaining a suitable distance so as not to be personally affected, means that the performance of emotional labour is often associated with stress.

## Stress, coping, and emotional labour

### Running case: 'all kicking off'

Simon Chance has arranged, through his football club directorship, some deals at the hotel for travelling away supporters. Jane Grimes can hear a set of supporters in the restaurant being drunk, loud, and generally abusive to the waiting staff—as if the waiters didn't get enough abuse from the head chef.

After dinner, the football party makes their way into the bar area. At first, the raucous behaviour—singing, chanting, and dancing on the table—is confined to their corner of the bar. Then, two of the party stagger up to the bar to buy a round.

As they slump against the bar, Grimes feels intimidated. They start to make lewd suggestions about what she might like to do once her shift has finished. She tries as hard as she can to smile and humour them, but, as it becomes obvious she will not be acquiescing to their requests, things turn nasty. Pointing at her, one of the men starts yelling at the top of his voice, shouting a stream of the worst insults and expletives possible.

Grimes can take it no longer, bursts into tears, and runs behind the bar into the staff room.

Imagine performing a job, day in, day out, where you are required to remain calm and pleasant in the face of abusive customers—a constant onslaught of unpleasant remarks, swearing, and even violent threats. How much of this could you take before you snapped back at the customer? How would you cope if you were not able to snap back for fear of how managers might react?

Visit the Online Resource Centre to listen to a recording of such a phone call in a call centre.

## Real life case: emotional labour in call centres

In a study of an airline sales call centre, Steve Taylor (1998) notes the difference between 'hard' and 'soft' targets that workers have to meet. Hard targets are the familiar numerical targets of calls handled per hour, for example, which can be monitored using the surveillance afforded by computerized monitoring of workers.

Soft targets relate to the way in which operators speak, and respond, to customers during calls. It is stated that agents should respond 'in a manner which upholds the commercial interests of Flightpath, rather than in a manner which expresses their own perception and feeling' (Taylor, 1998: 91). The targets can be monitored by listening into conversations—staff will be found out if they let their emotions get the better of them and shout or snap back at rude or abusive callers.

As described earlier, emotional labour often accompanies service sector jobs which are already subject to intensified forms of rationalization, such as the numerical targets in the case of the call centre. Pugliesi (1999: 134) describes this emotional labour as a 'hidden workload' on top of existing work.

Pugliesi (1999) further suggests that emotional labour is stressful, lowering job satisfaction and increasing psychological distress.

To what extent workers are expected to deal with unpleasant behaviour, even abuse, as part of their work, varies in different professions.

Korczynski and Bishop (2009) highlighted how workers in UK job centres faced regular threats, abuse, and often violence in their work. This, however, was 'normalized and routinized' (ibid.: 84) with neutral, euphemistic language used in training and by management—abusive customers became 'challenging customers', for example. At the same time, the workers were expected to perform emotional labour. Requirements to be helpful and friendly could be enforced by 'mystery shopper' visits.

In other cases, management might intervene more in protecting front-line staff. In UK railways stations, posters can be seen which uphold the right of staff to work 'without fear', stressing to passengers the unacceptability of abusive behaviour.

What responsibility do you think management have to help workers manage and cope with stress caused by performing emotional labour?

## Running case: backstage

Jane Grimes is in tears in the staff room, with a small group of staff gathered around to comfort her.

'Poor you,' said one of the bar staff. 'You're new, aren't you—not had anything like that before. Don't worry, you'll get used to it. You'll be able to keep that smile fixed pretty soon.'

'But why should I have to put up with that?' blubs Grimes. 'They were just horrible to me.'

'We shouldn't have to put up with it, but unfortunately we have to, otherwise we'd be out of a job,' is the reply. 'Look, we get no help on this from the management, so we have to help each other and help our-selves—don't let the punters get the better of us. When we are back here we can help each other and be ourselves—remember out there it's all an act.'

'Look over there,' says one of the bar staff, pointing at the now highly-inebriated man who had been making suggestive comments to Grimes earlier on, 'I mean, as if someone as gorgeous as you would go near him. He's in here a lot—we've all had those approaches from him. We're convinced that's a wig he wears.' Grimes peers through a gap in the staff room door to see another member of staff clearing glasses next to the supporter. She smiles at him as she takes the glass, then turns to the staff room, touches the top of her head as if to indicate a wig, and winks towards the others in the staff room.

Grimes starts to laugh and the women in the staff room join in, pulling apart the character of the football fan and imagining the inadequacies that lead him to behave in such a way. Feeling better, she thanks the other staff for helping her to cope.

'Don't worry,' replies one, 'we all have our ways of dealing with it.' 'Just remember,' adds another waitress, 'they have no idea who you are so don't take it personally. In fact, most of us put on an act, almost taking on a different personality in front of the punters. As long as you don't lose sight of who you are when you get back here then you'll be OK. Just think of yourself as an actor, and out there is your stage, and you can even begin to enjoy it, let alone cope with it.'

Rather than management helping workers to cope with the stress of emotional labour, a number of studies have shown how workers help each other on a more informal basis. Such emotional support among colleagues is often focused around camaraderie and the use of humour as a means of coping with the stress of such work (Bolton and Boyd, 2003; Bolton, 2005).

- Hochschild (1983) noted the use of 'upbeat banter' among cabin crew when in 'backstage' areas, out of sight of passengers. This may be to offer support to each other or may be to make jokes at the expense of passengers to help 'laugh off' the stresses of abusive or rude behaviour.

- Korczynski (2003: 58) studied emotional labour in call centres and used the term **communities of coping** to describe informal, backstage groupings that provide mutual emotional support and which become a 'crucial part of the social relations of the service workplace'.

  > **Communities of coping** Mutual support among co-workers to cope with stress and other negative factors of emotional labour.

- Livesy (2000) notes similar forms of 'reciprocal emotion management'—colleagues listening and offering emotional support—among paralegals in private law firms.

There would seem again to be a distinction between 'frontstage', where workers are in front of customers and required to perform emotional labour, and 'backstage', where workers are not on show and are thus more at liberty to 'be themselves'. However, as we will see, this distinction between frontstage and backstage is not always so clear cut.

## Employability skills: service sector experience

In Chapter 11 we examined transferable skills and how identifying such skills from your experience of work can enhance your employability. For many students, the service sector will be the main experience of work undertaken, with part-time and vacation jobs in bars, shops, and the like. Think ▶

▶ about the extent to which skills of emotional and aesthetic labour can be shown as transferable skills on your CV—dealing with people, for example. Furthermore, in interviews you may be asked to give examples of where you have solved a problem or worked under pressure—aspects of emotional labour that you have encountered in your own work may provide you with examples that you can present as evidence for these.

# Emotional labour and emotion management

The management of our emotions is not confined to what happens in the workplace when serving customers. When a casual acquaintance passes in the street and enquires how we are, we may smile and say 'very well, thank you', rather than reveal all of our tales of woe.

Hochschild (1983) made a distinction between emotional labour and other, wider forms of emotion work or **emotion management**. When saying 'very well' to an acquaintance, we are engaging in the management of our emotions, but we are not performing emotional labour—the reason being that we are not receiving a wage for that particular performance.

**Emotion management** Any management of personal emotional displays inside or outside of a working relationship.

Earlier in the chapter we saw performative labour, of which emotional labour is an example, located within the capitalist wage–labour relationship. Hochschild, too, located emotional labour within this relationship—it is work performed *specifically and explicitly for a wage*.

Emotion management is a general term for the control of emotions, of which emotional labour is one specific type that has an exchange value—it attracts a wage (Callahan and McCollum, 2002). The backstage banter and mutual coping strategies seen previously are a form of emotion management, but they are not emotional labour as they are not done for a wage. However, it is not a clear-cut distinction to say that emotional labour is that which takes place frontstage and emotion management is a coping strategy which takes place backstage.

Bolton and Boyd (2003), drawing from Goffman's earlier terminology, use the term 'presentational self' to describe the sort of emotion management that takes place not only backstage, but occasionally front of stage too—the nudges and winks that workers use to help each other cope with stresses of emotional labour: 'A put down comment, a secret smile—these are small, but important moments . . . offering important intervals in organizational control for the maintenance of organizational identities' (Bolton and Boyd, 2003: 102).

While such emotion management does not attract a wage, it does, nevertheless, play a part in the wage–labour relationship in the sense that it affects the balance of control in that relationship. The organization 'no longer controls the emotional agenda' (Bolton and Boyd, 2003: 291).

While management may wish to control workers into particular emotional performances in exchange for a wage, the emotion management of the workers can be seen as a form of coping with stress and, furthermore, as a form of collective resistance against these organizationally prescribed 'feeling rules' (Bolton and Boyd, 2003).

Taylor and Tyler (2000), like Hochschild, studied air cabin crew and noted a number of individualized acts of coping and resistance. Some attendants spoke of faking smiles, deliberately maintaining a personal level of distance behind the look that the organization required of them—a psychological act of distancing in order to maintain their own identities.

The suggestion is that workers maintain a degree of control, even when frontstage, such that control of emotions by management is not total.

By bringing in the role of emotion work in backstage areas, and its slippage into the behaviour and gestures of the team while in frontstage areas, we see that the boundaries between frontstage and backstage are not necessarily permanent. As Goffman (1959: 78) states: 'All the world is not, of course, a stage, but the crucial ways in which it is are not easy to specify.'

## Review questions

| | |
|---|---|
| **Describe** | What is meant by emotional labour? |
| **Explain** | What is the difference between deep and surface acting? |
| **Analyse** | How can emotional labour can be used as form of resistance by workers? |
| **Apply** | How does backstage emotion management help workers in the bar at Junction Hotel cope with the stress of their work? |

# Aesthetic labour

## Running case: dress code

**From:** simon_chance@junctionhotel.co.uk

**To:** bar_staff@junctionhotel.co.uk; restaurant_staff@junctionhotel.co.uk; reception_staff@junctionhotel.co.uk; porters@junctionhotel.co.uk

**Subject:** New uniforms

Dear colleagues

I am writing to you all as valued members of hotel staff, particularly as you are our front-line stars, the people that are on show to our customers. I know that your standards of service are great, but now we really want you to look the part, too.

Tomorrow, new uniforms will arrive for all customer-facing staff. I hope that you will like them and, when wearing the Junction Hotel uniform, feel that you are a living, breathing part of the brand itself.

It's not just the uniform which is important here—it's the way you are the look of the hotel. Service is sleek and professional, polite and unhurried, yet efficient.

May I here remind you of other aspects of our dress code which have been slipping recently, but which are important in presenting the look of Junction Hotel that you are here to perform.

- Women: wear make-up to be elegant—it is there to enhance your professional image. Too little and you look unkempt, but, at the same time, don't lay it on with a trowel. Hair is to be in a neat, professional style—nothing too extreme in colour or styling. Some jewellery looks good, but, as with the make-up, not too much.

- Men: hair should be neatly styled and short—full stop. Facial hair is absolutely discouraged. This is a slick, luxurious hotel, not a gathering of geography teachers. No jewellery is the preferred option—it is a distraction.
- For both men and women it goes without saying that basic levels of hygiene are required—nails and the like are to be clipped to appropriately professional lengths. And remember—absolutely no tattoos to be on show at all.

You will be called out from shifts tomorrow to collect your new uniforms—wear them proudly and exude the Junction Hotel image throughout your working day!

Best wishes,

Simon

Performance aspects of service work involve not just the management of emotions, but of appearance too—if work is like a stage, then costume is a part of the performance. An example might be dress codes, which specify what workers should wear, and other aspects of appearance, such as hair or fingernail length.

Witz et al. (2003) coined the phrase 'aesthetic labour' to describe those demands upon a worker's appearance which form part of the wage–labour relationship—just as there are demands on emotional performances front of stage in service industries, so it is that workers are also expected to dress and look the part. However, aesthetic labour goes beyond surface appearance—clothes and grooming—to bodily movements and comportment, almost the way that the look and image of an organization is performed.

## Workplace dress codes

Uniforms are common in many workplace environments. We might not think of a police officer, a professional footballer, or a nurse as adhering to a dress code, but they are being instructed what to wear while undertaking paid employment. At the most basic level, uniforms are thus an aspect of aesthetic labour.

**Dress code** Standards of dress and appearance prescribed by an organization to its workers.

However, **dress codes** often go further than just providing a particular set of clothes to wear. They provide guidance as to how a uniform should be supplemented with particular aspects of grooming. Thus, Lainsbury (2000), quoted in Bryman (2004: 124), notes appearance standards that might supplement uniforms at Disneyland Paris:

We have appearance standards that are a condition of being hired. For men it means no facial hair, a conservative haircut with no hair over the ears or the collar, no earrings, no exposed tattoos, and no jeans. For women, no extremes in dying hair or in makeup, and no long fingernails. We want a conservative, professional look; we want our employees to be warm, outgoing and sincere. We don't want guests to be distracted by oddities or mannerisms of the cast members.

With these conditions, would you be eligible to be employed at Disneyland Paris?

Even without there being a specified uniform, guidance on the type of clothing to wear, as well as grooming standards, might be given. This might be in routine service work or in professional jobs where workers deal with clients.

## Real life case: UBS dress code

Swiss bank UBS hit the news after publishing a 44-page dress code (BBC News, 2010), giving advice on appearance to its client-facing staff, both male and female. The guide was notable for its precise attention to detail (Bolshaw, 2010; *The Guardian*, 2010a). It also outlines reasons for a dress code, suggesting that the UBS dress code is there to communicate the bank's professional values and culture (*The Guardian*, 2010a).

Such a professional image would be conveyed by women wearing a plain tailored suit in dark charcoal, black, or dark blue, with a white blouse or shirt (*The Guardian*, 2010a). The code then goes into detail on the length of skirt (it should be mid-knee length) and how the jacket should remain smooth when the wearer is seated and should not rise up when walking (*The Guardian*, 2010a).

Further advice within the code, among many other points, suggests:

- shoes should fit properly as tight shoes create a 'twisted smile' (BBC News, 2010)

- wristwatches should be worn to signal trustworthiness and punctuality (*The Daily Telegraph*, 2011)

- glasses should be kept clean for the sake of optimal vision (*The Daily Telegraph*, 2011)

- detailed advice on how to apply make-up and the type of perfume to wear (*The Daily Telegraph*, 2011).

After giving advice on other pertinent topics, such as maintaining fresh breath, the code turns its attention to men. A similar professional style of dress is encouraged, with daily shaving recommended, and certainly no stubble over three days old (Bolshaw, 2010). Detailed instructions, including a diagram, on how to put on a tie were also included, with advice that a tie should complement the bone structure of the face (Kellaway, 2010).

The extent of detail in the dress code led to negative press coverage. UBS stated that it would review the code and, while a dress code for men, for example, of dark suit, white shirt, and red tie would remain, the extent of detail of other recommendations would be reviewed (BBC News, 2011; *The Daily Telegraph*, 2011).

Why do you think this dress code attracted so much negative publicity? Do you think this was deserved or do you think the dress code is useful?

While dress codes can set standards and advice for workplace appearance, they may also be used both to *preclude* people from gaining employment and *exclude* people from current employment. Nickson et al. (2003: 193) give a list of reasons for dismissal from work or the refusal of employment in the first place. They included a man refused bar employment for having a ponytail, people being dismissed for appearing too old, and a designer boutique manager not employing women who wore larger than a dress size 16. Such cases often form the basis of legal action.

- In the USA a woman employed in a property firm took action after claiming to have been sacked for refusing to dye her grey hair and wear 'younger, trendy suits' (Pilkington, 2011).

- In the upmarket Harrods store in London, a female member of staff took legal action after being sacked for refusing to wear make-up in line with the store dress code (Davies, 2011).

Dress codes thus make up an initial aspect of aesthetic labour. As we will see later in the chapter, often these requirements impinge unequally on women, as do the standards of appearance by which they are judged compared with those applied to men.

## Aesthetic skills and embodiment

While dress and appearance form a part of aesthetic labour, Witz et al. (2003), who originally coined the term, suggested that it is about more than just surface 'costume'. Rather, aesthetic labour is about how we 'embody' deep down a particular 'look' or aesthetic.

The suggestion is that service work requires more than the robotic fast-food worker repeating phrases at the till. Service work involves a lot of feeling in the interaction: for example, in a hotel or restaurant the interaction is judged a lot more, and it is in movements and looks, as well as costumes, that this is demonstrated—it comes from much deeper within the body.

---

**Theory in context:** Pierre Bourdieu and habitus

**Embodied dispositions/ habitus** Our natural way of acting and reacting—a deeply held repertoire of instinctive behaviours.

The idea of embodiment, or **embodied dispositions**, derives from Pierre Bourdieu (1984), whose concept of **habitus** described how aspects of our social being are deeply ingrained and are manifested in such things as our dispositions—the way we instinctively act and react in social situations. This is not just a product of the feeling and emotional mind, nor reducible to a product of learning—it is a product of much deeper levels of socialization.

Bourdieu's work is most strongly associated with social class. He suggests that our upbringing creates deeply embodied markers of class that are shown in our mannerisms and dispositions. It is when we try to adopt the mannerisms of a different class group that we betray our background.

You may hear people pour scorn on people for being 'new money'—lottery winners or self-made business people, for example. The implication is while they have the money, they do not have the 'breeding'—the tastes and mannerisms associated with the upper class. Despite having the money being associated with the upper class they give away their working class origins in their tastes and behaviours.

Such examples illustrate the idea of habitus—the social signs of class are so ingrained that it is difficult to achieve mobility between the classes while not betraying class origins in mannerisms and behaviour: in our embodied dispositions.

---

The concept of aesthetic labour, as outlined by Witz et al. (2003), suggests that aesthetic labourers do more than put on an act: they begin to embody the dispositions as demanded of them by their workplace.

---

**Real life case:** *Ladette to Lady*

The idea of whether or not people can adopt and embody the appearance, behaviour, and mannerisms of a different class is tested in television 'reality' programmes such as *Ladette to Lady* (ITV/RTF Media) or *Australian Princess* (Network 10/Granada Productions).

The concept of such programmes is that a group of women whose behaviour is deemed to be loud, raucous, uncouth, and of a lower class, is taken through a set of tasks which train them to adopt

▶ the mannerisms of the upper class. The competition is to see which of the contestants does this the most convincingly.

The degree of embodiment of class-related habitus is shown in the range of tasks and instruction that the contestants receive—dress, speech, and deportment (posture, walking, getting in and out of cars, etc.), for example. Using habitus we could debate what is achieved at the end of such a series. Has the winning contestant fully embodied the behaviours of a different class, or are they simply putting on the best act—a form of class transvestism where the surface appearance is adopted, but the mannerisms do not really reach deep down?

Think of nightclub bouncers. They don't just have to dress the part—wearing a dark suit and tie maybe; a key skill of their job is that they also have to *embody* the part. Thus we would not only expect a bouncer to have certain physical characteristics—emphasizing size and strength— but we would also expect them to 'carry' that body in a certain way, with an authoritative demeanour. Such a demeanour would also be carried through in interactions—the way in which a situation is responded to, for example. In the face of a fight, a calm authority can be displayed through bodily movements and mannerisms as much as words. Of course, such a performance also links with emotional labour, as described earlier. The bouncer would be expected to remain calm, even if others were in a heightened emotional state and, perhaps, being abusive.

Can you think of any other jobs where you would have expectations of the appropriate demeanour that a worker would display?

The suggestion of Witz et al. is that a similar set of embodied dispositions are expected more and more in service work—workers are expected to embody the image or 'look' of the company in their actions and movements. Workers arrive with a set of 'embodied dispositions'— those which are desirable will have been encouraged, for instance, through imagery in recruitment advertising. Such dispositions are never a completed project and so, through training, workers are 'corporately made up' (Witz et al., 2003: 37)—trained not just in appearance and social/emotional interaction, but also in the style of the service encounter or 'specific modes of embodiment' (ibid.: 44). Thus, the workers themselves become part of the organizational aesthetic that is presented to customers, part of the 'experience' created by service and leisure sector organizations as examined earlier in the chapter.

This embodied notion of aesthetic labour draws both on Bourdieu, to show the deep nature of embodied dispositions, and Goffman, to demonstrate how these are presented in 'action' when front of stage.

Nickson et al. (2003) note specific class issues in this type of aesthetic labour in service encounters, namely that the types of dispositions sought are increasingly those typical of the middle class. In areas where manufacturing industry has declined, those made unemployed, generally from a working-class background, have found themselves at a disadvantage in gaining employment in service work, where it is the characteristics of students from middle-class backgrounds performing part-time service work which are valued more by employers.

Class is not the only area where aesthetic labour has a disproportionate impact. In the following section we see how both emotional and aesthetic labour have a different impact when gender is considered.

## Review questions

| | |
|---|---|
| **Describe** | What is meant by aesthetic labour? |
| **Explain** | How does aesthetic labour go beyond surface-level appearance to embodied dispositions? |
| **Analyse** | How might aesthetic labour exclude people from certain jobs? |
| **Apply** | What dress and appearance codes have you had to follow, both in work and elsewhere? |

# Performative labour and gender

### Running case: 'sexing up'

Staff reactions to the new uniforms are mixed. The receptionists have business suit outfits, whereas in the bar and restaurant women are expected to wear outfits described by one waitress as 'a bit revealing'.

'Lucky you,' replies a receptionist, 'you get to be feminine, do yourself up a bit. We have to stand behind reception looking like we're working in a bank.' 'No, lucky you,' replies the waitress, 'those customers are like rampant tom-cats at the best of times—we're just going to be objects for their desires in these outfits.'

In contrast, the male staff in all areas have the same outfit: a regular fitting shirt, trousers and tie, with a jacket for any staff on duty in the reception area—certainly not an outfit that could also be described as 'revealing'.

In the bar, the first shift wearing the new uniform starts. While the male bar staff are allowed to get on with their work, Simon Chance calls Jane Grimes over. 'Come on love, do the outfit some justice,' he says in an encouraging tone. 'Go and have a bit of banter with them—it will make their night. You've got the outfit—go and sex it up a bit with them.'

Grimes has had enough—she already has to deal with the unpleasant behaviour of customers that often borders on harassment, and now she is expected to positively encourage it. She removes her name badge and throws it on to the floor in front of Simon Chance. 'I quit,' she shouts. 'I thought I had come to work in a hotel, but it seems like I'm working in a brothel!'

Statistically, service work is gendered (Kerfoot and Korczynski, 2005: 389) and the types of performative labour demanded in service work suggest that the burden of emotional and aesthetic labour impinges unequally on women rather than men.

 Are there any jobs where you would more than likely expect the person doing that job to be one gender rather than another?

For Steve Taylor (1998) the increase of women in the service workforce has been paralleled by an increase in emotional labour. As Hochschild suggests:

> Schooled in emotion management at home, women have entered in disproportionate numbers those jobs that call for emotional labour outside the home.
> (1983: 181)

Within the wage–labour relationship, emotional labour is not rewarded financially to the same extent as other workplace competencies. A worker might expect a qualification, such as a degree, to be rewarded financially as part of the wage–labour exchange, but emotional skills seem to be considered merely a natural part of being female, learned as a part of growing up. Women are employed as 'women' with various assumed natural resources (Adkins and Lury, 1999), but these resources are not rewarded in the market place.

As with emotional labour, many of the requirements of aesthetic labour seem to impinge more on women. Studies on appearance at work have focused on how it is often an unrewarded burden that falls upon women as part of a perceived 'natural femininity', an embodied knowledge, or habitus, about what 'feminine' behaviour and aesthetics entails. Taylor and Tyler (2000: 86) note how, in addition to norms of feminine 'aesthetically pleasing' appearance, flight attendants' emotional work in caring for and interacting with people were seen as 'natural' feminine abilities or as 'women's work'.

## Gender and sexual commodification

Furthermore, aesthetic labour, with its concerns with appearance, can lead to demands which lead to the sexualization and objectification of women in service work. Sexual attractiveness becomes a part of what is expected in return for a wage; in other words, sex sells. Examples of such uneven demands between the genders in different jobs include:

- emphasis on the physical attractiveness of (female) betting shop cashiers, enhanced by the uniform, in the face of (mainly male) clients (Filby, 1992)

- in tourist and hotel industries, standards of attractiveness may even be stipulated in person specifications in job advertisements, but tend to apply only to female employees (Adkins, 1995)

- grooming and weight checks being performed regularly on air cabin crew, but only on female staff (Tyler and Abbott, 1998).

In her original work, Hochschild (1983: 181) noted how female flight attendants were expected to embody both 'motherly' emotional qualities and more appearance-bound 'sexual' qualities. Or, as Tyler and Abbott (1998: 440) state more bluntly, the air stewardess combines three emotional, aesthetic, and sexually-commodified roles—'part mother, part servant, part tart.' Hochschild repeats a quote from one air hostess in her original study:

> You have a married man with three kids getting on a plane and suddenly they feel anything goes. It's like they leave that reality on the ground, and you fit into their fantasy as some geisha girl.
>
> (Hochschild, 1983: 93)

In such professions where smiles, ego massaging, and 'entering into the spirit' take place, Adkins suggest that women are being expected, as part of their paid work, to enter into a form of 'sexual servicing' of men. This involves not only maintaining an attractive appearance and complying with a dress code, but also engaging in sexualized jokes and banter, or 'giving men what they want' (1985: 133). In this respect, Adkins states that women become **sexually commodified**—it is part of the 'arrangement of service labour' (Adkins, 2000: 207). Brewis and Linstead (2000: 172) suggest that in some areas of service work, women may 'genuinely prostitute' themselves.

**Sexually commodified** The sexual attractiveness or desirability of a worker is used as part of the work they perform for customers or clients.

**Real life case:** Hooters

The marketing of theme restaurant Hooters is based around the attractiveness and sex appeal of the 'Hooters Girls'. This is stated on their own website, where they suggest that 'The element of female sex appeal is prevalent in the restaurants, and the company believes the Hooters Girl is as socially accept-able as a Dallas Cowboy cheerleader, Sports Illustrated swimsuit model, or a Radio City Rockette' (quoted in Ferrell and Hartline, 2011: 520). However, this aspect of marketing female sex appeal has led to protests and criticism when new Hooters restaurants have been proposed in both the UK and the USA (MSNBC, 2006; Bindel, 2008; Brown, 2008; *The Guardian*, 2010b; Walker, 2014).

The issue revolves around the role of the 'Hooters Girls', waitresses who are expected to wear a re-vealing outfit (MSNBC, 2006) based on the image of an American cheerleader. A contract from Hooters in the USA was leaked on to the Internet, which emphasized just how much such Hooters girls were expected to see their 'sex appeal' as a part and parcel of their everyday job for which they are paid, including signing an acknowledgement that they accept an amount of joking, banter, and sexual in-nuendo based upon this (Hyde, 2008; Bindel, 2008; Walker, 2014).

It is this explicit drafting of sexualized appearance and sex appeal into the labour process that angers protestors, with one commentator (Bindel, 2008) suggesting that the sexualized atmosphere is more akin to a 'strip club' than a restaurant.

Hooters, on their website, disagree with this, noting a vigorous anti-harassment policy. Further-more, they suggest that the marketing or use of sex appeal in work is justified and not limited to Hooters: 'Claims that Hooters exploits attractive women are as ridiculous as saying the NFL exploits men who are big and fast. Hooters Girls have the same right to use their natural female sex appeal to earn a living as do super models Cindy Crawford and Naomi Campbell. To Hooters, the women's rights movement is important because it guarantees women have the right to choose their own careers, be it a Supreme Court Justice or Hooters Girl' (quoted in *The Guardian*, 2010b; and Ferrell and Hartline, 2011).

Do you think that it is legitimate for a company to expect people to perform the type of work described at Hooters for a wage?

While Hooters might be a one-off case, women's aesthetic and emotional performances are commodified in frontstage service work, with differing degrees of sexualization required as part of the wage–labour relationship, in a way that is not expected of men.

Review questions

| | |
|---|---|
| **Describe** | What is meant by sexual commodification in service work? |
| **Explain** | To what extent are expectations for emotional and aesthetic labour placed more on women than they are on men? |
| **Analyse** | What do you understand by Brewis and Linstead's (2000) statement that some women 'genuinely prostitute' themselves in service work? |
| **Apply** | Are there jobs where emotional and aesthetic labour are expected mainly of men? |

# Chapter summary

This chapter has examined emotional and aesthetic 'performances' that take place in customer-facing service work in order to contribute to the 'experience' that is consumed in many service sector organizations. Such work sits alongside rational management techniques as part of the service sector labour process. Both rationalized working techniques and performances where the worker is 'on show' are aspects of the service sector working relationship for which a wage is paid. Such performative labour creates inequalities in terms of class and gender, for example, and can be seen as an extra element of control over workers by management. At the same time, it is also an area where worker resistance, which starts with strategies of coping in backstage areas of the organization, can find its way into frontstage workplace performances.

## Further reading

Bryman, A. 2004. *The Disneyization of society*. Sage: London.
Covers all aspects of Disneyization; the chapter on performative labour looks at both emotional and aesthetic labour.

Grugulis, I. 2007. *Skills, training and human resource development: A critical text*. Palgrave Macmillan: Basingstoke.
Chapter 6 covers emotional and aesthetic labour from a workplace and worker perspective.

Nickson, D., Warhurst, C., and Cullen, A.M. 2003. Bringing in the excluded? Aesthetic labour, skills and training in the 'new' economy. *Journal of Education and Work* 16(2): 185–203.
A case study of how aesthetic labour excludes certain sections of the workforce from service sector work.

Adkins, L. 1995. *Gendered work: Sexuality, family and the labour market*. Open University Press: Buckingham.
Two service sector case studies, from a hotel and a theme park, which show the uneven impact of service work on women.

## References

Adkins, L. 1995. *Gendered work: Sexuality, family and the labour market*. Open University Press: Buckingham.

Adkins, L. 2000. Mobile desire: Aesthetics, sexuality and the 'lesbian' at work. *Sexualities* 3(2): 201–18.

Adkins, L., and Lury, C. 1999. The labour of identity: Performing identities, performing economies. *Economy and Society* 28(4): 598–614.

Baker, M., Wild, M., and Sussmann, S. 1998. Introducing EPOS in Bass Taverns: A report of the case and an exploration of some of the issues. *International Journal of Contemporary Hospitality Management* 10(1): 16–23.

Baudrillard, J. 1970. *La société de consommation: Ses mythes, ses structures*. Denoël: Paris.

Baudrillard, J. 1983. *Simulations*. Semiotext(e) Inc.: New York.

BBC News 2010. UBS dress code scrutinizes staff underwear, 17 December. Available at: http://www.bbc.co.uk/news/business-12023033

BBC News 2011. UBS to revise 44-page dress code. 17 January. Available at: http://www.bbc.co.uk/news/business-12207296

Beardsworth, A., and Bryman, A. 1999. Late modernity and the dynamics of quasification: The case of the themed restaurant. *Sociological Review* 47(2): 228–57.

Bindel, J. 2008. It's more like a strip club than a restaurant. *The Guardian*, 11 April. Available at:

http://www.guardian.co.uk/lifeandstyle/2008/apr/11/women.business

Black Country Living Museum 2015. Available at: http://www.bclm.co.uk (last accessed 20 August 2015).

Bolshaw, L. 2010. La DressCode revisited. *Financial Times*, 23 December. Available at: http://blogs.ft.com/women-at-the-top/2010/12/20/la-dresscode-revisited/#axzz2DLktq GZ6

Bolton, S. 2005. *Emotion management in the workplace*. Palgrave Macmillan: Basingstoke.

Bolton, S.C., and Boyd, C. 2003. Trolley dolly or skilled emotion manager? Moving on from Hochschild's Managed Heart. *Work, Employment and Society* 17(2): 289–308.

Bourdieu, P. 1984. *Distinction: A social critique of the judgement of taste*. Harvard University Press: Cambridge, MA.

Brewis, J., and Linstead, S. 2000. The worst thing is the screwing (2): Context and career in sex work. *Gender, Work and Organization* 7(3): 168–80.

Brown, J. 2008. Hooters: Over the top, underdressed and over here. *The Independent*, 12 April. Available at: http://www.independent.co.uk/life-style/food-and-drink/features/hooters-over-the-top-underdressed-and-over-here-808160.html

Bryman, A. 1995. *Disney and his worlds*. Routledge: London, New York.

Bryman, A. 2004. *The Disneyization of society*. Sage: London.

Callahan, J.L., and McCollum, E.E. 2002. Obscured variability: The distinction between emotion work and emotional labor. In: Rafaeli, A., Ashkanasy, N.M., Zerbe, W.J., and Hartel, C.E.J. (eds) *Managing emotions in the workplace*. Sharpe: Armonk, NY, pp. 219–31.

*Daily Telegraph*. 2011. Swiss bank UBS changes much-mocked dress-code. 17 January. Available at: http://www.telegraph.co.uk/finance/newsbysector/banksandfinance/8265124/Swiss-bank-UBS-changes-much-mocked-dress-code.html

Davies, C. 2011. Harrods 'ladies' code' drives out sales assistant. *The Guardian*, 1 July.

Eco, U. 1986. *Travels in hyper-reality: Essays*. Harcourt Brace Jovanovich: San Diego.

Featherstone, M. 1991. *Consumer culture and postmodernism*. Sage: London.

Ferrell, O.C., and Hartline, M.D. 2011. *Marketing Strategy*, 5th edn. South-Western Cengage Learning: Mason, OH.

Filby, M.P. 1992. The figures, the personality and the bums: Service work and sexuality. *Work, Employment and Society* 6(1): 23–42.

Gabriel, Y. 2005. Glass cages and glass palaces: Images of organization in image-conscious times. *Organization* 12(1): 9–27.

Goffman, E. 1959. *The presentation of self in everyday life*. Doubleday: Garden City, NY.

Gottdiener, M. 1998. Themed environments of everyday life: Restaurants and malls. In: Berger, A.A. (ed.) *The postmodern presence: Readings on postmodernism in American culture and society*. Alta Mira Press: Walnut Creek, CA, pp. 74–87.

Guerrier, Y., and Adib, A. 2003. Work at leisure and leisure at work: A study of the emotional labour of tour reps. *Human Relations* 56(11): 1399–417.

Hochschild, A.R. 1983. *The managed heart: Commercialization of human feeling*. University of California Press: Berkeley.

Hyde, M. 2008. Buffalo duck wings and a dash of orange tempt Beijing palates. *The Guardian*, 12 August.

ICRTouch 2015. EPoS systems for pubs and bars. Available at: http://www.icrtouch.com/epos-solutions/icrtouch-pubs-bars (last accessed 20 August 2015).

Karabanow, J. 1999. When caring is not enough: Emotional labor and youth shelter workers. *Social Service Review* 73(3): 340–57.

Kellaway, L. 2010. Better to waste time at the office. *Financial Times*, 19 December. Available at: http://www.ft.com/cms/s/0/6240fe56-0a30-11e0-84bc-00144feabdc0.html#axzz2DLkxbaax

Kerfoot, D., and Korczynski, M. 2005. Gender and service: New directions for the study of 'front-line' service work. *Gender, Work and Organization* 12(5): 387–99.

Kirshenblatt-Gimblett, B. 1998. *Destination culture: Tourism, museums and heritage*. University of California Press: Berkeley, Los Angeles.

Korczynski, M. 2003. Communities of coping: Collective emotional labour in service work. *Organization* 10(1): 55–79.

Korczynski, M., and Bishop, V. 2009. Abuse, violence and fear on the front line: Implications of the rise of the enchanting myth of consumer sovereignty. In: Fineman, S. (ed.) *The emotional organization: Passions and power*. Blackwell Publishing: Oxford, pp. 74–87.

Korczynski, M., and Ott, U. 2004. When production and consumption meet: Cultural contradictions and the enchanting myth of customer sovereignty. *Journal of Management Studies* 41(4): 575–99.

MSNBC 2006. Hooters to change—but not what works, 14 December. Available at: http://www.msnbc.msn.com/id/16209446/ns/business-us_business/t/hooters-change-not-what-works/#.ULOvZ2f_1M4

Nickson, D., Warhurst, C., and Cullen, A.M. 2003. Bringing in the excluded? Aesthetic labour, skills and training in the 'new' economy. *Journal of Education and Work* 16(2): 185–203.

Office for National Statistics (ONS) 2015. *Index of Services: May 2015*. Available at: http://www.ons.gov.uk/ons/rel/ios/index-of-services/may-2015/index.html (last accessed 20 August 2015).

Pilkington, E. 2011. Woman 'sacked for having grey hair'. *The Observer*, 10 July.

Preece, D., Steven, V., and Steven, G. 2002. Quality management in public house retailing. In: Antony, J., and Preece, D. (eds) *Understanding, managing and implementing quality: Frameworks, techniques and cases*. Routledge: London, pp. 195–210.

Pretes, M. 1995. Postmodern tourism: The Santa Claus industry. *Annals of Tourism Research* 22(1): 1–15.

Pugliesi, K. 1999. The consequences of emotional labor: Effects on work stress, job satisfaction, and well-being. *Motivation and Emotion* 23(2):125–54.

Ritzer, G. 1996. *The McDonaldization of society: An investigation into the changing character of contemporary social life, revised edn*. Pine Forge Press: Thousand Oaks, CA.

Ritzer, G. 2015. *The McDonaldization of society*, 8th edn. Pine Forge Press: Thousand Oaks, CA.

Taylor, S. 1998. Emotional labour and the new workplace. In: Thompson, P., and Warhurst, C. (eds) *Workplaces of the future*. Palgrave Macmillan: Basingstoke, pp. 84–103.

Taylor, S., and Tyler, M. 2000. Emotional labour and sexual difference in the airline industry. *Work, Employment and Society* 14(1): 77–95.

*The Guardian* 2010a. UBS demands 'well groomed' employees, right down to their pants. 17 December 2010. Available at: http://www.guardian.co.uk/money/blog/2010/dec/17/ubs-well-groomed-employees

*The Guardian* 2010b. Feminist activists protest against Hooters in Cardiff, 11 August. Available at: http://www.guardian.co.uk/cardiff/2010/aug/11/cardiff-feminist-network-say-no-to-hooters-campaign-city-centre-protest

Tyler, M., and Abbott, P. 1998. Chocs away: Weight watching in the contemporary airline industry. *Sociology* 32(3): 433–50.

Walker, T. 2014. Grim second life of the 'breastaurant': The oft-loathed sector is booming in the States thanks to Hooters, Twin Peaks and Tilted Kilt. *The Independent*, 12 December 2014.

Ward, J., and McMurray, R. 2015. *The dark side of emotional labour*. London: Routledge.

West Edmonton Mall 2015. Available at: http://www.wem.ca (last accessed 20 August 2015).

Witz, A., Warhurst, C., and Nickson, D. 2003. The labour of aesthetics and the aesthetics of organization. *Organization* 10(1): 33–54.

Zonal Retail Data Systems 2015. Pubs and bars. Available at http://www.zonal.co.uk/sectors/pubs-bars/ (last accessed 20 August 2015).

# Corporate social responsibility, sustainability, and business ethics

*Can businesses act sustainably, ethically, and responsibly?*

## Chapter overview and learning outcomes

By the end of this chapter you should be able to:

- describe some of the key principles of corporate social responsibility, business ethics, and sustainability

- explain why Milton Friedman argues that firms have no corporate social responsibility

- explain the principles behind shareholder capitalism

- analyse what the key critiques of capitalism are.

## Key theorists

| | |
|---|---|
| R. Edward Freeman | Freeman is one of the leading proponents of stakeholder theory, which argues that successful businesses build their strategy around their relationships with key stakeholders |
| Karl Marx | Philosopher, economist, activist, and revolutionary, Karl Marx is famous for his hard-hitting critiques of capitalism and support for communism; his works continue to be widely read and debated today |
| Milton Friedman | The Nobel prize-winning economist who famously argued that corporate social responsibility is 'unethical' |

## Key terms

| | |
|---|---|
| Free market | A philosophy and economic system which argues that business works at its most efficient when open exchange can happen between businesses with minimal government interference |
| Business ethics | The application of ethical principles to organizations to either understand, judge, or direct individual and organizational ethical decision making |
| Corporate social responsibility | A perspective which stresses the responsibilities that corporations have towards society and other stakeholders |
| Sustainability | A complex term; it often stresses the long-term viability of the environment and/or the corporation |
| Capitalism | The dominant economic system, which is based on private ownership of the means of production of goods and services for the purposes of making profit |
| Philanthropy | Originally meaning 'for the love of humanity', it is now taken as meaning the giving of time or more commonly money for good causes |

# Introduction: corporations in the news

## Running case: expansion plans

With Junction Hotel now finally doing well, Simon Chance begins to think about expansion. Booking rates are near capacity, the hotel now regularly holds five weddings a weekend with, on average, 150 people for a full sit-down meal, and the bar takings have doubled. Profits are increasing and, for the first time, he is looking forward to writing the yearly report.

With this success Chance has started to consider building an extension at the front of the hotel. A new conservatory would add much-needed space and allow them to host 250 people per wedding and for the big Christmas parties—boosting potential profit. An architect has said it should be feasible, as long as they can get planning consent.

Flicking through his emails he notices a couple from Linda Wilkinson entitled 'Complaints from local residents'. In the email she explains how two of the local residents came in over the weekend, while the wedding was in full swing, complaining about the noise. Another email—'More complaints'—was, this time, about the aggressive behaviour of the guests as they left the wedding. While he wished such things didn't happen, he thinks, 'What can Junction Hotel do? People come to the hotel to have a good time and it is our job to give it to them.' With that, he goes back to the architect's plans.

Stories of corporate corruption and miscommunication have been commonplace in the news in recent years. For example:

- Fourteen Chinese workers committed suicide over bad conditions at the Foxconn factory
- 1,100 garment workers were killed when Bangladesh's Ran Plaza factory collapsed
- Bankers fixed rates on foreign exchanges, while in chat rooms calling themselves 'the players', 'the 3 musketeers', '1 team, 1 dream' and 'the A-team'
- Companies such as Tesco were accused of overstating their profits

Stories such as these have raised questions over the ethical status of businesses today. According to business consultants Portland Communications, 67% of people say levels of trust in business have decreased over the last five years (Portland Communications, 2014). As Andrew Witty, chief executive officer (CEO) of the pharmaceuticals giant GlaxoSmithKline, puts it, 'Trust in business has clearly eroded and needs to be reconstructed. It's very dangerous if a country doesn't trust the private sector' (cited in High Pay Commission, 2011). The financial crisis has now put the social responsibility of business firmly in the spotlight, and, along with climate change and human rights in developing countries, such concerns can be expected to exist for many years to come. Indeed, as we will contend in this chapter, corporate reputation is likely to form one of the biggest contemporary issues throughout your career.

## Real life case: KitKat and palm oil

When was the last time you ate a KitKat? Over a billion are made in the UK each year, and most of us think they are little more than a harmless pleasure. Yet Greenpeace say we should think more carefully about it.

▶ In March 2010, Greenpeace launched a campaign claiming a key ingredient, palm oil, was killing orang-utans. Palm oil was sourced unsustainably because to grow it large sections of rainforests were cut down, destroying the orang-utans' natural habitat. 90% of the world's palm oil is from Indonesia and Malaysia which, over the last 60 years, have lost a portion of rainforest three times larger than the size of the UK; this, according to the UN, is a significant reason why Indonesia is the third largest emitter of carbon in the world.

To highlight the issue, Greenpeace produced a short advert of an office-worker biting into a KitKat finger in the shape of an orang-utan, which then dripped blood on to his computer keyboard. The advert went viral on Facebook and YouTube, with tens of thousands of hits. Greenpeace campaigners posted messages on Nestlé's Facebook page and dressed as orang-utans to meet shareholders at Nestlé's annual general meeting.

At first, Greenpeace claim, Nestlé tried to censor the advert, but within three months, and after substantial public pressure, they promised to change. Their head of stakeholder engagement in sustainability says deforestation is complex but 'now we're seeing a wave of ambition to tackle this that is sweeping the industry' (cited in Gies 2014). Nestlé now state they are 'fully committed to ensuring that the palm oil in our supply chain is responsibly sourced and to ensuring that our suppliers comply with our Responsible Sourcing Guideline'. They stated that by the end of 2014, 82% of the palm oil they sourced would be traceable, and they were aiming to reach 95% by the end of 2015. They are seeking to support smallholders and have a 'no-deforestation' commitment (Nestlé 2015). KitKats are also Fairtrade—and so maybe it is now possible to eat them with a clear conscience?

**Sources:** Hickman (2009); Greenpeace (2010, 2012); Tabacek (2010); Greenpeace (2013); Nestlé (2015).

Why do you think Nestlé felt the need to respond to this campaign? Look through other ingredients of your food, and even cleaning products—do they include palm oil? How do you feel about this?

The humble KitKat, therefore, connects us to many of the key features that this chapter examines.

- Nestlé are not alone in being the subject of protest campaigns; many other companies have been criticized for using unsustainable palm oil (Bates, 2015). Indeed, recent years have seen numerous corporations under scrutiny about their practices. At stake is their corporate reputation and brand image, prevention of increased legislation, and the maintenance of ties with key stakeholders.

- Getting these features wrong, as we will see, can cost firms millions of pounds in fines (such as those that the banking industry has received) and, more significantly, goodwill from customers, suppliers, and the government. Getting it right can open up to new customers or give the firm a competitive advantage.

- As we will see later in the chapter, corporate social responsibility (CSR) statements have become standard practice and many organizations are now also producing sustainability reports. Business ethics and sustainability have become core aspects on many business degrees and are increasingly seen as critical competences for business leaders.

## A word on definitions and terms

Attentive readers will have noticed that so far we have used three key phrases: business ethics, sustainability, and CSR (Figure 17.1). We could also have used, among others, the phrases 'stakeholder theory', 'corporate govern-ance', and 'global citizens'. Each phrase captures a particular aspect of business practice.

**Business ethics** deals primarily with the prin-ciples that should be used to govern business conduct, how people should act, and the under-lying philosophies behind ethical actions. It is often taught using case studies, and one of its central aims is to sensitize students and manag-ers to the need for ethical awareness in business and (in some versions at least) to attempt to lay out a moral code of conduct for business people.

**Figure 17.1** The three overlapping theoretical frameworks. CSR, ethics, and sustainability.

**Business ethics** A form of ethics applied to business. It is the study and evaluation of decision making within businesses through various moral concepts and judgements.

CSR, also known as **corporate social responsibility**, looks at the wider responsibilities that businesses have and how they should meet them. Based on stakeholder theory (discussed later in the chapter), the CSR perspective argues that it is often in the firm's interest to meet the needs of its stakeholders in order to ensure its long-term survival.

**Sustainability** has come into vogue recently, in part because of increasing concerns with the environment (particularly climate change), but it has the wider meaning of the long-term sustainability of the firm itself. This can lead to confusion, but it does demonstrate the challenges of balancing environmental and profit concerns.

While each has their different meaning and focus, for the purposes of this chapter we will not spend too long distinguishing between these terms, rather drawing on the ideas from each area where appropriate.

**Corporate social responsibility** A contested term with different interpretations, generally taken to mean the social and environmental responsibility that corporations have towards their stakeholders.

**Sustainability** The long-term stewardship and maintenance of the environment and the prospects of the firm.

## Chapter outline

This chapter will begin by laying out why ethics matters before moving on to examine the four key ethical perspectives. This discussion will then lay the foundation for the central questions which preoccupy this chapter. Should privately-owned, profit-seeking compa-nies be concerned with acting in a socially responsible, moral, and humane way? Should they exist for their own purposes or for the good of society? The response that one makes to this question is moral and depends, to a large degree, on one's beliefs as to the central purpose and responsibility of businesses, which we have summed up in the following five categories:

- shareholder capitalism
- stakeholder capitalism
- ethical capitalism
- ethical within capitalism
- against capitalism.

While each category covers a particular perspective, they also overlap and do not necessar-ily capture all the views of each perspective. They therefore should be seen as **heuristic devices** which broadly capture these positions rather than as fixed categories.

**Heuristic device** Used to help simplify a theory and make it more understandable.

# The need for business ethics

**Real life case:** corporate scandals in the news

In 2015 Sweden was rocked by a series of resignations within Industrivärden, which owns companies including Volvo, Ericsson, and SCA (a Swedish forestry and paper company). In late 2014 it was revealed that SCA had been using private jets to fly around its chief executive, Jan Johansson. He was often flying alone: not a good impression for the company's sustainability image. What happened next was more worrying. Reports then started coming out of wives and children being flown to the SCA-owned hunting-lodge (which cost an estimated 100 million krona), the London Olympics and European football championships (Milne, 2015). These revelations showed a level of corporate extravagance at odds with the egalitarian values that Sweden holds (Crouch 2015).

Petrobras, the Brazilian state-run oil giant, is one of Latin America's most prominent firms. They are now involved in one of the largest corruption scandals ever in Brazil (Costas, 2014). The investigation started when investigators discovered that Alberto Youseff had given a Land Rover to Paulo Roberto Costa, the former Petrobras executive (Bawden and Sheffield, 2015). Prosecutors claim that in an arrangement commonly referred to as 'Operation Car Wash', Petrobras executives took bribes from construction firms and overpaid for contracts; other accusations include bribes to government officials and politicians and the fixing of contracts (Smith et al., 2015). They have also been accused of transferring $1.4 million to Europe by wrapping money into plastic packages and concealing them in clothing and socks and 'underneath a baggy suit' (Bawden and Sheffield, 2015).

In April 2015 Petrobras wrote off approximately $17 billion in corruption-related costs (Connors and Trevisani, 2015). Petrobras says that they are now tackling the problem. Petrobras chief Aldemir Bendine states 'Today is an important day, not only for us but for the whole company. We are cleaning up mistakes' (cited in Bawden and Sheffield, 2015).

Australian firm Woodside Petroleum announced in its annual sustainability report that in 2014 it sacked seven staff for 'fraud-related' incidents (Macdonald-Smith, 2015). It stated it had a 'zero-tolerance' approach to unethical behaviour and 'Woodside's Whistleblower Policy sets out our commitment to maintaining an open working environment in which employees and contractors can report unethical, unlawful or undesirable conduct without fear of retaliation or reprisal' (cited in Kakulas, 2015).

 Visit the Online Resource Centre to read other scandals.

**Oxymoron** A phrase that appears to contradict itself.

If you have a cynical attitude, then you might expect this chapter to be a very short one—the phrase 'business ethics' could be seen as an **oxymoron**. You might think that businesses are only worried about making a profit. Indeed, the phrase 'business is business' is often used to suggest that you have made a 'hardnosed', 'rational' decision where morals and feelings did not come into it.

But, on closer examination, all business at its most basic level requires some degree of ethical behaviour; otherwise business quickly becomes impossible. What would happen, for instance, if you knew that your university canteen, to save costs, were using ingredients that might kill you? Similarly, how likely would a business be to sell to someone they believe has no intention of paying? Also, given the choice, would you want to work for a company that you knew treated it workers badly and even physically abused them? All business activity, to be able to survive, requires a level of trust and moral action—otherwise the entire system quickly disintegrates.

The question, therefore, is not whether firms should act in an ethical way, but rather what is the ethical basis for their actions and how do they balance wider social responsibilities with concerns for profit?

---

**Real life case:** Taylor Swift makes Apple change their tune

Just hours after Taylor Swift posted a comment on Tumblr announcing that her new album '1989' would not be appearing on Apple Music, Apple executive Eddy Cue announced that it was reversing its policy and was now paying artists during the Apple's three-month free trial period (Trugman, 2015). Taylor Swift alleged that Apple were not going to pay artists for the trial period, which she said would harm independent labels in particular, likening it to customers wanting a free iPhone (Dredge, 2015). Even after this victory, many artists complain that they receive only 0.2 cents per track played on the free streaming service (Spence, 2015).

---

Have you ever streamed music for free or even downloaded a track for free? Do you ever think about what it must be like for the artists that do not get paid? See Chapter 14 for examples of how governments have tried to stop illegal downloading.

# Ethical decision making

As customers we face ethical decisions every day: from streaming music for free to choosing whether to pay more for organic food. At work we also face ethical decisions, from how we treat customers and colleagues through to being pressured to do things that go against our personal values. As many of the business scandals we have listed above demonstrate, ethical decision making is an important issue. Ethical issues at work do not just relate to large headline-hitting scandals; they can also be everyday and seemingly innocuous acts, as shown in Table 17.1.

Ethical dilemmas are therefore all around us. While we may think that unethical decisions are made by 'bad' people, John Boatright (2013) argues that ethically questionable actions are often carried out by people that do not set out to act badly. He claims that they often start on a 'slippery slope' where they convince themselves that so long as it is legal, it is acceptable. This can eventually lead to more substantial unethical acts. Boatright argues: 'Recent graduates just entering the investment profession are especially vulnerable to ethical missteps because they are often naive and may not see the ethical aspects of situations they confront' (2013: 8). They can feel pressure from middle managers to hit targets. Such middle managers might not have told them to act unethically, but 'they often turn a blind eye to how an objective is achieved so long as it is achieved' (2013: 8). Boatright argues that business ethics should be taught not to stop 'bad people' acting unethically but to sensitize good people to what might be unethical decisions.

However, individual awareness is not enough. Often such unethical acts are 'known' but collectively we chose not to see them. This is called 'wilful blindness' (Heffernan, 2011),

Table 17.1  Ethical dilemmas in the workplace

| Issue | Example |
|---|---|
| Cheating on the company | Leaving work early, stealing pens from work, or small-scale fiddling of expenses |
| Cheating on clients | Misleading customers about how good a product is in order to get a sale, hiding the true costs of a service agreement, or encouraging them to buy something that they don't really need so that you win your monthly bonus |
| Working in unethical industries | Companies spamming customers with fake PPI and 'accident claim' calls |
| Turning a blind eye to unethical acts of co-workers or managers | Seeing, but not confronting or reporting, a manager who over-reports figures to meet targets, or a fellow employee who treats a customer badly or takes short-cuts on product safety to get the job done on time |
| Selling products that are bad for the planet or people | A cashier at a petrol station selling products that will contribute to global warming, a customer service assistant at a discount retailer selling clothes made in sweatshop conditions, or a fast-food chef making burgers that are unhealthy |

where 'a group of people tacitly agree to outwardly ignore something of which they are all personally aware' (Zerubavel, 2006: 2). Ethics therefore needs to impact culture, and unethical acts need to be challenged by people (sometimes called whistleblowers, as discussed later in the chapter) who are prepared to say what everyone knows but does not feel able to say.

These ethical issues are important, not only for companies' reputations but also for the lives of the people that are affected by the decisions they make. Some of the most serious scandals have resulted in people losing their lives. Organizations therefore play a part in shaping our society.

As a response there have been a number of initiatives to put ethics on the agenda for business students. For instance, the Chartered Association of Business Schools have recently stated that business schools should be involved in 'educating future business leaders and ensuring they have an awareness of the ethical dimensions and responsibilities of business' (Chartered Association of Business Schools, 2015).

The United Nations have set up PRME (Principles for Responsible Management Education), which aims to develop the capabilities of students to 'be future generators of sustainable value for business and society at large and to work for an inclusive and sustainable global economy' (UNPRME, 2015). They aim to change the way that education works in business schools.

Visit the PRME website and read about the principles. How do you feel about them? Do you feel that they are reflected in what you have learnt so far at university?

To better understand how to make ethical decisions, we first have to turn to the field of business ethics (see Table 17.2).

Many business ethics texts seek to provide guidance for how to navigate the range of difficult choices that people face in organizations.

**Table 17.2** Key areas of business ethics

| Normative ethics | tells us what we *should* do. These ethical frameworks seek to separate out good from bad practice and make moral judgements on how people should act. |
| --- | --- |
| Descriptive ethics | tell us what people *actually* do and seek to provide an explanation of *why* they do it. |
| Managing ethics | are ways in which companies seek to manage the behaviour of their staff. This can be through a variety of techniques such as mission statements, codes of practice, and training. |

# An ethical framework

Business ethics is a complex field drawing on many different theories. The following sections will introduce the main ethical theories, which are summarized neatly in Figure 17.2.

## Teleological ethics

Taken from the Greek *telos* meaning ends, teleological ethics states that an action can only be judged by its consequences. For our purposes, the most important teleological perspective is utilitarianism, which was summed up by Jeremy Bentham (the inventor of the Panopticon—see Chapters 4 and 13) as 'The greatest happiness of the greatest number is the foundation of morals and legislation' (cited in Fisher and Lovell, 2009: 129).

Within this view, actions are not good or bad because of their character or intention; rather it is their effect on how much overall benefit they produce. For utilitarians, something is good if it increases the overall well-being of people. A moral act is thus one that increases pleasure (good) more than it produces pain (bad). Utilitarians therefore argue that

**Figure 17.2** An ethical framework.

**Source:** © Business Ethics & Values: Individual, Corporate and International Perspectives, Fisher, C. and Lovell, A., Pearson Education Limited, 2006

you can calculate the cost–benefit of a particular action. Bentham assumed all humans are motivated by the desire to create pleasure and avoid pain, and therefore they will do things that increase pleasure.

In a business sense, pleasure is often equated with profit maximization and is used to justify shareholder capitalism (see the following sections), the belief being that if everyone follows their self-interest, overall it will benefit the whole of society. A wider interpretation, however, might be used to justify stakeholder capitalism (see later in the chapter), as the impact on the whole of society needs to be calculated.

Consider an ethical dilemma that you had recently. How easy would it be to do a cost–benefit analysis?

## Deontological ethics

Taken from the Greek *deon*, meaning duty, deontological ethics asks whether the action is right, fair, and honest. It is not concerned with the consequences of an action, but the reasons behind it. Within this perspective, acts are ethical only if they are conducted based on duty and not if there is a reward.

**A priori** Independent of experience.

The deontological perspective looks to create universal rules and sees ethics as an end in itself. Ethical principles, particularly for the philosopher Kant, exist **a priori**; in other words, they exist independently of the particular circumstance or the outcome and are worked out on the basis of pure reason, and there is one universal code, regardless of culture and belief, that everyone should follow. Kant, in what he called the 'categorical imperative', argued you should always act based on the assumption your action will become a universal law of human behaviour. (For a review, see Fisher et al., 2013.)

Would you act any differently if all your actions became universal laws for human behaviour? Might you, for instance, recycle more or reduce your carbon emissions?

While this view might seem appealing, it is also seen as very rigid. For instance, while most of us would consider lying as wrong, what if you had to lie to save someone's life? For Kant, this then raises the question over which duty should come first (such as lying or preserving someone's life). However, it becomes difficult to come up with universal laws that fit all circumstances.

### Real life case: whistleblowers

A whistleblower is someone who reports what they suspect to be wrongdoing at work, which is officially defined as 'making a disclosure in the public interest' (Gov.uk, 2015). This can include reporting concerns that somebody's health might be in danger, damage to the environment, or a company not obeying the law or covering up wrongdoing. Whistleblowers act in ways that they think are in the public interest, often stating they are doing so because they felt that what they were being asked to do, or were witnessing, went against their personal values.

The most famous recent example is Edward Snowden, the CIA analyst who left his Hawaii home, travelled to Hong Kong, and leaked to journalist Glenn Greenwald many of the surveillance ▶

▶ practices that the US government was carrying out on its citizens, other countries, and their heads of state (Harding, 2014). Other famous whistleblowers include HMRC's permanent secretary Dave Hartnett, who revealed how US bank Goldman Sachs 'was forgiven £10m interest on a failed tax avoidance scheme' by the UK tax authorities (Leigh, 2011); Italian Hervé Falciani, who worked for HSBC and who is helping 'Spanish prosecutors pursue tax dodgers who are hiding their money in Switzerland' (Tremlett, 2013); and UK NHS cardiologist Dr Raj Mattu, who when working at a medical school at Warwick University raised concerns about patient safety, warning patients that their lives were at risk (Smith, 2014).

While many would defend their actions on ethical grounds, whistleblowers often personally suffer. At the time of writing, Edward Snowden was in hiding in Russia, Hervé Falciani had been arrested and faced death threats, and Dr Raj Mattu faced numerous investigations, suffered from depression, and was sacked (Smith, 2014). A recent report has stated that half of all whistleblowers who contacted the report's authors had either been dismissed or resigned after raising their concern (PCAW, 2015).

To tackle this problem around the world, calls have been made to protect whistleblowers. Unions in India have been calling for more protection in the banking industry (Muringatheri, 2015), and in the UK the Bank of England said that in the Libor rate scandal whistleblowers were largely ineffective (Grant, 2015). The NHS in Scotland will employ 'whistleblowing champions': 'Scotland's Health Secretary Shona Robison wanted all NHS staff to "have the confidence to speak up without fear" about patient safety' (BBC News, 2015a).

Dr Kate Kenny agrees that whistleblowers face a difficult time, often being seen as traitors within their organizations. Her research on whistleblowing in the financial services (Kenny, 2014b) highlights how the basic structural features of many organizations, such as the reporting systems, pay and bonus schemes, and corporate governance, make it difficult for people to speak out. Moreover, she notes that the relationships that workers in financial services firms naturally form with one another discourage people from breaking ranks and reporting wrongdoing.

She argues elsewhere that whistleblowers struggle to make their voices heard, and that the media play a crucial role in enabling some stories to reach the public while others remain unreported (Kenny, 2014a). For all these reasons, society must find new ways to support whistleblowers who risk their jobs, their well-being, and their incomes in order to speak up about dangerous and illegal practices (Kenny, 2015).

What would it take for you to become a whistleblower? How much would you be prepared to risk to speak out for what you think is right? How would you act differently if you knew that everyone would follow your actions?

Another deontological perspective is that of justice and rights. The **libertarian** view, particularly as developed by Robert Nozick, argues that the essential right people have is freedom, particularly freedom from government interference and for property rights. People, he argued, have the right to free choice and to act how they want so long as they are not breaking the law. In business, this justifies shareholder capitalism (discussed later in the chapter), as shareholders are seen as having the right to use their property in whatever way they like providing they act within the law.

An alternative deontological perspective is social justice. This perspective is most strongly associated with John Rawls and is linked to communitarianism (discussed later in the

Libertarian A perspective that stresses individual freedom above all other concerns.

chapter). Rawls asks us to imagine what a 'just' society would look like if we did not know our position in the world. In other words, you could be anyone, rich or poor, male or female, in the developed world or from a developing nation. From this position of 'total ignorance' we then need to imagine what we would like the world to be like. Believing that we are risk-averse individuals, Rawls thinks we would design a world of fairness based upon the same civil and political rights for all and a system of meritocracy (this supports the stakeholder approach).

## Virtue ethics

### Real life case: the MBA oath

In light of the financial crisis, questions began to emerge about the ethical and moral role that business leaders played in creating the crisis and, consequently, the type of education they received (Currie et al., 2010). MBA students from Harvard Business School (widely acknowledged to be one of the leading business schools in the world and a centre for training future leaders) began to ask: 'How did we get into this crisis? Why didn't business school professors sound the alarms in advance of the meltdown? Why were so many MBAs involved in the decisions leading up to the crisis? Are MBAs so concerned with increasing their personal wealth that they ignore ethics and their responsibilities to society?'

As a response to these questions, the graduates of the 2009 MBA created the MBA oath. Modelled on the Hippocratic oath, which doctors swear, its stated 'mission is to facilitate a widespread movement of MBAs who aim to lead in the interests of the greater good'. Among the pledges were to be aware of the impact the organization had beyond the business itself, not to be corrupt or do practices harmful to society, to provide economic and environmental sustainability for future generations, and to set an example to followers.

**Source:** http://mbaoath.org/about/

Visit the Online Resource Centre to read the MBA oath in full. Would you pledge an oath like this? Do you think that saying an oath will make you behave in a more ethical manner?

Virtue-based ethics focuses on the individual, particularly their personal characteristics. Drawing on Aristotle it looks at the individual character—how it is formed and develops to achieve 'eudaimonia' (life-long development of well-being, or human flourishing). (For a review, see Fisher et al., 2013.) It focuses on means, not ends (unlike teleological ethics), and personal characteristics rather than rules (unlike deontological ethics). Advocates of virtue-based ethics believe that if practised in the right way it will lead the individual to make the right choices.

In the business context, virtue ethics focuses on the character of the individual and their capacity to make the right choices (see MacIntyre, 1967). Proponents would argue that the moral education of managers is therefore vital to help them cope with the ethical complexity of modern life.

A related concept, drawing on feminist philosophy, is the 'ethics of care'. It argues that most philosophy (and therefore ethics) are written by, and based on, male ideals. For instance, Gilligan (1982) argues that women demonstrate a different way of moral reasoning, particularly due to early socialization, and tend to seek compromise and ways of avoiding blaming one side exclusively in a dispute so that everyone gets something, rather than looking for the black and white morals that men tend to look for (for a review, see Fisher and Lovell, 2009: 107).

Virtue ethics, however, can overemphasize the importance of the individual, either by praising heroic individuals or by blaming **bad apples** for immoral actions.

**Bad apples**   A phrase that dismisses an occurrence as just down to a few bad people or organizations, while claiming that others should not be judged as the same.

> ### Real life case: stronger penalties for 'bad apples', says deputy governor of the bank of England
>
> Recent years have seen numerous scandals within the financial services industry, with mis-selling and rate fixing being reported. To date, these scandals have cost the industry approximately £38.5 billion in fines and compensation.
>
> One of the solutions that has been offered is to punish the rouge traders and managers. There have been calls for prison sentences of up to 7 years for reckless managers of banks (Bowers, 2014). Minouche Shafik, the deputy governor of the Bank of England, said more should be done to punish what she called 'bad apples' (BBC News, 2014). Yet while many would welcome punishment for bad individuals, many others have questioned if it is really a result of a few 'rotten apples' or a product of a wider culture of corruption (Arnold and Binham, 2015).
>
> A report by Professor André Spicer of the Cass Business School states that what is needed is not necessarily punishment of a few individuals but wholesale cultural change. In an interview for this book, Professor Spicer told us that this should include changing
>
>> the symbols and signs which are prominently displayed within the banks. For instance some large banks prominently displayed the share price in the lobby of the headquarters. This reminded employees the only thing which counted was increasing the share price of the bank. Now they prominently display values and ethical statements in the headquarters—this communicates a different message. But symbolism is not enough. Banks have also had to transform day to day practices—this means encouraging people to engage in different ways of doing things. For instance, in the past interactions with customers were mainly based around a routine of sales. This has been replaced with routines based on customer support and educating the customer about the risks they are taking on when they get a loan. Finally, changing culture means shifting deeper value of people within the bank. Often senior management try to do this through inspirational speeches and training programmes. But this is often not enough—tone from the top counts for very little when it is not matched by 'message from the middle'. Getting the latter right is difficult—often because middle managers faced competing pressure to both cut costs and build a more ethical culture at once. The result is they find it difficult to change culture as quickly as regulators and senior management might like.                    (Spicer, 2015)

Should managers face prison sentences for wrongdoing in their company, particularly if they personally did not do the act themselves? Is the problem the result of 'rogue' individuals (rotten apples) or part of the wider culture?

## Individual growth and organizational learning

Our final ethical perspective emphasizes the importance of learning and development (see Chapter 10) as part of ethical development. It focuses on how to be more effective in one's job while developing an ethical character. A particularly popular (and inspiring) example is provided by Stephen Covey's *The 7 habits of highly effective people* (2004). On the surface, this book appears to be a conventional time-management and self-help book, with charts for how to plan a week and habits to be successful. However, it goes further by asking the reader to define what they consider being successful really means, and what sort of character and life they want. This stresses a number of things, including the importance of having a personal vision not just in work, but also in terms of balancing personal, family, and professional responsibilities. At the heart is developing an ethical character and focusing on priorities based upon principles rather than quick fixes. Having sold over 15 million copies, Covey's book has proved highly influential, particularly during the 1990s. It does, however, reinforce the image of the heroic ethical individual able to overcome all adversity.

What are your personal values, and how important are they in your daily decision making?
What would you like others to say about your moral character?

The second individual growth perspective is communitarianism. This perspective argues that the community should be considered more important than individuals or the state. Communitarianism stresses the importance of social relations and suggests that human life will improve if the community and public values guide our decision making. In other words, we do things for the good of the community rather than for ourselves. We will have more to say on communitarianism later in the chapter.

## Study skills: research ethics

Research ethics is becoming an increasingly important aspect of university life for both lecturers and students. Any significant piece of research now has to be passed beforehand for its ethical credentials, either by a supervisor (in the case of undergraduate students) or a committee (for most academics). Such aspects as how the data is collected, stored, and used all need to fit ethical guidelines. The primary aim is to reduce the risk of harm to participants and make sure that the data is not used in the wrong way.

Undoubtedly, this has brought a lot of benefits as it requires the researcher to consider the impact their research can have on their participants before the research is conducted. However, it might stifle some research. For instance, it is unlikely that some innovative research like Zimbardo's Stanford prison experiment (see Chapter 13) would be allowed to occur today due to the harm it might cause to the participants (Wilson and Hunter, 2010).

## Review questions

| | |
|---|---|
| **Describe** | What are the key principles of each of the ethical frameworks? |
| **Explain** | What are the strengths and weaknesses of each of the ethical frameworks? |
| **Analyse** | Which of the frameworks do you consider more useful when tackling business dilemmas? What is your reasoning for this? |
| **Apply** | In the 'bad apples' case (above), how much impact do you think it will make to change the symbols displayed in the bank from live share price updates to ethical statements? |

# The economic framework for ethical action

While ethical frameworks are important in guiding individual and organizational behaviour, the choices that we have and the possibilities for ethical action are also shaped by the economic system in which we live. For the rest of the chapter we will examine the five main perspectives that exist currently, at least within Western countries.

Karl Marx (1859/2012) argued that the economic structure (which he called the base) shapes the nature of society (which he called the superstructure), and society exists to maintain and legitimize the economic system (Figure 17.3). For instance, this Marxist framework argues that within our society schooling exists primarily to support the economy, not only in providing skilled workers but also in establishing the values and attitudes these workers should have (to accept authority, turn up on time, want to achieve high grades—like promotion at work—and accept discipline).

Consequently, for ethics, our central ideas are a product of the superstructure (our family, education, religion, reading of mass media, politics, etc.) and our actions are constrained by the base—the economic system in which we operate. According to this view, while it is important to look to individual organizations and people, our ethical beliefs and the choices (we think) we have are more political or ideological in nature than we tend to believe.

The first three frameworks accept the economic system of capitalism as their basis, although they have different interpretations and emphasis within it. The latter two could broadly be said to be against capitalism as an economic system, but they offer two different responses to the problems they perceive that capitalism creates (Figure 17.4).

For the purposes of this chapter, capitalism is understood to be the economic system in which we (in the West) live, where one group—the capitalists (shareholders or owners of the firm)—owns the means of production, and another group—labour (workers)—sell their labour. We have featured this in the capitalist working relationship.

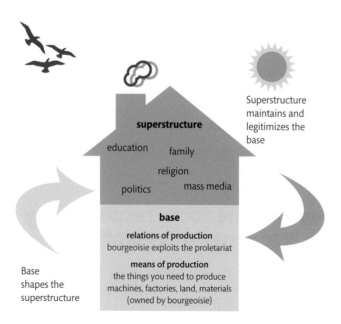

**Figure 17.3**  The base and superstructure model (based on Marx, 1859/2012).

**Figure 17.4** The five
frameworks featured in
this chapter.

Accept capitalism

Shareholder
capitalism

Stakeholder
capitalism

Ethical
capitalism

Challenge capitalism

Ethical
within
capitalism

Ethical
against
capitalism

# Shareholder capitalism

**Running case:** hitting the headlines

While Simon Chance is still musing over his hotel expansion plans, Linda Wilkinson comes rushing into his office looking flustered. 'Do we have an appointment?' Chance looks at her quizzically and with a slight sense of annoyance. 'Look at this,' Wilkinson cuts across him, pointing to the front page of the local paper. 'It's worse than I predicted.' Still not really understanding what is going on, Chance snatches the paper from her. 'What are you talking about? . . . Oh, I see,' Chance says, seeing the headline 'Junction Rubbish' accompanied by a big photo of the hotel with litter strewn across the road. '"Weddings at local hotel are causing mayhem, say local residents",' Chance reads to Wilkinson, '"drunken yobs making noise through-out the night . . . traffic blocking up local streets . . . guests being sick in neighbour's front garden . . . litter being dumped on the street". This is not good,' Chance declares, looking up from the paper. Chance's office door opens and in comes Weaver. 'Have you seen this?' Chance asks, handing the paper to Weaver. With only a quick glance, Weaver hands the paper back. 'Newspaper tittle-tattle,' Weaver declares. 'Look, the weddings make us a lot of money. Sure, they make a lot of noise, but, then, they are having fun.' Wilkinson looks shocked: 'But it's a really bad story—front page, too.' Weaver smiles at her. 'It's just paper talk. It will all blow over in a week and be forgotten about. News today, but tomorrow it's just fish and chip paper. You have to be strong and withstand these stories. When the profits come through the investors will be thanking you.'

# Milton Friedman: the social responsibility of business is to increase its profits

Nobel-prize-winning economist Milton Friedman is the most prominent and outspoken critic of corporate social responsibility and a defender of shareholder capitalism. In a widely discussed article published in 1970 he claimed 'there is one and only one social responsibility of business—to use its resources and engage in activities designed to increase its profits so long as it stays within the rules of the game, which is to say, engages in open and free competition without deception or fraud' (Friedman, 1970: 126). Anything else, he states, not only is not the purpose of organizations, but is actually unethical.

Drawing on libertarianism, Friedman argues that companies are the shareholders' property and therefore should be run exclusively in their interest. This interest, he stated, is 'to make as much money as possible while conforming to their basic rules of the society'. For instance, a company should not spend money 'on reducing pollution beyond the amount that is in the best interests of the corporation or that is required by law', as it would lower profit for the shareholders.

This libertarian perspective also calls for less control by the government, as people (including shareholders and therefore corporations) should be free to live their lives in a way that maximizes freedom. Finally, Friedman also argues that because managers are not trained in solving social problems, they should not be required to tackle them. Businesses, therefore, should not have responsibilities for solving society's problems because it dilutes what they are good at—being run in an efficient and profitable manner.

Visit the Online Resource Centre to read more about Milton Friedman's theories.

Do you think companies should be run exclusively in shareholders' interests? Can you see any problems with the position that Friedman outlines? Can you think of any examples that would question Friedman's assertions?

## Adam Smith: the invisible hand

The shareholder capitalism perspective also takes a particular reading of utilitarianism, using **ethical egoism**. This perspective claims that you should act in your own self-interest as doing so is the best way of promoting the maximum overall level of happiness. 'It is not from the benevolence of the butcher, the brewer, or the baker, that we expect our dinner, but from their regard to their own interest. We address ourselves, not to their humanity but to their self-love, and never talk to them of our own necessities but of their advantages' (*Wealth of nations*, I.ii.2; Smith, 1776/2012). Because trading is beneficial to both parties, it will increase the good for all. Collective interest, it is claimed, is best promoted through self-interest. Intentions reached individually will be the best decisions for the entire society.

> Ethical egoism   People acting in their own best interest is the best way to get a good society.

Smith argues that you are likely to work harder, spend your money more carefully, and invest it more wisely if it is for your own interest. Similarly, workers will seek to maximize their skills and work as hard as possible to maximize their wages, buyers will look to purchase goods for the lowest amount possible, and sellers will thus be forced to compete with each other to offer the best goods at the lowest price. Self-interest supports society as a whole, 'led by an invisible hand to promote an end which was no part of his intention . . . By pursuing his own interest he frequently promotes that of the society more effectually than when he really intends to promote it' (*Wealth of nations* IV.ii.9; Smith, 1776/2012). According to this view, the market has an 'invisible hand' that promotes the greatest good for all.

# Economic growth is good for all: the rising tide raises all ships

**Real life case:** Stephen Hester's bonus

In January 2012 Stephen Hester, the then CEO of Royal Bank of Scotland (RBS), turned down a bonus of just under £1 million. Hester had come under considerable public and political pressure, particularly because RBS are predominantly a government-owned company. Many members of the public considered his pay excessive, particularly at a time of austerity that meant the majority of public and private sector workers were experiencing pay freezes and even job cuts (Neate, 2012).

In our interview Hester said that although it 'may not be the job of a business person specifically', everyone needs to understand the issues surrounding high pay and inequality. However, he argues that capitalism is 'the most effective way of increasing the wealth and opportunities of most people'. It is effective because it increases the size of the 'economic pie' which 'unleashes different people's motivations and talents in different ways, which can accentuate financial differences. The biggest income differences on the planet at the moment are in China and India today, which are the fastest-growing, biggest producers of economic pie growth out there'.

'If you want, as a society, to have some wealth to go round, you need to allow, or even encourage, the efforts that lead to some people having a lot more money than others because of their business success. And then you need to rein some of that back through taxation in order to make acceptable to everyone the way that the pie is ultimately distributed . . . and that is the trick. So, if we were to instigate a rule that said that pay differences cannot be more than X, then, simply, we will be less successful economically and there will be less of the pie to go round for everyone. But, equally, if the people that do well out of the current system are ignorant of everyone else and offensive, then the system won't last either.'

**Source:** Author interview with Stephen Hester, former CEO of Royal Bank of Scotland, February 2012.

Visit the Online Resource Centre to read the full interview.

Hester's arguments draw from utilitarianism and libertarianism. Both hinge on the assumption that shareholder capitalism is the most effective way of increasing overall wealth and produces increased benefits for all. This argument is sometimes known as the 'trickle-down effect': in former US President Franklin D. Roosevelt's metaphor, 'the rising tide raises all ships'. This argument claims that although capitalism might produce more inequality (as the rich will get proportionally richer than the poor), it will 'drag up the poor people, because there are the resources to do so' (Robinson, 2012: 204), as Margaret Thatcher once famously claimed. According to this view, the goal of the economy should be wealth creation rather than wealth redistribution as, in the long run, everyone will benefit.

## Philanthropy: giving something back to society

**Real life case:** world's richest man gives away his fortune

In 1999, Bill Gates, the founder of Microsoft, and his wife Melinda announced that they would give away most of their $100 billion fortune. (In 2006, Warren Buffett joined them, giving away about $31 billion or 99% of his wealth.) According to their website, the charity they set up, the Gates ▶

> ▶    Foundation, has a mission to 'Increase opportunities for people in developing countries to overcome hunger and poverty'. They apply business techniques to invest in high-impact (therefore, they state, efficient) projects, looking for 'high-impact, sustainable solutions that can reach hundreds of millions of people'.
>
> In 2010, Gates and Buffett launched a campaign called The Giving Pledge 'to invite the wealthiest individuals and families in America to commit to giving the majority [at least half] of their wealth to philanthropy' (Carlyle, 2012; Giving Pledge, 2012). Many have signed up.
>
> Visit the Online Resource Centre for more detail about the campaign.
>
> **Source:** http://www.gatesfoundation.org/globaldevelopment/Pages/overview.aspx.

Why do you think these billionaires are giving away much of their fortunes?

The shareholder capitalism model argues that individual shareholders have the right, indeed in countries like the USA almost a duty, to give some of their wealth away. Gates and Buffett are not the first. Henry Ford, who set up one of the first foundations, and David Packard, the founder of Hewlett Packard, gave money to set up a hospital, university, and aquarium (Ford Foundation, 2012; Packard Foundation, 2012).

Philanthropy was at its strongest in the UK in the Victorian era, when many successful business people were often driven by Christian belief that money is the root of all evil and that it was a necessity to help the poor. Many were Quakers, including the founders of banks Barclays and Lloyds and chocolate manufacturer Cadbury's. They gave away vast fortunes to help the needy; they also set up schools and hospitals and funded the arts (Dellheim, 1987; Ackrill and Hannah, 2001).

Today, many corporations have a philanthropic arm, giving money back to society, investing in the arts and local community projects, sponsoring local sports teams, and allowing staff to volunteer their time and skills to local charities.

### Real life case: how much do corporations give?

In 2014 the American organization Committee Encouraging Corporate Philanthropy (CECP) surveyed 271 multi-billion dollar companies and discovered:

- median total giving in CECP's sample was $18.5 million, with the top quartile donating a minimum of $48.9 million
- 90% of companies offered at least one matching gift programme
- 60% offered paid-release time for employees to volunteer
- education, health, and community and economic development were top priorities for the typical company.

The report made clear that companies did not just give company cash, but also foundation cash and non-cash, including tapping the skills and resources of a company (e.g. pro bono and product donations), in addition to types of societal engagement that are not counted in total giving, such as employee volunteer hours.

**Source:** CECP (2015).

While such actions are highly commendable, questions remain about the role of philanthropy. Firstly, there is a concern that it is undemocratic, as certain causes might be more appealing to rich people, giving them more power than if the money was distributed through general taxation (BBC Television, 2011a). For instance, Victorian philanthropist George Peabody, who helped the poor of London to have somewhere to live, only wanted people he considered of 'excellent moral character' who he thought were worthy of help (BBC Television, 2011b).

Secondly, giving these large amounts diverts attention away from some of the potentially less ethical activities, for example donating money to a local good cause to gain public support for a potentially controversial activity. For instance, one of us went on a training day for artists in business and was told of a business that put on an arts event to give them some positive publicity when applying for planning permission. The impression they gave was that using the arts was a cheap way of buying public support for their new development.

## Problems with the shareholder capitalism model

While shareholder capitalism has been very popular with many politicians and business leaders, substantial questions remain over its ethical status and the assumptions on which it is based. Firstly, it is based on the assumption of the 'economic person' who always acts in a rational manner. As we discussed in Chapter 5, people do not always act rationally or seek to maximize their own interests. Secondly, it assumes that self-interest is good for all—an assumption that is challenged by the 'tragedy of the commons' (as discussed in the Research insight below). Thirdly, it assumes that acting in self-interest has no negative effects on others, something economists call *externalities*. Fourthly, challenges have been presented to the 'rising tide' thesis by arguments that income inequalities produce social problems. Finally, the supreme rights of shareholders are being challenged by placing more attention on them.

### Assumption 1: self-interest is good for all

**Research insight:** The tragedy of the commons
Hardin, G. 1968. The tragedy of the commons. *Science* 162(3859): 1243–8.

In this seminal article, ecologist Garrett Hardin describes a fictional situation where cattle herders graze their cows on common land. Hardin states that, unconsciously, each herdsman will ask 'What is the **utility** *to me* of adding one more animal to my herd?' By putting another cow on the land, a herdsman increases his personal wealth as he benefits from the proceeds of the sale of the cow, but it has a negative effect on the grass that will be spread across all the herdsmen. Therefore, by acting in his individual interests each herdsman will add more cattle to the land, which will ultimately destroy the quality of the land—thus the tragedy of the commons.

Self-interest versus common interest.
**Source:** Shutterstock.

> **Utility** The benefit that an individual might gain.

Hardin's work has been criticized for, among other things, historical inaccuracies (Hawkshaw et al., 2012). However, it does provide a powerful riposte to the utilitarian argument that everyone should act in their own self-interest, as it demonstrates that if they do, our common interests are not always served. As the KitKat example which opened this chapter demonstrates, while it might have been in Nestlé's private interest to obtain supplies from the cheapest possible source, the long-term interests of the whole of humanity would be better served by maintaining the rainforest. Such failures are sometimes called 'market failures', when negative effects of a transaction can fall on a third party—again, the occurrences that economists call *externalities* (Bakan, 2005).

## Assumption 2: individuals should be free to pursue their own interests

The premise of shareholder capitalism, that business leaders have responsibilities only to shareholders, is justified on the grounds that business activity is positive—creating jobs, goods, and services—or, at best, benign (not harmful) for society. However, upon closer examination, this position is hard to sustain in every instance.

To maximize profits, critics argue, businesses in fact transfer the *true* cost of transactions to society. For instance, firms do not pay for the pollution they cause, the unemployment benefit of workers made redundant, the building of new roads needed for a new factory, or the extra health costs caused by their products, e.g. smoking. These other costs fall on a third party who is not involved in the decision making process.

Economists call these costs *externalities* or spillover costs. These are the side effects—positive or negative costs on society, on other people, who have no part in the decision-making process (see Bakan, 2005).

---

### Real life case: climate change

While some still question human-made climate change, there is increasing acceptance that human activity (including business) is a significant cause of climate change and that intervention is rapidly needed to deal with it. A recent Intergovernmental Panel on Climate Change (IPCC) report has stated that if emissions of greenhouse gases continue at their current rate, it will result in 'long-lasting changes' that will have 'severe, pervasive and irreversible impacts for people and ecosystems' (IPCC, 2014). Drawing on worldwide scientific evidence, the report argues that global temperatures have risen steadily since 1880—the birth of the Industrial Revolution (Figure 17.5)—and particularly from the 1950s.

A rise in global temperatures of 2°C above pre-industrial levels might trigger the collapse of the Amazon rainforest, resulting in the release of trapped carbon, and the thawing of the permafrost, releasing trapped methane, which might start a potentially irreversible process of temperature growth. A rise of 3°C would lead to temperatures not seen for 3 million years. Lord Stern, from the Grantham Research Institute on Climate Change, argues that this could have profound effects on human life, causing droughts, famines, and mass migration (Stern, 2006; Schäfer et al., 2012). The IPCC state that, 'Climate change is a threat to sustainable development' and now argue that we cannot prevent some climate change and will have to adapt to survive (IPCC, 2014). ▶

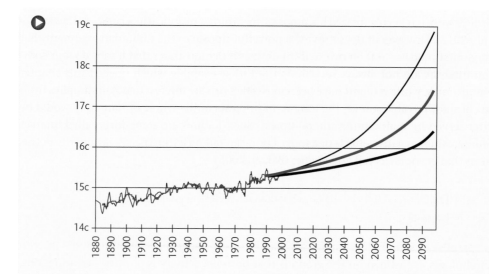

**Figure 17.5** The average rise in global temperatures.

**Source:** Based on research by the Intergovernmental Panel on Climate Change (IPCC).

In June 2015 the US and Brazil, some of the world's biggest polluters, pledged to increase the production from renewable energy sources to 20% of total production by 2030 (Worland, 2015). Similarly, by 2030 China aims to reduce its carbon emissions per unit of Gross Domestic Product (GDP) by 60% from 2005 levels (Briggs, 2015). Many state that this might be too little too late, but it does show some progress on a key issue (Robins, 2015).

As the real life case illustrates, governments are faced with the need to deal with externalities, such as reducing carbon emissions back to the socially optimal level. Either the government could impose regulation to overcome any negative effects on society, for instance making it more expensive to emit carbon by imposing a carbon tax, or it could make firms internalize the negative costs, e.g. the clean-up costs, which is an incentive to reduce pollution (for a critique see Böhm et al., 2012). Climate change, many critical theorists argue, is not simply a technical issue but one that requires political solutions (Wittneben et al., 2012), which require new ways of seeing the world (Levy and Spicer, 2013).

## Assumption 3: economic growth is good for all

### Real life case: executive pay

In recent years one of the strongest areas of criticism of large corporations has been the levels of executive pay (see Table 17.3). In a recent report by the High Pay Commission (2011), it is argued that some bosses' pay has risen more than 4,000% since the 1980s.

**Table 17.3** Percentage of UK national wealth received

| Top percentage earners | 1979 | 2007 |
| --- | --- | --- |
| 0.1% | 1.3% | 6.5% |
| 1% | 5.93% | 14.5% |
| 10% | 28.4% | 40% |

In the USA the top 0.1% take home over 7.5% of gross domestic product (GDP), whereas in Sweden it is less than 2.5%. Other statistics from the report include:

- the average income of a FTSE 100 CEO is estimated at £4.2 million

- The average CEO earns more in three days than the average employee makes in a year

- the former CEO of Barclays, Bob Diamond, earned over 75 times the pay of the average employee; in 1979 it was 14.5 times. In 2011, he received £16 million in salary, benefits, and previous years' share awards. He even had his £5.75 million tax bill paid (Schäfer et al., 2012)

- they predict, at current levels of increase, that by 2035 the top 0.1% will take home 14% of national income.

In a more recent report, the High Pay Centre (formally the High Pay Commission) argue that the more recent attempts to link the pay of CEOs to performance has failed. The pay of the FTSE 350 Company Directors has increased by 300% between 2000 and 2013, while the pre-tax profits of the same companies has only increased by 95% (High Pay Centre, 2014). They suggest that these long-term incentive plans do not work, even in their own terms, and argue that the system needs reforming.

Visit the Online Resource Centre to find links to the reports.

### Real life case: a tale of two CEOs

Sir Martin Sorrell CEO of advertising company WPP earned a reported £43 million in 2014, approximately 179 times more than the average employee. Sorrell defended his large pay, stating he made 'no apologies' for the pay he received. Chairman Philip Lader stated that 92% of the pay was performance-based and that it was supported by 83% of shareholders. It could also be argued that Sorrell has led the company from being worth £1 million in 1985 to £20 billion today (Burn-Callander, 2015)

Michael Wolf, the CEO of Swedish bank Swedbank, earned KR11,338,000 (around £861,461) in 2013 (BloombergBusiness, 2015) as head of one of the Nordic region's largest banks. As with other top executives in the region, he is not eligible for a bonus. He was recently ranked 13th among the Best Performing CEOs in the World by Harvard Business Review staff (2014). However, when questioned about his relatively low pay in comparision to international CEOs, he states 'I'm not underpaid—relative to many workers in Sweden, I am very well paid' (cited in Pollard, 2012).

 What do you think about the different perspectives of executive pay illustrated by these two examples?

The belief that as long as everyone gets richer the level of inequality does not matter has been challenged in *The spirit level: Why equality is better for everyone* (Wilkinson and Pickett, 2010). Drawing on large amounts of statistical evidence, Wilkinson and Pickett argue that it is not the overall level of wealth which matters (as shareholder capitalism has it), but the level of inequality.

Looking at societal issues, such as physical health, mental health, drug abuse, imprisonment, obesity, trust, and violence, they found that the countries with the highest levels of social inequality fared worse in these measures. For instance, on one hand, the USA is the world's richest country; they have vast inequalities of income, high crime, and even high

**Figure 17.6** The impact of income inequality on child mortality.

**Source:** From Wilkinson and Pickett, The Spirit Level, 2010. Reproduced by permission of Penguin.

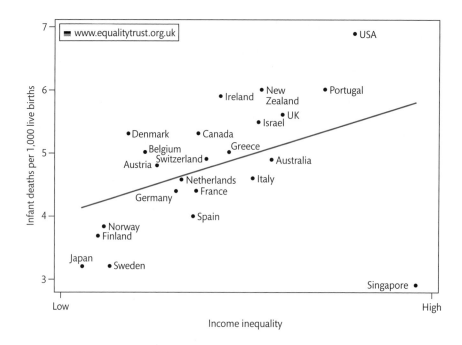

infant deaths per head of population (see Figure 17.6). On the other hand, Scandinavian countries have greater equality and lower social problems. Wilkinson and Pickett therefore conclude that the greater the gap between the rich and the poor, the higher the levels of crime, health problems, unhappiness, drug addiction, and environmental problems.

Wilkinson and Pickett therefore argue that developed countries have achieved about as much as they can from growth. Indeed, increasing growth now contains the potential to harm the planet as it requires more resources. Consequently, the goal of society should be to increase equality rather than focus on economic growth.

Greek philosopher Plato stated that the best paid in society should not receive more than five times the lowest in society. What would society be like if it that policy was introduced? Does the amount of money you have matter more, or the gap between rich and poor? How might equity theory (which we examined in Chapter 9) apply here?

## Assumption 4: shareholders' interests are the only important ones

The final underlying assumption of shareholder capitalism is that because they (the shareholders) own the firm, it is their property to do with as they like. The business should be run exclusively in shareholders' interests and the consequences for others are, at best, secondary and, at worst, disregarded if they harm the shareholders interest. As we will see later, however, it could be argued that from a moral point of view such a perspective is problematic and can even be detrimental to the long-term interests of the shareholders.

## Cases of harm to stakeholders

In recent years there have been numerous cases of the harmful impacts that large (and sometimes small) organizations have had—see Table 17.4 for details. Business supporters often reject them as examples of a few bad apples and state that we should also be aware of

**Table 17.4** Corporate social responsibility in the news

| Category | Headline | Description | Sources |
|---|---|---|---|
| Harm to workers | 1,100 garment workers die in factory collapse | In 2013 an eight-story factory building in Dhaka, Bangladesh, collapsed killing 1,100 factory workers with a further 2,500 being rescued alive, many with serious injuries. The Rana Plaza building, which was the production plant for many household names in the fashion industry, had been known for years to be unsafe. Brad Adams, Asia director at Human Rights Watch, stated 'The government, local factory owners, and the international garment industry pay workers among the world's lowest wages, but didn't have the decency to ensure safe conditions for the people who put clothes on the backs of people all over the world' (Human Rights Watch, 2013). Many of the factory workers knew the building was unsafe but 'they would lose their jobs if they didn't go to work at the unsafe factory building' (DuFault, 2013).<br><br>In June 2015 police charged the owner Sohel Rana and 40 other people with murder for ignoring warnings not to allow the workers into the building the day before it collapsed (BBC News, 2015b).<br><br>Many of the retailers whose clothes were made in the factory and others like it responded in July 2013, with 70 retailers signed a legally binding pact to conduct safety inspections at factories in Bangladesh (Mathew, 2013). Matalan, who only used Rana Plaza factory for a short trial period before the 2013 tragedy, have worked with charities to provide some income and health insurance for up to five year for some of those affected by the buildings collapse (Matalan, 2015). | DuFault (2013); Human Rights Watch (2013); Mathew (2013); BBC (2015b); Matalan (2015) |
| Suicidal workers | Xbox and iPad workers threaten mass suicide | Foxconn, who make Xbox and iPads in factories in China, have alleged that the working conditions are so bad that 300 workers threatened to commit mass suicide. Another report has stated that the workers even had to sign pledges that they will not kill themselves. Att least 14 workers killed themselves in 16 months.<br><br>They were paid only 65p an hour; they were doing excessive overtime—98 hours instead of the legal maximum of 36 hours a month; they slept in dormitories of 24 people; badly-performing workers were humiliated in front of colleagues.<br><br>In late 2014, the BBC's undercover *Panorama* reporter had to work 12 hour shifts for 18 days without a break. Apple responded by saying 'We are aware of no other company doing as much as Apple to ensure fair and safe working conditions. We work with suppliers to address shortfalls, and we see continuous and significant improvement, but we know our work is never done.' | *Daily Mail* (2011); *The Guardian* (2011); CBS News (2012); Bilton (2014) |

**Table 17.4** *(cont'd)*

| Category | Headline | Description | Sources |
|----------|----------|-------------|---------|
| Harm to customers | Car explosion | In *The Corporation*, Joel Bakan (2005) describes a court case where car manufacturer General Motors (GM) were sued after a car exploded. During the court case they discovered GM had not only put the fuel tank in a dangerous position to save costs but also calculated that the savings outweighed the risks of getting sued by 500 fuel-related fatalities they thought might occur each year. This produced a potential saving of $2.40 per car. The judge concluded GM's behaviour was 'morally reprehensible and against applicable laws because it had put profits above public safety' (2005: 63). | Geyelin (1999); Pollack (1999); Bakan (2005) |
| Harm to animals | Mega-cowshed | While we often like to think of our milk coming from cows happily grazing in the countryside, the reality can be very different. A mega-cowshed proposed in Nocton, Lincolnshire, was originally planned to house 8,100 cows (but was reduced to 3,770 after protests) who would have 'little access to pasture or sunshine'. With two milking cycles a day, the aim was to produce 387,000 pints of milk each day. The owners argued that this would produce milk more efficiently while still maintaining welfare standards. Responding to public concerns, Nocton Dairies stated: 'We do not feel there is a nutritional benefit for the cows to go outside. But we have listened to the concerns of welfare groups, the RSPCA and the public of what they feel is better for the dairy cows. If they feel happier with cows allowed to go outside we are going to offer our cows outside space' (BBC News, 2010). Despite these changes, at the time of writing, the planning application had been turned down. | *Daily Mail* (2010); BBC News (2010); *Daily Telegraph* (2011) |

the vast amount of good that businesses do (primarily in supplying jobs, goods, and services that people need, and also giving things back to society). However, for campaigners and anti-capitalism protestors, such cases are examples of fundamental problems with the structure of capitalism.

Visit the Online Resource Centre for links to further examples.

These sorts of cases challenge Milton Friedman's and Adam Smith's argument that unfettered self-interest produces good for everyone. They demonstrate that firms have an impact on, and many would argue a responsibility to, wider society. This is where stakeholder perspective comes in.

## Review questions

| | |
|---|---|
| **Describe** | What is the shareholder capitalism perspective? |
| **Explain** | What are the key arguments for and critiques of this perspective? |
| **Analyse** | What do you think of Andrew Carnegie's statement: 'The man who dies rich, dies disgraced' (quoted in Partington, 1998: 181)? |
| **Apply** | How would you advise Junction Hotel to deal with the negative newspaper headlines? Should the income from weddings be their main concern? |

# Stakeholder capitalism

## Running case: the letters column

Having hoped that the media storm would blow over, Chance is horrified to see that in the following day's paper the letters column is full of letters from the local community complaining that Junction Hotel is affecting their lives. Oliver Price from the local neighbourhood committee writes to complain of the 'loutish' behaviour of wedding guests and the 'excessive noise' made at weekends. Ronald Farley also writes in complaining that, despite his emails, the management of the hotel do not seem to care.

Thinking that nothing else could go wrong, Chance picks up his ringing telephone. On the other end is Ian Terry, one of Second-Chance Consortium's biggest investors and a local in the town. Terry has also seen the letters column in the paper and says that he is horrified that the hotel is receiving such negative publicity. Recalling Weaver's words, Chance tries to calm his fears by saying that the storm will quickly blow over and once the profits come in from the larger weddings all of this will be forgotten. 'I live in this community,' Terry protests, 'and, anyway, do you really think that we have a chance of getting the extension through planning with stories going on in the press like this? We will get kicked out at the first stage if this is kept up. You need to sort it out, and fast.' With that, he slams the phone down.

It is quickly apparent that the shareholders are not the only ones to be affected by an organization's actions. Many groups or individuals have a **stake** in any action a business takes and therefore, it could be argued, should be considered when decisions are made. For instance, a full-time employee spends a large part of their waking hours at work and is, generally, financially dependent on the job, so, arguably, has more at stake than an individual shareholder who might only have some of their savings tied up in the company. Similarly, many customers rely on the services a company offers. For instance, when care home provider Southern Cross ran into financial difficulties after their rents increased, not only were staff going to potentially lose their jobs but also the accommodation of thousands of vulnerable pensioners was at risk, causing anxiety for them and their families (Snell, 2011; BBC News, 2011). Equally, local communities can be impacted by issues such as noise pollution or an increase in traffic. In short, many other parties are impacted by the actions of a single organization. These groups include, but are not limited to, those shown in Figure 17.7.

**Stake** A claim or interest.

**Figure 17.7**
Organizations'
stakeholders.

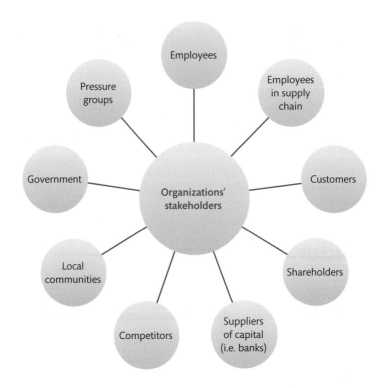

**Stakeholder**
Someone who has an
interest or claim in the
activities of the
organization.

Within academic literature and business terminology these groups are often called **stakeholders**. A stakeholder is a person or group who could be impacted by the actions of the organization. The challenge is to identify who the stakeholders are and what responsibilities the organization has to them, and to balance the competing interests of these stakeholders.

Some stakeholder theorists go further, arguing that firms have to act within the interests of society because otherwise society will withdraw its support and prevent them from existing. As Davis argues, 'Society gave business its charter to exist, and that charter could be amended or revoked at any time that business fails to live up to society's expectations' (1973: 314). This charter, often called the 'licence to operate', stated that any business need to make sure everyone's rights are respected in a community. Furthermore, governments impose or loosen controls, set investment in infrastructure, provide workers through training and education, and provide healthcare for sick employees and regulation against unfair competition. Indeed, in recent years, throughout the world, governments have even been bailing out banks because of the negative impact that their failure would have had on other businesses. As a consequence, businesses must maintain enough trust in order to not be put under extra legislation.

One of the central challenges, therefore, is to define who the stakeholders are and how much to privilege them. Different versions of stakeholder theory present alternative approaches to this issue. The legal view presents a narrow list of only the legal duties a firm has; the strategic view stresses what is good for the firm, therefore privileging the importance of customers or those whose actions will impact trade (e.g. maintaining a good relationship with a key supplier and paying them on time); whereas the full stakeholder view looks at everyone the firm can impact, even if they are not likely to trade (Figure 17.8). Even this wider view can have business benefits. Consider the KitKat case from the beginning of the chapter. The orang-utan is not a consumer of Nestlé products and the activists who campaigned against Nestlé were still a small minority of consumers, but the wider impact of this campaign had the potential to damage Nestlé's long-term reputation.

Stakeholder theory also draws on business ethics. From a social justice (deontological) viewpoint, it argues that business actions should be fair. Drawing on communitarian ethics, it stresses the importance of placing the community above individual interests.

**Figure 17.8**  How wide should stakeholder theory go?

Certainly, from an ethical viewpoint stakeholder theory offers the potential for a more well-rounded view of the ethical responsibilities than the rather narrow definition of shareholder capitalism because it asks businesses to consider the overall benefits to society. Yet questions remain about how much organizations fully apply these principles.

## Real life case: the Board Charter

A recent survey for the CBI said that only 53% of people think that business makes a positive contribution to society (CBI, 2014). This is significant, as stated by Katja Hall, the CBI deputy director-general: 'Businesses simply can't operate without their employees and consumers, and part of securing long-term sustainable growth will be about rebuilding public trust in business.' John Kay, economist and chair of a government review of UK equity markets and long-term decision making, goes further, arguing: 'Making a profit is no more the purpose of business than breathing is the purpose of living'. He asks 'Why should I allow organisations that believe in profits above all else to exist in modern society? There is no good answer to that question' (cited in Confino, 2014). Kay's view is not unique. A recent survey by global accountancy firm PwC states that four out of five investors consider sustainability issues to be relevant (PwC, 2014). Stephen Green, the former boss of HSBC, recently stated that the public have lost respect for businesses, particularly in financial services, and that there is a 'widespread public perception that some multinational businesses and some wealthy individuals play fast and loose with the tax rules, so as to squirrel away income into low-tax jurisdictions and avoid making their rightful contribution to the public wellbeing' (cited by Butler, 2015). He argued that businesses should be more responsible and that this should be led by the directors.

One response to this is made by Mazars, a global accountancy, audit, and tax advisory firm with headquarters in France. In November 2014 they published a report, *The Board Charter for sustainable success* (Carey and Herbinet, 2014). Fiona Woolf, the former lord mayor of the City of London, states that the report aims to 'help business leaders to navigate the difficult waters in which they have to sail'.

The report says that 'too great an emphasis has been placed on short-term shareholder value-maximisation at the expense of a more balanced focus on long-term sustainable success' (2014: 2). The writers argue for a need to move from simply focusing on profit towards a broader concept of wealth creation, taking into consideration the impact on stakeholders and the wider society. To help firms that want to do this, they have produced a Board Charter that seeks to guide and embed long-term thinking and sustainability into the decisions of senior business leaders. They state that a company's board members should act as role models, build relationships based on authenticity and trust, and be selected to provide a broader stakeholder approach, and that the firm itself should have a long-term strategy and culture for a wider stakeholder perspective. This long-term thinking will build a more sustainable firm by protecting the firm's reputation and its 'licence to operate'.  ▶

In an exclusive interview for this textbook, Anthony Carey, partner at Mazars and co-author of the report, states that while many boards, particularly within the financial services industry, have woken up to these ethical issues, good practices have not always been adopted throughout the rest of their organizations. To rectify this, boards need to be able to know more effectively what is going on within their company. Carey states there are a number of actions that boards can take; these include:

- conducting employee engagement surveys: this aims to establish, firstly, how important employees feel ethics are and secondly whether employees feel able to raise ethical issues with their manager

- integrating ethical issues into the recruitment process: is the firm recruiting people with the right ethical values, and does the firm take ethical issues seriously during the recruitment process?

- learning from employees that leave: conducting exit interviews to gain feedback about how employees felt regarding the ethics of the company

- ensuring that the organization has effective 'speak-up' procedures: is there a fair and transparent way for employees to raise concerns; would they feel protected if they did; and is there a helpline if they want to blow the whistle?

Carey also states that all stakeholders, particularly customers and suppliers, should be listened to and learnt from (Carey, 2015).

 Visit the Online Resource Centre to read the whole report and watch our interview with Antony Carey.

## Corporate social responsibility (CSR)

Few people and, in particular, few large-scale organizations today (at least publicly) support Friedman's claim that the only responsibility businesses have is to their shareholders. Increasing attention by the press, public awareness, and campaign groups have meant that firms have to respond to issues such as sweatshop labour and environmental pollution to protect their reputation and brand image. Consequently, it is increasingly important to consider CSR (Freeman and Liedtka, 1991).

Companies such as Ford now stress the CSR credential. In our interview, Joe Greenwell, the Chairman of Ford in Britain, states that Henry Ford saw his purpose as 'broader than just making money', but in 'serving mankind' (source: Author interview with Joe Greenwell, Ford in Britain, 2012). Ford paid for schools and hospitals and got involved in the local community—something that lives on in Ford as a company. Greenwell states that all leaders within Ford throughout the world are engaged in some aspect of CSR. Ford, Greenwell states, 'clearly went beyond Milton Friedman' as he 'wanted to make the world a better place'. The pillars of Ford today—'quality, green, safe and smart'—carry on this legacy. 'Ford has given us such good opportunities and we want others to think well of it'. This is not just to do social good, but there 'is a certain amount of enlightened self-interest about it'.

 Visit the Online Resource Centre to see the full interview with Ford's Joe Greenwell.

Why might it be in Ford's interest to be seen in a good light?

Indeed, Adam Smith, who we met earlier, as well as writing *The wealth of nations* (1776/2012), also wrote *The theory of moral sentiments* (1759/1976), a book which suggested combining ethics with capitalism. In the Victorian era many business owners, particularly because of their Christian faith, became concerned about the ethics of their wealth, resulting in them setting up charities or, like Cadbury's, running their firms in a way that also looked after their workers. However, it was not until the 1950s that CSR became a serious concern within business and academia, starting with Howard Bowen (1953).

Bowen is considered the founder of CSR (Carroll, 1999). He argued that because business leaders have decision making power which impacts citizens, they have a responsibility to act in ways beyond money making but 'which are desirable in terms of the objectives and values of our society' (Bowen, 1953: 6). Interestingly, when surveyed, 93.5% of businessmen agreed with this statement (Bowen, 1953).

Over the last sixty years CSR has grown enormously as an academic discipline and business practice. Most businesses now consider it an important part of their practice (Carroll, 1999)—essential for building (or protecting) their reputation and demonstrating the positive impact they can have on society. Thus it has now become almost an obligatory requirement for most medium and large companies to issue CSR statements and reports and even to establish departments dedicated to CSR.

Visit the Online Resource Centre to see some examples of CSR statements and reports.

CSR draws on the ideas of Scottish industrialist and philanthropist Andrew Carnegie, the founder of US Steel. He believed that business is a positive force as it increases society's wealth. However, it required two key principles to be in place in order to work: (i) the charitable principle, where the more fortunate help the less fortunate; and (ii) the stewardship principle, where the rich hold the wealth 'in trust' for the rest of society (Fisher et al., 2013). Belief in these basic principles, combined with the belief that acting appropriately results in limited government intervention (particularly rules and regulations), has given CSR considerable credence in business circles (Freeman and Liedtka, 1991).

Think of a medium-to-large-sized company that you know well and search on the Internet for '[company name] CSR statement'. What do you find out?

While there is no agreed definition of CSR (Carroll, 1999), there are a few common themes (Figure 17.9). Most definitions argue that businesses have obligations (something that an organization has to do) beyond their legal (following the law) and economic obligations (making money for shareholders), towards society (for a discussion, see Carroll, 1999.)

In this section we will argue that there are two main forms of enlightened self-interest. One is the damage limitation model, which sees CSR as a way of limiting the negative side-effects of the firm's activity. This view sees CSR coming into play only when there is a potential impact on the firm. The other is the view that we have called **ethical capitalism**, which tries to integrate CSR into the heart of the firm's activities and trade on the benefits

**Ethical capitalism**
A business approach which seeks to integrate CSR as central to the purpose and activity of an organization.

**Figure 17.9** Carroll's (1991) levels of corporate social responsibility (CSR).

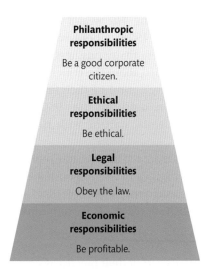

Philanthropic responsibilities

Be a good corporate citizen.

Ethical responsibilities

Be ethical.

Legal responsibilities

Obey the law.

Economic responsibilities

Be profitable.

(Figure 17.10). Firms such as Innocent Smoothies, Yeo Valley milk, and Ben and Jerry's ice cream set themselves up as being more ethical in their approach with the intention of customers buying into (and paying a premium for) more ethical and sustainable products.

These two positions can really be seen on a continuum, with many firms operating somewhere between them.

The minimal CSR perspective argues that it is in a firm's self-interest to act in a responsible way because it will save money, avoid legislation, and prevent the brand being stained. For example, the cost of BP's oil spill in 2010 was not only for the clean-up but also for the reputational implications (*The Guardian*, 2012).

**Figure 17.10** Minimal and integrated corporate social responsibility (CSR).

Minimal ⟵──────────────────────⟶ Integrated

Make money for shareholders          Core purpose of business

Prevent reputational damage          Positive social image

Legal compliance          Prevent further regulation

---

**Real life cases:** enlightened self-interest: companies responding to criticism

Many clothing retailers, such as Primark and Gap, have been accused of using sweatshop labour to provide cheap goods. As a response, they formed the Ethical Trading Initiative. They state: 'Our vision is a world where all workers are free from exploitation and discrimination, and work in conditions of freedom, security and equity. This year our corporate members' ethical trade activities touched the lives of over 9.8 million workers' (Ethical Trade Initiative, 2012).

TV celebrity chef Hugh Fearnley-Whittingstall launched a fishing campaign. He found that half of fish caught were thrown back, often nearly dead; there was over-consumption of cod, prawns, salmon, haddock, and tuna; and there were unsustainable practices for catching the tuna. The largest single tuna company, John West, was singled out from the rest of the industry for their use of fish aggregating devices (FADs) which indiscriminately catch sharks, rays, and endangered sea turtles. They recently announced they were stopping the use of FADs and would only use pole and line by 2016 (Greenpeace, 2012; John West, 2012).

Supermarkets like Sainsbury's have conducted a campaign to get people to eat alternatives to the big five fish (cod, prawns, salmon, haddock, and tuna).

Marks and Spencer's have launched a campaign 'Forever Fish—a major new campaign to help customers and their children learn more about fish, clean our British beaches and protect UK marine life' (Greenpeace, 2012; FishFight, 2012).

**Sources:** Ethical Trade Initiative (2012); Greenpeace (2012); John West (2012); FishFight (2012).

The rise of corporate social responsibility is said to produce numerous benefits for the firm. This is sometimes called the enlightened self-interest model. These benefits include:

- *attracting better employees*—as companies compete in a 'war for talent', top employees are more likely to go to a company with good CSR credentials. In a recent survey, almost 90% of respondents said they would be more likely to work for an organization that is considered ethically and socially responsible. Around 50% said they would be willing to forgo higher pay or promotion to work for a company with a good reputation, and 33% said global warming issues were 'very important' when deciding where to work (Kelly Global Workforce Index, 2012). Anthony Carey, a partner with accountancy and audit firm Mazars, argues that this makes good business sense. 'If you want the most talented team members then you need a good ethical reputation. The most talented employees want to work for ethical businesses' (Carey, 2015). This is particularly important for attracting millennials, he claims, who have ethical values 'hardwired' into them.

Would working for a more ethical company be important for you?

- *gaining more affluent customers*—having products that are Fairtrade, more sustainable, and ethically supported is often seen as attracting more affluent customers who can afford to pay more for ethical products.
- *attracting shareholders* who do not want to be associated with unethical companies. In recent times ethical investment funds have emerged: for instance, those that do not invest in arms companies or tobacco producers.
- *building long-term reputation*—speaking on BBC Radio 4 in 2011, Sir Martin Sorrell argued that if businesses are only interested in short-term profit then CSR does not matter. However, 'if you are in the business of building brands in the long term . . . you will not do things that offend society, the environment and other stakeholders'. CSR should not be an add-on or a separate department or statement. CSR should be 'embedded in the strategy of the company. CSR therefore is an essential prerequisite for the success, ensuring that the firm continues to be trusted by the public' (BBC Radio, 2011).
- *avoiding legislation*—for instance, firms avoid giving off too much pollution in order to prevent more stringent legislation from occurring. This is a critical reason for putting CSR in place and is seen in the long term as a way of reducing costs.

## Does being ethical reduce profits?

CSR scholars (e.g. Aras and Crowther, 2012) argue that CSR and profitability are not only compatible but essential. While unethical practice might, in the short term, produce a profit, in the long term they can have devastating impacts on a firm through negative implications on reputation, legislation, and employee commitment. Selfish interests and ethics coincide.

What evidence seems to suggest (see Capaldi, 2005) is that firms that apply *some* CSR to their practices do better than those that are completely unethical, but also do better than those that really try to integrate their ethical practices. Melvin Tumin calls this the 'principle of least morality' (1964). It costs to be seen as really bad, but it is also expensive to do very good activity. The most financially prudent and successful way is to do just enough to be seen as not negative.

It is arguable that enlightened self-interest is not really ethical at all. According to this view, doing a good act because it is for your own benefit could simply be considered as self-interest and does little to challenge the dominance of large-scale corporations (Banerjee, 2008).

## Greenwashing: do CSR statements really result in ethical practice?

While CSR statements are popular, there are substantial questions over whether companies are more concerned with presenting a positive image than changing their practice. This concern is illustrated by the next real life case.

---

**Real life case:** the corporate social responsibility of Walmart

Walmart is one of the world's largest companies (in the UK they own Asda), with a revenue of $482.2 billion (Walmart, 2015). The supermarket is famous for selling food, clothes, and many other consumer goods at low prices.

In recent years they have become increasingly focused on presenting a positive image about their CSR. Their CSR statement states they have a positive impact on society and many of their adverts stress the benefits to the customers' families, the community, and their employees. They state that they seek to integrate sustainability into every aspect of their business and are taking a global outlook on their responsibility to communities throughout the world. They now publish a Global Responsibility Report (Walmart, 2012a) detailing their activities. These include working towards zero landfill waste globally, expanding the use of local produce, commitment to sourcing $20 billion of products from women-only businesses, donating millions of dollars to support those experiencing natural disasters, and clearer labelling to help customers make more healthy choices.

They also state that integrity is at the heart of what they do. For instance, they state that they treat their employees, who they call associates, and all suppliers with respect and dignity. All new associates have to complete e-learning modules in ethics, which takes four hours. The company also complete global ethics education, which they are now rolling out throughout the world.

They also engage directly in philanthropy, giving $958 million annually ($500 million in-kind within the USA) and plan, by 2015, to donate $1.1 billion of food.

Robert Greenwald's documentary *Wal*mart: The high cost of low price* (2005) argues that Walmart are not as ethical as they present themselves to be. The film shows Walmart's CEO, Harold Lee Scott, speaking about the great economic and social benefits that the company brings, creating jobs and opportunities not only in the USA but throughout the world. However, Greenwald argues that the reality is somewhat different. He accuses Walmart of driving down wages, resulting in the employees being forced to rely on the state to support their families; promoting only part-time working, thereby avoiding the cost of benefits paid to full-time workers; union-busting activities; demanding unpaid overtime from staff; and lobbying for tax cuts.

One of the most notable examples in the film was an interview conducted with Jim Bill Lynn, Walmart's former global services operations manager. His job was to make sure that the factories making Walmart products in Mexico, Central America, and South America complied with the code of conduct that Walmart had to provide clean, safe, and humane working conditions. Lynn stated he was very loyal to Walmart, claiming if you cut him he 'would have bled Walmart blue blood'.

During his inspections, he states that he found 'female workers subjected to mandatory pregnancy testing, padlocked fire doors, a lack of available drinking water, workers that were locked in factory compounds until released by management, and other shocking conditions'. He also observed threats by management against employees for revealing these conditions. After his first factory inspection, he went home to his hotel room, phoned his wife and 'wept' (Greenwald, 2005).

He believed that once they were aware of these violations, Walmart would 'do the right thing' and enforce the code. However, Lynn claims that rather than welcoming this information, they in fact sacked him for doing his job. This, Greenwald implies, challenges Walmart's CSR claims.

Walmart vigorously attacked the film, arguing that it was biased and misinformed and was created by anti-Walmart activists. Walmart stress how they are making positive impacts on the lives of people in developing countries. They cite interventions such as the Women's Economic Empowerment Initiative in Bangladesh, where they support 60,000 women with basic numeracy and literacy schemes so they can calculate their overtime (Walmart, 2012b), and a scholarship in India to help women to develop retail skills in order to become more independent (Walmart, 2012c).

Visit the Online Resource Centre for links to the claims Walmart make and the criticisms that campaigners make about their impact, and make up your own mind.

# Sustainability

In recent years, particularly reflecting concerns over climate change, sustainability has risen on the agenda. While this is, in part, an environmental concern (using the earth's natural resources in a sustainable manner) it has also come to mean sustainability of the organization. It has therefore become quite a woolly concept and means different things to different people. However, a good working definition has been provided by former Norwegian Prime Minister Gro Harlem Brundtland: 'meeting the needs of the present without compromising the ability of future generations to meet their own needs' (World Commission on Environment and Development, 1987: 43).

## Real life case: Ford's EcoBoost

While for most environmental campaigners the car is the symbol of pollution and the destruction of the environment, over the last few years car manufacturers have increasingly been designing cars that have better environmental credentials. They have been working on cars that have lower fuel consumption, cars with lower carbon dioxide ($CO_2$) emissions per mile, hybrid cars, and, in the long term, fuel cell technology so that by 2050 we will have zero-emission cars (Greenwell, 2011).

The Ford Focus Econetic.
**Source:** © Ford in Britain.

Every car manufacturer is now producing more environmentally friendly cars. Joe Greenwell, Chairman of Ford in Britain, argues that the car industry 'bought the science [on climate change] a while back' and has been working on reducing the $CO_2$ emissions of cars for many years.

It is necessary to comply with European legislation, but in our interview, Greenwell states that it is 'not a compliance issue but a competitive race . . . as the customer in general sees the benefits'. He says climate change groups see the automobile industry as a good example of where 'regulation has been useful in encouraging us as a manufacturing group to compete with each other to get $CO_2$ emissions down'.

Customers, however, have not bought into all eco-cars, largely because some are expensive, and Greenwell states the industry believes there is more that it needs to do to convince them. 'The customer has to see value.' It has moved from compliance to competitive advantage as customers become more interested in eco-cars. He argues that low carbon technology is a tremendous opportunity for growth for car manufacturers.

**Source:** Author interview with Joe Greenwell, Ford in Britain, 2012.

Visit the Online Resource Centre for the full interview with Joe Greenwell, Chairman of Ford in Britain.

**Figure 17.11** The triple bottom line.

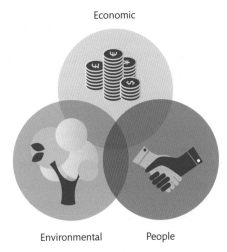

Economic

Environmental        People

## Triple bottom line

Whereas shareholder capitalism only looks to the 'bottom line' of profit, the idea of the 'triple bottom line' extends the organization's focus to include people and the planet (Figure 17.11).

Developed by John Elkington of consultancy firm SustainAbility, it works on the basis that by measuring performance it improves the focus on people and planet. It aims to create a set of measures, called metrics, for all of a firm's activities. By measuring them the belief is that it will change their behaviour. While profit is easy to measure, the impact on people and the plant is harder. Balancing the different bottom lines is also a challenge. However, this does represent an interesting way of putting into 'hard' terms (i.e. numbers) many of the social and environmental concerns that CSR and sustainability raise.

# Ethical capitalism

**Running case:** Chance needs to decide between money and reputation

Chance realizes that he is on the horns of a dilemma. Yes, the weddings are making a lot of money, but they are beginning to create a bad reputation for Junction Hotel, and this is hitting the business. He had heard that at a recent wedding fair at least two couples had said they did not want to get married at the hotel because of what they'd read in the papers about people getting drunk and aggressive. 'We need to turn this around,' he thinks, 'but how?' So, he calls in Linda Wilkinson for a meeting.

'We need to grab hold of the agenda and show that we are putting something back into the local economy,' Wilkinson suggests. 'How about we get all our food locally—sustainably, and seasonally. You know, local beef and pork, freshly-picked vegetables . . . people really go for that sort of thing. We could buy in local beer from the microbrewery and also start offering eco-weddings. Then, get it out in the paper to show that we are doing good things for this area—creating jobs and supporting the environment. You never know, we might even get a better class of customer and not have the same problems.'

Our third perspective extends the CSR/sustainability issue by arguing that rather than being an add-on to existing practice, ethics needs to be at the heart of business. A firm can no longer simply 'appear' ethical—they have to actually practise ethical behaviour; otherwise, in the world of social media, they will be found out. For instance, in *Who cares wins* David Jones claims that 'Consumers now know more about companies and expect more of them' (2012: 4). He argues that in the world of social media greater attention is placed on companies' ethical standards. It is not enough to appear ethical—they need to be ethical.

Similarly, in *Screw business as usual* Sir Richard Branson (2011) argues that businesses should be a force for good in the world. He asks his reader to imagine the potential of all the businesses in the world coming together to do good for society. He claims the boundaries between doing good and doing well are becoming merged. He writes that if he had 'one message' to help the next generation of entrepreneurs it is 'doing good can help improve your prospects, your profits and your business; and it can change the world' (2011: 2). The idea of a conflict between profits and being ethical is a 'false dilemma', Branson claims; 'business as usual isn't working. In fact, it's "business as usual" that's wrecking our planet. Resources are being used up; the air, the sea, the land—are all heavily polluted. The poor are getting poorer.' While capitalism has 'created economic growth in the world and brought many wonderful benefits to people [it has] come at a cost that is not reflected on the balance sheet' (2011: 20–1). Being ethical and making money is therefore seen as not only possible but desirable.

Jones (2012) provides a number of fascinating examples, including Levi's Water<Less Jeans, Marks & Spencer's Plan A, and Dove's Campaign for Real Beauty, all of which have sought to put ethics at the heart of their actions.

Visit the Online Resource Centre for more examples.

## Employability skills: put ethical actions on your CV

Both David Jones (2012) and Richard Branson (2011) argue that ethical capitalism is on the rise and, in the future, numerous jobs and businesses will focus on this emerging area of business. Branson claims that successful entrepreneurs will combine ethics and business, and Jones claims that consumers are driving businesses to greater social responsibility. These views are backed up by the professional services company KPMG, who state 'Business leaders are increasingly realizing the need to integrate environmental and social issues within the business strategy' (KPMG, 2011: 1). As we saw in the KitKat example and the MBA oath, many feel that there is a need for businesses to be more aware of the ethical dimensions of their actions. Therefore, CSR and employability do not, necessarily, have to be seen in opposition.

As you develop your CV, including something that demonstrates a good understanding of CSR can be very useful. As Lord Michael Hastings (2008), KPMG's global head of citizenship and diversity, states: 'I think that any of the big FTSE 100 companies is utterly and expectantly approachable on CSR'. He goes on to say that when putting together your CV you should highlight things that you have done that have done good, not as extras under CSR but that are integral to your CV. In doing so you will demonstrate that you 'love making a difference'. Finally, find a job where you feel you can make a positive impact on the world. This will turn your job from being a 'duty' to 'an opportunity to make a powerful difference in the world' around you.

## Review questions

| | |
|---|---|
| **Describe** | What are the key principles behind stakeholder capitalism? |
| **Explain** | What is meant by the 'triple bottom line'? |
| **Analyse** | Why do stakeholder capitalism and ethical capitalism see shareholder capitalism as unsustainable, both for the planet *and* for the businesses concerned? Which position do you consider stronger and why? |
| **Apply** | Consider a company that you know well and try to list all the stakeholders that you can think of (remember to include those in the supply chain and those who are indirectly impacted by the organization or might have an interest in it). Using the three models listed, which ones would fit in a legal, strategic, or wide definition of stakeholders? Which would you consider the most important and why? |

# 'Ethical within capitalism'

While CSR and ethical capitalism have brought with them a number of benefits, for many academics and campaigners they do not go far enough. They state that an organization's primary purpose should be not to make money but to do social good: for example, to help particular communities and the environment, to promote particular causes, or to create more humane work practices.

## Real life case: Sound Bites

Sound Bites in Derby are a local, organic, and wholefoods shop that specialize in providing sustainable and ethical food. Not only are the products they sell seeking to be ethical—organic, Fairtrade, and ecological—but the way that they run the business is integral to what they do. They are a workers' cooperative, which means that the workers run the shop—managing it day to day and through a weekly co-op meeting. Instead of having a boss that tells them what to do, they take collective decisions. They aim to bring about 'positive social change', not only through the things that they sell but also by being involved in boycotts and campaigns, being a hub for the community to promote social projects, and being a catalyst for increased support of socially and environmentally responsible producers and distributors.

> ▶ As Ruth Strange, one of their founders, states: 'We set up Sound Bites to make it easier for people shopping in Derby to support projects they could believe in, rather than increasing the wealth of the dominant and destructive food corporations' (author interview with Ruth Strange via email, April 2012).
>
> **Source:** Soundbites (2012).

Many of these alternative organizations are run on a not-for-profit basis, either reinvesting their surpluses back into the community or running things on a cost-only basis. Many are run as workers' cooperatives, which seek to make the workers central to the decision making processes (Parker et al., 2007; Radical Routes, 2009; Cheney et al., 2014).

Cooperatives have a long tradition. One of the most famous are the Rochdale Pioneers, a group of textile and other workers who came together to pool their resources in order to buy food and other household items. They were responding to the high prices that the mill owners charged and came together with a common goal of good service over profit. Their aims (BBC Manchester, 2010) were to have:

- open membership
- democratic control
- dividend on purchase
- limited interest on capital
- political and religious neutrality
- cash trading
- promotion of education
- sale of pure, unadulterated goods.

The Rochdale Pioneers were working-class people who came together to offer self-help and tackle their own problems (rather than receiving handouts from middle-class philanthropists). They offered an alternative model of production and exchange.

## Real life case: UK building societies

It is interesting to note that in the UK much of the financial services used to be run through mutual organizations called building societies and friendly societies. These were local, mutual societies where people would club together, often meeting in pubs, to buy their own houses. They would be run in the interests of their members, offering fairly cheap mortgages and reasonable savings rates. They were also very cautious with their lending. In the 1980s the UK Conservative government relaxed the laws to allow them to be converted into banks. Many did convert, and members of some received pay-outs of thousands of pounds each, particularly as 'carpetbaggers' (opportunists) joined them for as little as £100. Some of those that demutualized—Northern Rock, Bradford & Bingley, Halifax, Bank of Scotland (HBOs), and Alliance & Leicester—have struggled in the financial crisis.

**Sources:** BBC News (1999); Bowers (2008); Pollock (2008); Klimecki and Willmott (2009); Newcastle Building Society (2012); Nationwide Building Society (2012).

While it is impossible to predict what would have happened, many have argued that had the building societies stayed mutual then they would have had the cash reserves and safer lending policies to have weathered, or not even have landed in, the credit crisis of 2008. Have customers sacrificed long-term security for short-term profit?

'Ethical within capitalism' organizations are not only driven by social purpose but also run in a different way. One of the key ways this is done is by increasing participation in decision making. Often, one of their key principles is to be run in a non-hierarchical way in which power is distributed throughout the organization and decisions are based upon consensus rather than through orders from the leader (Parker, 2012). Consensus-based decision making is not based on voting but involves reaching a genuine, informed agreement which everyone supports or can live with. It aims to weave together the best ideas to allow the group to collectively formulate the most creative solutions. The Seeds for Change activist group is one of the key trainers and proponents for consensus-based decision making. A group that wishes to use consensus could aim to put in place the following qualities:

- *Common goal*: that everyone wants to be a part of.
- *Commitment to reaching consensus*: by honestly listening to each other and being willing to shift your position to accommodate others.
- *Trust and openness*: everyone respects each other's opinions and right to express them.
- *Sufficient time* given for consensus making so that the right decisions are made.
- *Clear process*: making sure everyone understands the process.
- *Active participation*: create a situation where everyone can feel involved.
  (Source: adapted from http://seedsforchange.org.uk/free/shortconsensus)

In doing so, these alternative organizations provide a direct challenge to many of the 'mainstream' practices that we have covered in this book (see Land and King 2014; Parker et al. 2014; Griffin et al. 2015). They turn the pursuit of profit on its head by making the ambition for the organization to work for social good or to create employment opportunities where, in conventional terms, they would not exist.

### Real life case: *The Take*

At the height of the Argentinian economic collapse in 2001, numerous factories were closed resulting in job losses and massive unemployment. Avi Lewis and Naomi Klein's film *The Take* (Lewis, 2004) tells the dramatic story of how one set of workers from the Forja car factory start occupying the factory in which they used to work and make it function again. Whereas the managers and accountants had abandoned it as a going concern, seeing it only for its scrap metal value, the workers started cleaning up the machines and turning it into a working plant again. They set up a workers cooperative, run on democratic lines, with the aim of giving them a livelihood (see also Lavaca Collective, 2007; Magnani, 2009).

The film is fascinating in showing how motivating this struggle for workers' control is and how shop-floor democracy works in practice (cf. Taylorism in Chapter 3), but also how challenging it is to run things in this way when it works against the interests of the banks and former owners who see the factory for its scrap metal value rather than as an opportunity to create jobs.

'Ethical within capitalism' models do not, therefore, focus primarily on what is most effective or efficient in traditional management terms (i.e. profit) but, instead, direct their attention to what maximizes human freedom, growth, and personal autonomy. They therefore offer a different model not only of what organizations can be, but also of the type of society and culture that they would like to create (Parker et al., 2014). The focus on mutual aid, community, personal growth, expression, and empowerment is often seen by their members as working in direct opposition to the consumerism of much of Western society (Parker et al., 2007; Radical Routes, 2009).

While small in number in comparison with the power and influence of large corporations that tend to dominate society and business, these organizations do cover a wide variety of areas including housing, food, transport, and even construction. Many work in education, often teaching people long-forgotten skills to help them become more independent in their lives and build up community bonds to become less reliant on large-scale corporations. In doing so they aim for more sustainable and ethical organizations and, with them, a reform of society.

Visit the Online Resource Centre for a list of alternative organizations.

## 'Ethical within capitalism' assessed

Non-capitalist organizations often aim for highly progressive principles. Their emphasis on community, empowerment, personal growth, and social change offers a fascinating and exciting vision of how organizations and society could be. However, sometimes they fail to live up to their ideals, having their own prejudices and blind-spots. For instance, Sherryl Kleinman (1996) describes a holistic health centre which, while run on alternative grounds, allegedly ends up reproducing the same practices of exclusion, power, and gendered relations that many accuse mainstream organizations of doing. This shows the challenges of really acting in an alternative way—at least within the existing capitalist society.

Often, things like organic, Fairtrade, or local and craft products are more expensive than their less ethical counterparts and so are sometimes only available for those who have more money.

# 'Ethical against capitalism'

### Running case: Chance tries to balance ethics and profits

Chance considers Wilkinson's views—they make sense. The more he thinks about it the more he begins to see possibilities for environmental and social improvements within the hotel. Some, he comes to realize, could actually save money: better loft insulation, eco-lights, reduction of food waste, key-cards for rooms to switch off electricity, and reducing the washing of towels. Others, though, might be more expensive, such as trying to get the hotel to reach zero carbon emissions (which would require refitting the whole hotel), insulating the whole building, or buying only organic food. 'There's only so far I can go, really,' Chance thinks to himself. 'It is a challenge balancing profits with ethics.'

While alternative business practices offer another, potentially more sustainable, humane, and ethical approach to running organizations, for many campaigners and some academics, particularly those of the critical management and Marxist perspectives, it is the economic system itself that is destructive and needs overturning. They argue that the problem is not individual people or even organizations, but capitalism as an economic system. They believe we cannot simply try to reform the system—we need to overthrow it.

Inspired by critics of capitalism, such as Marx and Engels, and anarchists, such as Proudhon (2011), many thinkers from Marxist tradition, the Frankfurt School, post-structuralist tradition, and libertarian tradition have long argued that the capitalist system is fundamentally exploitative and destructive. They argue that as an economic system, with its relentless focus on growth and profit, it is destructive to the environment, to people, and to society. It breeds inequality, exploitation, and social division and, through this, makes everyone poorer. It makes humans compete with each other rather than cooperate. According to this view, we are all trapped in an economic system that we have very little control over. It also holds us back from reaching our true human creative potential. Capitalism also perpetuates inequality by drawing wealth towards the rich and away from the poor.

### Real life case: 'Occupy' and other protest movements

The 'Occupy' movement sought to expose not only the vast profit and greed of the 'city', but the way that these institutions are intertwined to perpetuate the existing order. Proponents of this movement argue that the current economic system takes power, control, and money away from local communities and places it in the hands of large corporations, leaving individuals and communities feeling largely powerless.

They argue for alternative economic systems, like local money spendable only in local communities so that they can be allowed to flourish; local businesses rather than large-scale corporations; and economic activities to support human need rather than the other way round (OccupyLondon, 2012; How to Occupy, 2012).

Occupy was also interesting in the way that it was organized. It used social media to coordinate activities, but it also was based on continued discussion (Van Stekelenburg, 2012). The aim of movements such as Occupy was to reflect in their practice the values that they were espousing (Maeckelbergh, 2009, 2011). These included making the decision making process highly democratic and participative, where decisions were made through consensus rather than by a top-down leader. The movement was also highly diverse, with different groups and different countries acting around their own local concerns (Barker, 2012).

Central to their activity is to introduce more democratic and accountable ways of acting. They therefore operate without leaders, but work in a collective way focusing on collective decision making and empowering members to take ownership and control where they are. While they might not be overthrowing capitalism, they do offer a powerful image of an alternative (McDonald, 2006).

Anti-capitalist theorists argue that it is impossible, even when one sets out with good intentions, to act in a fully ethical manner (such as 'ethical within capitalism' models) within the current economic system—one would not be challenging capitalism as a system and therefore would face the dangers of being dragged back in. Business ethics, it is therefore suggested, acts as little more than a mask, deflecting attention away from what should be the actual target of capitalism as an economic system itself (Parker, 2002). It allows businesses to carry on in their usual practices without changing their underlying structure from a for-profit structure.

For instance, making more environmentally sustainable products might be commendable in that they are more sustainable and ethical; however, it could be argued that this does not overcome the deeper problem of consumerism and the pursuit of profit by capitalist firms. Capitalism as an economic system still drives firms to need to produce and sell more products, expand their sales, and have an economy based on increased growth. Anti-capitalists argue that capitalism as an economic system is therefore a driver towards economic growth rather than human need, and that more sustainable products do not really solve the problem. In other words, it is not just making products in an unsustainable way that is the problem: it is really our desire (created by marketing) for more products that we do not need (McDonald, 2006; Parker et al., 2007; Radical Routes, 2009).

Such views, while very interesting, require a fundamental overthrowing of the capitalist system which, except for the most optimistic of campaigners, does not seem that likely in the short-term (although the 'Arab Spring' of 2011 shows how quickly things can change). This conclusion does not, though, remove the ethical, social, and environmental challenges that exist today and therefore the need to still consider business ethics.

# Chapter summary and reflections for the future

It is easy to be cynical about the ethical and sustainable credentials of businesses, but, as we have seen, it is an area that has become increasingly high on the media, consumer, and business agenda. While shareholder capitalism is a powerful force, stakeholder theory—particularly through CSR and sustainability—is now a mainstream force within business and society; most people expect businesses, at least to some extent, to hold a certain level of responsibility.

Others, though, would like businesses to go further, arguing that the pace of change is too slow and that businesses largely act in order to protect their own interests. Ethical capitalism might present a growth area for the economy as increasing attention is placed on local, sustainable, and ethical products. However, these are often quite expensive and out of reach of poorer consumers.

Therefore, substantial questions remain about the nature of capitalism and whether businesses should be governed for the interests of the shareholders, consumers, and society as a whole. These are personal as well as societal issues, and worthy of strong debate.

## Review questions

| | |
|---|---|
| **Describe** | What alternatives to capitalism exist? |
| **Explain** | What are some of the key objections to capitalism that the 'ethical within' and 'ethical against' capitalism models hold? |
| **Analyse** | Is an alternative to capitalism possible and desirable? Would it bring its own problems? |

## Further reading

**Boje, D.M. 1998. Nike, Greek goddess of victory or cruelty? Women's stories of Asian factory life.** *Journal of Organizational Change Management* **11(6): 461–80.**
In this controversial article, David Boje describes some of the key criticisms made of a factory making Nike products, including physical and verbal abuse of the workers, long hours, and low pay. What is most fascinating is that it was originally withdrawn by the journal—visit the Online Resource Centre for links to Boje's own explanation of what happened and for links to the original article.

**Bakan, J. 2005.** *The corporation: The pathological pursuit of profit and power.* **Constable and Robinson: London.**
In this book, which also led to a popular documentary film, Bakan provides a challenging analysis of the legal foundations of the modern corporation, arguing that if judged against the World Health Organization's mental health criteria the corporation is a psychopath. This readable and interesting book provides some excellent case studies, as well as good theoretical contributions.

**Ngai, P. 2004. Women workers and precarious employment in Shenzhen Special Economic Zone, China.** *Gender and Development* **12(2): 29–36.**
This interesting article describes the difficult working conditions of garment workers in China. While it is a little dated, recent case studies have shown these conditions continue in many developing countries.

**Fisher, C., Lovell, A., and Valero-Silva, N. 2013.** *Business ethics and values.* **Prentice Hall: Harlow.**
This business ethics textbook provides an excellent introduction to many of the key business ethics theories with a number of interesting case studies.

## References

Ackrill, M., and Hannah, L. 2001. *Barclays: The business of banking, 1690–1996*. Cambridge University Press: Cambridge.

Alvesson, M., and Willmott, H. 1992. *Making sense of management*. Sage: London.

Aras, G., and Crowther, D. 2012. *Governance and social responsibility: International perspectives*. Palgrave: London.

Arnold, M., and Binham, C. 2015. City of London 'black book' is called for to track 'bad apple' traders. *Financial Times*, 19 February.

Bakan, J. 2005. *The corporation: The pathological pursuit of profit and power*. Constable and Robinson: London.

Banerjee, S. 2008. Corporate social responsibility: The good, the bad and the ugly. *Critical Sociology* 34(1): 51–79.

Barker, A. J. 2012. Already occupied: Indigenous peoples, settler colonialism and the occupy movements in North America. *Social Movement Studies* 11(3-4): 327–34.

Bates, D. 2015. The chocolate companies on the hunt for a sustainable Easter egg. *The Guardian*, 27 March.

Bawden, T., and Sheffield, H. 2015. Petrobras scandal adds to $16.8b losses: how gang allegedly used

Spanx and cling film to smuggle millions. *The Independent*, 23 April.

BBC Manchester 2010. How Rochdale Pioneers changed commerce forever. Available at: http://news.bbc.co.uk/local/manchester/hi/people_and_places/history/newsid_8838000/8838778.stm (last accessed 26 August 2015).

BBC News 1999. Building Society offers £1000 windfall. Available at: http://news.bbc.co.uk/1/hi/business/your_money/523936.stm (last accessed 24 November 2012).

BBC News 2010. Nocton super dairy cow numbers to be cut. Available at: http://www.bbc.co.uk/news/uk-england-lincolnshire-11747601 (last accessed 11 July 2012).

BBC News 2011. Southern Cross set to shut down and stop running homes. Available at: http://www.bbc.co.uk/news/business-14102750 (last accessed 24 November 2012).

BBC News 2014. Penalise 'bad apple' traders, suggests Bank of England. Available at: http://www.bbc.co.uk/news/business-29788270 (last accessed 2 July 2015).

BBC News 2015a. New measures pledge to make Scottish NHS whistleblowing easier. Available at: http://www.bbc.co.uk/news/uk-scotland-scotland-politics-33224516 (last accessed 2 July 2015).

BBC News 2015b. Bangladesh murder trial over Rana Plaza factory collapse. Available at: http://www.bbc.co.uk/news/world-asia-32956705 (last accessed 30 July 2015).

BBC Radio 2011. Desert Island Discs. *Martin Sorrell*. BBC Radio 4. Available at: http://www.bbc.co.uk/radio/player/b017vjlw (last accessed 28 November 2012).

BBC Television 2011a *Newsnight*. BBC 2, 13 June.

BBC Television 2011b When Bankers Were Good. BBC2, 23 November.

Bilton, R. 2014. Apple 'failing to protect Chinese factory workers'. Available at: http://www.bbc.co.uk/news/business-30532463 (last accessed 29 July 2015).

Bloomberg Business 2015. Michael Wolf M.Sc. Available at: http://www.bloomberg.com/research/stocks/people/person.asp?personId=8687570&ticker=SWEDA:SS (last accessed 30 July 2015).

Boatright, J.R. 2013. Confronting ethical dilemmas in the workplace. *Financial Analysts Journal*, 69(5): 6–9.

Böhm, S., Misoczky, M.C., and Moog, S. 2012. Greening capitalism? A Marxist critique of carbon markets. *Organization Studies* 33 (11): 1617–38.

Bowen, H. 1953. *Social responsibilities of the businessman*. Harper & Row: New York.

Bowers, S. 2008. Bradford & Bingley: Cast of characters, from demutualisation to nationalisation. *The Guardian*, 24 November.

Bowers, S. 2014. MP criticises HSBC for directors' threats to quit over accountability rules. *The Guardian*, 30 November.

Branson, R. 2011. *Screw business as usual*. Virgin Books: London.

Briggs, H. 2015. China climate change plan unveiled. Available at: http://www.bbc.co.uk/news/science-environment-33317451 (last accessed 4 July 2015).

Burn-Callander, R. 2015. Sorrell says high pay is for 'top-of-the-tree' performance. *The Telegraph*, 7 June.

Butler, S. 2015. Former HSBC boss speaks of 'deep regret' at Swiss tax avoidance scandal. *The Guardian*, 18 March.

Capaldi, N. 2005. Corporate social responsibility and the bottom line. *International Journal of Social Economics* 32(5): 408–23.

Carey, A. 2015. The Board Charter. Interview with Daniel King.

Carey, A., and Herbinet, D. 2014. *The Board Charter for Sustainable Success*. Mazars: London.

Carlyle, E. 2012. Meet the eight Forbes 400 billionaires who just signed the Giving Pledge. Available at: http://www.forbes.com/sites/erincarlyle/2012/09/18/forbes-400-billionaires-whove-signed-the-giving-pledge/ (last accessed 24 November 2012).

Carroll, A. 1991. The pyramid of corporate social responsibility: Toward the moral management of organizational stakeholders. *Business Horizons* 34: 39–48.

Carroll, A. 1999. Corporate social responsibility: Evolution of a definitional construct. *Business Society* 38: 268–95.

CBS News 2012. Xbox 360 workers reportedly threaten mass suicide. Available at: http://www.cbsnews.com/8301-205_162-57357444/xbox-360-workers-reportedly-threaten-mass-suicide/ (last accessed 11 July 2012).

CBI 2014. CBI launches campaign to boost public confidence in business. Available at: http://www.cbi.org.uk/media-centre/press-releases/2014/09/cbi-launches-campaign-to-boost-public-confidence-in-business/ (last accessed 30 July 2015).

CECP 2015. Giving in Numbers brief 2015. http://cecp.co/pdfs/giving_in_numbers/GIN_8x11_HighRes.pdf (last accessed 2 July 2015).

Chartered Association of Business Schools 2015. Ethics Guide 2015.

Cheney, G., Santa Cruz, I., Peredo, A.M., and Nazareno, E. 2014. Worker cooperatives as an organizational alternative: Challenges, achievements and promise in business governance and ownership. *Organization* 21(5): 591–603.

Confino, J. 2014. Society must call business' bluff on its fixation with profit maximisation. *The Guardian*, 5 November.

Connors, W., and Trevisani, P. 2015. World News: Brazil 'carwash' shrugs off ties to corruption scandal. *Wall Street Journal, Europe*, 23 June.

Costas, R. 2014. Petrobras scandal: Brazil's energy giant under pressure. Available at: http://www.bbc.co.uk/news/business-30129184 (last accessed 2 July 2015).

Covey, S. 2004. *The 7 habits of highly effective people*. Simon and Schuster: London.

Crouch, D. 2015. Swedish private jet scandal claims seventh scalp. *The Guardian*, 11 February.

Currie, G., Knights, D., and Starkey, K. 2010. Introduction: A post-crisis critical reflection on business schools. *British Journal of Management* 21(s1): s1–s5.

*Daily Mail* 2010. Battery farm for cows: 8,000 animals to be housed in milk factory. Available at: http://www.dailymail.co.uk/news/article-1254467/Battery-farm-cows-8-000-animals-housed-milk-factory.html (last accessed 11 July 2012).

*Daily Mail* 2011. You are NOT allowed to commit suicide: Workers in Chinese iPad factories forced to sign pledges. Available at: http://www.dailymail.co.uk/news/article-1382396/Workers-Chinese-Apple-factories-forced-sign-pledges-commit-suicide.html (last accessed 11 July 2012).

*Daily Telegraph* 2011. Plans for 'mega dairy' scrapped amid fears for the environment. Available at: http://www.telegraph.co.uk/earth/earthnews/8328927/Plans-for-mega-dairy-scrapped-amid-fears-for-the-environment.html (last accessed 11 July 2012).

Davis, K. 1973. The case for and against business assumption of social responsibilities. *Academy of Management Journal* 16(2): 312–22.

Dellheim, C. 1987. The creation of a company culture: Cadburys 1861-1931. *The American Historical Review* 92(1): 13–44.

Dredge, S. 2015. Taylor Swift criticises 'shocking, disappointing' Apple Music. *The Guardian*, 21 June.

DuFault, A. 2013. Can fashion companies use technology to connect with supply chain workers? *The Guardian*, 9 October.

Ethical Trading Initiative 2012. About ETI. Available at: http://www.ethicaltrade.org/about-eti (last accessed 24 November 2012).

Fisher, C., and Lovell, A. 2009. *Business ethics and values: Individual, corporate and international perspectives*. Prentice Hall: Harlow.

Fisher, C., Lovell, A., and Valero-Silva, N. 2013. *Business ethics and values*, 4th edn. Pearson, Financial Times: London.

Fishfight 2012. Available at: http://www.fishfight.net (last accessed 23 November 2012).

Ford Foundation 2012. History. Available at: http://www.fordfoundation.org/about-us/history (last accessed 23 November 2012).

Freeman, E., and Liedtka, J. 1991. Corporate social responsibility: A critical approach. *Business Horizons* 34(4): 92–8.

Friedman, M. 1970. The social responsibility of business is to increase its profits. *New York Times Magazine*, 13 September.

Geyelin, M. 1999. How a memo written 26 years ago is costing General Motors dearly. *Wall Street Journal*. Available at: http://online.wsj.com/article/SB9385366607816889.html (last accessed 28 November 2012).

Gies, E. 2014. Greenpeace report on P&G's palm oil sources could spur industry change. *The Guardian*, 31 March.

Gilligan, C. 1982. *In a different voice: Psychological theory and women's development*. Harvard University Press: Cambridge, MA.

Giving Pledge 2012. Available at: http://givingpledge.org/ (last accessed 24 November 2012).

Gov.uk. 2015. Whistleblowing for employees. Available at: https://www.gov.uk/whistleblowing/overview (last accessed 2 July 2015).

Grant, J. 2015. Bank of England acts to encourage whistleblowers. *Financial Times*, 11 June.

Greenpeace 2010. Ask Nestlé CEO to stop buying palm oil from destroyed rainforest. Available at: http://www.youtube.com/watch?v=1BCA8dQfGi0 (last accessed 28 November 2012).

Greenpeace 2012. Available at: http://www.greenpeace.org.uk/blog/oceans/and-then-there-were-none-john-west-changes-its-tuna-20110726 (last accessed 23 November 2012).

Greenpeace 2013. Certifying destruction. http://www.greenpeace.org/international/Global/international/publications/forests/2013/Indonesia/RSPO-Certifying-Destruction.pdf (last accessed 5 July 2015).

Greenwald, R. 2005. *Wal\*Mart: The high cost of low price*. Brave New Films: Culver City.

Greenwell, J. 2011. Responding to the twin challenges of global motor industry—sustainability and gridlock. Lecture at Nottingham Trent University, Nottingham, UK.

Griffin, M., Learmonth, M., and Elliott, C. 2015. Non-domination, contestation and freedom: The contribution of Philip Pettit to learning and democracy in organisations. *Management Learning* 46(3): 317–36.

Hardin, G. 1968. The tragedy of the commons. *Science* 162(3859): 1243–8.

Harding, L. 2014. How Edward Snowden went from loyal NSA contractor to whistleblower. *The Guardian*, 1 February.

Harvard Business Review Staff 2014. The best-performing CEOs in the world. *Harvard Business Review*, November.

Hastings, M. 2008. Everyone's talking about corporate social responsibility. YouTube. Available at: http://www.youtube.com/watch?v=TNKn93VViUc (last accessed 24 November 2012).

Hawkshaw, R., Hawkshaw, S., and Sumaila, U.R. 2012. The tragedy of the 'Tragedy of the commons': Why coining too good a phrase can be dangerous. *Sustainability* 4(11): 3141–50.

Heffernan, M. 2011. *Wilful blindness: Why we ignore the obvious*. Simon and Schuster: New York.

Hickman, M. 2009. Have a break—have an ethical Kit Kat. *The Independent*, 23 October. Available at: http://www.independent.co.uk/life-style/food-and-drink/news/have-a-breakndash-have-an-ethical-kit-kat-1835608.html (last accessed 11 July 2012).

High Pay Centre 2014. *Executive remuneration in the FTSE 350—a focus on performance-related pay.*

High Pay Commission 2011.*Cheques with balances: Why tackling high pay is in the national interest*. Final Report of the High Pay Commission.

How to Occupy 2012. A quick guide to revolution. Available at: http://howtocamp.takethesquare.net/2012/09/05/quick-guide-for-a-revolution-multi-language/ (last accessed 24 November 2012).

Human Rights Watch 2013. Bangladesh: Tragedy shows urgency of worker protections. Available at: http://www.hrw.org/news/2013/04/25/bangladesh-tragedy-shows-urgency-worker-protections (last accessed 30 July 2015).

IPCC 2014. *Climate change 2014 synthesis report*. Intercovernmental Panel on Climate Change: Geneva.

John West 2012. Available at: http://www.john-west.co.uk/sustainability (last accessed 23 November 2012).

Jones, D. 2012. *Who cares wins: Why good business is better business*. FT Publishing: London.

Kakulas, V. 2015. Oil and gas giant Woodside Petroleum sacks seven workers for fraud. *Perth Now*, 19 March.

Kelly Global Workforce Index 2012. The modern workforce: Acquisition and retention in the war for talent. Available at: http://www.kellyocg.com/uploadedFiles/Content/Knowledge/Kelly_Global_Workforce_Index_Content/Acquisition%20and%20Retention%20in%20the%20War%20for%20Talent%20Report.pdf.

Kenny, K. 2014a. What's luck got to do with it? Everything, if you are a banking whistleblower. https://theconversation.com/whats-luck-got-to-do-with-it-everything-if-you-are-a-banking-whistleblower-34689 (last accessed 29 July 2015).

Kenny, K. 2014b. Banking compliance and dependence corruption: Towards an attachment perspective. *Law and Financial Markets Review* 8(2): 165–77.

Kenny, K. 2015. We need to protect the whistleblowers who save our skins but pay the price. Available at: https://theconversation.com/we-need-to-protect-the-whistleblowers-who-save-our-skins-but-pay-the-price-41635 (last accessed 29 July 2015).

Kleinman, S. 1996. *Opposing ambitions: Gender and identity in an alternative organization*. University of Chicago Press: Chicago.

Klimecki, R., and Willmott, H. 2009. From demutualisation to meltdown: A tale of two wannabe banks. *Critical Perspectives on International Business* 5(1/2): 120–40.

KPMG 2011. *Corporate responsibility survey 2011: Marching towards embracing sustainability development*. KPMG: India. Available at: http://www.kpmg.com/IN/en/IssuesAndInsights/ArticlesPublications/Documents/Corporate-Responsibilty-Survey-Report.pdf (last accessed 24 November 2012).

Land, C., and King, D. 2014. Organizing otherwise: Translating anarchism in a voluntary sector organization. *Ephemera* 14(4): 923–50.

Lavaca Collective 2007. *Sin patrón: Stories from Argentina's worker-run factories*. Haymarket Books: Chicago.

Leigh, D. 2011. Goldman Sachs let off paying £10m interest on failed tax avoidance scheme. *The Guardian*, 11 October.

Levy, D.L., and Spicer, A. 2013. Contested imaginaries and the cultural political economy of climate change. *Organization* 20(5): 659–78.

Lewis, A. 2004. *The take*. Barna-Alper Productions: Canada.

Macdonald-Smith, A. 2015. Woodside Petroleum sacked seven staff for 'fraud-related' incidents. *Sydney Morning Herald*, 19 March.

MacIntyre, A. 1967. *A short history of ethics: A history of moral philosophy from the Homeric age to the twentieth century*. Routledge: London.

Maeckelbergh, M. 2009. *The will of the many*. Pluto Press: London.

Maeckelbergh, M. 2011. Doing is believing: Prefiguration as strategic practice in the alterglobalization movement. *Social Movement Studies* 10(1): 1–20.

Magnani, E. 2009. *The silent change: Recovered businesses in Argentina*. Editorial Teseo: Buenos Aires.

Marx, K. 1859/2012. *A contribution to the critique of political economy*. Forgotten Books: London.

Matalan 2015. Bangladesh update. Available at: http://www.matalan.co.uk/corporate/bangladesh-update (last accessed 30 July 2015).

Mathew, J. 2013. Rana Plaza Disaster: M&S, Tesco, Benetton and other retailers sign safety pact for Bangladesh factories. *International Business Times*, 8 July.

McDonald, K. 2006. *Global movements: Action and culture*. Blackwell: Malden, MA.

Milne, R. 2015. Sweden flies into a corporate storm. *Financial Times*, 21 January.

Muringatheri, M. 2015. Protect whistle-blowers, says bank union. *The Hindu*, 29 June.

Nationwide Building Society 2012. Membership matters. Available at: http://www.newcastle.co.uk/help/mutuality.aspx (last accessed 24 November 2012).

Neate, R. 2012. RBS boss Stephen Hester waives bonus: Reaction. *The Guardian*, 30 January. Available at: http://www.guardian.co.uk/business/2012/jan/30/rbs-stephen-hester-bonus-reaction (last accessed 26 November 2012).

Nestlé 2015. Response to author query from Nestlé. Customer Services. Enquiry 004374179D, August 2015.

Newcastle Building Society 2012. Mutuality. Available at: http://www.newcastle.co.uk/help/mutuality.aspx (last accessed 24 November 2012).

OccupyLondon 2012. Initial statement. Available at: http://occupylondon.org.uk/about/statements/initial-statement (last accessed 24 November 2012).

Packard Foundation 2012. Our history. Available at: http://www.packard.org/about-the-foundation/our-history/ (last accessed 24 November 2012).

Parker, M. 2002. *Against management: Organization in the age of managerialism*. Polity Press 250: Cambridge.

Parker, M. 2012. Super flat: Hierarchy, culture and dimensions of organizing. *Research in the Sociology of Organizations* 35: 229–47.

Parker, M., Cheney, G., Fournier, V., and Land, C. (eds) 2014. *The Routledge companion to alternative organization*. Routledge: London.

Parker, M., Fournier, V., and Reedy, P. 2007. *The dictionary of alternatives*. Zed Books: London.

Partington, A. 1998. *The Oxford dictionary of quotations*. Oxford University Press: Oxford.

PCAW 2015. The UK whistleblowing report: Public concern at work.

Pollack, A. 1999. $4.9 billion jury verdict in G.M. fuel tank case. *New York Times*, 10 July. Available at: http://www.nytimes.com/1999/07/10/us/4.9-billion-jury-verdict-in-gm-fuel-tank-case.html (last accessed 28 November 2012).

Pollard, N. 2012. Sweden, where CEOs come cheap and still deliver. *Reuters*, 14 June.

Pollock, I. 2008. Not such a good idea after all? BBC News. Available at: http://news.bbc.co.uk/1/hi/business/7641925.stm (last accessed 24 November 2012).

Portland Communications 2014. The situation is poor and getting worse. Available at: http://www.portland-communications.com/wp-content/uploads/2014/02/portland_bringing_business_home_polling.pdf (last accessed 2 July 2015).

Proudhon, P. 2011. *Property is theft! A Pierre-Joseph Proudhon reader*. AK Press: London.

PwC 2014. *Sustainability goes mainstream: Insights into investor views*. PwC: LondonPwC.

Radical Routes 2009. Aims and principles. Available at: http://www.radicalroutes.org.uk/aims-and-principles.html (last accessed 24 November 2012).

Robins, A. 2015. Obama's climate initiative—too little too late. *The Standard*, 5 August.

Robinson, N. 2012. *Live from Downing Street: The inside story of politics, power and the media*. Bantam Press: London.

Schäfer, D., Goff. S., and Parker, G. 2012. Barclays paid chief's £5.75m tax bill. *Financial Times*, 10 March. Available at: http://www.ft.com/cms/s/0/e1115196-69d8-11e1-8996-00144feabdc0.html (last accessed 26 November 2012).

Smith, A. 1759/1976. *The theory of moral sentiments*. Clarendon Press: Oxford.

Smith, A. 1776/2012. *The wealth of nations*. Wordsworth Editions Ltd: Ware.

Smith, A. 2014. 'There were hundreds of us crying out for help': The afterlife of the whistleblower. *The Guardian*, 22 November.

Smith, M., Valle, S., and Schmidt, B. 2015. The betrayal of Brazil. *Bloomberg Business*, 8 May.

Snell, J. 2011. Why a critic of institutional care is taking over from Southern Cross. *The Guardian*, 19 October. Available at: http://www.guardian.co.uk/society/2011/oct/19/interview-anne-williams-hc-one?newsfeed=true (last accessed 24 November 2012).

Soundbites 2012. Soundbites home. Available at: http://www.soundbitesderby.org.uk/. (last accessed 27 November 2012).

Spence, E. 2015. Apple loop: Taylor Swift's PR victory, new MacBook Pro review, Apple should delete the home key. *Forbes*, 26 June.

Spicer, A. 2015. Changing culture in the banking industry. Interview with Daniel King.

Stern, N. 2006. *Stern review on the economics of climate change*. Her Majesty's Treasury: London.

Strange, R. 2012. Author interview via email, 2 April.

Tabacek, K. 2010. Nestle stars in smear campaign over Indonesian palm oil. *The Guardian*, 18 March. Available at: http://www.guardian.co.uk/sustainable-business/nestleindonesian-palm-oil (last accessed 11 July 2012).

*The Guardian* 2011. Apple's Chinese workers treated 'inhumanely, like machines', 30 April. Available at: http://www.guardian.co.uk/technology/2011/apr/30/apple-chinese-workers-treated-inhumanely (last accessed 11 July 2012).

*The Guardian* 2012. BP adds $847m to Deepwater Horizon costs, 31 July. Available at: http://www.guardian.co.uk/business/2012/jul/31/deepwater-horizon-bp-847m-dollars (last accessed 24 November 2012).

Tremlett, G. 2013. Hervé Falciani to keep up fight against tax dodgers. *The Guardian*, 12 June.

Trugman, J.M. 2015. Taylor Swift's business plan outwits Apple executives. *New York Post*, 28 June.

Tumin, M. 1964. Business as a social system. *Behavioral Science* 9(2): 120–30.

UNPRME 2015. Six principles. Available at: http://www.unprme.org/about-prme/the-six-principles.php

Van Stekelenburg, J. 2012. The occupy movement: Product of this time. *Development* 55(2): 224–31.

Walmart 2012a *Beyond 50 years: Building a sustainable future*. Walmart Stores Ltd: Bentonville, AK.

Walmart 2012b Bangladesh. Available at: http://corporate.walmart.com/global-responsibility/womens-economic-empowerment/bangladesh-anju-ara (last accessed 25 November 2012).

Walmart 2012c India. Available at: http://corporate.walmart.com/global-responsibility/womens-economic-empowerment/india-amandeep-kaur (last accessed 25 November 2012).

Walmart 2015. Corporate and financial facts. Available at: http://news.walmart.com/walmart-facts/corporate-financial-fact-sheet (last accessed 30 July 2015).

Wilkinson, R., and Pickett, K. 2010. *The spirit level: Why equality is better for everyone*. Allen Lane, Penguin: London.

Wilson, J., and Hunter, D. 2010. Research exceptionalism. *American Journal of Bioethics* 10(8): 45–54.

Wittneben, B.B., Okereke, C., Banerjee, S.B., and Levy, D.L. 2012. Climate change and the emergence of new organizational landscapes. *Organization Studies* 33(11): 1431–50.

Worland, J. 2015. U.S., China and Brazil commit to new climate change goals. *Time Magazine*, 30 June.

World Commission on Environment and Development (WCED) 1987. *Our common future*. Oxford University Press: Oxford.

Zerubavel, E. 2006. *The elephant in the room: Silence and denial in everyday life*. Oxford University Press: Oxford.

# Conclusion
*Fond farewells*

## Chapter overview and learning outcomes

By the end of this chapter you should be able to:

- explain the importance of connecting organizational behaviour theories together

- describe some of the changes that have occurred in organizations over the last forty years

- analyse why it is important to develop your lifelong learning skills.

## Introduction

In organizations, topics such as motivation, culture, emotional labour, and rational work design are not isolated issues, but are interconnected. For example, carrying out repetitive, rationalized work in the style of Taylor is not just about the topic of *rational work design*. It may have an impact in areas such as:

- your level of *motivation*
- the *culture* of the organization you work in
- how you are *trained* to do your job
- the way that you are *led* and *managed*.

Similarly, when studying organizational behaviour (OB) we should see not a series of discrete, individual topics but a set of themes and topics that are interlinked. Therefore, as we will see, in order to really understand OB and to write strong essays or perform well in exams, it is important to understand how the themes connect together. This chapter draws together some of the key themes of the book.

How are you going to link the key themes together in your essay or exam?

This chapter also asks you to consider how organizations could change in the future. As we will see, the last forty years have seen considerable change in the nature of organizations and jobs, and the next forty years may be equally changeable. With developments in smart technology, the rise of such countries as China and India, and the emerging green economy, the nature of jobs is likely to change dramatically, with many occupations that will be common in the future not even existing in the present day.

# Pulling things together

**Running case:** Meg Mortimer's last day

'It is 6 am and you are listening to Calm FM,' Meg Mortimer's radio blurts out in the same way as it has every morning for the last forty years. 'The headlines today . . .,' the presenter drones on in his usual way, with Meg playing little attention. For her, today there is only one headline . . . it is her last day at work.

It feels surreal knowing that this routine, which she has come to know so well, is going to be her last: getting up at 6 am and having breakfast—two slices of toast; shower at 6:20 am; walking the dog at 6:40 am; driving to work at 7 am (she'll be pleased not to have to battle through the traffic and that queue on London Road again); in the cubbyhole-cum-office at 7.45 am reading her emails, seeing the reception girls, and catching up with the gossip with the cleaners; beginning her daily inspection at 9 am; looking at the daily statistics for room bookings at 10 am; attending the daily senior management meeting at 10.30 am; attending the restaurant meeting at 11.30 am; and having lunch at 12:30 am. Then, in the afternoons, tackling emergencies, dealing with maintenance issues, having meetings with staff to solve their problems, and—the bit that she really likes—listening to them as people. Today, though, will be different. Today she is having her leaving party.

Mortimer begins to reflect on the last year. It has been a year of changes, what with the new structure, all the new procedures, and the culture that the Second-Chance Consortium has tried to bring in.

She is surprised at how successful they have been. Occupancy rates are up, cleaning times are down, the restaurant has gone from strength to strength, and the new staff are certainly professional and hard-working. Yet some of the magic, the things that she really used to love about the hotel, seem to have been lost. Yes, they are more effective and efficient, more business-like in their approach, and have clearly-stated objectives, but it is somehow different.

With all these changes she wonders whether Junction Hotel, the one that she really loves, is still there.

Sometimes work and organizational life are presented as dreary and rational—devoid of emotions or feelings—in which people go to work only to be paid, longing for the weekend and, eventually, retirement. Yet, as we have seen repeatedly throughout this book, organizational life is far more complex that it appears. The informal or what is sometimes referred to as the hidden organization can have dramatic repercussions on organizational practice.

# The challenges of managing people and organizations

**Running case:** Simon Chance reflects on a year in charge of Junction Hotel

Today is also a strange day for Simon Chance, as it has been a year since he officially began running Junction Hotel. 'How time flies,' he thinks. It only seemed yesterday that he sat in this office and began what has proved to be one of his hardest, but also most interesting, years in management. Chance looks around his office again. 'Those wooden panels are still loose,' he thinks to himself. 'It is about time that I got them fixed.'

This last year has been hard—harder than he had ever imagined. It began with such optimism, a real sense of adventure. They had made all these plans, Weaver's A3s, new work processes, business reports, and targets for every departments. They had worked—well, if he was honest, they had sort of worked. The new systems for cleaning had certainly been successful. A few people had left, but you don't make an omelette without breaking eggs, as his mother used to say. Yet so much of what they had tried to do seemed so much more difficult than they originally had thought. When he and Weaver had worked on their plans prior to buying the hotel, he had thought there would be a few quick fixes achieved by bringing in a few tools he had used elsewhere, and off they would go—the hotel would become profitable again; another dose of the Second-Chance magic.

Yet, in practice, it all seemed so much harder. Things just did not fit the master plan. Indeed, things rarely seemed to go to plan. Numerous issues that disrupted things kept popping up that he and Weaver had not even considered. People did not react the way they expected, systems that had worked so well elsewhere seemed to fail here, and the usual ways they had used to get people motivated before seemed to stutter at Junction Hotel.

At first, he had got really frustrated with this and blamed the staff for not wanting to change. But, gradually, his respect for them began to grow. They cared about the hotel, he realized, not just their jobs. They just had different values and objectives from his.

At the heart of this was Meg Mortimer. At first, Chance had thought Mortimer was a silly old fool with all her talk that Junction Hotel was special. However, now, a year on, he really feels that he is beginning to understand what she meant. He has grown to love the place. Yes, it is a business, but he feels increasingly that it is more than that—that it has something special.

Ever since Fredrick Taylor and Henri Fayol, the belief that managers do the planning and create systems, and that workers just follow orders, has persisted. This has given the impression that organizational problems are fairly easy to solve—just implement a few simple procedures, steps, or theories. However, as we have seen throughout this book, in practice it can be far harder to do.

We have sought to stress how complicated and multifaceted management and working in organizations really is. To achieve even the seemingly simplest change can involve working with numerous people that have their own perspectives, with groups that have their established hierarchies and political agendas, and within (or sometimes even against) the established organizational culture. These are the sorts of realities that people working in organizations face on a daily basis. Therefore, as we have seen, it is the informal, or hidden, organization that often largely shapes the decisions and actions that people make within organizations.

To really understand what goes on within organizations and, importantly, to be able to implement change, you need to be able to appreciate the interconnected nature of OB. For instance, you cannot hope to understand motivation separately from personality, culture, or responses to leadership. OB is a highly inter-connected discipline.

## Study skills: the importance of connecting the themes together

It is tempting when completing an essay or exam question to just look at the topics closely associated with that particular question and only read the chapter concerned. However, in practice, and indeed to really understand the theory, it is important to understand how each aspect of organizational behaviour (OB) connects to other aspects. Strong answers show an awareness of the connection

▶ between themes. Intelligent management understands the connections between one intervention and other aspects of the organization.

It is therefore essential to appreciate the connections between the themes. By showing these connections you are able to present a stronger level of understanding of the particular topic, demonstrating an awareness of how the individual theory is impacted by the wider field of OB and the deeper issues that theorists are seeking to explore. Therefore, when you come to write an essay or study for an exam, do not simply focus on one topic alone, but try to make connections back to other themes.

## Review questions

| | |
|---|---|
| **Describe** | What is meant by OB being an 'interconnected' discipline? |
| **Explain** | Why is it important to link the key themes in OB together? |
| **Analyse** | What are the dangers of viewing a topic in isolation? What important organizational issues might be missed by doing this? |
| **Apply** | What themes from book can you identify in the reflections of Meg Mortimer and Simon Chance in this chapter so far? |

# The changing nature of organizational behaviour

## Running case: Meg's leaving do

As Meg walks nervously into the conference room she is greeted by a massive round of applause from Junction Hotel staff—past and present. 'Grab yourself a drink,' Simon Chance declares in a jovial way, greeting his adversary and friend. 'I want you to enjoy today.' It seems odd, but in many ways comforting, to Mortimer that through all their disagreements, at least Chance has been nice to her as a person—their disagreements are largely professional rather than personal.

As she picks up a glass of Merlot she looks around the room. 'I'm going to miss you lot,' she thinks. Sam from reception comes up to her and they exchange pleasantries for a while. 'I bet you can't wait to retire,' Sam beams, 'particularly putting up with him,' she says looking in the direction of Weaver. Weaver had certainly been difficult, or, in his management-speak, 'a challenge,' with all his systems and efficiency practices. Yet, she must concede, the hotel is now running better that it had ever done. However, in some areas it has gone too far, like those changes to the fitness centre. If Weaver had had his way, then the whole hotel would have been running on a great big flow-chart.

Then there was Chance himself. Meg has grown to respect him over the year. They did not see eye to eye on a lot of things and it had felt as though he was taking her hotel away from her. But, she has to admit it: ultimately, the guy seems to care about what goes on here. The way he tried to change the culture of

Junction Hotel and get them working in teams was different from how she would have done it, but at least it showed some awareness of the importance of people.

'I don't know how I feel about retiring,' Meg says more to herself than in response to Sam. 'I thought I would want to. I've been dreaming, longing for this day for a while. But now it's here I've come to realize that I like it here. I'm good at what I do, I know how everything works here, and I feel respected. Does that sound odd?' she said, noticing Sam. 'Now I'm retired, who am I?' Sam smiles in a puzzled, but sympathetic, way. Suddenly, she notices Simon Chance standing at the podium.

'Hello . . . hello everyone—if I could have your attention for only a few minutes.' A couple of people sigh, but in a friendly way. 'Today,' begins Chance, 'we are celebrating two major events: our long-serving and esteemed colleague Meg's retirement, and the first anniversary of the Second-Chance Consortium buying Junction Hotel. Now, we have been through a lot, all of us together, over the last year, and I wanted just to say a few words about what we have achieved, as well as how important Meg has been to this.

'When I walked into Junction Hotel for the first time just over a year ago I thought that we were buying just another hotel. How wrong I was.' Some of the audience laugh. 'You are unique and I mean that in a good way. We have been though a challenging journey over the last year and I am sure that we have all learned a lot. I thought I would share with you today a few things I have learned.

'Things have been tough and some tough decisions have been made. I know that they have not always been popular, but I think time will prove them to be correct.

'However, I have learned never to judge things by appearances. While this hotel might look ordinary, there are some extraordinary and talented people here. I have learned that what works well in other places will not necessarily work well here. I really hope that we can all grow together. Junction Hotel is a special place.

'Finally, I want to say a few words about Meg. As many of you will know, Meg began her life here as a cleaner and has worked her way up to the top of her profession. It is this attitude of hard work, customer care, and dedication to her staff that has made her the model professional and I, for one, will be sad to see her go. Although we have not always seen eye to eye on everything, I know that she is Junction Hotel through and through, and you can never doubt her dedication to the cause.

'So from all of us to you I would like to give you this . . .' At this point Chance hands over an enormous leaving card, a big bunch of flowers, a cheque, and, finally, a mug with a picture of Junction Hotel on the front '. . . for your world cruise, so you can never forget us.' 'And the mugs that work here!' Effingham pipes up to much laughter.

Then Meg begins to speak. She says how proud she has been to work at Junction Hotel and how much it has meant to spend so much of her time there. She is leaving with a heavy heart and thanks them for the great support she has received. 'Lots of things have changed over the last forty years,' she says. 'Who would have thought that we would now have all this technology and bookings coming from all over the world.' Then, with a subtle passing shot directed at Chance, Meg ends by saying 'Yet some things never change—the basics, listening to people, and good service—remember, keep the Junction Hotel spirit alive'. With that Mortimer sits down to her second round of rapturous applause of the day.

In many senses the nature of work has changed dramatically over the last forty years. Western economies have moved from manufacturing to a predominantly service-led industry, creating jobs and types of firms that would have been unthinkable in the 1960s and 1970s. The rising importance of information technology is an obvious factor. The mobile phone in your pocket is more powerful than many of the computers that took up whole floors in offices only a few decades ago, and your laptop can store and process more information than the computers that first sent man into space. But there have been numerous social changes as well.

The number of young people going to university has risen dramatically throughout the world. For instance, in the UK it has increased from around 400,000 in the 1960s to over 2,000,000 today (Greenaway and Haynes, 2003; Elias and Purcell, 2004). The types of jobs have also shifted as the 'knowledge economy' has taken off. However, with it, the hours that people work have increased, particularly with the advent of mobile phones, giving people the feeling that they never really leave the office.

Our relationship with our jobs and employers has also altered significantly. Our grandparents' or great-grandparents' generation often went into their first job thinking that they would have a job for life, and many stayed with the same employer throughout their entire career—such an occurrence is almost unthinkable in today's world. For some so-called 'portfolio workers' (Handy, 1994), even having one employer is not the case, as they work for two or three different employers at the same time, juggling different jobs (Van Buren, 2003).

There have certainly been some significant social advancements over the last forty years. The number of women in the workplace has dramatically increased and there has been some development in the number of women in senior positions. However, as we have seen, there is still a long way to go on this issue, as women and people from minority groups face significant hurdles on their way to the top of organizations.

This changing nature of the workforce has created the need for workplaces to be more flexible in their hours, as there is increasing recognition of the challenges that women and men face juggling family commitments alongside their work responsibilities. Work–life balance is, consequently, becoming a more significant issue as many workers have caring responsibilities (not only with young children, but, as we face an ageing population, elderly parents).

For all these changes, some of the optimism that existed in the 1960s, 1970s, and 1980s seems to have waned. Women and ethnic minorities still represent a relatively small minority on the boards of companies, social equality still seems a distant aspiration, and social mobility is still largely static (Hope, 2012; Thomson and Lloyd, 2011).

## Real life case: technology—the promise that was never delivered

As we have seen throughout this book, over the last 100 and particularly the last 40 years the rate of technological progress has been enormous as production processes have become more efficient and effective. One significant change has been the decline in numbers employed in agriculture from about 80% in 1900 to around 2–3% in 2000 (Jacques, 1996). This rate of change and the increasing efficiency elsewhere brought with it a concern that there would not be enough jobs to go round. So strong was this belief that in the 1970s and early 1980s, particularly with the birth of the 'micro-computer' (the forerunner to today's laptop and PC), many theorists were concerned about a workerless economy (Jenkins and Sherman, 1979; Rifkin, 1996) as production was taken over by robots (Levitan and Johnson, 1982). The concern that these theorists tried to explore was how people of the future (i.e. now) would cope with what they called 'serious leisure', where they only had to work a few hours a week (Stebbins, 1982). ▶

> ● Of course things have not turned out this way, with a long-hours culture continuing to be a major issue in developed economies. Managers work an average 46 days a year longer than in their contract (Worrall and Cooper, 2012). Jobs that barely existed in the late 1970s have become commonplace and technology seems to make more jobs, rather than reducing them. Moreover, as a way of covering pensions and the increased debt that people face, we are also working longer—into our late 60s and, potentially, early 70s. Interestingly, as a response to the recent economic downturn the New Economics Foundation (Coote, 2010) has even proposed that the three-day week would be a viable alternative, distributing jobs more widely and creating a fairer and more balanced economy. It would require a reduction in income but, they argue, a substantial increase in quality of life. Only time will tell if such a vision will be realized.

Would you accept a lower income for a higher quality of life and more leisure time?

The world of employment has, therefore, changed dramatically in the last few decades, bringing with it major changes in expectations, roles, and skills for graduates entering the workplace for the first time. The recent economic downturn has also played a significant role, meaning that many graduates are entering employment taking on quite different jobs from those that they were expecting when they started university, as a survey from PricewaterhouseCoopers demonstrates.

### Real life case: what do Millennium graduates want from work?

In late 2011, the accountancy and consultancy firm PricewaterhouseCoopers surveyed over 4,000 recent graduates throughout the world. Their results saw some interesting trends, particularly as a result of the recent global economic downturn. Their key findings were:

- loyalty-lite—a quarter expected to work for six or more employers over their lifetime, up from 10% in 2008
- 72% said that they had been forced to compromise in order to get a job
- 66% said they needed international experience to further their career
- 18% said that they expected to stay in their current job for the long-term
- development and work–life balance were more important than financial reward
- graduates wanted a good work–life balance, but 28% thought it was worse than they had expected
- 41% would rather communicate electronically than face to face
- CSR has decreased as a factor that graduates look for when searching for a job.

**Source:** PricewaterhouseCoopers (2008).

What do you think are going to be the most significant changes over the next forty years and why? How likely is it that your predictions will come true? What skills do you think you will need?

We can see here that the recent economic downturn has made it difficult for graduates to find the jobs they want, with many having to compromise and take jobs quite different in level and type than they originally intended, sacrificing location, pay, or even the level of job, just to get their first step on the career ladder. Even now that the economy has slowly picked up in some countries, many young people still need to make compromises in order to get a job. However, there are more substantial long-term shifts also occurring. The increasing expectation of traveling, working for various employers, and also being flexible in how work is done, but needing a better work–life balance, are all trends that have been growing over the last few decades. The way that we treat work is changing.

Indeed, it is not just our attitudes to jobs that are changing but the nature of the jobs themselves. As Vanessa Gough, professional development manager for IBM, states: 'most of the jobs that you will work in do not even exist yet'. She states that it is important to be open to the types of jobs that you will take in the future (author interview with Vanessa Gough via telephone, January 2012). This view is supported by Deborah Henretta, group president of the Asia and Global Specialty Channel, Procter & Gamble. She states:

> The workplace and workforce are going to change pretty dramatically as we look forward. The entire concept of work is going to become more flexible. The skills needed in the workforce are going to be less about IQ and a little bit more about EQ [emotional quotient], because if you think about it, a lot of IQ knowledge is going to be available at our fingertips through hand-held devices and the computer and technologies that we have at our disposal.

(Source: PricewaterhouseCoopers, 2011: 6)

**Emotional quotient (EQ), emotional intelligence** The ability to assess the emotions of yourself and others.

### Real life case: technology is taking away middle-class jobs

When we think of automation we tend to think of computers replacing large numbers of low-skilled jobs; we saw at the beginning of the book that technology had this impact with the Industrial Revolution and the changes introduced by Taylorism. However, a number of futurologists are predicting that the same thing is going to affect middle class jobs of the future. According to economists Frey and Osborne, approximately 47% of jobs in the US are under threat of being replaced (2013). Teaching is increasingly being replaced by computer-aided instructions. Computers are increasingly undertaking translation work, jobs such as book-keeping, and even legal work (Aeppel, 2015). Even a highly educated profession like medicine is under threat. In 2012 Vinod Khosla, an investor in Silicon Valley, predicted that 80% of doctors would be replaced within a generation (Khosla, 2012). Dr Pete Diamandis, the CEO of EX-PRIZE, agrees and argues that computers will not only do diagnostics but even perform surgery (Meltzer, 2014). While these changes will bring new and exciting technologies, Brynjolfsson and McAfee predict they will also bring high levels of inequality and the hollowing out of the middle class (2014).

Overcoming this challenge will require new ways of working and thinking. Brynjolfsson and McAfee argue that the situation 'is going to leave behind some people, perhaps even a lot of people, as it races ahead ... there's never been a worse time to be a worker with only "ordinary" skills and abilities to offer, because computers, robots and other digital technologies are acquiring these skills and abilities at an extraordinary rate' (cited in Meltzer, 2014). Skills that cannot be routinized or that require creativity will be far harder to replicate and replace with machines. So to survive, we will need higher levels of skills. New jobs will also be created as we become more released from these more routinized tasks. It will be an interesting, challenging but potentially rewarding future.

So, with this dramatic change in the nature and types of jobs that are available, and the skills and attitudes that will be needed to meet them, what can you do now to get ahead and how can your study of OB help?

One of the most significant factors is that you will not simply be able to learn a set of skills that you can then just import into your work. As we argued in Chapter 10, we cannot merely learn a set of skills and techniques from university to import into the workplace, as the nature of employment is likely to undergo substantial change over the next few decades. Any skills that you might learn could well be obsolete within the next few years. Rather, what you can learn is the process of learning: how to learn—being able to respond to new situations and to analyse and think critically about them.

> **Employability skills:** learning to learn—the importance of continuous learning
>
> As we have seen, the types of jobs that you are likely to be involved in and do over the course of your career may not even exist yet. Therefore, you cannot assume that at university you will learn a series of skills or gain knowledge that you can take into your job. If that was the case then within a few years your skills would become obsolete and you would, therefore, become ineffective in your job. Consequently, rather than facts, knowledge, or set skills that you can then use directly in your job, what university can most effectively give you is the capacity to learn. Learning to learn, developing the skills to develop yourself, identifying and building on your strengths, and overcoming your weaknesses will, therefore, be vital throughout your career.

How do you think changes in the nature of work will impact upon your future career? What can you do now to prepare for this?

# Predicting future trends

> **Running case:** Meg looks to the future
>
> Meg's replacement, so she is told, is beginning on Monday: a business graduate who has had five years' experience in an international chain of hotels, has worked throughout the world, and has a 'really good track record' of successful management. 'All very well,' thinks Meg, 'but he will not know the staff as well as I do or what makes them tick'.
>
> Reflecting on her time at Junction Hotel she wonders what the next forty years will be like for her replacement. Certainly, it is unlikely that he will be able to retire at 60 like she has been able to—will it be 67 or even 70 by then? She certainly hadn't even thought of the iPad, email, or Skype when she began working. 'What new technology will be in place when my replacement retires?' she thinks. 'Something we cannot even imagine now'.
>
> Meg has been working for Junction Hotel all her adult life. She wonders whether Steve, her replacement, will do that. 'Not likely,' she thinks. 'Young people don't seem to stick to firms like we did, but then there are far more opportunities than we ever had. Apparently, this guy, Steve, has just come back from working in America. America! Wow, I'd never have thought of working out there. Life for Steve will certainly be different than it has been for me,' she thinks.

As we have already seen, it is notoriously difficult to predict the types of changes that will be happening over the next few years, as things rarely work out as we expect. However, there do appear to be a few trends on the horizon that might become key areas for your future working life.

- Increased concerns over climate change have led to many calls to shift to a low-carbon economy (Stern, 2006). This may cause dramatic changes in the nature of the economy and with it the way that organizations need to operate (European Commission, 2011). It also has the potential to produce new jobs in areas that do not exist yet (BIS, 2012). Companies such as Ford are preparing themselves by developing products that can begin to respond to these challenges (source: Author interview with Joe Greenwell, Ford in Britain, 2012). If carbon emissions continue as a factor it will be not only manufacturing and design, but also the way the workplace is focused that will need changing. The move to a low-carbon economy will be a source of jobs and new ways of living that we are only beginning to imagine (Harvey, 2012).

- Another major change on the horizon is the rise of China and the potential decline of the West (Tselichtchev, 2012). As the recent 'credit crunch' has revealed, many commentators say that we are currently witnessing a dramatic realignment of the world's global economy from the West (USA, Europe) towards the East (China) and, with it, a shift in power and economic influence. This will bring with it new opportunities for Western companies as a new, emerging middle class in China will be interested in the products and services that the West provides, but it will also bring new competition and the need for other ways of working to respond to a different type of client group and culture.

- Related to the previous point, as we saw in Chapter 15, the world has been getting smaller and the issues of globalization and greater connectivity are becoming more important. This is reflected in the PricewaterhouseCoopers (2011) survey, where 71% said that they felt they needed international experience to further their career.

- The changing nature of technology will also open up new possibilities for employment, as well as destroying existing ones. New technologies can now quickly emerge, making predictions difficult.

However, many of the fundamentals remain. Central skills will include communication—listening to, understanding, and responding to people—as well as working in teams and being self-motivated.

## Review questions

| **Describe** | What sort of changes are predicted to occur in organizations over the next 40 years? |
|---|---|
| **Explain** | How will changes affecting organizations impact upon the nature of work and jobs in the near future? |
| **Analyse** | How might developments in technology impact upon the levels of skill needed by workers (see this chapter and Chapter 2 on Braverman's deskilling thesis)? |
| **Apply** | Think of specific jobs that people do now. How might technology and the changing nature of work affect the nature of these jobs in the near future? |

# Concluding remarks: the more things change, the more they stay the same

**Running case:** Meg writes a letter to her replacement

Dear Steve,

I am writing to you on my last day at Junction Hotel and you will read this on your first. I have had forty long, but happy, years at Junction Hotel. Along the way I've met some amazing and interesting people (as well as some difficult ones) and generally had a positive experience here. I hope that you have as positive a time as I have had.

As we may never actually meet I thought I would take this opportunity to write and tell you a little about why this is a special place and means so much to me. I really hope that you come to love the hotel in the same way as I do and come to appreciate why it is such a unique place.

This hotel means a lot to me; indeed, it has been my life. It has a character and charm that you can only really see from the inside. While on the surface they may have made a lot of changes, I hope that the spirit of Junction Hotel will live on long beyond me.

You see, Steve, what makes Junction Hotel special is that we care. We care about keeping the rooms clean, that the guests have a good stay, and that the food is made well. But, most of all, we care about each other. This place has been like a second family to me. When my son died five years ago, these were the people that cared for me and helped me get through the days. With all the talk of profit margins and room occupancy rates, the things that really matter are people.

I know others here might say that I am old-fashioned and sometimes do not keep up with the modern ways of doing things. Well, that might be the case, but this is because I believe that it is important to keep certain values alive. In our non-stop world of iPads, email, and the like I wonder if we are losing something important—the ability to really listen and respond to people, to care for them, and treat them as individuals. You might think I'm naïve or a relic from the past, but, to me, for all the changes that have happened in the last few years, the people are at the heart of this business. While Chance and Weaver might have all these systems and grand ideas, the real thing that keeps this hotel going, through the good and bad times, are the people. So, when you come in and make changes please be aware that, ultimately, people's lives are at stake. I have many good friends here; I hope that you look after them well.

And, most of all, I really advise that you enjoy your job. Money, status, and power are all well and good, but remember the key thing in the end is that you enjoy what you do. We spend so much of our time at work it is important that you feel you are enjoying it.

Yours

Meg

And, with a tear in her eye, Meg seals the envelope and puts it on the keyboard of her—well, what will soon be Steve's—computer.

What do you think of Meg's views? Do you feel that these values are realistic in the modern world?

As she does so, Meg wonders what her career has really achieved. She is proud to have made it all the way from the position of cleaner to the top of Junction Hotel—'I wonder if anyone will manage that again,' she muses. She is also proud of the way that she has held the hotel together at times of crisis. But she feels a little frustrated. The last ten years felt a little like treading water, going through the same routines day in, day out with little new to show for it.

Opening her leaving card, Meg is suprised by the comments in it. There are more than the simple platitudes that one normally writes in leaving cards: they are messages of genuine warmth and sincerity. Reading and re-reading, she finds that the recurring comments are of how much she has influenced the people around her, the little tricks of the trade that she had taught them, acts of kindness that she had long forgotten, and actions that she had performed which had helped them through difficulties. 'This is it,' she thinks, 'this is what the last ten years have been about—helping others'. Realizing that she has made a difference, she wells up. 'Yes, that's it. It was helping out those around me, that's what really counts. That's my legacy.'

What do you want to achieve in your career? What would you count as success? What sort of person do you want to be known as at work?

This chapter has sought to make two key arguments. Firstly, it is important, when studying OB, to understand that it is not a series of isolated topics, but is an interconnected discipline. To gain a strong understanding it is vital to explore how the topics connect together. This will give you a deeper appreciation of the subject, as well as the potential of a better grade.

Secondly, we have looked forward to the changing nature of organizations and, consequently, work, over the next forty years. As we have seen, the nature of work has changed in previously unimaginable ways over the last forty years and it is quite likely that the next forty years will be equally unpredictable. Therefore, instead of feeling that you can learn a series of skills or techniques of how to work in, and manage, organizations, it is more important to develop the capacity to learn, reflect, develop, and grow. Learning to learn, to think analytically and critically, will be more important to your future career than simply digesting a series of simple techniques.

A final note in our experience of having taught OB to thousands of students is that the issues that we have covered in this book are best understood when connected to actual practice. We have had many students approach us after a placement year or at graduation saying that the issues we have covered here have only really made sense to them after seeing them in practice. They have been grateful for the insights that they have gained, which have helped them understand themselves and others better, and enabled them to cope with the complexities of organizational life.

## References

Aeppel, T. 2015. What clever robots mean for jobs. *Wall Street Journal*, 24 February.

Brynjolfsson, E., and McAfee, A. 2014. *The second machine age: Work, progress, and prosperity in a time of brilliant technologies*. WW Norton & Company: New York.

Coote, A. 2010. 21 hours: A new norm for the working week. New Economics Foundation. Available at: http://www.neweconomics.org/blog/entry/

21-hours-a-new-norm-for-the-working-week (last accessed 26 August 2015).

Elias, P., and Purcell, K. 2004. Is mass higher education working? Evidence from the labour market experiences of recent graduates. *National Institute Economic Review* 190(1): 60–74.

European Commission 2011. A roadmap for moving to a competitive low carbon economy in 2050. *COM* 112(4).

Frey, C., and Osborne, M. 2013. The future of employment: How susceptible are jobs to computerisation? Available at: http://www.oxfordmartin.ox.ac.uk/downloads/academic/The_Future_of_Employment.pdf (last accessed August 2015).

Gough, V. 2012. Author interview via telephone, 17 January 2012.

Greenaway, D., and Haynes, M. 2003. Funding higher education in the UK: The role of fees and loans. *Economic Journal* 113: F150–F167.

Handy, C. 1994. *The empty raincoat*. Hutchinson: London.

Harvey, F. 2012. Switching to a green economy could mean millions of jobs, says UN. *The Guardian*, 31 May.

Hope, C. 2012. Plans for women's quotas on company boards dropped. *Daily Telegraph*, 28 May.

Jacques, R. 1996. *Manufacturing the employee: Management knowledge from the 19th to 21st centuries*. Sage: London.

Jenkins, C., and Sherman, B. 1979. *The collapse of work*. Eyre Methuen: London.

Khosla, V. 2012. Do we need doctors or algorithms?Available at: http://techcrunch.com/2012/01/10/doctors-or-algorithms/ (last accessed 13 August 2015).

Levitan, S.A., and Johnson, C.M. 1982. The future of work: Does it belong to us or to the robots? *Monthly Labor Review* 105(9): 10–14.

Meltzer, T. 2014. Robot doctors, online lawyers and automated architects: The future of the professions? *The Guardian*, 15 June.

PricewaterhouseCoopers 2008. Managing tomorrow's people: Millennials at work—perspectives from a new generation. Available at: http://pwc.blogs.com/files/millennials-at-work.pdf (last accessed 26 August 2015).

PricewaterhouseCoopers 2011. Millennials at work: Reshaping the workplace. Available at: http://http://www.pwc.com/en_M1/m1/services/consulting/documents/millennials-at-work.pdf (last accessed 26 August 2015).

Rifkin, J. 1996. *The end of work*. Putnam Books: New York.

Stebbins, R.A. 1982. Serious leisure: A conceptual statement. *Pacific Sociological Review* 25(2): 251–72.

Stern, N. 2006. *Stern review on the economics of climate change*. Her Majesty's Treasury: London.

Thomson, P., and Lloyd, T. 2011. *Women and the new business leadership*. Palgrave Macmillan: Basingstoke.

Tselichtchev, I . 2012. *China versus the West: The global power shift of the 21st century*. John Wiley and Sons: Chichester.

Van Buren, H.J. 2003. Boundaryless careers and employability obligations. *Business Ethics Quarterly* 13(2): 131–49.

Worrall, L., and Cooper, C. 2012. *The quality of working life 2012: Managers' wellbeing, motivation and productivity*. Chartered Management Institute: London.

# Glossary

**16 personality factor** A personality test which measures personality on a set of 16 scales of opposing character traits.

**Acquisition** The purchase of another company or business.

**Aesthetic labour** Usually found in customer- or client-facing service work where, in exchange for a wage, the worker is expected to manage their appearance and comportment in a manner directed by the organization.

**Agency** The capacity individuals have to act independently of the social structures and make free choices.

**Alienation** In capitalism, the estrangement of people from a number of human qualities, noted particularly by writers such as Marx and Braverman as a consequence of rational work design.

**Alternative models of organization** Workers' cooperatives and mutual organizations which seek for non-hierarchical modes of organizing and not-for-profit objectivities, often to bring about benefits to the members and society.

**Analyse** Widely associated with deeper intellectual thinking, it is the process of breaking things down into their constituent parts, investigating the underlying cause or basic principles.

**Anti-globalization movement** A collective term for protestors and critics of the power and effects of multinational corporations which they see as making the world less fair and more homogenized.

**A priori** Independent of experience.

**Assembly line** An automated conveyor that moves a product in front of workers who perform a small, repetitive task to each product that passes before them.

**Assessment centre** A recruitment strategy where different selection techniques are blended in a selection process.

**Autocratic** A command and control leadership style.

**Aversion therapy** A type of classical conditioning whereby a particular behaviour is continually accompanied by a punishment so as to discourage that behaviour.

**Backstage** A theatrical metaphor to represent areas of the organization where workers are out of view of customers and clients.

**Bad apples** A phrase that dismisses an occurrence as just down to a few bad people or organizations, while claiming that others should not be judged as the same.

**Banking education** Freire's critique of learning and teaching styles which see learners as being like bank accounts to be 'deposited' with amounts of knowledge.

**Behavioural psychology/behaviourism** An area of psychology which suggests that learning can be managed through the use of rewards and punishments.

**Behavioural theory** A psychological perspective which seeks to understand and change the behaviour of individuals.

**Big five personality scale** A personality test which measures personality according to a set of five traits: openness, conscientiousness, extraversion, agreeableness, and neuroticism.

**Binged** A phrased used during the Hawthorne studies meaning flicking the ear or arm of the person working too hard.

**Bolshevik** An insult indicating that a person is a Russian communist; in other words, that they are troublemakers who want revolution.

**Boundarylessness** Where the extent of sharing and dispersal of an organization's computer data gives a sense that there is no boundary to the organization.

**Bureaucracy** From the French *bureau*, meaning office; bureaucracy covers official, formal elements of rational organizational design, such as the hierarchical organization structure, the rules and procedures, and the official paperwork, which exert impersonal control over the organization.

**Bureaucratic** Describing the process of bureaucracy, sometimes used in a derogatory sense.

**Bureaucratic personality** A tendency to follow rules to the letter rather than seeing the wider picture and making more common-sense judgements.

**Business ethics** A form of ethics applied to business. It is the study and evaluation of decision making within businesses through various moral concepts and judgements.

**Butterfly effect** The suggestion in chaos theory that a small action can have unpredictable knock-on effects of a greater magnitude.

**Buzzword** A phrase which is a fad for a period of time.

**Call centre** An organization or department set up to handle a large volume of telephone calls, often managed efficiently using rationalized techniques.

**Camaraderie** A sense of togetherness and bonding.

**Capital** Investment in a business to set up the means of production, often used as a term to refer to business owners or capitalists who make that investment.

**Capitalist wage–labour relationship** The relationship between capitalists, who pay wages, and labour, who work in return for those wages.

**Ceremony** A public act, often planned and formal, which celebrates a particular event, achievement or anniversary, largely planned by senior management or part of the organizations established calendar. Ceremonies often have symbolic meaning that emphasizes important aspects of the organizations culture.

**Change** The process by which an organization makes changes in practices, processes, culture etc. in a planned or emergent fashion.

**Change agent** A manager, consultant, or other person who instigates and manages change.

**Change management** An effort or initiative undertaken to alter a particular aspect of the organization.

**Channels of communication** Ways in which a message is expressed, e.g. verbally or in written words.

**Chaos theory** A branch of science which sees natural systems as both ordered and, at the same time, unpredictable.

**Classical conditioning** A type of conditioning of behaviour where a reward or punishment accompanies and reinforces every instance of the behaviour to be conditioned.

**Classical Management School** A set of theories of management which draws upon rational methods of managing and organizing. Having developed from the early 1900s, it encompasses a number of theorists and practitioners who advocated 'one best way' of management. Examples of management styles and techniques which the school draws upon include Fayol and Taylor.

**Cliques** Exclusive groups.

**Coercion** Being forced in some way into performing a behaviour.

**Collective action** Any form of resistance against management taken by a group of workers.

**Colonization** Invasion and conquering of land, and enslavement of people, in Africa, the Americas, and Asia from the 1500s to the 1900s by European countries, such as England, Spain, Belgium, Portugal, France, and the Netherlands.

**Command and control** A top-down leadership style that emphasizes the importance of the leader who tells others what to do.

**Communication** A process whereby information is transferred from a sender (or senders) to a receiver (or receivers).

**Communication technology** Technologies which facilitate communication between people and the sharing of information.

**Communities of coping** Mutual support among co-workers to cope with stress and other negative factors of emotional labour.

**Communities of practice** Social groupings based around a common occupational practice and set of knowledge, who develop and share that knowledge among themselves.

**Complexity theory** The application of chaos theory to social systems, such as organizations, suggesting that small changes can have unpredictable and potentially limitless consequences.

**Conditioning** A change in behaviour brought about using stimulus–response techniques typical of behavioural psychology.

**Confirmation bias** A form of selective perception where people only tend to take note of information that confirms their already held perceptions.

**Conformity** Everyone in the group thinking and acting in the same way.

**Congruence** Corresponding or matching.

**Consumption** The purchase and use by customers and clients of goods and services created by an organization.

**Content theories** Theories of motivation which suggest that the content of work should be designed so as best to meet the needs which motivate workers.

**Contingency theory** Suggests that the best structure for an organization is determined by factors such as environmental uncertainty, the organization's size, and the technology that the organization uses.

**Corporate social responsibility** A contested term with different interpretations but generally taken to be the social and environmental responsibility corporations have towards their stakeholders.

**Control group** Used in scientific research, a control group does not receive any intervention and therefore is thus seen as representing the population as a whole. The control group is used as a standard of comparison to the research group who do receive intervention.

**Cost** The amount in wages and materials that it costs to produce a good or provide a service.

**Craft knowledge** Knowledge of a particular skill, often the result of a long period of training or apprenticeship.

**Critical (as in 'critical management studies')** A critical perspective, among other things, draws on Marxist theory and seeks to challenge the assumptions of mainstream management theory by stressing the impact that it has on employees and society.

**Critical analysis** To question the underlying assumptions of a perspective. In OB this may have particular emphasis on how power and inequality occur.

**Critical perspective** A perspective, drawing on Marxist theory, which seeks to challenge the assumptions of mainstream management theory by stressing the impact that it has on employees and society.

**Cross-cultural management** Managing a workforce from different national and cultural backgrounds.

**Cultural homogenization** A tendency for culture to become the same globally.

**Database** A computerized store of structured, organized data.

**Dataveillance** Surveillance brought about by examining electronic data which is held about individuals.

**Decoding** Converting a received message into the meaning perceived by the recipient.

**Deep acting** Emotional labour where the worker internalizes and believes in the performance in which they are engaged.

**Deep learning** Learning that tries to achieve a deeper understanding of, and engagement with, the material being learned.

**Dehumanization** Work that reduces people to part of a machine-like process, ignoring their human attributes. Widely associated with rational work design that was criticized by Harry Braverman.

**Delegation** Passing a job, task, or order down to lower levels of a hierarchy.

**Democratic** A leadership style which encourages the involvement of the group, but the leader ultimately makes the decisions.

**Description** A piece of writing that describes the theory or case study with little attempt at providing analysis. Often considered more superficial and therefore in student coursework results in lower grades.

**Deskilling** The obsolescence of workplace skills caused by rational work design or the introduction of new technology.

**Deutero learning** Bateson's conception of a higher level of learning whereby people are aware of how they 'learn to learn'.

**Digital divide** A divide between people who have access to computer hardware and network infrastructures, such as the Internet, and those who do not.

**Direct control** Face-to-face control of workers by a manager or owner.

**Discretion** The ability of an individual to act according to their own independent judgement, rather than being told exactly what to do.

**Discrimination** Where a person is treated negatively and unfairly because of their membership of a particular social group, e.g. because of race or gender.

**Disenchantment** For Max Weber this was a loss of 'magical elements' in society, and suggests some of the dehumanizing elements of bureaucracy.

**Disneyization** Term coined by Bryman which describes characteristics of the Disney theme parks that can be seen in other service and leisure organizations.

**Distributive leadership** An approach which emphasizes that leadership can occur throughout the organization by a wide variety of organizational members.

**Division of labour** Breaking down a job into more simple, individual tasks.

**Double-loop learning** Learning in organizations which goes beyond achieving a goal to question assumptions behind the goal being set, and that questions assumptions, values, and strategies more widely in the organization.

**Downsizing** Reducing the size of the workforce.

**Dress code** Standards of dress and appearance prescribed by an organization to its workers.

**Dysfunctions of bureaucracy** Unintended consequences of bureaucracy which lead to it not functioning in the efficient manner for which it is designed.

**Economies of scale** Cost reduction that comes from producing a product in large amounts.

**Efficiency** The minimization of cost, doing the same for less input of time and money.

**Electronic Panopticon** The ability to monitor our lives through the amount of electronic data and records held about us.

**Embodied dispositions/habitus** Our natural way of acting and reacting—a deeply held repertoire of instinctive behaviours.

**Emergent approach to change** An approach to change which sees the organization as being like a river, in constant flow, and suggests that in such an environment change emerges in the course of events rather than being planned in advance.

**Emoticon** Punctuation marks used in electronic communications, designed to simulate facial expressions.

**Emotional labour** Work where, in exchange for a wage, the worker is expected to manage their emotions to put on a particular emotional performance in front of customers or clients, especially in interactive service work.

**Emotional quotient (EQ), emotional intelligence** The ability to assess the emotions of yourself and others.

**Emotion management** Any management of personal emotional displays inside or outside of a working relationship.

**Empowering** The process by which the workers are given greater power and autonomy. Critics suggest this approach also places a greater burden on workers.

**Encoding** Converting the intended meaning of a communication into a form that can be sent as a message.

**Environment** The world outside of an organization which can have an impact upon that organization.

**Environmental leadership** A self-sustaining group where employees find gratification through the group and task.

**Equity theory** A process theory of motivation which suggests that people are either motivated or demotivated depending on how they are rewarded in the workplace compared with others.

**Equivocality** Situations where meanings are ambiguous and open to interpretation.

**Ergonomics** The design of workplace environments and tools to best fit the movements of the human body.

**Ethical capitalism** A business approach which seeks to integrate CSR as central to the purpose and activity of an organization.

**Ethical egoism** The belief that people acting in their own best interests is the best way to get a good society.

**Evidence** In academic writing, support for claims made.

**Expectancy theory** A process theory of motivation which suggests that people will be motivated into actions and behaviours that they can link with them achieving goals and rewards that they desire.

**Experience** Where consumption is of the organization itself rather than any product or service that it provides.

**Experiential learning** Learning which comes from experiences and reflecting on those experiences.

**Explanation** In academic writing, the ability to explain a theory or perspective.

**Explicit knowledge** Knowledge which can be expressed to other people as a set of words, facts, diagrams, or instructions.

**Exporting** Selling and distributing a good to another country.

**Extinction** Where a conditioned behaviour dies out because the reward or punishment is no longer provided.

**Extraversion** A tendency to focus and gain energy externally rather than from within the self.

**Extrinsic reward** A reward that a person receives which is provided by somebody else.

**False consciousness** A Marxist term—false beliefs held by the proletariat (workers) who do not know their true position in society as the revolutionary force to overthrow capitalism. Instead, they see the current structure of society as unchangeable and largely fair.

**Feedback** Reaction or response to a message.

**Fixed reinforcement** A reward or punishment provided at fixed time intervals or fixed instances of a behaviour to be reinforced.

**Flaming** Abusive messages sent to Internet forums and communities.

**Followership** In leadership theory: (a) the importance of looking at followers and (b) the ability to follow a leader.

**Followership theory** Stresses the importance of followers and seeks to emphasize their importance in theory and practice.

**Force-field analysis** A technique whereby triggers and resistance to change are plotted on a diagram in order to identify areas to focus on in a change-management programme.

**Fordism** The use of a moving assembly line to mass produce goods.

**Foreign direct investment** Setting up a production or office facility in another country.

**Formal communication** Official communication within an organization, following authorized pathways.

**Formal rationality** Technically efficient means of achieving particular ends without thinking of the human or ethical consequences.

**Founder** The person who established the organization.

**Four humours** The four elements that Hippocrates suggested made up the human body and which also divided into four personality types.

**Franchising** Granting the right to another company to operate an outlet or branch of a particular organization, subject to adhering to standards and conditions of the franchising company.

**Frontstage** A theatrical metaphor to represent areas of the organization where workers are in contact with customers and clients.

**Functionalist** A highly pragmatic theoretical perspective which takes an 'objective' view of reality. It looks at the elements that promote stability and within management theory it tends to promote the interest of shareholders and managers with less attention on the potentially negative effects on employees or other stakeholders or opportunities to promote creativity or freedom.

**Gaia hypothesis** A theory popular in environmental movements where the whole world is seen as an interconnected system.

**Gestalt psychology** An area of psychology which suggests that we perceive things as forms, patterns, and connections rather than as a set of discrete individual items.

**Glass cage** Gabriel's metaphor to represent the visibility of workers in service sector organizations, both from the surveillance of rational organizational control and the visibility of being 'on show' in front of customers and clients.

**Glass ceiling** An invisible barrier that minority groups and particularly women cannot pass through to get to senior positions in the organization.

**Glass escalator** Occurs when men enter female dominated professions and glide past them to more senior positions.

**Globalization** Defined in many different ways, globalization is where activities take place on an increasingly global scale.

**Global village** A metaphor to describe a perception of the globe shrinking in size as a result of the speed and global reach of transport and communications technologies.

**Glocalization** Adapting global practices and products to local conditions.

**Goal setting theory** An approach that argues that motivation is influenced by the difficulty, specificity, and feedback of reaching your goals.

**Gossip** Rumours and information communicated through informal means.

**Great man theory** A theory that certain individuals are born great and can lead organizations and societies.

**Group** A collection of people with a sense of shared identity and something in common but *not* with a shared purpose.

**Group dynamics** The processes involved in interaction between group members, with particular emphasis on the tensions, conflicts, and adjustments that occur.

**Group norms** The unwritten rules that shape behaviour.

**Halo/horns effect** The tendency for people to continually reaffirm their initial impressions of a person, whether good or bad.

**Hardware** Computer equipment and infrastructures through which computer networks operate.

**Hawthorne effect** The fact that the very act of observation changes behaviour.

**Hawthorne studies** A series of studies which ran from 1924 into the late 1930s. Widely credited with discovering the human side of the organization.

**Heuristic device** Used to help simplify a theory and make it more understandable.

**Hierarchy** The levels and ranks of an organization. Any one level reports to the level immediately above and commands the level immediately below.

**Hierarchy of needs** Maslow's theory which shows that individuals have a set of needs in hierarchical order, whereby people are motivated by the most immediate unsatisfied need.

**Hofstede's dimensions of culture** Four numerical scales on which national management cultures can be located.

**Horizontal/functional differentiation** The process whereby different parts of the hierarchy are grouped according to criteria, such as the function performed, the geographical area served, or the product or service provided.

**Horizontal loading** Increasing the scope of a job by adding elements of work of a similar nature and at the same level of hierarchical responsibility.

**Human Relations** A movement emerging out of Organizational Development that studies the behaviour of people in groups.

**Human resource management (HRM)** The part of an organization, and the study of organization, which concentrates on policies and procedures relevant to the management of people within the organization (sometimes known as personnel management).

**Hybrid consumption** Different types of consumption activity, which might otherwise take place in separate organizations, appearing together in one organization.

**Hygiene factors** For Herzberg, characteristics of a job which cannot bring about increases in the job satisfaction and motivation of workers, but which can cause demotivation if they are not addressed sufficiently.

**Hyper-reality** An artificial reality which is better than anything that could be experienced in the reality that it aims to reproduce.

**Hypothesis** A proposition that needs to be tested.

**Ideographic approach** An approach which sees personality as complex, unique to each individual, and dynamic.

**Impersonal control** Control of workers that is not done face to face, for example through delegation or through rules and procedures.

**Impersonal fairness** The idea that standardized bureaucratic procedures treat people equally and avoid the personal prejudice and preferences that individual managers might have.

**Implosion** Where a large amount of an organization's activity takes place through computer systems and is stored as computer code.

**Industrial action** Any action taken by workers in a dispute between capital and labour.

**Inertia** A tendency for an organization as a whole to resist change or lack the impetus for change.

**Informal communication** Communication in an organization not following official and formal guidelines.

**Informal/unofficial culture** Culture that is often not known or supported by management but one that many of the employees share. It can be in opposition to official, management-led culture.

**Informated organization** Where a large amount of an organization's activity and knowledge is stored as computer code in a database.

**Inputs** In equity theory, efforts and contributions made by an individual to their work.

**Intangible** Something that you cannot touch.

**Intangible space** Aspects of globalization that take place through intangible means such as media transmissions, data in computer networks, and imagery.

**Intensification of consciousness** Alongside the global village, an increased awareness of events and people worldwide.

**Interactive, customer-facing, front-line service work** Work in the service and leisure industries where the worker interacts with the customer or client, either face to face or by telephone.

**Interdisciplinary team/multifunctioning team** A team of people that is comprised of people coming from different disciplines. This approach can produce a wider perspective and knowledge but can also produce greater conflict.

**Internet community** A group which communicates together regularly on the Internet.

**Internet service provider (ISP)** An organization which provides a link to the Internet.

**Interpersonal perception** The way in which one individual perceives the personality of another.

**Interpersonal relationships** The way group members relate to each other.

**Interpretivist** A philosophical approach which seeks to understand how people interpret and make sense of the world.

**Intrinsic reward** A reward that a person senses for themselves, rather than it being provided by someone else.

**Introversion** A tendency to focus and gain energy more from within the self rather than externally.

**Iron cage of bureaucracy** Max Weber's observation of the increased presence of bureaucracy in society and its potential to trap people in its routines and procedures.

**Job description** A document which outlines the formal duties and activities that the holder of a particular office will be expected to perform, and their place within the overall organizational structure.

**Job enlargement** Where more tasks are added to increase the challenge and variety of the job.

**Job enrichment** Where the quality of work is increased through the provision of increased responsibility, autonomy, and variety of tasks.

**Job rotation** Where workers alternate between different tasks of a similar nature.

**Job simplification** Where a job is broken down into simple tasks, as with Taylorism or Fordism.

**Joint venture** Cooperation between two or more companies on a particular project.

**Just-in-time management** A form of management that tries to promote efficiency by reducing the amount of stocks that an organization holds, with components delivered as and when needed.

**Keirsey's temperament sorter** A personality-testing instrument which relates personality types to suggested occupational roles.

**Knowledge and learning** An aspect of organizational behaviour which emphasizes the importance of information, understanding, and practical skills for organizational success. In particular it examines the capacity of the organization to share this knowledge in effective ways.

**Knowledge clusters** Geographical areas where a number of knowledge-intensive organizations in a particular industry are congregated in close proximity.

**Knowledge-intensive firms** Organizations whose main business involves the development and innovation of knowledge.

**Knowledge workers** Workers employed for their specific knowledge and their ability to use this knowledge to innovate, and develop new ideas and products.

**Kolb's learning cycle** A model of experiential learning which suggests that people learn through different stages of experience and reflection, and that people have particular learning style preferences for different parts of that cycle.

**Labour** Work done in return for a wage; the term is also used to refer to such workers collectively.

**Labour process** How work is designed and controlled by management.

**Laissez-faire** A leadership style which leaves all decisions to the group.

**Leaderful** Where everyone has the capacity to be a leader or take a lead through doing activities.

**Leadership** The process of leading or influencing the behaviour of others. In the broadest definition, it can be carried out by anyone in the organization.

**Lean management** A contemporary form of Taylorist rational organization that attempts to eliminate waste or anything that does not add value from organizational processes.

**Learning organization** An organization which is set up so as to facilitate continual learning at individual and organizational levels.

**Learning styles** The different ways in which different individuals approach learning.

**Learning styles questionnaire** Based on Honey and Mumford's development of Kolb, a questionnaire which ascertains people's preferred learning styles.

**Libertarian** A perspective that stresses individual freedom above all other concerns.

**Licensing** Granting the right to another company to produce a particular branded good.

**Liquid modernity** Bauman's characterization of modern day society as dynamic, changeable, and flexible.

**Lottery question** A question which asks whether people would give up work if they had enough money to live on without having to work.

**Mainstream** The dominant or accepted view that emphasizes managers' right to manage and the central objective of organizations to make profits for shareholders.

**Management** The everyday practices of running the organization in a smooth fashion.

**Mass consumption** Large-scale purchasing of a product by consumers within society.

**Mass production** The production of a large volume of a standardized product, often making use of an assembly line.

**Matrix structure** An organizational structure that combines a traditional functional hierarchy with separately managed project teams that draw people from across different functional departments.

**McDonaldization (of society)** The principles of efficiency, calculability, predictability, and control by which fast-food restaurants are managed and organized, as applied by Ritzer to other contemporary organizations.

**McJobs** Deskilled jobs found particularly in service industries, such as the fast-food restaurant.

**Means of production** Tools, premises, and other property used to manufacture goods.

**Media richness theory** Examines the ability of different communications media to communicate rich, personal meanings rather than lean, impersonal information.

**Medium, media** A specific form of technology or technologies which convey and carry information.

**Merchandising** The image or brand of one company or organization appearing on other products.

**Merger** Two companies joining together to become one single entity.

**Message** An item of communication sent from a sender to a recipient.

**Metaphor** A figure of speech whereby we try to understand something by suggesting a resemblance to the characteristics of something else.

**Michigan studies** Early leadership studies which stressed the benefit of being employee-orientated rather than task-orientated to improve output.

**Miscommunication** Where some of the meaning of a communication is distorted.

**Mock bureaucracy** A situation where policies and rules exist, but are ignored.

**Motivating factors** For Herzberg, characteristics of a job which can bring about increases in the job satisfaction and motivation of workers.

**Motivation** The will and desire that a person has to engage in a particular behaviour or perform a particular task.

**Multiple intelligences** Gardner's theory that there are different types of intelligence that people possess in different combinations.

**Myers–Briggs Type Indicator** A personality testing instrument based on the personality types of Carl Jung.

**Naïve approach to change** An approach to change which sees the organization in simplistic terms, as if it were a set of building blocks which can be rearranged easily.

**Nature versus nurture** The debate about whether our personalities are something natural, i.e. that we are born with, or are nurtured and develop over time.

**Neo-Fordism** A form of rational organization which combines Fordist efficiency and control with the ability of computer technology to introduce flexibility into the work process.

**Networks** The sharing of data through linked computer systems or through the Internet.

**Neuroticism** Emotional instability.

**No-frills** A model of organizational cost reduction which offers a basic product, charging customers for anything extra to this basic offering.

**Noise** Anything which distorts the transfer of a message from source to recipient so that the intended and perceived meanings differ.

**Nomothetic** An approach which views personality as a set of measurable traits or types.

**Office** A defined role within an organization.

**Official** A person who fills a particular role in an organization. When working in that role, a person is said to be working in an official capacity.

**Ohio State studies** Conducted at a similar time to the Michigan studies and also considered leaders to be people- or task-orientated.

**One best way** Rational management techniques that propose one most efficient way to perform any task.

**Open source and online collaboration** A form of knowledge sharing and collaboration where computer code is made publicly available and developed collaboratively.

**Operant conditioning** A conditioning of behaviour which recognizes that rewards and punishments do not need to be continuous, but can be scheduled in a way to still condition behaviour.

**Organizational behaviour modification** The use of operant conditioning techniques in a workplace setting.

**Organizational justice** A concept that stresses the importance of the process as well as the outcome for the perceived fairness of a decision.

**Organizational knowledge** Knowledge which is a collective property of an organization rather than belonging to an individual.

**Organizational learning** Sharing and transfer of individual knowledge so that it becomes a collective property of the organization.

**Organizational structure** The roles and positions in an organization, often organized horizontally and vertically in the form of an organization chart diagram.

**Organization chart** A diagram of the structure of an organization.

**Organization development** A wide-ranging set of change management techniques, including techniques which derive from behavioural and Gestalt psychology.

**Orientations to work** A perspective which suggests that people have a predisposition to work that is influenced by our lives outside work and the meaning that we attach to work.

**Outcomes** In equity theory, the rewards and results of a person's inputs.

**Oxymoron** A phrase that appears to contradict itself.

**Panopticon** A prison design that allows surveillance to take place efficiently over all prisoners, used as a metaphor for surveillance and control in organizations as a whole.

**Paperwork** Official documentation and record keeping within an organization.

**Path-goal theory** Developed by Robert House, this theory argues that the leader's effectiveness is dependent on the motivation, satisfaction, and performance of her subordinates.

**Performative labour** Paid interactive service work where the worker is engaging in some form of performance, as if on stage. Refers, in particular, to emotional and aesthetic labour.

**Personality** A set of characteristics and behaviour displayed by any individual.

**Personality test** A written test whereby the responses to a set of questions are said to provide a measure of personality.

**Personality types** Broad personality groupings which are associated with a set of particular traits.

**Person specification** A formal list of the main requirements for a successful candidate for a particular job.

**PEST model** A model which breaks an organization's environment into four sectors: political, economic, social, and technological.

**Physical space** Aspects of globalization that involve goods and people moving across land.

**Placelessness** Where organizations exist in networks and seem to have no one fixed geographical location.

**Planned approach to change** An approach to change which sees change as planned over a series of long-term steps. Pays attention to human and social aspects of change, which are seen as 'hidden aspects' below the surface, as if the organization were an iceberg. Closely linked with organization development.

**Politics** A process of game playing and tactics that occurs within organizations often where different individuals jostle with each other to gain personal advantage.

**Post-bureaucracy/post-bureaucratic organization** A trend away from rigid, bureaucratic rules and structures in organizations towards more flexible and less hierarchical, rule-driven organizations.

**Post-Fordism** A break away from Fordism and towards management techniques which use the skill of workers and grant autonomy to workers, emphasizing communication and competencies, rather than command and control.

**Post-heroic leadership theory** A collection of theories that argue that traditional leadership over-emphasizes the importance of leaders and under-emphasizes followers.

**Post-industrial** A move in society and economy away from the dominance of manufacturing, towards a more flexible, service-based economy.

**Power** The capacity to get things done or to influence others.

**Power games and politics** The process where one individual or group tries to gain advantage or get another individual or group to do things that they might otherwise not intend to do.

**Predictive validity** The ability of a test to predict a candidate's job performance.

**Prepotency** One characteristic having dominance over others.

**Process theories** Theories of motivation which suggest that motivation is a result of individual processes of perception, comparison, and calculation.

**Processual** Always in a process of changing and developing.

**Processual approach to change** An approach to change which emphasizes the messy and political nature of change.

**Production** The work done in an organization by the workers within that organization.

**Professional knowledge** A common body of knowledge relevant to a particular profession or occupation.

**Pro-forma** A type of paperwork, sometimes called a form. It is a blank template with standard fields for different types of relevant information, which is filled in as a means of capturing information for the records of an organization.

**Psychodynamic** A description of Freud's approach to personality which sees personality as continually being developed and changed by various influences.

**Psychological** Arising from the mind or emotions.

**Punishment** In behaviourism, a negative response that is received for performing a particular behaviour.

**Quality circles** A group of workers who come together, often under the supervision of a leader, to identify, analyse and solve organizational problems.

**Radical change** A political and theoretical approach which emphasizes the need to radically transform the social and political structure of capitalism to overcome the contradictions of capitalism.

**Radical humanist** A radical change perspective which emphasizes the 'subjective' contradictions capitalism has on the consciousness of people, often outside their awareness, producing alienation and oppression.

**Radical structuralist** A radical change perspective which emphasizes the 'objective' contradictions of capitalism between the capitalist (shareholders and managers) and workers and society.

**Rationalization** Work that is designed to achieve maximum efficiency and reduce costs, encompassing aspects of bureaucracy and the scientific design of work.

**Rational–legal authority** According to Max Weber this is power that is legitimated by rules and procedures associated with an office rather than by traditional or charismatic means.

**Rational organizational design** The design of organizational structures and activities in order to achieve the organization's goals in the most technically efficient manner. Rational organization suggests an organization which is designed logically and systematically, even scientifically, so as to achieve its aims.

**Rational work design** The design of work tasks to achieve maximum efficiency and reduce costs.

**Recipient** The person that receives a message.

**Records** Information held by the organization relevant for bureaucratic functioning, including information about workers.

**Recruitment** The process of attracting a pool of candidates for a particular job vacancy.

**Red tape** An unintended consequence of bureaucracy, where rules and paperwork get in the way of work and activities, rather than helping tasks to be performed efficiently.

**Reflective practice** A form of professional development and training where workers reflect on actual workplace experiences and events.

**Reflexivity** Where an individual is connected in some way to a text they are reading about or writing, rather than simply looking at a text to which they are completely unconnected.

**Regulation** The sociology of regulation looks for the sources of stability and order rather than conflict, taking consensus at face value and seeing how social order can be preserved and strengthened. In organizational behaviour this perspective emphasizes the interests of managers and shareholders.

**Reinforcement** In behavioural psychology, the continued encouragement of a behaviour by the provision of a particular reward.

**Resistance** Drawn from critical theory, where marginalized and oppressed groups (such as workers and minorities) resist the aims and requests of more powerful groups, such as management.

**Resistance to change** Forces which resist a change taking place.

**Reward** In behaviourism, a positive response that is received for performing a particular behaviour.

**Rhizome** A mass of random, tangled connections which some people suggest is similar to the nature of the Internet and cyberspace.

**Richness** The amount and quality of information conveyed by any one message.

**Rite** A solemn act or procedure to observe an event or occasion.

**Rituals** Everyday habits that individuals do without thinking, which once had meaning but have gradually become part of the everyday activities of the organization.

**Rule of thumb** A rough estimate of the time needed to perform a task, based on a worker's expert knowledge of that task.

**Rules, policies, and procedures** Formal instructions that govern how particular activities in an organization are to be performed.

**Schedules of reinforcement** A blend of fixed and variable reinforcements designed so as best to reinforce desired behaviours.

**Scientific management** The use of scientific techniques to design work to be as efficient as possible.

**Scientific selection** Defining the precise characteristics of the ideal candidate for a job.

**Search engine** A website which allows users to search for items on the Internet.

**Search engine optimization** Techniques to increase the rank of a website on search engine results.

**Selection** The process of selecting the most appropriate candidate from a pool of applicants for a particular vacancy.

**Self-actualization** For Maslow, a realization, or actualization, of an individual's ultimate human and creative potential.

**Self-discipline** The process by which an individual trains and controls themselves usually for the purposes of self-improvement.

**Self-managed team** A team, often of professionals or highly qualified people, who manage themselves.

**Separation of planning and doing** Tasks designed by management, with workers having no input other than to perform those tasks.

**Servant leadership theory** A bottom-up perspective which sees the leader being the most effective where they support followers to enable them to do their jobs.

**Service sector** Non-manufacturing industries, such as retail, leisure, transport, finance, and media.

**Sexually commodified** The sexual attractiveness or desirability of a worker is used as part of the work they perform for customers or clients.

**Shirking or free-riding** An individual who does not pull their weight but is carried by other members of the group.

**Single-loop learning** Learning in organizations which merely adapts to achieving a particular goal.

**Situational leadership** A theory which stresses the importance of adapting the leadership style to meet the situation.

**Social** The human side of the organization, in particular the relations between people at work.

**Social facilitation** The tendency that individuals have to work harder when being watched by others, particularly on simple tasks.

**Social identity theory** Drawing from psychological theory, how an individual's identity is derived from being part of a group.

**Social loafing** A term which describes people who, when working in groups, do not work as hard because, often unconsciously, they rely on others to do the task.

**Social presence theory** Examines the degree to which the physical presence of the sender of a message can be felt in a particular communications medium.

**Social–radical approach** The view that organizations have an effect on the personality of their members.

**Social reward** A reward that comes from the feeling of being part of a group or team.

**Soldiering** Techniques used by workers to create time for themselves during the working day. Soldiering means that workers are not working at the most efficient level possible.

**Source** The sender or originator of a message.

**Span of control** The number of workers controlled by a manager at any one particular level in a hierarchy.

**Stake** A claim or interest.

**Stakeholder** Someone who has an interest or claim in the activities of the organization.

**Stereotype** Where a characteristic is attributed to a person because of their membership of a particular social group, e.g. because of race or gender.

**Stimulus–response** The underlying relationship of behaviourism, whereby a particular response, or behaviour, is the result of a particular stimulus.

**Strike** A form of collective action where workers withdraw their labour.

**Structure** Social life is largely determined by the social structure; the reoccurring patterns which influence the choices available. Structures are difficult to change.

**Structured interview** An interview with a set format and standard questions, based around job-specific questions.

**Subcontracting** Hiring another person or company to perform a particular process or service for an organization.

**Subculture** A localized culture with its own set of values and behaviours that reflects, but is distinct from, the wider culture.

**Substantive rationality** Rationality from a human and ethical perspective—if something is formally rational and efficient it does not make it substantively rational when considering its human and ethical consequences.

**Surface acting** Emotional labour that is performed by workers conscious of the fact that they are engaged in an artificial performance.

**Surface learning** Learning a set of facts in themselves, possibly for the purposes of a test or exam, rather than with any additional depth.

**Surplus value** Profit that capitalists gain over and above the wages they pay to workers.

**Surveillance** The observation, either overt or covert, of people to gain information about them or to exert order and control over them.

**Sustainability** The long-term stewardship and maintenance of the environment and the prospects of the firm.

**Synchronicity** The degree to which something happens immediately or after a delay.

**Systemic approach to change** An approach to change which recognizes the organization as an interconnected system whereby change in one area can have consequences and knock-on effects in other areas.

**Tacit knowledge** Knowledge which is personal, a form of second nature or knowing things 'off by heart', and which is difficult to explain to others.

**Task orientation** Focusing on tasks rather than on people.

**Taylorism** The work process designed by Taylor, associated with the division of labour into small tasks, which are then redesigned to be performed as efficiently as possible.

**Team** A group who meet together with a common purpose and some degree of mutual interdependence.

**Teleworking, telecommuting** Working away from a place of work by logging into a workplace's computer network.

**T-group (training group)** An activity which aims to get a group to understand and change its dynamics and attitudes.

**Theming** As with a theme park, this is where the image and identity of an organization, and the experience that it provides for consumers, is based around a particular theme.

**Therapy groups** A group who meet together with a trained counsellor or facilitator where the group members decide what to talk about.

**Three-step model of change** Lewin's model whereby a process of change goes through three stages of unfreezing, movement, and freezing.

**Time and motion study** Rational work design where tasks are measured and timed, and redesigned to maximize efficiency.

**Trade unions** Membership organizations which collectively represent the interests of a group of workers.

**Trained incapacity** Where people are so used to their behaviour being controlled by bureaucratic rules and procedures that they become inflexible and unable to think for themselves and show initiative.

**Trait** A characteristic of the person, often considered the behaviour, thoughts, and emotions that the person exhibits, considered stable over time.

**Trait theories** Nomothetic theories of personality which see individual traits rather than broad personality groups as the foundations of personality.

**Transactional leaders** Leaders who do deals with employees in order to get the task done. Seen in opposition to transformational leaders who offer a better vision of the world that employees can buy into.

**Transformational leadership** A leadership theory which stresses the leaders ability to transform the organization by offering a better vision for the future.

**Triggers** Factors which push towards a change taking place.

**Trolling** Messages sent to Internet forums and communities which deliberately aim to disrupt their normal functioning and norms of behaviour.

**Typologies** A system of classification of traits that organizations have in common.

**Uncertainty** A lack of knowledge about a particular factual issue.

**Unconscious** From psychology, particularly psychoanalysis, the area of thinking that is not directly available to the conscious mind, and is below the level of personal awareness.

**Unstructured interview** An interview with no preset formal structure.

**Utility** The benefit that an individual might gain.

**Value engineering** A form of cost analysis that compares the cost of an item or process against its perceived value.

**Variable reinforcement** A reward or punishment provided at varying time intervals or varying instances of a behaviour to be reinforced.

**VARK model** A model and questionnaire which places individuals into one of four preferred learning styles—visual, auditory, reading and writing, or kinesthetic.

**Vascular skin reaction** A white line on the wrist created by a blunt instrument which disappears more quickly when the person is fatigued.

**Vertical differentiation** The process whereby a hierarchy creates a number of different layers of management within an organization.

**Vertical loading** Where a job is enriched by adding tasks which would normally be associated with elements of responsibility linked to positions higher in an organizational hierarchy.

**Work-life balance** A balance between work and career on one hand, and wider aspects of life, such as family and leisure time, on the other.

**Work to rule** A form of industrial action where workers follow rules, regulations, and instructions precisely—this often results in the speed of work slowing considerably.

# Index